Making a New Deal

Making a New Deal

Industrial Workers in Chicago, 1919–1939

LIZABETH COHEN
Harvard University

PUBLISHED BY THE PRESS SYNDICATE OF THE UNIVERSITY OF CAMBRIDGE
The Pitt Building, Trumpington Street, Cambridge, United Kingdom

CAMBRIDGE UNIVERSITY PRESS
The Edinburgh Building, Cambridge CB2 2RU, UK http://www.cup.cam.ac.uk
40 West 20th Street, New York, NY 10011-4211, USA http://www.cup.org
10 Stamford Road, Oakleigh, Melbourne 3166, Australia
Ruiz de Alarcón 13, 28014 Madrid, Spain

First published 1990
First paperback edition 1991
Reprinted 1992, 1993 (twice), 1994, 1995, 1996, 1997, 1998, 1999

Printed in the United States of America

Typeset in Sabon

A catalog record for this book is available from the British Library

Library of Congress Cataloging in Publication Data is available

ISBN 0 521 42838 6 paperback

In memory of my mother
And for my father and Herrick

Contents

List of Illustrations	*page* ix
List of Tables	xiii
Acknowledgments	xv
Introduction	1
1 Living and Working in Chicago in 1919	11
2 Ethnicity in the New Era	53
3 Encountering Mass Culture	99
4 Contested Loyalty at the Workplace	159
5 Adrift in the Great Depression	213
6 Workers Make a New Deal	251
7 Becoming a Union Rank and File	291
8 Workers' Common Ground	323
Conclusion	361
Notes	369
Index	511

Illustrations

Maps

1 Five Chicago communities inhabited by industrial workers, 1919–39. *page* 22
2 Steel communities of Southeast Chicago, 1919–39. 25

Plates

1 Packinghouse workers demonstrate on streets of Back of the Yards in hunger march, 1932. (Courtesy of the Illinois Labor History Society.) 1
2 Steelworker at U.S. Steel's South Works with St. Michael's Church in background. (Courtesy of the Southeast Chicago Collection, Urban Culture and Documentary Program, Columbia College, Chicago.) 11
3 Cow grazing in South Deering back yard, circa 1926, from Mary Faith Adams, "Present Housing Conditions in South Chicago, South Deering and Pullman" (M.A. thesis, University of Chicago, 1926), p. 114. (Courtesy of the Southeast Chicago Collection, Urban Culture and Documentary Program, Columbia College, Chicago.) 27
4 Household possessions thrown from a house in the Black Belt during the race riot of 1919. (Courtesy of the Chicago Historical Society, Dn 71,301.) 37
5 Rally to organize Chicago's packinghouse workers, circa 1919. (Courtesy of the Illinois Labor History Society.) 44
6 Portrait of Croatian Falcons in South Chicago, circa 1924. (Courtesy of the Southeast Chicago Collection, Urban Culture and Documentary Program, Columbia College, Chicago.) 53

7 Banquet at the Jewish Home for the Aged located in the Jewish area of Greater Lawndale on Chicago's West Side, mid-1920s. (Courtesy of the Chicago Historical Society, ICHi 03011.) 59

8 Members of the Contursi family at the grave of Domenico Contursi, Mt. Carmel Cemetery, in the western suburb of Hillside, 1923. (Courtesy of the Italian American Collection, Special Collections, University Library, University of Illinois at Chicago.) 70

9 World War I Liberty Bond rally at the Pressed Steel Car Company plant in the Hegewisch section of Southeast Chicago. (Courtesy of the Southeast Chicago Collection, Urban Culture and Documentary Program, Columbia College, Chicago.) 78

10 Interior of the Silver Bank, private Jewish bank owned by Adolph and Max Silver, 1916. (Courtesy of the Chicago Historical Society, DN 67,025.) 81

11 Procession on the outskirts of an Italian village during a feast for Santa Maria Incoronata. (Courtesy of the Italian American Collection, Special Collections, University Library, University of Illinois at Chicago.) 89

12 Bearers of the statue of Santa Maria Incoronata along city streets during the celebration of an Italian feast in Chicago. (Courtesy of the Italian American Collection, Special Collections, University Library, University of Illinois at Chicago.) 93

13 Pastime Theater, West Madison Street, on Chicago's West Side, 1917. (Courtesy of the Chicago Historical Society, DN 68,755.) 99

14 Neighborhood grocery store owned by Antonio and Angeline Tortolano. (Courtesy of the Italian American Collection, Special Collections, University Library, University of Illinois at Chicago.) 111

15 Shopping at the Maxwell Street Market. (Courtesy of the Chicago Historical Society, DN 68,695.) 114

16 The Tivoli Theater, Balaban & Katz's picture palace at Cottage Grove and 63rd Street, South Side, 1927. (Courtesy of the Chicago Historical Society.) 122

17 WCFL Labor Day celebration, Soldier Field, 1927. (Courtesy of the Chicago Historical Society, ICHi 20832.) 137

18 Barbershop of Oscar J. Freeman in Chicago's Black Belt, 1942, by Jack Delano for the U.S. Office of War Information. (Courtesy of the Library of Congress.) 150
19 Assembly of men in the Black Belt from *Chicago Daily News*, 1930, with Walgreen Drugs sign in background. (Courtesy of the Chicago Historical Society, DN 92,921.) 153
20 Workers assembling telephone equipment at the Hawthorne Works of Western Electric during the 1920s. (Courtesy of the Illinois Labor History Society.) 159
21 A family picnic for International Harvester employees at Hinsdale, the company's experimental farm outside of Chicago. (Courtesy of International Harvester Archives.) 178
22 Workers at the South Works of U.S. Steel alongside a warning sign written in the many languages of this ethnically diverse work force. (Courtesy of the Southeast Chicago Collection, Urban Culture and Documentary Program, Columbia College, Chicago.) 203
23 Woman evicted from her Chicago home, July 15, 1939. (Courtesy of the Chicago Historical Society, ICHi 02029.) 213
24 Unemployed men being fed at Immanuel Baptist Church, 2320 S. Michigan Avenue, 1930. (Courtesy of the Chicago Historical Society, DN 91,443). 220
25 United States marshals and Chicago police try to keep order during a run on a Chicago bank in the early depression. (Courtesy of the Bettmann Archives.) 231
26 Oscar Mayer's Meatpacking Company giving away free sausages to those in need, 1932. (Courtesy of the Chicago Historical Society, DN 99,016.) 239
27 Protesters assembled for hunger march through Chicago's downtown, October 31, 1932. (Courtesy of the Chicago Historical Society, ICHi 20955.) 251
28 Rally to reelect President Roosevelt featuring poster "Roosevelt Helped Us Save Our Homes," October 1936. (Courtesy of the Chicago Historical Society, DN C-4,119.) 275
29 Blacks working on a WPA project in Chicago, April 1941. (Courtesy of the Library of Congress.) 280

30 Interior of Del Rio Italian Restaurant with portrait of Franklin D. Roosevelt over bar. (Courtesy of the Italian American Collection, Special Collections, University Library, University of Illinois at Chicago.) 284

31 Steel Workers' Organizing Committee motorcade in South Chicago, 1937. (Courtesy of the Chicago Historical Society, ICHi 20954.) 291

32 Noon rally organized by the United Packinghouse Workers of America outside Wilson & Company's Chicago plant, March 10, 1949, the day before a National Labor Relations Board election. (Courtesy of the Illinois Labor History Society.) 307

33 A mass memorial service in 1939 to commemorate the Memorial Day Massacre at Republic Steel two years earlier. (Courtesy of the Chicago Historical Society, ICHi 20951.) 323

34 A ration line outside the Great Atlantic & Pacific Tea Company store at 133rd Street and Baltimore Avenue in the working-class community of Hegewisch, 1941. (Courtesy of the Southeast Chicago Collection, Urban Culture and Documentary Program, Columbia College, Chicago.) 326

35 Daniel Senise of the industrial suburb of Blue Island, Illinois, bowling with his union bowling team, 1943, by Jack Delano for the U.S. Office of War Information. (Courtesy of the Library of Congress.) 342

36 Infant Welfare Society of Chicago nurse demonstrating bottle preparation to a mother in her kitchen, with radio in background. (Courtesy of the Chicago Historical Society, ICHi 20830.) 344

37 Delegates from locals all over the country assemble in Chicago for the National Policy Convention of the Packinghouse Workers' Organizing Committee – CIO, July 16, 1939. (Courtesy of the Chicago Historical Society, ICHi 20956). 361

Tables

1 Chicago manufacturing industries employing more than four thousand wage earners, 1923 *page* 14
2 Size of industrial establishments in Chicago by number of wage earners, 1919 16
3 Occupations of males ten years of age and over by race, nativity, and parentage in Chicago, 1920 18
4 Occupations of females ten years of age and over by race, nativity, and parentage in Chicago, 1920 20
5 Life insurance held by Chicago workers by nativity or race of family head, 1918 66
6 Annual expenditures on insurance by unskilled workers at International Harvester and Swift & Company, Chicago, 1925 74
7 Chain stores in Chicago 108
8 Chicago motion picture theaters by size and ratio of population to seats 130
9 Motion picture theaters in five Chicago neighborhoods inhabited by industrial workers, 1937 131
10 Radio ownership in selected working-class and middle-class Chicago neighborhoods, 1930 134
11 Welfare capitalism programs in selected Chicago companies during the 1920s 164
12 Mexican and black employees in three steel mills and two meatpacking plants in the Calumet region, 1918–28 166
13 Gainful workers unemployed in Chicago by occupational groups, 1930–1 241

14 Indexes of decline in employment and payrolls in Chicago manufacturing industries, 1929–33 243

15 Percentage of Democratic vote in Chicago elections among all voters, whites, and blacks, 1924–36 257

Acknowledgments

Since January of 1983 when I made my first research trip to Chicago, many people there and elsewhere have helped bring this project to fruition. Generosity with time, resources, and ideas has distinguished all the people I will acknowledge here and many others whose names I may have inadvertently omitted. Although this project is in the end my own, I feel that some of the collective spirit of the workers whose story this book sets out to tell has carried over to its production. Friends, family members, colleagues, and strangers all have left their mark, although not always in exactly the ways that they might have wanted. For what everyone of them has shared with me, I am sincerely grateful.

This book began as my dissertation at the University of California, Berkeley, where it was well nurtured by a committee made up of Paula Fass, David Brody, and Neil Smelser. My thesis director, Paula Fass, has been a constant source of inspiration and support since I began graduate school. Her brilliance has helped me at every turn, making my work infinitely better. Her unfailing commitment to me – as teacher, colleague, and friend – has been more important to my development than she can ever know. David Brody generously agreed to serve on my dissertation committee despite his affiliation with the Davis campus of the University of California. He gave me the benefit of his enormous critical faculties. I will always carry with me his counsel that complexity of analysis is best accomplished through simplicity and directness in writing and argument. Neil Smelser may have made history himself in being an outside reader who actually read the dissertation with great care and perception. I have appreciated his interest in me and my work since we read social theory together during my course work days.

Several friends and colleagues have at some stage read the entire manuscript and taken the time to share their criticisms with me. Given the length of this book, that was no simple task. Herrick Chapman, Frank Couvares, Gary Gerstle, Jim Grossman, Alice Kessler-Harris, Marjorie Murphy, Roy Rosenzweig, and Joe Trotter have all helped make this a better book. Over the years, many others have read and commented on specific chapters, which I have also appreciated. They include Ross Boylan, Sue Cobble, Kathy Conzen, Drew Faust, Mary Felstiner, Susan Glenn, Jim Gregory, Margo Horn, Becky Hyman, Mike Kazin, Ann Durkin Keating, Roland Marchand, Peggy Pascoe, Steve Ross, Debora Silverman, Judith Stein, Kat Weinert, Gavin Wright, and other members of the Berkeley Americanists Group and the Stanford Dissertation Writing Group. I have benefited as well from discussions of chapters presented to Gavin Wright and Paul David's Social Science Seminar at Stanford University in 1986, the Working-Class History Seminar of the Pittsburgh Center for Social History in 1987, and the Urban History Seminar at the Chicago Historical Society and the Chicago Area Labor History Seminar of the Newberry Library in 1988. I have not been able to deal adequately with all the criticisms and suggestions I have received over the years, but I hope these colleagues will recognize the ways that they have improved my book.

A large number of people assisted me with my research in Chicago, helping me to locate sources as well as overcome fears that I would be considered a carpetbagger from California. I would like to thank Archie Motley, Linda Evans, Ralph Pugh, Janice McNeill, and my many other friends at the Chicago Historical Society; Mary Ann Bamburger in Special Collections of the University of Illinois at Chicago; Bob Rosenthal and Dan Meyer in Special Collections at Regenstein Library of the University of Chicago; John Jentz and Richard Schneirov, both formerly of the Newberry Library; Leslie Orear of the Illinois Labor History Society; Dominic Pacyga and Jim Martin of the Southeast Chicago Historical Project, now of Columbia College; Greg Linnes at the archives of International Harvester; Diane Davorick at the Hawthorne Works of Western Electric, when it was still standing; Leonore Swoiskin at the archives of Sears, Roebuck; Bill Benedict of the Theater Historical Society; John Kok at Foote, Cone and Belding Advertising Company; Bob Marshall at the Special Collections of the Chicago Public Library; John McCutcheon at the *Chicago Tribune*; and Irwin Klass of the Chicago Federation of Labor. In addition, I would like to thank Lewis Erenberg, J. Fred MacDonald, Barbara Marsh, and Sidney and Shirley Sorkin for sharing their specialized knowledge of Chicago with me. Finally, I owe the greatest appreciation to the individuals who agreed to be interviewed for the book. As they gave me their memories, they truly brought this story to life.

Hunting down sources for this book took me to many places outside of Chicago. In New York, I received important help from Anna Marie Sandecki at the J. Walter Thompson Advertising Company Archives and Susan Werner, Editor of *True Story* magazine, at Macfadden Publications. At the State Historical Society of Wisconsin, Rick Halpern and Roger Horowitz shared their own research into the early history of the United Packinghouse Workers of America, including the wonderful interviews they did with former packinghouse workers. At the Labor Archives of Pennsylvania State University, Peter Gottlieb helped me weed through the voluminous archives of the United Steel Workers of America and identify sources relevant to the early history of steel organizing in Chicago. At the National Archives, I found all the curators I dealt with to be courteous and helpful, but I must single out Jerry Hess for his unusual willingness to mine the government records under his jurisdiction for sources that would help me and, I am sure, so many other researchers. The hospitality of Ann Billingsley and Jim Grossman, Suzanne Desan, Debby Leff, and Jerome Leonard made research trips to Chicago, Madison, and Washington, D.C., both fruitful and enjoyable.

This book has depended on many additional kinds of help. At Carnegie Mellon University, research assistance from Jennifer Keene, Tim Kelly, Steve Tripp, and Ruth Weening aided me at crucial moments. Lori Cole brought a sharp eye to the proofs. Here as well the staff of Hunt Library, particularly in interlibrary loan, went out of its way to help me acquire material I needed. Financial support from the Eugene Irving McCormak Graduate Traveling Fellowship of the University of California, Berkeley, a National Endowment for the Humanities summer stipend, and the Program in Technology and Society of Carnegie Mellon administered by Joel Tarr allowed me to spend concentrated time on research and writing. My department chair, Peter Stearns, helped in this regard as well by providing research funds and flexibility in scheduling. I am also indebted to my colleagues Kate Lynch and John Modell for help with tables and to Arden Bardol for such beautiful maps. Parts of Chapter 3 appeared as "Encountering Mass Culture at the Grassroots: The Experience of Chicago Workers in the 1920s," *American Quarterly* 41 (March 1989), and I thank the journal for granting permission for its use. Finally, I cannot imagine a better editor than Frank Smith of Cambridge University Press. He read the manuscript with intelligence and care and was willing to give me all kinds of advice without forcing me to take any of it. Also at the press, Russell Hahn saw the book through production with consummate skill.

Members of my family have sustained me both emotionally and, at times, financially, over the seven years that I have been at work on this book. As different as their own work lives are from my own, they have never wavered in believing I was doing something worthwhile. They have brought love and empathy to every step of the way that they have shared with me. My only sorrow as I complete this project is that neither my mother, Dorothy Rodbell Cohen, nor my mother-in-law, Katharine Eaton Leonard, both of whom cared so deeply about history and would have rejoiced at the publication of this book, are alive to celebrate with me. Nonetheless, I know that I owe much of this book to my mother. Her own political awakening took place during the 1930s, and she raised me on stories about the CIO, FDR, and the New Deal. Her social commitment and intellectual engagement are now, I hope, a part of me. In the three years that I have been transforming this project from a dissertation to a book, my life has been unalterably changed by becoming a mother myself. Although my two daughters Julia and Natalie may often have felt that this book was a third sibling to rival, the pleasure that they have brought to my life has made these happy, if not calm, years. Vicky Byrne, who helped to care for them, is probably more responsible than anyone for my ability to finish this book. I have left for last the person who has been my partner in every aspect of life during the more than fifteen years we have shared together. To Herrick, who has given me so much of himself, I give this book with all my love.

Introduction

Plate 1. In the midst of the Great Depression, workers in Chicago's packinghouses, steel mills, and other mass production factories, many of whom were unemployed, demanded that the federal government come to their rescue. These stockyard workers paraded down the streets of the Back of the Yards neighborhood in late 1932 agitating for more government relief. A few years later, industrial workers would successfully organize themselves into unions to make demands of their employers as well.

- Chicago workers of mass production factories demanded the federal gov't help. Would later organize into unions (industrial workers)

Popular folklore of the Great Depression often celebrates how Americans, as individuals, coped with the greatest economic calamity in the nation's history, how they delayed planned marriages, sustained themselves with home gardens, and perhaps most notoriously, sold apples on street corners. But all too often these tales overlook the more political and collective responses many people made. During the 1930s, in an industrial city like Chicago, workers who rolled steel, packed meat, and built farm tractors not only found personal strategies to deal with hardship, they also joined together to undertake new kinds of political action. Men and women who had tried in vain to organize permanent unions in mass production factories before or had been raised on stories of failure now prided themselves on building viable unions at the long-time bastion of the open shop, U.S. Steel; in the meatpacking houses of Armour and Swift, nearly as wretched as Upton Sinclair had described them three decades earlier in his muckraking exposé, *The Jungle*; and in the farm implement plants of International Harvester, the Chicago-based manufacturer that symbolized the marriage of the industrial and agricultural Midwest. Workers in these companies and in others finally managed with the help of the newly formed Congress of Industrial Organizations (CIO) to wage the nationwide offensive that was necessary to win union recognition from their powerful, national-scale employers. By 1940, one in three workers in Chicago manufacturing would be a union member where ten years earlier hardly any had been. Here, as in Detroit, Pittsburgh, Akron, and many other industrial cities in America, the men and women who made modern mass production possible were taking the risks to demand – and were winning – better pay, fairer working conditions, and recognition of their right to be represented by a union.[1]

Just as working-class Chicagoans – male and female, black and white, a large proportion immigrants from eastern and southern Europe or their children – were joining together to exert more control over their work lives, they were also asserting themselves in new ways in the larger political arena. During the 1930s, Chicago workers, along with men and women elsewhere in the nation, had begun to vote Democratic more consistently and in greater numbers than ever before, joining President Franklin Roosevelt's "New Democratic Coalition" to promote a notion of government that protected the well-being of ordinary Americans. Supporting the Democrats in Washington and Chicago, they felt, would ensure a more activist federal government committed to

*see highligted

* workers were voting Democratic

providing the benefits that over time have become associated with "the welfare state." On the job and at the polls, working people throughout the country were speaking in a collective voice and having it heard.

To better appreciate the significance of these political actions that in retrospect might seem quite moderate, it helps to consider how difficult it was for industrial workers to achieve them. Factory workers at these Chicago plants had tried before the 1930s to organize themselves in unions, but despite occasional short-term success, they had never managed to sustain broad-based unionization over a significant period of time. Workers' most recent, and successful, efforts had followed World War I. In Chicago's steel mills, packing plants, and agricultural equipment factories, manufacturing workers came close to building viable industrial unions, but they did not last. Fragmentation of workers along geographic, skill, ethnic, and racial lines – along with repression by employers and government and weak national union structures within the craft-oriented American Federation of Labor (AFL) – led to the defeat of workers' once promising challenge.

Even before the 1919 era of labor militance, Chicago workers had launched campaigns to demand better wages, hours, and working conditions from their employers and the right to organize in unions, but weaknesses in their own organizations, resistance by bosses, and recurrent economic recessions had conspired to doom their drives. In the steel industry, unionization had been a conservative movement of skilled men whose strength rested on their control over the supply of steelmaking skills. While for the last quarter of the nineteenth century the native-born and northern European steelworkers who dominated in skilled jobs managed to impose their own standards of wages, hours, and work rules through their craft union, the Amalgamated Association of Iron and Steel Workers, mechanization made their skills increasingly obsolete by the early twentieth century. Steel companies then had little trouble destroying the union and hiring nonunion, unskilled, eastern and southern Europeans to do more of the work. The mass of steel workers never enjoyed protection by a union, and even the skilled elite who were unionized had lost their advantage by the early years of this century.[2]

Craft unions of skilled butchers in Chicago's packing plants proved more successful in incorporating the unskilled, new immigrants who were finding increasing opportunities for work in packing as in steel, but even their best efforts to challenge the autocracy of employers in the period from 1900 to 1904 ultimately failed. Although union locals of the Amalgamated Meat Cutters and Butcher Workmen of North America for the first time cut across skill, ethnicity, and in a few cases, even race, persistent fragmentation by occupation, along with packers' ease in recruiting strikebreakers during the recession of 1904, meant defeat of the workers' strike and a return to miserable shop floor conditions.[3]

At the McCormick Company, the most important precursor to the International Harvester trust formed in 1902, an elite craft union of molders was also the dominant labor organization from 1862 until the issue of the eight-hour day rallied lesser-skilled workers to the Knights of Labor in 1886. For several months skilled and unskilled workers together carried out an effective strike. Then a bomb explosion at a mass meeting involving McCormick workers at Haymarket Square killed seven policemen and unleashed an enormous wave of employer repression and employee fear. As a result, unionization was effectively destroyed at McCormick by the end of 1886. Despite occasional reappearances, management's dogged determinism to exclude unions resulted in only one sixteen-month period during 1903–4 when the company recognized a union contract. When that labor agreement ended, International Harvester shut down for two weeks and reopened its doors on its own terms.[4]

The Chicago plants of U.S. Steel, Armour and Swift, and International Harvester all operated unhampered by labor challenges from these early years of the twentieth century until World War I, and then what workers managed to win during the war and its aftermath was mostly dissipated in the defeats of 1919–22. Although Chicago was one of the strongest union towns in the nation, with the Chicago Federation of Labor sheltering under its wing traditional craft unions and at certain times workers as unskilled as scrubwomen and box makers, mass production workers never managed to build lasting industrial unions there, or elsewhere, until the 1930s. Even the most famous victory of unskilled immigrant workers in the nation's history, the Lawrence Strike of 1912, did not survive as the model of solidarity among nationality groups that it had appeared to be during the three-month-long strike. Within a year after the radical strike leaders of the Industrial Workers of the World (IWW) had departed, union membership dropped to almost nothing, and employers were successfully playing one nationality against another as they made employment insecure for all workers in this Massachusetts textile town.[5]

Just as Chicago's factory workers did not have labor unions to voice their complaints and defend their rights until the thirties, so too most of them expected little from government, particularly the federal government. Many immigrant workers were not even citizens, and those who could vote often used their ballots to buy concrete services from the precinct captain and ward boss responsible to their particular ethnic neighborhood. Electoral politics was a local, at most a city, affair. The federal government, even as it grew in importance during the twentieth century, seemed of another world, having little significance for or interest in their survival. Voting in national elections during the 1930s for a political party they felt articulated their particular class interests represented a big change for industrial workers. Given this history of impotence at the workplace and in national politics, what may look today like only minor challenges to the status quo in capitalist industry or in the two-party system during the 1930s felt like real power to many working-class people. Their perceptions need to be considered alongside other kinds of historical analysis in making a full assessment of the strengths and limitations of workers' incorporation into American politics through the CIO and the Democratic Party.

This book is devoted to explaining how it was possible and what it meant for industrial workers to become effective as national political participants in the mid-1930s, after having sustained defeats in 1919 and having refrained from unionism and national politics during the 1920s. Why did workers suddenly succeed in the thirties as both CIO trade unionists and Democratic Party faithfuls? Certainly, changes in the larger political environment mattered; repressive measures like government's and employers' use of Red Scare tactics in 1919 and facilitating factors such as the Wagner Act of 1935 influenced whether workers' political efforts failed or flourished. But I will argue in this book that these external influences by no means tell the whole story, that their effectiveness in thwarting or encouraging workers' efforts depended as much on working people's own inclinations as on the strengths of their opponents or allies. This book will contend that what matters most in explaining why workers acted politically in the ways they did during the mid-thirties is the change in workers' own orientation during the 1920s and 1930s. Working-class Americans underwent a gradual shift in attitudes and behavior over the intervening decade and a half as a result of a wide range of social and cultural experiences. Daily life both inside and outside the workplace and factors as diverse as where workers turned for help in good times and bad, how they reacted to their employers' "welfare capitalist" schemes, and whether they were enticed by the new chain stores, motion picture palaces, and network radio shows or preferred the comfort of more familiar ethnic associations all are important in analyzing how workers' politics evolved. To understand why a bacon packer risked her job in the depths of the depression by joining a union or why a Polish immigrant steelworker registered and voted for the first time in 1936 requires investigation into many facets of workers' lives during the 1920s and the early depression that might not at first glance have seemed relevant.

In the course of taking a close look at the multiple ways that the lives of working-class people changed between 1919 and 1939, this book sheds new light on aspects of the social history of the interwar era that might not otherwise get attention or be considered in connection with each other. Chapters on the 1920s explore the fate of workers' ethnic identity after massive immigration stopped with World War I and the restrictive legislation that followed it, the way workers encountered the explosion of mass consumption and mass culture, and how large employers' ideological commitment to "welfare capitalism" was experienced by those at whom it was aimed. Similarly, for the 1930s, investigation into what the Great Depression meant to its working-class victims, how workers viewed the New Deal, and why they came to identify with the CIO gives a new perspective to phenomena that frequently are analyzed more in terms of institutional policy than popular experience. Historical study of the twentieth century at times, moreover, has erected artificial barriers between people's experiences at work, in the community, and with politics; between different ethnic and racial groups; and between decades such as the twenties and thirties. People's lives, however, cross over these boundaries. If we are to understand the complexity of those lives, we must strive to do the same.

Just as people's lives are not easily isolated in space and time, so their social identities are also multifaceted. It is my view that no simple affiliation with a particular social class, ethnic group, race, or gender alone determined behavior. People in Chicago combined identities as working class, immigrants or their offspring, black or white, and men or women in different ways at different times. Periods such as when these Chicago workers began to act politically during the 1930s involved subtle shifts in how people viewed themselves. This study will address itself to how people recombined their multiple identities in ways that led them to undertake new kinds of collective action, how, for example, workers' self-images as ethnic and working class became more compatible as a result of the upheavals of the Great Depression.

I have focused my investigation in Chicago. It became clear early in my research that the important factors to explore in understanding the sources of workers' politics during the thirties did not differ substantially by region. Despite minor variations, there was one national story to be told. The most revealing contrasts were not between one city and another but rather between worker communities and factories within a city like Chicago. This narrower focus, moreover, allowed me to investigate how workers constructed complex interrelationships between different spheres of experience – between their workplaces and neighborhoods, political and social lives, ethnic and mainstream cultures. A local study, which permitted me to probe diverse arenas of popular experience, seemed the most promising strategy.

Chicago's prominence made it an obvious choice. It was the second largest industrial area in the nation during the interwar period. Its multiethnic and interracial work force also proved to be an analytical advantage. Chicago's factories were staffed with people born in southern and eastern Europe and, increasingly as years passed, with their children. From World War I through the 1920s, moreover, these Poles, Slavs, Czechs, Italians, and Jews were increasingly joined on the shop floor by blacks and Mexicans. Rather than limit my scope, a focus on Chicago offered the opportunity to examine multiple races, ethnicities, work environments, and neighborhoods. Chicago presented the analytical possibilities of comparative history within its borders.

Furthermore, Chicago had a special advantage as the best documented city in the United States during the interwar period. With the University of Chicago as the major center of social science research, sociologists like Robert Park and Ernest Burgess, political scientists like Charles Merriam and Harold Gosnell, and social service professionals like Edith Abbott and Sophonisba Breckinridge – and hundreds of their students – investigated a vast range of issues in their urban laboratory of Chicago. Aside from Helen and Robert Lynd's *Middletown* and its sequel, *Middletown in Transition*, all major social science research during the 1920s and 1930s took Chicago as its locale. Even the Hawthorne studies, the pioneering investigation of worker–management interaction by Harvard Business School researchers under Elton Mayo, focused on a Chicago area plant of the Western Electric

Company. So long as their biases are recognized, these diverse contemporary studies of Chicago life can serve social historians like myself as revealing windows into working-class experience.

Despite the special advantages of a Chicago locale, a study like mine that seeks to understand changes in workers' attitudes and behavior faces inherent difficulties. Attitudes of nonelite groups are notoriously hard to document. And workers' behavior in ordinary rather than crisis moments is often invisible. In this investigation I was drawn, therefore, to what was visible, particularly to scrutinizing the way that workers related to the institutions that impinged on their lives. Patterns of loyalty to ethnic organizations, welfare agencies, employers, stores, banks, and theaters, to say nothing of more traditional kinds of allegiances to political parties and unions, revealed the choices that workers made in living out their lives. Whether a worker saved at an ethnic bank, bought company stock, preferred ethnic to commercial radio programs, or depended on the county for charity became a way of entering the often elusive territory of people's attitudes. When information was not available on patterns of workers' patronage, the changes that these kinds of institutions underwent in the course of the twenties and thirties suggested to me the kinds of pressures they were under to survive and in this way revealed something of the priorities of their patrons. Although I would have wanted to know what working people of the era actually said about their ethnic benefit societies, new chain stores, and the Democratic Party, I often had to tease out their attitudes by closely analyzing the institutions themselves.

This book tells the story of how industrial workers in one American city made sense of an era in our recent history when the nation moved from a commitment to welfare capitalism to a welfare state, from a determination to resist the organization of its industrial work force to tolerating it, and from diverse social worlds circumscribed by race, ethnicity, class, and geography to more homogeneous cultural experiences brought about by the triumph of mass culture, mass consumption, mass unionization, and mass politics. What these large changes meant for this particular group of Americans is the subject of this book. But in another way, the subject is broader. For the way steelworkers at U.S. Steel's South Works, packinghouse workers at Armour and Company, and tractor assemblers at International Harvester brought wide-ranging social and cultural experiences to bear on their political choices serves as a case study of the complicated process through which all individuals come to adopt new ideological perspectives. How people live, work, spend leisure time, identify socially, and do a myriad of other things shapes their political perspectives, with *political* understood in the broadest sense. It is my hope that this exploration into how one group of Americans came to act politically in new ways will make us more aware of the possibilities for other groups – as well as more sensitive to the subtle influences on ourselves.

1

Living and Working in Chicago in 1919

Plate 2. In 1919, Chicago's industrial workers lived in neighborhoods determined by their jobs and ethnicity. Here a worker at U.S. Steel's South Works plant in South Chicago is surrounded by the two most important symbols of his community, the steel mill and St. Michael's Polish Catholic Church. Fragmentation of workers' ranks by ethnicity, race, and geography impeded efforts to organize unions in the city's factories just after World War I.

In 1919, four million workers launched the greatest strike wave in American history. Boston policemen, New England telephone operators, textile workers up and down the East Coast, most of the workingmen and women in Seattle, 450,000 coal miners, and 365,000 steelworkers nationwide led an offensive in which more than one in five American workers eventually participated. Their goals were both material and ideological. Fearing retrenchment by management after World War I, workers fought to defend their wartime wages and hours but even more basically to protect their jobs. And inspired by America's war effort in Europe, they sought to bring the campaign for democracy back home, to their own shop floors and election wards.[1]

Chicago, with its history of labor militance and its location at the crossroads of transportation and communication, became a center of the strike movement, with more strikes than any other city besides New York. Here, too, some of the most important strikes took place, particularly in the mass production industries – steel, meatpacking, ready-made clothing, and agricultural equipment – that had made Chicago the second largest industrial area in the nation. Every day through the tumultuous summer and fall of 1919, Chicago's newspapers reported another event: a strike at Argo's Corn Products Company, a work stoppage at the Crane Company, a day-long general strike of 100,000 workers to free labor hero Tom Mooney, a walkout at International Harvester, conflict at all the major packinghouses, idle steel mills in South Chicago. And because the actions of Chicago's workers inspired others elsewhere, a national audience watched closely, particularly when they moved their challenge from the workplace to the polls and organized a labor party. The Labor Party of Cook County ran a full slate in the municipal election of 1919 and joined state and national labor parties in promoting progressive candidates for several years thereafter.[2]

Yet, despite what seemed at times irrepressible popular enthusiasm for new worker rights as laborers and citizens, by the early 1920s few could dispute that mass production workers in Chicago, as in the nation as a whole, had suffered almost total defeat. In each of the major industries, except the garment trade, workers' drive to sustain wartime gains and establish collective bargaining had failed. Likewise, the Labor Party's hope of giving workers their own voice in government had quickly faded, as its candidates were resoundingly defeated at the polls.

These debacles were substantial enough to silence further political stirrings by Chicago's industrial workers throughout the 1920s.

Analysts generally have blamed the political failures of industrial workers in 1919 on the strength of the forces that opposed them: the Red Scare tactics of government, employer combativeness, and the AFL's ambivalence about organizing non–craft workers into unions. These factors were undeniably important. But in singling out these external influences, historians have overlooked the extent to which obstacles within workers' own ranks contributed to their political failure. Isolated in local neighborhoods and fragmented by ethnicity and race, workers proved incapable of mounting the unified action necessary for success.

The typical industrial worker in Chicago around 1920 needed little prior training before securing a job in one of Chicago's mass production industries. Ability to endure long hours in tough conditions was the only requirement for most of the jobs the city had to offer. Work was available in a wide variety of industries, moreover, as Chicago's manufacturing economy was as diverse as it was strong (Table 1). The city's factories produced more food products, furniture, telephone equipment, agricultural implements, railroad supplies, and iron and steel than anywhere else in the country, with clothing and printing not lagging far behind.[3] The manufacturing establishments that made these products included large and small firms, but the majority of workers depended on large employers for jobs. In 1919 more than 70 percent of the 400,000 wage earners working in Chicago manufactures labored in the company of at least one hundred employees and almost a third of them in establishments employing over a thousand workers (Table 2). The typical Chicago mass production company was big not only in scale but in capital as well. Ninety percent of wage earners worked for corporations, not individuals, and almost 60 percent for employers with annual products worth at least $1 million.[4] A job seeker in Chicago looked toward giant employers such as Armour and Swift in the stockyards; Inland, Youngstown, Republic, Wisconsin, and U.S. Steel; the Pullman Company Works; International Harvester plants; Western Electric's Hawthorne Works; and Hart, Schaffner and Marx, maker of men's clothing. Despite their diverse jobs, Chicago's semiskilled and unskilled workers shared the experience of working in an enormous plant for a corporate employer.

Table 1. *Chicago manufacturing industries employing more than four thousand wage earners, 1923*

Industry	Establishments		Wage earners		Value of products	
	Number	Percentage of total Chicago	Number	Percentage of total Chicago	Dollars[a]	Percentage of total Chicago
Agricultural implements	4	0	7,267	1.9	29,534	0.9
Boots and shoes, not rubber	29	0.3	5,353	1.4	27,645	0.8
Boxes, paper and other, not elsewhere classified	91	1.0	4,499	1.2	24,146	0.7
Bread and other bakery products	1,052	11.3	9,926	2.6	80,123	2.4
Car and general construction and repairs, steam-railroad repair shops	23	0.3	16,396	4.3	47,193	1.4
Cars, steam and electric, not built in railroad repair shops	15	0.2	15,697	4.1	113,054	3.4
Clothing, men's	328	3.5	29,111	7.5	170,497	5.1
Clothing, women's	372	4.0	7,004	1.8	54,584	1.6
Confectionary	108	1.2	6,333	1.6	49,419	1.5
Electrical machinery, apparatus and supplies	180	1.9	16,777	4.3	127,308	3.8
Foundry and machine-shop products, not elsewhere classified	512	5.5	23,033	6.0	151,447	4.6

Furniture	255	2.7	10,956	2.5	61,331	1.8
Iron and steel, steel works and rolling mills	10	0.1	9,663	2.5	117,161	3.5
Lumber, planing-mill products not made in planing mills connected with sawmills	160	1.7	5,124	1.3	44,992	1.4
Millinery and lace goods, not elsewhere classified	163	1.7	4,541	1.2	23,664	0.7
Musical instruments, pianos	23	0.2	4,652	1.2	21,013	0.6
Printing and publishing	1,381	14.8	27,479	7.1	238,854	7.2
Slaughtering and meatpacking, wholesale	50	0.5	30,382	7.9	514,667	15.5
Steam fittings and steam and hot-water heating apparatus	20	0.2	7,336	1.9	41,821	1.3
Total Chicago industries employing more than 4,000 wage earners	4,776	51.2	231,529	60.0	1,938,451	58.3
Total Chicago including industries not listed	9,334	100.0	385,685	100.0	3,323,341	100.0

[a] In thousands.

Source: U.S. Department of Commerce, Bureau of the Census, *Biennial Census of Manufactures: 1923* (Washington, DC: U.S. Government Printing Office, 1926), pp. 1400–3.

Table 2. *Size of industrial establishments in Chicago by number of wage earners, 1919*

	Establishments		Wage earners	
Classes	Number	Cumulative percent	Number	Cumulative percent
No wage earners	1,576	15.0		
1–5 wage earners	4,131	54.2	10,065	2.5
6–20 wage earners	2,362	76.6	27,201	9.2
21–50 wage earners	1,226	88.2	40,001	19.1
51–100 wage earners	549	93.4	38,990	28.8
101–250 wage earners	434	97.5	66,366	45.2
251–500 wage earners	131	98.8	45,562	56.5
501–1,000 wage earners	87	99.6	57,543	70.7
Over 1,000 wage earners	41	100.0	118,214	100.0
Total	10,537		403,942	

Note: Number of wage earners represents average number of workers employed during the year.
Source: U.S. Department of Commerce, Bureau of the Census, *Fourteenth Census of the United States: 1920*, vol. 9, *Manufactures* (Washington, DC: U.S. Government Printing Office, 1923), p. 323.

Chicago's industrial workers also had their foreignness in common. In the early 1920s, more than half the white men and over a third of the white women working in manufacturing and mechanical industries were foreign born. Even a wage earner born in the United States was more likely than not to have had at least one immigrant parent. Only a very small percentage of industrial workers were native-born whites of native parents, and they tended to hold down the most skilled jobs. A small but growing number of blacks also worked in Chicago factories; concentrated in the steel and meatpacking industries, they held the lowest paying and least desirable jobs. Hence, the laborers and semiskilled operatives at work in Chicago's mass production plants were heavily foreign. And except for the garment and millinery trades, which were dominated by women, they were also mainly male (Tables 3 and 4).

Although a substantial portion of Chicago's total foreign-born and second-generation population came from Germany, Sweden, and Ireland, these were not the mainstays of industrial manufacturing. Rather, the "new immigrants" of the early twentieth century, those from southern and eastern Europe, prevailed in mass production work. A study of unskilled and semiskilled employees of twelve large firms who were "fully employed" during the year 1924, a particularly fortunate group, revealed that more than half of them were foreign born: 30 percent came from Poland, 16 from Italy, 7 from Lithuania, and another 7 from other Slavic countries. Of the remaining 40 percent native born, almost half were black.[5]

With the exception of blacks, mass production workers tended to live near their jobs. Although some traveled a long distance to work, the majority made their homes in the shadow of the steel mills, behind the stockyards, or a walk away from the garment factory. The neighborhoods around Chicago's plants reflected the needs of both employer and employee; jobs in the predominant industry drew and sustained people, but once there workers molded their own social worlds. This book will focus on five areas of Chicago where mass production workers lived and labored (Map 1):

1. the "steel towns" of Southeast Chicago;
2. Packingtown, consisting of Back of the Yards and other neighborhoods adjacent to the packing plants;
3. the old immigrant neighborhoods of the West and near Northwest Sides, where residents worked in the garment trades and in light industry;

Table 3. *Occupations of males ten years of age and over by race, nativity, and parentage in Chicago, 1920*

Occupation	Total number of males	Percentage native white: Native parentage	Percentage native white: Foreign or mixed parents	Percentage foreign-born white	Percentage black
Agriculture	3,236	17.8	29.4	51.3	1.3
Mineral extraction	588	24.1	22.8	47.8	5.3
Manufacturing and mechanical industry	411,574	13.9	28.2	53.9	4.0
Total laborers	79,171	5.9	15.5	67.3	11.0
Slaughter and packinghouses	6,781	3.6	10.6	67.5	18.3
Agricultural implements	1,680	2.3	10.4	83.5	3.8
Blast furnaces and steel rolling	8,279	3.7	11.2	64.2	20.9
Car and railroad shops	2,671	2.1	7.1	87.4	3.4
Other	11,301	3.9	13.8	69.2	13.0
Total semiskilled operatives	89,433	11.3	31.7	53.6	3.3
Clothing	11,678	4.6	22.8	71.8	.8
Slaughter and packinghouses	6,325	6.5	16.9	53.0	23.6
Agricultural implements	1,178	6.5	28.2	64.4	.9
Automobile	1,920	19.4	40.6	38.4	1.5
Blast furnaces and steel rolling	3,241	15.6	32.3	47.2	4.8
Car and railroad shops	3,699	7.5	17.5	73.8	1.2
Other	12,202	11.6	36.4	50.5	1.5
Transportation	98,510	24.1	37.1	35.2	3.5
Trade	172,264	23.8	31.5	39.6	4.9

Public service	22,682	19.6	36.8	39.3	4.2
Professional service	43,528	38.4	33.5	25.2	2.7
Domestic and personal service	55,798	12.5	13.5	48.8	22.7
Clerical	111,719	32.1	50.2	15.8	1.8
Total	919,899	20.3	32.0	42.6	4.9

Source: Ernest W. Burgess and Charles Newcomb, *Census Data of the City of Chicago, 1920* (Chicago: University of Chicago Press, 1931), pp. 59–63.

Table 4. *Occupations of females ten years of age and over by race, nativity, and parentage in Chicago, 1920*

Occupation	Total number of females	Percentage native white: Native parentage	Percentage native white: Foreign or mixed parents	Percentage foreign-born white	Percentage black
Agriculture	160	18.1	36.3	40.6	5.0
Mineral extraction	13	7.7	46.2	46.2	—
Manufacturing and mechanical industry	77,427	13.6	46.3	34.3	5.8
Total laborers	4,653	8.0	38.9	40.4	12.7
Slaughter and packinghouses	593	1.3	21.4	63.6	13.7
Total semiskilled operatives	51,403	11.6	48.5	33.9	4.9
Clothing	16,596	7.4	44.3	45.7	2.7
Slaughter and packinghouses	2,696	4.2	26.0	51.7	18.1
Iron and steel	2,147	14.4	50.4	31.6	3.5
Transportation	12,011	31.7	56.5	9.7	2.2
Trade	34,711	26.4	47.6	23.3	2.7
Public service	428	31.5	43.5	17.1	7.9
Professional service	27,663	42.6	41.8	13.0	2.5
Domestic and personal service	60,304	14.5	21.0	42.5	21.9
Clerical	98,818	30.8	58.5	9.5	1.1
Total	311,535	23.9	45.4	23.9	6.7

Source: Ernest W. Burgess and Charles Newcomb, *Census Data of the City of Chicago, 1920* (Chicago: University of Chicago Press, 1931), pp. 59–63.

4. the Southwest Side, stretching all the way to the working-class suburb of Cicero, a corridor encompassing McCormick Works (the central International Harvester installation) and the Hawthorne Works of Western Electric; and
5. the South Side Black Belt, where close to 90 percent of Chicago's black population lived and from where blacks traveled to their jobs in mills, stockyards, and other factories.

These five communities, home to the great preponderance of Chicago's industrial workers, had similarities as well as differences around 1919. Each community isolated workers geographically and culturally from other workers in the city. Each differed in ethnic character and in the extent of employer influence on neighborhood life. Taken together as well as compared, these communities illuminate why Chicago workers failed in their political offensive of 1919.[6]

THE STEEL TOWNS OF SOUTHEAST CHICAGO

Beginning 12 miles south of the Loop and continuing for 20 more into northern Indiana, a belt of steel mills lined the shores of Lake Michigan and the banks of the Calumet River, interspersed with grain elevators, chemical plants, and petroleum refineries. The southeastern corner of Chicago was part of the 196-square-mile Calumet region, which included such other steel towns as Chicago Heights, Illinois, and East Chicago and Gary, Indiana. At this crossroads of rail and water transportation, more than a half dozen major steel companies had staked their claims by the early twentieth century and built the blast furnaces, coke ovens, open hearths, and mills that would soon make this area the foremost producer of iron and steel in the nation. Iron ore, coal, and other raw materials made their way to the Calumet region via the Great Lakes and great railroad lines; finished products returned to the industrial heartland with equal efficiency. And during the 1920s, Chicago's strategic location would make it even more significant as a steelmaking center. U.S. Steel had the two biggest plants, South Works and Gary Works (the world's largest steel plant), and numerous other companies – Inland, International Harvester, and what would soon be known as Youngstown and Republic – operated mills nearby.

Just as steel dominated the economy of this area, so its plants overwhelmed the landscape. Except for the occasional park or bathing beach, the mills cut the residents of the Calumet region off from Lake

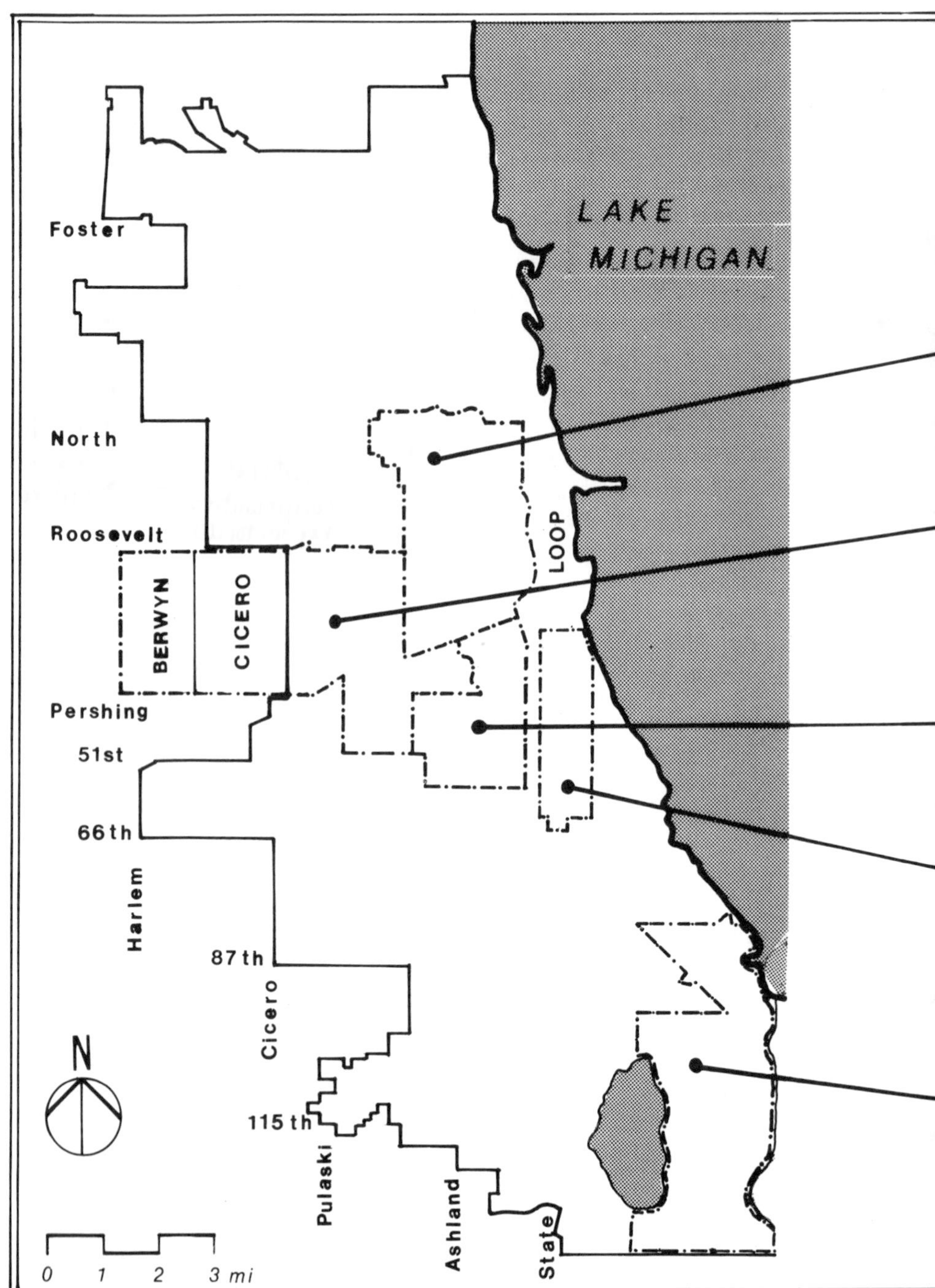
LAKE MICHIGAN
Foster
North
Roosevelt
BERWYN
CICERO
LOOP
Pershing
51st
66th
Harlem
87th
Cicero
N
115th
Pulaski
Ashland
State
0
1
2
3 mi

MAP 1
FIVE CHICAGO COMMUNITIES INHABITED BY INDUSTRIAL WORKERS
1919–1939

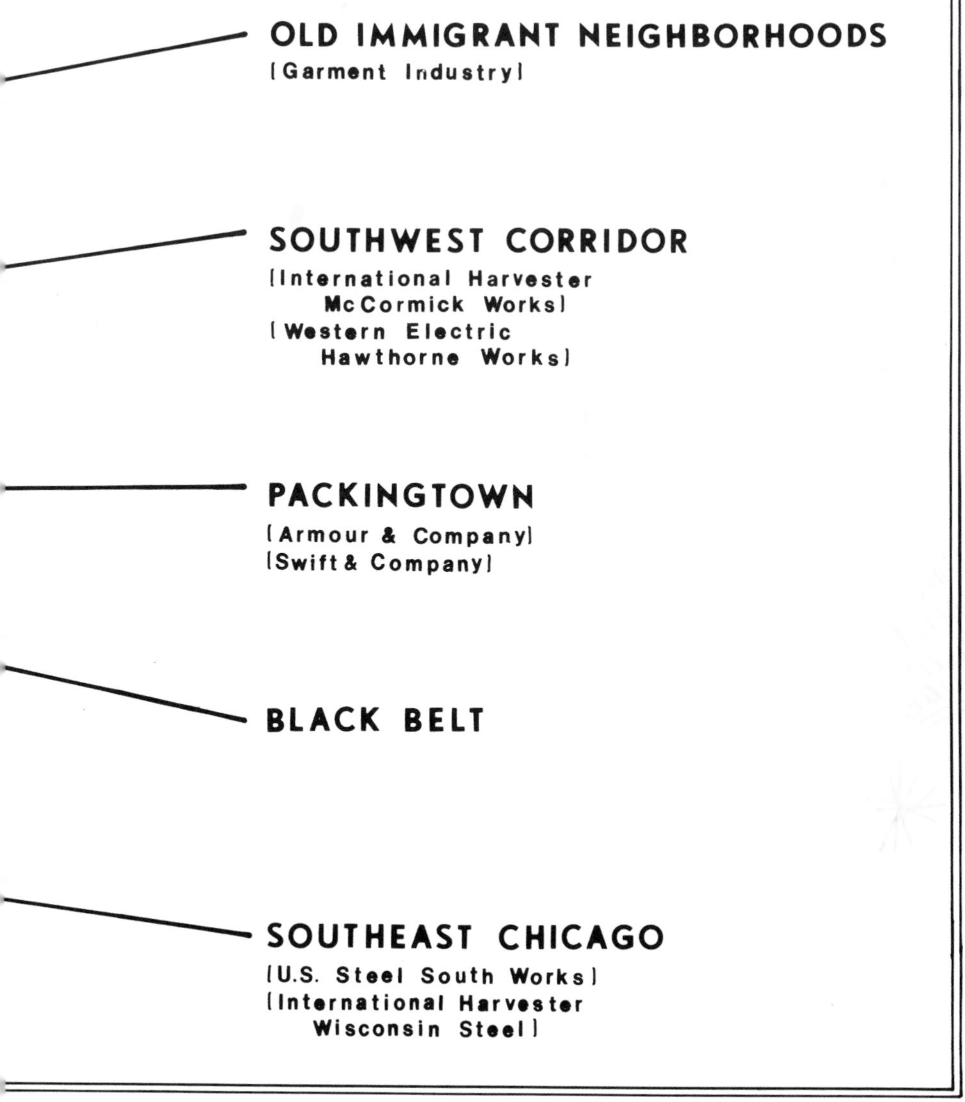

OLD IMMIGRANT NEIGHBORHOODS
(Garment Industry)

SOUTHWEST CORRIDOR
(International Harvester McCormick Works)
(Western Electric Hawthorne Works)

PACKINGTOWN
(Armour & Company)
(Swift & Company)

BLACK BELT

SOUTHEAST CHICAGO
(U.S. Steel South Works)
(International Harvester Wisconsin Steel)

Michigan. And within the region, the monstrous mills and their refuse – scrap yards, slag dumping grounds, industrial waste lands – isolated settlements from one another. An historically minded observer might have noted wryly that here was an industrial version of the pastoral New England landscape of a century earlier: nucleated villages clustered around belching factories instead of meetinghouses, while wide expanses separated one community from another. Four major settlements made up the Chicago part of the Calumet region: South Chicago, South Deering, the East Side, and Hegewisch (Maps 1 and 2).[7]

When a steelworker identified himself as a resident of the southernmost stretch of Chicago, he located himself in one of these four steel towns and usually in an even smaller neighborhood defined primarily by residents' ethnicity: typical were the Bush, inhabited mostly by Polish unskilled laborers; the brick bungalows of Cheltenham, reserved for skilled workers, more often than not the Swedes and Germans who had once dominated the labor force of the plants; and Greenbay, known as the vice district, with its rooming houses, pool rooms, and growing number of Mexican residents, the most recent immigrants to come to work in the mills. Neighborhood boundaries, at times invisible to the outsider, were well known and respected by those who lived here. But whether an ethnic enclave extended for one side of a street or for many blocks, individuals from other groups were rarely far away. Consequently, neither were ethnic tensions. Community life was filled with gang fights, sporting events that broke into ethnic conflict, and Irish churches that kept out Italians. It was not surprising to hear a native-born East Side man complain, "It is bad enough to work with Dagoes. I wouldn't think of living next to them."[8]

Ethnic conflict between American and northern European workers on the one hand and newer immigrant groups on the other began almost as soon as the latter began to arrive, near the turn of the century, and was rooted in job competition. As early as 1902, residents of South Chicago urged government investigation of the Illinois Steel Company's importation of four hundred Hungarians and two hundred Croatians; skilled workers continued for at least the next decade to complain that these immigrant workers brought unhealthy and overcrowded living conditions and, even worse, undersold native workers on the job. Still in 1919, the steeples of South Chicago's national churches – St. Michael's for Poles, Sacred Heart for Croatians, Our Lady of Guadalupe for Mexicans, St. Patrick's for Irish, St. Joseph for

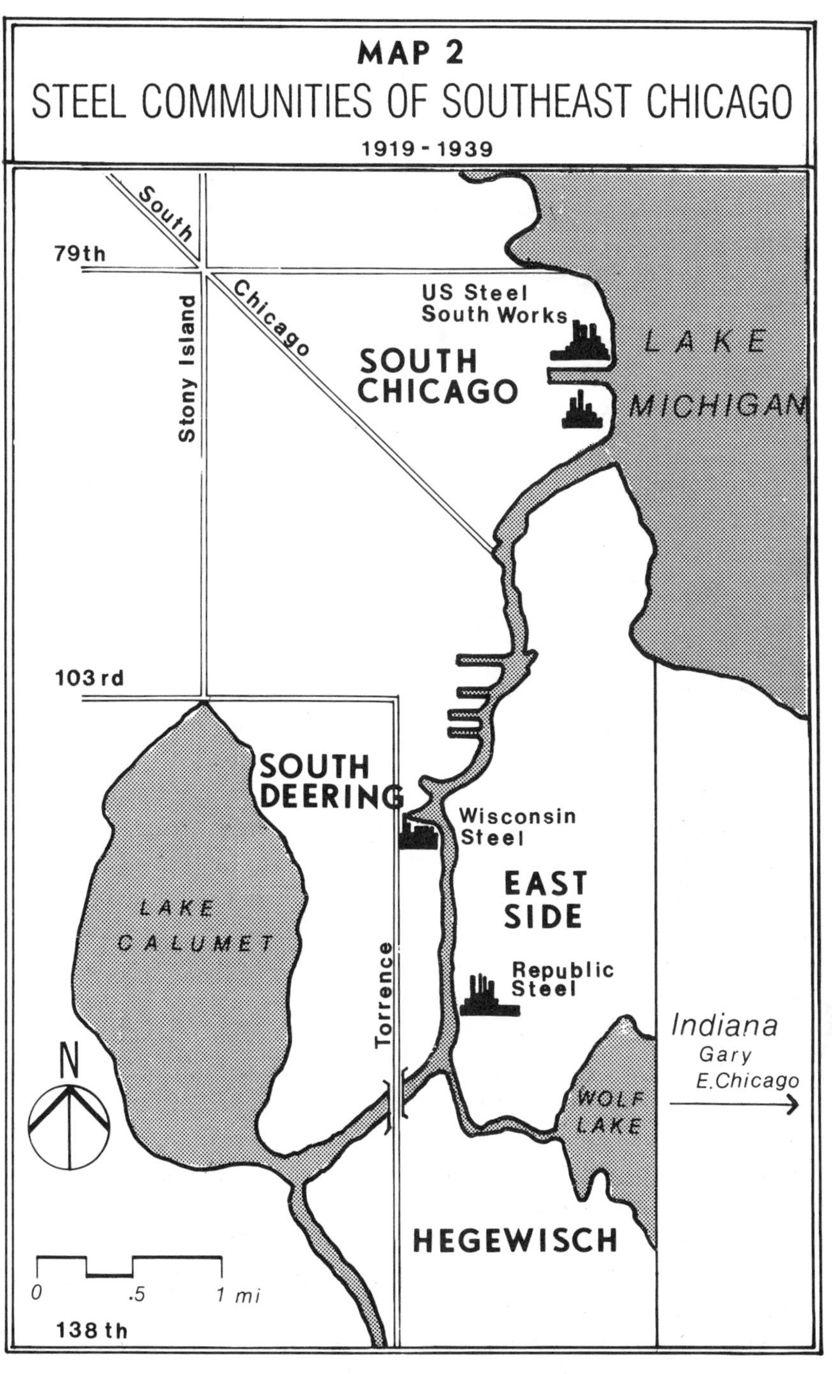
MAP 2
STEEL COMMUNITIES OF SOUTHEAST CHICAGO
1919 - 1939
South Chicago
79th
Stony Island
US Steel
South Works
LAKE
MICHIGAN
SOUTH
CHICAGO
103rd
SOUTH
DEERING
Wisconsin
Steel
EAST
SIDE
LAKE
CALUMET
Torrence
Republic
Steel
Indiana
Gary
E.Chicago
N
WOLF
LAKE
HEGEWISCH
0
.5
1 mi
138 th

Lithuanians, SS. Peter and Paul and East Side Baptist for Germans, St. George for Slovenians, Evangelical United Methodist for Swedes – vied with the smokestacks of the steel mills on the skyline and symbolized both the centrality of ethnicity to workers' sense of community and the way workers were divided among themselves.

The importance of neighborhood should not imply that the steel companies did not also shape their workers' lives. They drew them into this Calumet region, obligated them to "shift work" that switched from night to day in alternating weeks, and made them dependent on the corporation for financial security. But what today would be considered violations of people's well-being was viewed differently then: "When our back porch glistened from graphite, and orange ore dust belched from the enormous smokestacks," Estelle Uzelac Latkovich remembered of her childhood growing up next to South Works, "we knew times were good – the men were working!"[9] In most other ways, Chicago's steel employers intruded little on the private lives of their workers. Besides contributing financially to such "Americanizing" institutions as the local YMCA, they did little for their workers, not even helping them secure housing, which was often in short supply. While employees received few benefits, on the more positive side they were spared the company's meddling in their lives outside of work.

The one exception was Wisconsin Steel. Soon after International Harvester was created out of the merger of five producers of agricultural machinery in 1902, the new corporation bought a small steel mill and proceeded to expand it and the surrounding settlement of South Deering. This community became the closest thing in Southeast Chicago to a company town. As International Harvester involved itself in everything from providing utilities and parkland to contributing to local churches, residents in the neighborhoods surrounding Wisconsin Steel became more dependent on their major employer than workers in the other three steel communities. With at least three-fourths of the men who lived in South Deering working at the mill, a family like the Grandes was not unusual. The senior Mr. Grande came to work for Wisconsin Steel early in the century and remained for forty years; his son, Chuck, went to work at the mill as soon as he was old enough and stayed for fifty years, convinced to the end that Harvester, Wisconsin Steel, and South Deering "were a large and happy family."[10] Different kinds of relations with management were one more thing that differentiated Southeast Chicago's steelworkers, already separated by the formidable barriers of geography and ethnicity.

Plate 3. Back yards with vegetable gardens and grazing animals were not uncommon in the steel community of South Deering, where workers lived isolated in what was almost the company town of their employer, Wisconsin Steel. Of the steel companies in Southeast Chicago, this division of International Harvester was the most consistent in treating its workers paternalistically, and as a result it would have a very different history of industrial relations over the next sixty years.

PACKINGTOWN

The community isolation, ethnic insulation, and employer indifference that characterized life in most of the steel towns held true as well several miles northwest of the Calumet region, in the neighborhoods surrounding the Union Stockyards and their related meatpacking and by-products plants (Map 1). As with steel, Chicago's choice location at the crossroads of raw materials, labor power, and markets gave it special advantages. Railroads delivered millions of livestock a year to the yards and then carried them away as refrigerated meat, cured hams, lard, and glue. The Big Four packers – Armour, Swift, Wilson, and Morris – and their smaller competitors had made this industry the largest employer in Chicago and Chicago the center of meatpacking in the country. During World War I and shortly thereafter, the industry enjoyed particular prosperity, which boosted employment to over forty thousand people and attracted new sources of labor, primarily blacks and women. As in steel, workers in meatpacking inhabited neighborhoods encircling the workplace and cut off from the larger city – here by webs of railroad track, putrid city dumps, and huge expanses of freight yards and industrial plants.[11]

Also like steelworkers, packinghouse workers lived segregated by ethnicity. While the blocks of Back of the Yards, Canaryville, and Bridgeport, the neighborhoods where most white workers lived, displayed some ethnic mix, in general Poles dominated some quarters; Slovaks others; the Irish who had not already moved further south hung on to the north and east of the yards; and growing numbers of Mexicans were limited to two neighborhoods on either side. Blacks could not live in the area and generally arrived on the elevated line, which deposited them directly in the yards.

Steelworkers and meatpackers shared similar ethnic origins. The earliest butchers and packing workers, like steelworkers, had come from Ireland, Germany, and a little later from Bohemia. But as skilled work declined and the sources of immigrant labor changed, Poles, Lithuanians, and Slovaks, as well as blacks, filled the ranks of what had become a predominantly unskilled and semiskilled work force. Those of northern European birth or parentage who persisted in the stockyards did so as skilled butchers and foremen and lived in better neighborhoods to the south and southwest. In April 1921, the employment superintendent at Armour estimated that 25–30 percent of his work force was Polish, 20 percent Lithuanian, 27 percent black, and the rest of diverse nationality.[12] Some of these workers no doubt had been born in the United States (the 1920 census found slightly more native-born children of immigrants than foreign-born among the population of Back of the Yards). But workers' native birth easily escaped this Armour manager since even those born in America were likely to live in a world where English was not their first language, where they attended parochial school taught in a foreign tongue, and where social life revolved around family, a national parish, and the corner ethnic saloon or its substitute during Prohibition, the soft-drink parlor. When Arthur Kampfert began work in the packinghouses in 1914, he noted how these separate ethnic worlds carried over to the shop floor: "The vast majority of the workers could not speak the English language or neither understand one another. Profane language was easily learned by the foreign born, that was about the only English that one heard." Kampfert soon learned that the bosses encouraged this fragmentation of their work force: "As time went on I found out that in hiring new help the American born received $17\frac{1}{2}$ cents per hour, foreign born $12\frac{1}{2}$ cents per hour. Women received 10 cents per hour."[13]

In the years during and just after World War I, ethnic identification in Packingtown and in other working-class neighborhoods of Chicago intensified as homeland nationalism seized people, particularly those from newly created countries like Poland, Lithuania, and Czechoslovakia. Social workers at a settlement house noted, for example, that Polish, Bohemian, and Irish girls who had once mixed very well now seemed to emphasize their nationality differences. Also, immigrants increasingly played out Old World antagonisms within Chicago. In a number of neighborhoods, Jews and Poles clashed repeatedly during the spring and summer of 1919 in disputes over the anti-Semitic character of Polish nationalism. Jews held anti-Polish demonstrations, and Poles retaliated with boycotts of Jewish stores and attacks on Jewish peddlers. The most vicious case of Polish–Jewish hostility occurred in the steel community of South Chicago, where Poles accused a Jewish merchant of luring a Polish boy into his shop, killing him, and using his blood for religious purposes.[14] At the same time that old tensions were rekindled in a community like Packingtown, moreover, opportunities for inter-ethnic contact decreased. Prohibition closed down Whiskey Row, the daytime saloons near the packinghouses where workers of different ethnicities once mixed. The unions born during wartime reinforced division by separating workers into locals according to skill, nationality, and race rather than by department as they had done in the early twentieth century. Although Irish and German butchers, Slavic laborers, and black newcomers worked together in the packinghouses, at the end of the day they headed home to worlds segregated according to race, skill, and ethnicity.[15]

The lives of Chicago's steel and meatpacking workers conformed to a similar pattern around 1920. Work had drawn a heterogeneous group of primarily eastern and southern Europeans to Steeltown or Packingtown, where they forged distinctive ethnic communities around neighborhoods, national churches, and ethnic associations. At the factory, people came into contact with workers of different ethnicity, but they could not easily communicate. Outside of work, even though different nationality groups sometimes overlapped within neighborhoods, emotionally they inhabited separate ethnic worlds. In the years during and immediately after the war, moreover, tension plagued even the limited interaction between ethnic groups. And everywhere but in the South Deering neighborhood of Wisconsin Steel, workers' primary involvement with their ethnic communities faced little competition from employers. Company disinterest in the employees' private lives ensured that workers had even less to do with their employers outside of work than they did with people of other ethnicities.

As insular as ethnic life was in the steel towns and Packingtown, other areas where mass production workers lived were even more culturally isolated. In the remaining three working-class communities – the old immigrant neighborhoods close to downtown, the Southwest Corridor, and the Black Belt – not work but ethnic or racial affiliation initially attracted people to homogeneous settlements. Once there, workers sought employment in whatever nearby industries were popular among their group. These workers had even less contact with native Americans or individuals of different ethnicity than had Chicago's steelworkers and meatpackers.

OLD IMMIGRANT NEIGHBORHOODS

Traveling from north to southwest around the Loop in 1920, one still encountered, albeit in different stages of vitality, a ring of distinctive communities hugging the north and south branches of the Chicago River: Little Sicily; Stanislawowo, or Polish downtown; the West Town Jewish community; the Italian settlement around Grand Avenue; Greektown; the oldest and largest Italian colony of Little Italy; Jewish Maxwell Street, Chicago's Lower East Side; and Little Bohemia (Map 1). These were animated Old World ghettos where ethnic Chicagoans who lived elsewhere might return to buy authentic foods and goods not available in their neighborhood shops, to worship on a holiday or other special occasion, and to participate in ethnic societies and institutions. But for those who lived in these neighborhoods, the security of Old World language and customs often came at the price of poverty and the worst slum conditions in the city. For many, therefore, these were places to settle upon arrival in Chicago and places to leave as soon as possible.[16]

While in 1920 mention of the immigrant ghetto may still have summoned up popular images of the Jewish tailor or pushcart peddler, the Italian barber or vegetable grocer, and the Polish and Italian day laborer, in reality, a large proportion of the residents, particularly the young ones, were working in factories. A survey of young adults attending Friday night dances at the Chicago Commons Settlement in 1925, for example, found over 70 percent of the Poles holding manufacturing jobs, more than half of them within a mile of their homes.[17] No single industry organized the economic life of the community, as had steel and meatpacking, but the needle trades came closest to dominating the area, with branches of men's and women's clothing, millinery, gloves, knits, and furs. Unlike the national corporations that employed steel and packing workers, the owner of a garment workshop usually lived in Chicago, often in the same neighborhood as his employees, and owned no other factories elsewhere. But although these small-scale shops were generally the rule, a few major employers, such as Hart, Schaffner and Marx and B. Kuppenheimer, helped make Chicago nationally prominent in the clothing industry, particularly in the manufacture of quality men's garments. Although workers in the needle trades might still dislike the boss, he was local and, for the large number of Jewish workers, usually "one of them."[18]

Workers eventually left these original immigrant neighborhoods, but they did not abandon their ethnic communities. Rather, they moved with their compatriots. Poles headed farther northwest along Milwaukee Avenue, Italians pushed north and west, Jews went westward to North Lawndale and Humboldt Park, and Bohemians followed Blue Island Avenue to 22nd Street and continued west through South Lawndale to the suburbs of Cicero and Berwyn. In these new communities, Poles and Italians created national parishes, Jews transplanted synagogues and Hebrew schools, Czechs established sokols, churches, and Free Thought schools – and all brought ethnic shops and services with them as they resettled.[19]

THE SOUTHWEST CORRIDOR TO MCCORMICK AND HAWTHORNE

Two of Chicago's largest industrial employers, the McCormick Plant of International Harvester and the Hawthorne Works of Western Electric, dominated one of these areas of second settlement, a territory stretching westward from South Lawndale to Berwyn and southward to include the communities of McKinley and Brighton Parks (Map 1). What can be called the Southwest Corridor became the new home of Czechs and Poles who had moved out of Bohemian Pilsen and the stockyard neighborhoods. Many had left in search of better housing, and the fortunate bought small brick or frame bungalows on the new blocks, which mushroomed during the building boom of the twenties, or older brick two-flats that had once belonged to Irish and German workers. A Western Electric worker who bought a bungalow "on time" fifteen minutes away from the Hawthorne plant told a typical story: "When I first came to Chicago I lived out in a pretty bad district. I lost two children there, so my wife and I decided that we would get out of Chicago and move to a better place where the air would be fresher and we would be more independent."[20] Although these Czechs and Poles had left behind older industrial areas, most of them still looked to factories such as the McCormick Works of International Harvester and Western Electric to earn a living. Their new industrial employers, however, promised steadier and better-paying employment than the packing houses or the small plants of the West Side they had left behind.[21]

International Harvester and Western Electric were both national corporations like most of the steel and packing employers, but they developed contrasting approaches in dealing with the communities that supplied them with labor. International Harvester operated McCormick Works, the nucleus of its agricultural implement manufacturing empire, very differently from its Wisconsin Steel plant farther south. Rather than using paternalistic programs to cultivate a loyal work force in the neighboring community, management at McCormick took advantage of its central Chicago location to recruit not the choicest but the cheapest labor available, which by 1920 meant Slavs, Italians, and blacks. What worked economically also suited McCormick's industrial relations policy. Management felt that a socially atomized work force drawn from numerous ethnic communities would minimize militance at the company's most radical plant, still notorious for the 1886 strike that precipitated the "Haymarket riot."[22] So McCormick Works, in the center of Chicago, kept a businesslike distance from the diverse cultural lives of its workers.[23]

Western Electric's Hawthorne Works, in contrast to McCormick, developed relations with its community along the lines of Wisconsin Steel. Just as Wisconsin Steel had created the community of South

Deering, so Hawthorne Works fostered the working-class towns of Cicero and Berwyn. In 1905, Western Electric began to move its operations from old factories in Chicago and New York City to its newly built Hawthorne plant in suburban Cicero to centralize the manufacture of telephone equipment and, until 1925, electrical appliances for the home. In the ensuing years, Hawthorne management took great interest in Cicero and transformed it from a sleepy town of 14,000 in 1910 to a booming industrial suburb of 45,000 by 1920 and 67,000 by 1930. Likewise, the population of neighboring Berwyn reached 47,000 by 1930, an increase of 232 percent over 1920, promoting the *Chicagoan* to proclaim it "a lusty young city which builds whole new blocks overnight."[24]

But Cicero and Berwyn still shared much of the isolated character of the old immigrant neighborhoods downtown, from where many of their residents had come. With Cicero the next stop after South Lawndale on the Bohemian trek west, Czechs flooded the town. In 1920, among the 86 percent of Cicero's population that claimed foreign birth or parentage, Czechs dominated, followed by Poles. Hawthorne Works soon reflected this homogeneous population in its work force and became the largest employer of Czech workers in the Chicago metropolitan area. Unlike McCormick Works, Hawthorne cultivated a more ethnically homogeneous work force and actively involved itself in the affairs of the surrounding community where many of these workers lived. Whereas ethnically diverse workers made their way to International Harvester's McCormick Works each day from a multiplicity of neighborhoods, in Cicero fewer ethnic communities staffed Hawthorne Works to create a more integrated work and residential world around Western Electric.[25]

THE BLACK BELT

In these four communities – the steeltowns of Southeast Chicago, Back of the Yards, the old immigrant neighborhoods, and the expanding Southwest Corridor – mass production workers tended to be first- and second-generation immigrants with roots in southern and eastern Europe except for a small, although growing, Mexican population. This picture of Chicago's industrial work force is not complete, however, without mention of a group that increasingly filled its ranks. The city's black population more than doubled between 1910 and 1920, and again between 1920 and 1930, due to massive migration from the South.

Like the Jews, Italians, Poles, and Czechs of the old immigrant neighborhoods, newly arrived blacks first settled close to others of their race and then, when possible, looked for better housing en masse. But racial discrimination gave blacks many fewer options than European immigrants. They could rarely move where they chose or find jobs in any of the neighborhoods where they already lived.[26] As a result, almost 90 percent of black workers made their homes in the Black Belt of the South Side, with the rest in four or five smaller settlements; from these ghettos they traveled to jobs in steel mills, packinghouses, garment sweatshops, and factories. Race determined where Chicago's black workers lived, but more by coercion than the choice ethnic workers exercised.

Chicago's Black Belt took shape as the nation's second largest concentration of blacks, after Harlem, during the period from World War I to 1930 (Map 1). As late as 1910, blacks had been less segregated from native whites than were Italian immigrants; even in 1920, no census tract was 90 percent black. By 1930, however, two-thirds of all blacks lived in areas at least 90 percent black, one-fifth in tracts that were exclusively black. By the end of the twenties, white Chicagoans could point to a black city in their midst – an almost solidly black area from 22nd Street south to 63rd Street and between the CR & P railroad tracks on the west and Cottage Grove on the east – with its own commercial center, night life, dialect, and culture. As blacks pushed south and east in search of more plentiful and adequate housing, border skirmishes, house bombings, and other forms of white resistance eventually gave way to the redrawing of the "color line," and the belt grew a little wider and a lot longer. The Grand Boulevard neighborhood, 32 percent black in 1920, was 95 percent so by 1930; Washington Park went from 15 to 92 percent black during the same decade. By 1930, blacks had grown to number 234,000, almost 7 percent of Chicago's population, and yet they lived increasingly concentrated and isolated in the city.[27]

Even though blacks had to live a good distance from their jobs, work had nonetheless brought most of them to Chicago during and after World War I. The war had not only created more demand for the products of Chicago's industries, such as steel for armaments and packaged meat to feed Europe's armies, but it had also deprived these factories of the labor they needed. Men went off to fight, and the usual stream of new immigrants was cut off by war. This unprecedented economic opportunity attracted fifty thousand southern blacks to Chicago between 1916 and 1919. On their own or recruited by labor agents, they arrived to claim jobs at Swift, Armour, International Harvester, U.S. Steel, and elsewhere. Before the war, blacks had had few opportunities in manufacturing, except during brief stints as strikebreakers. After the strikes ended, they usually lost their jobs. Instead, blacks had supported themselves through domestic and personal service as waiters, porters, janitors, and servants. But by 1920, factory work rather than service provided the most important source of employment for black men, engaging more than 40 percent of them, and it was gaining among black women as well. By 1920, blacks were represented in the manufacturing labor force in greater strength than their 4 percent presence in the city's population and noticeably more so in large factories.[28]

Black workers made their greatest inroads in the stockyards and packinghouses, which were not far from the Black Belt, and succeeded almost as well in the steel mills of Southeast Chicago. During the war, more than half of all black men who held manufacturing jobs were packinghouse workers; in a few meatpacking plants the black work force went as high as 60 or 70 percent of total employees. By the end of World War I most adult black males in Chicago had worked in a meatpacking establishment.[29] Beginning with the war and continuing through the twenties, blacks made up 10–15 percent of the labor force in Chicago area steel mills. Steel employed fewer black workers than meatpacking, however, because more of the work required greater skill and continued to attract whites, the mills were far from where blacks could live, and many steel employers preferred to recruit Mexicans for the lowliest jobs.[30]

In the garment industry, the number of blacks was insignificant until 1917. In this case, however, the sweatshop doors opened not so much because of the war but because employers hired black women as strikebreakers in an industry that was already highly unionized. At the strike's end, five hundred blacks found permanent places in the needle trades, and their numbers grew as manufacturers set up "open shops" in the Black Belt.[31]

The only mass production plants important to this study that did not hire black workers during the war were Western Electric and Wisconsin Steel, the sole International Harvester facility in Chicago to hold out.[32] Situated far west and south, they were located a great distance from where black workers could live. But more important, both managements were extremely protective of their good relations with the communities in which they operated. While blacks might have provided a cheap source of labor, that profit would have been at the cost of other workers' good will. Because white employees feared blacks as co-workers – to say nothing of as neighbors – management at these plants respected community prejudice and did not hire blacks. In these "company towns," the reciprocity implicit in paternal relations gave employees real influence with employers on matters of race.

Life for Chicago's black workers was fraught with pressures resulting from the peculiar circumstances of their residential and work experiences. First of all, they were affected by the forced separation between home and work. Commuting to a job isolated black workers from colleagues in a more fundamental way than ethnic workers, who, despite their orientation toward ethnic communities, still came in some contact with each other outside of work. Even more detrimental to potential unity among black employees, blacks were isolated from co-workers of their own race. Because black community life was so removed from the workplace, it was built instead around other common experiences, such as church and leisure activities. Black packing workers, then, could not as easily deepen their work relationships at home in the Black Belt as Polish workers, for example, could in their neighborhoods adjacent to the plants.

It was also difficult for blacks to escape conflict with whites. At best, the search for decent housing subjected blacks to intimidation. At worst, it brought threatening mobs, bombings, and even murder to their doorsteps. Whites' fears over the expansion of the Black Belt, moreover, followed blacks into the workplace, deepening resentments about jobs already festering there. Despite the honest way that many blacks had found work during the war and their greater chance of being fired when economic recession hit in the spring of 1919, their earlier reputation as strikebreakers continued to make blacks suspect to white workers.

The strained atmosphere of competition between blacks and whites over housing and jobs finally exploded in July 1919 in a vicious, week-long race riot that left 38 people dead, 537 injured, and over a thousand homeless. The precipitating incident was the stoning of a

Plate 4. The wrecking of black homes like this one and other acts of violence during Chicago's race riot in the summer of 1919 deepened existing tensions between blacks and whites in the city, making it that much harder for workers to establish viable interracial unions in the factories where they worked together.

black youth whose raft drifted over an imaginary line extending out from contiguous black and white beaches on Lake Michigan. The Illinois National Guard and a severe downpour of rain helped to put an end to the hostile street fighting that ensued but not in time to prevent blacks from being blamed for the mysterious burning of forty-nine houses in Back of the Yards, which left 948 people, mostly Lithuanians, homeless and black–white relations permanently seared. While a third of the reported clashes occurred in the Black Belt, a greater number, 41 percent, took place in the white neighborhood just to the west, near the stockyards, and were aimed particularly at blacks traveling to and from work. Overt racial conflict had come to Packingtown. Race, like ethnicity, contributed to the fragmentation of the work force, in meatpacking especially but also in the steel and agricultural implement plants where a somewhat smaller number of blacks worked.[33]

Mass production workers and their families, whichever of these five communities they lived in, shared an orientation to "localism," both cultural and geographic. Race, ethnicity, job, and neighborhood served as boundaries, not bridges, among industrial workers in Chicago. In the immediate aftermath of World War I, when the city's workers sought to maintain the better hours and wages they had won in the crisis of wartime and when many of them hoped for larger political changes, their localistic orientation would conspire with the multiple forces that opposed them to bring on defeat. This is not to question the conviction or commitment that workers brought to their organizational efforts during that volatile year of 1919, nor to ignore the brutal repression practiced by those who opposed them – employers insisting on the open shop, government engaged in Red Scare tactics, and craft unions resistant to organizing industrial workers. But the hostility engendered by ethnic and racial fragmentation and workplace and neighborhood segregation undermined the best of intentions and the most promising of political challenges.

The ways that these five communities differed from each other also bore on workers' effectiveness in 1919. The more heterogeneous an area's population and an industry's work force – as in the steel towns, Packingtown, and around McCormick Works – the more ethnic or racial tension disrupted workers' ranks. And the more involved employers were in their surrounding communities – as at Wisconsin Steel and Hawthorne Works – the less likely it was that workers organized against them. Examining how these five communities and their industries fared during the turbulent days of 1919 will reveal how the barriers that divided Chicago's mass production workers also barred them from political victory.

1919 STRIKES CHICAGO

The steel towns and Packingtown felt Chicago's postwar strikes most intensively. In both the steel strike of 1919 and the packinghouse conflicts that continued until January 1922, community isolation and ethnic and racial tensions played into employers' hands to doom workers' struggles to defeat.

In steel, the disunity of workers – their difficulty in mounting a disciplined nationwide movement and in overcoming antagonisms between immigrant and native workers and between black and white workers – made their union drive vulnerable to steel employers and conservative craft unionists. Progressive leaders of the Chicago Federation of Labor launched a national campaign to organize the steel mills during the spring of 1918. Chairman John Fitzpatrick and his associate, William Z. Foster, had engineered a successful union drive of stockyard workers during the war and were convinced that the time had come to break the antiunionism of the steel trust and to do so for the benefit of all steelworkers, not just the most skilled who had long had access to exclusive craft unions. By August, they had established, under the auspices of the AFL, the National Committee for the Organization of Iron and Steel Workers, a collaborative effort of the twenty-four trade unions that claimed jurisdiction in steel. These craft unions officially cooperated. They could not afford to ignore the groundswell of support for unionization among the 350,000 rank-and-file steelworkers in fifty cities who rallied to the cause by the end of 1919, 90,000 of them from the Chicago district alone. Yet these unions hardly shared Fitzpatrick's and Foster's enthusiasm for industrial unionism. Throughout the campaign's year-and-a-half life, it suffered from the reluctance of craft unions to commit funds and organizers, particularly needed foreign-speaking ones, to the venture, which they feared threatened the traditional structure of craft internationals. By insisting on organizing steelworkers by crafts, moreover, the twenty-four trade unions that participated were disregarding whatever cross-ethnic and cross-racial relationships existed within shops and hopelessly trying to build bonds between "craft" mates in different shops who rarely knew each other.[34]

Although critics at the time and since have denounced the indifference of the Amalgamated Association of Iron, Steel, and Tin Workers and other craft unions, these traditional trade unionists should not shoulder all the blame for the steel drive's disharmony. To begin with, workers' inexperience with national movements and geographical isolation from each other also hurt the organizing campaign. Plant locals in different steel cities weakened the possibility of united action through their insistence on autonomy. Fitzpatrick and Foster recognized from the start that "to have even a ghost of a chance for survival" locals had to "pool their forces and make a joint effort. . . . To suppose that they can stand up individually and combat the gigantic steel corporations

would be childish."[35] Yet Fitzpatrick and Foster were soon frustrated as much by the threats of locals to act on their own as by the dawdling of the craft unions. Even when National Committee members knew that calling a strike vote was premature, they endorsed it to appease locals like the Johnstown Workers' Council, who wired: "Unless the National Committee authorizes a national strike vote to be taken this week we will be compelled to go on strike here alone."[36] "Spasmodic strikes," the Committee knew, could easily ruin the movement.[37]

The drive to organize nationally in steel was made all the more precarious because steel employers, who were experienced in coordinating efforts at the national level, exploited every opportunity to disrupt what they recognized was a fragile national campaign. When the committee at first limited its organizing to the Chicago area, steel companies proceeded to give workers elsewhere wage increases and the "basic" eight-hour day, still twelve hours work but at overtime rates after eight hours.[38] During the strike, employers in Chicago played on workers' ignorance and distrust of other steel production centers by spreading rumors like "they are going back to work in Pittsburgh" while Pittsburgh managers said the opposite.[39]

The deepest fissures in worker ranks from which the steel trust benefited, however, followed ethnic and racial lines. Immigrant workers – Poles, Lithuanians, Serbs, and others who labored long hours at the least skilled jobs for the lowest wages – were the bulwark of the battle in steel. Facing wage and job reductions at the war's end and frustrated by the ethnic barriers to job advancement, these workers were ripe for organization and swarmed into the new unions.[40] Politicized within their immigrant communities – in ethnic neighborhoods, associations, and sometimes even churches – they put the full strength of ethnic solidarity behind the campaign. In South Chicago, for example, striking Polish workers threatened other Poles who continued to work at Wisconsin Steel with expulsion from benefit societies and warned neighborhood ethnic grocers of attacks or boycotts if they continued to sell to scabs.[41] Even employers noticed that immigrants who lived together in ethnic communities were much more likely to strike than men of the same nationality working under the same conditions, whose homes were scattered and thus farther from ethnic peer pressure.[42]

Immigrant workers tried to overcome longstanding ethnic tensions and build alliances across national lines to secure collective bargaining and better working conditions for all, but their task was made harder by steel employers who exacerbated ethnic conflict.[43] A detective hired to fight the steel strike received orders, for example, to "stir up as much bad feeling as you possibly can between the Serbians and the Italians. Spread data among the Serbians that the Italians are going back to work. Call up every question you can in reference to racial hatred between the two nationalities." When the steel companies imported Mexicans as strikebreakers, they introduced another ethnic tension into the immigrant workers' ranks despite the fact that the small number of Mexicans who had been working in the local mills at the strike's inception had struck with their co-workers.[44]

By far the most troublesome barrier separated immigrants from native American workers. After the failure of the strike, both Foster and Fitzpatrick singled out the American-born workers for blame. Whereas natives tended to hold the skilled jobs and often shared the craft unions' antipathy to industrial unionism, that did not fully explain their reluctance to join with less skilled, immigrant workers. Rather, as Foster bluntly explained in his account, *The Great Steel Strike and Its Lessons*, "Everywhere American-born workingmen, unfortunately, are prone to look with some suspicion, if not contempt and hatred, upon foreigners, whom they have been taught to believe are injuring their standard of living." And now, they distrusted foreigners not only as co-workers in the steel mills but also as partners in the organizing campaign. English-speaking workers persistently told organizers, according to the director of the National Committee's Chicago district, "We are afraid of the foreigners, as they are hot heads and will want [an] immediate strike, which may lead to rioting and blood shedding."[45] Native workers, when they struck, were the first to return to work, some finding jobs in different plants to protect themselves against co-worker anger at their scabbing. Employers, of course, took pleasure in fueling the flames of this discord, doing whatever they could to incite the prejudices and fears of native workers. Characterizing the walkout as a "hunky" strike, they circulated handbills warning "Don't let the 'hunkies' rule the mills" and "WAKE UP AMERICANS!! ITALIAN LABORERS . . . have been told by labor agitators that if they would join the union they would get Americans' jobs."[46] Not above engaging in Red Scare tactics, the steel companies accused the striking immigrants of disloyal radicalism. The real issue in this strike, insisted the *Gary Works Circle*, was "Americanism vs. Bolshevism."[47] Already outnumbered in the mill and isolated in their own neighborhoods, such as Cheltenham in

South Chicago, native American workers more often than not were convinced to cast their lot with the boss, to fall back into the production line rather than the picket line.

Racial conflict among steelworkers also served as ammunition in the employer arsenal. Whereas blacks made up 10–12 percent of Chicago's steel force before the strike, they played only a minor role in union activities. Although most of the black workers at U.S. Steel's South Works walked out on September 22, the first day of the strike, they returned at the first opportunity. Partly, this reflected blacks' hostility to organized labor, which had long rebuffed them. But more importantly, their alienation resulted from the widening fissure between blacks and whites in the wake of the race riot and the deep isolation they felt as black workers. Living miles away in the Black Belt, it was not easy for them to attend union meetings, and the union made few special efforts to reach them. In fact, blacks got no assurances from union officials that they would be accepted without discrimination into craft unions, even if the strike succeeded.[48] When the steel companies began to hire blacks as strikebreakers in October, racial animosity intensified, just as employers had hoped. Before the strike was over, thirty to forty thousand blacks entered the mills nationwide as strikebreakers, eight thousand recruited right on State Street in Chicago and sent to the city's plants further south. There they were lucky to avoid strikers keeping a watch on the local Illinois Central Station and on cars that drove by, armed with bricks to pelt any blacks headed for the mills.[49] In Gary, U.S. Steel management paraded black strikebreakers along downtown streets to heighten workers' fears of losing their jobs and then locked them away in mills supplied with cots, meals, and motion pictures to keep the furnace fires burning.[50]

The fragmentation of the work force in steel gradually helped erode the strike. At Wisconsin Steel, as early as the end of October management influence over workers had made possible the reopening of the plant with 70 percent of the labor force back at work. Isolated in their "company town" of South Deering, Wisconsin Steel workers began defying the strike that many Southeast Chicago workers were still battling, intensifying conflict between neighborhoods and weakening the worker solidarity that Fitzpatrick and Foster knew was needed against the steel trust. By the end of November, 75 percent of the workers had returned in Gary, 80 percent in South Chicago, and 85 percent in Indiana Harbor. By December 10, only eighteen thousand out of the original ninety thousand in the Chicago district were still out.[51]

Once the Chicago strike collapsed in December, no one doubted that the struggle would be lost nationwide. On January 8, 1920, the committee officially called an end to the steel strike. Anyone who sought to learn lessons from the failure could see that a successful steel strike in the future would require a work force more capable of coordinating on a national level and more unified ethnically and racially. Without that, workers would remain their own worst enemies, constantly playing into the hands of strikebreaking employers. As defeat loomed, immigrant steelworkers repeatedly told their foreign-speaking union representatives, "We believe in the union and will remain loyal to it. However, you must organize the 'Americans' and negroes in order to make a success of the next strike." Years later, in the mid-1930s, *Fortune Magazine* would look back on the Great Steel Strike of 1919 and conclude that "the provincialism of steel workers" and the ethnic divisions among them helped create "an atmosphere in which undercover men worked more effectively than in any other major strike" to date.[52]

Strikers in Packingtown encountered many of the same problems as their comrades in steel, even though organizers had from the start made deliberate efforts to protect the movement from destroying itself through worker disunity. Nonetheless, despite impressive cohesion in the early stages of the campaign, workers' alliances were so fragile that employers and craft unionists still managed to exploit racial and ethnic conflict for their own benefit. Compared to the clash with the steel trust, the battle against the major packers lasted much longer, from the launching of organization drives in 1917 until the final strike defeat in January 1922, and underwent more complicated permutations, but the net result was much the same. The majority of packing workers, like Chicago's steelworkers, would enter the decade of the twenties disappointed in their effort to build a permanent industrial union and distrustful of the native and black workers whom they felt had betrayed them.

The Chicago Federation of Labor under Fitzpatrick and Foster had joined with leaders of the Amalgamated Meat Cutters and Butcher Workmen (AMCBW) to take advantage of labor's wartime strength and finally bring unionism to the stockyards and packinghouses, where previous efforts had been violently repulsed in 1894 and 1904. This early organizing campaign had succeeded so well that to avoid a strike threatened for late 1917, the president's mediation commission

Plate 5. Divisions between skilled and unskilled workers, natives and immigrants, whites and blacks plagued the campaign to organize the packinghouses during and after World War I. Despite its call for unity, this recruiting banner reflects the need to make special appeals to workers by craft, by language, and by race (Local 651 was reserved for black workers).

intervened and established arbitration machinery under federal Judge Samuel Alschuler that oversaw all labor–management disputes in the industry from March 1918 until September 1921. In the meantime, however, the workers' movement faced mounting problems so that by the time arbitration ended, it was no match for the packers. Much like steel strikers to the south, packing workers struggled, in the end unsuccessfully, to keep racial tensions under control as employers hired more and more blacks, to diffuse competition between locals of unskilled immigrant workers and the native, more skilled core of the Amalgamated, and to sustain rank-and-file support after the movement had been rocked by severe internal dissension. What had started as a glorious crusade to unify the skilled and unskilled, the native and immigrant, the white and black in Chicago's major industry never arrived at the promised land.[53]

Hostility between black and white packing workers most severely divided the work force. But unlike the steel unions, which ignored black workers, packinghouse organizers started off extremely sensitive to the importance of winning black support, having seen their unions destroyed in the past by the use of black strikebreakers. Even after the race riot, enlightened unionists did everything possible to keep harmony in the yards and convince blacks of the benefits organization would bring. But many blacks, particularly those newly arrived from the South in search of good jobs, had little understanding of unionism, and isolated in the Black Belt, they were easily influenced by community leaders arguing that unions were racist or self-serving. Packinghouse managers, moreover, did their best to reinforce black suspicions and to encourage loyalty to the boss by supporting welfare programs at the Urban League, local YMCAs, and black churches.[54] Gambling that paternalism toward black workers would keep reins on competing whites as well, the packing companies involved themselves in the social life of the Black Belt much more than in the white neighborhoods closer by.

Employer efforts coupled with white racism kept black workers away from the union. At the height of the organizing campaign in 1917, no more than a third of the black workers had joined. And by the end of the race riot in July 1919, particularly after the burning of Lithuanians' homes in Back of the Yards, white leaders no longer harbored much hope for racial unity.[55] It came as no surprise that by the time of the final strike in December 1921, only 112 workers remained in black Local 651, and the packers could look to the Black Belt for a steady supply of strikebreakers. An earlier idealism that had once prompted a unity parade marcher to carry a placard reading

> The bosses think that because we are of different color and different nationalities we should fight each other. We're going to fool them and fight for a common cause – a square deal for all

had deteriorated to the point where black strikebreakers were stoned and L trains arriving from the Black Belt attacked.[56]

In packing, as in steel, the split between skilled native, German, and Irish workers and unskilled eastern European immigrant workers also undermined the union cause, although here, too, organizers had sought to anticipate the danger. When the Chicago Federation of Labor created the Stockyards Labor Council (SLC) in July 1917 to coordinate the activities of the trade unions involved in slaughtering and packing, they organized unskilled, non–craft workers in locals according to neighborhood. This strategy was intended to avoid the departmental structure, used in 1904, that had reinforced a hierarchy of skill. Instead, they felt that by isolating immigrant workers in their own locals, they could build on the solidarity of ethnic communities to better discipline and empower the unskilled. One could see the validity of this position since many workers were politicized within neighbors' kitchens, ethnic clubrooms, and corner saloons. But in the end, this strategy backfired and contributed to ethnic tensions. In the case of blacks, the creation of a separate Local 651 in the Black Belt opened up the SLC to charges of Jim Crowism and maintenance of the color line. Among white workers, this arrangement institutionalized nationality divisions. When conflicts broke out within locals or in the SLC, even when they did not have ethnic roots, they were easily interpreted that way.[57]

A devastating schism between the Amalgamated and the SLC in the summer of 1919 widened this ethnic polarization. Although the AMCBW's attack on the SLC grew out of fear of losing control to an industrial union – which, it felt, would only confirm the displacement of skilled workers by the unskilled – the Amalgamated cast the split in xenophobic terms. Officers of the Amalgamated justified their union's actions with statements like Secretary Dennis Lane's that he could "speak but one language – the American language – and [had] no chance whatever to be heard" within the SLC.[58] By 1920, the Amalgamated presided over a much divided, demoralized effort to unionize the stockyards, just in time for the depression of 1920–1. Nonetheless, when the AMCBW finally called a strike late in 1921 against new wage reductions, a surprising number of immigrant workers rallied to the cause, testimony to how deep their antagonism to the packers ran. Here again, however, ethnic divisions sapped the strikers' strength, not only in the form of black and Mexican strikebreakers, but also in the defection of many skilled, native workers bought off by employers' regressive wage cuts, which penalized those with skilled jobs the least. Despite the fighting spirit of the immigrant packinghouse workers from 1917 through 1922, their isolation from blacks and native-born skilled workers, institutionalized in separate union locals and by residential segregation on Chicago's South Side, made a unified labor victory against united packers an impossible achievement at this time.

Workers at International Harvester's McCormick Works experienced

1919 much like steelworkers and meatpackers. The company's lack of paternalistic involvement in its workers' neighborhoods contributed to the ease with which employees organized that summer, but the heterogeneous work force that International Harvester deliberately had assembled to break ethnic and political solidarity succeeded in undermining worker unity. Here, too, managers shrewdly designed tactics to set native and foreign workers against each other and to convince American-born workers that their self-interest lay more with International Harvester management than with fellow workers.[59]

Harvester's approach to "divide and conquer" involved manipulating the Harvester Industrial Plan, a so-called democratic system of plant governance implemented the previous March to stave off unionism, to make it seem as if elected worker representatives had settled the strike on their own. The plan stipulated that only citizens could serve as worker representatives, which resulted in the virtual handpicking of representatives because at least half of the workers in Harvester's Chicago plants were foreign born and most of these were not naturalized. The workers who cooperated with the company's efforts to defeat unionism through employee representation tended to be natives, whereas those who struck in 1919 were primarily foreign born. The native representatives consented to reopen the factories as soon as it was deemed feasible and were given the authority to determine who would be rehired by interrogating, and no doubt intimidating, strikers. International Harvester thereby used the Harvester councils to deepen ethnic divisions within its own work force.

The garment industry proved to be the one place in Chicago where workers succeeded in their unionization drive in 1919, and a close look at that campaign confirms this analysis that fragmentation among workers weakened the union campaigns of the post–World War I era. Although the work force of Chicago's needle trades was more ethnically diverse than in New York, with Italians, Bohemians, and Poles almost as well represented as the Jews who dominated the industry in its major center, Jews still made up much of the leadership and active membership of a union like the Amalgamated Clothing Workers of America (ACWA). Jews may have comprised only 25 percent of the eight-hundred-member Chicago Coat Makers Local of the Amalgamated, for instance, but the active members were overwhelmingly Jewish. A strong Jewish labor consciousness continued to hold sway over an ethnically diverse constituency.

Jewish leaders, moreover, strongly committed to the concept of industrial unionism, would not allow nationality and skill divisions to fuel tensions in workers' ranks. They made deliberate efforts to recruit Poles, Italians, and even those blacks who worked in the trade through publishing weekly papers in numerous languages, employing organizers from these communities and encouraging representatives of different nationalities to serve as union officers. Strategies like these to single out workers of particular ethnicities, however, were carefully monitored never to interfere with the end goal of unity. Sam Levin, a leader of Chicago's Amalgamated, articulated the union's philosophy: "The bosses will try to play one race against another by one time giving preference in work to one nationality and at another time discriminating in favor of another. In this way they keep up a bitter feeling. . . . The Amalgamated tries to discourage separate nationality locals and insists on mixed locals. . . . What is [therefore also] necessary is rudimentary lessons in English, not in any other language since the Amalgamated must coordinate the different races in a harmonious whole." When, for example, employers set up nonunion shops on Chicago's South Side in 1917, the International Ladies' Garment Workers' Union (ILGWU), which shared much of the Amalgamated's perspective, neither fought the five hundred black women as scabs nor isolated them in a Jim Crow local but made every effort to integrate them into the union. Many of these successful garment union strategies, in fact, foreshadowed approaches that the CIO would take in the mid-1930s.[60]

Only for garment workers did 1919 mark a milestone, not a defeat. It signified the consolidation of the ACWA's control over the Chicago market and great progress for the ILGWU. A decade of activism that had begun with a spontaneous strike against sweatshop conditions at Hart, Schaffner and Marx in September 1910 closed on the acceptance of the forty-four-hour week by this same employer in January 1919. In addition to shorter hours, clothing workers now enjoyed higher wages, a preferential union shop, and a system of joint boards to make agreements and review grievances on behalf of all shops and locals. Garment workers succeeded because they avoided ethnic disunity, but their job was made easier, it should be noted, because they did not face national employers like U.S. Steel, Armour, or International Harvester. Although Chicago's clothing bosses were hostile to unionization, their local base meant that a complex, nationwide campaign was not required.[61] And employers' relative small scale made it easier for workers to focus their energies over a decade to build the kind of organization needed to win a major strike in 1919. The overwhelming concentration of garment workers in neighborhoods on Chicago's West and Northwest Sides, too, made residential isolation less the problem it proved in unifying steel, packing, and McCormick workers. The absence of similar conditions in other industries – of an ethnic union leadership that was politically progressive and able to unify workers of diverse ethnicity, race, and skill; of locally based employers; and of a residentially concentrated work force – made unionization elsewhere impossible in 1919, or at least premature.

The absence of a union struggle at Hawthorne Works of Western Electric suggests, however, that the hegemony of one group within a plant's work force did not alone ensure success or even the presence of a workers' movement. Here, there was no Czech labor tradition to match the Jewish one, and a more conservative tendency was accentuated by the new or aspiring homeowners who moved to Cicero. Most important, the company had kept a firm, paternal hand on neighboring communities. The isolation of Cicero and Berwyn only intensified the impact of a paternalistic employer like Western Electric and reduced the possibility that events elsewhere in Chicago during the stormy postwar period would be felt here. Despite the Chicago Federation of Labor's efforts to drum up support for a few employees who had been discharged for trade union activities, most of the mass production workers at Hawthorne Works chose to watch the fireworks of 1919 from afar.[62]

The isolation of Hawthorne workers from the larger struggle of mass production workers in Chicago was not unlike the difficulty more politicized workers had in unifying with other strikers in the city. Even when active in union drives, most workers' politics were deeply rooted in their own communities or industries. This parochialism contributed to the failure of Chicago's Labor Party in April 1919 to put Chicago Federation of Labor's Fitzpatrick in the mayor's office and popular packinghouse organizer John Kikulski at the city treasurer's desk. Federation leaders had founded the Labor Party because they felt the Democrats and Republicans had betrayed the workers to the corporations on the city's streets, in the Illinois state legislature, and in Washington. As the newsletter of the Illinois State Federation of Labor put it, "The workers of America were still waiting for that 'World Democracy' that they helped fight for."[63]

The Labor Party encountered all the obstacles confronted by third parties in a two-party system, especially because it was a new organization. From one perspective, Fitzpatrick's 55,990 votes (8.1 percent of those cast) was not a bad showing, particularly when added to the Socialist and Socialist Labor Party tallies to give the left 12 percent, or 81,557 votes. In several working-class wards, such as those surrounding the packinghouses, Fitzpatrick got 11, 12, 14, and in one case, 16 percent of the vote. On the other hand, one would have expected the Labor Party to have done better. Fitzpatrick's Chicago Federation of Labor alone represented 300,000–400,000 voters, and every day, labor unions were recruiting new supporters from mass production industries. The Labor Party, moreover, advocated just the kinds of things that industrial workers were calling for: the unqualified right to organize and bargain collectively, democratic control of industry, the eight-hour day and forty-four-hour week, and equality of men and women's wages. To ensure that the ticket was not viewed as representing the Irish and German old guard of the labor movement, the Labor Party assembled a slate that was ethnically mixed and distributed campaign materials in Polish, Bohemian, Lithuanian, and Yiddish along with English. The party also made a special effort to reach newly enfranchised, working-class women.

Yet in the end, the Labor Party could not translate the particular job concerns of Chicago's workers into support for a citywide, and later national, Labor Party campaign. Despite support for Fitzpatrick in some parts of the city, no aldermanic candidates were elected, and by the following year, when Fitzpatrick ran for U.S. senator, he captured only 0.5 percent of the vote. Working men and women were politicized within their "local" worlds of race, ethnic group, neighborhood, and job and were not oriented toward broader political alliances or solutions. Although some workers obviously did vote for the Labor Party of Cook County, many more saw little connection between fighting for a steel or packing union and voting new faces into government office. A large number of potential labor voters did not even cast ballots because they either were not citizens or were not registered. Others found it difficult to abandon their longstanding ties to the major parties, which, it will emerge in the next chapter, had a concrete presence in workers' neighborhoods through precinct captains of like ethnicity. Whatever their individual reasons, workers' reluctance to support the Labor Party led one steel worker from South Chicago to despair in 1920 that since "the workers did not have the sense to vote for Fitzpatrick," on top of their failure "to hold together" during the big strike, he saw "no way out." And indeed, it would not be until the 1930s that working-class people in Chicago would again look to electoral politics to achieve a class agenda, and this time their numbers, the party, and the circumstances would be completely different.[64]

Classwide strategies – the unionization of Chicago's major mass production industries and the staging of independent party politics – failed in Chicago during the era of 1919. Despite impressive demonstrations of workers' commitment, the obstacles to success proved too formidable. Without a doubt, employers were repressive. They often, moreover, had the government's power backing them up, granting injunctions against picketing, refusing permits for union marches, threatening alien strikers with deportation, and breaking up demonstrations with police force. But no less important, workers were divided. Fragmented into insular communities, the city's working-class population showed itself incapable of unifying across racial, ethnic, and territorial boundaries.

This is not to say that workers had no larger class consciousness. Some articulated classwide aspirations as they sought a better quality of life, and many recognized the necessity of a broad-based struggle that transcended narrow allegiances. In steel and packing, southern and eastern European immigrants tried to build coalitions with each other across national lines. And when ethnic community leaders denounced union activism, many immigrant workers found themselves rejecting those conservative newspaper editors and clergymen who feared any confrontation with employers. But some barriers, such as between immigrants and natives and blacks and whites, were not easily broken down. And because workers were politicized within their respective isolated worlds, transcending those boundaries was all the more difficult. Cohesive cultural communities both propelled working men and women to pursue ambitious political goals and kept them from the alliances necessary to accomplish them. Ironically, workers who did not see their ethnic and class identities necessarily in conflict in the end suffered from the difficulty of integrating them. The defeats of 1919, so traceable to racial and ethnic conflict, moreover, only served to increase suspicion among Chicago's various social groups and to make the possibility of a classwide political venture that much less likely during the following decade.

Just as cultural identity – as white or black, Irish or Pole, skilled or unskilled, resident of Cicero or Back of the Yards – mattered in how workers waged, and lost, the struggles of 1919, so cultural orientation continued to be pivotal to how people experienced the 1920s. Workers entered this decade in the wake of defeat and in the midst of a frightening economic recession. Dreams of a new unionism and a new politics were dead. But what happened to these workers during the 1920s? The twenties are often characterized as an apolitical era, a retreat from politics into all sorts of cultural experimentation – flappers, Fords, jazz, motion pictures, radio, religious fanaticism, chain stores, and more. This decade is also considered a period of political stagnation in workers' lives, those "lean years" caught between 1919 and the militance of the 1930s.[65] But what is missing in these standard renditions is an appreciation of just how politicized the realm of culture became over the decade. Whereas it is true that electoral politics and the union movement offered little promise and indeed cultural preoccupations dominated, workers were by no means living apolitical lives. Rather, political struggle over workers' loyalty continued, and culture itself became a contested terrain, as ethnic groups, the makers of mass culture, and employers all competed for workers' allegiance. Mass production workers were bombarded by cultural strategies designed to ally them with particular social and implicitly political communities. Ethnic leaders sought to keep them within the ethnic fold. Radio promoters, movie makers, and chain store operators desired consumers with uniform "American" tastes. Industrialists hoped to make them loyal, compliant employees. The choices workers made within this cultural contest of the 1920s reveal their state of mind as they stood on the precipice of the Great Depression and bear directly on their political actions during the 1930s.

2
Ethnicity in the New Era

Plate 6. Despite pressures to patronize more mainstream alternatives during the 1920s, workers continued to support ethnic institutions and organizations like this unit of the Croatian Falcons in South Chicago.

At a banquet celebrating the fifty-fifth anniversary of the Anshe Sholom Congregation in 1925, Rabbi Saul Silber expressed anxieties about the future that were shared by Polish, Czech, and Italian community leaders. On this seemingly joyous occasion, he lamented[1]:

> What will become of our children? Do we want them to grow up pinochle players and poker sharks, or do we want them to grow up men and women who have an understanding of the problems of life, who know the history of their ancestors, who are proud Jews, and who will be a credit to us? Our children are running away from us.... Let us build houses of worship, social centers and Hebrew schools, and let us provide the means for the coming generation to learn and to know.

During the 1920s, newspapers of the "new immigrant" groups, those who had emigrated from eastern and southern Europe in the decades between 1880 and World War I, were filled with concerns about the falling away of the flock. Czech "Jaroslavs" who became "Jacks," Poles who dropped the "wicz" or the "ski," Jews who intermarried, immigrants who packed away the once treasured handicrafts of the old country, all worried ethnic leaders. The move away from European customs, they feared, signified a decline in ethnic identity of consequence to their communities as well as themselves personally. For those who played leadership roles – small businessmen, heads of ethnic organizations, and increasingly, professionals serving ethnic clientages – status as well as economic survival depended on people's continued identification with their ethnicity and patronage of community institutions.[2]

Ethnic communities faced new pressures in the decade after World War I. The Immigration Acts of 1921 and 1924 so limited the numbers of eastern and southern Europeans who could emigrate to the United States that leaders feared ties with homelands would weaken when little new blood arrived to rejuvenate communities. The nativism responsible for the new immigrant quota system had also made many people cautious about public displays of ethnicity. This fear dovetailed with a general retreat from European nationalism. After initial enthusiasm for the new nations of Poland, Czechoslovakia, and Lithuania, it became apparent that their establishment could have an adverse effect on the vitality of American ethnic communities. The struggle for nationhood had long provided the focus for ethnic activity. Now, those who wanted to claim their new European citizenship could return home. When most ethnics realized that they preferred to remain here, new questions about the meaning of nationality arose.[3]

Change at home, in the city of Chicago, threatened ethnic identity as well. Although people still had fellow countrymen and women as neighbors when they moved from old immigrant centers to new neighborhoods, the intensity of the ethnic environment inevitably declined. In addition, during the 1920s, ethnic associational life faced a serious challenge as employers and commercial insurance companies began to offer alternatives to the death and sickness benefits long provided by ethnic mutual aid societies. Even the Catholic Church hierarchy contributed to the crisis by refusing to establish new national (or ethnic) parishes, promoting instead a perspective in which the world was divided between Catholics and non-Catholics, with no place for hyphenated Polish- or Italian-Catholics. Most frightening of all, the explosion of mass culture in the 1920s – chain stores, motion picture theaters, radio, and other forms of commercial recreation – threatened neighborhood shops and ethnically organized leisure such as society outings, sokols, and church affairs. Leaders like Rabbi Silber worried that young people particularly would find commercial culture an enticing alternative to socializing within the ethnic community.

Fear of losing their members to the pull of mainstream America motivated leaders to make deliberate efforts at keeping ethnic Chicagoans tied to national communities. They encouraged people to sustain traditional cultural practices and promoted holidays like Polish Day and Czech Independence Day to stir national pride. They revitalized schools and clubs to instruct the second generation in native language and culture.[4] Ethnic communities sponsored their own athletic teams as an alternative to leagues organized by the YMCA, settlement houses, or city parks. Ethnic teams would not only restrict social contacts, it was thought, but would also reinforce, through teamwork and competition, players' emotional commitment to the group.[5] Leaders even urged ethnic group members to become citizens in order to elect their own representatives to public and party office, as contradictory as that might seem.[6]

As Rabbi Silber's prescriptions indicated, however, leaders put their greatest energy into ensuring the survival of basic ethnic institutions. If put to the right purposes, the stability and prosperity of the 1920s could enhance, rather than undermine, the organizations that formed the bulwark of ethnic community. To this end, leaders made four major efforts. They worked to expand their communities' welfare programs, to put mutual benefit societies on firmer actuarial footing, to encourage ethnic alternatives to thriving mainstream institutions such as banks, and to defend ethnic parishes from archdiocesan attack.

That ethnic leaders tried to keep people invested in their national communities is one thing. How ethnic Chicagoans, particularly the industrial workers who are the subject of this book, responded is quite another. Whether the first- and second-generation southern and eastern Europeans who predominated in mass production work remained invested in the institutions of their ethnic communities as leaders hoped or began to look to alternatives provided by the larger society is a measure of workers' cultural loyalties during the 1920s. A Polish worker who abandoned the insurance of an ethnic mutual benefit society for a group policy offered by his employer or his friend who preferred a commercial bank over a neighborhood building and loan association signaled the kind of straying that ethnic leaders feared. In contrast, the worker who continued to depend on the Bohemian Charitable Association when hardship hit had good reason to value his ethnic affiliation.

Without obscuring important differences among the eastern and southern Europeans who labored in Chicago's factories or minimizing the diversity within each nationality group, common patterns in ethnic experience during the 1920s make it possible to generalize about Poles, Czechs, Lithuanians, Italians, and Jews. Black workers, who made up a growing proportion of the industrial labor force, on the other hand, had such different relationships to their community institutions that I will leave that investigation to the next chapter.[7]

HELPING THE NEEDY

Although the 1920s may have been a prosperous decade for the nation as a whole, few industrial workers escaped economic hardship. Unemployment always seemed to be lurking around the next corner, and family illness, unexpected death, or housing eviction could shatter an already fragile existence.

In an era before unemployment insurance or social security, ethnic groups tried as much as possible to care for their own. There were not many alternatives. Cities, counties, and states gave only minimal assistance during the twenties, whereas private philanthropic agencies often had limited resources, evangelical agendas, and little understanding of foreigners' needs, let alone their language. In some cases, agency discrimination against noncitizens required them to prove that they had taken at least the first steps toward naturalization before they could receive aid.[8] But ethnic populations shied away from outside help for their own reasons as well. In most ethnic cultures, there was a deep distrust of public assistance. "When work was slack many of the native American families had to apply for county 'charity,'" a Jugoslavian immigrant explained, "which was something none of the foreign-born families would even contemplate. In the old country there was no such thing as public relief. They didn't expect it or look for it in America."[9] Often the people of European countries that had state assistance, such as Italy, regarded dependence upon public charity rather than poverty itself as the disgrace. Those who went to the *ricoveri* (poorhouses) surely had no relatives or friends to care for them.[10] Anthony Sorrentino felt this shame as a young boy in Chicago when his family was forced to turn to "charity" after his father died in 1924: "This consisted merely of some staple commodities furnished by the county, some of which we could not use since we were not accustomed to such products, and occasionally clothing and a pair of shoes we detested wearing because of the inescapable 'charity style' they had. After a few months of humiliating experiences with 'charity,' we worked hard and never again had to resort to this form of support."[11]

In America, ethnic communities felt that the group as a whole shared the stigma that in Europe only the destitute individual had to bear. A visitor to a Polish neighborhood in South Chicago noted that Poles there viewed dependence on charity not only as their own failure but also as a poor reflection on all Poles.[12] To spare themselves the shame of watching their compatriots appeal to American institutions, ethnic groups found their own solutions. Many ethnic leaders would have agreed with the *Sunday Jewish Courier* when it asserted, "We are good citizens and good Jews, and, therefore, we do not burden the community with our helpless; we maintain charity institutions of our own."[13]

Although ethnic Chicagoans preferred appealing to the charities of their own communities over others, before turning to any institution they sought to exhaust the informal help available from relatives, friends, and neighbors. Aged parents could expect assistance from their children, and other relatives in need could usually appeal to family members who were better off. People could also count on aid from the neighborhood. In addition to odds-and-ends from the butcher, day-old bread from the baker, a free haircut from the local barber, the needy received donations of food and money from neighbors. For Italians in Chicago, collecting money door-to-door for someone in trouble became a ritual adapted from the Old World custom of *la pietà*, meaning charitable acts. Such donations were much like a gift: The giver derived satisfaction from aiding the recipient, who in turn did not feel indebted. Those who received today would give tomorrow.[14] Jews also were expected to assist their own, but they believed the giver should be anonymous. According to Mollie Linker, when women on the West Side saw a woman in the butcher shop or the grocery buying sparingly, they typically "would go to a few neighbors, collect money and bring food, and put it under the door and walk away."[15] Poles usually alerted their parish priest or church societies to neighbors in need.[16] In their own distinctive ways, people tried to watch out for their own.

Informal assistance, however, did not suffice. To meet the need, before World War I most ethnic groups began to create their own welfare institutions that, though modeled after American charities, respected traditional ethnic values. As late as 1925, a University of Chicago student observed members of a Slovak Church on the Northwest Side struggling to develop their own approach. Since charity work traditionally had little meaning within the Slovak culture, the pastor knew it would be hopeless to raise the issue directly. Instead, "he took a woman member into his confidence. . . . This woman soon spread the idea among other women. A few Sundays later the pastor announced in the church that a Social Workers Club was being formed."[17] An American environment had inspired the establishment of this Slovak Church charity, but Slovak culture determined the shape it took. Most ethnic groups had learned to take responsibility for their community's welfare before the 1920s. As early as 1910 prominent Bohemians in Chicago had founded the Bohemian Charitable Association.[18] Jewish Chicagoans took the welfare burden into their own hands even sooner. Although Jews had had some experience with organized charity in Europe, they made it flourish in Chicago, and elsewhere in America, more extensively than did any other ethnic group.[19]

The success Jews had in building their own agencies stemmed in part from a division within the American Jewish community. German Jews first established welfare agencies in Chicago during the nineteenth century, mainly to cope with the influx of Jewish immigrants from eastern Europe. Although ashamed of their "poor relations," German Jews wanted no Jew to become a public burden. Their charitable institutions

Plate 7. When they became poor, sick, or elderly, ethnic Chicagoans had few places to turn for help other than their community institutions, such as the Bohemian Charitable Association, the Polish Welfare Association, and the Jewish Home for the Aged pictured here sponsoring a banquet for residents.

soon bred others. The more Orthodox, eastern European Jews who were forced to apply to German–Jewish agencies resented their lax religious practices and their "scientific" approach to dispensing charity – the mandatory documents, inquests, and endless "snooping." In reaction, eastern European Jews started to build a charitable system of their own, more respectful of Orthodox religious values and dietary laws. By 1920, the Chicago Jewish community boasted a network of Jewish social services so extensive that some Orthodox Jews expressed dismay at how America had altered the way Jews helped each other. In an editorial, "Too Much Charity – Too Little Tzdokoh," the *Sunday Jewish Courier* chastised Chicago's Jews for having learned in America to give "charity": "Tzdokoh means to give anonymously; charity is a matter of publicity.... One can live in a large Jewish community in Europe for twenty years, and not hear a word about charity and institutions, but one can live no more than three days in a Jewish community in America without hearing a great to-do about charitable affairs, drives, institutions, etc."[20]

Despite such lingering misgivings about the institutionalization of charity in America, by 1920 ethnic agencies offered their clients cemeteries, hospitals, dispensaries, orphanages, day nurseries, old people's homes, employment services, and some relief benefits.[21] America had clearly taught ethnic communities to support charitable institutions as patrons as well as clients. Leila Houghteling's 1925 study of unskilled workers' budgets found few families who had not scraped together money to give to charity and proudly reported it to the investigator.[22]

After World War I, ethnic communities consolidated their assorted welfare services into larger, more centralized institutions. The fund drives that most immigrant groups ran during the war to support new homelands or to aid refugees had revealed enormous financial resources to be tapped. At the same time, the dislocations of war and the depression that followed put tremendous pressures on private charities in the city to take care of their own. The Harding administration insisted that local business and private social agencies, not public authorities, find remedies to the postwar depression, and Chicago complied, establishing a joint industry–charity Unemployment Conference Board.[23] To cope with growing demands, streamline services, maximize available wealth within their own communities, and present a united front for larger civic fund-raising, Jews and Catholics centralized welfare institutions under two umbrella organizations. The Jewish Charities of Chicago, with its twenty-six affiliated agencies, resulted from the merger of the Orthodox, eastern European Federation of Jewish Charities and the Reform, German–Jewish, Associated Jewish Charities. Likewise, the new head of Chicago's archdiocese, Archbishop Mundelein, organized the Associated Catholic Charities and its relief arm, the Central Charity Bureau, to centralize fund-raising as well as improve programs. Mundelein set out to apply modern business methods to "an efficient system" of Catholic welfare that coordinated the efforts of more than 25 institutions, 700 priests, 125 St. Vincent de Paul conferences, and thousands of volunteer laymen and women. Providing better for their people, both Jews and Catholics hoped, would keep them not only off the streets but also out of the hands of the county, the United Charities, and extremist "Bolshevik" groups.[24]

The consolidation of Jewish and Catholic social services sustained people's dependence on private, still often ethnic welfare by making these institutions financially more secure. Rarely did existing ethnic agencies disappear with the mergers. Orthodox Jews, for example, negotiated carefully to ensure that the newly created Jewish Charities would continue to fund Orthodox schools – Talmud Torahs and theological seminaries – and institutions like Mt. Sinai Hospital that respected dietary and other Orthodox traditions.[25] Similarly, under the Associated Catholic Charities, ethnic-affiliated institutions like the Polish Manual Training School and the Bohemians' Lisle Manual Training School survived. In fact, during the 1921 fund-raising campaign, the Chicago archdiocesan newspaper, *The New World*, published a weekly feature on the charity institutions of each ethnic group. The efforts of national parishes to care for their needy likewise were aided by the availability of funds from the Central Charity Bureau.[26]

Nevertheless, unified fund-raising campaigns and larger charity agencies established by the umbrella organizations planted the seeds of a broader sectarian identity beyond narrowly construed ethnicity. When the new Jewish Charities launched its drive for $4 million in 1925 under the slogan "Are You a Jew?" it hoped to encourage a common "Jewish" identity in place of the hyphenated ethnic Jews of the earlier era.[27] The confederation of welfare among Catholics similarly made people dependent on a larger community than the parish or ethnic group. Money for all affiliated charities was solicited once a year throughout the Chicago Archdiocese, and when in need, a person often turned to church-funded assistance. Catholics as well as Jews in the 1920s increasingly recognized that religious affiliation offered material, not just spiritual, salvation.

Neither ethnic nor the larger religious welfare networks could take care of all who needed help. When ethnic Chicagoans exhausted, or for some reason sought to avoid, the informal aid of family and neighbors as well as their own group's institutions, they had two major resources: the private, nonsectarian United Charities and the county. Official totals of charity cases in Chicago in 1928, for example, revealed that private agencies of all kinds handled almost three-quarters of them, with the United Charities alone handling more than one-quarter. But these numbers are extremely misleading. Only strict relief cases under the care of the Jewish Social Service Bureau and the Central Charity Bureau made their way into Jewish and Catholic case load totals, excluding the larger number of people helped through smaller programs such as parish-level societies.[28] More people than the official figures recorded looked to private ethnic or religious organizations rather than the United Charities. Furthermore, a close look at who received help from the United Charities between 1924 and 1926 indicates that at least half of the cases involved American-born families. Poles, Italians, and Czechs were underrepresented, for although they received a proportion of aid roughly comparable to their presence in the city's population, they made up a much larger portion of Chicago's poor. More revealing still are the very small numbers of people actually helped by the United Charities. For example, in the year 1924–5, of 4,202 people receiving assistance, 721 were Poles, 486 were Italians, and 110 were Czechs. Jews were buried in various nationality categories, but officials of the United Charities noted that the Jewish Charities coped with almost all of their needy.[29]

The county did not offer much of an alternative. For most people, relief offered by Cook County was at best a supplement to the assistance of private agencies. Most of those under the care of the Bureau of Public Welfare received only the meagerest of benefits: monthly grocery, milk and coal rations, and shoes for each member of the family. A much smaller number of people, 1500 in 1925, received more substantial support: the Mothers' Pensions, designed to assist women who were the sole support of children because they were widowed, deserted, or married to incapacitated spouses. Although more than twice as many people in Chicago appealed to the county as to the United Charities in 1925–6, the proportion of Polish, Italian, and Czech cases within that larger group was substantially smaller than among those helped by the United Charities, suggesting that here, too, native-born Americans made the most claims.[30] In short, foreign-born Chicagoans received little substantial help during the 1920s from welfare agencies outside their own communities.

Ethnic Chicagoans made greatest use of public welfare for securing medical treatment, which because of the cost and expertise involved was not easily provided by ethnic welfare services. About a third of the workers in Houghteling's budget study, for example, had sought help from some kind of public medical agency before or during 1924. These families, however, applied more often to clinics, dispensaries, the Infant Welfare Society, visiting nurses, and county doctors than to hospitals.[31] The preferred medical service operated on a neighborhood basis. Small in scale and frequently staffed by foreign speakers, it seemed less like a public institution. Even when seriously ill, ethnic Chicagoans avoided public hospitals. Transportation and language difficulties, preference for their own ethnic and religious hospitals, and general distrust of large public institutions kept them away. Eighty-five percent of the patients admitted to Cook County Hospital in 1925–6 were American, with Poles and Italians each making up only about 1 percent of users.[32] Even when faced with serious illness, ethnic Chicagoans sought alternatives to large-scale public welfare.

When people did seek welfare assistance outside of the usual neighborhood and ethnic channels, they often secured it with the help of the local precinct captain, who lived in the community and usually shared the same ethnic affiliation. The one-party machine politics long associated with Chicago did not take mature shape until the late 1920s and early 1930s under Czech Democratic Party leader Anton Cermak. During the 1920s, before the Democrats had firmly established the political base of their machine, Democrats and Republicans, including warring factions within both parties, contested for the loyalty of the city's ethnic population. Precincts fluctuated in loyalty to the point that it was not uncommon for a precinct captain to switch parties, bringing along his or her constituents to serve a different ward boss. Although some ethnic leaders at the time complained that weak ethnic party organizations deprived their groups of a fair share of political jobs and offices, on the local level at least the parties had to work hard to secure votes. Within this competitive system, the precinct captain provided the crucial link between the parties and the people. What the precinct captain delivered to voters 364 days of the year took on tremendous importance on election day, and offering people help in difficult times became a favorite way of ensuring political loyalty.[33]

Precinct captains played two welfare roles: They gave material and financial assistance directly and they served as liaisons to social service agencies. Half the precinct captains interviewed in 1928 reported providing food, coal, rent, clothing, and Christmas baskets to local families, with most of those furnishing this aid residing in poor and working-class neighborhoods. Yet precinct captains did more than deliver the occasional gift or favor. They mediated between agencies like the United Charities and the Cook County Bureau of Public Welfare and needy would-be clients, who were often intimidated by these organizations.[34] Branch office records of the United Charities tell the story of how precinct captains intervened, sending letters, escorting clients, even disguising themselves as the applicant's friend, to the point where social workers complained that they were using welfare agencies to further their own political ends by taking credit for the services rendered. Precinct captains' insider knowledge of the public relief system similarly allowed them to help widows apply for pensions, guide the sick to free medical facilities, and reduce the rigamarole and perhaps a little of the humiliation in applying for county aid.[35] Although the ethnic community did not provide the actual services, in the person of the precinct captain it still delivered relief to the needy.

Ethnic welfare survived the twenties, continuing to help industrial workers cope with the unpredictable tides of misfortune. Ethnic communities by no means satisfied every need, but they provided more assistance than other institutions, public or private, which were only viewed as a last resort. Few protested this arrangement. State and private social service workers wanted nothing better than for ethnic and religious groups to care for their own. They put energy into introducing higher professional standards to ethnic agencies rather than into creating alternatives. Ethnic Chicagoans, still harboring the fears of dependency that they had learned in Europe and that were reinforced in America, preferred to find their own solutions. By turning to familiar sources of support in the community, ethnic group members put little pressure on philanthropies and the government to provide greater services. During the 1920s, little conflict surfaced in Chicago over who should minister to the needy. For working-class ethnic people, ties to other Poles, Czechs, Italians, or Jews still served as lifelines to solace and safety in moments of crisis.

MUTUAL BENEFIT

Mutual benefit societies played an even more basic role in ethnic culture than social welfare agencies. Not waiting to turn to fellow countrymen at the point of desperation, ethnic Chicagoans early on had developed an extensive system of insurance within their communities through mutual benefit societies and fraternal organizations. Social and cultural changes underway during the 1920s, however, threatened this ethnic mutual insurance more than they did welfare by creating viable alternatives to ethnic solutions. Although there was no profit to be made from ministering welfare to suffering people, the same was not true of insurance. Commercial insurance companies launched massive campaigns to sell what they called "industrial insurance policies," with urban, ethnic workers representing their largest potential market. At the same time, the new welfare capitalist schemes of industrial employers, aimed at winning workers' loyalty and goodwill, offered increasing numbers of employees group insurance plans. Ethnic workers suddenly had choices in the twenties about how to handle their families' security. Because mutual assistance had long provided an institutional base for ethnicity, threats to its survival endangered the viability of ethnic communities.

Mutual benefit societies had long held a central place in American ethnic life. They formalized the help immigrants gave their countrymen in times of need and provided a link to the Old World while helping people adjust to the New. Some southern and eastern European immigrants had belonged to similar kinds of societies in Europe. More joined soon after arriving in America beginning in the 1880s and 1890s to ensure themselves a proper funeral in an alien land. Bohemians, Poles, Jews, and Italians, as well as other groups, joined with people from their home villages or regions, promising to contribute at a member's death toward burial costs and to send a delegation to the funeral.[36] An Italian woman, Nina Dal Cason, remembered the disgrace of people who had no insurance and thus were unable to hold a respectable burial for a loved one. To avoid a similar embarrassment, Lillian Cwik's Polish mother constantly reminded her daughter, "Work, work and earn for your grave."[37] Many benefit societies also provided money to help the deceased's family adjust to the loss of its breadwinner. In time, some societies added sickness benefits, a weekly allowance granted when a member encountered prolonged illness or serious injury, to compensate for loss in income. Assuring income during sickness was a realistic concern for immigrant men engaged in hazardous work. Along with these financial benefits, societies provided members with opportunities for sociability ranging from daily companionship in a lodge hall to special occasions such as picnics, dances, and feast days.

Mutual benefit societies continued to flourish well into the twentieth century. When the Illinois Health Insurance Commission investigated the insurance provisions of families living in working-class districts of Chicago during 1918, they were surprised to discover that four out of five families had protected one or more members with some form of life insurance or funeral benefit. Three-quarters of the male heads were insured, a majority with mutual benefit societies or lodges of larger, but still cooperative and sectarian, fraternal orders (Table 5). In fact, wage

Table 5. *Life insurance held by Chicago workers by nativity or race of family head, 1918*

Nativity or race of family head	Total number of families	Percentage with life insurance	Average amount of policy
All families	3,048	81.9	$419.24
United States, black	274	93.8	201.48
Bohemian	243	88.9	577.58
Polish	522	88.5	353.48
Irish	129	88.4	510.72
United States, white	644	85.2	535.56
German	240	85.0	416.49
Lithuanian	117	79.5	170.38
Scandinavian	232	75.4	401.58
Jewish	218	63.8	465.09
Italian	204	57.8	403.94
Other	225	75.1	410.96

Source: "Study of Representative Residental Blocks of Chicago's Wage-Earning, Population," *Report of the Health Insurance Commission of the State of Illinois* (Springfield: State of Illinois, 1919), p. 223.

earners and their families made up a majority of the total Illinois membership in fraternals. Among the immigrant groups involved in industrial work, Bohemians and Poles far surpassed the average of 82 percent, with 89 percent of their families holding life insurance; Jews and Italians, with 64 and 58 percent, respectively, held less than the average, although still a substantial number, of policies. This pattern persisted when the average amounts of death benefits for each ethnic group were compared, except that the Poles, among whom insurance was so prevalent, held only small policies and hence showed the lowest average amount of the four groups. Within an ethnic group, individuals' insurance holdings depended on their economic prosperity. The largest number of families without insurance and the smallest policies were found among those with the lowest incomes and, unfortunately, the greatest need.[38]

The commission recognized that despite its popularity, workers' insurance had limitations even for better-off workers. All policies were small, averaging $419, and in most cases were limited to death benefits. Only about a quarter of the workers had sickness and disability coverage, which left them vulnerable to unexpected expenses and loss of income. Women and children, the commission discovered, were insured less commonly than men and for lower amounts. Women nonetheless played a central role in protecting their families. Investigators remarked at how accurately housewives, their most frequent informants, reported insurance information and concluded that not only did women generally take responsibility for making payments but also they put great value on their families' investment. Although a financial burden, fraternal insurance remained highly prized.[39]

During the 1920s, mutual assistance changed in several ways of significance for the issue of ethnic identity. In 1919 the Illinois Health Insurance Commission stressed that foreign benefit societies and many fraternals, despite their popularity among workers, were actuarially unsound and regretted that Illinois was not among the thirty-eight states that had made efforts since 1910 to monitor such organizations. Most benefit societies had moved long before from passing the hat at a member's death to requiring regular monthly payments, and some had even instituted graduated assessments according to age. Still, too many avoided the reserve funds and mortality tables that insured the life of a society along with its members. Mutual benefit societies felt that their uniqueness as self-help organizations, after all, lay in their low rates, equitable assessments, and refusal to accumulate profits or encumber administrative expenses. "Keep your reserve in your pocket" became their motto. Without much financial backbone, however, mutual aid societies collapsed when burdened with an aging membership or too many claims. While the commission was drafting its report, the influenza epidemic of 1918–19, leading to an unprecedented number of deaths, proved the ruin of many small societies and validated the commission's concerns. As a result, many societies, particularly the large fraternal ones, became persuaded that they had to put themselves on sounder footing. They also realized that greater reliability would help them resist the growing threat of "industrial insurance," policies commercial companies had designed specifically for working-class families who paid small amounts weekly to salesmen collecting door-to-door.

By the time legislation mandating graduated assessments, reserve funds, and state audits was enacted in Illinois in 1927, the hundreds of societies and fraternals to which Chicago workers belonged had suffered years of institutional upheaval.[40] Increasingly during the 1920s, small societies with narrow European orientations and purely local constituencies stabilized themselves by merging with other related societies or joining large fraternals organized around national populations – Poles, Czechs, Italians, Jews – rather than particular villages or regions.[41] Whereas many people's involvement with their European homelands may have declined in the 1920s, the spirit of unity that had grown out of the nationhood struggle during World War I helped save these ethnic institutions. Members could imagine cooperating with countrymen and women in ways that they never would have before. As workers shifted their dependency to organizations representing national European communities, they began to participate in more nationwide American ones as well. When a local benefit society became a lodge in a nationwide fraternal, it subtly drew its members out of provincial and neighborhood isolation while still keeping them within the ethnic fold.

Although the European ethnic groups of concern here made this shift at different points, by the late 1920s the trend toward amalgamating community-level benefit societies touched them all. The Poles, with their history of intense but frustrated nationalism, led the move toward centralized fraternal organizations, establishing in Chicago two competing national-level associations by the end of the nineteenth century, the Polish Roman Catholic Union and the Polish National Alliance. Concerned with unifying immigrants as Polish Catholic "religionists" or as Polish "nationalists," both organizations at first embraced insurance half-heartedly as "a necessary cement with which to sustain the unity and coherence of the first thousands, and then tens of thousands of the members and groups of these organizations."[42] But when the achievement of an independent Poland left them floundering after the war, these associations found in the insurance business a new focus and way of retaining members. Without abandoning Polish aid and cultural programs, they intensified their attention to insurance. Other smaller Polish organizations – the Polish Women's Alliance, the Polish National Union, the Polish Alma Mater, the Polish Falcons of America – quickly followed suit.[43]

Even for ethnic groups more riven with conflict in the 1920s than the Poles, who had done much to overcome "nationalist" and "religionist" tensions, the move toward consolidation drew people into more national ethnic communities. Bohemians, for example, who had the oldest and most extensive benefit societies in Chicago, eventually had to choose between two major national affiliations demarcating rival camps in the American Czech community. Over time, the multitude of small, independent benefit societies became linked with either Catholic or free-thinking fraternal orders, bringing local communities into greater contact with like-minded Czechs throughout the country.[44] Jews, too, expressed political and cultural preferences in the process of consolidating. Soon after eastern European Jews arrived in America in the late nineteenth century, they founded *landsmanshaftn* according to their towns of origin, first to provide for synagogues and then for mutual aid and cemetery rights. When they began to affiliate with larger federations, some chose broader cultural identities as Polish, Galician, or Rumanian Jews; others created branches in political fraternals like the Socialist Workman's Circle or the labor Zionist Jewish National Workers Alliance; and still others preferred Jewish versions of traditional fraternal orders like the Independent Order Brith Abraham or the Progressive Order of the West.[45]

Italians in Chicago were latecomers to nationalism, but by the mid-twenties, after years of being treated in America as "Italians" and more recently having been inspired by the nationalist appeal of Benito Mussolini, they too began to consolidate small benefit societies into national ones. Soon after immigrants from Italy settled in Chicago neighborhoods alongside their *paesani*, they had organized mutual benefit societies in the spirit of *campanilismo*, or loyalty to their native villages. Beyond the death and sickness benefits, funeral arrangements, and services of an Italian-speaking society doctor that they offered, these societies served as the social center of men's lives, a substitute for the village piazza back in Italy. Members met to talk politics, play bocce, and sponsor an annual celebration in honor of their village's patron saint. In 1919 there were at least 110 such societies in Chicago. But during the 1920s and particularly with Illinois's requirement that societies either disband or incorporate under the new mutual benefit laws, most joined well-established fraternal organizations such as the Unione Veneziana, founded in 1923, the Grand Lodge of the State of Illinois–Order Sons of Italy in America, which appeared in Chicago in 1924, and the Italo–American National Union, originally the Unione Siciliana but renamed in 1925 to broaden its appeal, for "closer unity among those of our race into one homogeneous group, which would be a credit to ourselves, to America, and to Italy." By 1928, the Italo–

Plate 8. Workers of all ethnicities continued to belong to mutual benefit societies and fraternal associations during the 1920s, despite the greater availability of insurance through employers and commercial companies. A family like the Contursis considered it most respectable to entrust the burial of a loved one to an Italian society and cemetery and hence supported the consolidation of small societies into larger, more viable ones over the decade.

American National Union alone had taken under its wing more than twenty-seven smaller mutual aid societies in Chicago.[46]

Ethnic mutual aid associations designed other strategies beyond the amalgamation of small societies during the 1920s to fend off competition. Industrial insurance was not the only threat. Fraternals also feared the new group insurance being offered by Chicago's industrialists who prided themselves on being in the vanguard of welfare capitalism. As we will see in Chapter 4, International Harvester, U.S. Steel, Swift & Company, Armour, and Western Electric all offered employee benefits, including group insurance, to their workers. Fraternal organizations argued that getting insurance at work would lull workers into a false sense of security. Having canceled or failed to take out other insurance, workers would find themselves bereft of coverage when they quit a job or were discharged.[47] To distinguish themselves from these competitors, ethnic benefit associations began to promote their insurance as more dependable than any other sort. As the Polish Roman Catholic Union put it,[48]

> Above all things, we must remember that when it comes to the safeguarding of one's family, we should not seek it among "strange gods." . . . Has anyone heard of any other corporation besides the Polish offering assistance against strikes and other common mishaps? Never! Do these insurance companies offer aid to talented students who cannot afford to finance their career? Not at all. Do they try to see that we gain more influence in Chicago? Not in the least. When one does not meet the payment on the installment date, one is suspended.

Competition from employers inspired societies to broaden their appeal to family members who had previously not shared equal benefits under fraternal insurance and whom they knew would not be covered by employers' group plans. The annals of ethnic insurance organizations during this period are filled with the granting of new privileges to women members. The Jewish Progressive Order of the West acted typically when it decided in 1919 to grant women suffrage and allow them to elect female delegates to the national convention, at which point "women became very jubilant and men gave them a great ovation."[49] Other ethnic groups similarly reported women's increasing participation in fraternalism through separate organizations and auxiliaries or within previously all-male associations.[50] Given women's longstanding concern about insuring their families, ethnic benefit societies clearly sought to keep them vested in the fraternal model.

During the 1920s, children likewise became incorporated into the fraternal benefit system. For a long time people seeking protection on the lives of their children had to turn to industrial insurance companies, where coverage was often expensive, because fraternals could only write adult policies. Finally, in 1916, the National Fraternal Congress, concerned over the gains of commercial companies, drafted the Whole Family Protection Bill to permit fraternals to write juvenile insurance and lobbied for its passage in state legislatures. This bill passed in Illinois in 1917, although the next year the Illinois Health Insurance Commission found that most families insuring children still carried industrial policies. Societies undertook aggressive programs in the 1920s to build juvenile insurance departments, which they hoped would not only assure the survival of fraternal orders now but would also build a constituency for later by inculcating juvenile members with the spirit of fraternalism. The desire to attract members among second-generation immigrants frequently involved associations in heated debates over whether or not to permit English-speaking lodges or to publish parts of society publications in English.[51] Just as ethnic insurance drew diverse cultural and geographical groups into national communities during the twenties, so too it broadened along gender and generational lines those who might participate in them. Traditionally, fraternalism may have represented a patriarchal approach to protecting the family, but the effort made by associations during the 1920s to keep women and children invested in mutuality suggests that they recognized how much the survival of this ethnic institution rested on the continued support of other members of the family.

It is no simple matter to determine how loyal ethnic workers remained to fraternal insurance when faced with the new employer benefit plans and the aggressive salesmanship of commercial insurance companies. For the 1920s there is no source comparable to the studies the Illinois Health Insurance Commission had made a few years earlier. Statistics on the national level showed a decline in the number of fraternal societies after 1925, but this merely reflected mergers. National figures document a small increase in membership annually until 1929 as well as steadiness in the dollar amount of fraternal insurance until that too declined in the late twenties. But although fraternalism remained stable, enormous growth took place on the national level in industrial and group insurance. By the end of the decade, industrial insurance had twice the dollar value of fraternal insurance, with almost ten times as many policies, indicating that the average size of an industrial policy was much smaller. Group insurance matched fraternal insurance in dollar amount by 1928, although it lagged considerably in number of certificates.[52] On the national level, fraternalism stabilized in the 1920s while new business went elsewhere.

The Chicago situation did not necessarily reflect this national picture, particularly among industrial workers. While the Illinois Health Insurance Commission was finding a majority of working-class families holding society or fraternal insurance in 1919, national figures showed industrial insurance as smaller in amount but six times as prevalent. Chicago workers looked to industrial insurance primarily to insure their children. Since Chicago's working-class population, so closely tied to ethnic communities, gave greater support to fraternal insurance than the nation as a whole in 1919, it probably continued to do so through the 1920s.

The best source available on the insurance preferences of Chicago workers is Houghteling's 1925 study of the standard of living of semiskilled and unskilled employees in twelve large firms, including International Harvester and Swift & Company. The workers investigated represented the most privileged of industrial workers: They were all "fully employed" in 1924 and hence qualified for whatever insurance their employers, among the most welfare minded in the city, offered. Although there are inconsistencies in the data, a clear picture emerges of a working population where almost everyone held insurance; only 10 out of 282 International Harvester and Swift employees surveyed, or 3.5 percent, had none. Because International Harvester paid better wages, the workers there were able to buy more insurance than the workers in Swift's packinghouses. But in all other respects the purchasing patterns were similar in the two plants. The same proportion went without insurance. And the rank order in annual expenditures of blacks, Bohemians, Poles, and Italians was identical (Table 6).

Most workers surveyed by Houghteling took advantage of the group insurance offered at work, contributing weekly through wage withholdings, but they also retained other insurance. Whereas only occasionally did investigators indicate whether additional insurance payments went to a commercial company or a lodge, those notations when they do appear – "insurance for funeral expenses with Polish Society $3.04 a month" or "lodge sick benefit, $6.00" – alert us to the complexity of workers' choices. The family of Stanley and Natalie Cieslak, for example, paid $80.40 over the year for insurance. Stanley, employed at the Deering Works of International Harvester, paid $20.80 at work and $18.00 to a Polish Society. Natalie paid $1.20 a month to a Polish Woman's Society and an additional $0.15 a week, probably to an industrial insurance collector. Their two children were each insured for $0.10 a week, whereas an additional $1.20 bought them society insurance as well.[53] A similar persistence of fraternalism emerged in other studies of the period, such as an investigation of fifty working-class families in St. Casimir's parish in South Lawndale where almost all claimed to belong to lodges.[54]

To be sure, workers took advantage of insurance at work when it was available, and they bought industrial policies. As a result, their fraternal associations did not receive a fair share of the growing insur-

Table 6. *Annual expenditures on insurance by unskilled workers at International Harvester and Swift & Company, Chicago, 1925*

Nationality	Number of cases	Percentage of total cases	Percentage with no insurance	Average annual expenditures for policies
A. International Harvester				
Black	27	14.9	0	$119.05
Bohemian	5	2.8	0	87.36
Italian	14	7.7	14.3	27.16
Lithuanian	10	5.5	0	36.82
Polish	80	44.2	3.8	60.75
Other[a]	45	24.9	4.4	81.30
Total	181	100.0	3.9	72.54
B. Swift & Company				
Black	33	32.7	0	81.62
Bohemian	2	2.0	0	69.68
Italian	2	2.0	0	51.39
Lithuanian	8	7.9	12.5	30.07
Polish	36	35.6	2.8	61.45
Other[b]	20	19.8	5.0	59.23
Total	101	100.0	3.0	65.59

[a] Includes native white, Dutch, Irish, Croatian, Slovak, Slovenian, Hungarian, Norwegian, Swedish, Ukranian, German, Hollander, Armenian, Austrian, Russian, Serbian, and Mexican.

[b] Includes native white, Irish, Slovak, Slovenian, Hungarian, Swedish, Hungarian, and Austrian.

Source: Manuscript Schedules, "The Cost of Living Schedules of Unskilled Laborers in Chicago, 1925, by Leila Houghteling," 2 vols., Special Collections, Joseph Regenstein Library, University of Chicago. Data collected for Leila Houghteling, *The Income and Standard of Living of Unskilled Laborers in Chicago* (Chicago: University of Chicago Press, 1927).

ance wealth of the nation. There were indications, too, that younger people had less interest in fraternalism than their parents. Still, fraternal orders were surviving. They continued to provide funeral benefits and sickness pay, supplementing whatever other life insurance workers could afford. Moreover, in an effort to stay viable, mutual insurance societies, like ethnic welfare services, consolidated small-scale units into larger ones, in the process giving people a sense of affiliation with the institutions of a broader ethnic or religious community. Although workers in Chicago were clearly becoming less dependent on the fraternal order as a sole source of insurance, in the 1920s they by no means abandoned their allegiance to ethnic mutual aid. At a very basic level, mutualism helped sustain a family's sense of ethnicity.

BANKING ON THE FUTURE

When ethnic leaders fretted over the falling away of the flock, they recognized that members' economic success could threaten ethnic communities as much if not more than hardship. Prosperity, they feared, would usher people into a more American world. As the twenties brought stability, if not affluence, to many ethnic Chicagoans, pressure mounted to define ethnicity in a way that was compatible with achieving success in America and not as a stage to pass out of along the difficult road to assimilation. With few new immigrants to America, nothing less than the survival of ethnic communities and institutions was at stake. If ethnicity were cast as a vehicle, not an impediment, to prosperity, some ethnic leaders realized, people and financial resources would remain within the ethnic community. The creation of ethnic banking institutions during the 1920s served as the linchpin of this strategy.

Before the war, ethnic workers in Chicago largely were strangers to commercial banks. The little banking that they did took place in locales closely tied to the ethnic community: taverns, private banks, and building and loan associations. Taverns functioned as "miniature currency exchanges," according to one resident of South Chicago who recalled workers filing into their local drinking spots on payday in search of cash as well as libation. An intricate system evolved between the bank, tavern owner, and company around the safe negotiation of check into currency without workers having to enter commercial banks, which were rare in working-class neighborhoods anyway.[55] Ethnic workers who sought safekeeping and a little interest for their savings turned to private banks run by local businessmen. Lithuanians in Back of the Yards, for example, brought their savings tied up in handkerchiefs and stockings to their countryman Joseph Elias, whom they trusted because his father had been a farmer of some influence in Europe.[56] Yiddish novelist I. Raboy satirized Jews' similar preference for their own private over commercial banks. Whenever the protagonist Jacob walked into the big National Bank, "he was filled with fear. He gives them the money, they make a record of it, and Jacob leaves with the feeling that he is making the bank rich, and yet *he* has to thank *them*." In contrast, "Jacob loves to bring a small amount of cash into the Jewish bank. . . . The president of the bank himself stands behind the table, greets him cordially, and smiles."[57]

The comfort private, ethnic banks offered was often momentary, however. Unsupervised by any government agency, they failed at an alarming rate, leaving customers like Salvatore Cosentino penniless. He had saved $200 in a private bank owned by a West Side barber who ran it alongside his travel agency. When the barber–banker–steamship agent declared bankruptcy, Cosentino lost all his money.[58]

Building and loan associations provided a more reliable way for ethnic workers to save before the war. These cooperative organizations, like mutual benefit societies, provided an ethnic alternative to an otherwise commercial service and reinforced community solidarity at the same time. Most people participated in building and loan associations with the goal of saving to buy a home, although that was not a requirement. The Old World land hunger of immigrants translated into the desire for home ownership in America.[59] To finance the purchase, they joined with people from the same towns in Europe or neighborhoods in Chicago and established democratic savings associations that maximized investment by operating with little overhead. Elected officers received minimal salaries, and space in church and community halls or the rear of taverns was rented only for the weekly or monthly meeting. Members deposited as little as $0.25 or as much as several dollars at a time toward a down payment for land or house and then could borrow at low interest to finance the rest. By the end of 1918, 255 building and loan associations flourished in Chicago, a majority of them conducted and patronized by the foreign born. Czechs supported more than any other group with some 40,000 members, and Poles followed close behind.[60]

World War I transformed saving and banking experience for all Americans, most dramatically for ethnic workers. Suddenly, people who had never before owned a bond became investors in one or more of the U.S. government's five Liberty Loans launched between 1917 and 1919.

Many entered commercial banks for the first time to subscribe or redeem their interest coupons. Never before had the government issued bonds in such small denominations and payable in installments. It did so now not only to tap all available resources to finance the war but also to build as much public support for the military effort as possible. The Treasury Department's Liberty Loan compaigns penetrated deep into the communities and workplaces of the nation, encouraging patriotic rivalry among cities, employers, and particularly ethnic groups, who were eager to prove their American loyalty as well as help the United States secure the independence of their homelands. The Loan's Foreign Language Division "reached into almost every nook and cranny inhabited by foreigners," an organizer boasted, where it enlisted the help of national group leaders, pastors, priests, and the presidents of more than forty thousand organizations. The ethnic strategy worked. During the Fourth Liberty Loan drive in September 1918, the peak of the bond campaigns, 46.5 percent of all subscribers were of foreign birth or parentage, although they made up only 33 percent of the American population. This was a remarkable showing given the relatively small economic resources of the ethnic population, a factor that kept the dollar amount of their subscriptions to only 16 percent of the total collected.[61]

Ethnic groups in Chicago threw themselves into the Liberty Loan competition. The Bohemians subscribed the largest amount, but not without mounting extensive campaigns, which included canvassing all their people and demanding bond receipts to make sure subscriptions corresponded to ability to pay. They took pride that even the poorest Czechs had contributed their fair share.[62] Almost as successful was the Polish campaign, centered around the theme "He who buys a bond helps Poland." During the Third Liberty Loan drive, one Polish bank alone received over fifty thousand Polish subscriptions totaling more than $1.5 million.[63] All ethnic groups urged members to display Liberty Bond emblems in their windows, to make an impressive showing in the Liberty Day parades, and most important, to credit their bond purchases to their nationality, not their employer.[64] Given this pressure, it is not surprising that even the poorest of industrial workers participated. A survey of six hundred mothers who were working at unskilled jobs in the packinghouses during the summer of 1918, almost all foreign born, revealed that 84 percent of their families owned Liberty Bonds.[65]

Plate 9. During World War I, workers were under pressure at work and in their ethnic communities to prove their patriotism by subscribing to Liberty Bonds. For steelworkers like those who worked at the Pressed Steel Car Company plant in Hegewisch, it was usually the first time they had owned bonds paying interest, and afterward many became eager to continue their investing by patronizing banks.

Liberty Bonds created a new clientele for banks. Bond holders found they enjoyed participating in a world that previously had belonged only to the rich. Salvatore Cosentino, the man who had lost $200 in a private Italian bank, took tremendous pleasure right after the war when he paid for his wedding suite of furniture with $500 worth of Liberty Bonds rather than in installments, as the salesman expected.[66] Through their bond purchases, people became more comfortable with commercial banks. Beginning in 1918, savings account deposits in working-class neighborhoods increased.[67] Many ethnic Chicagoans also wanted to send money to their families in war-struck countries abroad and looked to the foreign departments of banks to handle it. Before the war, postal savings banks had provided the major alternative to ethnic banking schemes since they offered savings stamps in denominations as small as $0.10. But they paid very low interest and now began to seem less attractive to bond owners who had come to expect 4.25 percent.[68]

While working-class Americans were developing a new interest in banks, banks themselves were recognizing the potential of this new clientele. In a short period of time, it seemed to them, a whole nation had been converted from spenders to savers. Where once 300,000 had held bonds, now more than fifteen million did. As the war ended, banks hoped to redirect the savings power behind war bonds into banking institutions, "to get people who are unaccustomed to banking to come in and get acquainted," as the advertising manager for Chicago's Fort Dearborn Bank put it. Few groups escaped bankers' attention, and the president of the American Bankers' Association recommended trying "to get as close as we can to the foreign element," who had proven themselves so well during Liberty Loan days.[69]

Several other changes during and after the war reinforced the tendency for working-class Chicagoans to patronize banks. More and more employers like International Harvester and Western Electric were switching from cash to check payrolls for accounting and security reasons, just at the time when the enforcement of Prohibition put an end to legal taverns if not to drinking. Workers needed a new place where they were known to negotiate their pay checks. The private banks run by compatriots were also on the way out. To prevent so many banking failures and abuses, in 1917 the Illinois legislature passed a law abolishing private banks and forcing them either to take out state or national charters by January 1921 or to dissolve. And finally, simultaneously with the demise of private bank competition, a revolution of a sort was taking place within the banking community of Chicago. The postwar period witnessed phenomenal growth in outlying banks within Chicago's neighborhoods and expanding suburbs. Where in 1910 there were only thirty-three outlying banks and in 1914 sixty-five, by 1923, 173 of Chicago's total two hundred banks were scattered outside the Loop, most of them small state banks located at the center of neighborhood shopping districts. In cities like New York and Philadelphia branches of downtown banks serviced the new banking markets of the 1920s, but Illinois's prohibition against branch banking encouraged a proliferation of small and not always stable banks that had managed somehow to meet the state's minimal capital requirement. As a result, Chicago could claim more incorporated banking institutions than any other American city, 231 of them by 1928, not counting the 106 spread throughout suburban Cook County. In the postwar period, businessmen in outlying areas were investing feverishly in local banks that they hoped would boost their districts, and workers for the first time were finding commercial banks within easy reach of their homes.[70]

Ethnic businessmen were not about to let this banking opportunity pass them by or allow other bankers to heed the advice of the president of the American Banking Association and woo the foreign born. Building on the Liberty Loan message that the savings habit should be practiced within the ethnic community, they organized their own banks to keep ethnic dollars at home, expanding real estate opportunity and commercial enterprise within ethnic neighborhoods. Typical was the plea "Let Polish savings go into Polish hands and into Polish industry. Let these savings circulate among the Poles and we will all benefit."[71] On somewhat less pecuniary grounds, ethnic businessmen argued that the prestige of their communities was at stake. Banks testified to the thrift of a people, and as the founders of the Italian Schiavone State Bank phrased it, "among our immigrants there are men of high intelligence and education with the ability to compete with the best financiers of this country."[72] With great enthusiasm, ethnic bankers embraced the concept of the outlying bank and helped to promote it as "a decidedly Chicago institution," a network of "civic centers" serving the social and business needs of the city's many communities.[73] Prominent Poles from Milwaukee Avenue as well as South Chicago, Czechs in neighborhoods all the way west to Berwyn, Jews in North Lawndale, Italians on the West Side, all laid claim to the savings of their countrymen and in the process made banks even more a part of the lives of ethnic working-class people.[74]

Ethnic Chicagoans viewed their neighborhood banks as the civic centers promoted by bankers much more than natives did. Traveling south on Milwaukee Avenue, for example, bank buildings demarcated ethnic neighborhoods: first the Jewish State Savings and Commercial Bank at Western Avenue; then the largest Polish bank in Chicago, the Northwestern Trust and Savings; next the Slovak Papanek-Kovac State Bank; and finally the Italian Trust and Savings Bank at Grand Avenue. That the impressive building at the heart of the local shopping district belonged to their ethnic group and furthermore that they banked there inspired pride among community residents. Playing down the commercial side, ethnic Chicagoans gave these banks a place alongside other

Plate 10. Unregulated private banks like Adolph and Max Silver's bank, shown here in 1916 ready to serve its Jewish clientele, were required by an Illinois law passed the following year to take out state or national charters or to dissolve. The result, however, was not a decline in ethnic banking institutions during the twenties but a proliferation of chartered, though not always very stable, commercial banks in ethnic neighborhoods throughout Chicago. Saving at an ethnic bank became a new way to demonstrate one's ethnic loyalty. Identification of the men sitting behind the counter by their first names suggests that the Silver Bank was a family as well as an ethnic operation.

community institutions. Here they could speak their foreign tongue, send money to relatives abroad with ease, and for those groups, like Italians, with few building and loan associations, get help buying a home.[75]

A neighborhood bank knew its customers in the same familiar way as the corner store. When Thomas Perpoli's father died, his mother sent him to the Bank of Napoli a few blocks away to get the $80 his father had saved. A word with the clerk produced the money.[76] Angelo Patti remembered how his grocer father and the other neighborhood businessmen idolized the local Italian banker and gave him all their business.[77] When the state auditor closed the Sixteenth Street Bank in the Jewish Lawndale area because of a capital shortage, the depositors, who were small Jewish businessmen and workers, decided to take the matter into their own hands. Meeting at a local synagogue, they refused to allow the appointment of a receiver for the bank, pledged not to withdraw deposits for a year, and set out to raise $150,000 to enable the bank to function again.[78] Although coming to the aid of a crashed bank was unusual, this emotional investment in community banks was not. Ethnic bankers cultivated community allegiance by creating a favorable image in the neighborhood. Most noticeably, they contributed generously to ethnic welfare agencies, churches, and societies. The Czech Depositor's State Bank in Back of the Yards even went so far as to give money to needy families during the 1921–2 stockyard strike.[79] As a result, foreign communities became so invested in their own banks that they contributed greatly to what experts after the depression would conclude was a "bloated banking system" in the 1920s, where many unstable banks managed to survive.

Building and loan associations, far from suffering from the new ethnic banking competition, flourished during the 1920s with Chicago's boom in home building and the new stress on saving. The number and assets of Czech, Polish, Slovak, and Lithuanian building and loan associations grew, and other groups, such as Serbs, Croats, and Slovenes, established their own associations for the first time.[80] Increasingly, however, building and loans became less like community self-help societies and more commercially aggressive, buying advertisements in foreign-language papers and at times participating in real estate ventures. There were even cases where an ethnic land developer sponsored a building and loan association to help people finance home purchases. Nonetheless, those ethnic workers who managed to buy homes during the 1920s rarely had to leave ethnicity behind in the old neighborhood. Not only did they frequently move near others of their nationality, but also ethnic affiliation usually made the purchase possible thanks either to a building and loan association or a bank.[81] Buying a home – or any large purchase signifying "success," such as a car, for that matter – might have forced people into dependence on mainstream financial institutions and away from indigenous ones. Instead, the ethnic bank or association's help demonstrated the continued efficacy of the ethnic community. As leaders had hoped, ethnicity and economic success proved compatible in the twenties.

But as ethnic communities supported new banking institutions to share more fully in the economic growth of the city and to meet their populations' changing needs, they inevitably became more enmeshed in the commercial world. Unlike fraternalism, which remained an island of mutuality in a swelling sea of commercial insurance, the ethnic banks and building and loan associations of the 1920s moved away from the cooperativism and informality of earlier banking arrangements. In doing so, they introduced their patrons to the complexities of dealing with profit-making corporations. Nonetheless, to earn profits in ethnic communities, these financial institutions had to meet expectations ordinarily reserved for nonprofit services. Ethnic patrons thereby shaped their banks just as these banks influenced them. During the twenties, many workers began to buy homes and use commercial banks, in other words, to participate more centrally in American economic life. For a time at least, the ethnic banking institution and the ethnic banker succeeded in mediating this transition, guiding people into a more complex commercial world while ensuring the viability of the ethnic community in the postwar era.

HOW CATHOLIC A CATHOLIC CHURCH?

Ethnic welfare agencies, benefit societies, and banks all faced competition from nonethnic counterparts in the larger society during the 1920s. But challenges to ethnic institutions did not always come from such alien sources. From a most unexpected corner much closer to home arose one of the most vigorous assaults on Chicago's ethnic institutions. Soon after George Mundelein became archbishop in 1916, the Archdiocese of Chicago declared war on its national parishes.

The Catholic Church set out to centralize and strengthen its Chicago diocese out of many of the same fears that haunted ethnic communities. "At a time when amusements have been largely commercialized, there is danger in frequenting the palaces of pleasure," warned the Chicago archdiocesan newspaper *The New World* in 1922. The paper recommended that to compete with commercial recreation, churches must sponsor alternative social activities that kept people, particularly young ones, in the parish hall rather than on the street, even if it meant going as far as putting pool tables, bowling alleys, and even skating rinks in the church basement.[82] Like ethnic groups, the Catholic Church fought the attractions of "Protestant" settlement houses, YMCA's, and "Bible class" leagues by organizing its own citywide athletic team competitions.[83] Because the church also feared members' dependence on state and so-called nonsectarian welfare programs, it worked to strengthen Catholic social services, establishing the centralized Associated Catholic Charities ("to care for its children from infancy to grave") and developing new programs, among them training Catholic social workers and organizing Holy Name Society "Big Brothers" to save the Catholic juvenile delinquent both from vice and the "typical philanthropic worker – Protestant, Jew or agnostic."[84] No less concerned than Poles or Czechs to prove the loyalty of all Catholics in wartime, the Catholic Church urged Liberty Loan bonds on its parishioners, instructing clergy to promote bonds from the pulpit and even sell subscriptions in church vestibules.[85]

Whereas the church responded much like ethnic groups to these common threats, competition with ethnic communities also motivated its actions. Ethnic parish life, welfare programs, and notoriety within the city threatened Mundelein's vision of a powerful, Americanized Catholic Church in Chicago as much as non-Catholic rivals did. This American-born priest, descended from five generations of German–Americans, came to rule over an archdiocese in 1916 where almost two-thirds of the Catholics prayed in a foreign language – more than half in Polish – at a time when antagonism against foreigners and Catholics was on the rise. By the 1920s, nativists reigned in Congress, not just within extremist organizations like the Ku Klux Klan. The church, Mundelein believed, could best protect itself and its people from suspicion by becoming a force for Americanization: "The people of the United States must be Americans or something else. They cannot serve two masters."[86] Within months of his installation as archbishop, Mundelein abandoned the accommodationist stance of his predecessor Archbishop Quigley and launched a campaign to replace national parishes with territorial ones. To achieve this goal, he set out to prohibit any new national churches, to introduce English into existing ethnic churches (in a national parish, sermons, confessions, and activities took place in the relevant foreign language with only the mass in Latin), to build a new seminary to train all priests who would then be assigned to parishes irrespective of ethnicity, and to standardize and expand the parochial school system as a way of raising a Catholic, not hyphenated Catholic, new generation.[87]

Mundelein's assault on ethnic Catholicism within Chicago was one matter; his success in converting the church, once a bastion of ethnicity, into an Americanizing institution was quite another. Investigation into how the two largest Catholic ethnic groups among Chicago's industrial workers, the Poles and the Italians, responded to the archdiocese's reform efforts reveals whether workers ended the decade of the twenties any less "ethnic" and more "Catholic," as Archbishop Mundelein had hoped.

When the sociologists William Thomas and Florian Znaniecki immortalized the Polish community of Chicago in their massive study, *The Polish Peasant in Europe and America*, published between 1918 and 1920, they located the center of American Polish life in the parish. Assuming an importance it had not known in Europe, the Polish parish performed here as both village and church, the keeper of language and culture along with faith.[88] For the immigrant with memories of Poland, the church represented all that was left behind. A visitor to South Chicago movingly recounted that one day when he was talking to a group of soot-stained steelworkers, the bells of St. Michael's "began to ring the Aniol Panski. It was summertime. The conversation stopped immediately and one of the workers said to me, 'When these bells ring, it seems to me that the air is filled with the odor of fresh hay.'"[89]

For second-generation Poles, the parish defined their Polishness. In parish schools they learned native language and history as well as respect for traditional authority, be it parent, nun, or priest. As the church faced a second and even third generation that had never known Poland, the parochial school took on even greater importance as the guardian of the Polish parish's, and hence community's, future. From childhood through adulthood, an immense network of church societies, religious groups, as well as local lodges of Polish fraternal associations like the Polish National Alliance and the Polish Roman Catholic Union bound parishioners together. Daily life was punctuated by these society meetings, church duties, and morning and Sunday mass. Even special occasions bore the mark of the church, whether family christenings, name days, first communions, confirmations, weddings and funerals, or parishwide dances, outings, and bazaars. The Polish church did its best to manage all aspects of Polish life from baptism to last rites.

Although Mundelein's Americanization program threatened Polish ethnicity at its very heart, it inspired quite the opposite result from what the archbishop had intended. The battle with Mundelein, rather than weakening the Polish church, saved it from languishing once Polish nationhood had been achieved after World War I by introducing a new cause, a new enemy. Mundelein became the latest perpetrator of the

German *ausratten* policy to banish Polish culture. When the archbishop tried to implement his plans, Polish priests and parishioners fought back. Priests protested through church channels, taking their case all the way to Rome with their 1920 petition "I Polacchi Negli Stati Uniti Dell'American Del Nord." Lay Poles complained bitterly that "the Cardinal is not fair to the Polish people," "he is the greatest enemy of the Polish spirit." Even young ones chimed in with comments like "My dad you just ought to hear him hate the bishop!"[90]

Poles resisted Mundelein's efforts to centralize the archdiocese whenever they had an opportunity. The Reverend John Lange of St. Michael's parish near the steel mills in South Chicago, for example, reported that despite his great efforts, the 1919 fund drive for the Associated Catholic Charities proved unsuccessful "on account of the campaign launched against the Most Rev. Archbishop regarding his supposed opposition with respect to our Polish school."[91] Despite Mundelein's recurrent requests that all parishes establish Holy Name Societies as part of a diocesanwide network, Polish churches resisted, often not founding them until the late 1930s and 1940s. Again at St. Michael's, Reverend Lange struggled to carry out the archbishop's wishes but had to report poorly attended meetings, including a "smoker" that attracted more Irish Holy Name Society boosters and managers from the South Works of U.S. Steel than local Poles.[92] The most dangerous weapon in the Polish arsenal, however, was the threat to abandon the Roman Catholic Church altogether and join the schismatic Polish National Catholic Church. The creation of several new Polish National Catholic parishes in Chicago during the 1920s only sharpened that threat.[93]

The Polish defense against Mundelein's Americanization program succeeded both in neutralizing his assault and intensifying ethnic loyalty among Poles. After much agitation, Poles won four new national parishes during the 1920s and seven others that were officially territorial but Polish in actuality. Polish pressure also forced Mundelein to retreat on the parochial school curriculum issue and allow up to half a day of teaching, primarily catechism and Polish culture, in the Polish language.[94] The archbishop's plans to assign Polish priests to non-Polish parishes were also thwarted. But the invigoration of Polish ethnicity through Mundelein's Americanization attempts most powerfully frustrated his ambitions. When Joseph Chalasinski visited Chicago's Polish neighborhoods in the late 1920s, he still found insulated ghettos that seemed to him to differ little from the picture painted by Thomas and Znaniecki a decade earlier. The parish church, school, and priest still dominated the community. All who were not Poles were labeled "Jews," whether Baptist settlement workers, U.S. Steel managers, or public school teachers. Intermarriage, even with other Catholics, was not tolerated by the Polish church.[95]

Although Mundelein might not have acknowledged it, his efforts contributed to the survival of Polonia through the 1920s. To protect national parishes and keep territories Polish, pastors discouraged their people from moving out of neighborhoods.[96] Those who left for new subdivisions lobbied strenuously for additional Polish parishes and schools.[97] So what might have been a gradual dispersion of the Polish population became instead a politicized resistance to Catholic absorption. By 1930, more Poles worshipped in more national parishes than a decade earlier. Polish elementary schools, moreover, grew at a faster rate than territorial ones.[98] During the 1920s, Poles's faithful financial support allowed their churches and schools, particularly new high schools, to expand greatly. The church's vision of Catholic unity had only intensified Poles' commitment to preserving Polish identity.

The Italians who immigrated to Chicago before World War I could not have had a more different attitude toward the American Catholic Church than the Poles. Rather than grounding their ethnic identity in the church as the Poles had, they defined it in opposition. This was in contrast to Italy, where the village church had represented a civic community as well as religious one. Despite common grumblings against the privileges of the church, the aristocratic ties of the priests, and the labor and services expected of the community, Italians in Italy had associated the campanile of the church with the village it graced. As a result, they felt inextricably connected to the church, if not always strictly observant. Imagine, then, Italians' response when they encountered in America an Irish-dominated church, not only alien in language but also prejudiced against Italians for having violated the temporal authority of the Pope during Italian unification in the nineteenth century and for practicing what was considered an idolatrous, saint-oriented folk religion deeply offensive to devotional Irish Catholicism. Faced with worshipping in Irish or German churches or hardly less insulting at the Italian services sometimes permitted in church basements, many Italians in Chicago chose not to attend church at all. In some neighborhoods, particularly the Italian area near the McCormick

Works of International Harvester and in the steel town of Chicago Heights, a socialist anticlericalism reigned. Elsewhere, immigrants remained loyal to their village churches in Italy or carried on their very personal religion without a priest.[99]

By the early twentieth century, the American Catholic hierarchy spoke anxiously of "the Italian Problem," and in Chicago, Archbishop Quigley set out to meet it by establishing six Italian national parishes between 1903 and 1915. Recognizing that Italians were accustomed to a state-supported church where financial support from parishioners was unnecessary, Quigley underwrote the construction and operation of Italian national parishes in the hope of winning these reluctant religionists. Although the presence of national parishes improved the church attendance of Chicago's Italians before the war, problems persisted. A shortage of Italian priests and the Northern origin of these few when parishioners overwhelmingly came from the South kept many immigrants at a distrustful distance. Continued resistance to lending financial support to churches prevented the establishment of more than one Italian parochial school. Furthermore, local village and regional identities among Italians hindered the development of unified parishes. The community and religious integration that Poles achieved through the Polish Catholic Church in Chicago and that Italians had experienced within their villages in Italy eluded Italian settlers in Chicago.[100]

The way Italian immigrants adapted their Old World feasts in honor of village patron saints to New World urban neighborhoods revealed how extensively they were redefining the relationship between community and church. In Italy, the annual celebration of a town's special saint symbolized the union of commune and church. A solemn procession led by the local priest wound its way through the steep streets of a hilltop settlement, bringing the saint's statue out of the church and into people's everyday world. As villagers paraded behind the saint and joined in the celebrations afterward, they not only sought penance or favor, but also declared loyalty to this unified religious and secular community.[101]

Soon after Italian immigrants settled in cities like Chicago, they established societies to perpetuate valued aspects of village life, including neighborly sociability, mutual assistance, and annual celebrations of the patron saint. The *fratellanza* section of a society spent a year planning the rituals, entertainment, and street decorations for a feast to take place sometime between May and October. Given the difficulties

Plate 11. A solemn procession led by the local priest was the centerpiece of the annual celebration of a village's patron saint in Italy. Bringing Santa Maria Incoronata out of the church into the town and beyond signified a unified religious and secular community.

Italians experienced with the American Catholic Church, however, the feast took on a different meaning here than the union of church and community. Rather, Italians used the symbolic power of their traditional feasts to express their neighborhoods' rival claim on religious ritual and independence from the church hierarchy. Despite clerical disapproval, societies, usually based at Italian national parishes, organized weekend-long feasts that featured band concerts, dancing, *tombola* games, carnival rides, fireworks, and Italian culinary delicacies as a prelude to the special mass and spirited procession that traveled through the neighborhood. On Sunday, a motley parade made its way down festooned streets. Costumed bands heralded societies marching in formation; individuals carried tall candles, candle houses, or wax effigies of limbs afflicted during the year; the penitent walked barefoot or even crawled. Over all of this presided the saint from the heights of eight strong male shoulders. It should come as no surprise that clerics condemned almost every aspect of the event.[102] Not only did these "pagan rites" offend church teaching, but also the feast challenged priests' religious monopoly. The statue of the patron saint that had symbolized the unity of the secular and religious world as it went door-to-door in Italy now presided over a demonstration of defiance. Traveling up and down city blocks it sanctified a community more than a church.

When Mundelein began to implement his Americanization program in the 1920s, he confronted a dilemma in regard to the Italian community. If he impeded the organization of Italian Catholic institutions, he would only encourage further Italian withdrawal from the church. Nevertheless, footing the bill for Italian national parishes violated all the precepts of his Americanization ideology. Mundelein had no intention of paying for what he opposed. The archbishop at first tried to use the new tools of centralization – church social centers, Holy Name Societies, Catholic welfare services – to lure Italians. The only new Italian national parish he permitted during his twenty-one-year tenure, the West Side's San Callisto, had a lower floor equipped for social purposes to help the assigned Irish pastor, Reverend Murphy, "organize all the parishioners, men and women, young and old, into societies and clubs of various sorts."[103] When even these efforts did not save a number of Italian churches from financial crisis, the archbishop resorted to a new strategy: turning them over to Italian religious orders like the Scalabrini and Servite Fathers. For example, when the founding pastor of St. Anthony's resigned in 1922, having accumulated a debt of $77,000 over nineteen years, Mundelein passed the congregation over to the Scalabrinian order. San Rocco Parish in Chicago Heights came under the Franciscans' wing the same year for the same reason. By the end of Mundelein's reign in 1939, only two of the twelve Italian national parishes in Chicago were not run by religious orders.[104]

Mundelein's decision to turn Italian Catholic churches over to religious orders rather than support them himself did not help his Americanization campaign. The Italian orders understood better than the archbishop that attracting their compatriots to the church required the linking of religion and culture. In the churches and schools under their regime, Italian language flourished, images of Italian heroes like Dante and Columbus bedecked the walls, and Italian music reverberated in and out of the sanctuary. St. Philip Benizi, a Servite church in "Little Sicily," established a parochial school in 1920 that quickly became the largest Italian school in the city. A church bulletin that year promoted the school in cultural more than religious terms: "It is the school where your children learn that there does exist in this world a land called Italy, mother of every present civilization and center of Christianity. It is the school where they will learn not to be ashamed of being known as Italians, offspring of saints and heroes. It is the school where they will learn to speak the language of Dante, the sweet and beautiful Italian language."[105] For those attending Italian national parishes, Mundelein's commitment to Americanization ironically created more Catholic churches devoted to fostering rather than extinguishing an "Italian" identity.

Still, many Italians embraced the Catholic Church on their own terms. Although most Italian Catholics wanted the church's blessing on the ritual occasions of christening, marriage, and death, they were rarely reliable church members. The list of "don'ts" printed in St. Philip Benizi's parish bulletin of May 1924 suggests what Italian parishioners often did. For those who had managed not to profane the Lord's Day and had attended church, *Il Calendario Italiano* urged, "Don't be late for Mass . . . don't go to Mass without a prayer book or rosary . . . don't talk . . . don't leave the church until the priest has left . . . don't forget to bend the knee."[106]

Furthermore, alternative Italian cultures continued to compete with the church. Anticlericals still taunted priests and observant parishioners through the 1920s and not only in traditionally socialist neighborhoods. Father Luigi Giambostiani of the North Side received malicious letters accusing the priests of his church of being "con-artists" ("eggegi sfruttatori del popolino").[107] Even church goers remained independent minded, stubbornly rejecting the Holy Name Societies that the Fathers promoted, resisting calls for church contributions, and ignoring the priests' prohibition against sending their children to YMCAs and settlement houses.[108] Most aggravating to secular and religious order priests alike, Italians continued to boycott parochial schools, preferring tuition-free and ideology-free public ones. Although the 702 students in Italian Catholic elementary schools in 1910 had grown to 3,053 by 1920 with Quigley's building program, by 1930 enrollment stood only slightly higher, at 3,746. Thirteen times as many Polish children attended national Catholic schools than Italian ones by that year, even though Polish immigrants outnumbered Italian by only two to one.[109]

Also by the late 1920s, "pagan" feasts had been institutionalized among Italian Chicagoans, and several unique Italo–American characteristics had evolved. Free of church supervision and concerned with filling the coffers of the sponsoring societies, feasts became more materialistic. In place of the fruit offerings common in Italy, the devout in America pinned gifts of money to the flowing robes and ribbons adorning the saint. And people came to expect the leader of the procession to pause in front of a shop and cry out in Italian, "Who loves the Saint Maria Addolorata will give her money." Fireworks would explode when someone contributed five dollars, and the band would play the old Italian national anthem for fifty dollars.

Contrary to what many anthropologists have found in peasant festivals, where usual social structures break down and customary hierarchies of gender, class, and caste are inverted, these Italo–American feasts of the 1920s clarified the way the community was evolving.[110] Not only did people march behind their society banners, but also the emphasis on monetary donations reinforced economic distinctions of increasing significance. Rose Clementi complained how the desire to affirm status led some people to wear expensive clothes and drive cars in Santa Maria Incoronata's San Rocco procession: "They felt they were higher class people. Maybe they had a little more money than we did.... But they'd go all out.... And they were just common people like us, you know.... But they gave us an impression that we were... very, very humble."[111] As this ritual moved from celebrating unity to articulating Italian community, it could not avoid replicating the complexities of that secular world.

During the 1920s, the feasts also helped usher in a more national Italian identity. As a national parish usually brought together diverse Italian populations and sponsored several feasts, people in a neighborhood came to identify with these community events regardless of village origin. Similarly, as Italians began to travel easily to feasts around the city, whether to attend celebrations of their own San Rocco and Our

Plate 12. When Italian immigrants transferred the celebration of the village feast of Santa Maria Incoronata to Chicago, it came to symbolize the neighborhood more than the church as the Catholic clergy disapproved of such "pagan rites." As feasts such as this one became more enmeshed in the secular world, they grew to represent the nationalism and commercialism of the Italian–American community. Note, for example, the dollars pinned to streamers in the Madonna's right hand by contributors seeking favors or forgiveness. What had been Catholic in the Old World became Italian in the new one.

Lady of Mount Carmel patron saints in other parishes or to join relatives at their festivals, they came to recognize the feast as something meaningful beyond a Sicilian village or Chicago neighborhood, as something Italian.

Despite Mundelein's efforts to make them American Catholics, Chicago's Italians were becoming more aware of their larger ethnic community. Mundelein's Americanization program failed with them on two counts. To the extent that Italian Catholics participated in national parishes during the 1920s, Mundelein's passing of responsibility over to Italian religious orders unintentionally helped to bring more Italian cultural life into the church. To the extent that Italians rejected institutionalized Catholic religion and set nationalism against clericalism, Mundelein's program had little effect. Inside and outside the church, Italian prevailed over Catholic.

Poles and Italians took opposite approaches to the Catholic Church in Chicago: The Poles fought for the church and the Italians fought against it. Yet both strategies ensured community cohesion through the 1920s and strengthened ethnic identity. Nonetheless, the seeds of future instability lay dormant in these solutions. Nothing could redress the one-sided tally of nine national parishes to forty-two territorial ones created between 1916 and 1929. Likewise, Archbishop Mundelein's scheme for training priests, to "take boys born and raised in Chicago" and give them all "eleven years of training in the same courses under the same teachers," would inevitably influence priests' ethnic affiliations. The Most Reverend Abramowicz remembered seminary in the early 1930s most vividly for his first exposure to "boys of different nationalities . . . from other parishes."[112]

Within these ethnic communities, the extreme responses evoked by Mundelein's reforms would bring trouble later. For the Poles, the road of separatism led to ostracism in the larger archdiocesan community. As the church centralized under Mundelein, few if any Polish priests participated in the new agencies or gained high office.[113] For Italians, their ambivalence about the church prevented them from agitating for new national parishes as they moved farther north and west during the 1920s. Although families returned to former parishes for feasts and special occasions, any regular worship increasingly took place in territorial churches. If their children attended parochial school or catechism, they received a Catholic, not an Italian–Catholic, education. Here lay the roots of what Giovanni Schiavo predicted in 1928 would be a huge generational divide, as the next Italian generation grew "as staunch Catholic as the most fervent Irishmen."[114] Even though Mundelein's Americanization program for a time encouraged ethnic Chicagoans to assert their ethnicity in various ways, in the long run their ethnic identities would not escape unscathed.

As Chicago's industrial workers made their way through the rugged terrain of urban life, ethnic affiliation offered a crucial helping hand. Ethnic institutions continued to appeal to ethnic Chicagoans, whether as protector against poverty, illness, and death or as vehicle toward security and prosperity. But these institutions did not look the same in

1929 as they had in 1919. Pressure from ethnic group members, competition from mainstream alternatives, and historical events such as the passage of Illinois legislation monitoring mutual benefit societies and banks or the selection of George Mundelein as Chicago's archbishop, all demanded that ethnic institutions change to survive. Competition from institutions outside the ethnic community inspired members and leaders to adapt their welfare agencies, benefit societies, and banks to meet the pressures of change. As so often happens, these institutions came to resemble more closely the nonethnic institutions they opposed. This record of responsiveness to competition nonetheless suggests that during the 1920s ethnic culture was dynamic and adaptable, not a static bulwark of traditional, Old World ways.

In the course of adapting to change, ethnic institutions redirected people's sense of affiliation outward, beyond the narrow confines of the neighborhood. During the twenties, ethnic welfare agencies, mutual benefit societies, banking institutions, and church parishes all consolidated local and regional European loyalties into larger, national ethnic communities. What came to be defined as Jewish welfare agencies, Italian fraternal associations, Bohemian banks, and Polish parishes now serviced ethnic needs. Through some of these new nationally defined institutions, such as fraternal orders, Chicagoans began to connect to a more national community within America. Ethnic organizations introduced workers to the world outside their neighborhoods while ensuring that it was still an ethnic one.

As ethnic institutions competed more vigorously with mainstream counterparts, they grew to resemble them in crucial ways. Departing from many traditional values of mutual aid, self-help, and cooperativism, they became more commercial and bureaucratic. Seeking help from the Bohemian Charitable Association, insurance from the Polish National Alliance, a loan from an ethnic bank or building and loan association, and a favor from San Rocco were more complex experiences by the end of the 1920s than a decade before. At the same time, by continuing to patronize ethnic organizations, people protected themselves from the impersonality and atomization that often accompanied pure commercialism in the way that industrial insurance, for example, offered none of the social community of a fraternal lodge. Even though an ethnic bank may not have differed substantially from the native one downtown, banking here – close to home, in their native tongue, with familiar faces – allowed people to bring communal values and expectations to what otherwise would have been simply an economic exchange.

That industrial workers remained dependent on their ethnic communities bore implications for their larger social relationships during the 1920s. Getting help from a better off neighbor or a welfare agency supported by an ethnic elite kept workers tied to economic superiors within their communities. As ethnic institutions like fraternal associations consolidated, they encompassed people of different neighborhoods and economic statuses in ways that more narrowly defined mutual benefit societies had not. Now, workers and bosses could easily belong to the same fraternal order and at times even the same lodge. Similarly, appealing for help to a local banker on the basis of shared ethnicity and perhaps sitting next to him in church on Sunday reinforced the sense that ethnic loyalty transcended class differences within the ethnic community. Likewise, after the union defeats early in the decade, class affiliations outside the ethnic community, with other industrial laborers, offered workers little of the benefits and protections that their ethnicity did. In this way, dependency made working-class ethnics respectful of traditional authority figures within the ethnic community such as organization leaders, businessmen, and priests. At the same time, however, the legitimacy of these leaders rested on their continued ability to provide for all the members of their communities, including the lower classes.

Ethnic communities managed to stave off competitors in providing minimal social security to their members. Although they did not deliver a great deal by today's standards, in this era before welfare state programs the loose "safety net" that people could count on was furnished primarily by their ethnic group. But helping ethnic Chicagoans overcome adversity did not ensure that ethnicity would fare as well in other arenas. Accepting a Christmas food basket from a fraternal lodge surely required less commitment than choosing to attend an ethnic singing society meeting instead of a motion picture. Ethnic leaders knew that. They worried that if people went to the picture show, tuned in to the radio, partied at a dance hall, or shopped at a chain store for the latest American products rather than patronizing their local ethnic merchant, they would be lured away from ethnic culture. There was good reason for concern. The new, mass culture makers of the twenties – motion picture producers, radio broadcasters, chain store managers, and advertising executives – talked quite explicitly about the need to build a mass audience with uniform, middle-class tastes.

However, it would be a mistake for us to take the fears of ethnic leaders and the marketing ambitions of commercial moguls for fact.

Certainly, in one sense, Chicago's mass production workers entered the world of the new commercialism every day when they passed through the factory gates to make ready-made clothing, telephone parts, and packaged foods. Increasingly when they left work they encountered new temptations on how to spend their leisure. But we cannot assume that the "take-off" of mass culture and mass consumption in the 1920s required that everyone participate or that if people partook that they did so on somebody else's terms. Workers were not necessarily converted to middle-class values, nor were ethnics inevitably Americanized by the commercial triumphs of mass culture.

3
Encountering Mass Culture

Plate 13. The 398-seat Pastime Theater on West Madison Street typified the small neighborhood theaters that workers frequented during the 1920s. Admission was $0.25 in 1924, and most who attended were spared the additional cost of carfare as they lived within walking distance. Experiencing mass culture within theaters, stores, and radio stations tied to their ethnic communities kept workers from the cultural reorientation many expected would accompany their exposure to Hollywood movies, standard brands, and radio.

The J. Walter Thompson Company, the leading advertising agency in the country, devoted the July 1, 1926, issue of its in-house newsletter to the "New National Market." The newsletter claimed that because of a rising standard of living but more crucially because of the impact of nationally circulated publications, syndicated news features, motion pictures, automobiles, standardized merchandise, and most recently the radio, "we are fast getting to be a nation which lives to pattern everywhere." With each year, the "lines of demarcation" between social classes and between the city, the small town, and the farm had become less clear. For advertisers, this homogenization of American society – both vertically across classes and horizontally across regions – offered the opportunity of appealing to a truly mass market: "Millions of families regarded almost as recently as a few months ago as poor prospects for many kinds of merchandise, are now the best sort of prospects." Mass culture and consumption, the ad men argued, were standardizing the way Americans lived and cultivating them for future harvests.[1]

Confidence in the integrative power of mass culture did not reside just on Madison Avenue. The assumption was present everywhere in the 1920s. In 1924, the *American Mercury* proclaimed that "the man who knows his United States" knows that the radio, the comic strip, and the dance hall "have made us an homogeneous people."[2] A little while later in Chicago, the management of the local Balaban & Katz movie house chain steadfastly refused to sell reserved seats at a higher price, asserting that theaters were democratic institutions that should serve "all the people all the time" without class distinction.[3] Progressive employers like Henry Ford had so much confidence in the power of mass consumption to integrate workers into a middle-class culture that they advocated increasing workingmen's buying power and leisure time during the 1920s. The shorter work day and week would not only make workmen more content but also give them more time "to find out what is going on in the world" and, consequently, develop new consumer desires. Manufacturing companies in turn would benefit from the increased demand for products generated by this mass market.[4] Leaders of Chicago's ethnic communities struggling to bolster their own institutions were equally as convinced of mass culture's homogenizing power, although they feared rather than welcomed it. In the contest over workers' loyalty raging during the twenties, mass culture seemed to be a winner.

There were some, however, like the pioneering sociologist at the University of Chicago, Ernest Burgess, who remained skeptical that the growth of a national network of communication, commercial leisure, and consumerism heralded the end of cultural diversity. He told the Section on Neighborhoods of the Minnesota State Conference of Social Work in 1928 that he felt it was "entirely too early to predict what the full effect of the motion picture, the automobile, and the radio will be upon American and world civilization."[5]

Burgess was right to suggest that the impact of mass culture was not self-evident and that only with the passage of time would its effects be discernible. A longer view makes it possible to move beyond the prevailing contemporary assumption that the abundance of these new cultural forms meant that all people responded to them, and in the same way, and exposes the complex process by which mass culture and consumption entered different people's lives.[6] It is my contention that mass culture – whether chain stores, standard brands, motion pictures, or the radio – did not in itself challenge working people's existing values and relationships. Rather, the impact of mass culture depended on the social and economic contexts in which it developed and the manner in which it was experienced, in other words, how mass culture was produced, distributed, and consumed. As those circumstances changed by the end of the 1920s, so too did the impact of mass culture on Chicago workers.

BUYING INTO THE MIDDLE CLASS?

Twice a month in 1929, on Tuesday mornings, the publishers of *True Story Magazine* ran full-page advertisements in the nation's major newspapers, including the *Chicago Tribune*, celebrating what they called "The American Economic Evolution." Claiming to be the recipient of thousands of personal stories written by American workers for the magazine's primarily working-class readership, they felt confident reporting that since World War I, shorter working hours, higher pay, and easy credit had created an "economic millennium." Now that the nation's workers enjoyed an equal opportunity to consume, "a capital–labor war which has been going on now for upwards of three hundred years" had virtually ended. Twenty years before, Jim Smith, who worked ten to twelve hours a day in a factory and then returned home "to his hovel and his woman and his brats," was likely to resort to strikes and violence when times got tough. Not so his modern-day counterpart. Today, the magazine asserted, Jim Smith drives home to the suburbs after a seven- or eight-hour day earning him three to seven times as much as before, which helps pay for the automobile, the house, and a myriad of other possessions. Now an upstanding member of the middle class, Jim had learned moderation. Mass consumption had tamed his militance. So went *True Story*'s version of the fate of the factory worker in the 1920s.[7]

A truer story, however, remains to be told. To begin with, industrial workers in places like Chicago did not enjoy nearly the prosperity that advertisers and sales promoters assumed they did. All Americans did not benefit equally from the mushrooming of national wealth during the 1920s. Whereas workers' real wages climbed from prewar levels, their gains came mostly in wartime. Afterward, from 1923 to 1929, wages advanced modestly if at all in big manufacturing sectors such as steel, meatpacking, agricultural implements, and the clothing industry, particularly for the unskilled and semiskilled workers who predominated in this kind of work.

Still, if factory workers could have depended on these slowly rising wages from year to year and year round, they might have consumed more like Jim Smith. Instead, unemployment remained high throughout the decade, even for people with so-called steady work. More than half of the privileged, "fully employed," unskilled and semiskilled manufacturing workers interviewed by Leila Houghteling in 1924 found themselves out of work, most for more than a month a year, because of seasonal layoffs or illness. According to Houghteling's study, the uncertainty of work and the inadequacy of wages meant that more than half of the 467 families interviewed were forced to send mother or children to work, some even to take in boarders, just to live slightly above the minimum standard of living set for dependent families by the Chicago Council of Social Agencies. This finding was corroborated by two other investigations into the living conditions of Chicago wage earners. As a historian who recently evaluated the complex wage and price data for the 1920s wryly concluded, "the struggle for economic security, not the struggle to keep up with the Joneses, dominated working-class life in the prosperity decade."[8]

But people with commodities to sell worried little about workers' limited income. Instead, they trusted that an elaborate system of installment selling would permit all Americans to take part in the consumer revolution. "Buy now, pay later," first introduced in the automobile business around 1915, suddenly exploded in the 1920s, catalyzed by excess productive capacity in many industries during the depression of 1920–1. By 1926, it was estimated that six billion dollars' worth of retail goods sold annually by installment, about 15 percent of all sales. "Enjoy while you pay," invited the manufacturers of everything from vacuum cleaners to, literally, the kitchen sink.[9]

Once again, however, popular beliefs at the time do not hold up under closer scrutiny. Industrial workers were not engaging in installment buying in nearly the numbers that marketers assumed. First of all, workers had become savers during the 1920s at least as much as spenders. As we saw in the previous chapter, the Liberty Loan campaigns instilled in workers a savings habit that the depression of 1920–1 only reinforced, when many fell back on their wartime savings to survive the hard times following the war. When economic uncertainty failed to disappear during the twenties, workers saved in ever greater numbers through bank deposits, insurance policies, and building and loan associations, putting aside an increasing proportion of their incomes.[10] Opting for thrift over spending also made good economic sense to workers. Although some businessmen argued that high consumption would ultimately benefit workers by providing steadier employment in manufacturing, other industrialists contended that a high rate of investment and savings ensured a healthier economy. Chicago workers better trusted the advice to save, which allowed them to guard against adversity while contributing to more general prosperity.[11]

Workers certainly made purchases on credit, but less frequently than optimistic merchandisers liked to believe. Since 90 percent of a family's expenditures were for things not covered by installment credit, those with low incomes automatically had less to put toward the purchase of durables. Automobiles by far accounted for the greatest proportion of the nation's installment debt outstanding at any given time, more than 50 percent. But though *True Story*'s Jim Smith may have driven home from the factory in his new automobile, industrial workers in Chicago were not likely to follow his example. Leila Houghteling found that only 3 percent of the unskilled and semiskilled workers she interviewed in 1924 had cars. Even at the end of the decade, in the less urbanized environment of nearby Joliet, only 24 percent of lower income families owned an automobile, according to a *Chicago Tribune* survey.[12] Household furniture ran a not very close second to the auto at 19 percent of the nation's installment debt. It was this kind of purchase, along with small items like the phonograph, which made up about 5 percent of the total installment debt, that workers were likely to acquire on credit. Despite these commodities' minor share of the overall installment expenditure, 80–90 percent of all furniture and phonographs bought were purchased on installment.[13]

But even taking these items into account, the few contemporary studies that probed consumer credit experience suggest that it was middle-income people, not workers, who made installment buying such a rage during the 1920s, particularly the salaried and well-off classes who anticipated larger incomes in the future. According to an investigation of four thousand credit union loans taken by workers in Boston and Milwaukee during 1926, necessities like medical and dental bills or coal, not consumer durables, drove workers to borrow. A later study revealed that despite the doubling of national installment credit between 1929 and 1940, by the end of that period, middle-income people were still the most likely to buy on installment. And within the low-income group, the foreign born, the homeowner, and the family with three or more earners, all common characteristics of Chicago's industrial workers, bought even less on installment than those with low incomes as a whole.[14] Simply put, workers placed more value on paying cash than did those better off. After all, they, rather than the more prosperous, risked losing their investment by default or having their wages garnisheed to cover an outstanding debt. When relatively secure streetcar workers were asked in the late 1920s what they would do with extra income, most responded that a major priority was to have cash to avoid installment buying.[15]

When workers bought on credit, they were most likely to purchase small items like phonographs. But whether buying a phonograph or a washing machine changed workers' cultural orientation is unclear. Those who believed in the homogenizing power of mass consumption claimed that the act of purchasing a standardized product drew the consumer into a world of mainstream tastes and values. Sociologist John Dollard argued at the time, for example, that the Victrola revolutionized a family's pattern of amusement because "what they listen to comes essentially from the outside, its character is cosmopolitan and national, and what the family does to create it as a family is very small indeed."[16] We get the impression of immigrant, wage-earning families sharing more in American, middle-class culture every time they rolled up the rug and danced to the Paul Whiteman Orchestra.

But how workers themselves described what it meant to purchase a phonograph reveals a different picture. In story after story, Chicago Italians, for instance, related how buying a Victrola helped keep Italian culture alive in America. Recordings of Caruso singing Italian opera or of popular Italian folk songs enlivened home life once the family had saved enough to purchase a phonograph. Rather than the phonograph drawing the family away from a more indigenous cultural world, as Dollard alleged, many people like Rena Domke remembered how in Little Sicily during those years neighbors "would sit in the evening and discuss all different things about Italy," and every Saturday night they pulled out a Victrola "and they'd play all these Italian records and they would dance."[17] Far from symbolizing an individual's rejection of ethnic culture, a phonograph in fact helped Italians share in a collective experience as immigrants. Buying a Victor Victrola from the 12th Street Department Store at five dollars down, five dollars a month allowed Anthony Sorrentino's family to laugh along with Nofrio, a Sicilian comedian who told anecdotes dealing with "the everyday problems of living and with the frustrations of an Italian trying to express himself as he struggled to speak English – when he tried to use the telephone . . ., to order a meal in a restaurant, or purchase special articles in stores."[18]

Italians were not alone in incorporating the phonograph into existing ethnic life. Consumers of all nationalities displayed so much interest in purchasing foreign-language records that by the 1920s, Chicago had become the center of an enormous, foreign record industry. Big American companies like Victor and Columbia re-pressed recordings that had originally been made in Europe as well as opened their studios to immigrant artists recruited out of Chicago's southern and eastern European ethnic communities. These performers often went on to enjoy substantial fame, as their folk styles satisfied the former peasants now able to afford "talking machines" better than more sophisticated talent. The phonograph record made Pawlo Humeniuk, Franciszek Kukla, Jan Wanat, and Wladyslaw Ochrymowicz household names in Chicago's ethnic neighborhoods, if not on the city's well-to-do North Shore.[19] And some American-born workers also used phonograph records to preserve their ties to regional cultures. Southerners, black and white, for example, eased the trauma of moving north to cities like Chicago by supporting a record industry of hillbilly and "race records" geared specifically toward a northern urban market with southern roots.

But the major companies were not the only ones to supply this growing urban market. The establishment of independent pressing plants in the 1920s made it possible for small ethnic entrepreneurs to enter the record business with little capital. Even the small Mexican community in Chicago supported a shop that made phonographic records of Mexican music and distributed them all over the United States. Mexican immigrants reentering Mexico in 1927, whose return certainly suggests they had not totally assimilated to American life, brought with them phonograph records more commonly than any other object.[20] Owning a phonograph might have brought a worker closer to American middle-class culture, but it did not do so necessarily. A commodity could just as easily help a person reinforce ethnic or working-class culture as lose it. What mattered were the experiences and expectations that the consumer brought to the object.

Of course, when contemporaries spoke of a consumer revolution, they meant more than the wider distribution of luxury goods like the phonograph. They were referring to how the chain store – like A&P and Walgreen Drugs – and the nationally advertised brands they offered – like Lux soap and Del Monte canned goods – were standardizing even the most routine purchasing. "Mass selling has become almost the universal rule in this country," asserted a distributor of packaged meat, "a discovery of this decade of hardly less importance than the discovery of such forces as steam and electricity." Now that mass production had triumphed, it was only reasonable that more efficient methods of distribution would follow.[21] Doomed, everyone thought, were bulk, unmarked, or local brands and the small, inefficient neighborhood grocery, dry goods store, or drugstore that sold them. Wherever they lived, it was assumed, Americans increasingly were entering stores that looked exactly alike to purchase the same items from a standard stock.[22] Workers' limited incomes could not keep them from participating in a revolution of this scale.

The chain store of the 1920s bore little relationship to the huge K-Mart or Safeway supermarket of today. In appearance and size, it hardly differed from the independent grocery or drugstore nearby. When a customer entered, he or she still needed assistance from a clerk. The self-service approach, although tried by the Piggly Wiggly grocery chain during the 1920s, did not come into common use until the thirties.

More revolutionary was chain store management. Central headquarters made sure all branches looked the same, operated the same way, and sold the same stock. Chain stores specialized in products with wide consumer appeal, which made for quick turnover and high profits. Consumers benefited, as chains could sell these goods at a lower price than the independent store because their large volume of business allowed them to bypass middlemen and buy directly from manufacturers at a discount. Nationally advertised brands suited the system best since their manufacturers helped create consumer demand while also guaranteeing quality. A&P's slogan, "Quality you know by name," played on the crucial link between the standardized item and the standardized store. These "cash-and-carry" stores further reduced overhead by offering neither credit nor delivery. Chains built their image as suppliers of reliable merchandise sold in a no-frill, economical way.[23]

Although many of the big chains had begun in the late nineteenth and early twentieth centuries, they grew at an unprecedented rate during the 1920s, particularly within the nation's largest cities. By the end of the decade in Chicago, as in New York, Philadelphia, Los Angeles, and Boston, more than half of all retail products passed to the consumer through chain stores even though chains made up a much smaller percentage of store units than independents. "Mom and pop" stores survived, but their share of total goods sold declined. As in other big cities, Chicago's chains flourished best among grocery and variety stores but also did well as meat markets, auto-filling stations, cigar shops, restaurants, coal suppliers, confectioners, and shoe stores and drugstores (Table 7).[24] The chain fever soon infected other large distributors who feared their competition. In 1925, Sears Roebuck opened its first retail store in Chicago, the mail-order company's headquarters, launching its own national chain, which would reach 324 stores by the end of 1929 and would propel its main competitor, Montgomery Ward's, into the retail business as well.[25] Chicago department stores like Wieboldt's and Goldblatt's also began to open stores throughout the city, functioning as local, and eventually regional, chains.[26] By 1930, a customer could shop at the same stores even if he or she moved across town.

Sociology student Virginia Pattison was surprised, therefore, to find only two chain groceries when she visited the working-class neighborhood of Back of the Yards, and these on opposite corners of a major intersection. How could this heavily populated district have escaped the chain store invasion, she wondered. Had Pattison methodically investigated the location of chain groceries citywide, however, she would have recognized a pattern that made Back of the Yards no longer seem

Table 7. *Chain stores in Chicago*

Category of Store	1923			1929				1939			
	Total units, all stores	Number of units, chain stores	Percentage of units, chain stores	Total units, all stores	Number of units, chain stores	Percentage of units, chain stores	Percentage of total sales, chain stores	Total units, all stores	Number of units, chain stores	Percentage of units, chain stores	Percentage of total sales, chain stores
All Groceries	11,865	1,234	17.9	7,266	1,785	24.6	50.0	9,331	1,391	14.9	56.0
without meat	na	na	na	5,151	1,700	33.0	68.5	5,757	989	17.2	54.7
with meat	na	na	na	2,115	85	4.0	8.7	3,574	402	11.2	56.9
Variety, 5&10	na	na	na	383	150	39.2	93.8	333	172	51.7	96.1
Department stores	na	na	na	78	16	20.5	13.5	58	26[a]	44.8	67.2
Shoe stores	1,206	92	7.6	1,016	292	28.7	59.6	764	275	36.0	66.6
Confectioners	2,440	102	4.8	na	na	na	na	2,286	195	8.5	35.5
Restaurants	na	166	na	3,436	256	7.5	23.7	4,193	302	7.2	30.0
Cigar stores	1,204	216	17.9	1,380	249	18.0	44.1	751	177	23.6	60.7
Filling stations	na	307	na	1,255	476	37.9	36.4	2,161	190	8.8	19.0
Fuel dealers	na	111	na	761	61	8.0	21.9	1,243	57	4.6	15.6
Drugstores	1,283	90	7.0	1,969	231	11.7	35.2	1,903	237	12.5	41.2
Clothing	2,424	127	5.2	2,332	360	15.4	30.7	1,979	298	15.1	32.3
Furniture	na	na	na	501	73	14.6	27.3	420	40	9.5	29.3

Note: na, data not available.

[a] Includes mail order.

Sources: Ernest Hugh Shideler, "The Chain Store: A Study of the Ecological Organization of a Modern City" (Ph.D. Dissertation, University of Chicago, 1927), Chapter 4, pp. 18–20; U.S. Department of Commerce, Bureau of the Census, *Fifteenth Census, 1930: Retail Distribution* (Washington, DC: U.S. Government Printing Office, 1933), p. 633; U.S. Department of Commerce, Bureau of the Census, *Sixteenth Census, 1940: Retail Trade* (Washington, DC: U.S. Government Printing Office, 1943), pp. 218–19.

exceptional: two-thirds of the more than five hundred A&P and National Tea stores in Chicago by 1927–8 were located in neighborhoods of above-average economic status.[27]

The chain store that purportedly was revolutionizing all consumer behavior in the 1920s was mostly reaching the middle and upper classes. A walk down 71st Street between Jeffrey Avenue and South Shore Drive made this clear. The north side of the shopping street served residents of the elegant South Shore apartment houses built to the north during the twenties. The south side of 71st, cut off by Illinois Central tracks, which ran down the center of the street, served people who lived to the south, skilled workers and the lesser skilled who worked in South Chicago's steel mills. But more than railroad tracks divided these two shopping strips. Despite higher rent on the north side of the street and the fact that it was the sunnier and hence hotter side, thirty-three chain stores ranging from A&P and Piggly Wiggly to Fannie May Candies, Sinclair Gasoline, and Wyle's Hat Shop lined the sidewalk block after block. Here, a third of the stores were chains. On the south side, there were grocery stores, meat and vegetable stores, barber shops and bakeries but only four chains – Western Union, Bekker's Cleaners, a rug store, and a Cadillac dealer – all likely attracted to the low rent and large spaces available. Less than 8 percent of the shops on "the wrong side of the tracks" belonged to chains.[28]

An analysis of the location of chain stores in Chicago's suburbs reveals the same imbalance. By 1926, chains ran 53 percent of the groceries in prosperous Oak Park and 36 percent in equally well-off Evanston. In contrast, in working-class Gary and Joliet, only 1 percent of the groceries were owned by chains. As late as 1929, the industrial workers of Cicero found chain management in only 5 percent of this industrial town's 819 retail stores and in 11 percent of its groceries.[29] This was one revolution that workers seemed to have had little to do with.

By mutual consent, Chicago's working-class consumers and chain store executives kept chains out of industrial neighborhoods during the 1920s. For their part, workers were too tied to local merchants to abandon them for a small savings in price, estimated by experts to be 10 percent in Chicago. Having little refrigeration or storage space at home, most working-class people shopped every day. Stores on almost every block, open long hours, minimized the inconvenience, and families became regular customers of a nearby bakery, dairy, and particularly a combined meat market–grocery.[30] "If my dad had fifty customers, that's all he had, fifty," recalled Ted Pomorski, the son of a grocer in Back of the Yards. "If he got fifty-one one day, it would be an odd thing. Somebody from the next block was passing by or got mad at his butcher that day."[31] A customer joined a small, stable community when he or she patronized a particular store.

But customers selected a grocer like Mr. Pomorski for more than convenience; usually, he shared their ethnicity. When social worker Sophonisba Breckinridge surveyed ninety immigrant families in Chicago in the early 1920s, seventy-four said they purchased all their food from foreign-speaking grocers in the neighborhood.[32] A West Side grocer explained, "People go to a place where they can order in their own language, be understood without repetition, and then exchange a few words of gossip or news."[33] Indeed, the women who did most of the shopping in these neighborhoods were often slow to learn English; shopping in their native tongue sustained their control over family purchases. By following advertisements in foreign-language newspapers, housewives made informed decisions. And the ethnic store helped them perpetuate traditional dietary customs in America. Here Italian women found exotic fresh vegetables such as escarole and dandelion leaves and many varieties of macaroni, whereas Jewish women secured kosher meat, special fish, and challah bread.[34] Women, furthermore, depended on shopping as a way of socializing. The companionship that Italian men found in neighborhood barber shops, Mexican men in poolrooms, and Polish men in soft drink parlors, ethnic women found in the local store. Here, neighbors chatted together as they waited their turn and gossiped with the grocer. Just as women used their power over the household purse to keep their families tied to ethnic forms of insurance, so too they played a crucial role in sustaining working-class Chicagoans' dependence on another ethnic institution, the neighborhood store.[35]

The local store became an institution as central to an ethnic community as the church or bank and one that was visited much more often. Even when people of different ethnicity shared a neighborhood like Steeltown's Bush, they patronized separate groceries. On a practical level, patrons felt that they could best trust their own merchants: butchers of other "races" would certainly put a heavier thumb on the scale.[36] Beyond that, people considered it a matter of loyalty to patronize their own. When Bernice Novak's mother-in-law offered her a new

Plate 14. Antonio and Angeline Tortolano's store was typical of the family-owned groceries that ethnic, working-class people patronized during the 1920s. Here they could buy on credit and communicate in a familiar language with the shopkeeper. Customers bought bulk goods from barrels, crates, and sacks like those pictured in the foreground as well as learned about the packaged items so carefully displayed on the Tortolanos' shelves.

pair of shoes for her birthday in the late 1920s, she insisted Bernice buy them at the local Bohemian shoe store, not the more fashionable chain that had just opened in downtown Cicero.[37] Buyers were suspicious of a local shopkeeper who did not share their ethnicity, and Jewish merchants particularly suffered for it. One grocer trying to start a business in a neighborhood 90 percent Irish lost customers when they discovered he was Jewish; he finally gave up and entered the wholesale trade. A hardware store owner selling among Poles and Bohemians shaved his beard to hide his Jewish identity.[38] Ida Margolis, who managed to run a small general store not far from the stockyards for seventy years, had to content herself with the label "White Jew," an indication of acceptance, if not affection.[39]

Merchants encouraged ethnic loyalty by involving themselves in the life of their communities. Hardly a church anniversary book or dramatic club program lacked advertisements from local storekeepers. The neighborhood baseball team took the name of the corner grocer who bought its uniforms. During a community crisis like the stockyard strike in the winter of 1922, local merchants could be counted on to provide food.[40] As one ethnic merchant put it, "The Polish business man is a part of your nation; he is your brother. Whether it is war, hunger, or trouble, he is always with you willing to help. . . . Therefore, buy from your people."[41] A Piggly Wiggly or National Tea branch stood awkwardly outside this world where more than money was exchanged at the store.

Economic ties to the ethnic shopkeeper were no less important than cultural ones in keeping working-class families from shopping at the chain grocery. Most factory workers depended on a system of credit at the neighborhood store to make it from one payday to the next. When Adeline Milano Zappa's family shopped all week at their local Southeast Chicago store, the grocer would record their purchases in a small book. On payday, her father would settle their bill and be rewarded with a gift of fruit or candy.[42] In tough times, the loyal customer knew an understanding shopkeeper would wait to be paid and still sell her food. So when an A&P opened not far from Little Sicily, people ignored it. Instead, everyone continued to do business with the local grocer, who warned customers like Paul Penio, "Go to A&P they ain't going to give you credit like I give you credit here."[43] The chain store's prices may have been cheaper, but its cash-and-carry policy was too rigid for working people's budgets.

For their part, the directors of chain stores understood that working-class neighborhoods did not make good locales for their stores. Success for a chain rested above all else on location, leading chain managers to pioneer scientific methods of evaluating sites according to access, traffic, demographics, and local income.[44] Time and again in city after city, chains chose to expand in areas of high and medium purchasing power, not low.[45] Chain operators recognized not only that customers in lower economic areas had less to spend but also that other ties bound them to neighborhood merchants. The president of Reeves Stores, for example, acknowledged that "we know that we would fail in certain neighborhoods," particularly the foreign ones where people would come "for little else except sugar and coffee."[46] Although chains might have tailored their stock more to local or ethnic tastes, that would have compromised the economy of scale achieved through central purchasing of standardized items.[47] Instead, chains reached out to markets more amenable to their products, most notably the upwardly and geographically mobile, salaried middle class that was growing so fast in these years.[48]

Ethnic workers' preference for local over chain stores meant that although middle-class consumers were carrying home more national-brand packaged goods in the 1920s, working-class people continued to buy in bulk – to fetch milk in their own containers, purchase chunks of soap, and scoop coffee, tea, sugar, and flour out of barrels. When Sidney Sorkin entered his local store owned by Mr. Finkelstein, "the small man, our own big man, the independent merchant," he encountered "the mixed smells of coffees from burlap bags, beans, groats, rice, peas and buchshure, lined up along the floor. On the shelves the canned goods, with local labels . . . , fresh creamy cheeses and yellow butter, as well as the cookies and crackers in boxes with the hinged glass tops."[49]

That ethnic grocers like Mr. Finkelstein continued to sell bulk goods frustrated manufacturers of brand-name products. They sent salesmen into city neighborhoods to convince grocers that packaged items were more sanitary and required less time and overhead.[50] To better reach consumers, they hired advertising companies to study the buying habits of ethnic city dwellers and how to change them.[51] But more often than not, grocers responded to their entreaties as unenthusiastically as the storekeeper who told the Yuban salesman trying to promote elaborate display materials, "I have some under the counter that you left the last trip."[52] Not surprisingly, when the *Chicago Tribune* asked North Side Chicago residents of different income levels in 1929, "Do you prefer nationally advertised brands?" 53 percent of those with above-average income, 50 percent with average income, and only 38 percent of those with below-average income answered yes.[53] What standard brands working-class families did buy, furthermore, they encountered through a trusted grocer like Mr. Finkelstein or Mr. Pomorski – not an anonymous clerk at the A&P – which made the goods less suspect.[54]

Ethnic workers could not find everything they needed in neighborhood stores. But leaving the block in search of clothing or household goods did not transform them into J. Walter Thompson's ideal consumers. Many of Chicago's workers shopped on Maxwell Street, the West Side Jewish market where a buyer could bargain for anything from an overcoat to a mah-jongg set. By the late 1920s, a man who worked as a

Plate 15. On Maxwell Street Chicago's ethnic workers could shop as they had in Europe, haggling over prices in their native tongues and handling the merchandise to judge its quality.

"puller" on the street, aggressively soliciting prospective customers for a shoe store, reported that Poles, Italians, Bohemians, Lithuanians, and Russians who had been in America for many years had become the market's steadiest customers. Here they still shopped as in Europe, haggling over prices in their native tongue and comparing the quality of merchandise.[55] Although President Hoover's Committee on Recent Social Trends claimed that style consciousness was revolutionizing the retail trade during the 1920s, Maxwell Street customers were still opting for value and quality over style.[56] Because buyers cared more about how long an item would last than for its stylishness, Maxwell Street shops like Robinson's Department Store could keep prices low by buying end-of-season close-outs from mail-order houses.[57]

Even away from Maxwell Street, where working-class customers shopped at variety stores and inexpensive department stores, they disappointed manufacturers and retailers eager to encourage the latest fashion. "The Poles are very conservative," Milwaukee Avenue proprietors complained; "It is difficult to introduce a new article into the store. . . . They have a remarkable suspicion toward anything new. Likewise, they have very little confidence in brands."[58] The same merchants found it equally hard to break customers of the habit of haggling over prices. Some posted signs, "This is a strictly one-price store," whereas others gave in to their clientele and marked up the tagged prices to protect their profit when customers insisted on "chewing" down the price.[59]

Stores that Chicago workers patronized most frequently understood their priorities. Goldblatt's Department Store, with branches in the working-class communities of the West Side, Back of the Yards, and South Chicago by the end of the 1920s, let customers consume on their own terms. The Goldblatt brothers, sons of a Jewish grocer, applied what they knew about their neighbors' buying habits to establishing retail stores that quickly dominated the ethnic, working-class market in Chicago. They kept prices low, hours long, and stores close to where people lived. Aware that their immigrant customers were accustomed to central marketplaces where individual vendors sold fish from one stall and shoes from another, they adapted this approach to their stores. Under one roof they sold everything from food to jewelry, piling merchandise high on tables so people could handle the bargains.[60] The resulting atmosphere dismayed a University of Chicago sociology student more used to the elegance of Marshall Field's. To Betty Wright, Goldblatt's main floor was a mad "jumble of colors, sounds and smells." Amidst the bedlam, she observed

> many women present with old shawls tied over their heads and bags or market baskets on their arms. They stopped at every counter that caught their eye, picked up the goods, handled it, enquired [*sic*] after the price, and then walked on without making any purchase. I have an idea that a good many of these women had no intention whatsoever of buying anything. They probably found Goldblatt's a pleasant place to spend an afternoon.

Most appalling to this student, "Customers seemed always ready to argue with the clerk about the price of an article and to try to 'jew them down.'"[61] Betty Wright did not appreciate that behind Goldblatt's respectable facade thrived a European street market much treasured by ethnic Chicagoans.

The items that these working-class customers bought at Goldblatt's – or at the Leader Store, at Klein's, or on Milwaukee Avenue – were indeed the inexpensive, mass-produced goods becoming increasingly available during the 1920s. But contrary to the hopes of many contemporaries, a new suit of clothes did not change the man (or woman). Rather, as market researchers would finally realize in the 1950s when they developed the theory of "consumer reference groups," consumption involved the meeting of two worlds, the buyer's and the seller's, with purchasers bringing their own values to every exchange.[62] Gradually during the 1920s, ethnic workers came to share more in the new consumer goods but in their own stores, in their own neighborhoods, and in their own ways.

So long as Chicago's workers could buy their food from independent merchants in the neighborhood and shop as they wished elsewhere, "mass consumption" did not challenge ethnic or working-class identity. But beginning in the late 1920s and with increasing frequency during the Great Depression, Chicago workers found their customary market relationships disturbed. No longer could they depend on the neighborhood merchant or Maxwell Street shop in the same way that they had in the mid-1920s. Instead, chains and big downtown stores began to compete more aggressively for working people's business and eventually altered the consumer experience of Chicago's ethnic workers.

Flushed with success, chain stores continued to look for new ways to expand their share of the retail market. For much of the twenties, chains were satisfying unmet demand or competing among themselves. But toward the end of the decade, chain managers realized that sustained growth depended on reducing competition among themselves as well as cutting more sharply into the independent merchant's territory. With these ends in mind, chain stores engaged in several new strategies.

First, although big chains like A&P and Walgreen's Drugs continued to expand, they increasingly did so by merging with smaller chains.[63] Concentration, they felt, would diminish competition. Indeed, by 1931, an investigation of grocery chain competition in Chicago concluded that the ferocious advertising of 1923–8 had settled into a more "restrained" phase where stores felt more confident of their respective markets.[64] Chicagoans saw fewer chains more frequently around town.

Second, chains worked harder at crowding out independent stores. On the supply end, they pressured manufacturers and wholesalers to engage in "selective selling," which meant increasing special privileges to large purchasers and shunning stores with poor credit ratings.[65] At the point of distribution, chains widened their own scope, leaving less of the market to small stores. Whereas originally little but a more standardized stock had distinguished the chain grocery or drugstore from the independent one, by the end of the decade that changed as soda fountains, cigars, and sundries joined drugs at Walgreen's and baked goods, dairy products, vegetables, and finally meat found a place alongside groceries at the A&P, whose managers developed the "combination store" and later the self-service "supermarket" in the mid-1930s.[66] As early as 1930, an A&P district supervisor told the manager of one of his Chicago stores that had just begun to sell fresh produce: "There is a Fruit store (independently owned) in our block of stores which must go broke at any cost. . . . The Great A&P will last longer than those people."[67]

On an even more basic level, chains invaded the territory of neighborhood stores by helping to reorganize the commercial structure of the city. Over the course of the twenties, chains and big downtown stores allied with real estate interests and major outlying banks to decentralize the downtown shopping district, moving stores closer to the growing number of middle-class customers living at a distance. As a school textbook explained in 1930, "the retail section in the 'Loop' has put out its tentacles north, south, and west in outliers of the great district. They make shopping easier, especially for the mother of the family. Twenty-six shopping centers or neighborhood retail sections have developed which are so to speak centers of little towns within the city."[68] This centrifugal expansion of the downtown commercial district devastated small shops in its path. Faced with the tripling in value of major business corners between 1921 and 1928 and a corresponding increase in property nearby, many had to move or close down. But outlying shopping areas challenged small stores even more fundamentally because they upset the division of labor between the Loop and neighborhood shops. Rather than competing with a small chain store on the next block, the independent shop owner now faced a veritable downtown only a short walk or streetcar ride away. Here, emporiums of all sorts made the independent's enterprise seem all the more marginal.

Neighborhood storekeepers in working-class areas faced aggressive chain competitors also working hard to overcome their poor public image as "parasites" who deprived independent merchants of their lifeblood and drained money out of a community while giving little in return. Mr. J. C. Penney argued to other Chicago chain operators in 1930 that "the extent to which chain store units fulfill their obligations as citizens of the communities in which they operate is, to my mind, the measure by which their future success in these communities will be determined." He particularly promoted "good citizenship" as the way to win "the wage earning family" who was unwilling to favor "a savings of from one to twenty per cent on its daily outlay against a friendly feeling toward the merchants with whom the wife or husband may be doing business." Knowing how integral local merchants were to the life of a neighborhood, he urged his colleagues to develop "community personality." Get to know customers, involve yourself in local affairs, and support worthy charities.[69] Where the independent merchant had enjoyed an advantage – as community leader – chains mimicked him. Where he was limited – in size, stock, pricing, and location – they strove to surpass him.

The independent merchant began to feel the pinch from the chains in the years just before the depression. Small retailers, particularly the ethnic grocers who predominated in Chicago neighborhoods, had always led a precarious existence. According to a 1923 study, only five out of a hundred grocers stayed in business more than seven years.[70] By the late 1920s, added pressure from aggressive chains pushed more small stores over the edge and increased the difficulty of starting a new business, the dream of many an Italian grocery clerk or Polish delivery man. By the time Jean Brichke returned to a working-class Jewish neighborhood in 1931 after several years absence, she found four chain groceries where there had been only one, a Walgreen's that had pushed out a privately owned drugstore, two chain meat markets instead of local butcher shops, a couple of chain hat shops, a Grant's Dollar Store, and a Woolworth's. The National Tea Store long present in the neighborhood had recently added fresh fruits and vegetables, further threatening independent shops nearby.[71] In 1929, Louis Weinstein, a puller on Maxwell Street, expressed a similar pessimism about the small merchant's future as chains invaded that market as well.[72]

Independent storekeepers fought back. All over the country, they agitated for state legislation to restrict chains by taxing them or limiting their growth. But most of these lobbying efforts failed or resulted in laws soon found unconstitutional. More successfully, enterprising independent merchants and wholesalers organized what became known as "voluntary chains," associations to bring the independent retailer the advantages of quantity buying and sophisticated merchandising while retaining separate ownership and management. By the early 1930s, there were over four hundred such associations among grocers in the country operating in 60,000 stores, close to the 75,000 run by regular food chains. In Illinois, twenty-seven groups worked with 3,151 stores, almost as many retail units as the big chains operated in the state.

Voluntary grocery chains varied in structure. One organization based in Chicago, The Independent Grocers' Alliance (IGA), offered its fifty-eight wholesalers and nine thousand stores nationwide the benefits of centralized buying, standardized equipment, management advice, and a complete advertising program. As a result, an IGA appeared little different from a chain store. In contrast, the Associated Grocers of Chicago (A-G) only provided its six hundred local stores, predominantly owned by "foreign grocers," with merchandise delivered COD and advertising material like handbills, window banners, and newspaper copy. A mere sign in the window identified the A-G grocer. Nonetheless, by joining a voluntary chain, even small-scale ethnic storekeepers began increasingly to resemble the very enterprises they had set out to defeat. Ownership may have remained in private hands, but more standardized operations forced stores to favor national-brand goods and cater less to local and ethnic tastes.[73] Vincent Salamoni found Libby canned goods in his local grocery in Little Sicily by the early 1930s when previously he had only viewed them in an A&P window on Division Street. Now the future security of his grocer, like Mr. Pomorski or Mr. Finkelstein, rested on brand-name products. Similarly, the Midwest Grocery Company, a voluntary chain founded by thirty Polish grocers in Chicago, found it necessary to eliminate credit and conduct business on a strictly cash basis in order to prosper.[74] Over time, it would become less obvious what separated the IGA or the A-G store from A&P, whose onslaught it had survived in one respect but capitulated to in others.

Chain stores and national brands spread into workers' territory only gradually, starting in the late 1920s and intensifying during the Great Depression. For most of the twenties, these vehicles of mass consumption had only a marginal impact on Chicago's workers. Although workers' economic resources were limited, those fruits of mass consumption that they enjoyed – phonograph records, packaged coffee, or ready-made clothing – they bought in their own kind of stores from compatriot merchants. Most important, in contrast to what advertising executives had expected, Chicago's ethnic workers were not transformed into more Americanized, middle-class people by the objects they consumed. Buying an electric vacuum cleaner did not turn Josef Dobrowolski into *True Story*'s hero, Jim Smith. Instead, workers consumed on their own terms, giving their own meaning to new possessions. During the 1920s, the much heralded "mass consumption revolution" passed by most of working-class Chicago.

Workers' ability to sustain independent consumption patterns, however, depended as much on the way urban commercial life was organized as on their personal determination. During most of the decade, workers could depend on the small-scale enterprises in their communities to help them resist the homogenizing influences of mass consumption. So long as chain stores took little interest in the working-class market, foreign groceries and neighborhood drugstores thrived. Once chains and large commercial interests became more aggressive, though, alternative market arrangements became severely threatened. The same danger existed with forms of mass culture, like motion pictures and the radio, whose dissemination local communities could never control easily. The moving picture spectacle and a twist of the radio dial had the potential for drawing workers into mainstream mass culture more successfully than the A&P.

SCREENING OUT AND TUNING IN MASS MEDIA

Chicago's industrial workers may have had limited appetite for chain stores, but they indulged with gusto in motion pictures. Although movies had been around since early in the century, the number of theater seats in Chicago reached its highest level ever by the end of the 1920s. With an average of four performances daily at every theater, by 1929 Chicago had enough movie theater seats for one-half the city's population to attend in the course of a day, and workers made up their fair share, if not more, of that audience.[75] Despite the absence of exact attendance figures, there are consistent clues that picture shows enjoyed enormous popularity among workers throughout the twenties. As the decade began, a Bureau of Labor Statistics survey of the cost of living of workingmen's families found Chicago workers spending more than half of their amusement budgets on movies.[76] Even those fighting destitution made the motion picture a priority. In 1924, more than two-thirds of the families receiving Mother's Aid Assistance in Chicago attended regularly.[77] At the end of the decade, studies showed wage earner families spending a greater percentage of income on picture shows than families of either clerks or professionals. The $22.56 a year they put toward movies equaled that expended by clerks with a third more income and was twice as much as professionals spent who were earning salaries almost four times higher.[78]

Knowing that workers went to the movies is one thing; assessing how they reacted to particular pictures is another. Some historians have analyzed the content of motion pictures for evidence of their meaning to audiences; the fact that workers made up a large part of those audiences convinces these analysts that they took home particular messages decipherable from the films. But the variety of ways that consumers encountered and perceived mass-produced goods suggests that people can have very different reactions to the same experience. Just as the meaning of mass consumption varied with the context in which people confronted it, so too the impact of the movies depended on where, with whom, and in what kind of environment workers went to the movies during the 1920s.[79]

Chicago's workers regularly patronized neighborhood theaters near their homes, not the Chicago, the Uptown, the Granada, and the other monumental picture palaces built during the period, to which many historians have assumed they flocked. Neighborhood theaters had evolved from the storefront nickelodeons prevalent in immigrant, working-class communities before the war. Because of stricter city regulations, neighborhood movie houses were fewer in number, larger, cleaner, better ventilated, and from 5 to 20 cents more expensive than in nickelodeon days. But still they were much simpler than the ornate movie palaces that seated several thousand at a time. Local theaters in a working-class community like South Chicago, next to U.S. Steel's enormous South Works plant, for example, ranged in size from Pete's International, which sat only 250 – more when Pete made the kids double up in each seat for Sunday matinees – to the Gayety, holding 750, to the New Calumet, with room for almost a thousand.[80] Only rarely did workers pay at least twice as much admission, plus carfare, to see the picture palace show. Despite the frequent claims that palaces were "paradise for the common man," in the words of one architect, geographical plotting of Chicago's picture palaces reveals that most of them were nowhere near working-class neighborhoods. A few were downtown, the rest strategically placed in the outlying shopping areas taking shape during the 1920s to attract new middle-class audiences to the movies. Going to the movies was something workers did more easily and cheaply close to home.[81] As a U.S. Steel employee explained, it was

Plate 16. The 4,000-seat Tivoli Theater at Cottage Grove and 63rd Street on the South Side contrasted in almost every way with the Pastime which seated only 400 (p. 99). This so-called picture palace was owned by Balaban & Katz, the largest theater chain in Chicago. In contrast to the Pastime's $0.25 admission, tickets here were a dollar in 1924. That price plus the carfare required from most working-class neighborhoods ensured that middle-class people, not workers, were the picture palace's primary patrons.

"a long way," in many respects, from the steel towns of Southeast Chicago to the South Side's fancy Tivoli Theater.[82]

For much of the decade, working-class patrons found the neighborhood theater not only more affordable but also more welcoming, as the spirit of the community carried over into the local movie hall. Chicago workers may have savored the exotic on the screen, but they preferred encountering it in familiar company. The theater manager, who was often the owner and usually lived in the community, tailored the film selections to local tastes and changed them every day or two to accommodate neighborhood people who attended frequently. Residents of Chicago's industrial neighborhoods rarely had to travel far to find pictures to their liking, which they viewed among neighbors and friends.[83]

When one entered a movie theater in a working-class neighborhood of Chicago, the ethnic character of the community quickly became evident. The language of the yelling and jeering that routinely gave sound to silent movies provided the first clue. "The older Italians used to go to these movies," recalled Ernest Dalle-Molle, "and when the good guys were chasing the bad guys in Italian – they'd say – 'getem' – 'catchem' – out loud in the theater."[84] Stage events accompanying the films told more. In Back of the Yards, near the packinghouses, viewers often saw a Polish play along with the silent film at Schumacher's or the Davis Square Theater.[85] Everywhere, amateur nights offered "local talent" a moment in the limelight. At the Butler Theater in Little Sicily, which the community had rechristened the "Garlic Opera House," Italian music shared the stage with American films.[86] Across town, a small, local movie house seemed so much a part of her Brighton Park community that Anna Blazewicz could comfortably let Polish boys she met while ushering at the People's Theater walk her home afterward.[87] In the neighborhood theater, Hollywood and ethnic Chicago coexisted.

Neighborhood theaters so respected local culture that they reflected community prejudices as well as strengths. The Commercial Theater in South Chicago typified many neighborhood theaters in requiring Mexicans and blacks to sit in the balcony while reserving the main floor for the white ethnics who dominated the community's population.[88] One theater owner explained, "White people don't like to sit next to the colored or Mexicans. . . . We used to have trouble . . . but not now. They go by themselves to their place."[89] Sometimes blacks and Mexicans were not even allowed into neighborhood theaters. Dempsey Travis recalled being told, "Black boys are not admitted here," when he tried to buy a ticket to see "The Three Musketeers." And if he and his cousin did not move on, the ticket seller threatened, the big, blonde, burly usher at the door would "kick our nigger behinds."[90] Blacks were expected to go to the movies in black neighborhoods, Mexicans in whatever theater would have them. In Back of the Yards, the shabbiest theater, the Olympia, had the largest Mexican attendance, which led the rest of the population to scorn it. "That place attacts only 'hoodlums' and 'greasers.' I'd never take my girl there," was a typical Polish attitude.[91] The neighborhood theater reinforced the values of the community as powerfully as any on the screen. This is not to deny that working-class audiences were affected by the content of motion pictures but rather to suggest that when people viewed movies in the familiar world of the neighborhood theater, identification with their local community was bolstered, and the subversive impact of the picture often constrained.

Just as the neighborhood theater mirrored the parochialism of its surrounding community, so the centrally located movie palace aspired to a cosmopolitanism symbolized through its French Renaissance, Egyptian, or other exotic decor. In place of local owners who tailored programs to their audience, the picture palace's management reported to a regional or national theater chain, Chicago's largest being Balaban & Katz. Within a chain, programs were standardized; films and extravagant stage performances circulated from theater to theater, giving audiences all over town, and even the country, the same show. National stars, not amateur neighborhood talent or ethnic troupes, played the palace stage. "We are now producing certain acts in New York and routing them throughout the United States," Sam Katz explained in 1926, "so that the people in Dallas, Texas, are getting the same kind of theatre, the same film, the same character of service, and the same acts as the patrons of our theatres in New York."[92]

Professional distance also separated the audience from the palaces's off-stage employees. In a neighborhood theater, movie goers usually knew the owner or manager and the local kids who worked as ushers. One resident of South Chicago, for example, identified the community's theaters as Pete's International, which belonged to Pete "from up in Michigan . . . a great guy with the kids," the Lincoln, "owned by McGlocklin, a relative of Bill Rowan the dentist," and the Calumet Theater, where his friend Red Connors's mother and father made a living.[93] The picture palace, in contrast, operated like a corporation, with a bureaucratic hierarchy within each theater and throughout the chain. Viewers had contact primarily with ushers, who were not only strangers but were also instructed to treat the public as formally as possible. Chains like Balaban & Katz recruited college boys of specified height, weight, and "clean-cut" features whom they made appear even more official with military-style uniforms and training. Armies of ushers patrolled auditoriums seating several thousand to ensure that none of the familiarity of the neighborhood theater disturbed the awesomeness of the motion picture palace.[94]

In other ways the Balaban & Katz chain sought to create a standardized "American" atmosphere in all its theaters. The brothers Balaban and Katz, not long out of Chicago's West Side Jewish ghetto themselves, wanted nothing to do with the ethnic ambiance of the neighborhood theater; hence they prescribed in their managerial manual, "It has proven to be undesirable to use service employees who have very marked foreign accents." Blacks, they permitted, but only cast in stereotyped roles, as front door footmen ("approaching the old Southern coachman type"), as messenger boys ("of slight and slender build, well formed in good proportions, not markedly of the negro type with heavy features"), and as maids and porters in the washrooms.[95] Management's cosmopolitan ambitions did, however, lead it to reject the provincial admission policies of many small, neighborhood theaters. Balaban & Katz's doormen were instructed to let in whoever could pay. "Our type of service is broad and does not discriminate in any case of race, class, nationality, or creed," the company's manual stated.[96] In every way possible, the new Foxes, Paramounts, and Roxies sought to expunge the working-class, neighborhood character from the movie going experience to make it more respectable in the eyes of the middle class. Working-class and middle-class audiences may have viewed the same films during the 1920s, but they had distinctive ways of going to the movies.

In the mid-1920s, motion pictures in the United States were attracting an attendance of fifty million each week, equivalent to half the nation's population; by 1930, that figure would double, as even more people went more often.[97] But more than the size of the motion picture audience changed toward the end of the decade. Developments in the structure of the movie industry and the technology of film disrupted the equilibrium between the neighborhood theater and the chain-owned picture palace and by the early 1930s altered the way working-class Chicagoans went to the movies.

As the 1920s progressed, the neighborhood movie theater became an increasingly endangered species, not because working-class audiences abandoned it but because of the growing vertical integration of the movie industry. Where film producers, distributors, and exhibitors had once been three separate parties, now a "studio system" was evolving that gave producers control over every step from making to displaying movies. What began as a protective strategy to ensure studios a few prime showcases for their pictures turned into a vicious struggle to assemble nationwide chains once producers discovered that more money stood to be made in theaters than in movie making. By 1930, independent producers as well as exhibitors could hardly compete against the "Big Five" movie chains: Paramount, Loew's, Fox, Warner Brothers, and R.K.O.[98]

Chicago's home-grown Balaban & Katz theater chain exemplified the pattern. This partnership, which had pioneered the concept of outlying picture palaces featuring live stage shows, was operating a dozen movie palaces in Chicago by 1926 along with about ninety smaller theaters in and around the city. At that point, Adolph Zukor of Paramount, who had initiated Hollywood's move into theater ownership in the early 1920s, acquired controlling interest of Balaban & Katz and sent Sam Katz to New York to run the newly created Publix chain of almost a thousand theaters. This aggressive Chicago chain's formula for success would now spread nationwide.[99]

Although the "chaining up" of theaters, as one observer called it, resembled the growth of chain stores during the decade, it differed in an important way.[100] To a greater degree than independent theaters, independent stores were able to rival the chains because they had access to the same sources of supply, even if at greater cost. In the case of motion pictures, however, movie studio chains controlled production as well as distribution. Once chains felt they had saturated the market with picture palaces, they moved into the neighborhoods to profit from the local movie going that had become such a national habit. Wielding total control over film supply, the studio-affiliated chain threatened independent theaters much more than the chain grocery had its independent competition.

By the end of the decade, working-class communities had a hard time avoiding chain theaters. Although workers and their families had not often patronized chain picture palaces, now the chains had come to them, bringing into neighborhoods many of their standardized features. Neighborhood theaters did not close down; they were taken over and expanded by chain operations. Without chain affiliation, the independent theater had a difficult time gaining access to desirable films and competing with chain-associated houses nearby. Theaters of "the majors" enjoyed many advantages – first-run movies, the best play dates, and even protection from other chains, as the Big Five made agreements to minimize competition among themselves. Furthermore, owners who resisted integration and still tried to mount their own programs encountered a new obstacle known as "block booking" or "blind selling."[101] The unaffiliated exhibitor from the neighborhood movie house now found he or she had to take an entire block of a studio's releases at a fixed price; single rentals were prohibitively expensive. No longer could a theater owner easily shape his or her own program. Typical was the lament that in an area like Back of the Yards, "The films being shown today are much the same as those seen in small theatres in other parts of the city."[102] Chain theaters did not push working-class Chicagoans out of their neighborhoods but rather subverted the distinctive character of neighborhood movie going. By the beginning of the thirties, audiences at a Balaban & Katz or Schoenstadt theater in South Chicago and Back of the Yards encountered the same atmosphere, the same kind of management, and the same motion pictures as people in Chicago's more middle-class communities. Even theaters that managed to remain outside the studio system were feeling its influence, much like the independent stores forced into voluntary chains.

The arrival of the "talkies" in the late 1920s standardized movie going even more. The first movies with sound, "Don Juan" and "The Jazz Singer," premiered in Chicago's downtown picture palaces in 1926 and 1927. In no time, sound facilities became a requirement in even the most modest neighborhood theaters. By 1931, the talkies dominated the field so exclusively that a silent picture "had become almost an anachronism," in the words of one contemporary, to be found only in small towns and rural areas.[103] This revolution, however, exacted a special cost from small, neighborhood theaters. According to the same observer, "in recent years, many small houses have been discontinued because of competition from larger theatres and inability to meet the costs of installing apparatus for the production of sound effects."[104]

Whereas talkies attracted record numbers to the movies, the way they were merchandised and the technology they demanded left the public with fewer choices about where to view them. The chains, with the capital to convert theaters to sound and the aim of profiting from sound movies as much as possible, used the talkies to expand their hold over the nation's theaters. Warner Brothers, for example, whose investment in sound propelled it into first place among the Big Five overnight, expanded from one theater in 1927 to seven hundred in 1930. Publix, already far-flung in its theater holdings, acquired five hundred theaters in the mere nine months between September 1929 and May 1930. Over two million people could attend Publix theaters every day.[105]

Chicago's small theaters that had survived the silent era as independents now faced an even more precarious existence with sound. By January 1930, all of Chicago's theaters with 1,500 or more seats – without doubt chain owned – had been wired for sound, in contrast to a mere quarter of those with less than 350 seats and half of those seating between 350 and 1,000.[106] In an industrial neighborhood like South Chicago, at least four small theaters closed in the late 1920s, unable to make the transition to sound. When a group of eighteen teenage boys from this steel mill neighborhood told a University of Chicago researcher in 1934 where they went to the movies, they indicated that they almost always stayed nearby, much as they would have a decade earlier. But the theaters they now preferred showed how much the situation had changed since the mid-1920s. Asked where they went "most of the time," practically all of the boys listed Balaban & Katz and Warner Brothers theaters. The Gayety and Pete's International had managed to survive as independents. But only one boy patronized the Gayety "most of the time," about half the boys "sometimes." Tiny Pete's International Theater received mention for "infrequent" attendance. What had once been two of the most popular theaters in the neighborhood were now marginalized by chain competition and relegated to showing B westerns.[107]

More than chain ownership would make the theaters that Chicago workers patronized over the next decade less reflective of their local communities. The talkies themselves changed the theater atmosphere. No longer did the audience provide the spoken words, mediating between the film and the community as it commented and jeered. Now, movie actors talked directly to individuals in the audience, whose group affiliations received little reinforcement from the crowd, since with sound, audiences hushed all interjections.[108] As one film historian has aptly phrased it, "The talking audience for silent pictures became a silent audience for talking pictures." Sound also helped chains banish the live entertainment that had previously framed feature films. Taped shorts distributed nationally replaced ethnic troupes and amateur talent shows in neighborhood theaters and even eliminated stage shows at all but the largest picture palaces.[109]

In almost every respect, what had made for a neighborhood way of movie going disappeared with the vertical integration of the industry and the arrival of sound. By the mid-1930s, the four largest chains in Chicago – Balaban & Katz, Lubliner & Trinz, Schoenstadt, and Warner Brothers – would control a third of all theaters and as many as two-thirds of all seats. Between the heyday of the storefront nickelodeon and the peak of the chain theater age – before the U.S. Department of Justice brought antitrust action – the number of Chicago's theaters declined by one half, whereas despite population increase, the 9 to 1 ratio of people to seats held steady (Table 8). This meant that in the course of two decades, Chicago movie goers witnessed a major redistribution of seats from small, neighborhood movie houses to larger, chain-owned theaters.[110] Workers would still find theaters in their neighborhoods during the 1930s, but their ambiance had become as standardized as the films on the screen (Table 9).

Even if local communities did not control the production of motion pictures during the 1920s, they still managed for a good part of the decade to influence how residents received them. The independent, neighborhood theater in that way resembled the neighborhood store, harmonizing standardized products with local, particularly ethnic, culture. Both buffered the potential disorientation of mass culture by allowing patrons to consume within the intimacy of the community. Rather than disrupting the existing peer culture, that peer culture accommodated the new products. In both cases, too, aggressive expansion by competing chain enterprises, not the community's abandonment of these local alternatives, undermined their viability in the years shortly before the depression.

Shopping and theater going were easily mediated by the local community because they were public, collective activities. Radio, in contrast, entered the privacy of the home. At least potentially, what went out across the airwaves could transport listeners, as individuals, into a different world. But as it turned out, workers who listened to the radio did not have to forsake their cultural communities any more than did those who went to stores or motion pictures.

Radio broadcasting made its public debut when Pittsburgh's KDKA covered the Harding – Cox presidential election of 1920. Within a year, Chicago had its first radio station. Radio attracted Chicago's workers

Table 8. *Chicago motion picture theaters by size and ratio of population to seats*

Number of seats	1913 Number of theaters	1913 Cumulative percent	1916 Number of theaters	1916 Cumulative percent	1923 Number of theaters	1923 Cumulative percent
1–300	415	68.5	304	60.9	121	33.6
301–1000	175	97.4	171	95.2	162	78.6
1001–2000	16	100.0	24	100.0	64	96.4
2001–3000	0		0		9	98.9
Over 3000	0		0		4	100.0
Total	606		499		360	
Total seating capacity	251,044		224,403		275,446	
Ratio of population to seats	9 : 1		9 : 1		10 : 1	

Number of seats	1926 Number of theaters	1926 Cumulative percent	1937 Number of theaters	1937 Cumulative percent
1–350	116	29.9	49	15.5
351–750	92	53.6	82	41.5
751–1000	81	74.5	77	65.8
1001–1500	51	87.6	47	80.7
1501–1750	10	90.2	15	85.4
1751–2100	17	94.6	18	91.1
2101–2300	2	95.1	3	92.1
2301–2500	5	96.4	6	94.0
Over 2500	14	100.0	19	100.0
Total	388		316	
Total seating capacity	na		338,000	
Ratio of population to seats	9 : 1		9 : 1	

Note: na, data not available.

Source: Lois Halley, "A Study of Motion Pictures in Chicago as a Medium of Communication" (M.A. Thesis, University of Chicago, 1924), pp. 15–18; Arthur J. Todd et al., *The Chicago Recreation Survey 1937*, vol. 2 (Chicago: Chicago Recreation Commission and Northwestern University, 1938), pp. 31–2.

Table 9. *Motion picture theaters in five Chicago neighborhoods inhabited by industrial workers, 1937*[a]

Neighborhood	Population (1934)	Number of theaters	Number of seats	Average number of seats per theater	Ratio of population to seats
1. Southeast Chicago[b] (steel mills)	84,109	7	7,096	1,014	12 : 1
2. Packingtown[c] (meatpackers)	130,325	15	9,436	629	14 : 1
3. Old immigrant neighborhoods[d] (garment industry)	370,000	40	33,758	844	11 : 1
4. Southwest Corridor[e] (International Harvester and Western Electric)	244,751	25	21,188	848	12 : 1
5. Black Belt[f]	179,560	17	15,551	915	12 : 1

[a] See Map 1.

[b] Includes South Chicago, East Side, Hegewisch, and South Deering.

[c] Includes New City and Bridgeport.

[d] Includes West Town, Near West Side, and Lower West Side.

[e] Includes North Lawndale, South Lawndale, Brighton Park, and McKinley Park.

[f] Includes Grand Boulevard, Douglas, and Washington Park.

Source: Arthur J. Todd et al., *The Chicago Recreation Survey 1937*, vol. 4 (Chicago: Chicago Recreation Commission and Northwestern University, 1938).

from the start because it was affordable, in contrast to other modern technology like the automobile, and it appealed to people's mechanical interests. Early radio was much more of a hobby than our casual way of listening today suggests. Many people built their own radios. Basic mechanical skills and a few purchases at the ten-cent store were all that it took to construct a simple crystal set. Joseph Provenzano scrounged an oatmeal box from his mother and copper wire from the local dump, buying only the crystal, dial, and earphones.[111] Greater cost and effort went into making a more powerful vacuum-tube model, but there too a little ingenuity and a few bucks went a long way. Typical was the Mexican steelworker in South Chicago who put his night school English to work building a tube radio from a kit. Workers at Western Electric even got help from their employer; the Hawthorne Evening School offered courses in radio and the company store sold parts.[112] Radio retailers recognized that workers were particularly apt to build their own radios. "If the store is located in a community most of the inhabitants of which are workmen," a study of the radio industry showed, "there will be a large proportion of parts," in contrast to the more expensive, preassembled models stocked in the radio stores of fashionable districts.[113] That radio appealed to the artisan instincts of Chicago's workers was evident in their neighborhoods. As early as 1922, a Chicago radio journalist noted that "crude homemade aerials are on one roof in ten along all the miles of bleak streets in the city's industrial zones."[114]

Even workers who bought increasingly affordable, ready-made radios were active participants, spending evenings bent over their dial boards to get "the utmost possible DX" (distance) and then recording their triumphs in a radio log. "I've got 120 stations on my radio," one working man gleefully announced.[115] Beginning in the fall of 1922, Chicago stations agreed not to broadcast at all after 7:00 p.m. on Monday evenings to allow the city's radio audience to tune in distant stations otherwise blocked because they broadcasted on the same wavelengths as local stations. "Silent nights" were religiously observed in other cities as well.[116] In addition to distance, radio enthusiasts concerned themselves with technical challenges such as cutting down static, making "the short jumps," and operating receivers with one hand.[117] This early hands-on association, along with accusations of "low-brow" programming, earned radio the scorn of the "high-brow" elite and rooted its popularity in the middle and lower classes. Study after study revealed that despite efforts to attract their patronage, upper-class people listened least often, even when they owned one or more radios.[118]

Not only was radio listening active, but it was also far from isolating. By 1930 in Chicago, there was one radio for every two or three households in workers' neighborhoods, and people sat around in local shops and neighbors' parlors listening together. Surveys showed that, on the average, four or five people listened to one set at any particular time; in 85 percent of homes, the entire family listened together (Table 10).[119] In fact, in their study of Middletown, the Lynds noted that mothers often remarked that their families used to scatter in the evening, "but now we all sit around and listen to the radio."[120] In working-class communities radio listening came to resemble shopping and movie going in the way it brought neighbors and relatives together. Even before most people had loudspeakers on their radios, they shared earphones or, like Joseph Provenzano, "monkeyed around with the crystal until it got real loud. Then we'd take the earphones and we'd put them in a pot . . . and the sound there, you know, would reverberate in the pot and then we'd all listen to it."[121] The flat or shop with a radio became an instant center of social life. Communal radio listening mediated between local and mass culture much like the neighborhood store or theater.

But even more important to an investigation of the impact of the radio on workers' consciousness, early radio broadcasting had a distinctly grassroots orientation. To begin with, the technological limitations of early radio ensured that small, nearby stations dominated the ether waves. In 1923, half the stations in the United States broadcast at under 100 watts of power; in 1925, 38 percent still did. At 100 watts, a station could could count on no more than 3 miles of very good service, 15 of good, and 150 of fair. There were no stations above 5,000 watts until 1925, none above 10,000 until 1928. And even in that year, a survey commissioned by NBC found that 80 percent of the radio audience regularly listened to local, not distant, stations.[122] Furthermore, with no clear way of financing radio stations, it fell to existing institutions to subsidize radio broadcasting. From the start, nonprofit ethnic, religious, and labor groups put radio to their service. In 1925, almost a third of the 571 radio stations nationwide were owned by

Table 10. *Radio ownership in selected working-class and middle-class Chicago neighborhoods, 1930*[a]

Neighborhood	Number of households owning radios	Percentage of households owning radios
A. Radio ownership in five working-class neighborhoods, 1930		
1. Southeast Chicago[b] (steel mills)	10,927	53.0
2. Packingtown[c] (meatpackers)	14,579	46.1
3. Old immigrant neighborhoods[d] (garment industry)	34,491	34.6
4. Southwest Corridor[e] (International Harvester and Western Electric)	32,877	55.4
5. Black Belt[f]	19,673	46.4
B. Radio ownership in four middle-class neighborhoods, 1930		
1. Avalon Park	2,241	84.0
2. Chatham	8,262	81.2
3. Greater Grand Crossing	12,175	76.0
4. Englewood	15,386	67.6

[a] See Map 1.
[b] Includes South Chicago, East Side, Hegewisch, and South Deering.
[c] Includes New City and Bridgeport.
[d] Includes West Town, Near West Side, and Lower West Side.
[e] Includes North Lawndale, South Lawndale, Brighton Park, and McKinley Park.
[f] Includes Grand Boulevard, Douglas, and Washington Park.
Source: Louis Wirth and Margaret Furez, eds., *Local Community Fact Book, 1938* (Chicago: Chicago Recreation Commission, 1938).

educational institutions and churches, less than 4 percent by commercial broadcasting companies.[123] Even when newspapers, department stores, and radio shops sponsored stations, as they frequently did, they ran them as public services, not as commercial operations. The profit came from radio set sales. The local orientation of these sponsoring organizations coupled with the limitations of radio technology and an excessive demand for access to the airwaves gave radio broadcasting in the early years a strong local character, even in a major center of radio broadcasting like Chicago.[124]

Radio consequently brought familiar distractions into the homes of Chicago's workers: talk, ethnic nationality hours, labor news, church services, and vaudeville-type musical entertainment by hometown, often ethnic talent. More innovative forms of radio programming, such as situation comedy shows, dramatic series, and soap operas, only developed later. Sometimes listeners even knew a singer or musician personally since many stations' shoestring budgets forced them to rely on amateurs. Whoever dropped in at the station had a chance to be heard. Well-known entertainers, moreover, shied away from radio at first, dissatisfied with the low pay but also uncomfortable performing without an audience and fearful of undercutting their box office attractiveness with free, on-air concerts. Whereas tuning in a radio may have been a new experience, few surprises came "out of the ether." As a result, early radio in Chicago promoted ethnic, religious, and working-class affiliations rather than undermining them, as many advocates of mass culture had predicted.[125]

Almost from the start, ethnic groups saw radio as a way of keeping their countrymen and women in touch with native culture. By 1926, several radio stations explicitly devoted to ethnic programming broadcasted in Chicago – WGES, WSBC, WEDC, and WCRW – whereas other stations carried "nationality hours." Through the radio, Chicago's huge foreign-speaking population heard news from home, native music, and special broadcasts like Benito Mussolini's messages to Italians living in America. Radio, moreover, helped ethnic groups to overcome internal divisions based on European political geography and to become more unified ethnic communities of Chicago "Italians" or "Poles" by the late 1920s.[126]

Churches, likewise, quickly grasped the potential of radio as a tool of exhortation; within weeks of KDKA's first broadcast in Pittsburgh, a nearby Episcopal pastor was preaching on the air every Sunday morning. By the mid-1920s, Chicago radio audiences could hear innumerable Sunday services as well as daily morning worship and Bible readings. A religious holiday like the Jewish Yom Kippur or a special event like the International Eucharistic Congress, which the Catholic Church convened in Chicago during the summer of 1926, received extensive coverage on local stations.[127] Some clergy worried that broadcasting would diminish church attendance, but most agreed that any decline was more than compensated for by new recruits. "The radio has reintroduced religion in hundreds of thousands of American homes," proclaimed one church leader.[128] Even the minister of a small Slovak church in a working-class neighborhood on Chicago's Northwest Side professed enthusiasm about the radio as early as 1925 "as a medium through which religion can become or be made more popular."[129] Ironically, antimodern religionists, the Fundamentalists, proved the most aggressive in evangelizing through the radio. Chicago's WMBI, inaugurated in 1926 by the Moody Bible Institute, exemplified the spirit of revivalism on the air. Through preaching, devotionals, a weekly Radio School of the Bible, the "Know Your Bible," or KYB, Club, and plenty of gospel music, WMBI used new technology to incite "old-time religion."[130]

Ethnic and religious groups were not alone in recognizing that radio offered a new way of wielding influence. The Chicago Federation of Labor had failed after World War I in its political campaigns – in unionizing industrial workers, in mounting a successful Labor Party challenge, and in fighting off antilabor initiatives by business and government. But in the twenties, the federation seized radio as a new strategy for reaching Chicago's workers and articulating their concerns. If working people had retreated from explicitly political struggles, they might be reached on cultural ground. Radio would help "awaken the slumbering giant of labor."[131] Discussion about operating a labor radio station began as early as 1923, and in July 1926, the federation founded the first labor union station in the country, WCFL, to "influence or educate the public mind upon the meaning and objects of Trade Unions and of the Federation of Labor, correct wrong impressions by broadcasting the truth, and advance progressive economic ideas which when actually put into operation will benefit the masses of the nation."[132] Without the "Voice of Labor," Chicago labor leaders feared, radio could easily become the voice of capital.[133]

WCFL exemplified the grassroots character of early radio. Recognizing that not many workers could afford expensive, ready-made radio sets, the station actively encouraged people to make their own. The *WCFL Radio Magazine*, launched in 1927, devoted extensive space to articles on the latest techniques in building home sets. Listeners could also tune in weekly to the "Radio Study Club," where station engineers discussed how to make radio receivers along with new methods of radio transmission. For those less electronically oriented, WCFL engineers developed a low-cost, five-tube set that a local factory made and the federation sold on the installment plan.[134] WCFL programming, furthermore, epitomized noncommercial, community-sponsored radio

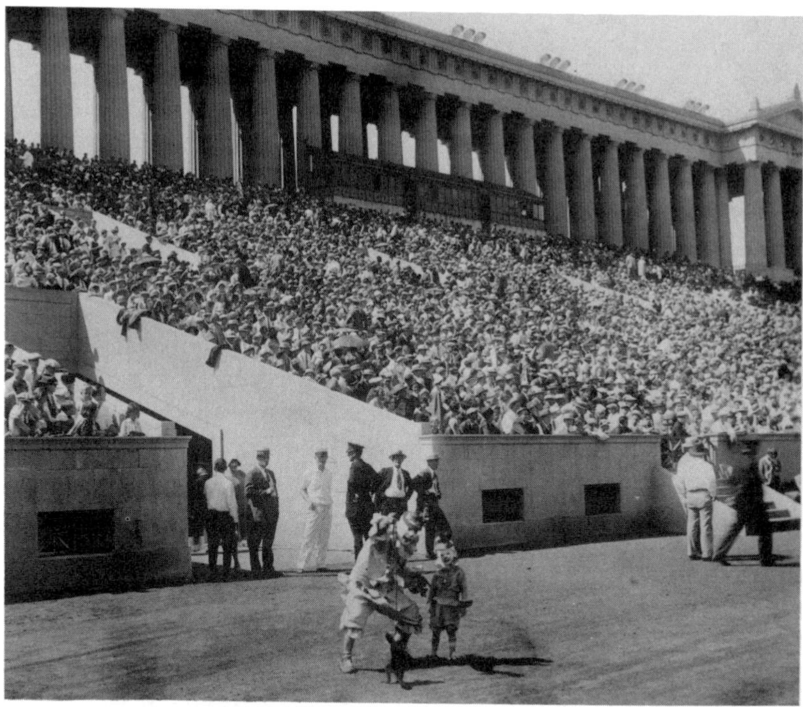

Plate 17. On Labor Day, 1927, thousands of Chicagoans assembled at Soldier Field in Grant Park for a celebration to benefit WCFL, the Chicago Federation of Labor's "Voice of Labor" radio station. In this early era before commercial, network radio came to dominate the airwaves, local nonprofit radio stations like WCFL were common. When Chicago workers turned on the radio, they heard familiar messages from labor unions, churches, ethnic societies, and other grassroots organizations.

broadcasting. Not only was the station supported by union donations and listener contributions, but also union locals sponsored particular shows. "Popular Program by courtesy of Carpenters' Local Union #54, Cicero, Illinois" was a typical weekly listing on the 1927 schedule.[135]

That Carpenter's Local 54 sponsored popular entertainment, not serious discussion of labor issues, is significant. Before WCFL began broadcasting, its founders claimed, "the program of this broadcasting station will be largely an educational campaign, consisting of speeches, lectures, reviews of the topics of the day, labor legislation, economics and so on."[136] Yet they soon recognized that to compete effectively for radio listeners, they had to offer amusement along with education. "Labor News Flashes," "Chicago Federation of Labor Hour," and "Labor Talks from the International Ladies Garment Workers' Union in New York City" went over best when alternated with entertainment like "Earl Hoffman's Chez Pierre Orchestra" and "Musical Potpourri." Ethnic programs like "Polish Hour" and "Irish Hour" and daily and Sunday church services further attracted working-class audiences to the station.[137] But however much like other stations WCFL seemed, when union miners went on strike, listeners heard nightly appeals for clothing and supplies. When the Chicago florists' organization locked out unionized greenhouse workers, listeners were urged not to buy flowers for Easter. When the American Federation of Teachers held their annual convention in Chicago, listeners shared many of their deliberations.[138] The public recognized that a serious mission underlied WCFL entertainment. In September 1927 Mrs. Mary Schultz wrote to WCFL asking how her truck driver son might enter a trade and closed her letter by saying, "We enjoy your programs very much and our Radio is seldom changed to any other station." Hers and other letters to the station testify that for many members of Chicago's working class during the "lean years" of labor activism, WCFL was the labor movement.[139]

Early radio listening neither enticed people away from habitual family and community circles nor undermined existing identities, as for example, Polish, Catholic, and working class. Instead, radio frequently reinforced these affiliations. No doubt radio exposed some people to new cultural experiences, to different ethnic and religious traditions, or to new kinds of music. But most important, workers discovered that participating in radio, as in mass consumption and the movies, did not require repudiation of established social identities. Radio at middecade, dominated as it was by local, noncommercial broadcasting, offered little evidence that it was fulfilling the predictions of some advocates and proving itself "the great leveler," capable of sweeping away "the mutual distrust and enmity of laborer and executive . . . business man and artist, scientist and cleric, the tenement dweller and the estate owner, the hovel and the mansion."[140]

The local, noncommercial structure of early radio may have nurtured ethnic, religious, and labor programming, but at the same time it raised the problems of who would pay for radio broadcasting and how the airwaves would be regulated. The resolution of these issues over the course of the decade would undermine radio's early grassroots character and thereby alter the listening experience of Chicago's workers.

The first of these issues, how to fund radio stations, troubled radio promoters from the start and continued to plague them as more than half the 1,079 stations established between 1922 and 1925 went bankrupt.[141] Operating a radio station proved too costly for many of the nonprofit organizations that undertook to do it. Leaders in the radio field debated different schemes for financing stations, from taxing owners or manufacturers of radios to selling public subscriptions, but most opposed involving the government or charging consumers.[142] In this vacuum, one of the most powerful broadcasting stations, American Telephone and Telegraph's WEAF in New York City, began experimenting with paid commercials and thereby launched a wave of "toll stations" all over the country. When the public, including Secretary of Commerce Herbert Hoover, protested that direct commercial advertising would contaminate the airwaves, a form of indirect sponsorship arose as a compromise in which a company underwrote a show in exchange for prestige and publicity.[143] By the mid-twenties, the big radio stations began featuring programs like the Eveready Hour, the A&P Gypsies, the Gold Dust Twins, and the Ipana Troubadours. As is obvious from this list, manufacturers and distributors of brand-name products were the first to appreciate the commercial potential of radio.[144]

Interest in advertising intensified with the emergence of network radio, which gave advertisers a national audience. It was not accidental that WEAF, initiator of commercial radio, became the home station of the National Broadcasting Company when it formed the first radio station chain in 1926. Almost from the start, the success of commercial radio and national networks were inseparably linked. The promise of national exposure attracted advertisers, whose fees made possible more elaborate radio productions. These first-rate network shows put independent stations at a disadvantage and expanded the audience for network radio. Those very same commercial interests who were competing during the 1920s for a larger share of the consumer market – companies like Metropolitan Life, Walgreen Drugs, Palmolive Soap, and Publix Theaters – seized radio as a new vehicle for making their appeal.[145] According to J. Walter Thompson's Radio Chief, William Ensign, "National advertisers find that radio . . . carries their names or the names of their products into millions of homes in a way which is not only conducive to good will building – but which stamps those names with a personality that makes them mean more than just something to be bought."[146]

By the end of the twenties, the distinction between indirect and direct advertising had blurred. Increasingly, advertising agencies were not only advising clients about radio campaigns but also were producing shows for them to be sold as "packages" to the networks.[147] These shows not very subtly plugged the products of their sponsors. Metropolitan Life Insurance brought radio listeners morning exercises, Aunt Jemima and A&P gave recipe advice, and the Hoosier Manufacturing Company broadcasted lectures on efficiency in the kitchen.[148] Radio had come a long way from featuring amateur talent on local stations. By solving its finance problem through advertising, American radio set itself on a course in which successful selling became the end purpose of programming.

Resolving how to regulate access to the airwaves also favored commercial, network radio over local, nonprofit stations. During the grassroots era of radio, chaos reigned on the airwaves, as more stations sought to broadcast than there were frequencies available. In the absence of any more recent legislation than the Radio Act of 1912, which required all persons operating wireless communications to get a license from the Secretary of Commerce, Secretary Hoover assigned wavelengths to radio stations. When the demand for air space and time surpassed the supply, Hoover also began limiting the power and hours of some stations while prohibiting others from broadcasting at all. By 1925, almost 600 stations were on the air for at least a few hours a week, while 175 applications remained on file. In Chicago, forty stations used channel space adequate for only seven full-time stations by sharing time and transmitting at different powers.

But this make-shift regulatory system was far from perfect and, many felt, far from fair. The Department of Commerce denied WCFL a license, for example, until the federation accused it of favoring large, corporate stations. Once official, WCFL continued to resent the limits on hours, power, and frequency set by Commerce. Finally in 1926, Chicago station WJAZ became so disgusted at being restricted to two hours of broadcasting a week that it defied the terms of its license to test the Secretary of Commerce's authority to regulate. In decisions that only exacerbated the crisis, the courts and the U.S. attorney general ruled that the Department of Commerce had no power to police the airwaves, leaving stations to regulate themselves. The result was increased chaos. Between July 1926 and February 1927, over two hundred new stations went on the air (sixty-five of them in Chicago) while old stations jumped to new frequencies and increased their power and hours. Radio broadcasting became even more of a free-for-all.

Congressional passage of the Radio Act of 1927 finally brought order to the airways, but at the expense of small, local stations. The Federal Radio Commission created by the new law revoked the license of every radio station and then required that stations reapply. Under the new regime, allocations of frequency, power, and hours rested on "public interest, convenience and necessity," which in the minds of the commissioners translated into technical and programming quality. Because commercial stations could mount superior productions with advertising revenue, they walked away with the strongest power, the clearest frequencies, and the longest broadcast periods. Of the twenty-four clear channels created by the commission, twenty-one went to network stations affiliated with NBC or the brand-new CBS. WCFL, on the other hand, suffered considerable loss of broadcasting time as it was required to share its frequency with two other stations. For years the Chicago Federation of Labor continued to fight for a clear channel at 50,000 watts, eventually taking its case to Congress. But few local nonprofit stations shared WCFL's pugnaciousness against what it termed "the Radio Trust." Many, instead, gave up. In the end the Radio Act of 1927 brought stability to American radio but accomplished it by consolidating the broadcasting industry along commercial and national lines. By 1930, fewer, more powerful stations, at least a third of which were commercial and a fifth affiliated with national networks, ruled the airwaves.[149]

Chicago workers experienced this consolidation of radio broadcasting very directly. When they turned on the radio in the late 1920s, they found more network programs, more advertising, and fewer local shows than just a few years before. By 1930, all the major radio stations in Chicago had affiliated with NBC or CBS, and many smaller ones, feeling pressure to broadcast more elaborate programs, negotiated to carry some network shows. Even WCFL worked out an agreement with NBC to purchase certain programs. Soon, "Rudy Vallee's Orchestra," "Roxy and His Gang," and "Squibb's Program" flanked "Labor News Flashes."[150] By 1930, hopes for a noncommerical system of radio had also died. Advertising seemed the only strategy to pay radio's way. Ethnic programming turned to ethnic merchants or outside businesses eager to penetrate ethnic markets, and soon even WCFL sold time to sponsors like the Ford Manufacturing Company who sought access to workers' pocketbooks. By the mid-1930s, a study of retail advertising on Chicago radio stations revealed that WCFL had become a prime recipient of local advertising dollars.[151]

Religious broadcasting made a similar transition to the commercial, network era. Many commercial stations carried nonsectarian religious programs like Chicago station WLS's "The Little Brown Church of the Vale, a lay-man's community church," designed to reach a broad audience. Networks also made programs with denominational appeal available to their affiliates, such as the pan-Protestant "National Religious Service," "The Jewish Hour," and Father Coughlin's "Radio League of the Little Flower." Commercial stations ran these religious broadcasts as a public service, without paying sponsors, to lure listeners and legitimate stations where advertising underwrote most everything else.[152]

Ethnic, religious, and labor programming by no means disappeared with the changes in radio at the end of the decade. Instead, much the way ethnic stores evolved into outposts for brand-name goods and neighborhood theaters became linked to movie chains, local radio stations became more national and commercial in order to survive. Where once radio had provided a voice for community groups, by the 1930s it treated these constituencies as potential markets for advertisers' products. Radio, furthermore, bolstered similar commercial trends in shopping and movie going by giving national standard brands and chain theaters exposure through advertising. And when stores piped in radio shows, movie theaters arranged schedules around the popular "Amos 'n' Andy Show," and radio stars made Hollywood pictures, some aspects of mass culture reinforced others.[153]

It is difficult to know how Chicago audiences reacted to the commercialization of radio. The little evidence we have suggests that people opposed it without having any realistic alternative. When the major Chicago broadcasters set out to discontinue silent night in 1927 because it interfered with radio's new priorities – earning advertising revenue and presenting network shows – the public opposed the move by more than five to one, according to a *Chicago Daily News* poll.[154] Apparently, listeners preferred "to fish" for obscure, distant stations than to know that nationwide everyone was listening to the same programs. Nonetheless, silent night was put to final rest in November of 1927. At just about the same time, a survey of Chicagoans' attitudes toward radio as an advertising medium revealed that people appreciated the high quality of network programs sponsored by national advertisers but not their advertisements. Half of those surveyed said they still preferred local Chicago programs to chain broadcasts originating in New York.[155]

But the trend was against local, amateur, noncommercial radio. Ironically, no one better articulated this transformation than a spokesman for NBC's Chicago station, WMAQ, when he testified before a Federal Radio Commission hearing in 1930: "We believe that the fundamental reason for the remonstrances to-day by the special interests, by religion, by education, and by similar groups is clear. The minorities, and they include many groups of educated and intelligent people, are to-day receiving little or no radio service from the average cleared channel stations. They have been lost sight of."[156]

Radio may have ended up, by 1930, in the hands of national, commercial networks, but that fate was by no means preordained. Through much of the decade, radio offered local ethnic, religious, and labor groups a new way to reach constituents and reinforced the cultural predilections of Chicago workers. As with standard brands and the movies, workers encountered radio first through the filter of their ethnic and working-class communities. Only when chain stores, chain theaters, and chain radio stations acted to expand their hold over the consumer market and set out to destroy independent competitors did mass culture force a more uniform message onto its audiences.

By having community stores, theaters, and radio stations disseminate mass culture during the 1920s, workers avoided the kind of cultural reorientation that Madison Avenue had expected. Working-class families could buy phonographs or brand goods, go regularly to the picture show, and be avid radio fans without feeling pressure to abandon their existing social affiliations. Participating in mass culture made them feel no more mainstream or middle class, no less ethnic, religious, or working class than they already felt. When a politically aware Communist worker asserted that "I had bought a jalopy in 1924, and it didn't change me. It just made it easier for me to function," he spoke for other workers who may not have been as self-conscious but who like him were not made culturally middle class by the new products they consumed.[157]

It might be argued that those working-class Chicagoans most changed by mass culture were not adult workers but their American-raised children, many of whom would not join the work force until the 1930s. Certainly, their parents often thought so. When Mary Shemerdiak lamented that "the people of this younger generation are of the shallow type who care for clothes, shows and dances" and not for Ukranian clubs or other ethnic activities, she voiced a complaint common among immigrant parents in Chicago.[158] During the 1920s, foreign-born industrial workers who had emigrated to American before the war often were distressed to find their children, growing into their teens and early twenties, attracted to what seemed the most mainstream forms of mass culture.

Ethnic, working-class parents were right to observe that their children craved stylish fashions, the latest motion pictures, popular tunes on the radio, and evenings at commercial dance halls. Among this first American generation, the normal process of emancipation from parental authority had taken on a larger cultural meaning. Young people's struggle for emotional autonomy from parents converged with efforts to assimilate into American society, making adolescence a time to escape the confining ethnic worlds of their families.

Mass culture provided an ideal vehicle for expressing independence and becoming more American. Whether a teenager belonged to a gang of "delinquents" who stole cars, shoplifted at Goldblatt's and snuck into the movies, or at the other extreme, joined the growing ranks of working-class youth attending high school, he or she participated in a peer society that celebrated the most commercial aspects of mass culture.[159] Fashion in clothes most visibly separated ethnic youth from their parents. Social worker Sophonisba Breckinridge noted that although immigrant mothers were accustomed to "unchanging fashions which were judged entirely by their quality," sons and daughters bought flashy clothing to last only a season. Interviews with men and women in their twenties who worked at Western Electric's Hawthorne Works revealed that they viewed earning money to buy "swell clothes" as a prime benefit of working.[160]

But a closer look at how the children of Chicago's industrial workers, some of whom were already employed themselves, partook of mass culture reveals that this attraction did not entail as much repudiation of ethnic identity as parents feared. Rather, more like their parents than was at first apparent, young people looked to their ethnic peer groups to mediate mass culture. Interests that seemed unorthodox at home were nonetheless pursued in ethnic company at neighborhood movie houses, club rooms, and dance halls. The way that they participated in mass culture did not so much tear ethnic youth from their roots as help them reconcile foreign pasts with contemporary American culture.

Young people spent enormous amounts of time at picture shows, but given the neighborhood structure of movie going during the 1920s, they created worlds of their own peers within local theaters. A study of the habits of ten thousand Chicago schoolchildren from all economic groups found the typical youth going to a neighborhood theater once or twice a week alone or with siblings and friends. Three-fourths of the young people did not go to the movies with their parents.[161] In ethnic working-class neighborhoods the situation was extreme: Theater audiences consisted of multitudes of unaccompanied youth.[162] There, laughing and yelling with their friends, young people were hardly lost at the movies. Polish adolescents in a North Side neighborhood went so far as to treat a nearby theater like a clubhouse and would arrange to meet there almost nightly. One youth explained, "There is about fifteen or sixteen of the bunch and we always go 'way down in front and sit down there under the clock.... We always sit over along the wall next to the door."[163]

When Chicago's working-class youth were not socializing in movie houses, they could be found at their neighborhood clubs. Whether Jewish, Polish, Italian, or Czech, whether from Lawndale, Back of the Yards, Little Sicily, or Cicero, young people built their social lives around clubs. Known as "basement clubs," "social clubs," or "athletic clubs" and dubbed a myriad of all-American sounding names (such as the Bluebirds, Aces, Spartan A.C., Lawndale Sportsman, Owls, East Side Wildcats, Wigwams, Yankees, and True Pals), these associations guided the cultural experimentation of young people from their mid-teens to mid-twenties. Here, in rented quarters away from parental eyes and ears, club members played cards, held "socials," and planned sports contests and annual dances. To the radio's constant blaring – the "prime requisite" of every club, according to one observer – club members practiced the ways of the larger world, its fashions, music, games, dance steps, social mores, and sex role stereotypes. Parents and ethnic associations often condemned these clubs for corrupting the young. In a typical expression of concern, the Jewish People's Institute located "the problem of 'basement clubs'" in their lack of adult supervision, non-Jewish programs, and "frequenting of commercialized recreation facilities where boys and girls do mingle freely."[164] These fears, however, prevented the Jewish People's Institute and its counterparts in other ethnic communities from appreciating the extent to which clubs kept their youth socializing within ethnic, neighborhood circles and encountering mass culture in familiar company.[165] Adults also overlooked another indication that young people's rejection of ethnicity was far from complete. When funds ran low, club members approached trusted neighborhood merchants like Calistro's Barbershop, Kantor's Delicatessen, Elfman's Funeral Parlor, Anton Balaty's Grocery, and Fuka's Men's Clothing to take out ads in dance programs and purchase team uniforms.[166]

As concerned as immigrant parents were about clubs, they disapproved more of the commercial dance palaces that had invaded the urban scene since the war and were enticing their children further from home. Critics shared with devotees an image of the dance hall as a place where young working people stepped out of their diverse pasts to become part of a new generation, all dressing the same, doing the same dances, conversing in the same slang.

But when young people left the shelter of a neighborhood club dance for one of Chicago's ballrooms (the Aragon, the Trianon, Guyon's Paradise, Dreamland, and the White City Ballroom, considered the city's best), they remained part of an ethnic social network more than the popular image conveyed or their disapproving parents understood. Although some youth no doubt thrived on the anonymity and sexual possibilities these big dance floors offered, most indulged in the famous bands and cosmopolitan atmosphere while still enjoying familiar company. Whenever observers penetrated beyond the surface uniformity of the crowd, they inevitably recognized that a fine-tuned social system was at work. Most attending were working-class people, from "the great hinderland of Chicago . . . the Stockyards, Steeltown, the West Side," in one commentator's words. Particular dance halls, by proximity to certain transport lines and by reputation, attracted people from some ethnic groups or neighborhoods more than others, and certain nights often were dominated by one group. Within a large pavilion like Dreamland, ethnic groups laid claim to different areas of the floor: the Italians by the door, the Poles and Bohemians at the extreme other end, the Jews in-between. These ethnic clusters, furthermore, were made up of cliques that arrived together or met there regularly: the Vernon Athletic Club, which attended en masse every Saturday and Sunday night to dance with its own girls; a crowd from Lane Technical High School; a group of Polish girl friends from South Chicago; eight steel workers from the same mill.[167] Florence Roselli and Margaret Sabella both frequented the Aragon with a group of Italian girls from the neighborhood: "The words would go around that Saturday night we're going to the Aragon." There they would dance with boys they knew from the neighborhood, away from parental vigilance, and even more importantly, they would meet young Italian men from other parts of the city.[168]

Whereas the social world of ethnic working-class youth expanded when they went out dancing, it grew in carefully circumscribed ways. Without a doubt, a night at the dance hall offered more interesting opportunities than a meeting of the local parish's Polish National Alliance chapter, but it more likely meant getting to know a Pole from across town than someone of totally different background. Mass culture in the 1920s helped Chicago's young people build bridges between isolated ethnic neighborhoods. While trying to be American, they learned to be Chicago Italians, Jews, and Poles.

Undeniably, members of the younger generation were more attracted to mainstream mass culture than their parents, but even then, their greater participation did not force them to abandon ethnic and class affiliations. Rather they used mass culture to create a second-generation ethnic, working-class culture that preserved the boundaries between themselves and others. That they felt alienated from their parents' world did not necessarily mean that they forsook it for a nonethnic, middle-class one.

BLACKS GO COMMERCIAL

The experience that Chicago's white ethnic workers had with mass culture was not shared by their black co-workers, who came north in huge numbers during and after World War I to work in mass production plants. Blacks developed a different and complex relationship to mass culture. Black more than ethnic workers satisfied those who hoped a mass market would emerge during the twenties. Unlike ethnic workers, blacks did not reject commercial insurance, chain stores, and standard brands. But blacks disappointed those who assumed an integrated American culture would accompany uniformity in tastes. For ironically, by participating in mainstream commercial life, which black Chicagoans did more than their ethnic co-workers, blacks came to feel more independent and influential as a race, not more integrated into white middle-class society. Mass culture – chain stores, brand goods, popular music – offered blacks the ingredients from which to construct a new, urban black culture.

Not that migration to northern cities disrupted all of the southern way of life among blacks. Many institutions and informal networks accompanied them on the journey and were transplanted in their new home, most important of which were churches. But in black Chicago, in contrast to ethnic Chicago, the church did not become an institution that held the community together. Whereas a Polish Catholic or Jewish worker might have worshipped in the same pew as his boss and Italian Catholics, whether bourgeois or proletarian, had their animosity toward the church hierarchy in common, the church in Chicago's black community reflected its fragmentation between old and new settlers, between migrants' places of origin, and particularly between social classes. Church membership served as an index to social and economic status, and membership change became part of upward mobility. Whether one worshipped at the establishment Olivet Baptist Church or in a storefront Baptist, Holiness, or Spiritualist congregation said a lot.[169] With religious life so fragmented, a unified culture for a "black metropolis" would have to come from elsewhere.[170]

Blacks' receptivity to mass culture grew out of a surprising source, a faith in black commercial endeavor not so very different from ethnic people's loyalty to ethnic businesses. During the twenties, a consensus developed in the black community that a separate "black economy" could provide the necessary glue to hold what was a new and fragile world together. If blacks could direct their producer, consumer, and investment powers toward a black marketplace by supporting "race businesses," the whole community would benefit. Less economic exploitation and more opportunity would come blacks' way. This was not a new idea. "Black capitalism" had been fundamental to Booker T. Washington's accommodationist, self-help philosophy, culminating in his establishment of the National Negro Business League at the turn of the century. What changed in the 1920s was that now blacks of all political persuasions, including the Garveyite nationalists and even the socialist-leaning "New Negro" crowd who spoke through Chicago's militant *Whip*, shared a commitment to a separate black economy. The "self-help" and "mutual benefit" concerns that within ethnic communities persisted in cooperative enterprises like fraternals and building and loan associations took on a commercial orientation among blacks. Black institutions would not cushion the shocks of mainstream white society. They would compete to replace it, claiming their fair share of twenties' prosperity. In the face of racial segregation and discrimination, the black community would forge an alternative black metropolis that rejected white economic control without rejecting capitalism.[171]

At the center of the separate black economy stood race businesses. Black consumers were told that when they patronized these businesses, they bought black jobs, black entrepreneurship, and black independence along with goods and services and bid farewell to white employment prejudice, insults, and overcharging. "You can strut as much as you want to, and look like Miss Lizzie [an upper-class white person], but you don't know race respect if you don't buy from Negroes," sermonized one pastor. "As soon as these white folks get rich on the South Side, they go and live on the Gold Coast, and the only way you can get in is by washing their cuspidors."[172] It was nothing less than an issue of life and death. When white merchants closed their doors during the race riot of 1919, starvation had threatened every home in the Black Belt.[173]

Black consumer dollars supported all kinds of black businesses in the twenties but benefited most those whose products or services were geared solely to black needs. Undertakers, barbers, and beauticians faced few white contenders for the right to perfect the appearance of blacks living or dead. In a related way, black cosmetic companies, among them a Chicago banker's Overton Hygienic Manufacturing Company, made millions marketing standard brands for blacks: Black-No-More cream, Cocotone Skin Whitener, and especially the Walker System, Madame C. J. Walker's hair growth and straightening program distributed through her nationwide chain of beauty parlors. Black newspapers, the most prominent of which was Robert Abbott's nationally circulated *Chicago Defender*, likewise faced little white competition over reporting black news. And advertisements of products and services geared to blacks kept these newspapers afloat.[174]

Marcus Garvey's black nationalist United Negro Improvement Association sponsored black-run commercial enterprises – a Black Star steamship line, hotel, printing plant, black doll factory, chains of groceries, restaurants and laundries, and the Negro Factories Corporation operating plants in industrial centers. In Garvey's project to cultivate race pride, commercial success in America was no less important than his better-known "Back to Africa" programs. Even this radical

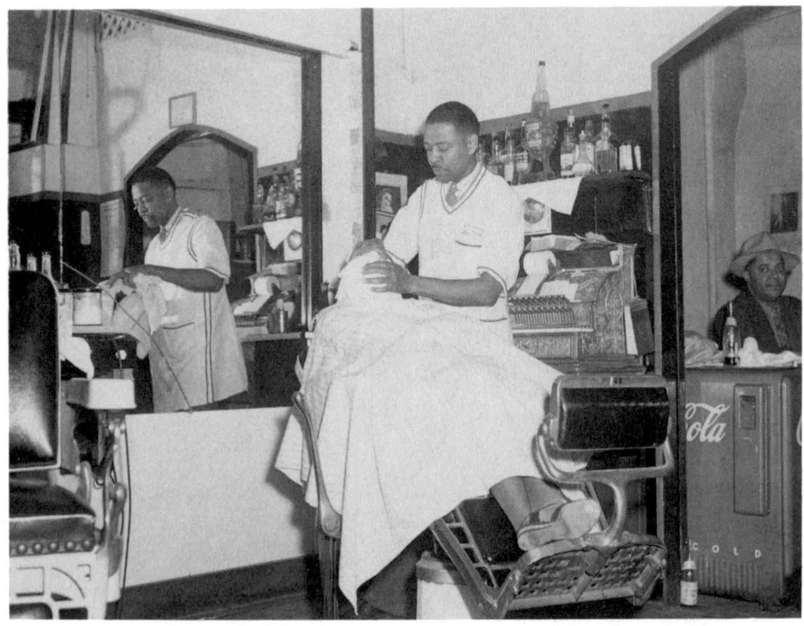

Plate 18. This photograph, taken by Jack Delano of the U.S. Office of War Information in April 1942, depicts the kind of small business that blacks succeeded in, since barbers, hairdressers, and undertakers faced little competition from whites with their superior economic resources. The caption reads, "Mr. Oscar J. Freeman, barber, owns the Metropolitan Barber Shop, 4654 South Parkway. Mr. Freeman has been in business for 14 years," which would put his shop's opening at 1928, during the heyday of the drive for a separate "black economy."

nationalist movement embraced capitalist standards of success, promising "every Black Man, Woman, and Child the opportunity to climb the great ladder of industrial and commercial progress," according to the Black Star line stock circulars.[175]

Black consumers made black-owned insurance companies the greatest business triumph of all. Although black companies faced aggressive competition from mainline insurance companies, they nonetheless captured a healthy share of the market by exposing that white firms charged blacks higher premiums and refused to hire black agents. The black insurance market was a profitable one. Blacks of every social status valued insurance for its promise of security in life and dignity at death. In 1918, the Illinois Health Insurance Commission found 93.8

percent of the black workers in its Chicago block study carrying life insurance, a rate surpassing all ethnic groups, even the insurance-minded Bohemians. Blacks' poor economic situation showed only in the low dollar value of their policies (Table 5). When Leila Houghteling surveyed unskilled and semiskilled workers steadily employed at International Harvester and Swift & Company several years later, every black interviewed had insurance. Job security made their commitment to insurance all that much clearer. These black workers spent more on policies each year than any other group, ninety-eight dollars compared to the Bohemians' eighty-two (Table 6).

Although blacks had a tradition of fraternals much like ethnic whites, by the 1920s commercial insurance companies had come to satisfy most people's insurance needs. Some black Chicagoans had left fraternal memberships behind when they journeyed north. Others recognized that fraternal benefit plans were actuarially unsound. The vertical social integration that characterized ethnic fraternals, moreover, was fast breaking down in the stratified black Chicago of the 1920s, directing black voluntarism into more class-specific organizations like social and business clubs. The lodges that remained active were locals of nationally organized fraternals – the Elks, Odd Fellows, Masons, Knights of Pythias, and Order of Eastern Star – where social and political functions often overshadowed benefit programs.[176] Seven black insurance companies sprang up in Chicago between 1919 and 1928, almost a third of the twenty-three companies nationwide that belonged to the National Negro Insurance Association. Two of them, Victory Life Insurance Company and Liberty Life Insurance Company, were among the most prosperous black business ventures in America. White companies, led by the Metropolitan Insurance Company, still carried more policies than black firms, but as the decade progressed, more and more Chicago blacks were choosing to insure the life of the black community along with their own.[177]

Despite the good intentions of many of its residents, Chicago's black metropolis could never boast a totally separate black economy. Often, no black alternative to a white business existed. In other cases, black companies did poorly, prompting some critics to blame black consumers for patronizing "the Jew" or "the chain" over their own small shopkeepers. As one black merchant complained, "I think that colored people will have to be educated to trade with each other. I notice that even now what you would call the most substantial people on this street pass my store on their way to 31st Street to trade with some Jew merchant. Of course, the chain stores offer a great deal of competition to any independent merchant, but having come in close contact with Jews, as I did, I know they feel they can 'jive' a Negro along and get his money."[178]

In fact, the causes of black business failure lay much deeper, in the insurmountable economic barriers that kept black entrepreneurs from competing viably. Most crushing was the lack of capital black businessmen had at their disposal. Only the two black banks in the city, the Binga State Bank and the Douglass National Bank, could be counted on for loans, and their resources were limited.[179] Under these circumstances, black merchants could hardly afford to offer customers the credit that ethnic shopkeepers gave their countrymen or Black Belt Jewish businessmen gave blacks. The short supply of cash in black stores, furthermore, kept wholesale orders small, retail prices high, and shelf stock low, all of which forced black customers to shop elsewhere. And the black businessman's lack of commercial experience made it that much harder for him to cope with his financial difficulties.[180]

Although in 1929 Chicago ranked first among cities in the number of black-owned stores, there were only 815 of them in the city. This meant there were 287 blacks per store, compared to 39 Poles per Polish-owned store and 40 Italians per Italian-owned store. The poor showing of black business made black consumers, even those deeply committed to a black economy, dependent on white business. But concern with black economic independence nonetheless left its mark. Within the white commercial world, blacks developed two preferences they pursued when they were financially able: standard brand goods and chain stores. Blacks shopping in nonblack stores felt that packaged items protected them against unscrupulous storekeepers or clerks. Not sharing the ethnic worker's confidence in his compatriot grocer, the black consumer distrusted bulk goods. Black consumption of standard brands became so prevalent that the Secretary of the National Negro Business League estimated that "in proportion to his income, [the Negro] buys more high grade, trade-marked goods than any other group in America."[181] This reliance on brand names only grew, moreover, when black customers who could survive without credit increasingly chose to patronize chain stores, attracted to their claims of standardized products and prices.

No less important, the chain store could be pressured to hire black

Plate 19. When this photograph was published in the *Chicago Daily News* in 1930, it bore the caption, "Race Riot, 51 St. and Grand Blvd." Whether it was in fact a race riot or simply an assembly of unemployed black men in the Black Belt is hard to say, but note the Walgreen Drugs sign prominent in the background, an indication of the prevalence of chain stores in black neighborhoods during the 1920s. Blacks favored chains over small independent stores run by whites for the standardized products and prices, and job opportunities, they offered.

clerks, whereas the Jewish, Greek, or Italian store in a black neighborhood was usually family run. If blacks could not own successful businesses, at least they should be able to work in them. By the mid to late 1920s, consumer boycotts to force chain stores to hire blacks – particularly those dark enough for their racial identity to be unmistakable – flourished on Chicago's South Side and in Gary's black neighborhoods. This spirited movement to achieve black economic independence through employment rather than entrepreneurship occurred on many fronts. In the fall of 1927, the *Chicago Defender* reported that "one of our progressive churches called a meeting of more than 400 members, and it was decided that all stores which would not employ our people should be boycotted. . . . This meeting will be continued every week.[182] Meanwhile, campaign literature flooded the South Side, blocks were organized, speakers circulated among clubs, ministers approached local merchants, pickets marched, and "flying squads" visited stores inquiring in a loud voice why no blacks worked there.

Even the sometimes anticapitalist Chicago *Whip* joined in, spearheading a "Don't Spend Your Money Where You Can't Work" crusade. By 1930, consumers had pressured Black Belt branches of the South Center Department Store, Sears Roebuck, A&P, Consumers, Neisner's 5 Cents to A Dollar, Woolworth's Five-and-Ten-Cent Store, and Walgreen's Drugs to employ blacks, some almost exclusively.[183] For their part, these chains lost no time posting signs and sponsoring advertisements in local black newspapers that avowed, "We Employ Colored Salesmen."[184] Good will radiated between accommodating chains and black consumers. With good reason: Blacks seeking equal employment felt they had more leverage over chain stores than over the family-operated shops of ethnic grocers. But inadvertently, consumers' endorsement of large retail chains made it harder for black merchants to compete and in time, as competition decreased, allowed prices in ghetto branches of chains to rise while product quality fell.

The failures of a separate black economy helped as much as its successes to orient urban blacks toward the mass consumption trends of the 1920s – commercial insurance, standard brands, and chain stores. Blacks more than ethnics fulfilled the hopes of the mass culture proponents who prophesied a unified consumer market during the twenties. But blacks disappointed those who assumed an integrated American culture would accompany uniformity in tastes. For ironically, participation in mainstream commerical life made blacks feel more independent and influential as a race, not more integrated into white, middle-class society. With strict limitations on where blacks could live and work in Chicago, consumption became a major avenue through which they could assert their independence. In time, purchased items – clothing, trinkets, cars – would take on special cultural significance within black society that was often unintelligible to whites.

Consumption was not the only aspect of mass culture to contribute to the making of an urban, black identity. Black musicians and audiences expressed race pride through jazz. In contrast to black commercial schemes that mimicked white examples or black consumption that contented itself largely with white products, here the trend setting went the other way. Black folk culture, black inventiveness, and black talent gave the twenties its distinctive image as the *jazz age* and dictated the character of mainstream American popular music for many years to come.

Chicago was the jazz capital of the nation for most of the 1920s. The push of northward migration, aided by the closing down in 1917 of New Orleans' Storyville red light district where many black musicians worked, and the pull of a "wet" city where racketeers and politicians collaborated to make sure Prohibition put no damper on night life drew southern jazz musicians to Chicago clubs. Zoning ordinances had isolated Chicago's "vice districts" on the South Side, far away from white middle-class neighborhoods.[185] Here, in the middle of the Black Belt, mixed audiences in "Black and Tan" cabarets tapped to the beat of King Oliver, Louis Armstrong, Lil Hardin, "Fats" Waller, Freddy Keppard, Jelly Roll Morton, and others. In segregated company, blacks relished Chicago's "hot jazz" at their own more modest clubs, black movie theaters, and semiprivate house-rent parties. Whites, meanwhile, danced black dances like the Charleston to black bands playing in palatial ballrooms that prohibited black patronage.[186]

The Chicago jazzmen's music reached far beyond the city's night clubs. Blacks, and some whites, all over the country bought millions of blues and jazz phonograph recordings known as "race records." With the exception of black-owned Black Swan Records, white recording companies like Paramount, Columbia, OKey, and Victor produced special lines for black customers. But because white companies depended on the profitable sales of race records as the phonograph business bottomed out with the rise of radio, they had little interest in interfering with the purest black sound. At record stores on Chicago's South Side, one store owner remembered, "Colored people would form a line twice around the block when the latest record of Bessie or Ma or Clara or Mamie come in . . . sometimes these records they was bottlegged, sold in the alley for four or five dollars apiece."[187] And as far away as the rural South, blacks kept up with musicians from Chicago and New York by purchasing records from mail-order ads in the *Chicago Defender* or from Pullman porters traveling south. [188] Race records helped unify black musical styles across regions, creating an increasingly national black sound. The radio, too, helped bring black jazz to a broader audience, white and black. An early Chicago station, WBBM, which the Atlass brothers launched in 1924 from the basement of their family's home, specialized in jazz. Other Chicago stations regularly broadcast Earl "Fatha" Hines with his band at the Grand Terrace Supper Club and groups performing at the Blackhawk Restaurant. Fletcher Henderson's Rainbow Orchestra played at New York's Savoy but in time was heard, over radio, in homes all over America.

Black jazz musicians shaped white mass culture even more profoundly than their frequent club appearances, recordings, and radio exposure might have suggested. Although Paul Whiteman's "sweet" sound and the big-band "swing" style that predominated by the 1930s may have seemed a long way from the bluesy improvisations of Chicago hot jazz, there was no denying the influence of black musicians. All jazz trumpeters learned from Louis Armstrong. The finest white musicians, like Leon "Bix" Beiderbacke and Benny Goodman, got started hanging out at black Chicago clubs. Black men – Duke Ellington, Fletcher Henderson, and Don Redman – turned the Chicago hot sound into the smoother, bigger, more tightly packaged "swing" that came out of New York. True, white bands often reaped more financial profits from jazz than did its black creators in Chicago's Black Belt clubs. Also true, by making a name for themselves in the music world, blacks fit right into white stereotypes of the "natural musician." Nonetheless, jazz gave black musicians and their fans recognition in the cultural mainstream for expressing themselves in a language they knew was their own. Long before Motown, blacks were molding American popular music in their own image.

Blacks listening to jazz on race records might on first take have seemed no different than Poles listening to Polish folk music on foreign-language recordings. Both were using Victrolas and records purchased from white phonograph companies to enjoy their own musical heritage. But on closer inspection, a crucial difference separated these black and Polish consumers. Because assimilation into the mainstream was possible for white ethnics, they used mass culture to stave it off by keeping their own culture alive. Ethnic records, like stores, theaters, and radio programs, set out to reinforce traditional culture in the face of threatening alternatives. Racial discrimination, on the other hand, kept blacks from the same opportunities, and pressures, to assimilate. Given that very different context, black jazz recordings, or black employment in chain stores, became a vehicle for making a claim on mainstream society that racism had otherwise denied. Mass culture, which offered ethnics a conservative retreat, became in the hands of blacks a way of turning blacks' vulnerability and dependence on mainstream society into a demand for respect.

When black workers patronized chain stores or bought packaged goods, they were asserting independence from the surrounding white society, not enslavement to cultural norms. No doubt their consumption of mass cultural products, ranging from standard brands to popular music, gave them interests in common with mainstream American society and subjected them to the vagaries of the capitalist market. But with mass culture as raw material, blacks fashioned their own culture during the 1920s that made them feel no less black.

Mass culture during the twenties did not have one predictable impact. Instead, its meaning changed as its production and distribution was reorganized. Ethnic workers had one experience with standard brands, movies, and radio when they encountered them through ethnic mediators, another when industry consolidation made commercial chains their disseminators. Similarly, people's own social circumstances inspired them to view mass culture in different ways. Ethnic workers watched their own children and their black co-workers value the most commercial aspects of mass culture, from which they themselves felt alienated. And although attracted to mass culture, ethnic youth and urban blacks constructed their own versions of it, which differed from the mainstream. Finally, mass culture was not always the invention of Hollywood and Madison Avenue. The case of jazz reveals how black folk culture made it to the top of the charts. The structure of delivery and the predilections of consumers interacted to shape mass culture's impact over the decade.

For most of the 1920s, Chicago's industrial workers displayed different relationships to mass culture according to their ethnicity, race, and age. By 1930, however, the emergence of larger commercial units, even in some cases monopolies, among retail stores, movie theaters, and radio stations limited the range of experiences with mass culture that were possible. Although they did not always recognize it, workers increasingly were shopping at the same chain stores, buying the same brand goods, going to the same chain theaters, and listening to the same radio programs on chain networks. Ethnic workers began to have more in common with their co-workers of different ethnicity and race and with their own children. Not only did they participate in more experiences that transcended Chicago neighborhoods, but also they were beginning to share a cultural life with workers elsewhere in the country. Later chapters will show how the Great Depression encouraged this national commercial trend, visible by the late 1920s, by further undermining small distributors of all kinds. It will also become clear that the way that workers first encountered mass culture during the twenties had a lasting impact on how they responded when it became more standardized during the 1930s. Whether they were ethnic workers who eased into mass culture through the local store, neighborhood theater, and ethnic radio program or black and young workers who refashioned commercialism to their own needs, mass culture would not make them feel any less Polish, Jewish, or black or any less of a worker.

The apprehension that ethnic leaders felt about mass culture, during the 1920s at least, appears unwarranted. Ethnic consciousness and race consciousness suffered little at the hands of the makers of Maxwell House Coffee, National Tea stores, Paramount Pictures, and NBC. But it is misleading to assume that workers' cultural identities in the twenties were only formed in the arenas of consumption and leisure. Steelworkers, meatpackers, garment sewers, and telephone and farm equipment makers spent by far the greatest amount of time every day and week at work. Here they encountered an additional competitor for their loyalty, employers who wanted workers to identify with their place of work, to be company men and women.

4
Contested Loyalty at the Workplace

Plate 20. Although workers did not often strike during the 1920s, they and their employers nonetheless came into conflict on the shop floor. These workers assembling telephone equipment at the Hawthorne Works of Western Electric, like their counterparts in other industries during the 1920s, approved of employers' new commitment to welfare capitalism but often resented the way it was implemented.

When Betty Piontkowsky refined lard at Armour and Company, Bernice Novak wired telephone switchboards at the Hawthorne Works of Western Electric, Phillip Janik pumped coke at Wisconsin Steel, and Moses Parker made parts for the latest model of McCormick reapers, they worried about more than completing the manual tasks laid out before them.[1] In innumerable ways every day at work, industrial workers like these four struggled with choices that exposed their deepest loyalties. Should they play up to the foreman in hopes of an easier or better-paying work assignment? Should they produce beyond the required quota to earn more money, even if it "ruined the job" for fellow workers who performed more slowly? Should they save through the company's thrift plan, not at the local ethnic bank, and sign up for the employer's group life insurance policy, letting their old mutual benefit association membership lapse? Should they spend leisure time participating in company sports teams, dances, and picnics or stick to their neighborhood friends? Was it worth complaining about – even quitting over – conditions at work or, more risky, joining with other workers in organized protest? Chicago's industrial workers had been soundly defeated in the labor battles after World War I. Nonetheless, in more subtle ways, the factory remained the site of employer and employee contests in the 1920s. At work as in their ethnic communities and as consumers, workers still made decisions that forced them to declare their loyalties.

Industrial workers' relationship to their employers was more complex in the twenties than ever before because they faced bosses who had undergone a kind of conversion experience after World War I. Large industrialists, motivated by fear of the working-class militance that had spread worldwide from 1917 through 1919, by resentment toward a Progressive Era state whose intrusions into corporate autonomy reached new heights during the war and by frustration at maintaining a work force during the labor shortages of wartime, had rethought the way they related to their factory workers. For a long time, manufacturers had assumed that the interests of management and labor inevitably conflicted: Workers had to be "driven" to labor efficiently and to respect the boss's authority. Even progressive firms like the National Cash Register Company, International Harvester, and the Pullman Company, which pioneered moralistic welfare work before the war, did little more than put a padded glove over an iron fist.[2] But when the war brought the doubling of labor turnover and an explosion of strikes, many large employers began to experiment with new strategies for gaining labor's good will, many of them specifically designed to satisfy workers' complaints. Even after the dangers of 1919 had passed and the severe depression of 1920–1 had changed the labor market from a sellers' to a buyers' market, employers expanded rather than abandoned their efforts.[3] What began as a response to worker demands became a new mission for manufacturers. In the era of welfare capitalism, the enlightened corporation, not the labor union or the state, would spearhead the creation of a more benign industrial society.

This was a far grander conception than what historians have viewed narrowly as the antiunionism of the "open-shop drive" and the "American plan" or as a simple paternalistic strategy for stemming employee turnover. In fact, employers in the postwar era went out of their way to avoid appearing paternalistic. Strikes in 1919 against "benevolent" employers had brought home the lesson that "employees are quick to resent paternalism."[4] As a big Chicago confectioner, the Wrigley Company, explained its approach during the 1920s, "We carefully avoid those things which have given welfare in general a bad name; we never pry into their [employees] private affairs nor home life."[5] Instead, progressive business leaders entered the twenties hoping that mutual interest at the workplace would unite management and worker. The ideal was encapsulated in a drawing that hung over Cyrus McCormick Jr.'s desk at International Harvester of two muscular arms, one labeled "Capital," the other "Labor," jointly supporting a globe entitled "Industry."[6] Industrialists like McCormick envisioned a new order where workers recognized that their own fate was intertwined with that of their employers and so struck a deal: loyalty to the boss in return for good treatment and security on the job. Swift & Company spelled out the new rules as clearly as any employer in its 1923 yearbook[7]:

> The goal toward which Swift & Company is working in its relations with workers may be summed up as follows: To make employment more secure, to pay fair wages, and to make this possible by avoiding waste and by improving the whole economic machine; to lead, not drive men, by having well-trained and sympathetic executives and bosses; to provide for self-expression on the part of our workers, and to keep the way wide open for their eduction and advancement; to bring about a closer cooperation and a better understanding between the workers and the management.

In the new order, moreover, industrialists' social responsibilities went beyond their employees. Outside the plant, in the community at large, they had a similar leadership role to play. Whether the problem was as national as the 1921 economic depression or as local as needy churches in the neighborhoods near their plants, businessmen were expected to intervene. Managers were to function as socially conscious "trustees" for interest groups far broader than their stockholders, obligated "to employees, to the public . . . , even to their competitors," according to the Chamber of Commerce's Committee on Business Ethics.[8]

That even the Chamber of Commerce, traditionally conservative, shared in this new vision testifies to its predominance in business circles during the twenties. Of course, not all manufacturers embraced these values. Small companies often lagged behind larger ones. And those who subscribed to the new agenda, including all of Chicago's large industrial employers, differed in how they chose to implement it.[9] Nonetheless, there is no denying that managerial ideology almost everywhere underwent a sea change during the 1920s. A report of the National Industrial Conference Board at the end of the decade described it as more than the sum of individual industrial relations programs, as "the outgrowth of a habit of mind, an attitude towards human relationships, a balancing of moral obligations, and a regard for practical results." Among managers and workers, the report went on to claim, nothing less than "a new attitude toward each other, born of better understanding and mutual respect" was flourishing.[10]

Chicago's industrial employers contested alongside ethnic leaders, mass culture promoters, and what remained of the labor movement for the loyalty of mass production workers during the 1920s. As in other arenas of working-class life, although the struggle was not overtly political, cultural issues such as the way workers spent leisure time, where they turned for help in adversity, and whom they worked alongside at the plant became charged with political significance. How Chicago employers implemented their new, harmonious vision and how industrial workers reacted to it, in other words, the extent to which Chicago's mass production workers put their own "welfare" in the hands of "capitalists," had important bearing on how these industrial workers reacted when capitalism failed them during the Great Depression.

THE EMPLOYER'S VISION

Understanding what welfare capitalism meant to industrial workers first requires reconstructing as well as possible how people encountered this ideology in concrete ways everyday at the plant. The industrial relations programs that Chicago's major manufacturers implemented differed in subtle ways that bore significance for their long-term relations with employees. But in general, U.S. Steel, International Harvester, Swift, Armour, and Western Electric all assembled comprehensive welfare capitalist plans involving five kinds of activity: restructuring interpersonal relationships at the plant, rewarding workers through wages and promotions, experimenting with industrial democracy, instituting welfare programs, and assuming community responsibilities. Chicago's large employers executed these five aspects of welfare capitalism so similarly that generalizations across firms are easy to make. Their differences in approach will become evident later (Table 11).

In laying the groundwork for this new era of harmonious industrial relations, welfare capitalists sought to restructure workers' interpersonal relationships at the plant. Top management hoped to secure employees' loyalty to the company by reforming the way they related both to peers and to superiors. Up to 1919, employers had assumed that the best way to keep their semiskilled work force from unifying politically was to divide it ethnically, each group doing a particular kind of work under the thumb of a foreign-speaking or at least foreign-comprehending foreman. In the steel mills of South Chicago, for example, certain nationalities were assigned to specific occupations: Italians were the unskilled laborers in bricklaying departments, Swedes manned the galvanizing departments, Poles provided the unskilled labor for the blast furnaces, and Croatians did the common labor in the finishing departments of rail mills.[11] Likewise, packing plants before the war hired different ethnic groups for different jobs. According to an employment agent at Swift, each week "we change about among different nationalities and languages. It prevents them from getting together."[12] But once the strikes of 1919 demonstrated that cohesive ethnic communities could in fact nurture militance within their own ranks, managers balked at policies that reinforced ethnicity at the workplace and shifted their strategy. "The present disturbance has made plain the extreme difficulties in dealing with non-Americans, who seem to be especially prone to trust a leader of their native tongue and to distrust any action on the part of the employers," International Harvester's Manager of Industrial Relations, Arthur H. Young, lamented. "They are particularly susceptible to the pleas of their countrymen and the newspapers printed in their own language, no matter how unscrupulous these leaders and organs may be."[13]

To break down these subversive ethnic subcultures, Young recommended that International Harvester step up its Americanization

Table 11. *Welfare capitalism programs in selected Chicago companies during the 1920s*

Program type	Western Electric, Hawthorne Works	International Harvester, McCormick Works and Wisconsin Steel	Swift and Company	Armour and Company	U.S. Steel, South and Gary Works
Wage incentives	Yes	Yes	Yes	No	na
Employee representation plan	No	Yes	Yes	Yes	No
Vacation plan	Yes	Yes	Yes	Yes	No
Benefits (sickness, disability)	Yes	Yes	Yes	Yes	Yes
Stock ownership	Yes	Yes	Yes	Yes	Yes
Group insurance	Yes	Yes	Yes	Yes	Yes
Pension plan	Yes	Yes	Yes	Yes	Yes
Recreation and social programs	Yes	Yes	Yes	Yes	Yes
Foremen's training	Yes	Yes	Yes	na	Yes
Company/plant magazine	Yes	Yes	Yes	Yes	Yes

Note: Most of these programs were instituted after World War I. The only exceptions were some of the stock, benefit, and pension programs, but even in those cases provisions became much more extensive in the 1920s. Approximate work size in the 1920s: Hawthorne Works, 22,000–30,000; McCormick Works, 4,000–7,000; Wisconsin Steel, 2,000–3,500; Swift, 5,000–8,000; Armour, 6,000–9,000; South Works, 8,000–10,000; Gary Works, 11,000–14,000. na, not available.

programs. His response was not unique. The Americanization and naturalization campaigns of employers during this period are their best-known strategies for wooing workers away from ethnicity. All of Chicago's large manufacturers turned corners of their factory floors into classrooms and substituted English primers for machine tools several hours a week.[14]

But the attack on ethnicity at Harvester and other Chicago industries during the 1920s went beyond the sponsoring of English and civics classes. Supervisors set out to isolate individual workers by breaking up ethnic and racial communities within the factory. They hoped to banish competitors for workers' loyalties and more basically to individualize the relationship between management and labor. Employers had learned that they invited more than militance when they allowed workers to cluster by ethnic group. "The first Mexicans that came to us came with a gang leader and insisted on going to work together in the 'freezer,'" explained a packing house executive. "Then as soon as the gang leader got a better job he moved them all away. So now we don't bunch them up any more."[15] Not only did ethnic shop teams increase worker turnover, but according to the Superintendent of Mill No. 5 at Wisconsin Steel, they also hurt efficiency. "You see here how it is arranged. We try never to allow two of a nationality to work together if we can help it. Nationalities tend to be clannish and naturally it interferes with the work and the morale of the place. You see here in this loading department, for instance, we have an Italian, an Irishman, a Pole, a Dane and two Mexicans working."[16]

Employers also employed blacks and Mexicans to diffuse ethnic solidarity among their other workers, which contributed to the increasing presence of these two groups within Chicago's factories during the decade. In many plants, their combined totals exceeded 30 percent (Table 12). For all these large industries, except Western Electric, which found women to do the cleaner, electrical assembly work at low wages, blacks and Mexicans were the cheap, immigrant labor of the 1920s, taking the place of southern and eastern Europeans who had been barred by immigration restriction quotas.[17] A University of Chicago student who worked one summer in the South Works of U.S. Steel was not surprised to find only blacks and Mexicans on the "relining gang," a team that worked amid terrible dust and heat to clean out the old bricks from caved-in furnaces and replace them with new ones. In the packinghouses, Mexicans and blacks were sure to be found in unbear-

Table 12. *Mexican and black employees in three steel mills and two meatpacking plants in the Calumet region, 1918–28*

	Mexicans		Blacks		
Year	Number	Percentage of total employees	Number	Percentage of total employees	Total employees
Steel mills: Indiana Harbor Works, Inland Steel; Gary and South Works, Illinois Steel (U.S. Steel)					
1918	104[a]	0.4	1546	5.3	29,089
1919	232	0.9	2699	10.7	25,115
1920	1228	4.6	2580	9.8	26,446
1921	438	2.6	1647	9.8	16,795
1922	1537	6.4	3432	14.3	23,966
1923	2919	11.3	3352	13.0	25,773
1924	3479	12.1	4096	14.3	28,680
1925	3837	13.2	3717	12.8	28,969
1926	4421	15.8	3261	11.6	28,067
1927	4042	14.6	3138	11.4	27,628
1928	4081	14.2	3203	11.1	28,757
Meatpacking plants: Armour, Swift					
1918	78	0.3	[b]	[b]	27,254
1919	79	0.3	[b]	[b]	23,642
1920	266	1.5	5110	27.8	18,361
1921	82	0.6	2928	20.3	14,460
1922	86	0.7	4236	32.7	12,952
1923	482	3.2	5148	33.6	15,311
1924	711	4.8	4840	32.4	14,956
1925	644	4.7	4244	30.6	13,851
1926	612	4.5	4068	29.6	13,748
1927	596	4.5	3864	29.0	13,317
1928	746	5.7	3894	29.5	13,194

[a] A few Mexicans employed at Inland Steel in 1918 do not appear here since no nationality report showing their number was available; probably they were employed after the report was made.

[b] Data available for one plant only: 1918, 1,624; 1919, 1,710.

Source: Paul S. Taylor, *Mexican Labor in the United States: Chicago and the Calumet Region*, vol. 7, no. 2, University of California Publications in Economics (Berkeley: University of California Press, 1932), p. 46.

ably cold freezers or in foul-smelling pickle, glue, and fertilizer departments.[18] Employers, moreover, were even known to use blacks and Mexicans against each other to ensure that neither group monopolized those jobs reserved especially for them. A supervisor at one foundry admitted that "the Mexicans were first employed here to dilute colored labor," whereas the employment manager of another plant, which at the time was increasing its proportion of Mexican employees at the expense of blacks, was even more candid: "We have Negroes and Mexicans in a sort of competition with each other. It is a dirty trick."[19] Nonetheless, although usually assigned to the dirty, poor-paying, and dangerous common laborer jobs, some blacks and Mexicans, particularly in packing and steel, rose to semiskilled and skilled work because bosses wanted to spread them around their plants as "strike insurance." A report by the Chicago Urban League in 1923 confirmed that blacks who had gained new skilled positions as a result of postwar strikes were retaining them.[20]

Employers did not worry that putting workers of different backgrounds next to each other in the plant would foster interethnic alliances. Communication among workers was difficult when 43 percent of the work force in packing and 54 percent in steel was foreign born and many workers born here spoke poor English. Furthermore, the conflicts between ethnic and racial groups that had deeply divided workers in 1919 seemed to persist in Chicago's shops and neighborhoods during the 1920s. Everyone told stories about tensions between "Polacks" and "Spicks" (Mexicans) and "Spicks" and "Niggers," while taking for granted comments like that made by a second-generation Polish youth: "I work in a place where there are three Mexican workers . . . on the third floor. I would quit if I had to work with them."[21] When employers played one group against another for jobs, they fed these antagonisms. More importantly, when employers tried to isolate workers from each other and orient them individually toward the company, they intended that no kind of peer community, ethnic or interethnic, would intervene. Employers wanted workers to depend solely on the boss.

Welfare capitalists recognized that peer loyalty among workers was not the only barrier to better relations with individual employees. Top management also conceded the need to patrol better the way employees experienced company authority daily on the shop floor. Under the prewar "drive" system, foremen and other shop supervisors had enjoyed almost total autonomy in running their departments, particularly in the hiring, firing, and disciplining of workers. In many cases, employers had given foremen this power as part of an earlier struggle to deprive skilled craftsmen of control over production. The foreman had become management's representative on the shop floor.[22] By "driving" workers, the foreman asserted the company's, and his own, authority. At a place like South Works, the reputation of a foreman rested on how well he drove his men to "beat the record." King Steelmaker of the Cinder Shore, alias Billy Field, demanded of his crew everything short of "being boiled in a Bessemer," according to one admiring contemporary.[23] For workers before the war, getting and keeping a job required responding constantly to "the crook of the finger" that beckoned for hard labor as well as bribes, kickbacks, and favors.[24]

But workers' complaints when they quit jobs or went on strike convinced employers of the danger of leaving employee relations unstandardized and in the hands of often arbitrary foremen. Hence, just as manufacturers set out to restructure the way workers related to their peers in the twenties' factory, so too they tried to improve relations between workers and their superiors, by taking authority away from foremen and turning it over to "experts" in employee management within newly created personnel and industrial relations departments. Employers recognized that the foreman's unsupervised interventions could jeopardize the company's hold over the worker much the way the ethnic peer group did. Typically, large manufacturing firms in the 1920s created new departments that centralized hiring and discharging, standardized jobs and wages, encouraged internal promotion, and administered company welfare programs, all at the expense of the foreman's power. Meanwhile, foremen were also losing control over production matters to expanding engineering and planning staffs.[25]

Robbed of much of their traditional authority, foremen were subjected to special training programs designed to improve their skills in handling workers on the shop floor. As the decade progressed, large employers everywhere began to offer foremanship courses. By June 1927, the U.S. Chamber of Commerce reported that almost a thousand courses had been conducted during the previous year, whereas many trade associations, like the National Metal Trade Association, prepared training materials for members. In Chicago, whether it was a course for Calumet area steel foremen at the South Chicago YMCA, the in-house "Foremen's Development Course" at Swift & Company and International Harvester, or Western Electric's morale-boosting, Saturday night bowling-and-dinner affairs for foremen, the message was consistent: "Hire-and-Fit, not Hire-and-Fire," "teach, don't boss," "be a leader of men," and "the modern supervision of labor is a psychological problem."[26] Employers had realized that if welfare capitalism was to work, foremen had to be brought along. "If the foreman does not feel invested in the executive viewpoint," the Illinois Manufacturers' Association reminded its members, "the most carefully laid plans, on the part of the management, may change color very radically at the point where they are actually put to work."[27]

Invading "the foreman's empire" and then reforming his ruling style became a cornerstone in management's strategy to improve company rapport with wage earners. Without that, the "old-style" foreman would continue to give workers common cause against the boss and prevent, as the ethnic group had, the development of a steady, individualized relationship between company and employee. But manufacturers did not stop here in their quest to win workers' loyalty. They turned to wages and promotions as additional methods of tying men and women to the firm.

During the 1920s, large manufacturers instituted wage incentive plans designed to maximize workers' efficiency by individualizing earnings. Most American employers had found full adoption of Frederick Winslow Taylor's "scientific management" schemes too rigid, but they were attracted to his advocacy of wage incentives as a way of pushing workers to produce to their potential. Replacing straight time or piecework remuneration, incentive pay systems spread over the decade until almost three-fourths of all manufacturing workers were paid this way by the early 1930s.[28] Whether known at Swift & Company as the Bedaux Point System, at Western Electric as the "Bogey" system of individual rating, or elsewhere as the "task-and-bonus" and "Halsey Premium Plan," the principle remained the same. With the help of time-and-motion studies, fatigue tests, and other measurements, company job raters set a standard for a particular job that they expected the average worker to produce. Whatever workers produced above that base rate comprised the "bonus," which usually was divided 75 percent to the employee and 25 percent to management for its role in providing adequate machinery and materials. Employers felt confident that workers, now rewarded for proficiency and extra effort while assured a base pay, would produce good quality work at their most efficient pace.

Because wage payment was calculated on an individual basis, workers would be freed from peer pressure to restrict output, a strategy previously practiced to protect jobs or to set a comfortable pace of work for the group. These new wage incentive plans reinforced employers' other efforts at isolating individual workers. As one manufacturer put it bluntly, "When each worker is paid according to his record there is not the same community of interest."[29]

By distinguishing jobs more systematically through the assignment of different rates, employers created another way of dividing their workers: Individual promotions became much easier to offer. Increasingly complex job ladders promised that the makeup of work groups would constantly change, and while together, members would view each other as rivals for management's favor rather than as colleagues. One industrial relations specialist also suggested that internal promotion ensured that "the hope of better things tomorrow [will] take their minds off the difficulties of today."[30] Whereas Western Electric encouraged workers to prepare themselves for future opportunities at the Hawthorne Evening School, more informal training at many other plants shared a similar aim.[31] When in 1922 the president of U.S. Steel, Judge Elbert Gary, instructed his subsidiaries in company policy, he could have spoken for most managements: "Positions should be filled by promotions from the ranks, and if in any locations there are none competent, this fact should be given attention and men trained accordingly."[32] Even when the mechanization of factory work diminished the differences between one job and another and made promotion not much better than a lateral transfer, companies still moved workers around the plant with questionable assurances like "practically every executive in the great plant of Armour and Company has 'come up from the bottom.'"[33]

Furthermore, employers endorsed wage incentives and job ladders for reasons other than just dividing the work force. They hoped that the opportunity to earn more money and enjoy more job security would discipline workers, making them more reliable in attendance and more willing to stick with the company rather than quit.[34] Work force turnover had long troubled American manufacturers, with factory hands constantly quitting over grievances or because they felt they could find a better job elsewhere. One study of plants nationwide from 1910 to 1919 found that average yearly separations were equivalent to a complete change of work force annually, as if the payroll had changed 100 percent. When the Bureau of Labor Statistics inquired into turnover in twenty-five Chicago establishments during the war period, with its enormous demand for labor, no firms proved to have an annual turnover of less than 60 percent and four-fifths cited turnovers between 100 and 336 percent. Meatpacking numbered among the worst.[35] The ready availability of immigrant labor before the war and black labor during the war meant employers could usually replace workers who quit. But by the twenties, few employers could afford to be cavalier about a bottomless labor supply.

Even more importantly, as factory work became more mechanized over the decade, machine operatives increasingly dominated the work process, squeezing out both skill at the top and brawn at the bottom. Employers began to discover that semiskilled operatives, not trained craftsmen or common laborers, were the most expensive to hire, train, and replace.[36] As electrification and labor-saving equipment entered Chicago's factories during the 1920s and workers suffered from "deskilling," employers nonetheless came to value a stable, company-trained work force all the more.[37] Plant magazines kept reminding workers "Don't Drift. Stay Aboard The Good Ship 'Steady Job' And Get Somewhere," "Find A Job and Stick With It," avoid your own "Story of 'Jumping Sickness' – By a Victim."[38] Chicago manufacturers sought to trade wage incentives, promotions, and respect for seniority for faithful, hard-working employees.[39]

The "great fear" of Chicago's employers, however, was not the weekly and monthly dissipation of employee ranks through turnover but the recurrence of the kind of labor militance that had plagued them during the World War I era. To ensure that 1919 would never happen again, International Harvester, Swift, and Armour implemented what they called "industrial democracy" in their plants. Dubbed different names – employee representation plans, works councils, conference boards, and company unions – and structured in diverse ways, the idea everywhere involved bringing worker and management representatives together to set company policies and respond to employee grievances. With industrial democracy in place, these progressive employers thought, the pressure for unions would subside. The same Cyrus McCormick, Jr. who worked daily under the framed image of "Capital" and "Labor" entwined wrote that industrial relations before and during the new era could be compared to "the difference between a feudalistic state – the government of which, however enlightened, contains nothing of the consent of the governed – and a democracy. . . . If people have a voice in the making of the regulations which affect them, they are more able to understand and accept law."[40]

The ideal that McCormick articulated, which was endorsed by hundreds of other employers who instituted these plans between 1919 and the late 1920s, promised that company decision making would truly be shared, that no issue was too privileged to escape joint deliberation. Not surprisingly, the reality in most plants hardly measured up. Managements protected their prerogatives through loopholes and exercised firm control over council activities. Soon after International Harvester established the Harvester Industrial Council Plan as an experiment in democracy, Harold Fowler McCormick revealed in a letter to his brother Cyrus how tactically the company viewed the Harvester works councils: "Mr. Perkins [vice-president] is considering the question of granting an eight hour day as a basis, or a vacation of one, two, or three weeks for all workmen on Company pay, as something to hand to them thru the new Industrial Council plan. We need something big and fine coming as a result of this to cement its value between the men and the Company."[41] Over the next months and years, International Harvester, Swift, and Armour allowed these bodies to validate the concept of industrial democracy by crediting them for attaining paid vacations, group insurance, and other welfare programs. No less regularly, they used them to legitimate firing strikers, reducing wages, and enacting unpopular policies. In most cases, joint councils found themselves doing the boss's dirty work amid running plant sports programs, administering company benefit plans, and educating employees in the merits of safety, quality, and efficiency.[42]

One might wonder why manufacturers continued to advocate employee representation plans once the fear of unionization had subsided since they granted councils so little power. True, concern that workers might take unauthorized collective action persisted. And the ideal, if not the reality, of industrial democracy continued to intrigue employers. But what gave employee representation continuing appeal was that it helped the progressive employer accomplish other goals close to his heart, the restriction of the foreman's authority and the individualization of employee–employer relations. By making the works council meeting the hub of management–worker interaction, employers further diminished the importance of what happened on the factory floor, where the foreman presided. The actions of foremen, moreover, were now subject to review by council committees and assemblies. Swift & Company executives justified industrial democracy to their stockholders in just these terms: "The Assembly Plan has also had the effect of making foremen more careful and liberal in their actions and decisions as they come in contact with the workmen from day to day."[43]

Employee representation plans advanced management's other goal of isolating workers as individuals by redressing grievances on an individual rather than collective basis. An observer of industrial relations at Wisconsin Steel concluded that despite the representational structure of the plant's works council, "the voice of self-organized workingmen is not recognized. The company is willing to listen to the suggestions of the individual workers but refuses to deal with them as a group."[44] Individuals might appeal inequitable wage ratings, unfair dismissals, or inadequate sanitation facilities, but these grievances were viewed as requests for special dispensation within existing policy guidelines, not challenges to those policies themselves with consequences for other workers. Swift & Company could boast in 1925 that about 70 percent of the eighteen hundred cases brought before its joint assembly over the previous three and a half years had been decided in favor of employees without feeling that management's authority was in the least challenged.[45]

The Hawthorne Works of Western Electric, the Chicago area's largest employer with a work force fluctuating between twenty-five thousand and thirty thousand employees, did not institute employee representation but took a "human relations approach" that shared many of the same goals. The personnel director of Western Electric explained in 1928 why his company had chosen a different path. Although acknowledging the value of employee representation, he argued that it was "predicated upon a conflict of interest. In that respect it doesn't differ in principle from the trade union relationship." Western Electric sought to avoid conflict entirely: "To do this . . . [management] must really know what the employee thinks . . . , what are the worker's satisfactions and aspirations, and . . . set up management policies that will synchronize with the worker's viewpoint and compel thereby his cooperation."[46] The Hawthorne experiments to identify factory conditions most conducive to worker productivity, which were carried out by Harvard Business School professors under Elton Mayo, are well known. Less so, though as serious a collaboration between company and academics, is the extensive interviewing program Hawthorne instituted toward the end of the decade "to find out what the worker thinks."

Originally initiated in conjunction with foremen training to identify common complaints shop workers had about their supervisors, the program quickly became an end in itself. Industrial relations experts at Hawthorne determined that by talking privately with every hourly worker at least once a year, they could keep employee grievances individual as well as nourish an alliance between laborer and top management that kept lower-level supervisors in check.[47] Whether Chicago manufacturers convened joint assemblies or spoke on a one-to-one basis with employees, they felt that they could strengthen their own authority by allowing their workers more of a voice.

All these welfare capitalist strategies – breaking up ethnic communities in the factory, restraining foremen, rewarding workers with wage incentives and promotions, respecting seniority, and "democratizing" plant government – were complemented by benefit programs offering workers such perquisites as sickness pay, pensions, and paid vacations. Managers hoped these welfare programs would mollify workers' complaints and encourage them to identify their personal futures with that of the company.

When firms offered workers benefits, they urged employees to entrust their long-term security to a steady employer. Promises of a down payment on a house, a sure income to retire on, help to families in hard times, even a vacation next summer encouraged workers to stick with the company. Employers sought to encourage faithful service all the more by awarding benefits according to a worker's tenure. The longer an employee stayed with the company, the greater the benefits. A man had to be sixty-five years old and have given Swift & Company at least twenty-five years continuous service to qualify for a pension; a woman of fifty-five needed twenty years.[48] At the Hawthorne Works, an employee earned sick benefits after two years, in amounts that increased over time.[49] Workers at International Harvester received a week of paid vacation after two years of continuous service with good attendance, two weeks after five years.[50] Just as bosses had come to value their investment in semiskilled operatives, so they hoped these workers in turn would learn to value the benefits that came with long-term service to the firm and find quitting too risky to their families' security. A cartoon parable on the back cover of Wisconsin Steel's employee magazine brutally warned workers against the dangers of independence. Responsible Alec had stayed loyal to Harvester's Employee Benefit Association (EBA), so when he was killed by a truck, his family inherited a "nest egg" that allowed his children to remain in school. Reckless John, on the other hand, had ignored the EBA and thus in dying sentenced his unfortunate offspring to a life of hawking newspapers on Loop street corners.[51]

Employee stock ownership plans, one of the most popular welfare programs of the decade, sought to bind the futures of manager and worker through a shared investment in capitalism. The enthusiasm that workers demonstrated during the war for buying Liberty Bonds gave employers the same idea that it had given ethnic bankers, to channel patriotic energy, and dollars, into the purchase of company stock. Employers justified the selling of their stock to workers at below the market price as a way of raising capital and giving employees a greater voice, even though workers held too small a share to make those goals very meaningful. Rather, when Western Electric let its employees buy stock on installment through wage deductions, when Swift & Company helped employees borrow on their stock when they needed a loan, when U.S. Steel, Armour, and International Harvester gave workers annual bonuses for keeping up stock payments, management was embracing a crucial dimension of welfare capitalism: the end of an industrial system that pitted proletarian against owner. "Stock ownership makes the wage earner an actual partner . . . a real capitalist," proclaimed Judge Gary of U.S. Steel. "They have as keen a desire to see the institutions of this country protected as those who have greater riches, and they may be relied upon to lend their influence and their votes in favor of the protection of property and person."[52] Within the factory, workers who identified as owners would "have an interest in seeing that things are done properly," Swift assured its stockholders.[53] Enlightened businessmen congratulated themselves that by making the men and women who labored in factories capitalists, they had found a way of both avoiding paternalism and getting employees themselves to provide the necessary bulwark against Bolshevism. "The Capitalist Has Shaved Off His Whiskers," announced Western Electric executives as they invited shop workers to become co-owners.[54]

Employers also used welfare programs to keep competitors for workers' loyalty at bay. Class-conscious labor militants remained one enemy. Although unions no longer posed a substantial threat, a company like International Harvester knew that there were radicals in its ranks and hence ran careful checks of absences each May Day and on Tuesday, August 23, 1927, the day Sacco and Vanzetti were executed.[55] Managers felt that welfare programs were their best defense against appeals to their workers' class consciousness. Harvester and other employers decided to grant hourly employees paid vacations, for example, "to remove the argument of class distinction which now prevails" when workers compared themselves to more privileged salaried staff.[56]

Another kind of solidarity that threatened employers was ethnic solidarity. At the same time that managers moved to dissolve ethnic communities in the workplace, they designed welfare programs to compete with ethnic services outside the plant. Employers recognized that if a worker could depend on an ethnic mutual benefit society in tough times or look to an ethnic building and loan association in better ones, he had less need to be loyal to his job. Nor had employers forgotten what they had learned in 1919 about how ethnic organization encouraged militance. As late as the summer of 1928, an employment manager in a large concern lambasted the mutual benefit societies of his latest recruits, the Mexicans: "The Mexicans have societies, and of course if they organize one way, it is but a step to organize another way."[57] Chicago companies directly challenged ethnic organizations. Western Electric founded its own Hawthorne Building and Loan Association; all of these large manufacturers offered sickness benefits; and Western Electric, Swift, Armour, and U.S. Steel developed group life insurance plans.[58] International Harvester spoke for them all when it openly defended its programs against competitors: "Comparison as to benefits, cost and regulations governing same with those offered by the best of relief and fraternal organizations has demonstrated that our association offers more to the employes [*sic*] than they can get elsewhere."[59] And a Princeton Industrial Relations Section memorandum argued that not only did company death benefits increase employee good will by offering help "at a time when it is most needed," but they also lessened "the necessity for 'passing the hat'" among peers, a euphemism for mutual assistance.[60] Promoting primary loyalty to the firm truly became a matter of life and death.

But working people did not make commitments to their ethnic communities simply for security. The day-to-day camaraderie they found there – whether playing sports, singing and dancing, or just hanging out with friends on the corner – contributed to their investment. This reality did not escape welfare capitalists and led them to expend a great deal of energy in intensifying the social side of work. When workers spent leisure time on company grounds, they not only broadened their involvement with the firm, industrialists believed, but they would have less time to indulge in the "drinking, gambling and brawling" so common in working-class ethnic communities – and so disruptive of good work habits. All Chicago manufacturers paid new attention to recreation, but Western Electric proved a particularly influential model. A worker at the Hawthorne plant found sports the cornerstone of the company's extracurricular program. Fourteen organized sports ranging from soccer to skating to shooting, facilities including a 10-acre track, a new gym, and a professional stadium, and Saturday afternoon athletic events were planned to appeal broadly. Sports at work, it was thought, would create less need for the sokol or the neighborhood team. Not only would workers participate themselves, but also they would turn out to root for Hawthorne's teams when they played against those of neighboring plants in Chicago's Industrial League. The league had been established by the Association of Commerce in 1920 explicitly to help employers use sports to rebuild morale in their factories. "When you start this (baseball team)," local bosses had been told, "your employees will begin to work six days a week and not five.... This ball club will be something they can rally around" as players as well as spectators.[61]

Much the way Hawthorne managers hoped company sports would divert workers' attention from the neighborhood playing field toward the workplace, they organized social events to compete with ethnic leisure. Despite the preponderance of Czechs and Poles in the work force, they avoided sponsoring activities that reinforced ethnicity, building company sociability around mass culture instead. Hawthorne workers could join a radio club, learn to construct their own receivers at the Hawthorne Evening School, and spend lunchtime listening to radio shows broadcasted over a loudspeaker. These included either popular entertainment or "educational" messages sponsored by the Illinois Manufacturers' Association as unsubtle as "The Adventures of a Bank Account" and "The Popular Man in the Factory."[62] Noon hour also featured motion picture viewings and outdoor dances.[63] The serious stepping, however, took place at company dances held each month at Chicago's most popular ballrooms, Guyon's Paradise, Harmon's Dreamland, and the Trianon, where all the biggest bands played.[64] During lunch or after work, a worker might stop off at the general store located at the Hawthorne Works, which discounted the latest appliances along with other brand-name goods and directed consumers to large dealers in the city who would sell to them wholesale.[65] No doubt company officials wanted to help workers buy carefully to avoid an ever-threatening

Plate 21. A caravan of buses transported International Harvester employees and their families to a day in the country at Hinsdale, the company's experimental farm outside of Chicago. Welfare capitalists organized outings such as this one to encourage workers to look to their employer rather than their ethnic communities or working-class peers during leisure as well as work time. Employers wanted no competitors for workers' loyalty.

spiral of debt. But they nonetheless created competition for the neighborhood ethnic merchant, which only worsened when Western Electric arranged with A&P and National Tea stores to honor company pay checks when they replaced cash in 1927.[66] It was fitting that businessmen who were profiting so handsomely from manufacturing the electrical equipment needed to advance radio, motion pictures, telephone communication, and the like should seek the solution to social conflict in mass culture as well.

Employers imported mass culture into the factory during the twenties not simply to compete with ethnic communities but also to unify a diverse work force across ethnicity and rank. Managers who wanted to individualize their relationships with workers when it came to wages and discipline had not lost sight of the importance of teamwork. Having undermined workers' ethnic peer groups inside and outside of the factory, they sought to reconstitute community along more acceptable lines. The "happy family," sharing a common cultural life but still respectful of those in authority, provided the ideal. As the personnel director for all of Western Electric put it, "People who have the opportunity to play together will work together in greater harmony and any industry today is a cooperative enterprise."[67] Weekly sings, which brought a movable piano and song leader into a different department of the Hawthorne Works everyday, sought to promote musical as well as social harmony through popular hits and songs like "America" and "Down Upon the Swanee River," not the Old World tunes more familiar to many employees.[68]

Departmental and companywide sports teams also aimed at developing an *esprit de corps* that transcended differences in ethnicity, age, and rank. Along with the usual baseball, track, and swimming teams, managers hit on bowling as a surprisingly suitable sport. A spokesman for the Chicago Association of Commerce introduced it at the city's first annual industrial bowling tournament in 1921 by saying, "The bowling game is one of the few strenuous games we have in which the middle-aged men may compete with the young fellow in the firm. Such a game makes it possible for all members of a firm to meet in competition, thereby becoming better acquainted and establishing a better ground for understanding."[69] Before long, hardly a large manufacturer in Chicago failed to sponsor a bowling team.

Chicago's industrialists promoted a "family feeling" as well by distributing company magazines to all employees. Every month workers either carried home from work or received by mail the *Hawthorne Microphone, Swift Arrow, Armour Oval, Harvester World,* and *South Works Review.*[70] Plastered with photos of John Lukaszinski's new baby and Mike Jurkas's fishing trip, news of Charlie Svoboda's secret date, Elsie Stabla's marriage and Horace Hornberg's retirement, and as many other employee names as could possibly be dropped, house organs assisted recreational programs in constructing a new kind of collective life at work that had nothing to do with employee grievances. When workers turned out to root for the "company team," managers felt confident that they were supporting more than the men on the field.

Enlightened industrialists crowned their vision of welfare capitalism with a call for employers to assume social responsibility beyond their own plants, in society at large. Manufacturers brought several motives to their concern for the welfare of the wider community. On the one hand, advertising had given companies by the 1920s a new appreciation for favorable public opinion. They dared not ignore the world outside the factory, filled as it was with potential customers, workers, stockholders, and citizens whose political support might be needed someday. Civic-minded companies would benefit in the long run from serving on charity boards or contributing generously to needy causes.[71] No less important, Chicago businessmen had noticed that manufacturers involved in their neighboring communities, like Wisconsin Steel in South Deering and Western Electric in Cicero, had survived 1919 with fewer bruises. Taking the lesson to heart, manufacturers took a new interest during the 1920s in what they considered the "stabilizing institutions" in their workers' communities, such as the YMCA, the Boy Scouts, parks, libraries, schools, and churches. Chicago steelmakers became so invested in the nearby YMCA, for example, that U.S. Steel–South Works paid for at least half the cost of constructing a new building, and Wisconsin Steel supported a full-time Y office on its grounds.[72] U.S. Steel, Wisconsin Steel, and Western Electric all improved parks in their communities to enhance the quality of life there as well as their own reputations.

Providing fuel for local churches was another strategy to bolster both a conservative community institution and the employer's image close to home.[73] Not accidentally, such largesse made friends where managers needed them. "I got the colored pastors to send colored men whom they could guarantee would not organize and were not bolsheviks," a steel works superintendent explained.[74] Several years later, in the depths of the depression, a steelworker trying to unionize the men at South Works asked the priest at nearby St. Michael's for help. "Do you want us to bite the hand that feeds us?" the priest reproached the organizer, pointing to piles of wood and a basement full of coke.[75] When Wisconsin Steel heated St. Kevin's Church, Armour and Swift gave children in Back of the Yards a safe place to play, U.S. Steel bought books for the new South Chicago branch library, Western Electric contributed to Cicero's new public high school, and International Harvester awarded prizes for the best vegetable gardens in the area, these Chicago companies laid claim to their communities. Employers who had encouraged workers to play at the plant rather than in the ethnic neighborhood were trying, at the same time, to make that neighborhood more an extension than escape from work.[76]

But businessmen did not just concern themselves with amenities in their neighborhoods or their reputations around town. Rather, their whole conception of welfare capitalism depended on viewing the corporation as the most responsible institution in society, more properly charged with the general welfare than was government. Much the way employers developed welfare programs to challenge the hold ethnic benefit associations had over their workers, they assumed civic responsibility to compete with state welfare. What welfare capitalists did not provide, government surely would, employers feared.

The antistatism of Chicago manufacturers grew out of resentment over government regulation during the Progressive Era. According to employers, these regulations had worsened with the war and persisted into the twenties. The meatpackers not only faced federal arbitration of labor relations from wartime through the early 1920s but also continued to struggle during the decade against Federal Trade Commission (FTC) charges that they had conspired in restraint of trade and with Department of Agriculture efforts to scrutinize their operations. International Harvester faced similar charges that it had cut prices to monopolize the market, whereas U.S. Steel fought government pressure to end the twelve-hour day.[77] The beleaguered industrialists found a spokesman for their opposition to government regulation in Secretary of Commerce Herbert Hoover. As he told the Chamber of Commerce at its national meeting in 1924, "The vast tide of these regulations that is sweeping onward can be stopped. . . . It is vitally necessary that we stem this tide if we would preserve that initiative in men which builds up the character, intelligence and progress in our people." The solution Hoover offered executives assembled in Cleveland and those who later read his speech in local journals like *Chicago Commerce* was that business must govern itself. "The conscience and organization of business" could go a long way toward keeping government out.[78] It was a simple move to apply this ideology to the realm of social welfare: develop enlightened welfare capitalism to avoid a welfare state.

Progressive employers advocated providing for the welfare of their own workers and communities to keep the state at bay. The depression of 1921 offered an early opportunity to put the idea into practice. President Harding set the appropriate mood in Washington when he told the National Conference on Unemployment, "I would have little enthusiasm for any proposed relief which seeks either palliation or tonic from the federal treasury." In Chicago, local businessmen and industrialists seized the president's words, joining hands with private charities to fight the postwar unemployment crisis.[79] Emblematic of their commitment to let business, and not government, pull Chicago out of depression was the "Pageant of Progress," an exposition city boosters organized on the shores of Lake Michigan to create jobs and stimulate recovery, "an answer to that suggestion that bread lines and other forms of charity be established for the relief of the unemployed."[80] For the rest of the decade, the Chicago Association of Commerce urged its members to take seriously the business of helping the city's needy. A conference of the city's best-known businessmen agreed that firms should underwrite the United Charities by assessing themselves according to the size of their employee ranks. When unemployment rose again in 1924, local employers including Western Electric, Swift, and Harvester met with social service agencies to handle the crisis.[81]

In the meantime, on a more defensive front, the Employers' Association of Chicago and the Illinois Manufacturers' Association lobbied in Washington and Springfield to make sure that old-age pension legislation or other kinds of "European parasitism" did not corrupt the American scene. Between 1911 and 1929, only one reform statute the Illinois Manufacturers' Association seriously opposed became law in the state.[82] Instead, to keep industry free of both government regulation and a larger tax burden, welfare capitalists argued that it was employers' job to provide for "the aged, the defective, and the indigent," in the words of P. W. Willard, Director of Personnel for Western Electric.[83] In the mind of the welfare capitalist, the "good employer" would earn its employees' loyalty and productivity by protecting them against economic uncertainty on the one hand and an un-American welfare state on the other.

Industrialists' rejection of social legislation was integral to a welfare capitalist program that aimed to make workers dependent on employers instead of their own communities and the state. A contemporary labor economist somewhat exaggerated what employers were prepared to do but nonetheless made the point that the company wanted no competition[84]:

> If the worker has a toothache, the company dentist will cure it; if he has a headache . . . he can get treatment from the company doctor; if he . . . needs an operation, the company doctor will help him find a competent surgeon; in some cases, the company optometrist will measure him for glasses, and the company chiropodist will treat his corns. If he has legal difficulties, he can obtain free advice from the company's lawyer; . . . if he wishes to save money, the company will act as agent for a bank, deduct the money from his pay check, deposit it in

the bank, and do the book-keeping for him; if he needs to borrow money, the company will lend it to him at a low rate of interest; if he wishes to own a house, the company will build one for him and sell it to him on easy terms, or help him to borrow the money to build it himself.

There is no doubt that large manufacturers like Western Electric, Swift, Armour, International Harvester, and U.S. Steel believed in a special relationship between boss and worker that transcended foremen, labor unions, ethnic communities, and the state. But their vision of the responsible capitalist protecting his employees' welfare did not necessarily become a reality for Chicago's workers.

WORKERS' RESPONSE TO WELFARE CAPITALISM

Industrial relations experts in Chicago's large manufacturing plants meticulously recorded just how many of their workers received company benefits. Their monthly tabulations must have pleased them. Workers and their families lined up for free medical care at Wisconsin Steel's clinic.[85] At Swift & Company by 1930, 91 percent of employees belonged to the Employee Benefit Association, and of these, 92 percent had subscribed to the company's group life insurance policy.[86] In Cicero, growing numbers attended the Hawthorne Evening School, and thanks to the Hawthorne Building and Loan Association, more and more workers were saying about their houses, "I bought it through the company."[87]

To employers' greatest satisfaction, a large number of workers in every one of these firms took advantage of the opportunity to become a stockholder. About a quarter of Swift & Company's employees owned stock. This made them about a third of Swift's total stockholders, although the higher echelon of employees, no doubt, was best represented and held the largest number of shares.[88] At U.S. Steel, stockholding prevailed more extensively among shopworkers. Almost 70 percent of eligible employees, those who had been on the payroll the required number of months, subscribed. "Great campaigns were going on to get the workers to buy steel stock; and lots of workers were trying to do it," recalled South Works steelworker George Patterson, by way of explaining his stock purchase in 1927.[89] Seventy percent of International Harvester's eligible employees subscribed to stock as well, and in some Harvester plants in Chicago the numbers were even higher. When Harvester announced an extension of its Stock Ownership and Investment Plan in 1928, almost 80 percent of McCormick Works employees signed on. An observer at Wisconsin Steel noted that "even the Mexicans invest their money and watch the daily stock quotations in the newspaper."[90] Across town at Western Electric's Hawthorne Works, 80 percent of those eligible also subscribed to AT&T stock. Not even the young, single girls who worked for low wages in Hawthorne's Coil Winding Department passed up the opportunity to become stockholders.[91] Without a doubt, Chicago workers were taking advantage of the new benefits that welfare capitalism had brought them.

Workers' participation in the welfare programs offered to them did not necessarily mean, however, that welfare capitalism was succeeding the way progressive industrialists hoped it would. The roll turner who subscribed to a share of U.S. Steel stock or the sliced bacon packager who received some money from Swift when she was ill did not have to promise unfailing loyalty to the company in return. Although workers' attitudes are difficult to know for sure, the evidence suggests that welfare capitalists succeeded in one respect and failed in another. Their accomplishment was to convince industrial workers of the 1920s that a fair employer should take responsibility for the welfare of his work force. But managers' actions proved less convincing than their rhetoric. Whether unable or unwilling, they rarely did what it took to allow workers to put full faith in the boss. Instead, their failure to deliver as promised frustrated employees, who took advantage of what benefits they could but often felt far different from the loyal, satisfied workers idealized in welfare capitalist ideology.[92]

One reason that Chicago's factory workers did not experience welfare capitalism the way the movement's theorists expected was that despite these new benefits, general conditions of work were still poor. The gravest problem was unemployment. Industrial workers suffered with repeated downturns in the business cycle, making the 1920s more a series of rises and falls than a "prosperity decade" for them. Unemployment in manufacturing was higher between 1923 and 1927 than for any other five-year period since 1900, excluding depression years. "First job I had with the company only lasted for three months and then I was laid off," a typical Wisconsin Steel worker recounted. "Then I got on again and worked for seven months and was laid off again. I've been here steady for three years now, but if I was young I sure as hell wouldn't work here."[93]

Equally as disruptive of an employee's confidence in the boss were seasonal layoffs which hit almost everyone sometime, even those with so-called steady jobs. A study of the steel industry confirmed that in "normal times" at least one in eight steelworkers was out of work.[94] A seasonal layoff not only threatened a worker's livelihood but also resulted in a forfeiture of benefits if it lasted long enough. In most companies, a break in service varying from a week to sixty days compelled a loss of accumulated benefits. Workers had to begin again counting time toward seniority or a paid vacation if they were lucky enough to be recalled. As Owensby Lee, an old-timer at Swift, explained the frustration, "We had to wait five years for one week's vacation. And I've seen men work four and one-half years and then get laid off."[95] To workers like Owensby Lee, the chance to enjoy a paid vacation the following summer or a pension in several years had limited power when they were not sure they would have a job the following day.

Few mass production workers escaped such seasonal instability since all Chicago industries experienced "rush" and "slack" seasons during the 1920s. Although some employers tried to regularize production over the year, they felt constrained by how the deflation of 1921 had altered the way their customers purchased. Consumers of industrial products avoided accumulating inventory, preferring what they called "hand to mouth buying." Manufacturers adjusted work schedules accordingly, fearing being caught with unsold products and unused raw materials. Rather than carry a full work force year round, they thought it more economical to invest in machinery that permitted high levels of production when needed.

Workers in the needle trades and manufacturing tied to agriculture, such as meatpacking and agricultural equipment, encountered the most seasonal unemployment.[96] In packing, in fact, seasonality intensified over the decade. One Chicago plant in 1923 employed two-thirds as many workers during the slack period as during its busy one, whereas in 1926 it retained only about half.[97] By the time investigators for the Women's Bureau of the Department of Labor studied employment among female packing workers during 1928–9, they found that 80 percent of them had experienced some unemployment over the previous years, each occasion bringing new trauma to their families. "You see the forelady coming with the yellow slips and you want to run before she reaches you. My mother scolded every time I had a lay-off," one young woman recounted bitterly.[98] Blacks and Mexicans, whose unskilled jobs made them easily expendable, were prime candidates for layoffs. "They are always putting on new men and letting them off," a Mexican worker complained. "They [the Mexicans] can barely live and they dare not leave because the only other place they can go to is the track or the beet fields."[99] But not even the privileged, "fully employed" workers that Leila Houghteling interviewed for her standard-of-living study in 1924 were spared. A majority of them lost substantial time from the job as well.[100] Welfare capitalist concern over turnover only went so far as keeping workers on the payroll, or available for call-up, when business warranted it. When there were orders, employers prized dependable, trained workers. But in more difficult times, managers expected employees, not the company, to absorb the loss. With eyes glued to the bottom line of the balance sheet, employers in the end showed more commitment to stabilizing their production than their work forces.

Even when employed, the typical industrial worker rarely found conditions at work the panacea that welfare capitalists promised. Wage rates were low, hours were long, and factory conditions were poor. Investigators at the time and observers since concur that despite employers' professed endorsement of a "doctrine of high wages" during the 1920s, the real wages of unskilled and semiskilled workers barely grew over the decade. Furthermore, because most of their gains came from declines in prices, employees did not psychologically feel indebted to their bosses. At International Harvester, for example, managers dropped wage rates once the militance of the 1919 era ebbed, increased them 10 percent for the unskilled and semiskilled in 1923 to a level still short of the 1920–1 high, and then granted no further wage increases between 1924 and 1929.[101] When over ten thousand Hawthorne workers met with interviewers at the end of the decade, they voiced twice as many complaints about wage payments than their next most common grievance.[102]

Workers were also dissatisfied with their long hours. Whenever given the opportunity, they asked for reduced hours of work with extra compensation for overtime. Rarely in the 1920s, however, did employers respect these wishes or make it financially possible for workers to limit their hours of labor on their own. The steady decline in working hours that began in the 1890s leveled off after 1920. Workers particularly resented the Sunday work that employers demanded during peak periods. One feisty woman at Hawthorne Works greeted news of a Sunday assignment with, "I suppose we'll be working on Palm Sunday and Easter Sunday. We won't call it Sunday any more, we'll call it Slave Day. Well girls, with this Sunday's pay I can make the last payment on my Rolls Royce."[103] Steelworkers at South Works who demanded "an eight hour day, one day's rest in seven" and "double rate of pay for overtime, holiday and Sunday work" in 1919 were still working an average of fifty-four hours a week in 1926, with no special compensation for unusual work demands. The abolition of the twelve-hour day in 1923 had not made a revolution.[104] Employers were no more eager to absorb the added costs of shorter working hours than to keep employees on the payroll during slack times.

Fringe benefits also could not compensate for the unhealthy and disagreeable environment that many workers found in the factory. Women who worked in the casings department of the packing plants discovered that the "pickle water causes salt ulcers and they're very hard to cure, nearly impossible if you have to keep working in the wet." Their husbands and fathers suffered from "hog's itch," rheumatism from the damp cold and, among the most unfortunate who labored in the fertilizer plants, a permanent body stench.[105] Steelworkers labored amid heat, dust, and continual noise and could never drop their guard against accidents. "It was like breathing after you worked in the mill a certain length of time," said Phillip Janik of his constant vigilance against the dangers of the open hearth.[106] Everywhere workers complained about the inadequacy of toilets, showers, lockers, and ventilation.[107] Some employers tried to make their workshops less hazardous. But really improving the overall conditions of work – keeping workers on the payroll year round whatever the job orders, granting workers the forty-hour week they consistently requested, and making the factory a decent place to work – would have cost employers far more than adopting adjunct welfare programs. Manufacturers found it easier to sweeten the icing than to enrich the cake itself. But it will become clear that they paid a price for promising a treat and then leaving their workers' appetites unsatisfied.

Deficient working conditions did not alone undermine worker support for welfare capitalist programs. Many of the programs themselves failed to operate the way employers intended. Manufacturers had developed schemes to restrain foremen's arbitrary authority on the shop floor, to individualize management's relationships with employees, and to make workers more dependent on the firm. These strategies, however, often fell short of the mark.

The "foreman's empire" survived the 1920s more intact than managers desired. They had sent foremen back to school to learn to become more enlightened supervisors and had tried to implement standardized systems like job ladders and seniority. But setting policy in the conference rooms of industrial relations departments was one thing, reforming entrenched behavior on the shop floor quite another. A well-developed foreman's culture opposed welfare capitalist reforms. Many foremen not only felt personally threatened but also denounced the effort to win the goodwill of labor through liberal treatment as futile or misguided. A visitor to the Wisconsin Steel Works the day of a Foreman's Forum meeting overheard a group joking about the last assignment, which none had read. One man spoke out: "That man D____ doesn't know as much about industrial problems as I do, and then his damn humanitarianism makes me sick. When he begins to talk about the right way to treat the men and the wrong way, he doesn't know what he's talking about. I don't believe he has even been inside a steel mill or he wouldn't come out with that soft soap bunk that he hands out at those meetings." If these particular foremen attended that evening's meeting, they were in the minority. The attendance by foremen had dropped during the course of six months from 250 to less than 75.[108]

Foremen also resisted other executive initiatives to curb their authority. Worker accounts of factory life during the 1920s dwell consistently on the way foremen played favorites, rewarding their relatives and those who pleased them and harassing those who did not.[109] Fearful workmen often felt obligated to offer their foremen tips, presents of alcohol, and such services as a car wash, grass cutting, or house repairs on a Sunday.[110] Some workers, most often Mexicans, Italians, and Poles, felt that not even doing that would win them the favor of a prejudiced Irish or native-born foreman like the one who claimed "the men working around here are dumb Bohunks who will never get any further than they are now."[111] Women felt a special kind of pressure to become the foreman's friend, for which he promised they'd "get the easiest work and make the big money" or else risk his displeasure. "You could get along swell if you let the boss slap you on the behind and feel you up," Armour canner Anna Novak complained.[112]

Foremen had little trouble skirting personnel systems like seniority and promotional ladders that supposedly protected workers from the foreman's power. They thereby kept workers dependent on them alone. "The foreman who had a pet would tell him to take off a week sick, instead of being in the plant on the day of the layoff. In that way, the foreman could avoid laying off by seniority one of his pets. There were no published lists," a packinghouse worker explained.[113] If a foreman claimed there was no work in his department and had a worker transferred to another one, that employee lost his seniority since seniority in meatpacking was by department, not plantwide.[114] Workers also knew that the Personnel Department was unlikely to come through with promotions for ordinary operatives despite company avowals to the contrary. Industrial relations expert J. David Houser, who investigated "what the employer thinks" in 1926, confirmed that "several employers became enthusiastic when describing the large opportunities offered subordinates for advancement in their establishments. In none of these cases, however, was any real promotional plan discovered. And those opportunities so glowingly described from above, employees regarded with indifference and lack of conviction. Contrary to the executive's belief, such workers usually had yet to be convinced that promotion was not largely a matter of favoritism or personal bias."[115]

This gap between the expectations raised by company officials for fairness and the arbitrariness of their immediate supervisors frustrated workers. "The company is all right but they never know what the foremen do," a steelworker grumbled. And if you complained to a higher-level supervisor that your foreman was treating you unfairly, "he gives the foreman hell and sends you back. But in four or five days the foreman may move you around and tell you there is no more work to do."[116] Industrial relations expert Houser concluded that chief executives had inadequate methods of learning how employees were treated. Some relied on the incidental reports of time study technicians who happened to observe the personnel methods of foremen. A few hired "undercover men" to tell them what went on in the shops.[117] But more than ignorance kept favoritism and authoritarianism alive in Chicago's plants. Although welfare capitalists denounced these practices in principle, if the old "drive" strategies led to profits, they closed their eyes. When an employment manager at one of the packinghouses was confronted with the obnoxious behavior of a particular foreman, he responded, "I know the foreman; he cusses them all. We have laid him off for a week several times." But was the company willing to do more than that? "He is one of the best foremen we have; he makes money for the company" was the reply.[118]

The strategies that employers had developed to create individual relationships with employees and thereby circumvent the foreman and workers' own peer groups did not work much better than their efforts to restrain foremen. Neither employee representation plans nor wage incentives succeeded in convincing workers that the company would reward fairly the initiatives of isolated employees.

Worker experience with employee representation plans followed a similar pattern at the three companies that had such plans. When Armour, Swift, and International Harvester initiated their plans in response to labor rebelliousness after the war, workers recognized them as antiunion tactics. But although the plans were submitted to an official vote, rejecting them was not easy. Workers nonetheless registered their objections by both voting and not voting. Even though a timekeeper at Swift kept a record of those who "did not vote right," the company had to admit several years later that "at first there were many employes [*sic*] who failed to vote when representatives were being elected, because they did not have confidence."[119] Although the Harvester Industrial Council Plan passed by a vote of 1,152 to 712 at Wisconsin Steel, many major departments rejected it. At International Harvester's largest and most radical Chicago plant, McCormick Works, employees managed to keep turning the plan down for two years.[120]

Once works councils had become a reality, workers in all these plants sought to use them to their own advantage. They tried to work around rigid company requirements for office holding to elect representatives who would be more than yes men. They requested wage increases and paid vacations, and they raised the individual grievances that the councils were best equipped to handle.[121] Yet within a few years it became clear that employee representation was little more than a facade. Employers only wanted the illusion of democratic decision making. By the mid-1920s, workers knew it was hardly worth bringing grievances to their representatives. As Swift worker Edward Hassett recalled, "You come up to him [the representative] with a case. He wouldn't take you to the foreman. He would go up an' talk to the foreman and come back an' say: 'Well there ain't very much we can do about it, but next time come up.'"[122] Employee representatives like Wisconsin Steel's Mike Quinn felt the same frustration at the council level.

> I'm supposed to be an employee representative from the mill and yet I don't dare do half the things I want to do. As soon as you begin complaining about safety conditions or promotions you are stepping on the toes of some fore-

man. . . . All hiring and firing and conditions according to the Constitution are affairs that should be dealt with jointly by the bosses and the employe [*sic*] representatives. But I have nothing to do with most of them.

Twice employee representatives tried to get wage increases. "Each time it has failed or was killed before being taken seriously."[123] As worker representatives on Harvester's councils reconciled themselves to their ineffectiveness, Cyrus McCormick credited the decline of conflict within the councils to unanimity between workers and managers: "Recently, after a lapse of over two years, I attended a meeting of this same body and was surprised to find that a meeting which used to take three or four hours . . . was now finished in forty-five minutes."[124] Employers' overwhelming desire to avoid contentiousness in the factory subverted their own strategy of dividing workers by responding conscientiously to their individual grievances.

Workers had no more reason to trust that the new system of wage incentives would reward them fairly as individuals. Whenever investigators visited Chicago factories during the 1920s, they walked away convinced that workers were at best confused and at worst angry about wage incentive pay schemes. The root of the problem was that employers, in carrying out these wage plans, consistently violated two crucial tenets of Frederick Taylor's prescription about implementing incentives: that employees must understand exactly how bonuses work and that, once set, rates must never be revised downward even if worker productivity increased.

In employers' defense, many of them tried to explain to workers how to figure their bonuses, but the systems were extremely complicated. When Alma Herbst investigated the Bedaux wage system at Swift, she was forced to conclude that "many, judging from their remarks, are utterly unfamiliar with it in spite of the fact that every morning the standard sheet which states the amount of premium earned by each is posted in the various departments. All they know is they usually receive two pay checks, one of which is the premium . . . [as] added encouragement given the workers to increase their premiums." But rather than perceive a relationship between the previous day's or week's special exertion on the job, "the premium, according to the workers, seems to rain upon them as a gift from the gods. . . . It does not incite envy or emulation, for each sees the system in terms of an opportunity which seldom comes to him, and when it does, he is unable to explain how or why."[125] Lest we be moved to dismiss Herbst's observation as reflective only of the particular workers she happened to meet, other investigators came to the same conclusion. Some reported that workers blamed their bosses for keeping the rates from them; others noted that even with a little knowledge of arithmetic, workers found the morass of figures that their foremen gave them impenetrable. Rather than increasing worker productivity through competition, as employers intended, more often wage incentives encouraged workers to philosophize much like packing worker Bill Voorhis: "The bonus is like playing the horses. You work hard an' you expect him. You get nothing. You work easy. You get a lot."[126]

Complications in the system of wage incentives made workers confused. Their suspicions that employers were abusing it made them angry. Employees appreciated the weeks when they made more money, but the costs of those profits rarely escaped them. Workers complained that the pressure to produce brought the quality of products down, while their risk of accidents and illness went up. They also resented the way a percentage of their bonus earnings went to the company, a kind of punishment where "the harder you worked, the less you got."[127] Their gravest criticism, however, was reserved for how employers used wage incentives to speed up production without compensating workers fairly and then tried to reduce the work force. "If we turn a job out in two hours," a Hawthorne worker told an interviewer, "next week the bogey will be cut to one and a quarter hours. . . . I keep reducing my time on the jobs in an effort to increase my efficiency, but it doesn't do any good, because the rates are cut accordingly. I don't know when we'll reach the limit, but it looks like we'll soon be working through the noon hour in order to get ahead."[128] This worker was not misreading his boss's intentions. At a meeting of a Supervisors' Conference Group at Hawthorne, the high bonuses earned by operators were considered grounds for changing the bogey.[129] In the end, workers feared, their extra exertions could cost them their jobs. If one worker did more than what once was considered a "fair day's work," soon there would be no need for his neighbor. It will become clear shortly that workers did more than suffer the wage incentive system individually, but for now suffice it to say that employer misuse of these wage plans for speed-ups and layoffs doomed them as the motivating tool that Taylor had intended.

Similarly, industrialists failed to put their full effort behind the welfare programs they had adopted to make workers dependent on the company. Employers intended that benefit plans, group insurance, stock ownership, and pensions would safeguard workers and their families from cradle to grave, thereby reinforcing loyalty to the firm. Welfare capitalists hoped their employees would forsake ethnic mutual benefit membership or industrial insurance policies and watch their investment in the company grow over the years by accumulating stock and tenure toward pensions. It is clear that workers took advantage of these welfare measures when they could. But just as employers undercut foremen training, employee representation, and wage incentives, so too they derailed welfare programs through their lack of sufficient commitment.

Workers appreciated company sickness benefits and group insurance plans when they were cost free, but if they required employee contributions, as they did in most plants, these welfare provisions raised problems. The concept of an employer insuring the health and life of his workers only made sense when the relationship between boss and laborer was a stable one. If a worker faced frequent layoffs, he preferred to have his financial investment in his family's future welfare accrue through a more dependable organization. Hence, workers kept memberships going in their ethnic mutual benefit societies while still taking advantage of welfare programs at work. Gab Elson of Wisconsin Steel was typical. Elson needed both his Harvester sick benefits and his Knights of Pythias fraternal insurance to pay the $99.50 bill for twelve days in the hospital. In a similar position was an anonymous Ukrainian worker at Harvester's Tractor Works who told an interviewer that keeping up his membership in the Ukrainian National Association Lodge still was his top priority on pay day.[130] When workers like these faced pressure to contribute to company plans beyond what they felt they could afford along with their other ones, they balked. Group insurance particularly provoked this reaction. Most insurance companies required that at least 75 percent of the employees in a firm subscribe before a group policy could be activated. Employers, eager to deliver group insurance as part of their welfare package, put tremendous pressure on their employees to sign up and then saw to it that the insurance company got its premiums, even when working hours were reduced, by unfailingly deducting this payment from worker wages.[131]

A dispute between workers and management over group insurance at U.S. Steel's South Works provides a rare view of worker resistance. Soon after management announced a new group insurance plan to U.S.

Steel employees in 1926, an editorial appeared in the company newspaper, the *South Works Review*.[132] "There appears to be a misunderstanding among some of our employees with reference to the new group insurance plan," the column began. It seemed that employees had accused their bosses of having a financial interest in the company insurance. "I wish to assure our employees that neither the E. J. & E. Railway Company [a division of South Works] nor any of its officials are interested in it, in any way, shape or manner," declared the writer, "other than the interest it has in helping its employees to secure some additional protection for their families if they desire." The next part of the editorial reveals that workers interpreted taking the new group insurance as a threat to their existing insurance commitments and refusing it as a danger to their employment status: "It is not the thought or the intent that employees will cancel any other insurance they now carry in order to secure this insurance, but merely gives them an opportunity to secure additional insurance at a low rate if they so desire. . . . *Standing with the Company* will not be affected, one way or the other."

The next month, U.S. Steel announced a change in regulations designed to allay workers' fears about the effect of layoffs on group insurance. A worker who was laid off was now permitted to continue his group insurance payments for three months, and then month to month thereafter as arranged, not to exceed twenty-four months. U.S. Steel was trying to make its group insurance more competitive with plans less contingent on continuous employment. But managers still could not resist demanding loyalty as their price. The worker who was not working and wanted to keep up his insurance could only do so providing "he holds himself in readiness to return to Illinois Steel Company any time called."[133] Trading loyalty for benefits did not make sense to workers when the company pledged little loyalty to them in exchange. Workers could not afford to be dependent only on their employers.

Welfare capitalists' failure to convince workers that they had a long-term future with the company also doomed stockholding and pensions as methods of tying employees to the firm. Employers had hoped that workers who bought stock would become capitalists willing to make a long-term investment in the company. They took heart at the outpouring of enthusiasm that greeted every sale of shares. In time, however, employers began to notice a disturbing pattern. Workers bought stock, but they did not hold onto it. Once again Cyrus Mc-

Cormick put his finger on the problem, although he passed over it with his characteristically sanguine air: "At the time our new plan was announced we had some 29,000 employes in all departments of the business. Of these, 22,000 subscribed for stock to the astounding total of over $14,000,000. During the following twelve months many, of course, dropped out, either because of departure from the Company or because they needed the money for other purposes; but others have come in to take their places."[134]

In truth, workers eagerly bought stock at the discounts offered but not because they were making a commitment to their employers. They merely considered it a good way to save and perhaps make a little money on the side. Welfare capitalists did what they could to alter workers' motives. U.S. Steel paid stock bonuses if employees kept shares at least five years while regaling workers with tales of stock subscribers who had held onto their shares and now were getting extra income.[135] In 1928, Western Electric chastised the hundreds of their employees who were selling AT&T stock to take advantage of high market values for "killing the goose that lays the golden egg."[136] Workers nonetheless kept selling. By the end of the decade, employers estimated that at least half the employees who subscribed failed to retain their stock.[137] An ethnic newspaper like the Polish *Dziennik Zjednoczenia* regretted that employees did not forsake all stock purchases in favor of deposits in ethnic banks.[138] Employers knew by 1927, according to an economist who studied employee stock ownership in Chicago, that even when employees bought stock, stockholding had not bred "a sense of identity of interest with a particular firm."[139]

Workers' recognition that they had uncertain futures with any particular company made them skeptical as well of employers' promises of pensions. So many factors could intervene between hiring and retirement. One labor critic caricatured the impossible terms of a typical pension[140]:

> If you remain with this company throughout your productive lifetime; if you do not die before the retirement age; if you are not discharged, or laid off for an extended period; if you are not refused a pension as a matter of discipline; if the company is in business; and if the company does not decide to abandon the plan, you will receive a pension at the age of _____, subject to the contingency of its discontinuance or reduction after it has been entered upon.

Such cynicism was not unwarranted. Both U.S. Steel and International Harvester changed their pension provisions over the course of the 1920s when too many workers began qualifying.[141] Moreover, rather than observing contented pensioners among their families and neighbors, workers were more likely to see either people fighting to hold onto a job way beyond a reasonable retirement age or people in their late forties and fifties finding themselves obsolete. The first group, like the old bent-over ladies in their seventies that Anna Novak watched struggle to work everyday at the stockyards, had not accumulated a sufficient number of years for a pension.[142] The latter were victims of a new phenomenon that increasingly frightened industrial workers during the 1920s, age limits for workers. As skill became less important, employers were opting for the endurance of the young over the experience of the old. In 1929, Western Electric, for example, modified its personnel policy so that men past their thirty-fifth birthday or women past their thirtieth "should be considered carefully to insure that their employment will be mutually advantageous."[143] Employers' promises of a pension seemed empty when tested against the overwhelming human evidence workers observed every day in their own communities.

Neither for retirement nor for long-term investments, insurance, or sick benefits did workers feel they could depend solely on their employer. Welfare capitalists did not put enough resources behind their rhetoric to convince workers that it was safe to put all their eggs in the boss's basket.

Industrial workers in Chicago did not just passively endure employers' irresponsibility while taking whatever company benefits they could get. True, they did not mount the kinds of work stoppages and strikes that had been possible during the more politically open, immediate postwar years. Except for a brief revival of organizing activity in Chicago area steel mills during 1923, union drives and dramatic shop floor action belonged to the past.[144] What little radical activity had survived the government's Red Scare tactics, employers' open-shop drives, and the left's own internecine conflicts was barely visible. A handful of *Daily Worker* distributors persisted at packinghouse gates, and occasionally Communist shop papers like the *Harvester Worker* appeared in plant locker rooms.[145] Yet it would be a mistake to conclude that workers mounted no defense. A closer look at factory workers' behavior during the 1920s indicates that both as individuals and in groups they took advantage of flaws in welfare capitalism to minimize their vulnerability to employers.

So long as employers had passed the burden of absorbing the ups and downs of the business cycle onto their employees, workers tried their best to use job market fluctuations to their own advantage. More often than manufacturers would have liked, individual workers continued to quit jobs and to be absent from the ones they held. Although employers were reluctant to carry employees during slack periods, they had hoped welfare capitalist programs would keep workers loyal when there was work and on-call at other times. Instead, they encountered a work force that turned seasonality into stubborn independence.

Work force turnover declined in the course of the 1920s, but analysts agree that high unemployment was more responsible than workers' satisfaction with their jobs. Except for a short time during 1923 when workers were in great demand and consequently quit jobs in record numbers, a slack labor market prevailed in industry that worked to employers' advantage. True, quotas had halted most foreign immigration during the twenties, which should have made workers already here more valuable. But the combination of an increased flow of labor from farm to city, a rise in worker productivity, and fewer jobs in manufacturing conspired to preserve a "buyers' market," in the words of labor economist Sumner Slichter.[146] Given a climate so unfavorable to workers, it is remarkable that a very high percentage of workers still left jobs voluntarily, not because they were laid off or discharged. Industrial workers, skeptical of job security, asserted their independence. When workers heard that another company had entered a seasonal rush and was hiring at better pay, they quit the jobs they had. If rumors circulated that an employer would soon be laying off, they did not wait to get the official news. When a worker became angry at his foreman, he left if he had anywhere else to go. Tony Caruso, foreman at Wisconsin Steel, complained that over 75 percent of the men working in his no. 5 mill, particularly the young ones, had no intentions of remaining there permanently: "They work there to make a little money or just until they can find something better. Some are trying to get a job on the Police Department, others on the Fire Department, and some even as street car conductors," all of which promised steadier work.[147] If seasonality could not be overcome, workers would at least take advantage of it by seeking out the best jobs available that season. Employers who refused to protect workers' jobs in slack times would just have to cope with workers' abandonment in better ones.

International Harvester's careful record keeping and conscientious record saving preserved an extraordinary picture of turnover within a large manufacturing company. During most of the 1920s, in a large majority of Harvester's plants, fewer than half of all employees had been with the company for more than two years, and a large portion of the newcomers had been there for less than a year. In a way that may be hard to imagine given today's expectations of stable work, Harvesters' shops were a constant whirl of workers coming and going. Depending on the economy, 14–40 percent of workers were forced to leave on account of discharges and layoffs in any particular year. Between 1923 and 1929, an average of 70 percent of those who left departed voluntarily.[148]

These mass exits by workers did not please Harvester executives. As late as 1930, the Industrial Relations Department wrote Cyrus McCormick, Jr., "We feel our figure of 82% [total turnover] is way too high." The memo went on to review that each departure cost the company between fifty and one hundred dollars, taking into account everything from the initial interview, physical exam, record keeping, and introduction to the new job to the newcomer's effect on the foreman's time, production levels, and broken tools. Harvester's industrial relations experts clearly felt that the company was not doing enough to stem the tide of workers' departures. "We question whether sufficient attention has been paid to the costliness of labor turnover," they stated, and then went on to make recommendations aimed particularly at holding onto recent arrivals, the most apt to leave: "Among the corrective measures to be adopted should be a better and more careful selection of new employes [*sic*], better introduction to the new job, proper and adequate training and instruction by department heads and their assistants, closer contacts with the new employe during the early days of his employment, to make sure he is supplied with proper tools and equipment, understands his work and is able to make a fair day's pay for a fair day's work."[149] At the tail end of the twenties, even as a worsened economy made employment all that much harder to get, workers were still quitting jobs they did not like.

Workers not only angered employers by quitting but also aggravated them with their lack of work discipline when on the job. Sluggish productivity, tardiness, and absences were subtle ways that individual workers asserted their independence without resigning. Once again, International Harvester records demonstrate that an undercurrent of protest went on every day in the factory. To cope with poor discipline among its workers, Harvester finally agreed to implement a long-requested vacation plan in January 1929. Management told workers that paid vacations were an experiment pending proof that employees would work harder to compensate for comrades who were off while also curbing their own tardiness and absences. Specifically, more than six unexcused and thirty sick days a year – none of which the company paid for – would deprive a worker of a week's vacation. Everyday the company sent out a representative to make the rounds of absent workers' homes, verifying their excuses.

Harvester executives thought they could discipline workers with a bribe as well as provide a new welfare benefit without any additional cost. To their frustration, however, the first year the vacation plan went into effect absences persisted at almost the same rate as before in a plant like Wisconsin Steel. At every monthly works council meeting in 1929, management representatives ranted and raved over worker absenteeism. "We have a lot of hot jobs in the plant. It seems that the men on these jobs are the ones that can't get up in the morning," said one representative at an August meeting. "They say, 'Well, it's pretty hot out there today, guess I will take the day off and rest up a bit.' There is no question but what at least two-thirds or perhaps more of the absenteeism is absolutely unnecessary."[150] Some employee representatives responded by voicing their constituents' request for more legal days off. But Harvester officials would hear nothing of it. Nor did they like hearing that workers were resisting pressure to increase their efficiency despite warnings that the vacation plan might be abandoned. One employee representative from the Blast Furnace Department recounted at a works council meeting how defiant his men were[151]:

> I said, "Now when you get this vacation you will have to put a little more pep into your work." They said, "How will we do that?" I said, "You will have to wheel more ore." They said, "How are you going to do that?" I said, "Well, in your spare time you got to do a little more." They said, "Well, I do have spare time, but at the present time I am speeding up to get this spare time." I said, "That's all right, that's good, but you will have to make up for your vacation somehow."

At International Harvester, as at Hawthorne Works, U.S. Steel, and the packinghouses, workers responded to being at their employer's beck and call by keeping the boss waiting on occasion.[152]

Another way that individual workers shielded themselves from the vagaries of industrial work was to turn to their families for help. Much more than might be expected, the urban working-class family of the

1920s depended on a family economy. Although in a twentieth-century city like Chicago family members went off in different directions to work, they were not so very different from the nineteenth-century family who labored together in the local mill. All contributed wages to the family budget. The employment of one protected the family in case of reduced earnings or the unemployment of another. When Myra Hill Colson investigated the persistence of home work within black households in Chicago, she discovered that even in 1927 there was a strong relationship between a woman's work and the irregularity of her husband's earnings. One woman had been making artificial flowers at home for the previous three years because her steelworker husband's wages were sporadic. Another woman, Mrs. Y, shared an apartment with her cousin and both their steelworker husbands; the women went out to work or made lamp-shades when the men's unemployment necessitated it. Mrs. Z's husband "shaved backs" in the stockyards, but his wages in slow periods could be ten dollars or more below what they were in busy ones; at those times, Mrs. Z also made lamp-shades or worked as a waitress.[153] Another investigator uncovered a similar situation among steelworkers at the mill. One man told him, "The only reason they [he and his wife] did not separate . . . was because they were both earning money and were able to support the other when one was out of work."[154] Study after study revealed that the ability of a working-class family to make ends meet during the 1920s depended on the extra income generated by multiple earners. In more than two-thirds of Leila Houghteling's steadily employed workers' families, for example, the chief wage earner's income was not sufficient to maintain a standard of living equivalent to the "Chicago Standard Budget for Dependent Families." Women particularly – single, married, widowed, or abandoned – did someone else's laundry, scrubbed other people's floors, made clothes for others' children, and prepared and served food for tables not their own. All this they did not for "pin money" or to save for a house but to meet the monthly bills.[155]

Chicago's wage-earning families packed members off to work because they needed all the income they could get. But no less important, because mother worked at night cleaning office buildings in the Loop, daughter sewed pockets on men's suits, and oldest son worked in the steel mill alongside "chief breadwinner" father, each worker was less dependent on an employer's whim than he or she otherwise would have been.

Workers coped with the imperfections in their jobs not only in individualistic ways, by quitting, staying away from work, or depending on family financial help, but also by subtle forms of collective action. In the packinghouses, when the foremen were out of view, women workers sometimes changed jobs with old ladies who had been assigned back-breaking tasks.[156] On other occasions, to avoid layoffs, women in a work gang or a department took turns staying home for a week.[157] At South Works, Mexican steelworkers made themselves more independent of the employment office by selling their work numbers to other Mexicans when they wished to leave their jobs.[158] But workers' most common and influential strategy involved turning the wage incentive system to their own advantage through what was called "output restriction." Through this tactic workers demonstrated that they trusted their peer community with their personal futures more than their employer.

Although workers did not always understand the finer details of wage incentive plans, they knew enough to realize that working at top speed could lead to lower rates, speed-ups, and layoffs. Consequently, as their bosses implemented these new wage plans during the 1920s, workers drew together to mount a common defense. Their goal was to take advantage of higher pay whenever possible without losing ground. Their strategy was to carefully monitor their own productivity. Day to day, this meant that workers in a particular area followed rules of their own making. As a starting point, they agreed upon a fair level of productivity and permitted no one to surpass it. In the sliced bacon department at Swift's, for example, one worker confided that "the women themselves had gotten together and they would turn out a hundred and forty-four packages an hour of bacon. . . . A new girl would come in and the oldtimers would train her. They would help her out so that gradually by the end of a certain period of time she was doing the 144. But they would never let anyone go beyond that 144 packages." Anyone who defied the limit was punished. In the same Swift department, "one smart-aleck girl came in there once and she was going to show them and go beyond that number because she wanted to earn more money: all the bacon that she got from the girls further up the line was messed up and scrappy and she'd have to straighten it up to put it in the package. She couldn't make a hundred packages an hour.[159] At Western Electric, workers not only took similar action to keep "over achievers" in line, but they also exerted group pressure to ostracize them. Top performers were ridiculed with nicknames like "rate-buster," "chiseler," "runt," "slave," "speed king," "Phar Lap" (the name of a race horse), and "4:15 Special," meaning that they worked until quitting time.[160] Workers who had trouble figuring out how to maximize earnings under the wage incentive system had no problem comprehending how to restrict them.

Workers manipulated the wage incentive system to their benefit in other ways. In the presence of the rate setter, packinghouse workers learned "to wrap a package of bacon using a lot of extra motions.... When he wasn't there we eliminated all those motions and did it simply."[161] An interviewer at Hawthorne Works discovered in an amusing way that a similar system to beat the time study expert operated there. One day, unobserved, he entered a department where the men seemed to be working at a good pace amid a buzz of conversation. Suddenly, he heard a sharp hissing sound, all talk died, and the men noticeably slowed up in their work. Later the interviewer learned that the "lookout" had mistaken him for a rate setter and stepped on a valve releasing compressed air to signal the men to slow down.[162] Workers at Hawthorne and elsewhere also regularized their earnings by "banking," holding back finished work or job tickets for a slow day or week. Workers were known as well for using output restriction to communicate their dissatisfaction with a foreman to higher levels of management. Out of self-protection, foremen negotiated with shop staff far more than they would have by choice.[163]

In short, the wage incentives that employers implemented to set workers apart as individuals instead laid new ground for workers to come together. The Hawthorne studies demonstrated this point much more convincingly than their more frequently cited finding, the so-called Hawthorne effect, which argued that workers' productivity was primarily a function of the attention given them by supervisors. A more compelling though less publicized discovery of the Hawthorne researchers was that workers' own networks of social relations, not management attentiveness, regulated productivity. The Relay Assembly Test, and even more so the Bank Wiring Test, demonstrated that the working group had become a force to contend with on the shop floor.[164]

Although employers failed to realize it, their determination to mix ethnic groups in the factory broadened the new alliances that output restriction had created among workers. This does not mean that work groups of mixed ethnicity were without strains. In the bank wiring observation room at Hawthorne, twelve of the fourteen men were born

Plate 22. As this sign warning of danger in five languages indicates, workers at U.S. Steel's South Works, as in many other Chicago industries, were of many national origins. Employers who had previously assigned workers to specific jobs by their ethnicity began during the 1920s to mix work gangs in order to break up ethnic subcultures that might subvert managerial authority. When employees in the twenties joined together to resist certain aspects of welfare capitalism, by, for example, restricting their output in response to new wage incentives, this mix on the shop floor encouraged them to make alliances across ethnicity and race.

in the United States, but of these, one identified as Irish, two as Polish, three as German, and four as Bohemian. A powerful group identity helped them restrict output, but ethnic jostling nonetheless permeated daily life in the shop, ranging from long-standing animosities fueled by prejudice to constant cracks about Polacks to arguments over the comparative merits of the Masons, the Knights of Columbus, and the Catholic Church.[165] In many mills, the lunch whistle sent workers scurrying off to eat with friends of their own nationality. In Mill No. 5 of Wisconsin Steel, the Mexicans claimed the stairway, the older Croatian workers took one corner, second-generation Poles another, and several Americans ate alone.[166] But because workers depended on each other to keep wages up and jobs steady, it is likely that trust began to develop between members of groups that previously had been suspicious of each other at work and often still were outside the plant. Factory workers in the 1920s were by no means the first to restrict their output. But the new ethnic mix on the shop floor diversified the co-workers they were forced to depend on, just as new wage incentive schemes and labor-saving strategies increased the necessity of controlling productivity.

Mechanization and other employer tactics to streamline production during the twenties also helped to make output restriction an effective strategy among co-workers. By the end of the decade, for example, workers at International Harvester's Tractor Works were more likely to be working alongside each other on an assembly line than performing independent custom work, making cooperation more feasible.[167] Furthermore, employers' growing interest during the 1920s in more sharply differentiating work tasks by gender facilitated the creation of cross-ethnic work cultures on the shop floor, particularly in departments of Swift, Armour, International Harvester, and Western Electric that exclusively employed women. In contrast to managers' efforts at integrating workers along ethnic and racial lines, they felt greater efficiency would result from segregating the sexes by particular operations. But in doing so, employers encouraged new kinds of bonds across ethnicity and even race. The many examples of female solidarity cited in this chapter, of women secretly doing hard jobs assigned to older ones, taking turns staying at home to avoid layoffs, or restricting output in a department like sliced bacon, are no accident. By increasingly isolating women in the plant, managers allowed a woman's culture built on the common experiences of family – celebrations of births and marriages, exchanges of recipes and remedies, empathy for the ditched girlfriend and the overworked grandmother – to help women of diverse ethnic backgrounds come together to protect themselves. A shared interest in a more public kind of culture, professional sports, began to serve the same unifying function among male workers.[168]

Welfare capitalism had given manufacturing workers new reason to communicate with each other as well as new ways. Not only were people now likely to cooperate with persons of different ethnicity on the factory floor, but they might also deepen that relationship by playing with them on the department baseball team or chatting at the company dance. Once workers had their own interests in common, employer-sponsored recreation could function to intensify employees' collective identity as easily as to diffuse it. Workers who still lived apart from each other gained new opportunities to mix now that their employers were organizing activities outside of working hours. Male and female employees ended the twenties sharing more than the "family feeling" that welfare capitalists had intended.

By the late 1920s, as signs of depression became more apparent, it may even have begun to dawn on blacks that they had more to gain by allying with their co-workers than their bosses. Blacks had employers to thank for their entry into Chicago's industries during and after World War I. In 1919 and through most of the following decade, they repaid that debt with their loyalty. Employers like Swift and Armour could count on blacks, for example, to play active roles on employee representation councils. Black workers participated not just to keep on the boss's good side but also because, as one representative honestly explained it, there was a great amount of "prejudy" against colored men in the unions, whereas with employee representation, they did not feel this prejudice.[169] Indeed, memories of the postwar race riot and strikes were vivid enough during the twenties so that most blacks remained more suspicious of the whites they worked alongside than of their employers.

It is a sad commentary on the racial realities of the 1920s that black workers staked so much on management. For evidence abounds that employers frequently mistreated their black employees. Black workers predominated in the poorest paying, most unpleasant jobs, and managers' prejudice kept them there. This was most blatant in the packinghouses. At both Swift and Armour, management made a rule that no finished products could pass through black hands. They rationalized this disciminatory practice by arguing that plant visitors on tour would be offended to see black workers handling food that whites might eat.[170] As white worker Mary Hammond explained, "I'm in sliced bacon. That's supposed to be the lightest, cleanest place to work. They wouldn't take on a Negro girl if she was a college graduate."[171] Demsey Travis's Aunt Mary, married to a black packing worker, might scoff that "black folks have been handling food for white folks as long as I can remember," but racial prejudice irrationally circumscribed black employment in industry.[172] Blacks consistently earned less in industrial jobs than whites.[173] Moreover, International Harvester, the packinghouses, and steel mills all carefully monitored quotas on the number of blacks that could be hired. Supervisors insisted time and again that blacks had a higher incidence of quitting and absences whereas all evidence contradicted that. Not even when Harvester's Industrial Relations Department assembled data demonstrating that blacks were more disciplined than whites on the job did management loosen its quotas.[174]

By the late 1920s, blacks began to realize where faith in their employers was getting them. As the job market deteriorated, they found their overall presence in industry declining from the mid-1920s (Table 12). Many felt their jobs were going to Mexicans because they would work for less. At Armour and Company, black stars marked the time cards of black workers to ensure that foremen pulled them first when layoffs were necessary.[175] Bonds between white and black workers would prove much harder to build than between one ethnicity and another. But by placing at least some blacks side by side with whites in the factory, welfare capitalists were facilitating cooperation between workers of different races for their mutual survival. When black and white workers on Swift's cattle-killing floor became angry at their foreman's refusal to place extra help on the gang, they joined together in a work stoppage. "We had a close working relationship – the blacks and the whites – strange as it may seem," recalled a black leader of the protest.[176]

Workers rebelled against what they perceived as shortcomings in welfare capitalism. But it is important to recognize that they acted out of disappointment that reality had not measured up to expectation. Workers were not dissuaded of the value of welfare capitalism, only frustrated by employers' mishandling of it. By responding to workers' desire for more stability in their lives with new industrial relations policies in the twenties, enlightened industrialists provided workers with a new set of standards for evaluating a good job: steady work, high wages, opportunity for advancement, decent conditions, generous benefits. When layoffs, low wages, little job mobility, poor conditions, and inadequate benefits prevailed, workers were indignant. How deeply working men and women believed in welfare capitalist values emerges from the distinctions they themselves made between companies. Despite frustrations with program failures, workers considered some employers to be better welfare capitalists than others. The criteria they used to make those judgments were derived from welfare capitalist ideals.

Chicago industrial workers singled out three of the plants under discussion for upholding welfare capitalist standards better than others. Workers arrived at such judgments by comparing their employers to others nearby, often in the same industry, to other jobs they had held, and to other plants owned by the same company. The general consensus in Packingtown, for example, held that Swift was more fair than Armour. Most of the problems of packinghouse employment remained, but at least here work was steadier, wages were better, and in the words of worker Elizabeth Washington, "They're more for their employees than any other company. They try to do the right thing for them .... Armour hasn't got nothin' like that. We're privileged to talk to the superintendent. At Armour you got to have a committee."[177]

Likewise, in the steel communities of Southeast Chicago, residents viewed Wisconsin Steel as a better place to work than neighboring U.S. Steel. The most important factor was Wisconsin Steel's eight-hour day, implemented in 1918 and retained.[178] Additional factors made workers here appreciate their plant's superiority to others in the area. For instance, despite the establishment of a central employment office at U.S. Steel in 1919, shop foremen still wielded tremendous power.[179] At Wisconsin Steel, in contrast, workers felt their foremen were better kept in check. Employee Frank Jacovich might still complain about low wages and the ineffectiveness of the plant works council at Wisconsin Steel, but overall he felt, "It's a damn good company to work for. They give us eight hour day.... we have steady work. Ford [who had a plant in Hegewisch, farther south], that son of a bitch, he's hell to work for. Soon as work slack, lay off, doesn't give a damn for men."[180]

Wisconsin Steel workers also recognized that their mill compared favorably with International Harvester's other plants, particularly the gigantic McCormick Works. Not only was the steel mill the only one to retain the eight-hour day into the 1920s, but also it paid men better for work in what turned out to be a safer place.[181] Likewise, although workers ignored many of Harvester's community outreach programs, they appreciated management's respect for their neighborhood life, which was expressed through the plant's refusal to hire blacks, the only one in Harvester's Chicago operation to do so. Because workers had to live nearby this isolated steel works, black co-workers would have meant black neighbors as well. It was one thing to work alongside blacks, quite another to have them living next door.[182]

Western Electric's Hawthorne Works, also surrounded by the prized bungalows of frugal employees, earned the respect of its workers with a similar discriminatory hiring policy. Like the relatively satisfied workers at Wisconsin Steel, those at Hawthorne were quick to compare their company favorably with other employers. As one Hawthorne worker put it, "When you work for other companies, you appreciate the Western Electric. Take Westinghouse for instance. They only give one week's vacation for ten years of service." Equally as impressive to this worker were Hawthorne's stock plan, savings provisions, and building and loan association: "I think this company has more to offer its employees than any other large industrial concern which I know of."[183] Moreover, the interview program that Hawthorne management implemented in the late 1920s helped convince workers that the company was on their side against autocratic supervisors. Instructions to interviewers told them to convey to subjects that the company needed their help in making Hawthorne a better place to work, particularly in reforming foremen's behavior. Tell them "you are acting as the eyes and ears of the management and the management of this company wants to know what the employees think of it."[184] The Hawthorne worker who confided to an interviewer that "the company as a whole, I think, is the best place in the world to work. But the individuals who are supposed to carry out the policies of the company are a bunch of skunks" only demonstrated the success of management's strategy of allying itself with workers against foremen.[185] But Western Electric's greatest advantage in appeasing workers was the health of the telephone industry. Demand for equipment grew over the decade, whereas seasonal slack periods were rare. Hawthorne employees could expect the most regular work of any of Chicago's industrial workers. At Western Electric, as at Swift and Wisconsin Steel, workers rewarded capitalist ideals by quitting less often.[186]

Welfare capitalists succeeded in having an impact on their workers, although not always in ways they anticipated. Workers took advantage of many of the new programs offered them. They came to expect benefits along with the job. And they judged a good company, in contrast to a bad one, by how close it came to meeting welfare capitalist standards, offering the steady, well-paying, decent work that workers could reward with their loyalty. But welfare capitalist programs did not go far enough in most plants for employers to earn the undivided loyalty of their workers. Although workers accepted the values of welfare capitalism and wanted employers to provide more for their welfare, workers were frequently disillusioned. Employers were unwilling – and possibly, as in the case of seasonality, unable – to restructure their operations extensively enough to offer their employees adequate security. Without that, workers had no choice but to sustain other, often ethnic affiliations. Employer sickness benefits, group insurance, and stock plans continued to have rivals in ethnic charities, mutual benefit societies, and banks.

By promoting a new set of expectations and then failing to fulfill them, employers frustrated their workers. People who never before would have turned to their boss for help in hard times now noticed that he was not there. Welfare capitalists had hoped their schemes would encourage men and women to identify with the firm as individuals. Yet their failure to deliver widened the gap between workers and employers while narrowing the gap between individual workers on the shop floor. Mixing workers by ethnicity and race and segregating them by sex, moreover, drew workers out of the ethnic isolation long characteristic of Chicago's factories and gave them a new sense of a common fate as workers. In a related fashion, new employer concern about machine operative loyalty handed workers a new weapon to wield. Being absent, quitting, and limiting productivity sent a sharper message to a boss well aware of the cost.

Welfare capitalism, although falling short of its goals during the 1920s, set an agenda that workers carried into the 1930s. By starting the process of bringing workers together in the workplace through mixing them ethnically and encouraging their collaboration in work groups, it helped equip them to challenge their employers several years later. No less important, it legitimized standards workers would seek to institutionalize in the thirties. Job security, high wages, and benefits would never again be dismissed as the pipe dreams of industrial workers. Although an acceptance of welfare capitalism did not necessarily imply approval of capitalism as an economic system, most workers in the 1920s probably were convinced that if employers assumed responsibility toward employees, capitalism could serve workers' as well as owners' interests. As will be clear later, survey data for the 1930s indicates that the majority of workers, even in the midst of the Great Depression, were unwilling to jettison capitalism. Welfare capitalism had taught workers that capitalists could act morally under the right conditions. This belief in the potential for a "moral capitalism," born out of the promise of employers' welfarism in the twenties, would shape the political character of workers' union movements in the thirties.

Once employers decided to bid for workers' loyalty by offering security "from cradle to grave," unions already existing in the 1920s were propelled in this direction in order to compete. The Chicago Federation of Labor began to offer its craftsmen members insurance plans (the Union Labor Life Insurance Company), vacation retreats (Valmar, By the Lake), and home ownership schemes (the Progressive Home Buildings of Illinois, Inc.).[187] The only major mass production union to survive the decade in Chicago, the Amalgamated Clothing Workers, became a model of the welfare-oriented union that would take full shape in the thirties. With its own Amalgamated Trust and Savings Bank, medical programs, credit unions, insurance plans including the Chicago Unemployment Insurance Fund, and cultural activities at the Amalgamated Centre, it offered members the kind of security welfare capitalists had promised and the CIO would later seek.[188] Welfare capitalism ironically set the terms not only for the "good employer" but for the "good union" as well.

Ethnic leaders of the 1920s had less to fear than they might have thought. Ethnic institutions remained at least as responsible for workers' welfare as corporations and were valued by members all the more. Furthermore, although ethnic groups may not have always appreciated it, workers' receptivity to the concept of paternalism at the workplace safeguarded it in the ethnic world as well. Benevolent, hierarchical authority became an accepted part of workers' lives on the job as it was in the community. At the workplace, employers neither weaned employees from other loyalties nor satisfied all their expectations. But they succeeded in convincing them that workers' welfare was part of their business. The only possible alternative to the corporation or community institutions that a working person could look to in the 1920s was the government. The wife of a fifty-one-year-old molder despaired that her husband "often wonders what he'll do when he gets a little older. He hopes and prays they'll get the State old-age pension through pretty soon." But there were few signs that government would come through.[189] In fact, Prohibition had made many Chicago workers suspicious of the state's intervention in private life. The European immigrants and their children who still predominated in the city's factories considered Prohibition an attack on their cultural traditions, an un-American assault on their freedom. At a Czech mass meeting against Prohibition, women costumed as Liberty served refreshments, while the Liberty Bell, the Spirit of 1776, and other such symbols of independence from tyrannical government paraded through the crowd proclaiming "the personal rights of man."[190] Resentment over the state's intrusion was more than a matter of principle. Everyday, police broke into private homes in working-class neighborhoods looking for bootleg liquor. In referendum after referendum during the 1920s, ethnic voters called for repeal of the Volstead Act.[191]

But although workers entrusted their welfare to their ethnic communities and their employers, inadequacies in both were contributing to the rise of another phenomenon. By the end of the twenties, ethnic groups were losing the battle over controlling mass culture, and welfare capitalists were revealing their limitations. The combination gave workers of different backgrounds more in common. The Polish and Bohemian worker laboring side by side at a factory bench were now living more similar lives than they had in 1919. Not only were they more likely to speak English, but they also could talk about seeing the same motion pictures, hearing the same radio shows, and buying the same brand-name products from the same chain stores. They also shared problems about the job that, even more important, they had begun to solve together, not just within their own ethnic work enclaves as in 1919. Thanks to welfare capitalists, ethnic provincialism was breaking down at the workplace, as it was in the larger world. Strong racial prejudices, of course, still prevailed, but even whites and blacks were starting to grapple with problems together on the job. By the end of the 1920s, Chicago's industrial workers were not "political" along conventional lines. Chicago's factories were far from the violent battlegrounds of the Western Pennsylvania coal fields or the Piedmont textile towns. But in subtle ways, a peer community of workers was emerging in the city's steel mills, packinghouses, and other mass production plants. For now, it existed side by side with workers' loyalty to traditional institutions like the mutual benefit association and deferential social relationships such as with ethnic elites and the boss. But when the Great Depression hit, shattering many of the institutional and personal arrangements that workers had counted on during the 1920s, workers would fall back on the one other support that they had had some experience with, each other.

5

Adrift in the Great Depression

Plate 23. Eviction scenes like this one were common on Chicago streets during the Great Depression. Not only did people often lose their homes, but they also found themselves bereft of many of the institutional supports, once provided by ethnic and racial communities and welfare capitalists, that they had depended on during the 1920s.

Looking back at the Great Depression from the vantage point of half a century later, it can be difficult to grasp how extensively working people's lives were disrupted. Historians' tendency to reduce the crisis of the thirties to a series of impersonal events – the stock market crash, unemployment, mortgage foreclosures, bank failures – obscures the reality of these disasters as people experienced them. The following portraits recapture some of the ways that the early depression materially and emotionally devastated Chicago workers and their families, as it undermined the survival strategies that they had developed during the 1920s.

For John Norris, a structural iron worker, the Great Depression meant the ruin of his carefully laid plans for retirement, to say nothing of his family's present livelihood. In 1927, Norris had invested his life savings in a two-apartment building costing $17,500. He put every penny that he had saved into the down payment and planned to pay off the rest over the next ten years from his earnings, his wife's boarders, and the rent from the second apartment. But by the later 1920s, Norris began to face more frequent layoffs from work. In no time, he lost his job entirely. The boarders were in no better shape and finally left, owing $300. With Norris unable to meet his payments, the mortgage was foreclosed in October 1930, depriving this fifty-year-old worker of all his equity of $8,100. His family remained in the house for eighteen months before they were "put out" to wander from friend to friend, stopping wherever someone had a room to give them in return for work.[1]

In August 1932, Mr. Goich and his two sons were barely subsisting with the help of at least three different charity organizations. In their small flat in Southeast Chicago near Wisconsin Steel, where Mr. Goich had worked until he lost his job three years earlier, this Yugoslav family did its best to manage despite Mr. Goich's current illness and the recent death of Mrs. Goich. Although Mrs. Goich had left an insurance policy worth a thousand dollars, the costs of her doctors and funeral quickly depleted that money. Mr. Goich was dependent on outside help for some time and became increasingly bitter about the way that social workers from the various charities were interfering in his life. "They're always snooping around," he complained. "They make me do everything their way. They tell me what time I should make the kids come in.

I think George and Dannie should be home at nine, but they say it's all right for them to be out till ten. What can I do about it? They tell me what I can and dassn't eat. They said I should give up smoking, and won't give me any money for tobacco. . . . They tell me how I oughta cook stuff. I can't even peel potatoes my own way. They meddle around with my clothes. . . . No, I wouldn't dare tell 'em to mind their own business. I ain't had two nickels to rub together in my pocket now for over two years. If I wuz to sass 'em, they might stop giving me stuff, the things the kids and me need. Christ, I couldn't even get up the $17 a month for the rent, let alone the food and coal. They got me by the balls. I gotta do what they tell me. But if I ever get to work again, I'll tell 'em all to go to hell quick enough."[2]

By the early 1930s, the Great Depression had already had a discernible impact on the life of eleven-year-old Dempsey Travis and his Chicago Black Belt family. His favorite Uncle Otis was laid off his job on December 22, 1929, only to be hit even harder seven months later when Illinois bank examiners closed the doors of the Binga State Bank, the financial rock of the black community. "Thrifty Uncle Otis became destitute with the turn of the examiner's key in the front door of the bank. Otis Travis died in 1933, broke and broken-hearted, without having recovered one penny of his savings," Dempsey recalled. Dempsey's father and his Uncle Joe, both packinghouse workers, had been cut from six ten-hour days a week to three eight-hour days. And even Dempsey lost his job as a *Chicago Defender* newspaper boy after "Black Thursday," October 24, 1929, the day the stock market crashed. His school career was also affected a few years later when the Willard Elementary School went on a double shift that cut school days almost in half. Other relatives took to the freight trains as "Hoover Hobos," moving from city to city, town to town, "looking for the prosperity their President had promised was just around the corner."[3]

Mrs. Rose Majewski, age 39, was born in Poland. Although she had lived in the United States for many years, she had neither taken out citizenship papers nor learned to speak English. When her husband deserted her and their five children in 1925, Mrs. Majewski kept her family going by scrubbing floors at the First Trust and Savings Bank for $21.50 a week until she was laid off in 1929. For another year she was able to find work, though at steadily declining wages, scrubbing in the

Merchandise Mart Building at $18 a week and cleaning chickens at a packinghouse for $10–12 a week. After June 1930, Mrs. Majewski could find no more work, so her sixteen-year-old daughter began doing housework in a private home for $4 a week and food. The Majewski family's $50 in savings was quickly depleted, and debts with the landlord and the grocer began to mount until further credit was refused. Payments on the family's fourteen insurance policies, for which they normally paid $2.70 a week, lapsed, as did those on the radio that they were buying on installment. Finally, they were forced into cheaper living quarters, four rooms on the top floor of what had formerly been a barn, for $14 a month. Mrs. Majewski felt she had no choice but to turn for help to local charities. Soon, the family was trying to make do on cash payments of $5 a week from a private welfare organization and a monthly box of food staples from the Cook County Bureau of Public Welfare.[4]

Steelworker George Patterson and his wife were unprepared for how hard the depression would hit them. Despite the October stock market crash, "We in the steel mills didn't feel that we were going to be too badly affected. The average worker didn't and I especially, being a prima donna roll turner you know, said that the roll shop was one of the last places that would feel the pinch. My wife and I got married in 1931 and I had said, 'Don't worry about it. We'll always do all right.'" But by 1932, Patterson was working at U.S. Steel's South Works plant only one day a month. To get more work than that was a game of "who you knew," whether or not you could win the foreman's favor. By the time his son was born later that year, Patterson and his wife had moved in with her parents, and he "couldn't buy a bottle of milk." To make things worse for steelworkers like Patterson, the U.S. Steel stock they had scrimped to purchase as an investment in the future under the company's employee stock ownership plan, worth $259 a share in October 1929, had tumbled fifty dollars within six months and continued to fall steadily until a share was worth less than $20. The job and stock that had offered Patterson security just a short time earlier now appeared worthless.[5]

Mr. Severino, twenty-eight years old in 1931, had come to the United States from Italy eleven years before. He first worked at Swift & Company slicing bacon and then found a better job as a millwright's apprentice at Western Electric, where he remained until he was laid off. When he tried to get his old job back at Swift, he discovered it was impossible without a recent "lay off card." Severino was able to find some short-term jobs – building the Chicago stadium, working as a laborer for a construction company, even returning to Western Electric for a few months – but the family survived mostly on the wages Mrs. Severino earned at the Union Bag Company. When she too was laid off, the family fell into debt. They lived directly over a grocery store, the proprietress of which was an old friend of Mrs. Severino's parents. By the end of 1931, the Severinos owed her nine months' rent and $250 for groceries. Although Mrs. Severino was ashamed to ask for more credit, knowing she could not pay, she saw no alternative. As it was, the family ate mostly bread and macaroni. Mr. Severino had tried a job with the National Advertising Corporation selling calendars on commission to small shopkeepers. In three days, however, he took only one order for fifty calendars. The sale ended up costing him a dollar since he charged the storekeeper seven dollars and the company charged him eight dollars for the minimum order of a hundred. He discovered the hard way that shopkeepers had no interest in buying calendars "when business is dead."[6]

These six family tragedies typify the troubles that thousands of Chicago workers encountered in the early years of the depression. Of course, industrial workers had faced economic downturns before. Many remembered vividly the hard times that followed World War I and the periodic unemployment that became almost a way of life during the 1920s. The Great Depression, however, took place on an unprecedented scale. Hardly a working family escaped its grasp. Workers routinely found their working hours and their pay cut when they were lucky and lost their jobs when they were not. Only half the people employed in Chicago manufacturing industries in 1927 were still working in 1933, whereas company payrolls had shrunk to an astounding one-quarter of what they had been five years before. Outside of work, families like the Norrises, the Goiches, the Travises, the Majewskis, the Pattersons, and the Severinos found themselves unable to meet bills, insurance payments, rents, and mortgages. With a cataclysm of such magnitude overtaking Chicago, the nation, and even the world, people began to doubt that their lives would ever return to normal.

But to understand the impact of the Great Depression on working-class families in Chicago, it is important to do more than measure the magnitude of their hardships. It is necessary to ask how the very structure of people's lives, particularly their relationship to basic institutions and authority figures in their ethnic communities, workplaces, and families, was transformed during the crisis. Earlier chapters established that during the twenties, workers in Chicago manufacturing looked to their ethnic communities for security. They accepted as well whatever assistance they could get from their welfare capitalist employers, though it was frequently less reliable. This chapter will investigate how well the strategies that workers depended on in the 1920s weathered the storms of the 1930s.

THE ETHNIC COMMUNITY IN CRISIS

Understandably, people first tried to handle the new crises that were engulfing their lives in familiar ways. When chief breadwinners lost their jobs early in the depression, other family members went looking for work, much as they had done in the 1920s. If the immediate family could not cope on its own, it turned to established networks of relatives and friends within the ethnic community.

But the magnitude of the city's economic crisis severely limited the help that family and friends could give intimates who were in trouble. These informal networks had worked before because people suffered their ups and downs at different times. In the 1920s, if a man was laid off during a slack season in one industry, chances were his wife or daughter or brother could find employment in an industry at more peak operation. When one family faced an emergency like illness or death, neighbors and other close associates could usually afford to help. But the effects of the Great Depression were so pervasive that people could no longer count on much assistance from these old networks. In the 1930s, spouses and children had a much harder time finding work when chief breadwinners lost their jobs. When Mr. Severino was laid off from Western Electric, his wife managed to find temporary work at the Union Bag Company; but when that job ended, she could find nothing more. Workers' relatives and friends helped when they could, but more often than not they were already pushed to the limit coping with their own problems. A study of one hundred applicants for relief in the winter of 1933 documented that relatives and friends had been willing to assist many of the needy at first, in some cases to avoid the "disgrace" of having the family on charity. But as the circle of unemployment widened, intimates became less able to help, engrossed as they were in their own difficulties. The Pulitzer family, for example, got aid from relatives on both sides of the family when Mr. Pulitzer first lost his job and home. But by February 1933, an investigator found that all the relatives, with only one exception, were themselves unemployed or working part time with incomes far lower than two years earlier. They were no longer able to assist the Pulitzers.[7] As time went on, Chicago's industrial workers could hardly manage their own problems. Despite their concern for those outside their immediate families, they could offer little material help.

As their troubles increased and they exhausted the informal networks available to them, Chicago workers looked, as was their habit, to the ethnic- and religious-affiliated community institutions that had long supported them in good and bad times. When the Great Depression made it harder for workers to hold jobs, to pay bills, rents, and mortgages, and to cope emotionally, they looked for salvation to their old protectors.

As workers reeled from one bewildering crisis, such as losing a job or a home, to another, the welfare agencies that had served their ethnic group or religious faith in the past seemed the obvious place to seek help. Even those who had managed without much assistance in the 1920s now turned to these organizations to cope with their troubles. "We had a number of people come to us, for assistance and advice, who for years have not identified themselves with the Polish-American group," acknowledged Mary Midura, a staff member of the Polish Welfare Association. "When they found themselves in financial distress, they sought contact with people of the nationality group from which they themselves emanated."[8] In search of money, jobs, food, and clothing, needy workers and their families called upon the Slovenian Relief Organization, the Polish National Alliance Benevolent Association, the Bohemian Charitable Association, the Jewish Charities, the Catholic Charities, and other sectarian welfare organizations.[9] Local churches were particularly swamped by appeals for charity. The parish priest of a Catholic Church in Back of the Yards found himself bombarded night and day with calls from the needy of his congregation, including many of his thriftiest families. They came, he said, "often bathed in tears – and [they] pleaded inability to help themselves any longer."[10]

Ethnic and religious welfare institutions were committed to deliver-

Plate 24. In the early years of the depression, private welfare agencies such as churches and ethnic organizations tried to cope with the massive need. But serving meals to the unemployed in church basements like the Immanuel Baptist Church pictured here or distributing occasional checks to people who had regular rents and bills to pay proved grossly inadequate. Even these services, moreover, quickly exhausted the limited financial resources of ethnic and religious welfare institutions.

ing the services that their constituents expected. Just as they had aimed to keep "their own kind" from being a public burden during the twenties, so they struggled to care for them now, even in the midst of a severe depression. "Let's have pride enough *not* to sponge upon public support when Catholic charity is still able to care for its own interests," one priest urged his flock.[11] The depression in fact impelled the Chicago Archdiocese to establish a comprehensive relief structure that rivaled the widely acclaimed Jewish Charities of Chicago. The Catholic Charities' Central Charity Bureau coordinated a decentralized operation that at its peak in the 1930s oversaw six thousand volunteers working in 325 St. Vincent de Paul Conferences organized on the parish level. Catholics were proud of their volunteer-staffed relief organization for minimizing overhead costs and blessing the souls of the saviors while sustaining the needy.

Along with delivering relief, the establishment of a citywide network of St. Vincent de Paul Societies had political significance. Many "national" (ethnic) parishes like the Italian Our Lady of Pompeii and the Polish St. Mary Magdalene had resisted archdiocesan efforts throughout the 1920s to encourage the establishment of St. Vincent de Paul Societies, viewing them along with Holy Name Societies as intrusions by the central Church hierarchy. When faced with the depression's staggering problems, however, they quickly fell in line; they needed financial assistance from the Central Charity Bureau. In parishes all over the city, St. Vincent de Paul Conferences met weekly with their pastors to assist as many in their communities as possible.[12] Local Catholic Churches assisted thousands of their congregants in these early depression years. But no less significant, Cardinal Mundelein's church used the great need for charity among Catholics to further its drive to bring national parishes under more central control. St. Vincent de Paul Conferences gave the archdiocese the foothold in the ethnic parish that it had sought throughout the 1920s.

For the Catholic Church hierarchy quite blatantly, and for other groups more subtly, the Great Depression presented a challenge to their authority. Legitimacy rested on continuing to meet their constitutents' needs and on protecting their group's good name in the larger community. Mayor Kelly, addressing the Catholic Slovak Day Fundraiser at Pilsen Park, congratulated the Slovaks for "taking care of their own hungry and destitute," in other words keeping them off the county rolls.[13] Less successsful groups felt the sting of public condemnation. Mexican leaders, for example, urged their community to take more responsibility for the suffering of Mexican immigrants in Chicago: "Due to our own negligence, either willingly or forcibly we are compelled to join the public charities. Therefore, we say that only through a strong organization we can, to a certain extent, overthrow the hostile propaganda voiced in some of the newspapers who accuse us of being a burden to the Relief institutions, a menace to the public health, and a hindrance to the stability and advancement of the life of the native worker."[14]

Yet despite the commitment of ethnic- and religious-affiliated agencies to serve their own people, these private charities could not handle the enormous demand for assistance. Church soup kitchens, ethnic fund-raising bazaars, and used clothing drives went only a small way toward meeting the huge demand. Observers repeatedly noted the inadequacy of private relief, claiming that organizations like the St. Vincent de Paul Conferences were less effective in practice than in theory. At St. Adelbert's Church, the St. Vincent de Paul Society met every Friday night from 7 to 8 p.m., "and if people do not go at that time they do not get help." The situation was not much better at nearby St. Casimir's, where "they say they have no money and they possibly give $3 a week to a family of ten people for a time and then refuse to give any more."[15] The difficulties of the Jewish Charities, long proud of its ability to care for Chicago's needy Jews, demonstrated the severity of the crisis for private agencies. By 1932, the organization was supporting fifty thousand Jewish unemployed, but not without running a huge deficit. Even then, the Jews who came for help received only the minimum in assistance. "Our waiting rooms are full of people.... But our pocket books are empty. Relief stations reach a point where they can give only food and coal, and pay rent only when eviction is threatened," agency staff fretted. Executive Director Samuel A. Goldsmith testified to a U.S. Senate Investigating Committee, "We insist that persons who come to our agencies shall have used up all of their resources and come to us empty-handed. We even ask that they borrow on their life insurance policies. These dependents on charity now are people who actually have been reduced to destitution."[16]

At the same time that the depression increased the demand for welfare services, it also undermined the financial resources of many religious and ethnic welfare agencies. When the Polish Welfare Association, for example, lost funds in two bank failures early in 1931, its program and staffing had to be sharply curtailed. Since most of the prominent Poles of Chicago who supported welfare services were in real estate, banking, or the insurance business, all of which were severely affected by the depression, the usual providers of financial support could not be counted on.[17] As the elite of an ethnic group tightened its belt, the effects were felt all the way down the social ladder.

It did not take long for clients, agencies, and civic leaders alike to recognize that the traditional voluntary approach to relief was floundering in an economic crisis of unprecedented magnitude. Still, the depth of popular commitment to a system of private welfare serving particular populations of needy was evident in the emergency measures cities like Chicago embraced. Rather than calling for an alternative system of state-supported relief to bail out beleaguered private charities, business and community leaders followed the advice of President Hoover's Emergency Committee for Employment. Much as they had done on a smaller scale during the depression of 1921–2, they collaborated to raise special funds to replenish the depleted treasuries of existing social agencies. Prominent Chicagoans orchestrated two drives for emergency money. The Cook County arm of Governor Emmerson's Committee on Unemployment and Relief raised $5 million in 1930, and the Joint Emergency Relief Fund of Cook County came up with more than twice that amount the next year. These dollars went directly into the separate coffers of the United Charities, the Jewish Charities, the Catholic Charities, the Salvation Army (serving mostly Protestants), and the American Red Cross (which helped disabled veterans). Lesser grants were also available to smaller ethnic agencies that the Chicago Association of Commerce had endorsed, like the German Aid Society, which recorded "$2,273.63 from Governor Emmerson's Commission" in its annual report for 1931.[18]

Chicago's private charities hoped that this system of subsidy would help them serve the clients they felt were rightfully theirs without interference by other agencies or the state. No one else, they felt, was better prepared to meet the material and emotional needs of Chicagoans in distress. The only people who repeatedly criticized this approach were professional social workers who argued that review of program quality should accompany funding. Although Cardinal Mundelein applauded the subsidy approach for sparing Catholics "fear of any discrimination" by non-Catholic relief agencies, United Charities' social workers despaired that Catholics were left to their parishes "where we feel that they will probably not receive the attention they should have."[19] The territoriality of existing agencies, not the highest standards of social service, drove the welfare system of the early 1930s, critics pointed out. Increasingly, professional social workers advocated a system of relief that had public funding and universal standards.

The public relief that existed in these early depression years was organized on the county level and offered few alternatives to private agencies. Although the Cook County Bureau of Public Welfare spent millions between 1929 and 1931, the money went not for general relief but to pay for Mothers' Pensions, Blind Pensions, Aid to Ex-Service Men, and commodity orders of food, milk, shoes, and coal intended to supplement the contributions of private agencies. Moreover, an extremely high rate of tax delinquency in Cook County further limited the funds available for relief.[20] Out of a total of $2.7 million spent on public and private relief in Chicago during 1928, before the Great Depression hit, 64 percent was expended by county agencies, 36 percent by private. By the end of 1931, however, when $12.5 million was being spent due to the emergency fund drives, the balance had completely shifted. Now private agencies accounted for 64 percent of relief expenditures, reflecting a 718 percent increase over 1928, whereas public agencies were only spending 162 percent more than they had in 1928.[21] Those Chicagoans who did not receive adequate relief from the welfare organizations of their cultural communities were far more likely to go to the private, nonsectarian United Charities than to the county.

To the frustration of Chicago's supporters of local, private welfare, even the emergency fund drives failed to solve the relief crisis. Within months of the completion of both drives, the money was exhausted, causing relief stations to close, monthly allowances to be cut, "no-rent" policies to go into effect, and most crucially, client disillusionment with existing agencies to grow. By trying to keep their claim on their communities amidst the upheavals of severe depression, sectarian social agencies inadvertently invited rejection when they failed to provide adequately for their clients.

The dissatisfaction that Chicago's Catholics displayed with the church's efforts to help them cope with the depression illustrates this development. Many needy church members criticized the way the Catholic Charities handled their applications. For example, Mr. and Mrs. Horbatcz were a young, married couple with two small children who lived in a four-room apartment until Mr. Horbatcz was laid off in

1930. Soon after, they were forced to move in with Mr. Horbatcz's mother and her two unmarried sons. When Horbatcz applied to the church's Central Charity Bureau for assistance, however, he was refused on the grounds that the family lived with his mother. Mr. and Mrs. Horbatcz told an investigator from the University of Chicago Settlement that they had learned too late that they should never have been truthful with a Catholic charity that bore such an unrealistic attitude toward family responsibility.[22]

Some unemployed Catholics mistrusted not only the Central Charity Bureau but also their local St. Vincent de Paul Societies and their parish priests. By early 1932, the pastor at St. Augustine's parish in Back of the Yards felt obligated to defend the reputation of his St. Vincent de Paul Society volunteers from community attack. Acknowledging that cuts in the weekly allowance had been necessary, he added, "The people of St. Augustine's have no reason to complain. In fact our St. Vincent de Paul men are deserving of the highest praise. They are working and slaving incessantly to aid our families. It has been said that some of our men are being paid. This is a mean lie."[23]

Catholics' resentment over the church's inadequate relief soon spread to other aspects of church policy. Parishioners expressed anger that the church still expected them to pay parochial school tuition, and many moved their children to local public schools. People also resented the fees that the church charged for performing ritual acts. In working-class neighborhoods of the city, baptisms, first holy communions, confirmations, church marriages, and burials declined noticeably during the depression.[24] One parish in South Chicago became so incensed that in July 1931 it demanded that in the case of "anyone who is poor and cannot afford to pay ritual fees for baptism or funerals, the priest must perform the ritual without any fee."[25] Teenage boys in St. Michael's parish next to U.S. Steel's South Works blasted the church's avarice, echoing their Polish parents' sentiments in bolder fashion. "These fuckers over here at St. Michael's, all they think about is *money*. You should *see* it when the money wagon comes around! They have to wheel it out in wheelbarrows! . . . Anytime you *want* anything, all they think of is, 'Do they get a fin for it?' They'd *never* give a Guy a break!"[26] Miles away, on the North Side of Chicago, another observer noted a similar attitude among Italian children who voiced publicly the views that their more discreet parents reserved for home: "There is a definite feeling that the church is always after money, money and more money. Children, ordinarily too young to make such observations, say when passing the Cardinal's house, 'See what a swell place we pay to keep up.'"[27] The Catholic Church, by taking responsibility for the worldly needs of its parishioners, could no longer get by with just offering spiritual solace to its suffering. Needy Catholics were increasingly judging it as a social institution.

The Catholic Church was not the only religious institution in Chicago to lose favor through its failure to provide members with adequate relief. Black Protestant churches had long played an important welfare role in black communities. Prior to 1929, for example, St. Marks Methodist Episcopal Church, a large established congregation at Wabash and 50th Street, kept its doors open every day and six nights a week for worship, socializing, and welfare activities. A staff of five social workers assisted parishioners with their problems. By 1934, however, the church's income had dropped 40 percent; the building was closed four days and four nights a week, three of the social workers had left, and the number of active church members had greatly declined. According to the Reverend J. B. Redmond, "As the church became less able to render financial support to its members, they turned more and more to the relief agencies."[28] The Reverend W. C. Petty of Mount Messiah Baptist Church several blocks away concurred. He admitted to a drop in attendance of 50 percent, which he attributed largely to the dramatic decline in his church's social service work. He sadly characterized the previous several years as "a turning away rather than toward the church."[29]

St. Clair Drake and Horace Cayton, in their investigation of the "black metropolis" during the depression, documented more broadly the observations of these two ministers. They found that throughout the Black Belt people were accusing the old-line churches of being "rackets," constantly demanding money without delivering much in return.[30] In contrast, the churches that flourished in black neighborhoods during the depression were Holiness and Spiritualist storefront congregations, which offered worshippers an intense, emotional experience and took little responsibility for anything but their souls. The Reverend Mary Evans, pastor of the revivalist Cosmopolitan Community Church, for instance, reported an increase in attendance of 40 percent from 1929 to 1934. Observers noted that by the mid-1930s there was hardly a block of the Black Belt without a Holiness or Spiritualist church.[31] For relief help, blacks increasingly turned to the United Charities, the county, and whatever other agencies on which they could prevail. Chicago relief statistics always reported the highest number of recipients in black neighborhoods. Here, of course, unemployment was unusually high, but no less important, the overwhelming poverty in the community meant that indigeneous welfare institutions, particularly the established churches, had an even harder time than their white counterparts relieving community distress.[32]

By the time desperation drove Chicago's Joint Emergency Relief Service to demand help from the Illinois state legislature in the winter of 1932 and the State of Illinois in turn to request federal assistance the following July, there was much less opposition in the city to the notion of public-supported relief. The failure of private welfare agencies to meet Chicago's needs ensured that. Even Edward Ryerson, the steel industrialist and important Chicago philanthropist who had long defended private welfare, finally recognized that a new era had arrived. In February, he went to Springfield and demanded $12 million to help the needy. When that ran out, he called on Hoover himself. "I got for the State of Illinois, the first federal money for relief ever granted," he reported. "It was a curious thing for me to do. I was bitterly opposed to federal funds at that time. But I realized the problem was beyond the scope of local government."[33] Times were changing for elites like the Ryersons as well as for working people like the Norrises, the Goiches, the Travises, the Majewskis, the Pattersons, and the Severinos.

Private welfare was not the only pillar of ethnic life to collapse under the pressure of the depression. Other institutions that ethnic workers had depended on during the 1920s failed them as well, most importantly ethnic benefit societies, ethnic banks and building and loan associations, and ethnic neighborhood stores. The fraternal insurance policies, bank accounts, mortgages, and credit arrangements that had once symbolized security or even success had less and less to offer workers.

The mutual benefit and fraternal insurance societies that had served as anchors of ethnic community life through the 1920s encountered rough seas during the Great Depression. Begun as self-help organizations by immigrants from the same region of the Old World or a common corner of America, these societies had assured members a proper burial. During the 1920s, small local societies had consolidated into national ones and new state regulations had mandated more stringent and less cooperative-style operations. But even as their societies changed, ethnic Chicagoans remained loyal, retaining memberships despite their group policies at work or supplementary industrial-type insurance purchased from commercial companies. Those other policies might come and go with a job or fortune, but fraternal insurance could always be counted on. Under the pressure of the depression, however, many workers began to have trouble keeping up insurance payments, which in no time threatened the stability of fraternal associations. For instance, when many members of the Unione Veneziana found themselves unemployed and thus no longer able to make monthly payments, the organization could not keep up its mortage payments and lost its hall. Shortly after, the Unione itself disbanded.[34]

Even societies that survived the depression had hard times. According to the history of the Slovene National Benefit Society,

> the economic crisis had come on, bringing hardships to the members. It had a direct influence upon the sick benefit fund and the fund for special benefits. Members continuously lost their positions, and turned to the benefit funds for aid. Conditions became worse in 1931. Members increasingly reported on the passive list. The sick benefit department was depleted of funds and a general referendum was necessary to decrease benefits and separate the various funds. The situation produced much disturbance and dissatisfaction among the members.

Membership that had peaked in 1930 at 63,945 decreased to 53,252 by early 1932, with the passive list reaching 5,000 members. By spring 1933, when the tenth annual convention met in Chicago, the membership had fallen to 48,295, with 8,000 members on the passive list. The convention was forced to adopt many far-reaching reforms to save the society. It discontinued the practice of lending money to members on their property, which had amounted to almost $1 million over the previous four years. It decided that all future investments, up to a total of 20 percent, should be placed in government bonds. It drastically reduced benefits for sickness, injuries, and operations.[35] Fraternal associations like the Slovene National Benefit Society that made it through the depression did not offer members the same kinds of benefits afterward that they had before.

To make matters worse, many fraternal associations had invested a large percentage of their assets in real estate, either by lending money directly to members or by purchasing mortgages from banks and building associations. For example, the Polish Women's Alliance in 1927 had tied up $1,350,000 of its total assets of $1,540,000 in mortgages. In the same year, the Polish National Alliance had $14,207,000 in assets, with

$12,545,000 invested in mortgages, the bulk of which were properties in the Chicago area. When the housing market collapsed with the Great Depression, the fundamental weakness in the investment policy of the fraternals was revealed. Many societies were left holding foreclosed property, now reduced in value and yielding little return.[36]

The crisis among fraternal associations had severe implications. Losing assets and members could jeopardize an ethnic society and, some even felt, an ethnic community itself. As one of the largest ethnic fraternals, the Polish National Alliance, argued in its weekly newspaper in January 1931, "the insurance scheme has been introduced into our Polish organizations as a necessary cement with which to sustain the unity and coherence of the first thousands, and then the tens of thousands of the members and groups of these organizations. Experience and practice have proved that without such cement, without such financial constraint to pay, there could not exist and prosper among the Polish immigrants any organization." As that cement weakened, many began to wonder what would happen to the strength of the ethnic community it had once bonded together.[37]

Most people went to great lengths to keep their policies active. They made other sacrifices before they were forced to borrow on their insurance, to take the cash surrender value if there was any, or in the worst cases, to just let the policy expire because there was no monetary compensation. One woman in South Chicago viewed keeping up insurance on her mentally ill and hospitalized husband as a top priority after paying rent and buying minimal food despite the fact that she earned only $7.50 weekly as a hotel maid. Once, when it looked like she could not make a monthly payment, "I thought she'd go crazy," her son recounted. "If she hadn't got it from my uncle, I was gonna go out and thieve it somehow!"[38] Mr. and Mrs. Hindelwicz kept up payment on four policies with a Polish insurance society despite Mr. Hindelwicz's layoff from Morris & Company Meatpackers in 1930, a $100 grocery bill, seven children to clothe and feed, and a large loan from a cousin to pay off.[39]

But even with scrimping and saving and letting other debts accumulate, it was often impossible to keep up insurance payments. Every study of unemployed families in Chicago during the early years of the depression recorded that large percentages, usually around 75 percent, had been forced to let some or all insurance policies lapse.[40] Not only was insurance a burdensome expense, but also many welfare agencies would not give relief to clients who still held insurance.[41] People in need often had no choice but to give up their long-cherished protection for tomorrow in order to survive today.

Not all the lapsed policies, of course, were fraternal ones. But when they were, the shock to the holder was particularly severe. If a commercial or employer's insurance policy failed them, workers considered it all the more proof that the capitalists had let them down. But when forced to abandon an investment in their own community organization, the betrayal hit closer to home. One investigator noted in the understated, unemotional language of official reporting that nonetheless betrayed the disillusionment of six families who had lost fraternal insurance: "their insurance had failed to provide the present and future security which they had been led to believe it would furnish them in emergency."[42] Workers who could not keep up their insurance payments often felt as if they had been let down by an old friend.

Chicago's industrial workers did not depend on their ethnic communities only in times of trouble. At more prosperous moments, as when saving money at the bank or buying a home, they looked to ethnic banks and building and loan associations. As described in Chapter 2, ethnic banks popped up all over Chicago during the 1920s, most of them small, state-chartered institutions located in the new, outlying shopping districts that boomed during the twenties. Because Illinois law prohibited branch banking, what in other major cities were outposts of downtown banks were in Chicago small, often ethnically owned financial institutions that somehow had scraped together enough capital to meet the state's minimum requirements. As a result, by 1928 Chicago could claim 231 incorporated banking institutions, more than any other American city, with 106 others spread throughout suburban Cook County. Almost every ethnic community in Chicago had at least one bank where people could transact business in their native language.

These small outlying banks were more numerous than stable, however. Illinois prohibition of branch banking and lax requirements for state banking charters had permitted many minimally capitalized and poorly managed banks to operate. In the bank failures that swept the city from 1929 to 1933 and were particularly intense after June 1931, these outlying banks were the first to collapse. By the time of the national bank holiday in March 1933, 163 of the 199 Chicago banks located outside the Loop had closed their doors. Only 16 percent, or 33 outlying banks, weathered the Great Depression. Far more than deposi-

Plate 25. Here, frantic customers participate in a run on a Chicago bank in the early depression. For many working people, the failure of what was often a local bank owned by a member of their ethnic group meant more than the loss of hard-earned dollars. It also meant loss of faith in the ability of their ethnic communities, particularly their leaders, to support them in times of trouble.

tors' lack of confidence caused these bank failures. Chicago's ethnic banks not only suffered from low capitalization; most of them also invested heavily in local real estate. The collapse of that boom brought a sudden depreciation in the value of banks' assets.[43]

Within a few years, disbelieving Chicagoans watched the downfall of such prestigious neighborhood landmarks as the Binga State Bank in the Black Belt, the First Italian State Bank, the Slovak Papanek-Kovac State Bank, the Czech Novak and Stieskal State Bank, the Lithuanian Universal State Bank, the Jewish Noel State Bank, and the largest Polish bank, the Northwestern Trust and Savings Bank, known familiarly in the Polish community as "Smulski's Bank." The *Chicago Defender*'s description of the scene outside Binga's Bank in the Black Belt captured the community tragedy of a bank closing: "Crowds of depositors gathered in front of the bank. Two uniformed policemen were out on guard for several days. There were no disorders. Instead, there was a deathlike pall that hung over those who had entrusted their life savings to Binga.... It was pride – that pride of seeing their own race behind the cages, that led them to 35th and State Street to do their banking. For years, the Binga Bank was pointed out to visitors as something accomplished by our group."[44]

When these banks failed, even more than when ethnic welfare agencies and ethnic benefit societies faltered, working-class people felt let down by the elites of their communities. Ethnic bank owners and managers had been local heroes, helping individual customers with mortgages and loans and providing leadership and financial assistance to the community. To ethnic workers, it was a scandal that bankers abandoned those who depended on them in a time of crisis. Stanley Kell's father, a machinist, organized a committee of depositors of closed Polish banks to try to get some return on their lost dollars. At a public demonstration outside one of these banks in the early 1930s, young Kell carried a sign that revealed how far from grace this previously admired banker had fallen: "I am a boy. You have taken my money. Does money mean as much to you as it does to me in your bank? If you need this money take the keys to this bank, throw 'em in the lake and stay in jail."[45]

The managers of an Italian bank in another Chicago neighborhood tried to ward off a run on the bank by calling on someone with even more stature in the community, Father Pavero, the local priest, to calm depositors down. The bankers gave Father their word that nothing was wrong and put him on a soap box to assure those who had assembled in the bank lobby that their money was safe, along with the church's. Most people went home convinced there was no danger. But when the bank closed the next day, Father Pavero found himself "cursed all over the place" along with the once esteemed bankers.[46] Homeowners felt even more betrayed when they discovered that the failure of their local banks created a loss of confidence and concomitant decline in neighboring property values.[47] Father Brazinski, Pastor of the Polish St. Marina's Catholic Church, despaired that the bank collapse had disillusioned Poles in his parish to such an extent that the "celebrated habits of thrift and savings are almost destroyed.... All banks around (seven of them) crashed and people lost their life savings and homes. The only attitude is 'There is no use of saving, spend everything otherwise you will lose it.' For years to come there will be no banking for the Polish family."

The National Urban League concurred that disillusionment from bank failures would have far-reaching ramifications for communities, as the closing of the Binga State Bank was bringing a "tremendous loss of confidence in Negro business enterprise and Negro financial institutions" in its wake.[48]

Ethnic building and loan associations, like banks, had facilitated workers' economic advances during the 1920s only to preside over their downfall in the 1930s. The same building and loan society in the Back of the Yards neighborhood that had helped the Dennison family buy a small building containing three apartments foreclosed on the mortgage in January 1931. Being allowed to rent the apartment they were already occupying was only small compensation to the Dennisons.[49] Many societies, like the Italo–American Building and Loan Association, the Lithuanian Dollar Savings, Building and Loan Association, and the Polish Nasza Chata Building and Loan Association, actually collapsed in the depression.[50] But even when they did not close, like their close cousins the ethnic benefit societies, building and loan associations failed members like the Dennisons who could not keep up payments.[51] No building and loan association enjoyed abandoning its members; many tried to extend deadlines and bend rules for a time.[52] But before too long, they had to foreclose on unpaid mortgages in order to stay afloat. Even then, damage from the depression remained. As late as 1940, a study by the federal government's Home Owners' Loan Corporation found only a fraction of Chicago's predepression building and loans in business, and very few of these still healthy. According to S. C. Mazankowski, a director of the Polish–American Building and Loan Association League of Illinois, irresponsible directors were most at fault. Selected for their wealth and prestige in the ethnic community rather than their brains and experience, and notorious for their unprofessional banking practices, they deserved, and got, the brunt of the public's blame.[53]

Even when owners did not face foreclosure and managed to hold onto their property, owning a home did not offer the kind of security during the depression that it had in the 1920s. Many welfare agencies barred homeowners from receiving relief. At the same time, moreover, homeowners who were landlords had a difficult time collecting rents from their tenants. Mary Rupcinski and her husband had unemployed tenants who went for long periods, once as long as eighteen months, without paying any rent. "They cheated me till I could not pay my interest on my mortgage and lost my house," she recalled bitterly.[54]

Because relief agencies refused to contribute to clients' rent payments until tenants were faced with eviction, small landlords, who were often workers trying to make a little extra money, had to choose between letting renters stay on free or paying the city to initiate eviction. They lost money either way.[55] The dilemma of the Barczak family of South Chicago was typical. When the Barczaks bought their home in the late 1920s, they thought they would soon be well-off, with three flats to rent, a father working in the steel mills, the eldest son old enough to join him, and the next son not far behind. But things did not work out as planned. By November 1932, only one flat had been rented and the payments on it were erratic; Mr. Barczak was working only two days a week; neither of the sons had a job; and the family could not get help from charity because they owned their own home.[56] For the Barczaks and thousands like them, all the things that had seemed wise in the twenties, like buying a home, keeping up fraternal insurance, and saving at the neighborhood bank or building and loan association, only caused trouble in the thirties.

Not even the faithful neighborhood merchant whose credit had sustained many an ethnic working-class family through bouts of unemployment during the 1920s could be counted on, to the dismay of customer and shopkeeper alike. Many tradesmen tried to keep up their old patterns of extending credit despite the depression. After all, they knew that credit was one of the main reasons customers patronized their stores over the cheaper chains. But as more customers were unemployed and not paying up, giving too much credit could bankrupt a store. "People would come to the store with little books and they would charge everything," Theresa Giannetti remembered angrily. "We'd keep track of what they would buy and if they had the money at the end of the month, they'd give us some; if they didn't, we just extended the credit. It got to the point where my Dad gave so much credit that he lost everything he had for giving the credit. . . . The people who owed us the money never bothered to pay it."[57]

Ethnic merchants like Mrs. Giannetti's father who had managed to survive the onslaught of the chains during the late 1920s were going broke meeting the traditional expectations of their customers. Some customers ran up more credit than they could possibly pay back. Still, if a storekeeper refused credit to a family with a large bill, he risked losing the entire sum owed. Then, too, merchants had to beware of what was known as "grocery cheating," getting all the credit you could from nearby grocers and then moving where people did not know you. Worst of all, when customers had money, small shopkeepers often watched them turn to the cash-and-carry chain store where their money-in-hand bought more. Many independent store owners, fearing bankruptcy, resorted to limiting credit, requiring customers to pay off the previous week's account if they wanted credit the following week. But in doing so, they minimized all the more what distinguished the small store from the chain and further drove customers away.[58]

Independent shopkeepers also fell victim to aggressive chain expansion during the depression. After some initial faltering in the early thirties, many chains figured out how they could make the depression work for them, often taking advantage of their size in ways that were not possible for the small store. Chain stores, ranging from A&P to Woolworth's consolidated units, closing inefficient and unprofitable ones and modernizing others since "the comparatively low cost of modernizing stores in times like these offers an advantage too great to be ignored," according to chain executives. In addition, new stores in better locations could be opened more cheaply than before given the low rentals of the post-1929 real estate market. Chain stores also developed new advertising and merchandising strategies and lowered operating costs by introducing self-service and increasing the number of products sold under their own label. Even when the number of chain stores fell during the thirties, chains' share of total sales in a particular market tended to grow (Table 7).[59]

The relief system contributed as well to the difficulty independent stores had competing with chains during the 1930s. Relief agencies run by the private United Charities, Cook County, and eventually, the state of Illinois and the federal government preferred recipients to buy food at chain stores where prices were lower. At first, agencies tried to enforce this by writing grocery orders only for chain stores. When small shopkeepers, ethnic groups, and relief recipients protested, they relented and authorized purchases from "the retail grocer of the client's choice."[60] As one irate citizen complained to officials in Washington, the National Tea Company, with its almost one thousand retail grocery stores in Metropolitan Chicago, has "in the past three years . . . acquired the bulk of the business of furnishing 150,000 destitute families . . . with the necessities of life, through the medium of contracts awarded to them by the Illinois Emergency Relief Commission." The writer went on to argue that this special treatment of the National Tea

Company hurt independent grocers in more ways than just depriving them of business. "Out of these profits . . . they [National Tea managers] installed 210 meat market units in connection with their grocery units in the Chicago area. Such meat market equipment cost them millions to install, and during this modern period of merchandising methods, which they boast about introducing, has wiped out hundreds of independent Grocers and meat dealers, forcing them into bankruptcy" [*sic*].[61] Not only had grocery chains like National Tea used the relief system to take dollars out of the small grocer's pocket, but they also had then spent the money to modernize and diversify chain operations in ways that hurt independents all the more.

Even after the policy of relief agencies was changed to allow all merchants to compete for the business of relief clients, the independent merchant still felt at a severe disadvantage. Many customers stayed with the chains. "We have lost about twenty-five customers through charity slips on the chain stores. When a customer owes you money, he does not like to come in when he cannot pay you," complained one grocer who after twenty-nine years in business found himself $3,500 in debt.[62] Furthermore, although he or she could now legally fill recipients' grocery orders, the small shopkeeper felt burdened by the relief bureaucracy in ways that the chains, with their professional bookkeeping, did not. Anna Blazewicz, who ran a grocery in a Polish neighborhood of Brighton Park, recalled that processing "charity tickets" was difficult: "They got food from the store like credit and every month we had to go and file and the city or county would pay back and it had to be just so because if you were a penny short or a penny over, then they would send the whole thing back to you."[63] If that was not hassle enough, the storekeeper had to cope with caseworkers who persisted in favoring chains, like the one who angered relief recipient Mrs. Carl Doyle so much by changing her grocery slip from the independent grocer she had selected to a Consumers' chain store – arguing "we'd get the most for our money" there – that Mrs. Doyle wrote to New Deal administrator Harry Hopkins in Washington to complain. At the other end, storekeepers felt squeezed by customers who threatened to have their grocery orders from the relief agency changed to another store if they did not receive additional credit.[64]

Other New Deal strategies to deal with the crisis of the depression intentionally or not worked to the disadvantage of the independent neighborhood storekeeper. Despite the Roosevelt administration's rhetorical commitment to safeguarding the small businessman, the National Recovery Administration (NRA) controlled prices for retailers and minimum wages and hours for their employees in ways that favored the chains. The chain store, able to buy products more cheaply from wholesalers, could sell them for less than the independent competitor. Small dealers who tried to meet the chain's sale price by selling below their own higher cost found themselves cited by the chain or large store for violating the NRA code for the retail food and grocery industry in the Chicago area. To make matters all the worse, the small storekeeper who hired a clerk or two to help in the shop had a hard time meeting the NRA code's strict wage and hour regulations.[65] It was no wonder that between overextending credit, competing with the chains, and coping with the relief system and the NRA, many small stores were forced to close.[66]

By the mid-1930s, working-class people were finding more chain stores near their homes and patronizing them more frequently. Even when the corner store survived, ethnic workers could less afford to indulge their preference for its familiar food products and comfortable atmosphere. People who may have opposed the chain store in principle found economic realities changing their buying habits. As early as 1931, the major trade journal of chain store executives predicted that "one of the most constructive features of the depression, so far as the chains are concerned, lies in the fact that it operates to make more people chain store conscious, a fact that will undoubtedly work to the advantage of the chains when better conditions return and consumer buying power increases. Thousands of people throughout the country have patronized chain stores this past year who never before felt it necessary to test the economies they claimed to offer."[67] By the end of the 1930s in Chicago, that prediction had come true. In the winter of 1936, when a DePaul University marketing professor conducted an extensive survey of the attitudes of Chicago housewives toward chain food stores, he found that chain stores had become much more popular in recent years, particularly among factory workers. By 1939, a survey by the A. C. Neilsen Company confirmed that 93 percent of what were labeled "lower middle" and 91 percent of "lower" income buyers now paid by cash, not credit, an indication that they were patronizing chain stores.[68]

As the corner grocer offered less credit than usual or closed down entirely, customers were forced to turn elsewhere. Loyalty to the local storekeeper of one's ethnicity had once been greatly valued, but now people felt that he or she had let them down, just when they needed help most. One more aspect of the "safety net" that their ethnic group had previously provided had collapsed with the Great Depression.

Workers' feeling that they could no longer depend on their neighborhood merchants or on other ethnic leaders like the mutual benefit society director and banker suggests that the depression threatened the class harmony of ethnic communities. Through the 1920s, when working-class Poles or Bohemians or Italians felt protected by successful businessmen and civic leaders of their own ethnicity, ethnic communities had remained integrated across class. But as the upheavals of the depression undermined ethnic institutions, particularly the credibility of their leaders, class tensions grew within Chicago's ethnic communities. The local businessman who once had supported ethnic welfare agencies or provided mortgage money was now perceived as only watching out for himself. As workers became more aware of class differences within their own ethnic groups, they were on their way to becoming more sensitive to them in the larger world and more likely to recognize their common fate with workers of other ethnicities.

WELFARE CAPITALISM IN DECLINE

When industrial workers looked beyond their ethnic community institutions for support during the 1920s, they turned to their welfare capitalist employers. Chapter 4 demonstrated how Chicago manufacturers developed welfare programs explicitly to encourage employees to depend on the boss. Welfare capitalists believed that they could create loyal, efficient workers by offering them job security and benefits. Workers, it had turned out, took advantage of these company welfare programs and even came to expect benefits along with the job. But they soon recognized that frequent layoffs and employer mismanagement made welfare capitalism undependable.

The Great Depression replayed this dynamic of employer promises and worker disillusionment in even greater intensity and left workers surer than ever that employers only valued welfare capitalism when it was convenient and cheap. As the depression deepened, many employers felt it was their responsibility to assist their workers, the natural fulfillment of their mission as welfare capitalists. In these hard times, it was important that the private sector, not the state, turn things around.

Plate 26. In giving away sausages to hungry people, many of whom were probably present or former employees, meatpacker Oscar Mayer (third from right) was a typical welfare capitalist in the early depression. Although welfare capitalists were ideologically committed to having business, not government, solve the problems of the depression, they abandoned many of their welfare programs when they decided the cost was too great.

"The industry tákes care of its own," the association of iron and steel companies characteristically asserted. Myron Taylor, soon to become president of U.S. Steel, elaborated in 1930: "Let it be said of the steel industry that none of its men was forced to call upon the public for help." Just to make sure, U.S. Steel, along with other companies, forbade employees to apply for relief to any charitable organization so long as they were still officially employed by the firm. To aid the larger community of unemployed, businessmen rallied to raise emergency funds for traditional charities to distribute, while they organized relief operations in their own plants for workers who had been laid off or were forced to work fewer hours at lower pay. Armour and Swift sent boxes of food and supplies of coal to former employees in the early 1930s.

International Harvester made interest-free loans and plowed garden plots available to their workers. U.S. Steel provided food baskets, rent subsidies, and cash loans, while Western Electric helped people find supplementary work.[69]

Before long, however, most companies began cutting back these relief programs, pleading unmanageable costs. At the same time, workers found that the welfare programs employers had so ardently proselytized during the twenties were disappearing as well. Some programs, like paid vacations, were deliberately cut to save money, whereas others, like stock plans and group insurance, atrophied with the depression or became irrelevant to workers no longer on the payroll. Nine families who had held group insurance until unemployment left them with neither protection nor an asset complained bitterly to an investigator that their many years of regular contributions had been "money thrown away." Even workers who officially held jobs had complaints. Employees at U.S. Steel's South Works, for example, found their group insurance cut, their stock worth only a fraction of its original value, relief gifts converted to loans, and dues to the company's welfare arm, the Goodfellows' Club, still deducted from their wages even when they were working only a day or two a week. Workers on U.S. Steel pensions saw their monthly checks reduced by as much as 25 percent.[70] If workers had held out any hope that welfare capitalism could be counted on when times got tough, they now had proof that it could not. Armour workers cynically joked that their employer's charity was made possible by the unpaid labor of employees forced "to work for the church," meaning that they were required to stay on the job after punching out.[71]

At even the most basic level of job security, welfare capitalists showed themselves to be untrustworthy. The layoffs that had been an unpleasant fact of life for workers during the 1920s became more menacing in frequency and duration. In many cases, temporary layoffs slid almost imperceptibly into unemployment. By 1931, the evidence was indisputable that manual laborers, skilled and unskilled, were suffering much more than white collar workers from the depression (Table 13). By 1933, more than half of U.S. Steel's mill hands were totally unemployed, and by the company's own admission there was not a single full-time worker on its payroll. The situation was not much better in Chicago's other manufacturing plants. Workers who managed to remain on the payroll found themselves working less often with each

Table 13. *Gainful workers unemployed in Chicago by occupational groups, 1930–1*

Occupational groups	Gainful workers	Unemployed workers, 1930		Unemployed workers, 1931	
		Number	Percent	Number	Percent
Men					
All occupations	1,152,108	141,065	12.2	353,980	30.7
Total, specified occupations	1,075,533	137,778	12.8	345,435	32.1
Proprietors and managers	123,926	4,084	3.3	8,752	7.1
Professional workers	35,171	2,795	8.0	5,158	14.7
Clerks and kindred workers	227,392	15,353	6.8	41,107	18.1
Skilled workers	260,818	43,939	16.8	105,305	40.4
Semiskilled workers	197,894	28,650	14.5	72,414	36.6
Unskilled workers	167,313	37,308	22.3	95,749	57.2
Domestic servants	63,019	5,649	9.0	16,950	26.9
Women					
All occupations	406,750	26,869	6.6	96,264	23.7
Total, specified occupations	393,275	26,474	6.7	95,214	24.2
Proprietors and managers	9,702	171	1.8	481	5.0
Professional workers	34,700	1,492	4.3	2,114	6.1
Clerks and kindred workers	176,160	9,413	5.3	31,173	17.7
Skilled workers	7,447	450	6.0	1,502	20.2
Semiskilled workers	87,801	8,879	10.1	31,057	35.4
Unskilled workers	8,463	784	9.3	2,853	33.7
Domestic servants	69,002	5,285	7.7	26,034	37.7

Note: The Bureau of the Census defined gainful employees as "all persons who usually follow a gainful employment even though they may not be employed at the time the census was taken."

Source: U.S. Department of Commerce, Bureau of the Census, *Fifteenth Census of the United States: 1930*, vol. 2, pp. 125, 437; table compiled by Grace Lee Maymor, "An Analysis of the United States Census Figures on Unemployment in Chicago, 1930 and 1931" (M.A. thesis, University of Chicago, 1934), p. 12.

week and month and for 10 percent, 15 percent, and even larger cuts in hourly wages. U.S. Steel and several other major firms heeded President Hoover's request that they not lower wages for just so long. Beginning in September 1931 they made the first 10 percent cut, which precipitated an avalanche of further wage reductions (Table 14).[72]

Blacks and Mexicans, who had been particularly loyal to employers during the twenties, found themselves singled out for more than their fair share of layoffs in the thirties. A combination of low-skilled jobs, lack of seniority resulting from frequent layoffs, and vulnerability to employer racism doomed them to "first-fired" status. As early as 1929, the industrial secretary of the Chicago Urban League reported, "Every week we receive information regarding the discharge of additional Race workers who are being replaced by workers of other races." Cases like the Gary Works of U.S. Steel, where the percentage of black steelworkers had already fallen by 1930 from 17.4 to 14.7 percent, were all too common. The unfortunate truth was that for a plant like International Harvester's McCormick Works, where management had complained throughout the twenties that blacks were becoming too numerous in the ranks, the depression offered the opportunity to bring black employment down from a 1920s high of 18 percent to 10 percent by 1940. Elmer Thomas, a black packinghouse worker, complained that blacks lost out in the Yards as well, as the depression expanded the pool of white workers willing to take unpleasant stockyard jobs: "They were hiring young, white boys, sixteen and eighteen years old, raw kids, didn't know a thing," in place of black workers. Between 1930 and 1940, the percentage of blacks in low-skilled meat industry jobs dropped from 31 to 20 percent. These declines in different sectors added up. By the end of 1932, 40–50 percent of Chicago's black work force was unemployed.[73]

Mexican factory workers did not receive much better treatment. Mexican employees of U.S. Steel's South Works, for example, fell from nineteen hundred in 1930 to three hundred two years later. The experience of one Mexican packinghouse worker was typical: "A 'white man' applied for a job in the place where I was working and the foreman, finding no vacancy, laid me off and gave my job to the applicant." Mexicans not only faced job dismissals but repatriation back to Mexico as well since few of them were citizens and many were accused of being illegal aliens. Almost half of Chicago's Mexican population was forced to leave the city during the depression years, as local relief agencies

Table 14. *Indexes of decline in employment and payrolls in Chicago manufacturing industries, 1929–33*

Year	Index of employment	Index of payrolls
1927	100.9	99.0
1928	93.3	88.9
1929	97.8	100.5
1930	90.9	86.0
1931	74.3	59.8
1932	56.5	35.9
1933	49.3	26.4

Note: Figures for the month of April of each year. Monthly average for 1925–7 is 100.
Source: Illinois Department of Labor, *Labor Bulletin* 12 (January 1933), p. 143. Reprinted in Homer Hoyt, *One Hundred Years of Land Values in Chicago: The Relationship of the Growth of Chicago to the Rise in Its Land Values* (Chicago: University of Chicago Press, 1933), p. 269.

routinely rounded them up and shipped them south to the border. Those who remained in Chicago with hopes of working often found themselves targets of animosity from their non-Mexican neighbors. In the area near Wisconsin Steel during the spring of 1934, for instance, several Mexican residents were assaulted by "an enraged mob of Polish people," according to a Mexican newspaper, "because there is an atmosphere of ill will against the Mexicans." Mexican workers felt caught. Laid off more frequently than other workers, they were then blamed for being an unwanted, if not illegal, burden on society when they sought relief. Staying in Chicago often proved as difficult as leaving.[74]

It should be noted, however, that the two plants that had distinguished themselves as the most dependable paternalists during the 1920s, Hawthorne Works of Western Electric and International Harvester's Wisconsin Steel Works, continued to demonstrate their good faith during the depression. Western Electric built on its human relations approach to employee management by making every effort to treat employees fairly. Rather than single out certain workers for firing, Western Electric implemented a "work sharing" program that moved everyone from a five-and-a-half-day workweek to a five- and then a four-day one. All workers also were requested to add an extra week of unpaid vacation to their paid two weeks. Although many companies officially endorsed the principle of work sharing, Western Electric was among the few who implemented it equitably. In addition, to keep workers occupied and on the payroll, when the reduced demands of the telephone industry had been met, the Hawthorne Works set up wood shops in the plant to produce such saleable items as bridge tables, jig-saw puzzles, radiator covers, and table lamps. A store was set up in the factory to sell these and other homemade goods to co-workers as well as outsiders. When some workers had to be laid off, the company tried to keep on those who were the sole support of families. Married women with more seniority, for example, often lost jobs to single women providing for their parents as well as themselves. Those workers who were let go, moreover, got assistance finding other jobs in the community and received termination allowances based on their length of service, a rarity in the depression.[75]

It is not clear why Western Electric went to such lengths to cushion the impact of the depression on its employees. It seems likely, however, that the firm's traditional paternalism toward its "company town" of Cicero managed to survive the depression not only because of management's commitment but also because the demand for Western Electric's telephone equipment, although slowed by the depression, never entirely disappeared. Nineteen twenty-nine set a record for sales and it was not until 1932 or 1933 that the depression really hit the Hawthorne Works hard. The fact that Western Electric had a monopoly, moreover, allowed the company to pass on the costs of a continued commitment to welfare capitalism to its customers. As John Mega, a long-time Hawthorne employee explained it, "Actually, it didn't cost them nothing. Really, the company had a monopoly on telephones. They were guaranteed a certain profit over and above the costs of operating the company. . . . The government guaranteed them that more or less."[76]

The management of Wisconsin Steel was not as exemplary as that of Western Electric, but as in 1919 and through the 1920s, it benefited from being favorably compared with U.S. Steel's neighboring South Works plant and with other International Harvester installations in Chicago. The Harvester administration demonstrated much more commitment to its employees during the depression than U.S. Steel did. To the extent that work sharing occurred at South Works, for example, employees saw it as an invitation to foremen to play favorites even more than they had in the 1920s. At Wisconsin Steel, in contrast, management still seemed to be making efforts to respect seniority, to rotate work among long-established employees, and to keep foremen under scrutiny. International Harvester also sponsored more extensive relief measures, like a no-interest loan program. "At the time of Depression when the world stood still as far as we're concerned here," a life-long resident of the neighborhood around Wisconsin Steel recalled, "They would loan money to their older employees. They'd have the kids come in and get their dental work done . . . and would clothe them and give them shoes. That was quite unusual to me because they were the only corporation that did that. People didn't have to repay that money until they went back to work, and to me this was wonderful."[77]

Furthermore, being isolated in South Deering allowed Wisconsin Steel to more effectively implement company relief programs than the more centrally located Harvester plants could. For example, because McCormick Works employees lived in center city neighborhoods, the garden plots at 55th and Cicero Avenue provided by the company were often too far out of the way to be convenient. In contrast, the open stretches of cultivable land near Wisconsin Steel directly benefited the large employee population that lived near the mill. More than two thousand employees farmed quarter-acre plots, equipped with seed kits and fertilizer supplied by the company. Most important, Wisconsin Steel workers experienced fewer layoffs and less extensive wage cuts than their peers at Harvester's implement and tractor producing plants. As Harry Bercher, a former chief executive of International Harvester who spent the 1930s in management at Wisconsin Steel, explained, "If you laid off these people, goodness only knows. They were pretty skilled people. You're not going to pick them off the street." Bercher also noted that because the steel works were so unique within the Harvester empire, managers at Wisconsin Steel enjoyed more autonomy in pursuing strategies such as keeping on workers during the depression.[78]

Wisconsin Steel also enjoyed an economic advantage over International Harvester's agricultural equipment plants that made its continued commitment to welfare capitalism possible. Although not in as privileged a financial situation as Western Electric, as a basic industry within the Harvester manufacturing empire sending about 60 percent of its steel to Harvester's equipment factories and selling the rest on the open market, the steel works proved less vulnerable than the equipment plants that depended solely on the evaporating consumer demand of farmers. The small batches of high-quality rolled and bar steel that this mill produced continued to find some specialized customers.[79] Although Western Electric and Wisconsin Steel were still laying off men and women, cutting wages and hours, and eliminating welfare programs during the depression, they managed to convince many of their workers that if they were not "good" employers in these difficult times, they were at least "better" ones. Philosophical conviction combined with the economic advantages that these plants enjoyed made their managers still seem dependable as welfare capitalists.

Despite these two exceptions, the majority of industrial workers felt abandoned by the welfare capitalists, much as they had been by ethnic institutions and their leaders. Traditional elites at the workplace and in the community, on whom workers had depended during the previous decade, both seemed to be letting them down. Nor were these the only long-established paternalistic relationships endangered by the depression. Within the family itself, traditional hierarchies, of father over mother and parent over child, were also threatened.

FAMILY LIFE DISRUPTED

During the depression, unemployment hit particularly hard at middle-aged men, those between thirty-five and fifty-five, just at the time in their lives when their family responsibilities were greatest. "A man over forty might as well go out and shoot himself," one despairing Chicago worker wrote President Roosevelt in 1934.[80] Manufacturers' tendency to prefer hiring men under forty-five, forty, or sometimes even thirty-five increased with the depression, when so many young people were available for work: "fatal forty," one Chicago caseworker labeled it; "too old to get work," a black laborer in his mid-forties complained; "a stranded generation," newspaperwoman Lorena Hickok wrote back to Washington from a fact-finding mission.[81]

Workers still depended on a "family economy" during the depression in the sense that the contributions of various members helped the family survive, but the delicate economic and psychological balance that had characterized it in the 1920s was upset when grown men could no longer carry their weight. Unemployment among husbands forced many wives and children into the work force during the 1930s as the sole support of their families. Women found it easier to find and hold work in the depression than their husbands. A government study of workers on relief in 1934 demonstrated that men were out of work longer than women in Chicago, in fact in all but one of the seventy-nine cities surveyed. Women's labor was cheaper. They worked in service occupations as clerks, maids, and waitresses, which survived the hard times better than manufacturing jobs.[82] Working-age children also were better able to find jobs than their unemployed fathers, and even when they were laid off, they could count on being called back to work sooner. Many young people who were used to contributing a fair share of their wages to the household now found they had to turn over everything. Clothes and recreation, to say nothing of schooling and marriages, had to be put off. Children did not always volunteer their help. Relief agencies usually required that children contribute all their earnings to the family's living expenses before they would provide any assistance. Children who resisted often had no choice but to abandon their families entirely.[83]

When the male breadwinner suffered prolonged unemployment, traditional authority relationships within the family, between husbands and wives and between parents and children, began to break down. Evidence abounds that men suffered severely from their loss of status as the family's chief breadwinner. One investigator of a large group of unemployed families concluded that most husbands felt deeply humiliated: "In his own estimation, he was failing to fulfill the central duty of his life – the very touchstone of his manhood – the role of family provider. . . . Every purchase of the family – the radio, his wife's new hat, the children's skates, the meal set before him – all were symbols of their dependence upon him. Unemployment changed all that."[84] Male responses varied. Some men withdrew emotionally. Others became angry, even violent. There were those who put on work clothes and pretended to go to work. A few even committed suicide.[85]

The fear of husbands and fathers that they were losing authority within the home was not irrational. Plenty of testimony survives that wives and children did lose respect for the head of the household when he was unemployed. From the perspective of Father Victor, Principal of Holy Trinity High School in a Polish neighborhood of Chicago, instability was besetting the Polish family. As a result of women rather than men earning wages, he observed, "The autocratic domination and importance of the wage earner is profoundly shaken. You should remember that the Polish family is based on authority, not on love. . . . The prestige of the former wage earner is lowered by asking working children or women for spending money – for beer, for cigarettes, for carfare."[86] A Chicago social worker, Clara Odeski, concurred. Since it had become easier for women to find employment than men, she claimed more women were assuming dominating roles in the family, while their husbands grew resentful over their loss of status.[87] One Polish wife exemplified perfectly Miss Odeski's claim. She had been supporting her family with the help of her oldest son for the four years since her husband, an unskilled laborer, had lost his job: "I am the boss in the family for I have full charge in running this house. You know, who make the money he is the boss." She also honestly felt that "the children are getting more fond of me than their father," a point her daughter substantiated by declaring, "I certainly like my mother lots more, for she buys me everything."[88]

The husband's emasculation within the family was not only symbolic. Social workers reported frequently that friction between husbands and wives manifested itself in sexual problems. One common pattern was an increased resistance among women to intercourse with their husbands. One woman stated her position quite clearly to a social worker: "When her husband was working and supporting her, she supposed it was his right to have sexual relations and she therefore acquiesced. Now she avoids it."[89] Not surprisingly, University of Chicago sociologist Ernest Burgess concluded in a study of the effect of unemployment on the family that there was a strong correlation between unemployment and marital unhappiness among men.[90]

Children also lost faith in their unemployed fathers. Many people recounted to Studs Terkel in his oral history of the Great Depression, *Hard Times*, that father–child relationships suffered in the depression environment. Particularly poignant testimony came from a worker's son: "One of the most common things – and it certainly happened to me – was this feeling of your father's failure. That somehow he hadn't beaten the rap. Sure things were tough, but why should I be the kid who had to put a piece of cardboard into the sole of my shoe to go to school?"[91]

A caseworker from a Chicago relief agency summed up the situation in 1934: "Family relations are becoming strained; fathers feel they have lost their prestige in the home; there is much nagging, mothers nag at the fathers, parents nag at the children. Children of working age who earn meager salaries find it hard to turn over all their earnings and deny themselves even the greatest necessities and as a result leave home."[92] The Great Depression was disrupting authority relations in the family, much as it had in the ethnic community and the factory.

What made the depression so catastrophic for Chicago's working-class families was not simply the loss of a job, a home, or insurance. It was that these losses called into question the sustaining institutions of the 1920s, threatening the patterns of loyalty that working people had taken for granted, in their families, in their communities, and at work. Ethnic benefit societies, churches, banks, building and loan associations, and neighborhood stores, workers' welfare capitalist employers, and paternalistic families were so damaged by the depression that they could no longer sustain the level of support on which people had relied. For workers already overcome with material deprivations, the loss of faith in these traditional organizations and authority figures – the ethnic leader, the priest, the boss, the father – created a crisis. Where should one turn now for protection and to ensure a future for one's family? As new competitors for workers' loyalty came to the fore in the course of the depression, workers would look in new directions for the security that their ethnic groups, employers, and even families had previously provided.

6
Workers Make a New Deal

Plate 27. These people were among the twenty-five thousand who participated in the hunger march of October 31, 1932, jointly sponsored by Chicago's Communist Unemployed Councils and Socialist Workers' Committee on Unemployment to protest cuts in relief payments. Despite more radical rhetoric, left-wing movements among the unemployed taught workers the same lesson as electoral politics in the 1930s, to look to the federal government for solutions to their problems. Workers began to depend on Washington for the security that their ethnic institutions and welfare capitalist employers had once provided.

In 1935, Mrs. Olga Ferk wrote a letter to President Roosevelt in which she complained that she was mistreated at her relief station, that she was only $19 behind in her government HOLC mortgage payments, not three months as accused, and that her son's Civilian Conservation Corps (CCC) paychecks were always late in arriving. "How long is this rotten condition going to last," she demanded of the president. "I am at the end of the rope. The Rich get Richer and the poor can go to – H – that is what it looks like to me.... Let's have some results."[1] What is most striking about Mrs. Ferk's letter is that only a few years earlier, her expectation that the federal government should provide her with regular relief, a mortgage, and a job for her son and be efficient and fair about it would have been unimaginable. In the midst of the Great Depression, families like the Ferks were depending on the national government as once they had looked to their ethnic institutions and welfare capitalist employers.

Two years later, Sociology Professor Arthur W. Kornhauser and his assistants at the University of Chicago interviewed several thousand Chicago residents of diverse occupations to learn their opinions about the great controversies of the day. Their findings indicate that Mrs. Ferk's discontents were typical of semiskilled and unskilled workers. Three-fourths of them felt that working people were not treated fairly, whereas in the minds of almost everyone, wealthy businessmen had too much influence in running the country. Although these workers were not asked directly how they would solve the depression crisis, their point of view can be pieced together from responses to other questions. Chicago's industrial workers blamed the capitalist system, and particularly big businessmen, for the economic depression, yet for the most part they were unwilling to abandon capitalism in favor of a socialist system where government owned industry. At the same time, however, they advocated the strengthening of two institutions to rebalance power within capitalist society: the federal government and labor unions. Ninety percent of the sample of unskilled workers and 81 percent of the semiskilled favored Roosevelt's New Deal, whose programs represented to workers the expansion of federal authority. Three-fourths of these workers even went so far as advocating that the government play a role in redistributing wealth in the society. Clearly, Chicago's working people were seeking a powerful federal government that would work for them, not their bosses. The other institution that workers thought would bring about a more equitable capitalist society was the labor union.

More than four-fifths of them endorsed strong labor unions to which all workers would belong. If workers were organized in unions and protected by a strong federal government, the "moral capitalism" that they had hoped for under welfare capitalism during the 1920s might finally prevail, these Chicago working people seemed to be saying.[2]

Having lost faith in the capacity of their ethnic communities and welfare capitalist employers to come to the rescue, Chicago's industrial workers had found new solutions. By the mid-1930s, they, and their counterparts elsewhere in America, were championing an expanded role for the state and the organization of national-level industrial unions. State and union, workers hoped, would provide the security formerly found through ethnic, religious, and employer affiliation as well as ensure a more just society. Although most workers interviewed did not call for revolutionary change, it would be a mistake to assume that their commitment to a moral capitalism did not challenge the status quo. Too often retrospective analysis of workers' responses to the Great Depression falls into the trap of pigeonholing them as either radical or not, according to some external standard, without evaluating in a more subtle way how workers changed their attitudes over the course of the 1930s. Newfound faith in the state and the unions was not preordained. It required workers to make significant breaks with previous values and behavior and to adopt new ones.

In this and the next two chapters we will probe how Chicago's factory workers, who had been isolated from the federal government and unorganized on the eve of the depression, came to hold the view that a strong state and strong unions could remedy the failures of capitalism so glaring in the Great Depression. This chapter will show how and why workers turned to the federal government. Chapters 7 and 8 will investigate the way they became invested in a national union movement. Each will seek to reconstruct the political mentality of Chicago's industrial workers by the late 1930s and how they came to it.

VOTING IN THE STATE

It was not at all obvious that when Chicago's working people suffered misfortunes in the depression they would turn to the federal government for protection. During the 1920s, these workers had put little faith in government, particularly at the national level. As we have seen, to the extent that working people's social welfare needs were met at all, they were met in the private sector, by ethnic communities and welfare capitalist employers. Many workers looked warily on the expansion of state power, as they felt it was already interfering with their cultural freedom by legislating and enforcing Prohibition.

Most indicative of their disinterest in government, large numbers of Chicago workers failed to vote. In wards with high percentages of foreign-born workers, less than one-third of the potential electorate (people over the age of twenty-one) turned out for the presidential election of 1924, in contrast to 65 percent in native, middle-class wards.[3] Many of these nonvoters could not vote because they were not citizens. Stiff citizenship requirements and a disinclination to naturalize kept them away. Others qualified to vote but did not bother to register or to vote even when registered. They simply did not find national party politics relevant to their lives. "I had cast maybe one ballot in a national election, before the mid-1930s," recalled steelworker George Patterson, an immigrant of Scottish birth who had become a citizen easily in the twenties with no new language to learn.[4]

Even those ethnic workers who voted during the 1920s did not often identify politically beyond their local community. The kind of machine politics that flourished in Chicago during the twenties kept people dependent on a very local kind of political structure not tightly bound to any one major party. In the city at large, not only did the Democrats and Republicans fight each other, but also factions within each party warred for supporters. Alliances developed around personalities, not policies. This volatility carried over to the local level, where ethnic groups, ward leaders, and precinct captains evaluated candidates and then delivered their votes to the ones they felt would best serve their needs even if they came from a political party not usually supported. Political parties were most visible in a community right before election time and then often disappeared. There were general patterns, of course, in the voting of blacks and "new immigrant" groups who dominated Chicago's industrial work force – blacks and Yugoslavs strongly Republican; Poles, Czechs, Lithuanians, and eastern European Jews frequently Democratic; Italians often split – but no party could count on a particular group's votes, except the Republicans on the blacks. It was a rare ethnic worker in Chicago who had a strong identity as either Democrat or Republican before the late 1920s.[5]

All this changed at the end of the decade. Workers became drawn into an interethnic Democratic machine in Chicago under the leadership of Czech politician Anton Cermak that connected them not only to a unified Democratic Party on the city level but also to the national Democratic Party.[6] The issue that made Cermak's political career, and drew Chicago's diverse ethnic communities together behind him and the national Democratic presidential candidate in 1928, Alfred E. Smith, was Prohibition. In referendum after referendum in Chicago, in 1919, 1922, 1926, 1930, and 1933, Chicago voters demonstrated that they were anywhere from 72 to 92 percent opposed to Prohibition. Sentiment in the city probably ran even higher as those workers most resentful of Prohibition were likely not voters.[7]

Ethnic populations for whom production and consumption of alcohol were central to cultural life opposed Prohibition most vehemently, and within these groups, contemporary analysts like Harold Gosnell concluded, those with lower incomes were most committed. Working-class ethnics felt discriminated against by the selective way that Prohibition was enforced in the city. A rich family could have a cellar full of liquor and get by, it seemed, but if a poor family had one bottle of home-brew, there would be trouble. To add insult to injury, workers' industrial employers embraced Prohibition as a holy cause. Indeed, employers made few efforts to hide their desire to destroy the tavern, "the workingman's club" where discontent traditionally blossomed, and to "improve" the moral habits of their employees. Prohibition served not only to unite ethnic Chicagoans around Democratic politics but also particularly to attract the workingmen and women among them. Here was a political issue that roused the masses. By 1928, Cermak had succeeded in unifying this anti-Prohibition sentiment sufficiently to make himself top Democratic boss in the city, the first foreign born and non-Irishman to run the party, whereas Smith, the party's Catholic and "wet" presidential candidate, had become the first Democrat at the top of the ticket to come close to carrying Chicago in years.[8]

The creation of a Democratic machine in Chicago under Mayor Cermak and his successor Mayor Kelly (who took office in 1933 after Cermak was killed by an assassin's bullet intended for President Roosevelt) has drawn much attention for how it paved the way for years of undemocratic rule by the Daley machine. What is lost in hindsight, however, is how voters actually felt about joining a citywide and national Democratic Party at the time. First- and second-generation immigrants still made up almost two-thirds of Chicago's population, and a large proportion of these came from eastern and southern Europe.[9] After years of having little voice in either party, new ethnic groups finally felt that they had a party that represented them. When Republican candidate "Big Bill" Thompson made an issue of Cermak's eastern European origins in the mayoral race of 1931, a multiethnic alliance for the Democrats was clinched. Thompson's taunt,

> Tony, Tony, where's your pushcart at?
> Can you picture a World's Fair mayor
> With a name like that?

and Cermak's retort ("He don't like my name.... It's true I didn't come over on the Mayflower, but I came over as soon as I could") crystallized for ethnic Chicagoans how the Democratic Party had become the only party for them.[10]

The best evidence that Chicagoans were becoming increasingly committed to the Democratic party is that the Democratic vote in both local and national elections mushroomed (Table 15). By 1936, 65 percent of Chicago voters favored the Democratic presidential candidate, three times as many as had in 1924. In wards with large numbers of first- and second-generation ethnics, 81 percent supported Roosevelt in 1936, in contrast to 38 percent for Davis in 1924. Even more significant, these new Democratic voters, when white, were less often converted Republicans than new recruits, ethnic working-class people who had not voted during the 1920s. In their wards, there was a two-thirds increase in voter turnout between 1924 and 1936, with essentially all of these new participants voting Democratic.[11]

Several factors explain why Chicago's ethnic workers were voting in record numbers, and overwhelmingly Democratic, during the depths of the Great Depression. To start with, more people were eligible to vote. In an immigrant district such as the one surrounding the Chicago Commons Settlement on the West Side, two-thirds of those over age twenty-one qualified to vote in 1930, in contrast to only one-third in 1920. Both the coming of age of the American-born second generation and the more than doubling of the numbers of foreign born who had become citizens, particularly women, were responsible.[12] But eligibility is one thing, actually turning out to vote quite another. Starting in 1928, Chicago's ethnic workers participated more actively in the political process, and as Democrats, because of ideology not just demogra-

Table 15. *Percentage of Democratic vote in Chicago elections among all voters, whites, and blacks, 1924–36*

Election	All voters	Whites	Blacks
Presidential 1924	22	na	8
Presidential 1928	49	na	30
Presidential 1932	57	59	23
Congressional 1934	65	64	42
Mayoral 1935	82	83	81
Presidential 1936	65	66	49

Note: na, data not available.
Source: Elmer William Henderson, "A Study of the Basic Factors Involved in the Change in the Party Alignment of Negroes in Chicago, 1932–1938" (M.A. thesis, University of Chicago, 1939), p. 25; *The Daily News Almanac and Yearbook for 1925, 1929, 1933–1937*; Kristi Anderson, *The Creation of a Democratic Majority, 1928–1936* (Chicago: University of Chicago Press, 1979).

phy. Finally by the 1930s, they felt like legitimate players in the political game. However undemocratic the one-party rule of Chicago's Democratic machine may have later become, it began as a democratic experience for many Chicago workers, giving them for the first time the feeling that the political process worked for them.

Most crucial in explaining the commitment to federal power that Kornhauser discovered in 1937, ethnic workers were becoming invested not only in Cermak's local Democratic party. Beginning with Smith's campaign as a wet candidate in 1928 and increasingly with Roosevelt in 1932 and particularly in 1936, workers felt that the policies of the national Democratic party were making a difference in their lives. "Before Roosevelt, the Federal Government hardly touched your life," explained one man. "Outside of the postmaster, there was little local representation. Now people you knew were appointed to government jobs. Joe Blow or some guy from the corner."[13] For jobs, and a myriad of other services once provided by others, it soon became clear, workers looked increasingly to the state. John Mega, a worker at Western Electric who grew up in a Slovak family in Back of the Yards, watched this transformation in his own family's political consciousness: "Our people did not know anything about the government until the depression years." His father never voted. In fact, he stated, "In my neighborhood, I don't remember anyone voting. They didn't even know what a polling place was." Suddenly with the depression, all that changed. Mega's relatives were voting to send Democrats to Washington and counting on them for relief and CCC and Works Progress Administration (WPA) jobs.[14] Because the Kelly machine identified itself so strongly with the New Deal, voters like Mega's family and neighbors did not feel they were favoring national over local government. They saw the Chicago Democrats as the conduit for Washington's largesse.

It is important to recognize, however, that the promise and impact of New Deal programs alone cannot explain workers' reorientation to the federal government. That they had personally helped put in power the Democrats in Chicago and in Washington mattered enormously. Voting was a gradual process teaching them that national politics was reciprocal. As workers took credit for electing the nation's political leadership, the state seemed less remote. Over time Chicago workers came to feel like national political actors who had earned rights by their political participation. When Celie Carradina's estranged husband refused to share his WPA pay with her in late 1935, this resident of Back of the Yards wrote to President Roosevelt for help on the grounds that "I hope you every way that I could doing election and I am going to do my best again" [*sic*].[15] Likewise, a WPA worker once employed by Western Electric asked Mrs. Roosevelt, "How can a worthy Democrat, with a family of 8 children and wife to support Support them civilized on $55.00 a month" [*sic*].[16] Many others like Mr. and Mrs. Memenga threatened the president that if relief benefits did not improve, "we will think twice the next time [we are asked to vote for you]."[17] Working-class voters in Chicago were coming to feel not only that their fate increasingly lay in the hands of New Deal officials but also that national office holders and bureaucrats owed them something for their votes. Chicago workers who ten years earlier had felt removed from the federal government would tell Professor Kornhauser by the late 1930s that they expected more from the state.

Black workers in Chicago were also voting in record numbers and more Democratic than ever before by 1936, but they arrived at this same destination via a very different route than did ethnic workers. Rather than being newcomers to the political process, blacks had participated actively in elections during the 1920s. When only a third of

Chicago's ethnics were voting in 1924, over 50 percent of blacks did. At the most basic level, it was easier for blacks to vote in Chicago. The longest residency requirement they faced was a year to vote in state elections, whereas the minimum requirement for naturalization was over five years, and it usually took immigrants at least ten years to become citizens. No less important, voting mattered to blacks who had been kept from expressing their full citizenship rights in the South. Many immigrants, in contrast, were former peasants from eastern and southern Europe who had never even had the expectation of voting.[18]

Blacks not only voted more than ethnics in the twenties but also displayed a strong loyalty to one party, the Republicans. In fact, Mayor "Big Bill" Thompson built his political career on the support of Chicago's black wards. Few blacks had been in the North long enough to forget the southern lesson that the Republican Party was the black's friend, the Democratic Party his racist enemy. The National Democratic Party had done little in recent memory to alter that image. The first blacks to attend a Democratic convention were seated as alternates in 1924, whereas at the 1928 convention in Houston, black delegates were segregated behind chicken wire. In Chicago, the two major parties kept up their reputations. Thompson rewarded blacks with city and party jobs, and the Democrats tried to win white voters by appealing to their racial prejudice. As late as the 1927 mayoral election, for example, flyers circulated depicting Thompson conducting a trainload of blacks from Georgia with the warning that "this train will start for Chicago, April 6, if Thompson is elected."[19]

Yet despite Chicago blacks' unfailing loyalty to the Republicans during the 1920s, by the late 1930s they were securely in the Democratic camp. Nothing demonstrates so well the extent to which working people reoriented themselves politically during the 1930s as this shift of black voters from Republican to Democrat (Table 15). Dependable voters in the twenties, blacks turned out in still larger numbers in the thirties. The 61 percent of eligible blacks who voted in 1932 grew to 70 percent by 1940. And blacks increasingly voted Democratic. With them as with ethnics, New Deal programs alone did not make Democrats. Local and national Democratic administrations complemented each other. Cermak, and even more so Kelly, wooed black supporters with traditional lures of the machine, like patronage jobs and benign neglect of illegal gambling, as well as with symbolic actions such as banning the film "Birth of A Nation" and ceremoniously naming boxer Joe Louis "mayor for ten minutes." In time, Kelly would even defend integrated schools and open housing, much to his own political detriment.

Blacks rewarded Kelly by filing into the Democratic Party. In fact, they demonstrated more support for the local Kelly machine in the mayoral election of 1935 than they ever did for Roosevelt, giving Kelly a record-shattering 81 percent of their vote. One year later, a slight majority of Chicago's blacks still favored the Republican presidential nominee. But what is lost in these national election results from 1936 is the magnitude of the shift nonetheless underway. Although Chicago's black national Democratic vote lagged behind other northern cities, Chicago blacks increased their support for Roosevelt 132 percent over 1932, more than blacks in any city but Cleveland. Already with the election of Arthur Mitchell in 1934, Chicago blacks had sent the first black Democrat to Congress. To the extent that black people in Chicago were slow to endorse the Democratic Party nationally, it was because of their success as Republicans in the 1920s. Blacks had enjoyed more influence in Chicago politics than in any other city, making Chicago the " 'seventh heaven' of Negro political activity," according to commentator Ralph Bunche.[20]

There is no denying, however, that Kelly and Roosevelt's efforts to make Democrats out of Chicago's blacks were helped by New Deal programs. Despite charging that the NRA functioned more as a "Negro Removal Act" than a "National Recovery Act" and that relief and job programs discriminated against them, blacks found themselves dependent on whatever benefits they could wring from federal programs as they tried to cope with the ravages of the depression. "Let Jesus lead you and Roosevelt feed you" replaced "Stick to Republicans because Lincoln freed you." The following ditty, which won the thunderous applause of black audiences in Chicago during the 1936 campaign, would have been inconceivable a decade earlier[21]:

> Millions a folks got to eat and sleep;
> Millions of us settin' on the anxious seat.
> Yo'all better vote right on 'lection day
> And keep this good ole WPA
> Ain't no ifs ands about it
> How you gonna get 'long widdout it?
> How you can take a little Republican jelly,
> But I ain't messin' wid my belly.

> You got relief, ole age pensions and WPA,
> But not if the Republicans coulda had they way.

By 1937 black workers were giving Professor Kornhauser the same message as their ethnic peers: Our survival depends on a strong federal government, and the Democrats, both in Chicago and Washington, are the only ones who can give it to us.

RADICAL BOOSTERS OF THE STATE

Not all workers in Chicago believed electoral politics could solve the crisis of the depression. A relatively small number joined the Communist Party, and many more, particularly in the early 1930s, enlisted in radical movements of the unemployed, organized by Communists and Socialists. But these left-wing crusades taught working-class recruits the same lesson as electoral politics, to look to the state for the solutions to their problems.

Unemployed and partly employed workers were frustrated with conditions in America in the early 1930s, but few went as far as joining the Communist Party. Chicago had been the birthplace of the American Communist Party in 1919, but Communist membership in the city declined during the twenties and New York became the party's national center. By the fall of 1931, the Chicago Communist Party claimed only two thousand registered members, although it managed in the presidential election of 1932 to attract 12,000 votes for its candidate, William Z. Foster, who in 1919 had teamed with John Fitzpatrick, president of the Chicago Federation of Labor, to try to organize steel and packing workers. A report that appeared in a February 1932 issue of *The Communist*, the party's theoretical journal, lamented how poorly industrial workers, particularly ones working in large factories, were represented in the Communist membership. Those who belonged were more likely than not foreign born. Nationally in 1931 two-thirds of party members were born abroad; in Chicago 53 percent were foreign born, with only one-half of those citizens. Not surprisingly given Chicago's ethnic make-up, the party there was made up mostly of Jews, Russians, South Slavs, Lithuanians, Hungarians, and Poles.

The Communist Party went out of its way to attract blacks by consistently agitating against white racism and for black equality.

Efforts ranging from sponsoring interracial dances to nominating a black man, James Ford, to run with Foster in 1932 to tenaciously defending the Scottsboro Boys – nine young blacks wrongly accused of raping two white girls on a train in Alabama – won the party black members, but uncomfortable in the party, they usually did not stay long. By the end of 1931 there were still less than one thousand black members nationwide, with half of those in Chicago. More than these five hundred Chicago blacks sympathized with the party, however. The Communists' battle against rent evictions in particular won them black votes. Seventeen percent of those who voted for Foster in 1932, over a thousand voters, came from the Black Belt's second and third wards.

As the thirties wore on, the party's influence on workers, black and white, grew, reflected somewhat in larger membership totals but much more so in the way the party cooperated with the mainstream institutions that workers most identified with, the Democratic Party and the CIO unions. Under the party's popular front strategy initiated in 1935, fascism loomed as a greater enemy than capitalism. American Communist Party members, seeking alliances with other progressive reformers, became supporters of Roosevelt and the New Deal, as well as crucial players in the CIO's drive to use collective bargaining legislation to organize America's factories. By the latter half of the thirties, workers who earlier had been wary of Communist disruption found that the party had joined the chorus exhorting the federal government to be more responsive.[22]

Although relatively few workers joined the party or voted Communist in the early 1930s, many thousands more were inspired by Communist and Socialist organizers to take to the streets in protest against the lack of jobs and relief and the prevalence of hunger and deprivation. Chicago, in fact, was an important national center for the organization of the unemployed. Here in 1930 the Communist Party held its founding convention of the National Unemployed Councils and established some of its first community councils. A year later Socialist activists affiliated with the League for Industrial Democracy founded a more moderate alternative, the Workers' Committee on Unemployment, which soon spread from Chicago to other cities. From their initiation through 1933, a period when local relief efforts were inadequate and disorganized, both groups rallied thousands of Chicago's unemployed of all races and ethnicities, along with sympathizers, to protest rent evictions, meager public relief provisions, and unfair treatment by social service agencies.[23]

Because these unemployed groups were not traditional political organizations with precise membership records, it is extremely difficult to determine how many workers belonged. In all likelihood, only a fraction of the city's population, at the most fifty thousand, considered themselves loyal rank-and-file members in the Communist Unemployed Councils or in locals of the Socialist Workers' Committee for Unemployment. But when an event like the October 1932 hunger march through downtown Chicago took place, many more joined in. Even those who stood on the sidelines, because they were employed or wary of joining a "radical" cause, were influenced by the strategies and demands of the more militant.[24]

In principle devoted to promoting Communist and Socialist alternatives to the political order, members of neighborhood locals of both organizations in practice were committed more to putting pressure on the existing system than to overthrowing it. Although famous for theatrically moving tenants and their furnishings back into apartments from which they had been evicted, unemployed groups were equally concerned with influencing the activities of the State of Illinois's Unemployment Relief Service established in the winter of 1932 to dispense the state and, by summer, federal money finally allocated for relief. Locals staged demonstrations almost daily outside relief stations but also worked tirelessly negotiating with case workers on behalf of neighborhood people with relief grievances. Securing rent and rations for someone like Mrs. Mary Brown, who had been refused relief on the false grounds that she still owned an insurance policy, was the nonsensational kind of activity that occupied a local. Some members surely participated out of ideological commitment to revolutionary politics, but with only a small number of Communist Party members in the city, these unemployed groups appealed far beyond that circle. A party organizer described honestly the attitude that was most common: "So what? Even if they are Communists, they are trying to help us help ourselves and no one else is doing that."[25]

The Communist Party learned quickly that to attract supporters to Unemployed Councils it had to subordinate its more radical agenda to the practical concerns of the rank-and-file unemployed whose dissatisfaction with capitalism tended to focus more on securing a better break today than promoting an alternative system for tomorrow. Sectarian issues like U.S. recognition of the Soviet Union and the "imperialist war danger" had to take a back seat. Steve Nelson, secretary of the Chicago Unemployed Councils for a time, recalled how Communist organizers had "spent the first few weeks agitating against capitalism and talking about the need for socialism." They observed quickly, however, that working-class people in the communities were more concerned with their daily struggles: "We learned to shift away from a narrow, dogmatic approach to what might be called a grievance approach to the organizing. We began to raise demands for immediate federal assistance to the unemployed, and a moratorium on mortgages, and finally we began to talk about the need for national unemployment insurance." When the Communists led protesters in a song like the "Life Insurance Racket Song," with its refrain of "They'd rob the old man of his burial right so we're fighting in the picket line," for example, they were appealing to one of the deepest anxieties of all working-class people, that they would lose their insurance.[26] The less confrontational Workers' Committee, which was founded by prominent Chicago progressives and operated out of the settlement houses and churches that they were affiliated with, was even more oriented toward mobilizing its more than twenty-five thousand members, organized in about sixty locals by mid-1932, to pressure the government to solve their immediate predicaments.

In their roles as watchdogs, both groups attracted several hundred, and at times even thousands, to mass rallies called over particular issues. By 1932, there were an average of ten relief protests a week in Chicago. In a rare and often tense collaboration, the Unemployed Councils and the Workers' Committee together drew 25,000 in the pouring rain, while thousands more watched, to a dramatic silent march through the streets of Chicago's Loop in late October 1932 to denounce a 50 percent cut in relief grocery orders. An observer described it as the biggest parade that Chicago had seen in years: "Rank after rank of sodden men; their worn coat-collars turned up, their caps – most of them seemed to be wearing caps – pulled down to give as much protection as possible.... Eight abreast. Closely massed. Stretching as far as the eye could see through the rain." "We want bread!" "We want work!" "Don't starve; fight!" read the placards of these determined marchers; the observer assured a by-stander who thought violence might erupt, "it wasn't a dynamiters' parade." Organizers claimed victory when a $6.3 million loan from the federal government's Reconstruction Finance Corporation staved off the cut. That a grant from the federal government constituted success testifies to the statist orientation of the unemployed groups.[27]

By 1934, for a variety of reasons, fewer workers were looking to these unemployed groups to express their discontent. Shrewdly, the state's Unemployment Relief Service and the Cook County Bureau of Public Welfare had centralized their grievance procedures into one public relations office in order to protect local stations from "harassment" by the organized unemployed. This action deprived locals of neighborhood targets for their protests. Locals were further neutralized through a new requirement that all complaints be submitted to a committee. Even more important, the New Deal's Federal Emergency Relief Act (FERA), in operation by the summer of 1933, channeled additional funds into the city and relieved the desperateness of the situation in a way that many of the unemployed had advocated. By the mid-1930s, the unemployed movement would itself become more centralized and bureaucratized under the aegis of a national coalition, the Workers Alliance of America. As the alliance lobbied for relief programs and represented the interests of WPA workers, who were, in effect, government employees, it increasingly forsook city streets for state legislatures and Washington.[28]

The decline of these radical groups by the mid-thirties, however, should not detract from their significance in the early years of the depression. Much more influential among workers than their small official memberships or sectarian affiliations might at first have indicated, they taught an important segment of Chicago's depression victims that being unemployed was not their fault and that they should join together to demand help, a lesson these workers would put to good use when they began to organize their factories several years later. Many organizers in the CIO would come directly out of the unemployed movement. In urging workers to ally with people of other races and ethnicities, the unemployed organizations gave a message not so different from the one delivered by Cermak's Democratic Party.

Organizers of both the Unemployed Councils and the Workers' Committee on Unemployment discovered early on that they were most successful when they structured locals around neighborhoods. Meetings could then be held in foreign languages and the memberships of ethnic organizations consistently tapped. In South Chicago, for example, a local of the Workers' Committee grew from its seven founders in March 1932 to over three hundred in a few months by drawing in members of Polish, Czech, and other national fraternal lodges and churches; it even mimicked the ladies' auxiliaries that existed in many of these organizations by establishing its own. Yet, at the same time that unemployed groups depended on narrowly defined community networks to recruit members, some locals and certainly the citywide organizations unified different racial and ethnic groups as "workers" around a common set of political goals. When the jobless from South Chicago, Back of the Yards, Little Sicily and most remarkably, the Black Belt marched shoulder-to-shoulder in October 1932 along downtown streets lined with Chicago's largest banks and corporate headquarters, they began to see with new clarity who were their allies and enemies and glimpsed as well the potential power of their collective action.[29]

Even more important than the actual relief increases and eviction suspensions that the unemployed groups won, they proved to dependent citizens that it was possible to get your way with government authorities. As one client temporarily "saved" from eviction by the "direct action" of his neighbors put it, "The Unemployed Council is built for action, not promises. The eviction was stopped. For three weeks, we could wait for recognition from a relief office. Our committee got it for us in fifteen minutes."[30] Even the police backed off in the face of organized, determined citizens.

Chicago's blacks felt particularly empowered by the movement. They were most drawn to the Unemployed Councils, where they attracted special attention from their Communist organizers. According to a study of the demographic makeup of Chicago's Unemployed Councils and Workers' Committees in 1934, blacks constituted 21 percent of the leadership and 25 percent of the membership of the Communist movement but only 6 percent of the leadership and 5 percent of the membership of the Socialist movement. Black participants gloried in standing up to landlords and police while singing the old spiritual "I shall not be moved" and in thwarting the efforts of the utility companies to turn off gas and electricity when bills went unpaid. With pride, they asserted their rights before social agencies that had long intimidated them. "It was a period of great learning," black Communist leader William Patterson remembered.[31]

By targeting the government as the solution to people's troubles, unemployed organizations helped workers look beyond their narrow communities and beyond private industry for their salvation. In the end, despite what the labels Communist and Socialist might at first have suggested, these unemployed groups served more to make people feel that the existing government could be made to work for them if they were unified than to channel dissent into radical alternatives. Although these workers may have marched when others merely voted Democratic, all of them became more oriented toward the federal government by the mid-1930s.

FROM WELFARE CAPITALISM TO THE WELFARE STATE

Voting in national elections and participating in the unemployed movement gave workers greater expectations for the state. Benefiting from New Deal programs made them dependent on it. Living as we do today in a world so permeated by the federal government, it is easy to lose sight of how much people's lives were changed by the expansion of federal responsibility during the 1930s. Even the conservative politicians of the late twentieth century who repudiate a strong federal government take for granted that working people will receive Social Security benefits upon retirement, that bank accounts will be insured by the Federal Deposit Insurance Corporation (FDIC), and that anyone who works will be assured a nationally set minimum wage. A world without these protections is hardly imaginable.

Despite the indisputable expansion of federal authority engendered by the New Deal, critics at the time, and even more so historians since, have nonetheless emphasized how improvisational, inconsistent, almost half-hearted the New Deal was. The reasons were varied. The Roosevelt administration was politically cautious, more oriented toward meeting emergencies than solving long-term problems, and most importantly, ambivalent, sometimes even fearful, about the growth of federal power that it was orchestrating. Critics rightfully point out that New Deal reforms failed to make the major social transformations, like the redistribution of wealth, that many progressives, including the workers Kornhauser interviewed, hoped for.[32] The American welfare state born during the depression turned out to be weaker than that of other western industrial nations such as England, France, and Germany. But a new direction nonetheless had been set. Most significant, workers made a shift from the world of welfare capitalism, where employers and voluntary associations cared, however inadequately, for their needs, to a welfare state, a reorientation that they would not easily reverse. This transition was particularly powerful for Chicago's workers because the basic services that they had looked to their ethnic communities and bosses to provide – welfare, security, and employment – and the depression endangered were taken over by the federal government. Although the New Deal may not have gone as far as many workers hoped it would, by providing welfare services, securing their homes and life savings, and offering them new jobs or reforming their old ones, the federal government played a new and important role in the lives of Chicago's working people.

The New Deal provided workers with federally funded relief programs, and eventually a permanent Social Security system, to take the place of the welfare previously dispersed by private organizations, often sponsored by their ethnic and religious communities. Federal assistance actually had begun through loans to the beleaguered states under Hoover's Reconstruction Finance Corporation. But it was the Federal Emergency Relief Administration (FERA), one of the first and most expensive creations of Roosevelt's New Deal, that regularized the national government's role in relief. Illinois was in such dire straits by the time Roosevelt took office in March 1933 that it became one of the first seven states to receive FERA funds. By the end of 1933, more than a third of Chicago's working population, including 44 percent of the city's blacks, looked to Washington for at least some of their keep, which put slightly more Chicagoans "on the dole" than was typical nationally.

It is true that FERA was designed as a shared undertaking between the federal government and the states. Of the $500 million first appropriated, half was intended to match dollars spent by the states, the other half as a discretionary fund for FERA's use wherever the need was greatest. But without a doubt, the national government shaped, and underwrote, this relief program. Between 1933 and 1935, the federal government provided 87.6 percent of the dollars spent on emergency relief in Chicago, in contrast to contributions of 11 percent by the state and 1.4 percent by the city. Even though state and local authorities administered the federal funds, everyone knew that the power lay in Washington. From the many relief recipients and unemployed organizations that lodged complaints against local relief operations directly with FERA chief Harry Hopkins or President Roosevelt to the caseworkers who feared Washington's reproof enough to beg clients not to write "as it causes... [us] a lot of trouble," it was generally agreed that the national government ruled relief. Mayor Kelly, in fact, fought efforts to return more of the administration of relief back to Chicago. The added patronage jobs were not worth the increased financial and social responsibility.[33]

The alarm of the Catholic Church in Chicago over this expanded relief role for the federal government testifies to its radical implications. The church recognized just how undermining of previous loyalties workers' new dependence on the federal government could be. Beginning in the summer and fall of 1932 and with increasing intensity over the next year as federal funding of relief grew, private charities withdrew from offering the kind of welfare they had struggled to provide before the national government stepped in. With FERA requiring that only public agencies could distribute its funds, private expenditures for relief in Illinois declined from a high of $8.3 million in 1932 to only $942,500 in 1935. Most agencies were grateful to be relieved of carrying a burden they were ill equipped to handle and redirected their energies toward helping families with specialized, often psychological problems such as domestic discord, vocational maladjustment, and parent–child conflict.[34] They were willing, moreover, to pay a price for their reprieve: that people would depend on the government the way they once had depended on them.

The Catholic Church, however, resisted this retrenchment. The Church hierarchy, which had long been working to consolidate its hold over Chicago's diverse Catholic population, mustered the considerable political clout it wielded in the city and in Washington, partly thanks to Archbishop Mundelein's friendships with Mayor Kelly and President Roosevelt, and in August 1933 had its Central Charities Bureau and Society of St. Vincent de Paul named a unit of the Illinois Emergency Relief Commission (IERC), the state's distributor of FERA funds. In other words, the church became an agent of the government in distributing federal and Illinois relief dollars. Disregarding the outrage of Chicago social workers, who denounced the ploy as a violation of both professional standards and the constitution's separation of church and state all the way up the relief bureaucracy to FERA chief Hopkins, the archdiocese took comfort that needy Catholics would benefit from new government aid while still being accountable to the Catholic Charities, the St. Vincent de Paul Society, and the priest.[35] The lengths to which the Chicago Catholic Church was willing to go to coopt this new federal welfare presence suggests how undermining it potentially was of workers' old dependence on private welfare agencies and benefit societies.

It has become almost an axiom among analysts of the Great Depression that Americans were ashamed to be on government relief because they saw dependency as one more sign, along with loss of work, that they had failed. The testimony of unemployed and underemployed workers that has survived from the Chicago experience, however, suggests a different story. Although some claimed to be too proud to go on relief and many preferred work relief to hand-outs, the vast majority defended the propriety of looking to the government for help. In the months before the federal government bailed out the struggling local relief effort, Thomas Jablonski complained bitterly, "America! What does America care for its children that it allows them to go hungry?" Another Polish-born Chicagoan argued for government intervention, "We are citizens of the United States, have been paying taxes . . . and are in dire need."[36]

Chicago workers felt that their American citizenship, voting records, and even military service so entitled them to relief benefits that their letters to Washington often revealed anger against foreigners who had not "earned" the privilege. For example, William Bowles, "an unemployed ex service man" who served his "Country and State since 1916, in the Regular Army and National Guards until August 1932 . . . born a Republican, Democrat by choice" wrote Roosevelt to complain of poor treatment at his Black Belt relief office: "Foreigners go there and get anything they ask for. . . . I think I am entitled to a little more justice from these people."[37] Likewise, Edward J. Newman, who had worked thirty years for employers including U.S. Steel and International Harvester, asked the president for help securing the "food, coal and cloathing and the necessity of life which we are deserving of as good Americans citizen. . . . I cannot see where Americans comes first you say this in your speeches why dont we Americans get what we are intitled to" [*sic*].[38] John Walsh asked President Roosevelt to prevail upon his Democratic ward committeeman or to write city hall: "They will take care of me Mr. President they are putting all forners [*sic*] to work and letting all the men of this Country Walk the streets."[39] Even the foreign born were not immune from claiming privileges; those who were citizens often demanded that they be treated better than those who were not.

These Chicago workers, like many others, were voicing new expectations for the state along with their prejudices. A social worker who had long held jobs in working-class districts of Chicago observed the change in attitude by 1934: "There is a noticeable tendency to regard obtaining relief as another way of earning a living. The former stigma attached to a family dependent on relief is gone and each family in a given neighborhood knows what, when, and how much every other family in a given neighborhood is obtaining from an agency. The men spend most of their time in the relief offices where they gather for recreational purposes while they await their turn to discuss their needs with the case workers." A truant officer who worked in the Black Belt concurred. When public relief meant being on the county rolls, many blacks had demurred out of pride. But now "this attitude had undergone a radical change. These people now demand relief and become indignant when a worker presumes to question their eligibility." Rather than feeling like beggars, workers felt they deserved benefits as citizens and more specifically for supporting FDR and the Democratic Party. It became more common for people to complain about the inadequacy and unsteadiness of relief benefits than to lament their own dependence on them.[40]

Working-class people were more likely than middle-class ones to feel justified taking government relief during the thirties. An extensive survey of the Indianapolis population completed in 1941 indicated that a greater orientation toward independence made middle-class citizens more resentful of their need for relief than workers. An aide to Hopkins made a similar observation in a letter to him in 1934: "Clients are assuming that the government has a responsibility to provide. The stigma of relief has almost disappeared except among white collar groups."[41] This situation concerned rather than pleased New Dealers, however. Ironically, the Roosevelt administration, which made federal relief possible, also began to teach people that they should feel ashamed to take it. Hopkins once admitted that in order to win acceptance of a work program to replace FERA, New Dealers "overemphasized the undesirability of relief." By the time recipients of federally funded WPA jobs got their official *Workers' Handbook* in 1936, they were being instructed[42]:

> What happens to us when we are on the dole?
> We lose our self-respect. We lose our skill. We have family rows.
> We loaf on street corners. Finally, we lose hope.

No sooner had workers shifted their dependence from the institutions of their local communities to the federal government than they began to be told that the state that offered them a hand could also bite. That the government went out of its way to teach working-class people to feel ashamed for being "on the dole" suggests that workers felt differently.

The federal government's new involvement in providing welfare was not limited to emergency relief measures. The Social Security Act, signed by Roosevelt in August 1935, established a permanent system of unemployment compensation, old age insurance, and aid for disabled and dependent children. Despite all the limitations of the act – the exclusion of many kinds of workers, the regressive payroll tax method of funding it, the small benefits, the administration of much of the system by the states – it is important not to lose sight of the strong impression it made on workers who had never before been offered any security by the government.[43] Social workers at the Chicago Commons Settlement were convinced that the residents of their neighborhood felt inspired by the creation of Social Security. "As the Social Security laws have begun to operate through the unemployment insurance act, the old age annuity and the old age pension, there has come to each individual a sense that he is joining with government and industry in an effort to build for the future," they wrote in the Commons Annual Report for 1937.[44]

Social Security also influenced people's day-to-day decisions about their lives. For a worker like Florence Parise, the prospect of benefits sent her back to work at the Kennedy Laundry in 1937, a job she had left several years earlier. Suddenly there was a future in the job. According to *Survey Magazine*, wage earners like John Pryblzka were realizing that Social Security provided them with a steadily increasing death benefit, making obsolete their "nickel-a-week" industrial insurance or ethnic benefit society policies.[45] Before the New Deal, a family with someone out of a job, old, disabled, abandoned, and even dead was at the mercy of family, friends, and community charity. In contrast, under Social Security, with all its limitations, a family had the right to benefits from the government.

Welfare was not the only responsibility of Chicago's ethnic communities that the federal government took over during the 1930s. In the 1920s, workers had entrusted their future security, in the form of savings and home mortgages, to ethnic banks and building and loan associations. People had felt confident that their investment was safe with the neighborhood banker or association officer. When these institutions encountered rough times during the depression, however, anxious depositors saw many of them fail, and the federal government come to the rescue of those that survived.

The banks that managed to endure Chicago's banking crisis of the early 1930s and reopened after the "national bank holiday" called by the president and Congress were all licensed as solvent by federal or state authorities. Customers, moreover, were assured of the federal government's continued backing through the FDIC, established under the Emergency Banking Act of 1933. "I was saved 'cause Roosevelt that time was elected" was how Salvatore Cosentino remembered the banking crisis of the 1930s.[46]

Many Chicago workers were so frightened by the failure of their local banks that they secured the federal government's protection of their hard-earned money in another way, by depositing it with the U.S. Government Post Office which was the only nonprivate thrift institution in America before the introduction of Social Security in 1935. The number of depositors with postal savings in Chicago grew from 13,614 in 1925 and 9,285 in 1929 to 121,091 in 1932 and 199,088 in 1935; between 1929 and 1935 those with postal savings increased more than 2,000 percent. Chicago and Detroit, moreover, had the highest amount of deposits per capita in the nation. A government report written in 1940 attributed Chicago's high rate to its ethnic population: "It would seem apparent that these large foreign elements are responsible for the unusually high total of Postal Savings in the area and that further these foreign persons are going to maintain their savings in 'Uncle Sam's' depository as a reserve against possible further banking troubles." The same report noted that people in Chicago were investing in U.S. savings bonds in record numbers as well. Having felt betrayed by the small banks and building and loan associations of their local communities, Chicagoans were now putting their savings where Uncle Sam could protect them.[47]

Salvatore Cosentino, whose bank savings were preserved by government action, was also among the many Chicago people who had government help holding onto another valuable asset, his home. Cosentino's home was one of the more than a million in the nation saved from foreclosure by the Home Owners' Loan Corporation (HOLC), which offered long-term, low-interest mortgages to eligible homeowners in urban areas who were unable to meet the terms of mortgage holders and faced loss of their property. Between 1930 and 1936, one in every four nonfarm dwellings in the Chicago area had been foreclosed or refinanced by the HOLC, which saved more than half of the threatened homes through granting 45,500 loans between June 1933 and June 1936. The HOLC was relatively active in the Chicago area compared to other cities. It refinanced twice as many homes in Chicago as in Philadelphia and San Francisco, the same amount as in Los Angeles and New York, but only half as many as in Detroit and Cleveland.[48]

Some critics have assumed that the HOLC was only helpful to the middle classes. A closer look proves that assessment incorrect. In a city like Chicago, many workers were homeowners, and in the midst of the depression, many of these people faced foreclosure. The HOLC, moreover, went out of its way to lend to owners of small and inexpensive homes. Sixty percent of the loans given in Chicago were in neighborhoods rated C or D in a system where A represented the most prosperous.[49]

Chicago's factory workers, who had sacrificed so much during the 1920s to buy their homes, were very grateful to the federal government for protecting them from foreclosure. Their reaction when they were turned down for HOLC loans, moreover, reveals how quickly they came to expect this government intervention as a right due them, much like relief. "My children served in the recent World's War, to make our United States a safe place to live in and protect our homes," complained Anna Cohen, a widow whose property was refused a HOLC loan because it included a store she rented out. Flory Calzaretta, disqualified on some other technical grounds, made a similar defense to President Roosevelt: "I am an American citizen for the past 30 years and my children were born in America, and as such I believe I am entitled to some consideration. Your Excellency made these loans possible for destitute cases just like mine." Barbara Ann Carter blamed foreigners for depriving her of a fair shake: "When we first applied and tried to get this loan over two years ago we found, by sitting there hours and hours that no one was getting any attention of loans but foreigners on the South Side."[50] No sooner had the federal government entered the mortgage business than Chicagoans counted on it being there.

As the national government stepped in to help workers protect their homes, ethnic institutions charged with that function became even weaker. It has already been established that ethnic building and loan associations suffered terribly in both reputation and finances during the

Plate 28. Many Chicago voters like those depicted here rallying for President Roosevelt's reelection in 1936 felt indebted to him because he "helped us save our homes." The federal government's Home Owners' Loan Corporation (HOLC) protected many workers' homes from foreclosure by offering long-term, low-interest mortgages. FDR and Uncle Sam were assuming a responsibility that previously had belonged to ethnic banks and building and loan associations.

depression. But the HOLC helped make the limping building and loan association even lamer. Building and loan associations accused the HOLC of hurting their recovery by overlooking their distressed loans and bailing out larger, more established banks instead. "The HOLC is ruining some of our institutions by prejudice against foreign people operating them," S. C. Mazankowski, Secretary of the Father Gordon Building and Loan Association and a director of the Polish American Building and Loan Association League of Illinois, complained bitterly. A more likely explanation, however, was that the HOLC rejected many association loans on the grounds that they were poor risks, having mortgages with inadequate security behind them or reflecting too high a percentage of the appraisal. Mazankowski confirmed this when he further grumbled "Our institution received from the HOLC about 46 cents for every dollar we had in property."[51] The source of the problem was that ethnic building and loan associations had served more effectively as community institutions with a social responsibility to their membership than as sound financial institutions. When the federal government began refinancing mortgages, it preferred the business practices of more stable, usually larger banks and thereby contributed to the demise of these smaller, often ethnic competitors.

In another way, the HOLC helped workers in the short run while hurting their ethnic and black communities in the long run. As part of its program, the HOLC sponsored a massive project rating all neighborhoods A through D or 1 through 4 so that property values could be easily assessed. Although the HOLC, with its government backing, was willing to give loans to people living in C and D areas, these ratings were later picked up by banks and used to discriminate against "declining" neighborhoods in granting mortgages and assessing property. Faced with fewer alternatives after the depression to the big banks that respected these ratings, workers became victimized for years by a "redlining" that originated with these HOLC classifications. My perusal of the Chicago HOLC Area Descriptions and Residential Security Maps indicates that judgments about neighborhood stability depended very heavily on race and ethnicity. Whenever foreign or black populations were observed, areas were automatically marked as "unstable." For example, a "blighted area of Poles and Lithuanians" near the stockyards received the lowest rating of 4 even though the report acknowledged that the "Lithuanian element" was thrifty and hence the neighborhood would probably "remain in a static condition for many years." Further deterioration was also unlikely, the report went on, because of "no threat, yet, of colored infiltration."[52] Many Chicago workers saved their homes in the thirties thanks to the HOLC, but the biases of its rating system ensured that many workers would have the HOLC to blame when the property values in their ethnic and black neighborhoods later deteriorated.

Whereas once people had consigned their most valuable assets to the care of ethnic community institutions, they now sought protection from the state. A large group of unemployed families interviewed shortly before many of these federal programs went into effect universally expressed rage at the local bankers who had lost their money, urging that "they be treated like crooks." They exhorted the government to take their place in safeguarding savings and mortgages: "If things keep up like this and the government doesn't realize it, there's going to be trouble. It doesn't feel good to be kicked out of your house."[53] Workers like these found tremendous comfort in the government's new activities. A hundredth anniversary book celebrating Polish contributions to Chicago, published in 1937, recognized that now Poles had someone outside their own community to thank for whatever economic success they could still claim eight years into the Great Depression: "With the aid of our splendid President, Franklin Delano Roosevelt, whose humanitarian interests resulted in HOLC and other security laws pertaining to homes, investments and savings, many thousands of homes and millions of dollars have been saved."[54]

Industrial workers found the federal government not only ensuring their welfare and security during the New Deal but also entering a third area that had long been outside the provenance of the state, employment. This was territory that previously had belonged almost exclusively to private employers. In the first phase of the New Deal, the Roosevelt administration tried through the National Industrial Recovery Act (NIRA) to get employers to voluntarily submit to industrywide "codes of fair competition," setting shorter hours of work and compensatory wage rates for their workers in return for production quotas, higher consumer prices, and a relaxing of antitrust restrictions for themselves. The hope was that government–business cooperation would promote national economic recovery by stabilizing production and keeping as many people working as possible.[55]

The voluntary character of the program, however, ensured that Chicago workers' experiences under the NRA varied tremendously. Some workers reported an improvement in working conditions. One of those, Agnes Castiglia, worked a forty-hour week instead of her usual forty-eight and earned two dollars more at the Traficanti Noodle Company. But others concluded that the NRA only legitimized hour and wage reductions. "I was getting 44½ cents an hour. The NRA came into effect, we got cut to 41½ cents an hour. That's the NRA," Frank Bertucci said cynically. And Antonio Palumbo, a cook at Brachs Candy Company, agreed: "NRA helpa the capitalist; didn't help the working-a people" [*sic*].[56] Many workers shared Bertucci's and Palumbo's experience that spreading the work around meant less for each individual worker. To a large extent, people's feelings about the NRA depended on how committed their industry was to the program. Employer enthusiasm ranged widely from electrical manufacturers like Western Electric who cooperated to the meatpackers who never even adopted an industry code.[57]

Overall, the NRA probably did more to heighten worker awareness that government could, and should, intervene in the private sector than to achieve concrete improvements. Letters from steelworkers in the Calumet region to President Roosevelt and NRA officials, for example, are filled with angry complaints of employer violations of the NRA and pleas for more direct intervention by Washington. In many cases, workers asked the government for protections, like minimum weekly hours and wages, that NRA legislation did not authorize. Before the NRA, it was unlikely that these steel workers would have brought complaints against their employers to the government.[58] Similarly, it will become clear in the next chapter that Section 7a of the NIRA, which required employers to let employees organize and bargain collectively through representatives of their own choosing, proved more meaningful for giving workers confidence that the government was behind them as they tried to organize than for establishing successful new unions. The NRA experiment in government–industry collaboration served mostly to whet workers' appetite for more state regulation of their working lives.

The federal government's involvement in employment extended to the creation of actual jobs, first as a part of relief and then, after 1935 with the WPA, in place of it. Job programs for the unemployed included the CCC, the Civil Works Administration (CWA), the Public Works Administration (PWA), the WPA, and the National Youth Administration (NYA). Although these programs are often remembered best for their contributions to the nation's cultural life – to art, theater, music, folklore, and so forth – the majority of the federal dollars went to employ manual laborers to renovate public facilities like parks, streets, sewers, and schools.[59] Factory workers who had been let down by private industrialists now found themselves working for the government. Observers commonly reported that the unemployed preferred these federal job programs to straight relief payments. "It is *work* we want, not *charity*," Mrs. Ellen De Lisle told President Roosevelt in requesting jobs for herself and her sons to supplement her husband's WPA check.[60] The government's job programs were not perfect. Workers vociferously complained about low salaries, uninspiring job assignments, and poor administration, including corruption. But as with relief, their gripes related more to these shortcomings in the programs than to their own dependence on them. A typical attitude was, "I gave the best part of my life to the American country, and I spent every cent I made here. They owe it to me to take care of me. If there is no regular work that I can pick up, they should find something for me to do."[61]

A wide cross section of Chicago workers flocked to job programs – seventy thousand assembled before sunrise on November 23, 1933, to register for the CWA – but blacks were particularly eager. Blacks suffered from higher unemployment than whites and knew they would be the last recalled to jobs in private industry. The typical WPA wage of fifty-five dollars a month, purposely low to discourage workers from remaining too long on the government's payroll, was welcomed by blacks who had few other options. Grace Outlaw, a writer with the Federal Writers' Project, captured this sentiment in her reconstruction of a conversation she overheard in the waiting room of the Illinois Employment Service in April 1939[62]:

Mae: You know something, us colored folks is losing ground every day . . . I been listening to that woman over there in the office and five outa every six calls she answers, wants whites only.
Miss Smith: It's the God's truth! . . . same way in the papers . . . all the ads but a few asking for white only . . . and on jobs where we used to always work too.
Mae: Lookit all the hotels . . . ain't hardly no colored boys in 'em no more and the red caps at the stations . . . ain't no such thing as colored folks work no more.
Miss Smith: I'm gonna get myself a a'phabet job just as soon as I can . . . they just as good and last longer than this private work . . . and you show don't work as hard neither.
Mae: You got something there, girl . . . my boyfriend's got one and he ain't work but six hours a day and ain't never work on Saddiys and Sundays . . . now you know that's a sender.
Miss Smith: But they ain't got no salary much . . . fifty-five dollars a mont.
Mae: When is you made fifty-five dollars in one mont?
Miss Smith: Well, come to think of it . . . I show ain't.

By 1939, a third of all people employed by the WPA in Chicago were black.

Blacks depended on the government for jobs, but they complained bitterly to WPA officials that they were discriminated against, always being dealt the most menial work. A group of WPA workers reassigned to common labor while their white colleagues got clerical jobs wrote President Roosevelt, "In all of your speeches, you have given us the impression that you are a God-fearing man and believe in the equality of men. If that be the correct diagnosis of your character, then we would like for you to know that the officials of the W.P.A. of Chicago, Ill are not treating us as God's children, but a God's step-children."[63] For many blacks the government proved no less discriminatory than

Plate 29. By 1939, a third of all people employed by the Works Progress Administration (WPA) in Chicago were black, suggesting how important federal programs like the WPA were to blacks' survival during the depression and to their political reorientation toward the Democratic Party and the national government.

private employers, except for one important difference: Blacks working in a federal job program had recourse. They could write to Washington to lodge complaints about their treatment locally, and in a surprising number of cases, action was taken. In many ways, being employed by the government during the New Deal gave blacks a taste of the kind of leverage they would demand during World War II when government and defense industries were compelled to practice fair employment. An anonymous black worker felt confident enough of his rights under the WPA to question Harry Hopkins "if it is legal for a Supervisor to descreminate [*sic*] the men working on W.P.A. Projects. Today the Supervisor came to a group of men working on Project 776 and asked for twelve men to water grass at night and said they must be white men. Do you think that is giving all men a square deal?" It was testimony to the sense of entitlement the WPA fostered among blacks that this man demanded an equal right to work at night in Marquette Park, a bastion of Chicago's Lithuanian community very hostile to blacks.[64] Consequently, even though working on the WPA was far from perfect, it was one of the New Deal programs most responsible for orienting blacks toward the federal government. As Frayser T. Lane of the Chicago Urban League put it, the WPA revealed to black citizens "just what the government can mean to them."[65]

The same way that the WPA recruited urban blacks, the CCC, and less so the NYA, made the state a concrete reality for a significant group of working-class young people from cities like Chicago. Although it may be hard to believe that youth from neighborhoods like South Chicago by the steel mills or Back of the Yards were the core of the two and a half million young men who went into CCC camps in rural Wisconsin, Oregon, and Washington to replant forests and conserve the soil, the evidence suggests it was so. The program was aimed at low-income boys with little educational or vocational background. Nationwide in January 1937, 37 percent of a sample of CCC enrollees had fathers who identified themselves as working in manufacturing and industry. Another 10 percent of the fathers did WPA or other emergency government work, making about half of the recruits boys who might have lived in Chicago's working-class neighborhoods. When a group of teenagers from South Chicago heard a rumor in September 1935 that the minimum age for entrance into the CCC camps had been lowered from eighteen to seventeen, they were jubilant. In no time the news spread like wildfire through the neighborhood, inspiring reactions like Harry's: "I wanna get in right away, by the first of October, if I can! We're getting help from the city and the county, so's I oughta have no trouble gettin' took." Upon their return from a year at camp, two Chicago youths testified to how much the experience had changed them, particularly how it had exposed them to different kinds of people from all over the country. They claimed that these "jobs" they had gotten with the national government had broadened their horizons beyond their families, neighborhoods, and even cities.[66]

Fortune magazine asked Americans of all income levels in 1935, "Do you believe that the government should see to it that every man who wants to work has a job?" Yes, replied 81 percent of those considered lower middle class, 89 percent of those labeled poor, and 91 percent of blacks, whereas less than half of the people defined as prosperous shared this view. The editors of *Fortune* concluded somewhat aghast, "public opinion overwhelmingly favors assumption by the government of a function that was never seriously contemplated prior to the New Deal."[67]

Workers were all the more enthusiastic about the government's new role in employment because their bosses deeply resented the state's intrusion into matters they considered their own prerogative. The evidence from Chicago argues powerfully against the "corporate liberal" analysis that the New Deal represented an effort by clever corporate capitalists to revitalize the economy with the help of a state that they dominated. Although industrialists may in the end have figured out ways of benefiting from reforms like the WPA, Social Security, and even the Wagner Act, they fought their introduction every step of the way. Organized business in Illinois managed to hold off the state legislation needed to implement various components of Social Security as long as possible. When the New Deal's most proindustry program, the NRA, was declared unconstitutional in May 1935, most employers breathed a sigh of relief, though they were to become much more antagonized by the next round of reforms, which included such hated legislation as the Fair Labor Standards Act of 1938. This law banned child labor and set a minimum hourly wage of $0.25 (gradually to be increased to $0.40) along with a maximum work week of forty-four hours (to be reduced within three years to forty hours) with time-and-a-half for overtime for all work related to interstate commerce. It was not so much these relatively low standards that bothered businessmen, but rather that the federal government was now empowered to intervene in matters that had long been out of its purview. "You have in these government attempts to control labor a tendency in the direction of a Fascist control of the worker, and through him of the industries, and through both control of the economic life of the country, and therefore control of its political life," an article in *Chicago Commerce* warned. Workers, however, viewed the state's growing involvement in their employment not as control but as needed protection against autocratic industrialists.[68]

When workers needed welfare, security for their savings and homes, and better jobs during the 1930s, they increasingly looked to the government they had put in office, not to their old community institutions or bosses. The situation of a family like the Ferks, which opened this chapter, would have been unheard of in the previous big depression of 1921. Fourteen years earlier, rather than writing to President Roosevelt about their government relief, mortgage, and job, the Ferks would have been begging for handouts from family, friends, neighborhood shopkeepers, former employers, and ethnic or religious welfare agencies. President Harding's government would have offered them nothing, and they probably would never have thought to ask. The decline of community institutions with the Great Depression and the rise of an activist welfare state that people felt had a responsibility to them profoundly changed the survival strategies of families like the Ferks.

THE MEANING OF WORKER STATISM

Chicago workers felt they were making a new deal during the 1930s when they became invested in national party politics and a national welfare state. In is important to consider, however, just how new that deal was and exactly what it meant that they made it.

Workers' faith in the state grew out of old as well as new expectations. On the one hand, they wanted the government to take care of them in much the same paternalistic way as they previously had hoped their welfare capitalist employers and their ethnic communities would do. This dependence on a paternalistic state is most clearly seen in the way workers viewed President Roosevelt. For many workers, FDR was the federal government. In the election of 1932, people voted against Herbert Hoover. By 1936 they were voting for Roosevelt on the grounds that "He gave me a job" or "He saved my home."[69] One unhappy husband who complained that his wife was now "wearing the pants" in the family reported that she rejected him on the grounds that now "F.D.R is the head of the household since he gives me the money."[70] As evident in the testimony presented in this chapter, distraught Chicagoans frustrated by the relief bureaucracy often appealed to Mr. and Mrs. Roosevelt for help. In enough instances to keep them asking, their appeals to "father" and "mother" Roosevelt were rewarded with action. Henrietta Malone was not alone in getting winter clothes out of her Chicago caseworker only after she had written the president. The files of New Deal agencies abound with letters, many on tattered pieces of paper in barely literate English, appealing to President Roosevelt for assistance.[71] People found it easy to look to him, moreover, because he went out of his way to cultivate an image as a fatherly figure concerned for the needy.

Workers' feeling that Roosevelt was caring for them in much the

Plate 30. When the owner of the Del Rio Italian Restaurant gave this portrait of President Roosevelt a privileged place over his bar, he joined many citizens in declaring a special relationship to FDR. Roosevelt went out of his way to cultivate an image of a fatherly figure, and people who had never before identified with a national political party or government found that FDR's paternalism made it seem less abstract.

same ways as their local communities and welfare capitalist employers had once promised to do helped personalize "federal power," which might otherwise have seemed so abstract. The woman who thanked the "government" for helping her out, saying "it sure is a blessing, too, to have sech [*sic*] a good government!" no doubt pictured Roosevelt personally making it all possible and rewarded him with her vote.[72] Even when people became frustrated with specific New Deal programs, they retained their faith in government by remaining confident of the president. Lorena Hickok reported back to Harry Hopkins in May 1936 that FDR enjoyed what today might be called a "can't lose" status among workers and even the unemployed. They gave him credit for any effort to improve conditions while absolving him of responsibility for problems ("he means right").[73] A Chicago man wrote FDR that he was sure the president could not "know whats going on around here."

Treatment of relief clients was extremely unfair, but "we know that it is not your falt but is the foult of those who are working in the relief stations" [*sic*].[74]

Workers in Chicago and elsewhere in the nation were looking to the federal government as they never had before, but the shock of that transition was cushioned by the way that they used the president to personalize the state. It was a rare worker's home where a portrait of Roosevelt, whether a torn-out newspaper image or a framed color photograph, did not hold an honored place. Eleanor Roosevelt later commented that after the president's death, people would stop her on the street to tell her, "They missed the way the President used to talk to them. They'd say, 'He used to talk to me about my government.'"[75] Martha Gellhorn's field report to Hopkins captured this strange and moving phenomenon, as true for industrial workers in urban Chicago as for the mill workers she visited in a southern textile town[76]:

> And the feeling of these people for the President is one of the most remarkable phenomena I have ever met. He is at once God and their intimate friend; he knows them all by name, knows their little town and mill, their little lives and problems. And though everything else fails, he is there, and will not let them down.

At the same time that workers projected their old paternalistic expectations of ethnic community and welfare capitalism onto the state, however, they were developing a new and somewhat contradictory notion that they were entitled to benefits from the government. Alongside a pattern of dependence grew a new claim to legitimate rights. By voting, by becoming Democrats, by supporting Roosevelt, by being citizens, by serving in the military, by spending their money in America, for all these reasons and more that workers quoted in this chapter have articulated, working people felt justified in their new sense of entitlement. With this notion of rights, moreover, workers were moving beyond the hierarchical authority relationships implicit in paternalism, which made them dependents. As contributing members of society, they made no apologies for taking relief, social security, FDIC insurance, HOLC mortgages, and CCC and WPA jobs from the state.

This sense of entitlement lay at the heart of the social vision that workers endorsed during the 1930s, a vision that is easily overlooked when the only tests applied to worker politics are capitalist or anticapitalist, moderate or radical. As Kornhauser discovered in 1937, workers advocated a form of political economy that can best be characterized as "moral capitalism." They did not reject private ownership of property but favored a form of capitalism that promised everyone, owner or worker, a fair share. A *Fortune* survey in 1940 was surprised to learn that "the man on the street wants more income than he has, but no more than that of many a government clerk." Apparently, American workers were dreaming neither of a dictatorship of the proletariat nor a world where everyone was a successful capitalist.[77] Rather, they wanted the government to police capitalism so that workers really would get that "new deal" they deserved. Kornhauser reported that the majority of workers favored empowering the government to redistribute wealth. The files of the WPA likewise are filled with letters from workers who felt it was legitimate to expect the state to apply moral standards of need in compensating WPA workers. "Do you by any means think that by giving a family of seven or eight, the same amount of money as family of one or two is being fair?" demanded one Chicago worker of the president. Interestingly, the form letter that the WPA sent in response to the many appeals it received for a more need-centered pay system explicitly rejected workers' moral capitalist perspective: "The Federal government, in superseding the program which included direct relief with a work program for eligible employable relief clients, took the position that all persons in a given occupation on a project should in general receive the same wages regardless of size of family, in accordance with traditional policies underlying employment, whether public or private."[78] In many ways, by urging the state to assign wages according to the standards of a moral capitalism, workers were advocating more of a new deal than did Roosevelt and his advisors.

Contrasting workers' expectations of the New Deal with those of the policymakers who created it introduces the issue of how distinctive working people's politics actually were. Workers' integration into the mainstream, two-party system could suggest that they had little ambition for a class-conscious politics. Indeed, industrial workers in Chicago were far from revolutionary; few voted Communist, and fewer still joined the Labor Party of Chicago and Cook County, which had a strong affiliation with the traditional craft unions of the Chicago Federation of Labor.[79] But that does not mean that workers had no sense of themselves as members of a working class distinct from the middle and upper classes. As a worker told an investigator in another city during the 1930s, "Hell, brother, you don't have to look far to know there's a workin' class. We may not say so. But look at what we do. Work. Look at who we run around with and bull with. Workers. Look at where we live. If you can find anybody but workers in my block, I'll eat 'em. . . . Look at how we get along. Just like every other damned worker. Hell's bells, of course, there's a workin' class, and its gettin' more so every day."[80] Chicago workers showed the same recognition of their class distinctiveness when they sent innumerable letters to Roosevelt and his advisors explicitly on behalf of "the working class people."[81] By voting Democratic and supporting the New Deal, many workers felt that they were affirming rather than denying their class status. American society was polarized enough in the midst of the Great Depression that workers could feel that supporting a sympathetic mainstream party like the Democrats was a way of pursuing their class interests. Many even went so far as to consider the Democratic Party a workers' party.

One might wonder if workers were deceiving themselves in believing that the Democratic Party really had their interests at heart. But many of their experiences reinforced that view. Foremost was the political language that Roosevelt used. It was the president of the United States, for example, not some rabble-rousing radical, who pledged himself when accepting his party's nomination in 1936 to take on the "economic royalists" who were fast creating a "new industrial dictatorship" that autocratically set the conditions of labor. "Private enterprise" had become "privileged enterprise." At many other times as well, workers heard Roosevelt lash out at their bosses and commit himself to protecting "the common man" and woman. The Republicans only helped FDR's image as the working person's president, determined to turn things upside down, by lambasting the New Deal as a dangerous break with the past, "one that is alien to everything this country has ever before known."[82]

This political rhetoric affected workers so powerfully because it fit well with the world they knew in Chicago. By the election of 1936, Chicago was polarized into political camps with definite class identities. In their factories, workers and their bosses were almost always on opposite sides. "Thes companys shure dont want you President" [*sic*], one steelworker wrote Roosevelt.[83] Eva Barnes learned that lesson the hard way. She arrived at her job assembling radios one day wearing a big Roosevelt button. When she was told to take it off and refused, "they said, 'You're for Roosevelt, you get out, you don't get a job.'"

Other Chicago employers made their preferences clear from the start by putting Alf Landon leaflets, which denounced FDR, into workers' pay envelopes.[84]

As workers took stock of political allegiances beyond their workplaces, in the city as a whole, they could not help but notice that even a place as Democratic as Chicago divided along class lines. In 1936, 81 percent of those with family incomes under a thousand dollars a year voted for Roosevelt, as did 79 percent of those earning one to two thousand dollars; in contrast, only 46 percent of people with family income over five thousand dollars pulled the lever for Roosevelt. Cutting it another way, FDR won 82 percent of unskilled and semiskilled worker votes and only 32 percent of major business executives and 39 percent of a white collar group like engineers.[85] Neighborhoods where well-to-do native whites resided were conspicuous Republican strongholds. A soloist at the elite Fourth Presbyterian Church of Chicago recalled getting up to sing at services the Sunday before election day in 1936 and looking out into a congregation of a thousand: "It was a sea of yellow. Everybody was decorated with large yellow Landon sunflower buttons. Just the impact of the thing suddenly made me realize there is such a thing as class distinction in America."[86] It was even obvious to eleven-year-old Dorothy Flowers, who told the president in a letter that "some people dont like you because you try to help poor people."[87] Few could dispute that Roosevelt was the worker's hero when Chicago Republicans, among them the city's most powerful newspaper editors, were regularly attacking the "dole," disparaging relief recipients as "parasites" and denouncing the WPA as "a shameless boondoggle."[88]

Workers' identification with the Democratic Party does not mean that they did not recognize some of the limitations of the New Deal and try to push it farther to the left. In many ways the National Labor Relations Act, Social Security, and other prolabor legislation like the Fair Labor Standards Act were testimony to the power of working-class voters who pressured for progressive state action. Even after favorable legislation was enacted, lobbies like the Workers Alliance and Labor's Nonpartisan League continued to seek improvements such as broadening those covered by Social Security, building more low-cost housing, and expanding public works jobs. But workers' ability to achieve much of the relief and security they sought through the Democrats, as limited as some of that legislation turned out to be, reinforced their sense that they had an important voice in the party. Though workers were participating in mainstream politics, they felt they were joining with men and women of other ethnicities and races to get themselves, as workers, a new deal.

Of course, the Democratic Party was not a labor party explicitly committed to pushing an essentially anticapitalist trade union agenda in the political arena. The Democrats had to keep happy a broad-based coalition, including conservative southerners and antiurban rural interests, which made all their programs less progressive than they might have been. And Roosevelt, despite a rhetoric of class carefully tuned to scare some people and win others, had some very traditional ideas about who should hold power in American society. The result, as mentioned earlier, was that the New Dealers showed more ambivalence toward using the state for reform than their working-class supporters and explicitly rejected – through, for example, the regressive way they structured new tax laws and social security – workers' vision of a moral capitalism that would redistribute American wealth. The paradox of workers' politicization through the Democratic Party during the 1930s was that they became invested in a party that they felt served their interests much more than it did. Workers learned to live in the American version of the welfare state so well that they accepted inequitable programs like unemployment insurance, which let states set variant and inadequate benefits, without voicing much criticism of the New Deal. To the extent that the New Deal perpetuated inequalities and offered some people more of a "raw" than a "new" deal, workers themselves bear some responsibility.

Workers nonetheless made an enormous shift during the thirties from the world of welfare capitalism to a welfare state. When their welfare capitalist employers and ethnic communities who had promised to care for them in the 1920s let them down in the crisis of the Great Depression, workers found a new protector in the state. In time, as they began to participate more in national politics, they grew to feel that that protection was something they deserved. The depression, rather than turning workers against the political system, as many at the time feared it might, tied workers to it more tightly than ever as they became party voters and the beneficiaries of government programs. It is very possible that the New Deal's impact should be measured less by the lasting accomplishments of its reforms and more by the attitudinal changes it produced in a generation of working-class Americans who now looked to Washington to deliver the American dream.

7
Becoming a Union Rank and File

Plate 31. The CIO's Steel Workers' Organizing Committee orchestrated this motorcade through the streets of South Chicago to celebrate its first contract with U.S. Steel in March 1937. Already, thousands of workers had joined this new industrial union, hoping it would deliver the prosperity, security, and job control they felt was possible under a more moral capitalism. Over the next few years, many other industrial workers in Chicago succeeded in establishing CIO unions in their factories until most of the city's mass production plants were organized by the end of World War II.

By the mid-1930s many of Chicago's manufacturing workers were involved in building a new institution of their own, a network of national-level industrial unions designed to make demands of the employers they held responsible for much of their suffering. Drastic hour and wage cuts, total disregard for seniority in layoffs and rehiring, deterioration of benefits, and rejection of any real collective bargaining despite the federal government's pledge under the National Industrial Recovery Act and later the Wagner Act to protect it – these and other abuses drove Chicago's factory workers to take action. Thousands of steelworkers, meatpackers, and makers of agricultural machinery bravely put their signatures on union cards, smuggled union material into their plants, met secretly to strategize, and orchestrated work stoppages and strikes when necessary to force their bosses to bargain collectively for better working conditions. Workers acted despite fear of reprisals from employers whose power over them had grown as the depression shut off the "safety valve" of quitting utilized in the 1920s.

By 1940, one in three workers in Chicago manufacturing had become a union member. In plant after plant, workers won contracts from their employers, or at least demonstrated their support for the new unions affiliated with the national Congress (initially Committee) of Industrial Organizations (CIO). In a show of remarkable unity, workers joined with their co-workers of different races, ethnicities, ages, and sexes as well as gave support to peers organizing in other factories in Chicago, in the sister plants of national corporate giants like U.S. Steel or International Harvester, and in competing firms within an industrial sector such as meatpacking. This time, a decade and a half after the last unsuccessful effort to organize Chicago's mass production plants, workers would not let their opponents conquer them by dividing them. Well-organized, national-scale corporations would at last meet their match.

Workers looked to their new unions under the CIO to complement the state in providing them both with the security that ethnic groups and welfare capitalists had once promised and the equity that their vision of "moral capitalism" was leading them to expect. In this way, their ambitions were both material and ideological. The first president of the Steel Workers' Organizing Committee (SWOC) local at Inland Steel recognized that by the end of the 1930s workers had accomplished something much more fundamental than the achievement of any simple policy or demand. They had dramatically changed the way they related to the state and their employers: "A movement of the kind that we had in the Steelworkers Union and in the CIO was a movement that moved millions of people, literally, and changed not only the course of the working man in this country, but also the nature of the relationship between the working man and the government and the working man and the boss, for all time."[1] The men and women who produced the essential materials of modern American life – steel, automobiles, packaged food, and the like – had demanded, and were beginning to receive, a say in the two institutions that wielded the most power over their lives: the state and the corporation. In some of Chicago's factories, it would take the return of prosperity during World War II and, even more importantly, the government's intervention with wartime controls to force recalcitrant employers to recognize CIO unions organized by their workers. But in all plants where the CIO would represent workers by the end of the war, the groundwork was laid during the 1930s. Understanding how, why, and to what end workers succeeded in organizing themselves during the thirties is, therefore, of crucial significance.

Each Chicago plant that workers organized had its own complex and often dramatic story of how the majority of ordinary people working there became willing to put themselves on the line for a union, breaking the "industrial peace" of the previous fifteen years. Among the first plants organized in Chicago were ones we have been following throughout this book, U.S. Steel's South Works and Gary Works, Armour and Company, and International Harvester's Tractor and McCormick Works. In each of these plants, a unique scenario unfolded out of the convergence of specific individuals with particular industrial contexts. Although the bulk of this and the next chapter will move beyond these cases to generalize more broadly about the CIO's experience in Chicago, some background about the union drive among steelworkers, meatpackers, and agricultural implement workers is necessary.

STORIES OF STRUGGLE

The CIO's first Chicago success was in the mills of U.S. Steel, its South Works in Southeast Chicago and its Gary Works several miles away in northern Indiana. The push for a new union grew out of the company union that management had instituted in 1933 when the NIRA went into effect. U.S. Steel, like many other employers, had hoped that by resurrecting the old welfare capitalist strategy of the Employee Representation Plan (ERP), the company would satisfy the new requirement in the NIRA's Section 7a that workers be allowed to bargain collectively through representatives of their own choosing. It did not take long, however, for a core of employee representatives at both plants to recognize how biased the company unions were in management's favor. At these mills, as at others in the country during 1933 and 1934, disenchanted employee representatives and other rank-and-file workers turned to the moribund AFL craft union that had sponsored the unsuccessful organizing drive of 1919, the Amalgamated Association of Iron, Steel and Tin Workers (AAISTW), in hopes of reenergizing it. After this effort failed primarily because of AAISTW intransigence, frustrated representatives at South Works formed their own union, the Associated Employes of South Works, to push for what workers were demanding, and not getting, from the company union. By this time, discontent was so rife in the plant that when the Associated Employes called its first public meeting at South Chicago's Bessemer Park in the fall of 1935, almost a thousand workers showed up.

By June 1936, the Associated Employes of South Works claimed a majority of the elected employee representatives, a membership of three thousand steelworkers (about a quarter of the work force), and an active women's auxiliary of wives, daughters, and other female supporters. At just about this time, the CIO, which was established the previous November by labor leaders disgusted with the AFL's refusal to endorse industrial unionism, made its own move to organize the nation's steel mills. CIO leader John L. Lewis, who built his career running the United Mine Workers (UMW), struck a deal with the impotent AAISTW to pass its organizing mission as well as its legal lodge chartering authority to a new CIO-affiliated entity, the Steel Workers' Organizing Committee (SWOC), in return for a UMW contribution of $500,000 to the campaign. Lewis entrusted this first CIO drive, with its ambitious goal of organizing the largest of the basic industries, to his long-time deputy, Philip Murray, vice-president of the UMW.

Miners had long vilified the big steel companies for being vicious antiunion operators in the coal fields, and Lewis was determined to make the organization of steel a priority of the newly formed CIO. He knew, moreover, that steel was ripe for the CIO's harvesting because of how prevalent the kind of grassroots, rank-and-file activity that had taken place at the South and Gary Works was throughout the nation's mills. Workers had been agitating within their own plants for higher wages, shorter hours, seniority rights, paid vacations, union recognition, and grievance procedures. Now the CIO's SWOC promised a more coordinated effort so needed against the "Steel Barons."

In July, the Associated Employes of South Works voted to affiliate with SWOC, becoming Lodge 65, its first local. The next month, at a meeting in Gary, the Calumet Council of Employee Representatives, drawn from all the steel plants in the area, followed suit, increasing immeasurably the momentum of the CIO's campaign in the Chicago area. Those whom U.S. Steel had hoped would placate the rank and file were instead becoming its rebel leaders. As journalist Mary Heaton Vorse put it, the company unions had proved "a Frankenstein's monster to the employers who created them."[2] Though U.S. Steel tried to undermine the SWOC's appeal in the fall of 1936 by granting workers paid vacations and a 10 percent wage increase, membership in SWOC continued to grow. By early 1937 the leaders of the SWOC could claim that half of the workers in South Works and Gary Works were members, along with increasing numbers in neighboring Calumet district mills and over 100,00 nationwide. In the Chicago region, as elsewhere, over thirty groups of women's auxiliaries were assisting the drive, testimony to how deeply committed steelworking families were to the fight for a union.

Acknowledgment of the strength of the new steelworkers' union came in March of 1937, when Myron Taylor, president of U.S. Steel, announced that he had met secretly with Lewis and the company was ready to sign a contract. The surprising news came a month after the CIO's auto workers won a hard-fought victory over General Motors. Convinced of SWOC's tenaciousness, U.S. Steel dared not risk a lengthy confrontation with workers just when precious orders were coming in from a Europe preparing for possible war. Without having to call a strike or sit-down but with a show of force that grew even stronger once the steel contract was signed, workers at the largest steel company in the nation, employing almost half of all steelworkers, and bastion of the open shop achieved many of the demands they had been seeking: wage increases of about 10 percent on a scale where minimum pay was now five dollars a day, a forty-hour week with time-and-a-half for overtime, a week's paid vacation after five years, seniority rights in promotion and work force increase or decrease, a grievance procedure with arbitration when necessary, and most important in many minds, a recognition of the union and a commitment to bargain collectively with it. It would take several more years, bloodshed, and the pressure of wartime to break "Little Steel" – such firms in the Calumet region as Republic, Youngstown Sheet and Tube, and Inland – and for the SWOC, renamed the United Steelworkers of America in 1942, to be allowed to represent all workers, not just its members, in U.S. Steel plants. But until then the SWOC–U.S. Steel contract generally set the terms for all steelworkers. In the Chicago area, for example, firms like Republic and Inland matched many of U.S. Steel's new standards immediately, even though they held out against signing a contract with the CIO until 1942. What had begun as a small grassroots effort within several Calumet area steel mills and in other steel regions such as Pittsburgh mushroomed over several years into a powerful movement of national proportions.[3]

The relative ease with which steelworkers won a contract at U.S. Steel contrasts sharply with the experience of packinghouse workers at Armour and Company and agricultural equipment makers at International Harvester. But greater resistance by these employers only resulted in more militance on the part of their workers who had to fight all that much harder to win a union.

The CIO battle in meatpacking began later, lasted longer, and was a nastier fight than the steelworkers had faced. While steelworkers were carrying on their grassroots organizing in 1933–4 with the stimulus of the NRA, there was some equivalent early activity in the stockyards. The Amalgamated Meat Cutters and Butcher Workmen of North America, the long-established AFL craft union that had betrayed unskilled packing workers in the early 1920s, made some effort to exploit worker discontent during the depression. But the Amalgamated remained essentially uncommitted to industrial unionism in packing, much like the Amalgamated in steel. What successful organizing took place could be credited to a reborn Stockyards Labor Council, whose antecedent had represented the unskilled in the 1919 era, and a Communist union, the Packinghouse Workers' Industrial Union, part of a union drive resulting from the party's move above ground in the early 1930s. The ranks of all of these movements, however, were small, particularly in the big packing plants of Armour and Swift. More activity took place in the smaller packing companies, where veterans of the 1919 era had retreated after being blacklisted by the big employers and were now allying with

tion Plans, which had been around since 1921, long enough for packinghouse workers to be convinced of their ineffectiveness.

It took the organizing activity during 1935–7 in nearby steel communities and reports from labor "hot spots" further away like Akron and Flint to arouse the mass of packinghouse workers. As the excitement of building a real industrial union spread to Packingtown, a delegation committed to organizing the stockyards solicited help from Van Bittner, the CIO official running the SWOC campaign in Chicago. When Bittner asked for proof that the rank and file of packinghouse workers would be behind the effort, organizers collected two hundred signatures within just two days on small mimeographed cards inscribed, "I want a union in the packing industry." Within a month's time during the winter of 1937, over a thousand had signed. Later that year, on October 24, the Packinghouse Workers' Organizing Committee – CIO (PWOC) was officially established at a meeting of delegates from plants all over the country. The CIO's Bittner was named chairman.

Over the next four years, the PWOC battled against packers determined not to recognize unions, despite work stoppages, National Labor Relations Board (NLRB) elections, and federal orders. In the process, however, the rank and file of packinghouse workers became all the more committed to the union. The PWOC decided to target Armour first, since it had both the largest work force and the most repressive industrial relations practices. By October 12, 1938, the PWOC won a majority in an election and, thereby, certification from the NLRB, but Armour refused to recognize the results. The fight got dirtier, with the company firing union members, promoting company unions in various guises, and even sponsoring violent assaults on union leaders, while workers on the floor fought a guerilla war of slowdowns and work stoppages over grievances. Finally, in November 1939, another NLRB election demonstrated that the CIO had an overwhelming margin in the main Chicago Armour plant, and with the PWOC threatening a national strike and the Department of Labor pressuring for a settlement, the company relented. But it only agreed to sign a plant-by-plant contract, not the master contract covering all Armour plants that the PWOC was seeking. That would not come until 1942.

Meanwhile, however, Armour workers in Chicago won the same kinds of benefits as the CIO's steelworkers had, along with special protections that they felt they needed given the irregularity of work in packing: a guaranteed thirty-two-hour week, survival of seniority rights for a year rather than sixty days in the case of a layoff, and a commitment to equal pay for equal work. Before the battle was won at Armour, moreover, workers in the "Little Six" Chicago packing plants and the Union Stockyards streamed into the CIO and gained contracts, some with such advanced provisions as the dues checkoff and the closed shop. At the larger Swift and Wilson, workers would not get contracts until the early 1940s, but by 1938 the PWOC was already the organization to be reckoned with there. Locals in these plants had large and active memberships that made it possible for the PWOC to establish grievance machinery before official recognition. By July 1939, the PWOC would claim that about two-thirds of the 128,000 packing workers in the nation were CIO members.

The bitter battle that these rank-and-file packing workers fought against employers deadset against unionism carried over to the kind of union they eventually created for themselves. In 1943 the PWOC demanded its own international, the United Packinghouse Workers of America (UPWA), to gain independence from the CIO's controlling cartel dominated by former miners. Whereas the United Steelworkers of America became increasingly conservative politically and bureaucratic administratively, the UPWA for many years remained a left-wing union deeply committed to union democracy and racial equality.[4]

The third stronghold of the CIO in Chicago was the Farm Equipment Workers' Organizing Committee (FE), which orchestrated the union struggle at International Harvester. Here victory was as hard to achieve as in packing, and an equally militant, left-wing union resulted. Whereas Armour fought the PWOC with strong-arm tactics, International Harvester, the McCormick family firm long proud of its welfare capitalist tradition, tried to inject new life into its old commitment. Soon after the NRA went into effect in 1933, management did such things as reinvigorate the Harvester Works Councils (its ERP plan), liberalize vacations, resurrect its Extra Compensation Plan of cash bonuses, grant wage increases, promise time-and-a-half for overtime, begin a new series of plant magazines, and organize foremen's conferences to discipline supervisors. The company was determined to show that workers could get what they wanted through their works councils, without "outside" unions. When the Supreme Court finally ruled the Wagner Act constitutional in April 1937 and Harvester was forced to abandon company turned to so-called independent unions started by loyal employee representatives who were very much under management's thumb. U.S. Steel and Armour had tried the same strategy, but with less ideological commitment than Harvester. Despite several NLRB rulings that International Harvester unfairly fostered and dominated labor organizations in its plants, the company persisted in favoring "inside" unions over the FE.

But in all of Harvester's plants except Wisconsin Steel, an important exception to be examined later, this new wave of welfare capitalism could not keep workers from embracing the unionism rampant throughout the nation's mass production factories. As early as 1933, energized by FDR's election and the possibilities of the NRA, rank-and-file workers pressured their previously quiescent council representatives to demand wage increases and other benefits. At Harvester's Tractor Works, employee representatives to the works council even formed an underground union, the ABC Union, which became a vehicle for organizing the plant much like the Associated Employes of South Works. By late 1936, a majority of Tractor employees supported the ABC Union, but Harvester's management refused to recognize it. Undaunted, the ABC Union turned to SWOC for help. By summer 1937 Bittner had assigned SWOC organizer Joseph Weber to establish a separate arm to organize the farm equipment industry, which became the FE. Finally, when two-thirds of Tractor workers voting in an NLRB-supervised election in 1938 chose the FE over the company's so-called independent union, Harvester relented and recognized it, making Tractor Works the first International Harvester plant to win a CIO union. It would take several more years, however, for Tractor employees to pressure management into giving them the wage increases, fairer piecework rules, and seniority protections that had driven their campaign for a contract. But workers at least had won the first battle of union recognition. Two nights after the NLRB victory in February 1938, euphoric employees of Tractor Works celebrated with a mock funeral procession past most of Harvester's Chicago plants. Two black hearses bearing the sign "The Death of Company Unionism at International Harvester" carried a warning to the company's other installations in Chicago.

From 1937 until 1941, FE gained members at Harvester's other plants, but the layoffs that accompanied the recession of late 1937–8 made the prospect of winning more NLRB elections uncertain. The giant McCormick Works, kingpin of the Harvester empire, was the prize most sought after by FE organizers, but there, for example, workers' ranks were decimated from a high of 8,343 in 1936 to 4,841 in 1939. Unionists feared that job insecurity would dampen political commitment. The struggle at McCormick Works came to a head in 1941 when the NLRB finally ruled on charges filed three years earlier by the FE, finding, not surprisingly, that the company had consistently interfered with employees' rights to organize themselves and ordering the dissolution of the so-called independent unions. The FE, nervous that it would lose NLRB elections, opted instead to close down four large plants including the McCormick Works, positioning itself to demand recognition as the price of reopening the plants. The strike did not last, however, and a vote became unavoidable when the AFL, providing a new cover for the challenged independent union, called the FE's bluff and demanded an election. When elections were held in six Harvester plants in June and July of 1941, to its own surprise the FE won in four of them, the central McCormick Works included. The rank and file's CIO sympathies ran deeper than even the union's organizers had dared hope. Fifty-five years after a union had been crushed at McCormick Works following the Haymarket tragedy, workers had finally brought one back. This complex campaign against a union opponent as indefatigable as International Harvester had required a union strategy of persistence and militance. The FE continued to deliver both in the years that followed as contentiousness with Harvester management, and even within the CIO as a less radical United Auto Workers battled the FE for jurisdiction in many plants, became a way of life.[5]

The narratives of these three union organizing campaigns in Chicago manufacturing raise more questions than they answer about how and why they happened, the relationship between rank-and-file workers and CIO organizers, and the meaning of these union struggles to the workers themselves. It is much easier to reconstruct events than to recapture the meaning of those events to the workers who participated in them. Moreover, although there are consistent patterns in all three stories, there are also important differences, such as that packing and agricultural equipment workers ended up with more radical unions than the steelworkers. The diversity in workers' experiences does not stop there. Two manufacturing plants in the Chicago area where the CIO never got a footing, despite its efforts, constitute the other, more conservative end of the spectrum. The Hawthorne Works of Western Electric and the Wisconsin Steel Works of International Harvester had stood out as [illegible] capitalism since the 1920s. Characteristically, workers in these plants continued to support so-called independent unions founded with management's backing after company unions were outlawed by the Wagner Act, even against CIO opponents in NLRB elections. When the bulk of Chicago's industrial workers were represented by CIO unions by the early 1940s, employees at Hawthorne and Wisconsin Steel stood apart. As spotty as the evidence is about what industrial workers actually thought, there is enough of a record left to probe first the attitudes and actions of those who joined the CIO and then why other workers chose the more accommodating path of supporting the "company unions" favored by their bosses.

HOW AND WHY THE CIO

The major question to be answered is how the bulk of Chicago's factory workers, who tried valiantly before but in the end always failed, managed during the 1930s to organize themselves into unions that their bosses, by the early 1940s, were forced to recognize. The narratives of these three union campaigns make one thing clear. Workers did not succeed because their employers were obliging.

Two kinds of factors explain workers' success in organizing. First, there were facilitating factors that created a favorable environment for unionization in the 1930s, specifically the support of the state and the assistance of a skilled union leadership. Second, changes occurred in the attitudes and behavior of rank-and-file workers. Many analyses of the CIO's triumph in the thirties stress the former, the importance of new external forces that broke a long-standing deadlock between workers and employers. A New Deal state more favorable to labor and a new generation of union leaders determined and able to organize industrial workers nationwide are often seen as the crucial catalysts behind the CIO's success. It is my contention, however, that without new kinds of commitment by ordinary factory workers, the help of neither the state nor union organizers would have been adequate to achieve such a major breakthrough.[6]

There is no denying that government support of the unionization drive made a huge difference. It gave legal assistance and legitimacy to industrial workers' long-standing efforts to organize. Rather than being thwarted at every turn by local police intimidation or state court injunctions or unfavorable federal legislation, workers for the first time found government at many levels and in its many branches on their side against the autocracy of employers. The Norris–LaGuardia Act of 1932 severely limited the use of injunctions against unions. The NIRA of 1933 asserted the right of workers to organize unions of their own choosing in its celebrated Section 7A and made some provision, although inadequate, for enforcement, through such bodies as the National Labor Board and the industry-specific National Steel and Auto Labor Relations Boards. Most importantly, the National Labor Relations Act (NLRA, also known as the Wagner Act), enacted July 5, 1935, fully institutionalized the government's commitment to workers' rights. The act established a National Labor Relations Board (NLRB) and granted it the power to investigate and prohibit any efforts by employers to "interfere with, restrain or coerce employees in the exercise" of their "right of self-organization." For workers, this meant that they could not be fired for joining a union, that the government would go after employers engaged in illegal, union-busting activities, and that they had a clear mechanism for selecting their bargaining representatives, a majority vote in an election that the NLRB, not the employer, would supervise. Industrial workers and their organizing committees, SWOC, PWOC, and FE, among others, lost no time taking advantage of this new legal structure for securing a union. By mid-1941, the NLRB had held nearly six thousand elections and petition cross-checks, involving nearly two million workers.

Other governmental action also facilitated workers' organization. In the legislative branch of the federal government, Senator Robert LaFollette's Senate Sub-Committee Hearings on Violations of Civil Liberties exposed the prevalence of corporate-sponsored spying and other sorts of illegal repression of workers' rights. In the judicial branch, the Supreme Court's ruling in April 1937 that the Wagner Act was constitutional forced those employers who had been holding out against the NLRB in the hope that it would be found unconstitutional to surrender to it. "When the Wagner Act was upheld," a Swift organizer recounted, "I knew that the CIO for the first time had the chance of success it deserved." In the executive branch, the Department of Labor under Frances Perkins put pressure on resistant companies like Armour and International Harvester to come to the bargaining table. When CIO organizers told industrial workers that "the President wants you to organize," they were referring to all the ways that Roosevelt's New Dealers demonstrated their commitment to labor.[7]

Even on the state and local levels of government there was a change. When Inland Steel refused to sign a contract directly with the SWOC during the "Little Steel" strike of spring 1937, Governor Townsend of Indiana maneuvered on labor's behalf and convinced Inland to sign an agreement with him that the union, too, endorsed. Townsend's state government also assumed responsibility for settling disputes that the plant's grievance procedures could not. Mayor Kelly of Chicago, after making the mistake of backing up Republic Steel with Chicago police pistols when the company refused to let SWOC strikers picket, a confrontation that led to the bloody Memorial Day Massacre of 1937, repented and gave the CIO so much support that a victim of the massacre, a steelworker who had lost his eye, publicly proclaimed during the mayoral campaign of 1939 that Kelly now deserved labor's votes. The year before, for instance, livestock handlers finally had gotten a contract out of the Union Stockyards when the mayor threatened to shut off the company's water if it didn't respect an NLRB election.[8] The state that workers were becoming increasingly invested in as Democrats and as citizens was standing by them at the workplace as well.

But this "whig" history of the state's growing role in industrial relations on behalf of labor overlooks the extent to which the pressure of rank-and-file workers brought about the support of the New Deal state as well as how mixed in impact much of this governmental action was, necessitating additional pressure from the rank and file to achieve its promised ends. In short, to a large extent it was the actions of workers that ensured these new protections by the state.

It took strikes and other agitation by rank-and-file workers to move Roosevelt's administration from a symbolic but unenforceable acknowledgment of workers' right to organize under the NRA to the establishment of real machinery to facilitate unionization through the Wagner Act. Although the NRA "had no teeth," in the words of PWOC unionist Arthur Kampfert, it unleashed a torrent of pent-up enthusiasm for organization and thereby created pressure for more coercive legislation like the Wagner Act. Widespread work stoppages in the months after the passage of the NRA made 1933 a more militant year than any since 1921. To be sure, the violent strikes initiated by auto workers in Toledo, teamsters in Minneapolis, and longshoremen in San Francisco during 1933 and 1934 most alarmed FDR and his lieutenants, but so too did the calmer grassroots organizing of industrial workers like those who made steel and tractors in Chicago. Steelworkers' strategy of threatening a national steel strike in June 1934, in fact, was designed specifically to force the president to intervene, which he minimally did when he established a National Steel Labor Relations Board. When that agency proved as powerless as all the other NRA labor boards, steel activists tried their best to keep pressure on Roosevelt and NRA chief General Hugh Johnson, while turning most of their attention to coopting the company-dominated Employee Representation Plans within their own plants.[9]

Refusing to be constrained by the NRA's limitations, workers like those at U.S. Steel's South Works and Harvester's Tractor Works transformed the ERPs that proliferated under the NRA into launching pads for more genuine unions. "When management came along with what I call the bastard child – the company union – when they handed us that, that opened up my eyes . . . and they didn't realize that a guy like me might someday turn on them, which I did," recalled South Works leader George Patterson proudly.[10] The NRA proved more powerful in raising workers' expectations and inciting them to demand further government assistance than in delivering significant state support in itself. As Herbert March, a leader in the effort to organize the packinghouses, put it, "While the workers had no rights [under the NRA], the illusion that they had rights had its impetus on their moving and fighting and stirring. People by that time had had it up to here – up to their ears. They had come through a real period of suffering and oppression and they were ready to revolt."[11]

Workers also used their electoral power to pressure New Deal policymakers. The upset of the 1934 election, when conservative Republicans were effectively voted out of Congress, proved beyond a doubt the power of new, working-class Democratic voters. By 1936, organized labor had come up with a strategy to maximize the bargaining power of workers' votes, establishing a Non Partisan League to rally behind government policies and policymakers deemed worthy of workers' support. "Every worker owes it to himself, his family, his union and his country to go to the polls himself, and to see that his fellow workers go too, to cast their votes in organized fashion for the labor-endorsed candidates," the *CIO News-PWOC Edition* instructed packinghouse workers in November 1938. At the city level, the Chicago CIO's threats to withdraw workers' votes from Mayor Kelly after the Memorial Day Massacre made him a much more prolabor mayor thereafter. Workers related to the state as unionists much as they did as citizens. Their growing political participation made them feel entitled to government help. The limitations of legislation like the NIRA inspired rather than disillusioned them to seek more effective state intervention. In the words of Leslie Orear, an early CIO activist in Chicago's packinghouses, "Before the New Deal people thought of the government as somebody else's. Part of the rich world's affairs. Then, this sudden notion that 'By God, the government can do something for us!' was a sensational revelation. The sense of empowerment that came with the Wagner Act was absolutely stunning."[12]

Although the Wagner Act was a big improvement over the NRA, it still had limitations that required rank-and-file workers to keep the pressure on employers at the shop floor. To begin with, it remained too easy for companies to ignore NLRB rulings. Armour refused to recognize the results of NLRB-supervised elections while International Harvester persisted in illegally promoting "independent" unions that it dominated. Companies like these also took advantage of the legal maneuverings possible under the act to stall for time. Harvester's well-paid team of attorneys deserves part of the credit for the more than three years it took for the NLRB to rule on charges brought by the FE.[13] As a result, at these packing and agricultural equipment plants, as at many others throughout the country, workers resorted to slowdowns and other kinds of shop floor actions to keep the heat on their employers. When, for example, Armour refused to recognize the PWOC after a fair election, workers responded with a plant wide "whistle bargaining" strategy of meeting every grievance with a secret signal to stop work. Another approach, called the "Rizz-ma-tizz," gave the illusion that workers were producing normally while in actuality they were slowing down to keep their foreman from making his quota. "Stop and Go" strikes similarly foiled company efforts to plan production. One week workers in a department would lower their output, the next week they would work beyond expectations so supplies would run out. An Armour unionist explained that these work slowdowns, stoppages, and walkouts had a crucial symbolic value: "This demonstrated to all . . . that the CIO had plenty of stuff on the ball and that there was no such thing as 'waiting for something to happen.'" Even simple acts of defiance, like throwing old washers into the sugar barrels scattered throughout U.S. Steel plants by company unionists hoping for monetary evidence of workers' loyalty, sent an unmistakable message.[14]

The Wagner Act necessitated shop floor activism not only because of weaknesses in its bureaucratic procedures but also because of its supposed strengths. By requiring unions to win by majority vote, the NLRA forced them to gain widespread support in the plants they were organizing. As FE leaders at the McCormick Works knew well, a small group of militant workers could close down a plant like the McCormick Works and make demands of management on behalf of all employees much more easily than they could win the sentiments of a majority of workers. In February 1941, eight FE organizers supported by a hundred or so union reliables in strategic departments managed to carry out a carefully laid plan to shut down the giant McCormick Works. They feared it would be much harder to convince a majority of McCormick workers to vote for the FE in an NLRB election.[15] Under the NLRA, then, organizers were constantly encouraging shop floor strategies to broaden their base among the rank and file. When militants involved fellow workers in collective actions like slowdowns and whistle stopping, they helped them overcome individual fear or inertia without risking employer reprisal.

Organizing success so depended on rank-and-file action that a top-down union like the SWOC found itself anxious to suppress the rank-and-file participation it had previously encouraged once a contract was signed. Joe Germano, who served as director of Chicago's District 31 from 1940 until his retirement in 1973 and did as much as anyone to curb rank-and-file input into decision making, openly acknowledged that the SWOC drive in Chicago was "helped tremendously by the real rank and filers who accepted this thing, were so joyful about it coming that they did everything they possibly could."[16] But the ink was hardly dry on the contract with U.S. Steel when the SWOC's national office circulated a letter to all lodges pleading with them to avoid more strikes: "For the sake of the future welfare of our Union and its members we urge all to remain at work pending our efforts to get the contracts signed in good faith."[17] Over the months that followed national SWOC leaders struggled to discipline rank-and-file members at U.S. Steel to respect prerogatives from the top and still pay their dues. Significantly, at steel mills where the SWOC did not yet have contracts and hence could not control the rank and file, shop floor agitation persisted. According to a grassroots leader at Inland Steel, workers "never had it so good" as before they got a contract, when the rank and file ran the show. Locals at mills like Inland, he claimed, remained more autonomous and "the workers developed the most militant and the

Plate 32. This rally organized by the United Packinghouse Workers of America the day before a National Labor Relations Board election at Wilson & Company indicates the importance of the national government's intervention in industrial relations to the CIO's success. However, although the National Labor Relations Act of 1935 was crucial for protecting workers' right to organize independent unions, rank-and-file activism was still required to make the government's machinery work on labor's behalf.

most inspiring type of rank-and-file organization that you can have .... As a result of the enthusiasm of the people in the mill you had a series of strikes, wildcats, shut-downs, slow-downs, anything working people could think of to secure for themselves what they decided they had to have."[18] Even in packing, where the PWOC was fairly responsive to the rank and file, worker proclivity toward shop floor militance forced the union to discipline the ranks once a contract with Armour was signed. Over three hundred workers in Armour's pork-killing department walked off the job in January 1940 when they learned that management had increased the number of hogs to be slaughtered daily. Under the terms of the union's agreement with Armour, they should have followed the grievance procedures established under the contract. Union officials were forced to concede to management that the stoppage was unjustified "and proclaimed that such stoppages would not be tolerated in the future."[19]

The machinery of the NLRA, therefore, cannot alone be credited with bringing mass production workers into unions during the 1930s. The big breakthrough at U.S. Steel took place before the Wagner Act was ruled constitutional, and the union struggles that followed elsewhere required at least as much shop floor support from rank-and-file workers. Often, it mattered more that workers could use the threat of government intervention against their employers than that the government in fact intervened, as when a Swift worker fought off his bosses' illegal harassment by yelling, according to a June 1939 issue of the Swift shop paper, that they "either give him a discharge card or get the h____ away from him, unless they wanted to sit in the witness chair and tell the government what they were trying to do."[20]

The other factor that facilitated the organization of factory workers during the depression was the support of a committed, skilled leadership capable of coordinating a national union campaign. The absence of such a cadre had hindered organization in the 1919 era, when there was little effective coordination between unreliable craft union internationals like the Amalgamated Associations in steel and packing, on the one hand, and enthusiastic but isolated workers at the local level, on the other. National-scale corporations like U.S. Steel, Armour, and International Harvester had found it easy to take advantage of this geographical and organizational fragmentation among their striking employees.

Now in the mid-1930s, a newly established national entity, the CIO, proved capable of directing broad-based organizing drives that made it easier for steel workers in Chicago to support auto workers in Flint, Armour workers in Chicago to coordinate with Armour workers in Sioux City, and U.S. Steel workers in Chicago to communicate with Harvester workers across town. "This time, instead of standing alone, isolated, repudiated even by their own International, the workers know that the might of the CIO and the power of John L. Lewis are behind them," journalist Mary Heaton Vorse wrote in 1936.[21] Masterminded and underwritten by successful industrial unionists such as John L. Lewis, Sidney Hillman of the Amalgamated Clothing Workers, and David Dubinsky of the International Ladies Garment Workers' Union, the CIO assembled professional teams of organizers drawn primarily from these unions and the Communist Party. Under the Popular Front launched in 1935, the Communist Party had abandoned its "dual union strategy" of organizing its own unions such as the Steel and Metal Workers Industrial Union at South Works and the Packinghouse Workers Industrial Union in the stockyards. Instead, the party returned to its old "boring-from-within" approach, but with a more immediate purpose. Communists were supporting reformist strategies as a beachhead against fascism. Fighting for the CIO was like supporting FDR and lobbying for social insurance. Lewis, faced with the awesome task of bringing a union to millions of unorganized industrial workers laboring for some of the nation's most determined antiunion bosses, turned to the party to supply him with experienced and dedicated organizers. Of the approximately two hundred full-time organizers on the SWOC payroll nationally in 1937, almost a third were known to be Communists.[22]

By 1936, the CIO had in place a national structure staffed by deeply committed individuals who were used to functioning within disciplined political organizations. Workers at the grassroots level, eager for representation, generally welcomed this outside help, although not, of course, without some tensions. When organizers from the CIO like Chicago Regional Director Van Bittner, SWOC's Nicholas Fontecchio, and FE's Joe Weber arrived on the job, they quickly tried to assimilate plant-level leaders like George Patterson, a roll turner at South Works, or Gerald Fielde, a machinist at McCormick Works, into the CIO's national structure, recruiting them as paid or volunteer organizers to help with the task of establishing lodges of the SWOC, PWOC, and FE that would be accountable to both local workers and national union administrators alike.[23]

Once again, however, as with the issue of state support, focusing on the contribution of organizers can result in overlooking the role rank-and-file workers played in making this national CIO structure work on a plant-by-plant basis. Sorting out the complex power relationships between rank and file and union leadership is never easy. Erring in one direction often creates too romantic a view of rank-and-file autonomy. Erring in the other direction makes workers out to be passive pawns of skillful organizers. The issue is made all the more complicated by the ambiguity of the labels "union leader," which can be applied to shop floor stewards all the way up to officers of an international, and "rank and file," which can include militant as well as more reticent workers.

At the local level, the line between rank and file and leadership was often far from sharp. For my purposes, I use *rank and file* to refer to the mass of workers whose foremost concern was with their particular jobs and *leader* for those who identified primarily with the trade union movement. Overall, I am stressing that the coordination and discipline of a well-structured national campaign helped the union drive of the 1930s succeed where previous ones had failed. But from all that has emerged so far about the actions of factory workers in the 1930s, it should be clear that organizers benefited from deep-rooted and fairly widespread rank-and-file commitment. Without that they could not have succeeded. Where it was lacking, as in the Wisconsin Steel Works of International Harvester to be examined in the next chapter, SWOC's most concerted organizing efforts got nowhere.

Rank-and-file workers did more than back up their national leaders. They helped shape the strategies of their CIO organizers. The SWOC leadership, for instance, knew that steelworkers feared an all-out strike in the fall and winter of 1936–7 and tailored its planning accordingly. CIO organizers everywhere built their campaigns around grievances articulated by the workers they were assisting. Shop stewards at Armour, for example, demanded special check-cashing windows to free workers from having to make purchases at the company's retail market in order to get cash because workers wanted them very badly.[24] But analyzing more extensively the influence that workers had on union organizers is difficult. One approach is to look at the way that rank-and-file workers in Chicago related to CIO organizers who were Communists since workers talked more explicitly about their relationship to them than to others.

The majority of Chicago's manufacturing workers were not Communists, much, of course, to the party's regret. When workers at South Works or Tractor Works launched their grassroots unions out of employee representation plans during the NRA period, the party had little to do with them. Several years later, even the House Committee on Un-American Activities was forced to conclude, after exhaustive investigation into Communist agitation, that in the strike at International Harvester during the winter of 1941, "there was no denying the Communist leadership but there was also no ground for believing that the overwhelming majority of the striking employees were even slightly Communist inclined." Likewise, in the stockyards, where a union as Communist influenced as the PWOC ruled, there were only a few hundred party members. A few years later, on the eve of the war, the numbers were even smaller, according to rank-and-file organizer and Communist Party member Vicky Starr, with about 125–150 actual members.[25]

Despite the unwillingness of mass production workers to commit themselves ideologically to communism, however, they recognized how useful experienced and dedicated Communist organizers could be to their battle for a union. "People didn't give damn if you was actually a member of the Communist Party, it was what you were doing in there. If you were contributing toward the cause, good," Clarence Stoecker, president of the FE local at McCormick Works and a party member, remembered. A PWOC activist recalled that packinghouse workers had a similar attitude. They loved Herb March because of everything he did for them despite the fact that he was a Communist. George Patterson recalled how he learned from party members in the South Works mill once he realized that there were a few steelworkers "who had much more knowledge of unions and history of the labor movement than me. I sought some of them out and found that indeed, they did read the *Daily Worker* and said they were keeping abreast of the current events in the labor movement from such papers as *New Masses*, a recently published magazine." Even Philip Weightman, a hog header on Swift's killing floor who became president of his PWOC local and a leader of the anti-Communist movement within the packing union took this view: "In all I've said about the Communist Party, I don't want to take anything away from them [Communist organizers], because they contributed. . . . I may not have been as aggressive as I was if it hadn't been for them, you see. The fact that they were talking and urging this and the other, that I thought was for the wrong reasons, but they were good things they were suggesting. That makes the difference."[26] When red-baiter congressman Martin Dies brought his House Committee on Un-American Activities to Chicago three days before the crucial NLRB election at Armour in November 1939 in hopes of discrediting the PWOC, packinghouse workers let him know what they thought of their "red" union leaders by voting overwhelmingly for the PWOC. Ordinary factory workers were using Communist organizers as much as they were used by them.[27]

Even more revealing of the rank and file's influence over organizers, workers made clear to Communists in the CIO what they had previously told Communists enlisting them in the unemployed movements of the early 1930s, that there were limits to their support. "You didn't talk about socialism per se," explained organizer Vicky Starr of the constraints. "You talked about issues and saw how people reacted. You talked about how one could attain these things."[28] Communists organizing in the factories of Chicago were so sensitive to what rank-and-file workers would put up with that their caution frustrated the Party leadership. In a 1938 critique of shop papers issued by Communist Party units in the South Works and Gary Works of U.S. Steel, International Harvester, and the packinghouses, Jack Martin, the party's Illinois State Educational Director, concluded that "all the papers suffer from one common and major weakness: they do not speak as a political organ which answers all questions, not only of building the union, but of national and local politics, questions of war and peace, the high cost of living, taxation, the revolutionary goal of socialism. The papers remain on the whole only good trade union papers." He particularly lamented that "the Party still does not appear before workers in the shops as the leader and organizer, as the political party of the working class . . . What is lacking in th[ese] papers is our own Party program which goes beyond that of the C.I.O."[29] While Martin chastised party militants for their lack of a larger political program, Communist organizers in Chicago like Herbert March, Vicky Starr, Hank Johnson, and Joe Weber knew that these were the terms that rank-and-file workers themselves had set. When questioned about his view of ideological struggles within the Communist Party during the 1930s, March scoffed, "That was a world removed. I was busy dealing with day to day struggles with the employers."[30]

Organizers like these Communists and rank-and-file workers were not only locked in combat with employers, they were also locked together in an embrace. Workers needed organizers to orchestrate a national campaign, to support them when they took risks, and to help them maneuver in the new bureaucratic waters of union organizing 1930s-style. Organizers needed workers who voted the right way in NLRB elections, went out on strike or stopped work when it was necessary, and were willing to put loyalty to a union above loyalty to a boss. Contrary to common assumptions that the CIO's success in the thirties must have come about either because of radical rank and filers at the bottom or persuasive strategists at the top, the new rules of union organizing that the New Deal ushered in required both plant-level enthusiasm and bureaucratic skill. Appreciating how much a powerful, national CIO leadership facilitated workers' organization does not demand as a corollary that rank-and-file workers let themselves be herded like meek sheep. Partnership with CIO organizers helped ordinary factory workers feel confident that they faced their employers backed by the political savvy, the legal smarts, and the bountiful billfold of "the mighty CIO." That made them more, not less, assertive at the workplace. A steelworker in Pennsylvania could not have explained his relationship to organizers more succinctly than when he compared his father's generation to his own: "The immigrant generation, they did not realize too much that they were exploited, or [if they did], it was natural for them. Even in 1919 [during the steel strike], many of them were [simply] led by the organizers. Us. We were different. [During the 1937 strike] we knew what we were fighting for."[31]

RESURRECTING THE RANK AND FILE

The role that rank-and-file workers played in getting the state and union organizers to work so effectively for them makes it that much more important to consider the mindset of ordinary industrial workers in the mid-1930s. It is possible that even with the critical assistance rendered by the New Deal state and this new cadre of union organizers, the CIO's unionizing drive might have met the same fate as earlier ones if workers had not themselves undergone some key changes. Rank-and-file workers in Chicago industries differed by the late 1930s from what they had been in the era of 1919 in two major ways. First, common experiences during the 1920s and the Great Depression made them more capable of unifying against employers who long had tried to defeat them by dividing them. Second, the CIO built on this new common ground with organizing strategies designed to unite workers even further.

The attitudes of the industrial workers who brought the CIO to Chicago's manufacturing plants by the late 1930s had been shaped by their day-to-day work experiences over the previous two decades, the first a decade dominated by the philosophy of welfare capitalism, the second dominated by the reality of searing depression. Workers in the 1920s had accepted the concept of welfare capitalism, although their bosses had rarely lived up to workers' expectations. As the Great Depression prompted a further deterioration in employers' commitment to welfare capitalism, workers turned increasingly to the state, and eventually the union, to ensure their welfare.

But despite workers' disillusionment with the practice of welfare capitalism, they harked back to its premises in the kinds of demands they made of their employers as they organized unions. Workers in steel, packing, and agricultural implements in Chicago sought the kinds of ameliorations they had been promised but rarely received under welfare capitalism through their union demands: better working conditions – higher pay, shorter hours, safer conditions, predictable and steadier work schedules, paid vacations, and an end to unjust piecework and bonus schemes; fairer work rules – seniority considerations for promotions in good times, for layoffs and rehiring in bad, and the curbing of arbitrary acts by foremen and other supervisors through grievance procedures; and real employee representation in negotiations with employers. In time, CIO unions also would press industrialists to provide more comprehensive welfare packages featuring medical and pension benefits to supplement Social Security. At the most basic level, these demands shared with welfare capitalism a faith that the work environment could be made fair within a capitalist economic structure and a managerial authority structure.

The way the CIO organized in a company like Swift, where management had been somewhat truer to welfare capitalism's tenets than at Armour, reveals the extent to which rank-and-file workers were seeking similar benefits through the union as they had expected from welfare capitalist employers. Philip Weightman and other PWOC leaders within Chicago's Swift plant, knowing the hold company paternalism still had over these workers, stressed that a union contract would codify and guarantee benefits now granted by the company as well as improve on them: "We said to employees Mr. Swift or whoever the Superintendent is, when he shuts his eyes, what happens to the benevolence? Who knows about it? It's not a policy agreed to with employers, not a contract, it's just something they're giving you. These good things you know about the union can improve upon with your help. If you don't get the union, the company can take them away anytime and you have nothing to say about it."[32]

It is easy to look at the nature of workers' demands and conclude that industrial workers in the 1930s had only nonideological, "bread-and-butter" concerns as they fought for a union. What that view misses, and the larger context of welfare capitalism helps establish, however, is that workers were very much ideological in their goals; they were just not anticapitalist. As Kornhauser's study of Chicago's industrial workers in 1937 suggested, workers might be called moral capitalists. They looked to the state and the union to create a more just society within a system that still respected private property and many managerial prerogatives. Although workers showed their strength on the shop floor, they did not demand a fundamental redistribution of power such as a role in hiring, firing, work and wage assignments, and production decisions. It is extremely difficult to know just where workers' orientation to moral capitalism came from. Long-standing expectations about America, particularly workers' own desire to acquire property, likely contributed. But certainly employers' message during the 1920s, that capitalism can be and should be fair to its workers, played an important part in shaping working people's world view.

That workers were pursuing something "moral," not simply economic, comes through from a close look at their demands.[33] So many of them concerned equity: equal pay for equal work; the end to job discrimination on the grounds of age, race, or sex; seniority in place of favoritism. A fascinating document, the word-for-word minutes of grievance committee meetings at Inland Steel from the governor of Indiana's truce to end the strike in July 1937 until 1941, reveals how much a desire to create a fair working environment motivated the complaints that SWOC representatives brought up with the superintendent of the plant, Fred Gillies. Spreading out overtime, rotating day and night shifts, following seniority religiously in making layoff decisions, punishing workers equally, whether Mexican or American, for infractions like quitting early: these were the kinds of issues frequently discussed. In another example, a PWOC pamphlet designed to respond to the proindustry Chicago press – admittedly a piece of union propaganda but still instructive – went so far as calling the packers "feudal lords of the middle ages" and "the Packerbund" (with its monopolist and fascist connotations), accusing the bosses of violating the true spirit of democracy and capitalism.[34]

Workers were frustrated with employers' unreliable implementation of welfare capitalism in the 1920s, and they expressed it by restricting their output and quitting, which frustrated their bosses in return. But the Great Depression changed the rules of this cat-and-mouse game. Not only could workers no longer afford to quit, but also they felt employers were violating the tenets of welfare capitalism so extensively that their basic rights were in danger. In the wake of the economic crisis, jobs were lost, benefits cut, security totally gone, and in many places, the hand of the foreman strengthened as work sharing and layoffs encouraged favoritism. As if this were not bad enough, managers angered workers with business decisions that undermined whatever remnants of credibility as welfare capitalists they still had. The handling of company profits was one outrage. During the years of 1930–3 when workers at Armour faced three large wage cuts, for example, Armour made a total operating profit of over $51 million and paid dividends amounting to $23 million. "Somehow, that didn't look fair to us," worker Clifton McKinney commented drily, revealing once again workers' expectations. Steelworkers expressed similar frustration with the spending priorities of their employers. When Mr. Stevens, manager of industrial relations at U.S. Steel, told employee representatives in December 1935 that they could expect vacations with pay as soon as the corporation "begins to show a profit," he was angrily reminded that "the iron and steel industry made twenty-six million nine hundred thousand dollars net profits in the first nine months of 1935, as compared with a net loss of ten million dollars for the same period in 1934, yet no two weeks vacation with pay was forthcoming."[35]

Rank-and-file workers also resented their bosses' introduction of more mechanization into factories during the depression, which by contributing to speed-ups and hiring cuts further undermined the spirit of welfare capitalism. As soon as a South Chicago steelworker heard about plans to increase production by putting more rod lines into Republic Steel's Merchant and Rod mills, he complained to General Johnson of the NRA, "Instead of working once in a while well just figure it out for yourself Gen." For black workers in Gary, mechanization had special meaning. Whites got the jobs operating the machines whereas blacks were demoted to common labor.[36] In general, businessmen justified this new concern with rationalizing the work process as an antidote to falling profits. The many corporate mergers that took place in the wake of economic crisis only further fueled the drive to streamline production.

Particular industries had special motivations for implementing technological innovations in the midst of the depression. In steel, for instance, the profitable market for steel products was switching fast from capital to consumer goods like tin cans, automobiles, and refrigerators, requiring major innovations in sheet and strip steel production. According to U.S. Steel's own calculations, by the end of its major rehabilitation program in 1937, scarcely one-quarter of its production was of the same composition or made in the same way as in 1928. By this time as well, American steelworkers were turning out a third more steel per hour worked than in 1929. The story was much the same in packing. The Stockyards Labor Council estimated that improved machinery and the speeding up of workers meant as early as 1934 that forty thousand were doing work that fifty-two thousand had done in 1929. The process could be seen clearly on the shop floor. Swift worker Mary Siporin testified in 1939 that where twenty girls had once sliced bacon, there now were six.[37] Disillusioning workers further, when the NRA ended in 1935 many found themselves back with the wages, hours and working conditions of pre-1933. A steelworker who had grown accustomed to one wage rate found it difficult to return to a lower one.[38]

Inland steelworker Nick Migas spoke the truth when he said about the CIO era, "We were pretty ripe for organization."[39] Rather than depend any longer on unreliable bosses, workers sought recognition of their own unions to bargain collectively with employers. But the welfare capitalist dialogue of the 1920s about what constituted a good employer and a good workplace continued to shape workers' expectations, even as they challenged one of its basic tenets by establishing independent organizations of workers to hold employers to their promises. Although there were plenty of outspoken people around – some of them at the next bench in the factory – who argued that workers' lives would never improve until capitalism was overthrown, the mass of workers continued to believe that capitalism could be made fair.

Workers also applied the strategies they had developed coping with the limitations of welfare capitalism during the 1920s to their CIO organizing. Most importantly, they built on the gang cooperation developed through output restriction to carry out the rank-and-file shop floor actions such as slowdowns and work stoppages that were so crucial to the CIO's success. Workers at Harvester's Tractor Works, for example, were motivated in their campaign first for the secret ABC Union and then the FE by a long-standing dissatisfaction with the plant's group piecework system, which in addition to rate cutting and other wage inequities rarely took into account the obstacles to a person "making out," such as machine breakdowns, stock shortages, and resupplying a work area. The Tractor Works had been International Harvester's model plant for scientific management and assembly-line production since 1922. Workers who had already united in opposition to the company's piecework system during the 1920s now put their shop floor strategies to work for the union.[40]

Similarly, when management at South Works sensed that disenchantment was growing among roll turners in 1934, they introduced the Bedaux system of bonus payments. That, however, only "gave our group impetus to do more organizing," George Patterson remembered, and led eventually to workers cooperating in a work stoppage. Opposition to bonus and piecework plans continued to fuel the union drive in steel.[41] At Swift, the Bedaux system also propelled organizing. In only one of many examples, "solid support of all the workers on the floor" in pork cut helped the PWOC's grievance committee cut the speed by one hundred hogs an hour. "Workers all through the plant are realizing that the 'Bonus' is a slave driving system which must be brought under control," the *CIO News-PWOC Edition* proclaimed.[42]

Even when the issue was not rejection of a bonus-type pay system, workers built on their tradition of gang solidarity against the boss's wage and productivity schemes and against fellow workers who were "rate busters," "chiselers," and "squealers." The women who worked in sliced bacon at Swift turned the cooperation they had developed through a tradition of output restriction into unionization overnight when one of their number died suddenly from an illness caused by the freezer's chill. Likewise, Jesse Perez, a beef lugger on the cutting floor and a CIO steward, recounted to a WPA interviewer in 1939 how "the boys on the gang" first asked him "what you gonna do?" about a terrible speed-up and then came up with their own solution of all stopping work one day in protest.[43]

Clinton Golden and Harold Ruttenberg, early leaders of SWOC who wrote an important tract on industrial relations in 1942 entitled *The Dynamics of Industrial Democracy*, claimed that in steel as well, work gangs became the forerunners of the union: "In going about the task of organizing a group of workers in a given plant into a labor union, we have consciously sought out the leaders of these informal groups throughout the plant, interested them in taking a lead in forming the union, and found that their joining the union invariably caused the members of the informal organization to follow suit. In labor–union parlance these leaders are called 'the men with a following.'" Work gangs were such a good recruiting ground for the CIO that twenty years later, a few workers at Inland Steel admitted that they had joined the union simply because of informal pressure within their work group. One worker who was and remained opposed to unionism yielded to avoid constant peer pressure: "It was like compulsory – you had to. They approached you, kept after you, hounded you. To get them off my neck I joined." The work group that had monitored welfare capitalism in the 1920s became a crucial vehicle for unionization in the 1930s.[44]

Welfare capitalism, of course, was not the only training ground workers encountered over these two decades. Some, particularly militants, remembered the dreams of the 1919 era of unionizing and even earlier struggles. This was particularly the case in packing, where government arbitration from 1918 to 1921 had prolonged the benefits enough to make it a positive memory. Founders of the reborn Stockyards Labor Council explicitly claimed that past when they resurrected the earlier labor organization. They even consulted with William Z. Foster and Jack Johnstone, leaders of the previous organizing drive who were now important figures in the Communist Party. Many ordinary packinghouse workers, however, harbored negative impressions of 1921, particularly of black strikebreakers taking white jobs.[45]

Workers in steel and agricultural implements also seemed little inspired by memories of the past. Golden and Ruttenberg remarked in *The Dynamics of Industrial Democracy* that memories of previous militance had worked against SWOC because they had taught steelworkers "not to join unions rashly, as that meant strikes, and hardships, and losing out in the mill." Rank-and-file leader George Patterson's experience at South Works corroborated this report that memories of 1919 played a limited inspirational role twenty years later. As a newcomer to the United States in 1924, Patterson learned little from other steelworkers about the 1919 strike. They talked about it so rarely that he claims not to have been aware that there had been such a serious strike until the CIO campaign, when the comparison became apparent. Even then, "it was the old story. They [fellow workers] tried to say that the organizers of that time of 1919 had run away with the money, they had sold the workers out, that the union was something that could not be trusted."[46]

More important than old, often painful memories of labor struggles for making workers more assertive were their fairly recent experiences coping with the Great Depression, particularly dealing with relief agencies. The various unemployed groups had shown people, whether they were actively involved in relief appeals or not, that the dependent had a right to voice grievances. According to organizer Herbert March, who himself had been active in the Unemployed Councils, a crucial core of the PWOC was younger workers who had come into the packing industry after passage of the NRA with "experience fighting for their rights as unemployed for relief." Even before Armour recognized the PWOC, March felt the union's steady growth took place because, like organizations of the unemployed, "we were aggressively pressing for the many, many myriad of grievances that the workers had." One strategy the union employed that came right out of the confidence and experience people gained making demands of relief agencies involved forcing the company to set aside one evening a week to handle employee complaints. Beginning at 4 or 4:30 p.m., one by one a hundred or so aggrieved workers would take their turn confronting the plant bosses with their problems. March recalled occasions when they kept the managers there until 9 p.m. Veterans of the battles over relief benefits, they felt they could say, "Nobody's getting out until we settle all these cases. These guys have all been waiting here all this time and you can't treat us this way."[47]

It is interesting to note that by the late 1930s, the cross-fertilization was going the other way as relief recipients brought the new strategies of the shop floor to their struggle for better relief benefits. A small item in *Survey Magazine* of December 1937 reported that several Chicago district relief offices recently had faced sit-in strikes of clients lasting as long as two days: "Eating lunches, climbing in and out of windows, community singing and other disturbances made acute difficulties in operating the relief office."[48] In an even more direct link, the FE, SWOC, and PWOC all took a leadership role in handling complaints and orchestrating protests against relief agencies. Members of the FE organized a march on Cicero's relief headquarters and town supervisor's office in September 1938 to demand higher relief allotments. The SWOC turned its skills at mobilizing demonstrations for union contracts to running rallies against cuts in WPA jobs. During the recession of 1938, the PWOC set in motion a special unemployment committee to assist those who had lost packing jobs in claiming relief benefits or WPA positions.[49]

The Great Depression left another legacy to the CIO organizing campaign worth mentioning. The humiliation that many middle-aged men underwent during the depression, losing jobs to younger, less experienced men, helped make seniority rights a major union demand.

Some companies that had been disinclined to hire old workers during the 1920s seized the depression as an opportunity to dismiss those already on board. At one steel mill where older men with good service records (many of them immigrants who could not read English) were fired, the company justified its actions on the grounds that a state safety law required that all workers operating cranes be able to read English. Clarence Stoecker was outraged that younger men like himself got work in 1935 whereas the more experienced older men in his forge shop at Harvester's McCormick Works were being laid off for long periods. After experiences like these, workers were willing to fight for seniority rights more vigorously than ever.[50]

In sum, the goals and strategies of the CIO did not come out of the blue, nor were they rooted in some mystical militant past. Workers brought their experiences with welfare capitalism and the depression directly to bear on their struggle for a union. Sometimes employers had a hard time believing that the CIO was not the work of corrupting, outside agitators, that the rank-and-file workers who were combatting them now were the same ones who had seemed more accommodating earlier. When Armour's pork division grievance committee complained to the plant superintendent about a speed-up and the lack of a relief man, Superintendent Renfro responded, "You've been getting along for a good many years this way. What's the difference now?" Crawford Love, hog-kill steward, told him frankly, "The difference is this. I've been up there for eighteen years, and for eighteen we've been breaking our hearts for the company, but now we've got a chance to say something about it." Although Love and his fellow workers may have appeared to be suffering in silence those long eighteen years, they were collecting resentments and perfecting strategies that, whether they had realized it or not, readied them to confront their employers head-on when given the opportunity.[51]

8
Workers' Common Ground

Plate 33. Steelworkers and their families and friends throughout the Calumet region gathered for a mass memorial service in 1939 to commemorate the Memorial Day Massacre. Two years earlier, the Chicago police had killed ten demonstrators and wounded more than a hundred others as they peacefully protested Republic Steel's refusal to recognize the Steel Workers' Organizing Committee. The mix of faces assembled here – men and women, white and black, of all ethnicities – reflected the new unity among industrial workers that helped make the CIO a success.

Rank-and-file workers' success in organizing unions during the 1930s reflected more than common lessons learned on the training grounds of welfare capitalism and the Great Depression. Even more fundamentally, those who worked in Chicago's factories had come to share a similar cultural life that helped them unite against their bosses as they fought for a union. In the World War I period, workers' disunity, particularly along skill, racial, and ethnic lines, had contributed to their defeat. Employers played one group against another while workers lacked ways of transcending the cultural isolation that kept them apart. By the mid-1930s, however, workers, whatever their skill and whether born of immigrant or native parents, white or black, simply had more in common on which a united union movement could be built. Most crucially, the CIO, recognizing the importance of a shared culture to the organizing process, reinforced workers' new common ground with a deliberate cultural strategy, the construction of what I call a CIO "culture of unity."

Skill divided manufacturing workers less and less over the course of the twenties and thirties. Workers' decision to restrict their output during the welfare capitalism of the 1920s and the speed-ups of the 1930s had taught them to cooperate better on the shop floor, often across skill lines. The increased mechanization over these two decades, moreover, narrowed the gap between the skilled and unskilled and linked workers in a more integrated production process. As *Fortune Magazine* put it in 1940, in contrast to the World War I era, "the immigrant's sons (who talk and are American) and the skilled worker's sons were now working side by side at machines." But as this quotation from *Fortune* suggests, workers now had more in common than their machine tending. Fundamental social and cultural changes made workers less different culturally than their fathers had been in ways that made it easier to cooperate in fighting for the CIO.[1]

On the simplest level of demographics, more workers were English-speaking, second-generation ethnics or blacks who had lived in the North for years. Although it is difficult to figure out exactly who was working in Chicago's manufacturing plants in the mid-1930s, the few statistics available suggest they tended to be younger than forty and hence likely to have been American raised if not American born, given that massive immigration had come to a halt by the early 1920s. In the case of the one group that continued to immigrate during the 1920s, the Mexicans, the story was not much different. A study of Mexicans in

Chicago concluded that those who became active in the CIO were men who had come to the United States as boys or were born here. Workers who had been increasingly mixed together by ethnicity, race, and skill on the shop floor since the early 1920s were having an easier time communicating with each other.[2]

Not only could factory workers talk to each other better, but also similar experiences outside of work gave them more in common to talk about. Even though many continued to live in separate ethnic and racial communities, what happened in those neighborhoods was becoming less distinctive. We have seen how the ethnic institutions that workers so depended on during the 1920s had themselves been changing, gradually drawing workers into more national ethnic communities and more mainstream commercial culture through, for example, banks and building and loan associations and ethnic stores distributing brand-name goods. Many industrial workers of the 1930s had as second-generation ethnic youth in the twenties integrated mass culture like the radio into their neighborhood lives. As the Great Depression eroded local and ethnic institutions, mass culture expanded its reach even further. Chain movie theaters were displacing small, independently owned movie houses and thereby attracting more working-class people to their feature pictures; chain stores were becoming more appealing to penny-pinching working-class customers as their credit-giving neighborhood merchants were folding; and national, commercial, network radio shows were overwhelming the local, nonprofit, often ethnic programs that had been so popular during the twenties. Workers in the 1930s were more likely to share a cultural world, to see the same movies and newsreels in the same chain theaters, shop for the same items in the same chain stores, and listen to the same radio shows on network radio, a situation very different from that of 1919 when workers lived in isolated cultural communities (Tables 7–10).[3]

Radio, probably more than any other medium, contributed to an increasingly universal working-class experience. By the mid-1930s, radios were a staple in Chicago workers' homes. A University of Chicago student working in a recreation program in a working-class Polish neighborhood estimated that only one out of ten girls came from homes without radios. Another community worker in a steelworkers' area of South Chicago concurred: "Despite their limited financial resources, the families of nearly all of these boys possess radios," he claimed, an observation that was further documented in a survey of 1,093 seventh-

Plate 34. Even in the most isolated working-class community of Chicago, Hegewisch in Southeast Chicago, workers could shop at a chain grocery store like the Great Atlantic & Pacific Tea Company by the 1930s. These Hegewisch workers and wives lined up with wartime ration coupons in 1941 to purchase the same items from the same kind of store as people in working-class neighborhoods all over Chicago,. regardless of race and ethnicity. Experience with mass consumption became part of workers' shared culture during the thirties.

and eighth-grade boys from South Chicago that found that less than 1 percent of them had no radios in their homes in 1939.[4] Manufacturers had introduced inexpensive table-top and even pocket-sized radios in the early 1930s, making it possible for almost everybody to listen at home rather than go to a neighbor's or hang out at the local store. By 1940, moreover, 40 percent of Chicago workers surveyed had two radios in their homes, allowing individuals to listen away from other family members. As a result of the increasing isolation of the radio listener, the local community mediated less between the program and the audience than it had in the 1920s when families, neighbors, and friends listened together.[5]

As radio programming became more established in the 1930s, people listened to the radio more often. A *Fortune* survey found that by 1938 listening to the radio was the nation's favorite pastime, just edging out movies and holding a clear lead over reading. The editors estimated that on a typical winter evening people were listening to radio programs in around 40 percent of homes. The increasingly sophisticated field of market research revealed that lower-income families particularly listened frequently. Another *Fortune* poll indicated that twice as many people on the lowest income level preferred radio to books and magazines, whereas on the highest income level the relationship was almost inverse.[6] By the end of the thirties, it had become common knowledge in the trade that radio owners of low income and education level spent much of their time tuned in to the radio.[7]

Among all Americans, but particularly workers, the radio was displacing the newspaper. A *Fortune* survey of 1939 revealed that 70 percent of Americans relied on radio as their prime source of news, 58 percent thinking that it was more accurate than the press. The lower a person's economic status, the more likely he or she preferred radio over print.[8] Working people were less likely by the mid-1930s to learn about world events from diverse Chicago or ethnic newspapers than from a network newscaster.[9]

Entertainment on the radio by the mid-1930s also tended to be less local and more national in origin. Rather than familiar, Chicago-bred musical performers or other locally known personalities, workers heard a greater variety of shows packaged for a national audience, as more and more of Chicago's independent stations, in order to survive the depression, were bought by or affiliated with one of the four networks, the Red and Blue Networks of NBC, CBS, and the Mutual Broadcasting Company after 1934. Even WCFL, the Chicago Federation of Labor's "Voice of Labor," wanted a greater affiliation with NBC but was refused because of its strong AFL identification. This concentration in radio toward larger, network stations can be seen in the decline in total number of Chicago stations from nineteen in 1930 to thirteen in 1938, leaving only half as many small stations under 1,500 watts whereas those broadcasting at 20,000 watts or more almost doubled.[10]

Listening to more national, network radio exposed workers to more standardized programs. Beginning in the early 1930s, radio exploded with new programming forms: the dramatic play written for radio, the variety show, the soap opera, the children's program, and the quiz show. Jack Benny, George Burns and Gracie Allen, Bing Crosby, Edgar Bergen and Charlie McCarthy, the Lone Ranger, Rudy Vallee, the Shadow, Helen Trent, Little Orphan Annie, Major Bowes, and a host of others were now fixtures in Chicago workers' households whatever residents' race, religion, or ethnicity. Local ethnic programming persisted in Chicago during the 1930s, even enduring to the present day, and industrial workers continued to listen, as surveys showed that the small stations that broadcasted these shows were patronized by people of lower income and "cultural level." But ethnic radio too was becoming more commercial in the 1930s as it looked farther afield for advertisers. It increasingly was serving an older audience, as younger people in these communities preferred tuning in to network programs.[11] A sign painter told a WPA writer in 1939 of his surprise at the incongruous ritual he observed every morning while he worked in a Lithuanian bar. At a certain time, the owner's wife would "come out with pail and mop, but before she started to work she'd park her fanny behind the bar. There's a little radio there. She'd turn it on and listen, with her head almost on top of it. By God, I thought her ears were glued to that loudspeaker. But always the same programs, two of them. . . . They were 'Dan's Other Wife' and 'Road of Life.' Ain't that a bitch, though? And as soon as those two programs were over, always the same two, she'd turn off the radio and begin work like hell, moppin' up that floor."[12] Ten years earlier, this Lithuanian woman more likely would have listened to a Lithuanian hour, if one was on that early in the morning and if there was a radio in the bar. Ethnic culture was also becoming a part of everyone's listening experience as network offerings, such as the Goldbergs, Amos 'n' Andy, Eddie Cantor with regular guests the Mad Russian and the Greek restaurant owner Parkyakarkas, and the first soap opera, "Painted Dreams," which focused on Mother Moynihan and her shop clerk daughters, presented stereotyped, ethnic characters, some borrowed from the vaudeville and minstrel shows now in decline.

Network radio also reinforced the gender cultures that helped bring workers of diverse backgrounds together at the plant. Among male workers, professional sports was a constant topic of conversation, as baseball and particularly prize fighting attracted huge listening audiences during the CIO era. The largest radio audience to date, 63.7 percent of potential listeners, tuned in to the Max Schmeling – Joe Louis bout over two networks in June 1938. It is not hard to imagine Chicago workers exchanging news and opinions about the latest White Sox loss or Joe Louis victory, much as photographs of the sit-down strikers in Flint showed them charting baseball scores as they occupied General Motors plants. Among women workers, radio characters like

Stella Dallas and Fibber McGee and Molly easily found a place within the female shop floor culture that had blossomed during the 1920s, as surveys revealed that over 70 percent of women at lower economic levels, 10–15 percent more than higher-income women, listened to the radio each day.[13]

In sum, by the time Chicago's factory workers were fighting for the CIO in the late 1930s, they owned more radios, listened more frequently, and enjoyed a greater but more standardized range of programs than they ever had before. Market researchers concluded in the mid-1930s that people were gradually moving toward selecting particular programs rather than being steadily tuned to a certain local or ethnic station, as was common in the 1920s. In 1939, a pathbreaking study sponsored by the Office of Radio Research under sociologist Paul Lazarsfeld entitled "Social Stratification of the Radio Audience" identified more precisely just which shows people of different social classes preferred. People in the C and D income groups, on the lower end of the economic scale, the study concluded, favored general entertainment and drama while eschewing classical and semiclassical music and educational programs.[14]

As marketing research made it clear that people's listening tastes differed by their social group, and that those at the lower end of the income scale made up a significant portion of the listening audience, broadcasters were taking their preferences into account as they programmed. As a result, workers were finding more of what they liked on network radio as time went on. So even though radio was pulling workers out of their isolated cultural communities and giving them more experiences in common with other workers, radio was not necessarily absorbing them into one homogeneous culture, as early promoters of mass culture had predicted in the 1920s. As the research manager of NBC realized by 1940, "radio offers a 'class' as well as a 'mass' market."[15]

The unity that radio offered workers did not just depend on their distinctive tastes. The way workers used radio to bring them together mattered as well. When a South Chicago steelworker reported that men in his plant were beginning to doubt the company's promises in 1935, he invited other co-workers to join in with an allusion to the shared culture of radio: "So if you are beginning to be a doubter too, pack your lunch and 'Come up'n see us' at the next meeting, and as Amos and Andy say, We'll talk the sichyation over."[16] Several months later, the Associated Employes of South Works held their first organizational meeting the same night that Joe Louis unofficially established himself as world heavyweight champion against Max Baer, rank-and-file leader George Patterson remembered. When the one thousand assembled steelworkers adjourned early to hear the 9:30 p.m. broadcast sponsored by the Buick Motor Company over network radio nationwide, it is not hard to imagine that this popular culture that they shared as working-class Americans contributed to the spirit of their own battle to start a union. That they were rooting for Louis, a black man, may have had a particular meaning for these workers whose success against U.S. Steel depended on building alliances across race. This is not to claim that white workers who supported Louis had overcome their racism, but sharing a black hero clearly had an impact on their attitudes. A month earlier, Al Monroe of the black newspaper the *Chicago Defender* had written about accompanying Louis "to a festival that had never welcomed Race guests.... When we entered the place there was an air about it that did not seem free from discrimination. The little fellow who met us at the door appeared a bit bewildered." But in no time, "we had the best of everything about the place – they had discovered the presence of Joe Louis, the bomber." Furthermore, although it is difficult to know for sure if, and how, these working people understood the contest symbolically, Louis and Baer did have social class images in the popular media of which fans like these steelworkers likely were aware. Louis was a fighting symbol in the Great Depression, a man of simple roots who nonetheless was managing to accomplish great things. A long-time resident of industrial Detroit, Louis had not long before labored like themselves as a worker at Ford. Baer, in contrast, was the "rich guy." In the words of sportswriter Jonathan Mitchell, "Baer ... made wisecracks and went to parties and was a harbinger of the return of the old days. He was Broadway, he was California and Florida, he represented the possession of money once more and spending it." It did not take much of a leap to see the Louis–Baer fight as a metaphor for industrial workers' own struggle against their bosses.[17]

Not only did radio give workers in the same work group, department, and factory more common cultural experiences, but also it made them feel part of a larger, citywide and particularly national culture. Although this is a difficult contention to prove, the observations of social scientists at the time support it. Robert and Helen Lynd concluded when they returned to study Muncie, Indiana, in 1935 that network broadcasting was carrying "people away from localism" and giving "them direct access to the more popular stereotypes in the national life." The same year, two social psychologists who studied extensively the "psychology of radio" suggested how radio in the network age might be helping workers feel part of major movements like the New Deal or the CIO. They concluded in their study that "the listener has an imaginative sense of participation in a common activity. He knows that others are listening with him and in this way feels a community of interest with people outside his home.... Only in a vague sense is the printed word a social stimulus, whereas the radio fills us with a 'consciousness of kind' which at times grows into an impression of vast social unity. It is for this reason that radio is potentially more effective than print in bringing about concerted opinion and action."[18] If the CIO succeeded in the late 1930s partly because workers had become more cosmopolitan, network radio helped make them that way. The expectations that radio enthusiasts had held for this new technology in the early 1920s, that it would unify Americans, did not come true until programming was consolidated through the network system in the 1930s. But even then, it was not clear that radio was creating the homogeneous mass audience for which Madison Avenue had hoped. Rather, at the same time that radio listening was bringing working-class people closer together, it was providing a new way of delineating differences between them and the middle and upper classes.

Workers' sense that they had experiences in common with other working people in Chicago and throughout the nation was being reinforced in two other ways worth mentioning. First, they felt that they shared a common fate as victims of the Great Depression, which made it easier not to blame themselves for their financial troubles. Hard times escaped few working-class families, whether white or black, Polish or Irish. This recognition was particularly significant for blacks in Chicago. The depression had destroyed their special relationship to welfare capitalist bosses who had cultivated blacks' favor as "strike insurance" during the 1920s. With the depression, these workers found themselves laid off in greater numbers than white workers as well as the last to be rehired. The NRA, with its promise to spread out the work, only made things worse. In the hands of many employers, blacks accused, the NRA had become a "Negro Removal Act," responsible for replacing blacks with white workers. That industrialists responded to the weak economy by cutting back on black, and Mexican, workers had important implications for workers' unity, as we shall see. Whereas employers in 1919 had encouraged divisions among their employees by using these groups as strikebreakers, they invited a very different scenario in the 1930s when they risked alienating black and Mexican workers.

Second, workers had in common their new identity as Democratic voters. All over the country, as in Chicago, workers were supporting Democrats in local elections, but of even greater consequence was their support for the national Democratic Party, particularly for its standard bearer, Franklin D. Roosevelt. CIO organizers in the steel industry of the Calumet region reported at their weekly meetings in November and December 1936 that "sentiment is very good since the reelection of FDR." Union recruitment improved as workers felt the power of their numbers. As a newsletter of employee representatives in steel expressed it soon after the election, "We are all free men now that President Roosevelt has been reelected by our vote – by labor's vote." The radio helped rally industrial workers for Roosevelt. Listening to the president on the radio reinforced workers' sense that, in the words of steelworker George Patterson, "it seemed FDR was on our side, organizing with us." Roosevelt understood the power of the radio to build a constituency. He broadcasted forty formal and informal speeches between the spring of 1933 and the spring of 1935, and his wife, Eleanor, became a regular on the NBC variety show "Vanity Fair." An important byproduct of his strategy was that his working-class supporters came to feel a solidarity not only with him but also with the other FDR faithfuls they knew as well.[19]

In sum, rank-and-file workers were communicating better in their work groups and factories and feeling more akin to each other within Chicago and across the nation. But workers' sharing of more social and cultural experiences and greater identification with a national workers' community were not enough to ensure the success of the CIO. Job differences, ethnic and racial prejudices, and political disagreements between, for example, Communist and non-Communist workers persisted in the Chicago of the 1930s despite greater similarities in people's cultural lives. Those organizing in the city's factories knew that like a smoldering fire these animosities had the potential if provoked of destroying a rank-and-file union movement as they had in 1919. It took a CIO, aware that workers' common cultural ground offered new possibilities for national unity, to turn promise into reality by orchestrating a campaign that very deliberately drew workers into what I call a CIO "culture of unity." This strategy differed significantly from the approach of AFL unions, which typically had built on the distinctive culture of a trade. The CIO in this regard resembled more the labor movements of the late nineteenth and early twentieth centuries, the Knights of Labor and the Industrial Workers of the World (IWW), which emphasized what all workers had in common. Recognizing the danger of worker disunity and understanding the potential of shared culture to overcome it, those organizing the CIO's national union campaigns set about to build on workers' common cultural experiences to cultivate a culture of unity among the rank and file of America's factories. As a consequence, for the first four or five years of the CIO's existence, ordinary workers in mass production industries underwent an intensive socialization that affected almost every aspect of their lives.

THE CIO'S CULTURE OF UNITY

The CIO's effort to create a culture of unity that brought workers of different sexes, races, nationalities, and locales together was so basic to its organizing philosophy that it permeated all CIO union activities in Chicago on and off the shop floor. Solidarity, of course, was the age-old cry of labor movements, but it had a very particular significance to the industrial unionists trying to organize America's factories in the 1930s. If any theme prevailed in this historic drive to bring unions to manufacturing workers throughout the vast United States, it was the recognition that workers themselves must change to prevent the kinds of divisions that had doomed similar efforts to organize them in the past.

The chasms that CIO unions devoted themselves most intensively to closing separated workers of different races and ethnicities. In 1933, when the NIRA was enacted, packinghouse workers' enthusiasm for a union had been dampened by fear "that it would not be possible to achieve unionism because you had the split of black and white and too many nationalities . . . that they [employers] would play against each other," according to PWOC organizer Herbert March. As late as January 1935, a steelworker at Inland Steel similarly despaired that "WE WORKERS ARE THE FOOLS! Before you can hope to further your interests you must forget that the man working beside you is a 'Nigger,' Jew or 'Pollock.' The man working beside you, be he Negro, Jew or

Pollock is a working man like yourself and being exploited by the 'boss' in the name of racial and religious prejudice. You work together – FIGHT TOGETHER!!!" By 1939, after four intense years of CIO campaigning and education, unions like the PWOC felt they could justifiably claim that the situation today looked very different from the past, "when the packers were able to separate the different nationalities and use the Negro and the immigrant workers as strikebreakers. The union has been ironing out the differences between different national groups of workers whom the packers had been playing off against each other, and between Negro and white workers, and *today these groups stand united within a strong industrial union*." To a remarkable degree, this PWOC boast that workers had learned to see commonalities where once they had seen differences was true.[20]

CIO organizers from the grassroots to the national office made reaching out to black workers a top priority of the union campaign. Aware that the depression had destroyed blacks' privileged connection to the boss, unionists did whatever they could to win the confidence of black workers who long had been suspicious of AFL unions they felt were discriminatory. At the national level, the SWOC organized the National Conference of Negro Organizations To Support the Steel Drive in February 1937, bringing together in Pittsburgh black leaders and steelworkers from Birmingham to Chicago "to make it perfectly clear," according to a press release, "that the issue of black versus white will not arise in the CIO campaign to organize a steel union." Philip Murray promised the 186 delegates representing 110 organizations with more than 100,000 members, many of whom were prominent black community leaders, that with a union blacks would have the same opportunities for advancement and would earn the same pay as whites. He pointed to the success of the United Mine Workers' Union against the "race differential" as proof. The conference responded by pledging to set up local committees to help SWOC organizers, to run mass meetings to report on the conference, and to use black pulpits, press, and radio to urge all black steelworkers to join.[21]

In organizing campaigns within Chicago, organizers lost no time responding to black concerns. SWOC field workers set up a union headquarters in the Black Belt, so as to avoid the situation of 1919 when blacks who lived far from the steel mills felt isolated from the union drive.[22] The PWOC, which needed black support desperately to win a union in an industry where so many blacks worked, took up black causes on and off the shop floor. The union pushed for black job promotions, removal of black stars on time cards, integration of all-white departments like sliced bacon, and hiring of black workers in proportion to their presence in Chicago's population while pressuring Mayor Kelly to give blacks wider opportunities in the city at large by hiring them as streetcar and bus conductors.[23]

The CIO's determined effort to woo black workers succeeded. Blacks responded with tremendous enthusiasm to the CIO's drive. Everywhere, observers reported that blacks were among the first to rally to union campaigns. In the packing plants, the killing floors where blacks predominated became the most militant departments, and their centrality to the packing process proved invaluable in implementing the PWOC's workplace strategies. If this department went down, the whole plant went down. Packinghouse worker Sophie Kosciolowski speculated that "maybe because they felt they didn't have too much to lose, they seemed to have so much courage. . . . I think if it weren't for the . . . enthusiasm of the Negroes to join the union . . . we could[n't] have done it."[24] While Kosciolowski attributed black workers' support for the CIO to their desperation, Clarence Stoecker offered a somewhat different explanation for why blacks proved more receptive to the CIO than whites in the early stages of the drive at Harvester's McCormick Works, many going so far as opening their homes on the South Side for weekend meetings. He concluded that whereas young white workers preferred to see their factory jobs as temporary until they managed to fulfill dreams of opening a tavern or filling station or going to school to learn a trade, blacks cared about improving their working conditions at Harvester because they aspired to higher paying jobs there, even to becoming foremen.[25] Probably desperation and ambition both contributed to blacks' championing of the CIO, though blacks making agricultural implements at Harvester may have felt somewhat more eager than those laboring in the wretched packinghouses to stick with their present employer in the future.

A fascinating set of documents has survived that provides insight into black steelworkers' attitudes toward the CIO. In the summer of 1936, as SWOC was gaining a foothold in the Gary and South Works of U.S. Steel, black journalist Claude Barnett was hired by the industrial relations department of the company to learn what he could about black attitudes toward the CIO. Barnett organized a team of interviewers to surreptitiously go into the neighborhoods of black steelworkers and assess both the CIO's strength and the possible strategies U.S. Steel might employ to keep blacks loyal to the company. They discovered more hesitation among black steelworkers than in packing and at International Harvester, but overall the interviewers reported that "the arguments of the CIO were taking effect on the men," particularly because "the presence of Negro organizers and the reputation of the UMW are tending to allay the old ideas as to discrimination by labor unions against [Negroes]." In steel it was the nature of the CIO itself – opposed to the antiblack AFL, committed to sending blacks into the field as organizers, sympathetic with black steelworkers' unique grievances, and led by people like John L. Lewis and Sidney Hillman with solid track records – that won the confidence of black workers. The CIO's appeal was all the more effective, Barnett had to tell U.S. Steel managers, because among black workers, "the attitude of the company has been characterized by an almost total lack of regard for the workers":

> The Negro workers feel that the Company "double crossed" them. Even though they stood with the Company in the strike of "19" they did not benefit. A few men were kept in good jobs – but over the years these Colored men have been replaced with white – and no recognition of Negro "loyalty" was actually granted.

With the depression, moreover, U.S. Steel had even tried to push them out of what hard, dirty, hot, and low-paying jobs they still held, black workers felt. To make matters worse, Barnett concluded, any actions management might now take were likely to be construed as "just a sop." In a report filed in the winter of 1937, Barnett urged the company to take steps to meet blacks' principal demands – better working conditions, opportunity for advancement, and permanency of employment – but it is possible that the pessimism of Barnett's report may have contributed to U.S. Steel's decision that March to sign a contract with the CIO.[26]

Whatever their motivation, black workers made a dramatic shift from the apathy and, worse, opposition, to the unionization of steel and packing they had exhibited in 1919 and now looked to a multiracial union movement for their economic survival. From the individual black worker in Chicago to the politically powerful National Negro Congress, an organization of 585 black organizations founded in 1936, blacks conveyed that their hopes for the future rested with the CIO.[27]

With the CIO's encouragement, whites also made progress overcoming deep-rooted prejudices against blacks. "Overcoming prejudice didn't mean anyone got invited to somebody's house for Christmas dinner," PWOC unionist Leslie Orear explained, "But so far as on the job and in the union. . . . See, we were making a *religion* of racial unity," and with time, people really learned to respect each other. One black worker, Jim Cole, felt the CIO was making nothing short of revolution in the once racially polarized packing plants: "I don't care if the union don't do another lick of work raisin' our pay, or settling grievances about anything. I'll always believe they done the greatest thing in the world gettin' everybody who works in the yards together, and breakin' up the hate and bad feelings that used to be held against the Negro." Steelworkers made similar comments about how race relations had improved in the mills. South Chicago had long been known as a difficult place for blacks to be in, forcing black workers, for example, to avoid certain spots at night for fear of being attacked by white gangs. With the union, the situation improved noticeably. A few white steelworkers even went so far as inviting black co-workers home to dinner.[28] Racial unity became a watchword of the CIO's campaign in the 1930s, and to an astonishing degree in those early years – given both the long history of prejudice in industrial communities and many of the racial conflicts that would later erupt – it became a reality in locals everywhere. A black butcher in Armour's sheep kill, filled with optimism, boasted to a WPA interviewer in 1939 that whereas once "the white butchers hated the Negroes because they figured they would scab on them when trouble came and then get good-paying, skilled jobs besides, . . . with the CIO in, all that's like a bad dream gone. Oh, we still have a hard row, but this time the white men are with us and we're with them."[29] The CIO hardly created a racially integrated society, but it went further in promoting racial harmony than any other institution in existence at the time.

CIO unions also made sure that employers would never again take advantage of another potential division within the industrial work force – nationality. So that all ethnic groups as well as natives would participate, organizers worked closely with the ethnic and religious communities feeding workers into Chicago plants. Whereas by now many younger workers did not have strong ethnic identities, other Chicago workers still spoke Croatian or Polish or Spanish as their first language. Speakers, signs, and literature were prepared in all the appropriate languages and special events such as Polish dances, Mexican fiestas, and Irish ballad singing aimed to attract people of different ethnicities to union events. Staffs were painstakingly set up to include representatives of all the locally important ethnic groups. The staff of the PWOC, for example – Hank Johnson (black), Frank McCarty (Irish), Joseph Barrett (American), Sigmond Woldarozyk (Polish), Herbert March (Jewish), and Refugio Martinez (Mexican) – covered almost all the bases.[30] Moreover, ethnic institutions, although weakened by the depression, could still provide good recruiting grounds for the CIO. Union leaders consequently called on ethnic and religious organizations to lend their halls for meetings and to encourage their members to join. SWOC events at Croatian Hall or the Italian Cooperative Society and solicitations at Holy Name Society gatherings were standard fare.[31]

CIO organizers were ever mindful of how ethnic conflicts had disrupted similar unionizing efforts in the past. SWOC headquarters sponsored a national meeting of fraternal orders in Pittsburgh, whose success, *Steel Labor* claimed, marked "a fundamental change that has been taking place in American life . . . that some half a million Americans of foreign birth or extraction . . . all agreed to unite for a common purpose, the improvement of the lot of the nation's steel workers by union organization." CIO Regional Director Bittner followed suit with his own Chicago area convention of fraternal organizations in late November 1936 to "checkmate any Steel Trust plots to set steelworkers against each other on racial and religious lines, as they did in the 1919 strike," according to steel organizer George Patterson.[32]

The CIO's effort to preempt the ethnic conflict that it knew could easily resurface was particularly successful in the case of Mexicans who, like blacks, had served as strikebreakers in the 1919 era. Long banished to the most menial jobs in steel and packing plants and laid off more than their fair share during the depression, Mexican workers welcomed the CIO's attentions, quickly recognizing how seniority and a grievance structure would bring them more equality in pay, in promotions, and in treatment on the job. Mexican enthusiasm added a good deal of fuel to the CIO's fire. A Mexican Club in Packingtown, the Lazaro Cardena Club, delivered hundreds of signed union cards to the PWOC by taking on the job of collecting them itself. By 1939, organizers claimed that almost every Mexican in Armour was a member of Local 347. At Inland Steel, Nick Migas went so far as to claim that "the union spread like wildfire" because of Mexican support, and in steel more generally,

Mexicans became the first foreign-language group to organize 100 percent.[33]

As workers like these Mexicans came to share CIO leaders' commitment to ethnic unity, the CIO took every opportunity to advertise what a multiethnic community it had become. Polish and Italian organizing committees conspicuously welcomed each other at rallies, and SWOC locals flaunted their internationalism with activities such as "language days" on the picket line, when demonstrators marched in colorful European peasant garb. George Patterson's amusing account of the new tastes that reached his palate within the first few years of building a steel union reflected the celebration of ethnic diversity that the CIO promoted: "I, who had been confined to the four walls of a steel mill, now found out . . . about Hungarian goulash, minestrone soup, lox and blintzes of creamed cheese, corned beef on hard rolls or rye bread, gefilte fish, and other exotic dishes."[34]

Appealing to workers' ethnicity was a means, not an end, however, for CIO organizers. They sought just the right balance between acknowledging ethnic difference and articulating worker unity. Their strategy was to meet workers on their ethnic, or racial, ground and pull them into a self-consciously common culture that transcended those distinctions, so as to avoid what happened in 1919 when workers remained politicized within isolated ethnic communities. CIO leaders were aware that workers were increasingly sharing interests outside of their ethnic worlds, and they encouraged those experiences on and off the shop floor that brought workers closer together. At the workplace, the CIO reinforced unity among workers by applauding collective rank-and-file actions such as slowdowns and work stoppages but also through a strategy that we are apt today not to take seriously enough as it has lost much of its significance. The CIO utilized union buttons to create an alternative, and unified, workers' community within the factory. When workers dared to wear CIO buttons in the intimidating, tense plants of the mid-thirties, they powerfully asserted their independence from the boss and their alliance with all other union loyalists. This "emblem of freedom," as PWOC's Arthur Kampfert called it, was more than an innocuous symbol. Some workers like Stella Nowicki got fired for wearing one, and hundreds of others found that their CIO buttons incurred the wrath of their supervisors. Displaying a CIO button on the shop floor became a ritualized way for workers and shop stewards to openly declare their new allegiance. When black worker Phil Weightman was elected steward early in the organizing campaign at Swift, he accepted but challenged the other union members in hog kill to "come out in the open with him" and wear their union buttons the next day: "The next morning union buttons blossomed all over the hog kill."

Buttons carried so much significance that they became ammunition in the battle between the CIO and company unions on many shop floors. At South Works, for example, the company union, the Steel Employees Independent Labor Organization, fought the SWOC by distributing its own red, white, and blue buttons, "to make believe our union was foreign and didn't belong and they were the true blue Americans," steel unionist Al Towers remembered with disgust. Likewise, when a few company union men at Armour came to work in December 1938 wearing buttons of the Amalgamated Meat Cutters, evidence that they would try to fight the PWOC under another name now that their Mutual Association had been outlawed, three thousand workers from twenty-six departments responded to the provocation by stopping work. Once a contract was signed at Armour, workers there took pleasure in continuing to wear their CIO buttons so that people coming through on tours of the packing plant would be confronted with a sea of union buttons up and down the production lines. Buttons marked union members as sisters and brothers regardless of ethnic or racial origins.[35]

Outside of work, the CIO also recruited workers into a culture of unity by establishing common grounds for all workers. Thanks to the end of Prohibition and the reopening of taverns near plants, the unions gained a neutral ground free of territorial and ethnic associations to carry out a crucial mix of socializing and agitating. The Chicago CIO's history is filled with bars like Sam's Place next to Republic Steel, which served as workers' headquarters during the Memorial Day Massacre, and the famous saloon on Ashland Avenue, where the PWOC was founded. On a more routine basis, taverns provided regular meeting places for union members in particular departments as well as a central location for stewards to collect dues. To ensure the availability of such neutral territory, the PWOC took it upon itself to integrate many of the taverns and restaurants surrounding the stockyards, using the pressure of a white boycott against establishments refusing to serve blacks.[36]

Even more important, CIO unions put great efforts into developing social and recreation programs where workers who had little contact inside or outside the plant could develop stronger ties to each other through sharing leisure time. The pages of all CIO newspapers were filled with reports of dances, picnics, summer camps, softball teams – the new game of the thirties that "everyone could play" – and bowling leagues, the old game of the twenties that welfare capitalists had favored for the same reason. Recreation could provide a glue to bind workers of different races, ethnicities, and ages together.[37] One unionist was particularly convinced that sports carried the key to involving young people in the PWOC: "Now, when the lads at Illinois Meat want to bowl, instead of going to any alley with some neighborhood gang and forgetting all about the union, the union members bowl together. People who never bowled before are learning this sport and having plenty of fun, and all because the union made it possible for them to get into the game. We work together on the job. Now we are playing together at night. It's making us all better friends so that we'll stick together in the organization whatever comes." A good game could also introduce CIO workers in different plants to each other. SWOC lodges in the South Works and Gary Works of U.S. Steel spent Labor Day of 1937 battling each other on a baseball field and then picnicking together afterward. The PWOC regularly entered teams in the Labor Sports League and, in 1940, established the CIO Softball League of Chicago to encourage some friendly feuding among packing and nearby FE locals.[38] The CIO competed for workers' loyalty in much the same way that welfare capitalists had during the 1920s, when they had used company sports and social activities to make their culture of paternalism predominant over workers' ethnic and neighborhood commitments.

In promoting this culture of unity, the CIO used a tool that it observed was already bringing workers together: the radio. When William Z. Foster, veteran of the organizing drives in packing and steel in 1919, wrote a pamphlet entitled *Organizing Methods in the Steel Industry* to suggest how the effort in the mid-1930s might improve on earlier failures, he stressed what a big difference the radio could make: "In an industry such as steel where the company maintains terrorism to prevent the workers from attending open meetings, the radio takes the union message directly into the workers' homes."[39] John L. Lewis and Philip Murray lost no time following Foster's advice. Typical was the SWOC memo that circulated in late December 1936 asking all field workers to publicize the fact that Lewis would deliver a radio address between 7:30 and 8:00 EST over the Red Network of NBC.[40] Even on the local level of the Calumet district, employee representatives from all

Plate 35. Here, Daniel Senise of Blue Island, Illinois, an industrial suburb of Chicago, bowls with his union bowling team. In an effort to build solidarity among workers in the late 1930s, the various organizing committees of the CIO developed recreation programs that would bring members together outside of working hours. Much the way welfare capitalists had used social activities to foster loyalty to the company during the 1920s, CIO organizers hoped that by encouraging workers to socialize together, union loyalty would supplant more divisive cultural affiliations along the lines of ethnicity, race, and neighborhood.

the area mills who met in November 1936 to unify their organizing efforts decided to use the radio to reach their collective constituents. Two weeks later, however, SWOC leader Bittner, who was struggling to exert SWOC control over these grassroots worker movements, announced at a District 31 field workers' meeting that "there will be no radio talks," testimony to his recognition of the radio's power. From his point of view, it was all right for Chicago steelworkers to hear national leaders like Lewis, Murray, and even Bittner on the radio but certainly not independent-minded local organizers like George Patterson and Michael Ostroski.[41]

By 1939, the CIO's use of radio in organizing had progressed far beyond the occasional Lewis or Murray speech. That spring, the Chicago PWOC put on a weekly radio program that featured ordinary packinghouse workers talking about the union drives in their departments. To reach a larger audience of packing workers, the PWOC also inaugurated a series of radio broadcasts over the most powerful radio stations in the Midwest.[42] Not only did CIO unions put the radio to direct use in their organizing campaigns, but also they recognized that radio listening would indirectly benefit their cause by expanding the interests workers had in common. CIO newspapers featured regular columns filled with the latest gossip about radio stars, professional athletes, and network shows. In using radio to unify workers of different backgrounds, CIO unions intentionally or not reinforced the attractions of network radio.[43]

Network radio contributed to a third kind of unity that the CIO sought. Workers had to be unified not only racially and ethnically but also geographically. Steelworkers in 1919 had suffered for their local orientations. At the very height of the strike, steelworkers in some communities were persuaded that strikers had already returned to work in other strike centers. To avoid similar manipulation, it was clear that workers needed to be well informed about the activities of their peers elsewhere and to coordinate strategy as much as possible. If employers could manage to keep track of union activities in all their own plants as well as their competitors', so could workers. It was fear that the grassroots organizing activity within the Calumet region during 1935 and 1936 would fragment in the same way it had before, in fact, that prompted George Patterson, President of the Associated Employes of South Works, to write John L. Lewis in January 1936, urging him to "tie all the unions of the Calumet Region together" in a national "drive

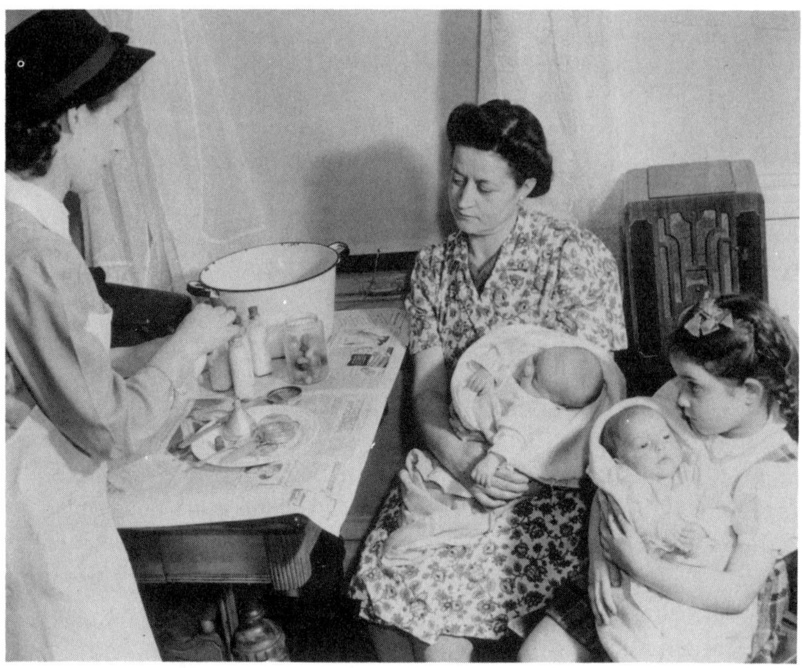

Plate 36. This photograph from the files of the Infant Welfare Society of Chicago was intended to show a trained nurse demonstrating to a poor mother how to prepare bottles for her twin baby boys. It also illustrates that by the mid-1930s radios were standard equipment in even the poorest homes in Chicago. Union organizers, recognizing what an important role the radio played in factory workers' lives, used it in their effort to build a CIO "culture of unity" that cut across region, race, ethnicity, and gender.

on steel." "Unless something is done shortly by a great power stepping in and welding the multitude of independents together," Patterson warned, "all the ground gained will be lost in organizing the steel workers into an Industrial Union, this because of the reason that the independents are all working at loose ends, and not co-operatively."[44]

Once it launched its organizing drive, the SWOC tried not only to unite workers within a steel region like Calumet or Pittsburgh but also to develop ties between these areas. One of the first things that SWOC's research department did was to ferret out wage inequalities between U.S. Steel plants. Golden and Ruttenberg reported that this information was quickly sent out to organizers, so they could blare through the loudspeakers at a mill gate, "Who said a craneman is worth twenty cents more in Pittsburgh than in Chicago? Does a craneman eat any more in Pittsburgh? Does he have any more children to clothe? . . . No! No! A thousand times No! Join the union and bring justice to all workers."[45] To further expand workers' national consciousness, CIO newspapers like the *CIO News* and *Steel Labor* gave extensive coverage to organizing activities nationwide in all the industries where the CIO was active. At meetings of CIO locals, members heard similar reports. A call for the December 18, 1936, meeting of the South Works SWOC lodges urged people to come and "hear about the settlement of the Bendix Plant and Midland Steel sit down strikes. You must hear about the March of Steelworkers, in Gary, Indiana Harbor and Pittsburgh and Youngstown, Pennsylvania." Organizers also made good use at rallies and in union literature of patriotic symbols, such as the American flag and portraits of President Roosevelt, to reinforce workers' shared national identity.[46]

The CIO's campaign to get workers in one plant to empathize and cooperate with workers in another worked. Even before the CIO came to Chicago, steel unionists demonstrated their increasing cosmopolitanism by establishing the Calumet Council of Employee Representatives and communicating directly with their Pittsburgh peers. By the time of the Little Steel Strike in spring 1937, a year after the CIO came into existence, all the steel lodges in District 31 routinely sent "solidarity auto caravans" to each other's demonstrations, and steelworkers in the Calumet region kept such close tabs on the steel towns of Pittsburgh's Monongahela Valley that they felt almost like neighbors.[47] Workers at Harvester, Armour, and Swift also kept careful track of company policies and union activities at other plants within their own industries. Both the PWOC and the FE held founding conventions where delegates from all the packing and agricultural equipment centers in the nation met in Chicago, and thereafter locals kept workers informed of events elsewhere. On a more local scale within Chicago, "flying squads" of organized workers at Armour and smaller unionized packing plants paid evening visits to the homes of Swift and Wilson workers to lobby for the union.[48]

Workers in different industries within Chicago similarly had come to understand that their fates were intertwined. Stockyard workers made regular trips to South Chicago to join their union brothers and sisters on the picket line, and Swift workers supported the strike at the

McCormick Works in 1941, realizing that if Harvester workers won a 75 cents an hour minimum wage, it would be that much easier for Swift workers to get 20 cents more per hour "instead of that killing Bonus System."[49] A Chicago reporter was so struck in 1939 by how much more solidarity existed among Chicago workers than ever before that he wrote, "Years ago, the worst place in the country for a mass meeting was Chicago. The people would stay in their own neighborhoods and not budge, but now. . . ." After an event like the massive CIO rally at the Chicago Coliseum that July, crowds of workers waited for trolleys to take them home in every direction – to the West Side, to South Chicago, to the Black Belt. Furthermore, it was reflective of Chicago working people's sense of participating in a movement that transcended any one particular plant, industry, or city that they usually spoke of being a member of the CIO, not the SWOC, PWOC, or FE.[50] The days when U.S. Steel could play workers in Gary against workers in Pittsburgh, or when people in Back of the Yards were oblivious to the troubles of people in South Chicago, finally seemed gone.

The last prong of the CIO's culture of unity consisted of developing a family-oriented union culture. Because workers of all races, ethnicities, and regions shared the experience of family, activities that "bring families closer together in a strong bond of friendship," in the words of the FE Women's Auxiliary, provided another source of unity.[51] Even the SWOC, which one might have expected, as a steel union, to celebrate male culture, was family oriented, with Christmas parties and "Junior Lodges" for SWOC children, family spaghetti dinners, and special children's and women's days on the picket line. Beginning in December 1937, moreover, the SWOC newspaper, *Steel Labor*, was mailed to workers at home with the addition of a women's page to keep wives and daughters involved in the union.[52] SWOC organizers, as others in the CIO, had gradually come to recognize the key role women played in decision making within the working-class family, although it took a while for some of the old-line UMW leaders to admit it. Increasingly, *Steel Labor* featured articles and cartoons like the one depicting a steelworker's wife ordering her husband and son as they left home for the mill, "You pay your dues today. If there had been a union in the mill twenty-five years ago, we'd be a lot better off."[53]

Hundreds of women in the Calumet district performed a serious organizing service through the eleven women's auxiliaries they founded. Steelworkers' wives did the traditional female work of raising money, operating strike kitchens, and organizing social activities to foster fellowship, but they did not stop there. They also went door to door in steelworkers' neighborhoods to convince other wives that they should encourage their men to join SWOC. Their printed magazine, *Women in Steel*, helped spread the message even further. Wives and soon organizers knew that the approval or disapproval of a steelworker's wife could determine his loyalty. "Once you convince the women, and they convince the men, then everything's fine, you know. We were able to sign a lot of cards that way," Dorothy Patterson, a founder of the Women's Auxiliary at South Works, explained. Women like Patterson also knew that if the wives took the lead in breaking down racial, ethnic, and neighborhood barriers, the men would follow. The roster of the Calumet district's SWOC auxiliaries read like a league of nations. Increasingly common were events like the birthday party for a black member of the auxiliary held in the home of an Italian woman and attended by whites and blacks. And no one was in a better position to prevail upon the Catholic priests, who had long benefited from the faithfulness of steel wives and daughters. Women in steel proved they were powerful even as they remained auxiliary.[54]

In packing, where many more women actually worked in the plants, this family agenda led the PWOC to endorse women's auxiliaries as well as to organize women working in the packinghouses by making their grievances a major part of the PWOC's demands. Female packinghouse workers, of course, shared male workers' discontent with speedups and unsanitary conditions, but they also felt specially victimized by their bosses. An Armour worker, Sophie Kosciolowski, ennumerated women's common complaints: "Some of us are required to do extremely heavy work.... Then there are those who do skilled work yet receive no extra pay for their skill.... Still others of us do the sort of work that men do, yet their pay is far below a man's.... If Armour and Company has taken advantage of the men employees, the company has taken twice as much advantage of the girls. Bossy foremen seem to be always trying to push the girls around." The union's call for "equal pay for equal work" rallied many female packing workers to the union. When Eva Barnes promised the women she was organizing, "We're gonna get the same wages" as the men who were paid 31 cents more an hour for identical work, "I had forty women the first day I went out."[55]

Despite the PWOC's concern about pay equity for women, however, its family orientation reinforced traditional female roles. The equal-pay demand won the support of many men less for what it offered women than as a protection against employers replacing male with female workers, which had become a prevalent practice during the depression.[56] Many of the appeals to working women, although acknowledging the necessity of their labor for family survival, gave a double message. A leaflet aimed at young women working in the packing plants, "For Women Only: The Perils of Packinghouse Patty," for example, told a story through poem of overworked, sixteen-year-old Patty whose life was made even more oppressive by her boss's sexual advances. She finds the solution to her problems in the union, which delivers both unity against the boss and "a handsome and brave CIO steward."[57]

The bulletin of the PWOC Women's Auxiliary, "We Women: Wives and Friends of Packing House Workers," encapsulated the prescribed role for women. Under the motto "We Aim to Assist" women reported their activities as enlightened consumers of union labels and fair-priced goods, educators, fund-raisers, party givers, and especially social progressives. "Women, young and old, regardless of their race, color or nationality" were encouraged to participate and were featured in articles breaking down customary barriers. The Armour Women's Auxiliary traveled all the way to South Chicago to visit a "sister club" at U.S. Steel, Mexican wife Aida Martinez received a layette for her new daughter from fellow auxiliary members, and a black woman told of how the PWOC helped her overcome a prejudice against unions born during her childhood in the South.[58] Working-class women in Chicago had frequently taken part in union activities before the mid-1930s. Their militance in the 1921 packing strike, when they threw rocks, bottles, and red pepper at mounted policemen while shouting "Cossacks! Cossacks!" had become lore in Back of the Yards. But the CIO's conviction that recruiting the family's male breadwinner was not enough, that women needed to guide a family union culture, institutionalized the family unit in the union in a new way that both encouraged women's participation and restricted their turf.[59]

Chicago's industrial workers made good unionists by the late 1930s because of what they had learned from this CIO culture of unity as well as from their frustrations with welfare capitalism and the Great Depression during the previous decade and a half. When employers tried pulling out their old tricks of "divide and conquer," they were frequently met with workers' scorn, which seemed to surprise them. The following story conveys how unified Chicago's rank-and-file factory workers had become and how little many employers understood that. A black worker at Armour sought to take advantage of the company's credit union, established in the mid-1930s to keep people loyal to the firm and out of the CIO. "They knew he was a union man, so they made it hard for him," the worker telling the story recalled. He was told he could not get a loan unless another worker who had a bank account in the credit union signed for him. The black worker asked Charlie, a white man who had been in the yards a long time and had an account:

> Charlie walked into the office and signed them papers, and them in charge of the loans with their eyes popping like a fish out of water. Manager was so upset he asked Charlie to step into his private office. He said to him, "You really mean you want to sign for that man, and he a colored man! I hate to think a white man would want to take on that responsibility." Charlie – he's Irish – looked at this manager and grinned. He said, "Well, sure now, I do appreciate that bit of advice, seein you ain't chargin nothin for it. But that black boy's my friend. He works with me. He's a union brother and I guess maybe you're surprised to hear that I'm in the union, too! So just save that advice of yours for somebody don't know no better." Walked out of there and slammed the door.[60]

All over Chicago and elsewhere in the nation small moments like this testified to the social revolution that the CIO, at least for a time, was making.

WHY DIVERSITY?

The last two chapters have stressed the experiences that helped rank-and-file workers become more effective unionists in the late 1930s than they or their predecessors had proved in 1919. They learned lessons coping with welfare capitalism and the Great Depression, they developed greater potential for carrying out a unified campaign as they shared more of a cultural world, and they were inspired by the culture of unity that the CIO promoted. The importance of these changes for explaining the rank and file's mentality and behavior by the late 1930s becomes even clearer when one tries to account for the diversity in workers' responses to the CIO, both among workers who supported the CIO and those in two major Chicago factories, the Hawthorne Works of Western Electric and the Wisconsin Steel Works of International Harvester, who resisted it.

In factories organized by the CIO, individual workers varied in their commitment to the union, but no simple formula predicted across industries who would be the rabid union booster, who the more reticent supporter. The kinds of work people did, their insecurity about losing their jobs, their history with the company, these and other factors made each working population and job situation unique. In packing, for example, observers commented that blacks and young people flocked first to the union and that women were often slower to join. Workers on the killing floors signed on early, moreover, not only because many of them were black, according to Leslie Orear, but also because of the kind of control they collectively felt over the product: "There was a sense of solidarity on the killing floor where people up and down the line were looking up and down the line themselves and their product was coming from up there and you're all a part of this thing. When the line is fast, everybody has to work faster." The perishability of meat made these workers all the more powerful. In steel and agricultural implements, similar factors related to the demography of the work force and the subtleties of the work process dictated who in the rank and file rallied to the union from the start.[61]

It is easier to explain diversity among Chicago's different CIO unions than to predict which individuals would become staunch CIO advocates within any particular plant. How well employers had implemented welfare capitalism over the previous decade and a half and how they now reacted to the CIO explains much of the variation in CIO union militance. One can place the CIO unions within the Chicago plants we have been following along a continuum from left (militant) to right (moderate) that corresponds to the effectiveness of employers' welfare capitalism: McCormick Works and Tractor Works of International Harvester, Armour, U.S. Steel, and Swift. In other words, workers who felt more rewarded by welfare capitalism, as at Swift, became less militant unionists than workers at Armour or McCormick Works. PWOC activists constantly complained that workers at Swift were much harder to organize than at other packing plants where the boss had a poorer reputation. Mary Hammond described how her own brother exhibited this frustrating loyalty to the company: "He never joined the union. He's just a suckhole for the company. He sticks up for Swift and Company like he owned the damn place." Even when the PWOC finally amassed enough support at Swift to win a contract, the local there remained a thorn in the side of union leftists, leading an anti-Communist movement within the PWOC.[62] Although U.S. Steel was certainly no model welfare capitalist, management's early cooperation with SWOC helped to keep the union moderate, reinforcing the conservative bent of the UMW's leadership. Because U.S. Steel proved so accommodating, SWOC leaders felt able by 1938 to purge the steel union of Communist organizers. The continued resistance of Armour and International Harvester, meanwhile, meant that SWOC sent these Communist organizers on to the PWOC and the FE where it knew difficult and dirty work still needed to be done. There, company intransigence and union militance became mutually reinforcing.[63]

The role that the success or failure of welfare capitalism played in motivating rank-and-file workers to organize is all the more evident when one investigates why workers at Hawthorne Works of Western Electric and Harvester's Wisconsin Steel Works chose to stick with so-called independent unions rather than join the CIO. By the early 1940s, when workers in Chicago's other major industries had endorsed CIO unions, moral capitalist workers at Hawthorne and Wisconsin Steel believed their employers had come close to creating "fair" places to work, particularly in comparison with surrounding factories, and instead favored the Western Electric Independent Labor Association and the Progressive Steelworkers' Union, both of which had close ties to management.[64]

As earlier chapters have shown, managers at Hawthorne and Wisconsin Steel had proved themselves trustworthy paternalists during the 1920s, offering good benefits and limiting layoffs as much as possible. In the Great Depression, although their workers still suffered cut-backs and lost jobs, they made a more serious commitment to work-sharing, alternative production schemes and relief programs than managers at other plants did, facilitated, as we have seen, by their more advantageous market conditions. When the CIO came to town and tried to win over the labor forces at Hawthorne and Wisconsin Steel, these workers rewarded their employers by choosing to stay loyal to less contentious "company unions."[65]

The choice of Wisconsin Steel workers to reject the CIO, despite SWOC's repeated efforts to organize them, is all the more interesting because they were the only manufacturing workers at International Harvester not to join a CIO union, whether the FE or UAW. (The company's coal miners also supported an independent union over the UMW.) As noted earlier, Wisconsin Steel workers felt more positively about their jobs during the 1920s and 1930s because they compared them to those both at the neighboring U.S. Steel mill and at other Harvester plants. Most importantly, because Wisconsin Steel's management valued them as a labor force, workers faced fewer layoffs, particularly during the depression when workers at other Harvester plants were losing their jobs. Workers did their share, too, to keep Wisconsin Steel's work force stable. The large percentage of workers coming from the surrounding community of South Deering had displayed little interest during the interwar years in quitting and moving on. The comment of one long-time resident of South Deering epitomized the attitude common among residents: "That was a good place to work years ago; . . . always work, work, work, continuous. Other plants would have strikes, but never Wisconsin Steel."[66]

Welfare capitalism, moreover, was more effective within the insular community of South Deering than among the more dispersed workers of McCormick or Tractor Works. For example, contrary to management's intentions, the gardens supplied as a relief measure during the depression offered McCormick workers a rare opportunity to get together outside work and share complaints about the company as they hoed. Years later, an article in a 1950 issue of *FE-UE News* reminded workers of the "tenant farmers" of the depression, "men whom Harvester couldn't provide a full weeks work for, so they were given a piece of worn-out land in the suburbs and told to raise enough cabbage to make out." "Out of the talks in the cabbage patches," the paper claimed, came dreams of a real union. In contrast, at Wisconsin Steel gardens close to the "company town" of South Deering served to reinforce workers' already favorable feelings toward Harvester. Assured that management would meet the wages the CIO negotiated at nearby steel plants, workers at Wisconsin Steel felt they had nothing to lose in trusting their fate to the Progressive Steelworkers' Union.[67]

Although harder to pin down, the experience of workers at these two plants demonstrates not only how germane workers' experience with welfare capitalism was to the CIO's success but also how much it mattered that workers shared a common culture. Whereas workers at plants that signed on with the CIO were increasingly participating in national "mass culture," workers at Hawthorne and Wisconsin Steel were living more traditional cultural lives in their isolated communities of Cicero and South Deering. Care must be taken not to exaggerate the differences, but some intriguing evidence suggests noteworthy comparisons. When chain stores were taking business away from independent, ethnic merchants in other working-class neighborhoods, the storekeepers of Cicero and Berwyn, many of them Bohemian, were effectively keeping them out. They launched a successful "Trade on Roosevelt Road" campaign in 1933 and continued to benefit from antichain sentiment in the community in the years that followed. As recently as 1972, in fact, a visitor to Cicero was shocked to discover that "Cermak Road [Cicero's main street] is a wide-berthed street, which runs for blocks and blocks unscarred by chain store shopping . . . Kobzinga Furniture, Novak Sporting Goods, Old Prague Restaurant, Richard J. Talsky: Doctor of Chiropractic, Hraska Bakery . . . Pavlicek Drugs . . . Klaus Restaurant, Bohemian–American Food – Cermak Road's storefronts offer as useful an index to Cicero's demography and character as is perhaps to be had anywhere." Not surprisingly, Cicero in the 1930s was also the home of radio station WHFC, a low-powered station that continued to broadcast ethnic programs in the Chicago area.[68]

South Deering was if anything more isolated than Cicero, allowing its residents to also ignore some of the national cultural trends that elsewhere unified workers across ethnic communities, and with peers in other plants in the city and country. In 1937, it was the only community in Southeast Chicago not to have a movie theater, indeed the only working-class neighborhood in the city surveyed in Table 9 that had none. Not surprisingly, a survey in 1939 of the movie-going habits of seventh and eighth graders living in South Deering and the Bush, the South Chicago neighborhood bordering U.S. Steel's South Works plant, revealed that girls and boys in South Deering were more than twice as likely not to have attended the movies during the previous week than their cohorts in the Bush. If this was the case among the age group usually most involved in mass culture, one can only guess when their parents last went to the movies or what radio programs they preferred.[69] The insularity of this South Deering community differed greatly from the residential experiences of McCormick workers. CIO unionists observed that organizing workers at the McCormick Works required them to use special tactics like home visits because employees lived so dispersed throughout the city. To the extent that there was an adjacent community feeding workers to the McCormick plant, it was a neighborhood filled with Italian Socialists and other radicals, a sharp contrast to South Deering's conservatism.[70]

Western Electric and Wisconsin Steel also assured employees living in their respective surrounding communities that traditional race relations could continue. Hawthorne only began to hire blacks in 1941 when its status as the largest single producer of communication and electronic equipment for the war effort required it, and Wisconsin Steel first let in a small number of black workers when it too became involved in war production. Roosevelt's Executive Order 8802 prohibited racial discrimination in defense industries. The absence of black workers throughout the 1920s and 1930s not only made it easier for residents of Cicero and South Deering to keep their provincial worlds intact but also deprived these plants of a population that had catalyzed unionization elsewhere.[71]

The socially and culturally isolated communities of Cicero and South Deering were a conservative force in the lives of their workers. By continuing to reinforce the ethnic insulation, racial exclusiveness, geographical separatism, and employee dependency of an earlier era, they equipped workers poorly to challenge paternalistic relationships with their employers. At the same time, however, it should be noted that corporate paternalism had helped these workers preserve the kind of community life they wanted. Because workers at Wisconsin Steel, for example, were able to use Harvester's welfare capitalist commitment to protect their community of South Deering, it resonated for them in ways it never did for workers at McCormick or Tractor Works. It should come as no surprise that when the Wagner Act made unionization almost mandatory in American mass production industries, workers at Hawthorne and Wisconsin Steel preferred the more traditional, deferential option of the company union.

The limited impact of the CIO in these plants and communities meant, furthermore, that its culture of unity did not penetrate deeply enough to provide a unifying force of its own. It is revealing that these two communities became the settings for two of the worst race riots to take place in Chicago since 1919. Significantly, the Cicero Race Riots of 1951 and the Trumbull Park Riots two years later both took place when blacks tried to move into housing in the back yards of these factories where traditional racial divisions had rarely been challenged, either by employers or workers. That the war brought a small number of blacks to work in these plants was worrisome enough. The possibility that they actually might move next door was unbearable to many residents. Without the CIO, these communities had no indigenous institution capable of moderating racial fear.[72]

This diversity both among CIO-affiliated unions and between CIO and non-CIO unions suggests that more than anything else, the interaction of two factors determined what kind of union workers in any particular plant would support: first, the employer's behavior, particularly his commitment to welfare capitalism and his reaction to unionization when it arrived; second, the strength of a unified workers' culture, both inside and outside the CIO, to bring employees together to participate in a national union movement. Employers and rank-and-file workers together shaped the particular variant of the union story that emerged in each one of Chicago's mass production plants.

UNIONISM CIO STYLE

Chicago's industrial workers turned to CIO unions during the 1930s for much the same reasons that they had come to depend on the state. As employers' welfare capitalism and the organizations of their own communities were failing them in the Great Depression, they had to look elsewhere for survival and for the kind of equity they felt they deserved as citizens and workers. By 1940, many of Chicago's factory workers had become invested in two "new" institutions, government and union. As both new Democratic voters and new rank-and-file union members, workers felt like proud and powerful participants. They had made the New Deal and the CIO possible.

A very particular kind of unionization emerged during the 1930s through the CIO. By focusing on rank-and-file workers, this chapter brings to light some divergences from the usual generalizations made about the CIO. Chicago's factory workers were aided by a friendly New Deal state in their struggle for a union, but their own assertiveness helped make it so. Likewise, workers were assisted by organizers, but they disciplined those organizers, particularly Communist ones, to respect the rank and file's own values. Whereas workers made bread-and-butter demands through the union, these grievances were ideologically based in workers' commitment to moral capitalism, a belief that capitalism and its factory outposts could be made fair and just for all.

The majority of industrial workers obviously were not anticapitalist revolutionaries, but they did demonstrate militance in their union campaigns, particularly on the shop floor, that suggests they had a clear sense of themselves as a "class" apart from their employers. Work stoppages and slowdowns, sit-down strikes that challenged the property rights of employers, confrontations with police on picket lines, and a myriad of other actions that called for worker solidarity against the boss all demonstrated workers' awareness of their distinctive class interests, albeit within a larger framework of accepting capitalism. Steelworker George Patterson acknowledged how much bolder union leaflets were in defaming the boss in the late 1930s than they are today: "It was nothing for us to draw the body of a man and put a rat's head on him and say, 'Well, here's one rat and this is what he says. What do you say, mister worker?'"[73] If one accepts the approach of sociologist Rick Fantasia, that workers' class consciousness is better revealed through their collective actions at crucial moments of militancy than through static questionnaires probing for "disembodied mental attitudes," then those who labored in Chicago's steel, packing, and agricultural implement plants surely displayed a kind of "class consciousness" as they struggled to establish CIO unions.[74]

At the root of this class consciousness, moreover, was a worker culture that unified workers across race, ethnicity, region, age, and sex and made their common action possible. To make this issue all the more complex, however, this worker culture owed a lot to mainstream culture, to the unfulfilled promises of employers' welfare capitalism, and to the unifying powers of mass culture. Experiences workers shared going to the movies, shopping at chain stores, or tuning into the radio tied them tighter to each other than when they had lived in more insular cultural communities. If workers were becoming more like each other, inevitably, of course, they were becoming more like other Americans. But as advertisers and marketers were learning to make distinctions within the "mass market" and were gearing products specifically to this working-class audience, total cultural homogenization as it had once been imagined never became a reality. Advertising agencies lost no time in recognizing the profits that would result from factory workers making a more decent living once they were unionized. In the October 1937 issue of the J. Walter Thompson Company monthly bulletin, *People*, the lead story, "Your Customer, the Worker: With New Wants and a Fattening Purse, He Enlarges Many Markets," probed the distinctive tastes of American workers. The trade journal *Chain Store Age* began in this period to speak of serving three markets, with "the price customer" and "the quality customer" at either end of the class spectrum. A&P made the unique shopping needs and cooking habits of a working-class family, the Steinmillers, the subject of an early issue of *Woman's Day* magazine, which the store began to publish in 1937 as a way of showcasing its own Ann Page label and other standard brands, to convince working-class customers that the chain grocery was adapting to suit their lives. Earlier in the chapter, we saw that radio broadcasters in the mid-1930s made the same adjustment to a segmented market.[75] Although workers were becoming more integrated into mainstream mass culture, that "mass culture" was altering to accommodate their distinctive tastes. A working-class version of mass culture was taking shape in both the experience of working people and the consciousness of promoters.

It should also be noted that contrary to the usual assumption that mass culture was depoliticizing, the experience of industrial workers in the 1930s suggests that even as workers shared more in national commercial culture, integration enabled them to mount more effective political action, specifically to overcome the cultural fragmentation that had hindered them earlier. Workers who partook of mass culture did not become passive politically, even as they led lives that on the surface at least may have looked increasingly like those of the middle class. Chicago steelworkers who organized unions as they listened to Joe Louis fights over network radio were inspired to assert themselves as workers, not to identify with middle-class America. Much as was the case in the 1920s, the context in which workers experienced mass culture in the 1930s helped shape its impact on them. At a time when they were all suffering from the depression and searching for collective solutions, talking about a boxing match on the radio or the latest bargain at the A&P helped workers to maintain their group identity. Ironically, the broader dissemination of commercial culture that accompanied its consolidation in the 1930s may have done more to create an integrated working-class culture than a classless American one. In a divergence from the frequent claims of labor history, it was not the artisan worker tied to a "traditional" face-to-face community who built a union this time around. Rather, it was his or her more "modern" neighbor, working the assembly line at a factory and enmeshed in all the commercialism of mass culture, who brought the CIO to Chicago.

The particular course that CIO unionization took, however, did have some costs. A national-level CIO seemed the only way to compete with large employers who were themselves national entities. The failures of 1919 had proved that. But grassroots spontaneity and local concerns often were subordinated to the national CIO agenda. This imposition of "top-down" control happened first and most dramatically in steel, where the national leadership of SWOC began very early to tie the hands of its locals. At the start, district officers were appointed, not elected, and even after elections were held starting in 1944, it became virtually impossible to unseat District 31's director, Joe Germano. Locals also had little fiscal independence. Member dues went directly to the steel union's central office. As early as January 1937, Bittner was telling his organizers in Chicago, "We are dictating policy of all lodges until steel is organized. Democracy is important, but at this time collective bargaining and higher wages are the issues." When Bittner decided to divide South Works Local 65 into four, more controllable locals, staff organizer George Patterson, who deeply respected the will of the rank and file from whose bosom he had risen, despaired: "Democracy from the bottom up, that we had practiced in Local 65, was now difficult to pursue. We had different conditions to face. Four local unions in South Works, each from a different geographical area of the plant." Steelworkers who had managed to overcome the fragmentation their employers had encouraged now had to contend with a union leadership also bent on dividing them. Similar frustration over lack of autonomy arose when the grievance committeemen elected by the different departments of South Works decided they would rather meet with the company's managers alone: "lo and behold, they found that there was always going to be a [SWOC] staff member coming into the meetings in order to see that the union would be guided." It did not take long for Patterson and other veterans of the grassroots Associated Employes to realize that "what *we* wanted" was not of concern to the men at the top: "They were hand-picking what we would call 'yes-men': anybody that could stand and talk and didn't bow to their thinking was gradually eliminated."[76] Although CIO leaders were less personally invested in the packing and farm equipment unions and hence did not tend as much to impose their authority on these locals in the early years, when the larger political environment became more anti-Communist, these left-wing unions found the CIO's top leadership interfering more.

A second cost of the CIO's organizing strategy was that its family orientation kept women from gaining much of a role in union leadership. Even a progressive union like the PWOC expected that the male breadwinner would represent the family's interests in policy making, that in its power structure the union would replicate the social relations of the traditional family. Although women made up a large percentage of packinghouse workers and union members and equal pay for equal work concerned union leaders, women received little official recognition by the union. Stella Nowicki complained bitterly, "I did the shit work, until all hours, as did the few other women who didn't have family obligations. And then when the union came around giving out jobs with pay, the guys got them." The PWOC, like most other unions, wanted women to join unions, organize auxiliaries, and even shape union culture, but they did not make much room for them on center stage. Real power was left in the hands of the men in their lives. The worst of it, according to Nowicki, was that women soon internalized these union values of challenging class but not gender relations; it was difficult to get women who "looked upon the union as a man's job" to demand to be stewards and office holders. Consequently, by reinforcing the patriarchal family, the CIO did not encourage workers to challenge traditional gender relationships as much as ethnic and racial ones, even as women's presence in the industrial work force increased substantially with the war and its aftermath.[77]

Finally, a third choice made by the CIO that cost workers concerns the union's relationship to government. The decision of workers and their unions to look to the government for protection ultimately compromised union independence. Rank-and-file steelworkers had become so dependent on FDR, for instance, that when the president responded unsupportively to the tragedy of the Memorial Day Massacre during the effort in the spring of 1937 to organize "Little Steel," the strikers' militance dissipated. Workers who had rallied demonstrators to Republic Steel with posters that declared "Roosevelt Gave It, Republic Is Trying to Take It Away" were devastated when the president denounced both company and union with the words "A curse on both your houses." Roosevelt's condemnation proved more lasting than popular outrage at the Chicago police for firing on peaceful demonstrators. Within a few months, workers at Little Steel were back at work and the SWOC had to cancel the strike despite the ten dead and over a hundred wounded. Industrial workers had so much invested in their alliance with FDR and his government that when these authorities backed off from supporting labor in direct confrontation with business, it was extremely difficult for CIO leaders to defy them.[78] John L. Lewis learned this lesson the hard way when he endorsed Wendell Wilkie for president over Roosevelt in 1940. This beloved leader of labor found himself personally sacrificed on the altar of government. According to

Leslie Orear, Lewis went from being "number one hero to number one clod" overnight among Chicago's packinghouse workers.[79] When government took a stronger regulatory hand to labor in wartime and in the postwar period with the restrictive Taft–Hartley Act, this kind of union movement, as dependent as it had become on the state, would not have the autonomy to mount an effective resistance.

Over time, rank-and-file workers would find themselves freer of the employer autocracy and paternalism that had ruled their lives for decades – certainly a blessing. But they would also be subjected to new tyrannies that their CIO industrial revolution had precipitated and that continued CIO decisions in the 1940s and 1950s would further reinforce. New elites would soon try to run workers' lives: union officials, government administrators, and in the case of women, male unionists. Chicago's industrial workers and their colleagues around the country had realized that their futures depended on centralized, national political movements like the CIO and the Democratic Party. What they had only begun to comprehend amid the euphoria of the late 1930s, however, was that succeeding as national actors could be imprisoning as well as liberating. It is beyond the scope of this book to investigate how these latent tendencies of the early CIO toward union bureaucracy, male oligarchy, and state cooptation grew more powerful and, many would say, more damaging to the spirit of industrial unionism. But as we come to the end of this story, it is important to remember that nothing in the CIO's development was inevitable and that in the early 1940s rank-and-file factory workers all over the country were still feeling proud that they had created a "mighty CIO" that embodied the values, needs, and hopes of working people like themselves.

Conclusion

Plate 37. An event like the National Policy Convention of the CIO's Packinghouse Workers' Organizing Committee in 1939 marked how far the organization of meatpacking workers had come in the twenty years since the union agitation after World War I. Workers from Jersey City to Denver, male and female, black and white, native and Mexican, skilled and less skilled, Communist and non-Communist assembled in Chicago to demand national contracts from their bosses. Nothing short of broad social, cultural, and political changes in the lives of working people over the previous two decades account for the change.

Chicago's factory workers inhabited a far different political, social, and cultural world in 1940 than they or their predecessors had twenty, or even ten, years earlier. Whereas once many had not voted, particularly in national elections, and often had harbored fears of the government infringing on their freedom, by the late 1930s most were loyal Democrats invested in an interventionist national government. Similarly, whereas previously, most recently in the 1919 era, factory workers' efforts to organize industrial unions had rarely survived for long, workers at last succeeded in organizing unions under the umbrella of the national CIO. Whereas earlier, working-class families had depended for their welfare needs on the informal networks and formal organizations of their ethnic communities and less reliably on their welfare capitalist employers, they now looked to government and unions for protection against threats as diverse as job layoffs, illness, and unstable banking institutions. Whereas once distinctive ethnic communities had circumscribed the cultural life of their members, workers' exposure to mass culture, the Democratic Party, and the CIO gave them more cultural experiences in common. National affiliations ranging from network radio fan to Democrat to CIO unionist had replaced workers' local, more parochial dependencies on neighborhood, ethnic group, and employer.

Workers' ethnic loyalty did not so much disappear with this reorientation as change. Rather than ethnic communities and their leaders actually delivering independent services to members through welfare and benefit organizations, banks, and stores, by the late thirties they served as mediators between their members and mainstream institutions. Ethnic politicians established such entities as the Polish Democratic Club of the 7th Ward or the Lithuanian Democratic League to help their constituencies exact their due from the party and the new agencies of government like the WPA and HOLC. Ethnic organizations proved to be crucial conduits providing new members and resources to the CIO. And as ethnic benefit societies declined with the Great Depression, individuals within ethnic neighborhoods frequently funneled their communities' insurance dollars into commercial companies by becoming insurance agents.[1] In these ways, ethnic elites managed to regain some of the credibility they had lost when working-class members of their ethnic communities felt abandoned by them in the crisis of depression. But ethnic workers would never again accept so easily the hierarchical authority of the ethnic community. Cross-ethnic working-class institutions like the union and the Democratic Party, which seemed under FDR to represent their class interests, offered them a more advantageous alliance. Nonetheless, ethnic identity continued to have meaning in the daily lives of Chicago workers during the 1930s, even though ethnic institutions no longer satisfied members' needs on their own. At best they served as liaisons to mainstream alternatives, helping to ease ethnic Chicagoans into a world of nonethnic unions and government and commercially provided services, where ethnicity became more a sensibility than a support system.

The good proportion of Chicago's industrial workers who were black also shifted their allegiances over these two decades so that they too ended the era as enthusiastic Democrats and CIO unionists. Blacks' progression, however, differed somewhat from that of ethnic whites. Despite how white racism isolated them in Chicago's Black Belt and restricted them to the worst industrial jobs, blacks had embraced more of mainstream culture in the 1920s, such as mass consumption and national Republican Party politics, although giving them special meaning as part of a new, northern, urban black culture. As blacks overcame their long-standing distrust of Democrats and labor unions in the 1930s and joined with white workers in supporting the New Deal and the CIO, they were in some ways abandoning less of an alternative culture than ethnics but in other ways risking more. By casting their fate so much with other workers, they gave up protectors like Republican Party leaders and employers and grew dependent on the egalitarian commitments of government, union, and fellow workers. The decades that followed the thirties, filled as they were with continued discrimination, would only demonstrate how limited these commitments were.

Diverse factors played out over two decades combined to bring about this dramatic shift in workers' political orientation. During the 1920s, the legendary transformative forces of Americanization, consumerism, mass culture, and welfare capitalism had not integrated Chicago's workers into the homogeneous and compliant "middle-class mass" that many had hoped for, where workers were indistinguishable from Chicagoans of other classes and ethnicities. Rather, during the twenties ethnic communities proved remarkably adaptable in their confrontation with such homogenizing forces. They strengthened their ethnoreligious institutions in the face of the Americanizing intentions of the Chicago Catholic Archdiocese. They adapted their fraternal organizations to compete with the alternative insurance schemes of commercial companies and employers and in a way that broadened workers' ethnic identity beyond narrow geographic or cultural boundaries. They set up ethnic commercial banks to accommodate the huge amounts of money that workers had invested in Liberty Bonds and that otherwise might have drawn them closer to mainstream institutions. For much of the 1920s, moreover, most working-class Chicagoans continued to shop at their neighborhood, ethnic-owned "Mom and Pop" stores, not at the new national chains; to listen to radio programs produced locally, often by members of their own ethnic and religious communities; and to watch motion pictures at their neighborhood theaters rather than in the great movie palaces of the era. Finally, even as Chicago workers came to embrace the basic premise of their employers' welfare capitalism, that capitalism could be fair to workers if employers lived up to their moral responsibility, its limited achievements ensured that few workers lost sight of the continuing antagonism between capital and labor. Workers' efforts to influence the way welfare capitalism functioned in the factory, furthermore, strengthened alliances among workers of different ethnicities and races. Workers found themselves by the end of the 1920s cooperating increasingly across ethnic, racial, and skill lines on the job while still depending upon the institutions of their ethnic communities outside of it.

The Great Depression upset the survival strategies workers had developed during the 1920s and forced new solutions. As it weakened the welfare and financial institutions of workers' ethnic and racial communities and drove employers to eliminate most of their welfare capitalist programs, workers had to look beyond their ethnic networks and bosses for help. In the late 1920s hatred of Prohibition had finally galvanized ethnic workers to unify as Democrats and had helped them recognize the usefulness of state action in alleviating that oppression. When local and private welfare efforts failed to meet the depression crisis, turning to the national government seemed the best way of redressing this wrong as well and offered an assistance to workers that they felt they had rightfully earned through their increased participation as Democratic voters. To complement the welfare state in protecting their interests, moreover, workers enlisted in the battle to create strong industrial unions. Beginning in the mid-1930s they laid the groundwork, with the help of the New Deal and national CIO leaders, for the organization of most of America's mass production plants by the end of World War II.

An important reason why workers of diverse ethnicities and races succeeded in asserting themselves collectively as Democrats and as unionists by the 1930s was that they had more in common culturally from which to forge alliances. More of them were second-generation Americans, they had come to trust each other in mounting collective responses to employers' welfare capitalist schemes in the twenties and early depression, and the particular way that mass culture reached workers during the 1920s and 1930s did not absorb them into a classless cultural mainstream. By the thirties, consolidation in the dissemination of mass culture through fewer and stronger chain stores, chain radio networks, and chain theaters combined with the hardships the depression brought to their smaller competitors meant that workers came to inhabit a more similar cultural world regardless of their race or ethnicity. No less important, the CIO recognized how much the success of its effort to unionize the nation's mass production factories depended on workers' new common ground, and it developed an organizational strategy that built on this new potential for unity. The social integration that mass culture and welfare capitalism had failed to achieve in the 1920s was accomplished by workers themselves and turned toward their own working-class ends in the 1930s. Here as in most cases of politicization, multiple influences encouraged people to espouse new values and take new kinds of collective action. Chicago workers' experiences as citizens, ethnics or blacks, wage earners, and consumers all converged to make them into New Deal Democrats and CIO unionists.

During the 1930s American industrial workers sought to overcome the miseries and frustrations that long had plagued their lives neither through anticapitalist and extragovernmental revolutionary uprisings nor through perpetuation of the status quo of welfare capitalism but rather through their growing investment in two institutions they felt would make capitalism more moral and fair – an activist welfare state concerned with equalizing wealth and privilege and a national union movement of factory workers committed to keeping a check on self-interested employers.

This way of incorporating industrial workers into the political process was unique to American workers in many respects. In Europe, where workers were more anticapitalist, they supported unions and political parties that demanded more radical changes, helping in some cases, such as Sweden, Britain, and West Germany, to establish welfare states that were more Socialist in orientation, and in others, notably

France and Italy, to make workers less integrated into mainstream political parties. American workers, in contrast, even when they harbored a "class" agenda as in the 1930s, turned to an existing mainstream political institution like the Democratic Party to achieve it. As a result, although at the time many individual workers and CIO officials hoped to accomplish working-class objectives through the Democratic Party, the reality of the party's broad base early on committed it to multiple, and ultimately less progressive, goals. Similarly, the CIO's union structure was innovative only in addressing itself to the organization of industrial workers. In many other ways, such as its larger political strategy of working through existing parties and its bureaucratic structure, it differed little from the AFL. Hence, American workers' idealistic but nonetheless conservative economic loyalty to a "moral capitalism" circumscribed the political alternatives they could imagine supporting. The crisis of the Great Depression, moreover, made it easier for the Democrats, as the party out of power, to project themselves as a political alternative. It is true that in the process of coping with a depression that drew them deeper into national politics and of organizing CIO unions that successfully challenged the autocracy of employers, American workers became more aware of their distinctive class interests. But paradoxically, by choosing to carry on their struggle through the Democratic Party and the CIO, workers became tied more than they ever intended to the status quo. What resulted was worker investment in a political party, a welfare state, and a union movement that rarely proved as responsive and democratic as workers had originally hoped.

The years that followed the 1930s, marked by World War II and its Cold War aftermath, confirmed the conservative path to which workers had committed themselves. Despite the new CIO contracts won and the new heights in CIO membership reached, the way the business of the thirties was completed during the forties reinforced the most conservative trends of the earlier decade. The Democratic Party came out of the war committed to using the powers of government to ensure economic growth and no longer as concerned about balancing that goal with efforts to tame capitalism's excesses. For labor, this meant that during the biggest strike wave ever, in 1945–6, the Truman administration intervened on the side of employers, and the next year congressional Democrats cooperated in the passage of the Taft–Hartley Act, which deprived workers of many of the benefits they had gained under the NLRA. Government intervention in industrial relations that in the

1930s had protected workers' rights now presided over their restriction. It became harder for workers and their unions to strike, to establish the closed shop, to influence employers' hiring and firing, to take sides in federal elections, and to tolerate political diversity within their own ranks. During the war years, moreover, the CIO itself became increasingly entrenched in bureaucratic politics that served to reinforce the power of the leadership over the grassroots and the power of political centrists over progressives. Although the historic unity of the early CIO period between workers of different backgrounds, between blacks and whites, and between Communists and non-Communists continued to leave its mark on the CIO, racial and particularly ideological conflict convulsed CIO unions in the course of the 1940s.[2]

To view the events of the thirties in light of what followed after 1940, however, distorts reality. Rather than interpret the struggles of the 1930s to account for these later developments, it is important to see them for what they meant at the time. This book has examined workers' politics during the thirties as connected not to what was then an unknown future but in light of the experiences people had already had, particularly during the previous decade of the 1920s. From that vantage point, the struggles of the 1930s marked substantive changes in working people's political lives. Stopping the clock before 1940, moreover, puts a new cast on the events of the thirties in another way. Although the situation would alter by the forties, the unity of industrial workers and their collective rank-and-file action emerge as major ingredients in the CIO's success. This is not to imply that the CIO was purely a grassroots movement or that there were not significant limitations to its accomplishments during the early phase of its history. This book has tried to present a balanced picture. Nonetheless, examining the late 1930s on their own terms exposes what is easily lost in the longer view, that many involved in fighting for the CIO at the time felt they were participating in a political movement that was made by, and for, average working people. When black packinghouse worker Jim Cole told an interviewer in 1939 that the CIO "done the greatest thing in the world gettin' everybody who works in the yards together, and breakin' up the hate and bad feelings that used to be held against the Negro," the important point is not that subsequent history shows that workers never fully overcame their racism but that it looked as if they had to workers like Cole at that moment in time.[3] He could not know how tensions would grow between white and black workers in the CIO when the government in wartime backed blacks in their battle against job discrimination and when union rules like seniority eventually brought blacks into more direct competition with whites (although Cole's own packinghouse workers' union would remain the strongest advocate of black civil rights within the CIO). The racial conflicts, the ideological divisions, and the centralization of authority that would come to characterize CIO unions later have led many postwar labor analysts to minimize the achievements of ordinary workers in the 1930s. By keeping its focus on the interwar years, this book has tried to recapture what rank-and-file workers accomplished in building a successful CIO movement, without romanticizing who they were or denying the imperfections in what they achieved.

Notes

Sources and organizations frequently cited in the notes are identified by the following abbreviations:

BAR	Claude A. Barnett Papers, Chicago Historical Society, Chicago, IL
BUR	Ernest W. Burgess Papers, University of Chicago Special Collections, Joseph Regenstein Library, Chicago, IL
CAP	Chicago Area Project Papers, Chicago Historical Society, Chicago, IL
CFLPS	Chicago Foreign Language Press Survey, compiled by the Chicago Public Library Omnibus Project, WPA, 1936–41, University of Chicago Special Collections, Joseph Regenstein Library, Chicago, IL
CHS	Chicago Historical Society, Chicago, IL
COM	Chicago Commons Settlement House Papers, Chicago Historical Society, Chicago, IL
FERA	Federal Emergency Relief Administration Papers, RG 69, National Archives, Washington, DC
FITZ	John Fitzpatrick Papers, Chicago Historical Society, Chicago, IL
FWP	Federal Writers' Project Papers, Works Project Administration, Library of Congress, Washington, DC
HOLC	Home Owners' Loan Corporation Files, RG 195, National Archives, Washington, DC
HSMF	Hawthorne Study Microfiche, Joseph Regenstein Library, University of Chicago, Chicago, IL
IC	Italian American Collection, oral histories and miscellaneous materials pertaining to Chicago's Italians in the twentieth century, Special Collections, University Library, University of Illinois at Chicago, Chicago, IL
IH	International Harvester Company Archives, Navistar International Transportation Corporation, Chicago, IL
JWT	J. Walter Thompson Advertising Company Archives, New York, NY (relocated to Duke University, Durham, NC)
LC	Manuscript Division, Library of Congress, Washington, DC

MCD	Mary McDowell Papers, Chicago Historical Society, Chicago, IL
NA	National Archives, Washington, DC
NLRB	National Labor Relations Board Files, RG 25, National Archives, Suitland Branch, Suitland, MD
NRA	National Recovery Administration Records, RG 9, National Archives, Washington, DC
PAT	George Patterson Papers, Chicago Historical Society, Chicago, IL
ROHP	Roosevelt University Oral History Project in Labor History, Roosevelt University Library, Chicago, IL
SECHP	Southeast Chicago Historical Project Archives, Urban Culture and Documentary Program, Columbia College, Chicago, IL
SHSW	State Historical Society of Wisconsin, Madison, WI
UCSC	University of Chicago Special Collections, Joseph Regenstein Library, Chicago, IL
UICC	Special Collections, University Library, University of Illinois at Chicago, Chicago, IL
UNCH	United Charities Papers, Chicago Historical Society, Chicago, IL
UPWA	United Packinghouse Workers of America Papers, State Historical Society of Wisconsin, Madison, WI
USWA	United Steelworkers of America Papers, Chicago Historical Society, Chicago, IL (copies at Labor Archives, Pennsylvania State University)
WC	Welfare Council Papers, Chicago Historical Society, Chicago, IL
WE	Western Electric Company Archives, New York, NY (relocated to AT&T Bell Laboratories Archives, Warren, NJ
WPA	Works Progress Administration, RG 69, National Archives, Washington, DC

INTRODUCTION

1 To simplify matters throughout the book, I use *U.S. Steel* instead of naming its major subsidiary, which ran the South Works and Gary Works in the Calumet region. That was the Illinois Steel Company until 1935, when U.S. Steel merged it with the Carnegie Steel Company to create one operating unit responsible for steelmaking in Pittsburgh, Youngstown, and Chicago, the Carnegie–Illinois Steel Corporation.

2 David Brody, *Steelworkers in America: The Nonunion Era* (New York: Harper Torchbooks, 1969).

3 James R. Barrett, *Work and Community in the Jungle: Chicago's Packinghouse Workers, 1894–1922* (Urbana: University of Illinois Press, 1987).

4 Robert Ozanne, *A Century of Labor–Management Relations at McCormick and International Harvester* (Madison: University of Wisconsin Press, 1967); "Haymarket, 1886!" *Chicago History* 15 (Summer 1986): 21–35.

5 Melvyn Dubofsky, *We Shall Be All: A History of the Industrial Workers of the World* (New York: Quadrangle/The New York Times Book Co., 1969), pp. 255–8.

1. LIVING AND WORKING IN CHICAGO IN 1919

1 For general discussion of the 1919 era, see Jeremy Brecher, *Strike!* (Boston: South End Press, 1972), pp. 101–43; James R. Green, *The World of the Worker: Labor in Twentieth-Century America* (New York: Hill and Wang, 1980), pp. 93–9. On the labor and farmer–labor parties, see Nathan Fine, *Labor and Farmer Parties in the United States, 1828–1928* (New York: Rand School of Social Science, 1928), pp. 377–97. For labor's linking its demands with a larger ideological commitment to democracy, see "Labor Day 1919," *New Majority*, 30 August 1919.

2 On Chicago in 1919, see "Strikes and Lockouts in the United States, 1916 to 1922," *Monthly Labor Review* 16 (June 1923): 1386; Graham Taylor, "An Epidemic of Strikes in Chicago," *The Survey* 42 (2 August 1919): 645–6, quoted in Brecher, *Strike!*, pp. 115–16; William M. Tuttle, Jr., *Race Riot: Chicago in the Red Summer of 1919* (New York: Atheneum, 1970), pp. 137–42; "Workmen's Interests," *Daily Jewish Courier*, 9 July 1919, CFLPS, Box 23.

3 For information on the Chicago economy, particularly the manufacturing sector, see Irving Cutler, *Chicago: Metropolis of the Mid-Continent*, 3d ed. (Dubuque, IA: Kendall/Hunt Publishing Company for The Geographic Society of Chicago, 1982), pp. 159–99; Homer Hoyt, *One Hundred Years of Land Values in Chicago: The Relationship of the Growth of Chicago to the Rise in Its Land Values, 1830–1933* (Chicago: University of Chicago Press, 1933), pp. 196–8; Harold M. Mayer and Richard C. Wade, *Chicago: Growth of a Metropolis* (Chicago: University of Chicago Press, 1969), pp. 226–50; U.S. Department of Commerce, Bureau of the Census, *Census of Manufacturers: 1920, 1923, 1925, 1927, 1930, 1937, 1939, 1940* (Washington, DC: U.S. Government Printing Office).

4 U.S. Department of Commerce, Bureau of the Census, *Fourteenth Census of the United States: 1920*, vol. 9, *Manufactures* (Washington, DC: U.S. Government Printing Office, 1923), p. 317; Chicago Daily News, *The Daily News Almanac and Year-book for 1926* (Chicago: Chicago Daily News, 1927), p. 782.

5 Leila Houghteling, *The Income and Standard of Living of Unskilled Laborers in Chicago* (Chicago: University of Chicago Press, 1927), pp. 20–3.

6 For residential distribution of workers in Chicago's largest industries, see *Report of the Chicago Traction and Subway Commission on a Unified System of Surface, Elevated and Subway Lines* (Chicago: Chicago Traction and Subway Commission, 1916).

The only large groups of manufacturing workers listed in Table 1 of the appendix and omitted in my treatment are printing and railroad car workers. Although there were some semiskilled workers in printing and publishing, essentially this work called for skilled employees. Railroad car shops handled a combination of construction and repair work and entailed a wider range of jobs than the typical mass production factory. Janice Reiff and Susan Hirsch are presently engaged in a major project to analyze the employment records of the Pullman Company repair shops in the collection of the Newberry Library, Chicago. See Janice L. Reiff and Susan Hirsch, "Reconstructing Work Histories by Computer: The Pullman Shop Workers, 1890–1967," *Historical Methods* 15 (Summer 1982): 139–41.

7 For general discussion of Southeast Chicago and its four "steel towns," see John Ashenhurst and Ruth L. Ashenhurst, *All About Chicago* (Boston: Houghton Mifflin Company, 1933), pp. 170–2; William T. Hogan, *Economic History of the Iron and Steel Industry in the United States*, vol. 3 (Lexington, MA: D.C. Heath Company, 1971), pp. 811–12; Ron Grossman, *Guide to Chicago Neighborhoods* (Piscataway, NJ: New Century Publishers, 1981), pp. 153–67; Mayer and Wade, *Growth of a Metropolis*, pp. 186–8, 234–46; Chicago Plan Commission, *Forty-Four Cities in the City of Chicago* (Chicago: Chicago Plan Commission, 1942), pp. 49–50, 53–5; William Kornblum, *Blue Collar Community* (Chicago: University of Chicago Press, 1974); Dominic Pacyga, "South Chicago," *Chicago Journal* 5 (15 April 1981); Marcia Kijewski, David Brosch, and Robert Bulanda, "The Historical Development of Three Chicago Millgates: South Chicago, East Side, South Deering," Illinois Labor History Society, 1972 (mimeo); Mary Adams, "Present Housing Conditions in South Chicago, South Deering and Pullman" (M.A. thesis, University of Chicago, 1926), pp. 15–91; Ernest W. Burgess and Charles Newcomb, *Census Data of the City of Chicago, 1920* (Chicago: University of Chicago Press, 1931), pp. 559–62, 565–7, 575–80, 587–8, 612–13.

On life in the community of South Chicago near U.S. Steel's South Works plant, also see "Fifty Year Graduate Shares Fond Memories of the Past," *Daily Calumet*, 23 May 1983; Edith Abbott, *The Tenements of Chicago, 1908–1935* (Chicago: University of Chicago Press, 1936), pp. 144–51.

On South Deering where Wisconsin Steel was located, see Dominic Pacyga, "Story of Wisconsin Steel Is Story of U.S. Industry," *Daily Calumet*, 13 December 1982; Newton I. Zemans, "South Deering," Paper for Sociology 269, 12 June 1929, BUR, Box 185, Folder 6; David Bensman and Rebecca Lynch, *Rusted Dreams: Hard Times in a Steel Community* (New York: McGraw-Hill Book Company, 1987), pp. 39–40, 43–4.

On the East Side community, see Adeline Milano Zappa, "East Sider Recalls Life in the Old Days," *Daily Calumet*, 19 July 1982; Dominic Pacyga, "Swedes Played Important Role in History of Southeast Side," *Daily Calumet*, 18 April 1983; Interview with Frank Stanley by Jim Martin, Chicago, IL, 17 September 1981, SECHP; Interview at Baumann family picnic by Jim Martin, Edgars Grove, IL, 27 June 1982, SECHP.

On the community of Hegewisch, see Jim Martin, "Southeast Area History Is Painted with Words," *Daily Calumet*, 10 August 1981; Dominic Pacyga, "Hegewisch Community Has Long, Rich Industrial History," *Daily Calumet*, 2 August 1982; "Hegewisch Community Celebrates 100 Years," *Daily Calumet*, 19 March 1983; Note cards for Hegewisch study, c. 1924–5, BUR, Box 190A; Ruth Pearson, "Ford City," Paper for Sociology I, Summer 1924, BUR, Box 50, Folder 2; "Hegewisch Community

Committee Files, 1957–58," Community Fund of Chicago Papers, Box 85, Folders 4 and 5, UICC; Memos on Hegewisch, c. 1939, CAP, Box 83, Folder 1.

8 "Document X," pp. 26–7 in Paul Frederick Cressey, "The Succession of Cultural Groups in the City of Chicago" (Ph.D. dissertation, University of Chicago, 1930), p. 256. Also, "Fitzgibbons Was Important Part of Southeast Historical Project," *Daily Calumet*, 13 June 1983; Arthur Itterman, "The Southwest Section of the East Side," Paper for Sociology 265, March 1933, BUR, Box 159, Folder 2; William J. Demsey, "Gangs in the Calumet Park District," Paper for Sociology 270, n.d. but c. 1928–9, BUR, Box 148, Folder 5; *St. George's Church Seventy-Fifth Anniversary Book, 1903–1978* (Chicago: St. George's Church, 1978); Phyllis Bate, "The Development of the Iron and Steel Industry of the Chicago Area, 1900–1920" (Ph.D. dissertation, University of Chicago, 1948), pp. 128–30.

9 "Fifty Year Graduate Shares Fond Memories," *Daily Calumet*, 23 May 1983.

10 Bensman and Lynch, *Rusted Dreams*, pp. 39–40.

11 For general discussion of the stockyards and packinghouse industry, particularly the surrounding neighborhoods, see Glen E. Holt and Dominic A. Pacyga, *Chicago: A Historical Guide to the Neighborhoods: The Loop and South Side* (Chicago: Chicago Historical Society, 1979), pp. 113–39; Robert A. Slayton, *Back of the Yards: The Making of a Local Democracy* (Chicago: University of Chicago Press, 1986); James R. Barrett, *Work and Community in the Jungle: Chicago's Packinghouse Workers, 1894–1922* (Urbana: University of Illinois Press, 1987), pp. 64–117; Dominic Pacyga, "Village of Packinghouses and Steel Mills: The Polish Worker on Chicago's South Side, 1880 to 1921" (Ph.D. dissertation, University of Illinois at Chicago, 1981), pp. 1–5, 8–11; Chicago Plan Commission, *Forty-Four Cities*, pp. 56–8; Cutler, *Chicago Metropolis*, pp. 160–3; Ashenhurst and Ashenhurst, *All About Chicago*, pp. 154–8.

12 Norman Sylvester Hayner, "The Effect of Prohibition in Packingtown" (M.A. thesis, University of Chicago, 1921), p. 7. Another source for the ethnic breakdown of packinghouse workers is the 1918 study by the Stockyards Community Clearing House of six hundred women workers who had children under age fourteen. Although the narrowness of this criterion and the exclusion from the study of black mothers keeps the data from being representative of the overall work force, the findings are still extremely interesting. These women, who worked at Armour, Libby, Morris, Swift, and Wilson, were 40 percent Polish, 20 percent Lithuanian, 8 percent native, and 27 percent combined Slovak, Irish, Russian, Roumanian, Swiss, Canadian, Italian, German, and English. Eighty-seven percent of all the mothers were foreign born; two-thirds of the women and one-third of their husbands could not speak English; 37 percent of the women and 32 percent of the men could neither read nor write. Only a quarter of the men were American citizens, and 43 percent of them had not even taken out their first papers toward citizenship, although the average length

of time spent in the United States was fifteen years. Two-thirds of the women's nine hundred children of school age were attending parochial, not public, school. The extremely foreign character of these women's lives suggests that wartime work attracted the least assimilated in the community, who may have also been the most needy since the great proportion of these women indicated that they were obligated to work for financial reasons. Despite a sample skewed toward the foreign born, we gain from this study a sense of how culturally isolated many packinghouse workers were. Report by Stockyards Community Clearing House, 1918–19, MCD, Box 40, Folder 20.

13 Arthur Kampfert, Manuscript, UPWA, pp. II-96–7.

14 Report on "The Pre-Adolescent Girl Study," Gads Hill Center, February 1917, in Lea Taylor Papers, Box 17, Folder CFS 1917–19, CHS, p. iv; Ann Friedman, "Life Among the Poles in Old South Chicago," *Chicago Jewish History* 12 (June 1989): 4–5; excerpts from Jewish newspapers, 11 May 1919 to 25 July 1919, CFLPS, Box 23.

15 Most commentators of the period noted the ethnic fragmentation of neighborhoods and social life. See Lindquist, "Study of Lithuanians in Chicago, 1922," BUR, Box 190A; William J. Blackburn, "A Brief Report of a Study Made of the Organization, Program and Services of the University of Chicago Settlement, 1927–28," MCD, p. 21; Alice Mae Miller, "Rents and Housing Conditions in the Stockyards District of Chicago 1923" (M.A. thesis, University of Chicago, 1923), pp. 17–22; Interviews with Rosemarie McIrny and Father Joseph Lynch, Chicago, IL, n.d., ROHP.

16 For general information about these immigrant neighborhoods, see Cutler, *Chicago Metropolis*, pp. 66–91, 97–107; Louis Wirth, *The Ghetto* (Chicago: University of Chicago Press, 1928); Abbott, *Tenements*, pp. 77–112; Harvey Warren Zorbaugh, *The Gold Coast and the Slum: A Sociological Study of Chicago's Near North Side* (Chicago: University of Chicago Press, 1929), pp. 159–81.

Even when neighborhoods were not totally homogeneous ethnically, a particular ethnic group set the tone for a settlement and served as a cohesive force over a long period of time. Because these communities were in flux over time and geographic space, ethnic mixing was greatest at the shifting borders of neighborhoods, such as between Italians and Jews on the West Side, between Jews and Poles in West Town, and between Italians and Poles on the Northwest Side. Rudolph J. Vecoli, "The Formation of Chicago's 'Little Italies,'" *Journal of American Ethnic History* 2 (Spring 1983): 17. Esther Crockett Quaintance, "Rents and Housing Conditions in the Italian District of the Lower North Side of Chicago, 1924" (M.A. thesis, University of Chicago, 1925), pp. 42–4; "A Study of Association House, Chicago, Illinois, Made by the Chicago Council of Social Agencies, 1922," WC, Box 249, Folder "Association House, 1922–66," pp. 28–33; "Survey of Off-the-Street Club by Northwestern University, February 11, 1929–June 21, 1929," Off-the-Street Club Records, Folder 97, UICC, pp. 4–8, Table 11.

17 William Rutherford Ireland, "Young American Poles" (written but not

submitted as M.A. thesis, University of Chicago, 1932), UCSC, pp. 3–27. Other sources on employment in this area include "A Study of Association House, Chicago, Illinois, Made by the Chicago Council of Social Agencies, 1922," WC, pp. 22, 33, 48, 64–5; "Survey of Off-the-Street Club by Northwestern University, February 11, 1929–June 21, 1929," Off-the-Street Club Records, Folder 97, UICC, Chart 5; "The Lower Northwest Side," n.d. but c. 1928 (Report by University of Chicago student under Burgess), COM, Box 23, pp. 31–3; "Annual Report, September 30, 1929," COM, Box 5, Folder "Annual and Other Reports, 1929–32," p. 2.

18 Barbara Newell, *Chicago and the Labor Movement: Metropolitan Unionism in the 1930's* (Urbana: University of Illinois Press, 1961), pp. 29, 54–70; "A Study of Association House, Chicago, Illinois, Made by the Chicago Council of Social Agencies, 1922," WC, pp. 64–5; Giovanni E. Schiavo, *The Italians in Chicago: A Study in Americanization* (Chicago: Italian American Publishing Company, 1928), p. 52.

19 Hoyt, *One Hundred Years of Land Values,* pp. 312–14; Humbert S. Nelli, *Italians in Chicago, 1880–1930: A Study in Ethnic Mobility* (New York: Oxford University Press, 1979), pp. 204–11; Wirth, *The Ghetto*, pp. 201, 244–57; Chicago Plan Commission, *Forty-Four Cities,* pp. 27–8, 81–2; Irving Cutler, "The Jews of Chicago: From Shtetl to Suburb," in *Ethnic Chicago*, Peter d'A. Jones and Melvin G. Holli, eds. (Grand Rapids, MI: William B. Eerdmans Publishing Company, 1981), pp. 60–71; and from the CFLPS, Box 26: "Jewish Albany Park," *Daily Jewish Courier*, 22 February 1924; "Show Shifts in City's Jews," *Chicago Herald and Examiner*, June 1931.

20 Interview with Male in Technical Branch, 21 August 1930, Fiche no. 184, HSMF. More than 100,000 single-family bungalows were built in Chicago during the 1920s. Hoyt, *One Hundred Years of Land Values*, pp. 245–6; Mayer and Wade, *Growth of a Metropolis*, p. 326; Cressey, "The Succession of Cultural Groups," pp. 187, 210–11, 277. On McKinley and Brighton Parks, see Holt and Pacyga, *Historical Guide*, pp. 140–55, and Paul F. Cressey, "Survey of McKinley Park Community," 20 October 1925, BUR, Box 129, Folder 7, pp. 1–5. On Cicero, see John T. Reichman, *Czechoslovaks of Chicago* (Chicago: Czechoslovak Historical Society of Illinois, 1937), p. 16.

21 Lindquist, "Study of Lithuanians in Chicago, 1922," BUR, Box 190A, Interview with Dr. Graicunas on Lithuanians in Cicero. For the residential distribution of Hawthorne workers all along the Southwestern Corridor, see Miller McClintock, *Report and Recommendations of the Metropolitan Street Traffic Survey* (Chicago: Street Traffic Committee of the Chicago Association of Commerce, 1926). An Italian colony centered around 24th and Oakley Avenue regularly provided workers to the McCormick Works of International Harvester. One long-time resident of the neighborhood recalled that at least one or two members of every family worked at Harvester. Interview with Sylvio Petrio, Chicago, IL, 8 June 1981, IC, p. 17.

22 Cyrus McCormick II, Report to directors and his mother, 5 June 1916,

Cyrus McCormick II Papers, File 185, quoted in Robert Ozanne, *A Century of Labor–Management Relations at McCormick and International Harvester* (Madison, WI: University of Wisconsin Press, 1967), p. 107.

23 International Harvester Company, "McCormick Works" (Chicago: International Harvester Company, c. 1920).

24 *Chicagoan*, 1928, quoted in Mayer and Wade, *Growth of a Metropolis*, p. 330.

25 Western Electric Company, "Hawthorne – Its Life and People" (n.p.: Western Electric Company, c. 1980); "Cicero Survey, 1937," WC, Box 292, Folder 60, pp. 18, 20–1, 24; Joseph Wagner, "Berwyn: A Short Study of a Residential Suburb of Chicago," Student paper, Winter quarter 1933, BUR, Box 159, Folder 3, p. 2; Jakub Horak, "Assimilation of Czechs in Chicago" (Ph.D. dissertation, University of Chicago, 1920), pp. 26–33.

26 The difference between the housing opportunities of immigrants and blacks in Chicago was noted as early as 1913 by Sophonisba Breckinridge in "The Color Line in the Housing Problem," *Survey* 40 (1 February 1913): 575–6. Examination of how systematic racial discrimination has kept blacks more ghettoized and poorly housed than whites has continued in more recent work. Allan Spear, *Black Chicago: The Making of a Negro Ghetto, 1890–1920* (Chicago: University of Chicago Press, 1967); Thomas Philpott, *The Slum and the Ghetto: Neighborhood Deterioration and Middle-Class Reform, Chicago, 1880–1930* (New York: Oxford University Press, 1978); Arnold R. Hirsch, *Making of the Second Ghetto: Race and Housing in Chicago, 1940–1960* (New York: Cambridge University Press, 1983).

27 Spear, *Black Chicago*, pp. 11–27; Chicago Plan Commission, *Forty-Four Cities*, pp. 32–44; Holt and Pacyga, *Historical Guide*, pp. 49–65, 87–101; St. Clair Drake and Horace R. Cayton, *Black Metropolis: A Study of Negro Life in a Northern City* (New York: Harcourt, Brace and Company, 1945), pp. 8–13; Hirsch, *Second Ghetto*, pp. 3–4.

28 For a thorough treatment of the "Great Migration," see James R. Grossman, *Land of Hope: Chicago, Black Southerners, and the Great Migration* (Chicago: University of Chicago Press, 1989).

29 Alma Herbst, "The Negro in the Slaughtering and Meat Packing Industry in Chicago" (Ph.D. dissertation, University of Chicago, 1930), p. xiv; Walter A. Fogel, *The Negro in the Meat Industry*, Report no. 12, Racial Policies of American Industry Series (Philadelphia: Wharton School of Finance and Commerce, University of Pennsylvania, 1970), p. 30; Paul Taylor, *Mexican Labor in the United States: Chicago and the Calumet Region*, vol. 7, no. 2, University of California Publications in Economics (Berkeley: University of California Press, 1932), p. 46; Catherine Elizabeth Lewis, "Trade Union Policies in Regard to the Negro Worker in the Slaughtering and Meatpacking Industry of Chicago" (M.A. thesis, University of Chicago, 1945), pp. 11–12.

30 Taylor, *Mexican Labor in Chicago*, p. 46; Spear, *Black Chicago*, p. 163.

31 Sterling D. Spero and Abram L. Harris, *The Black Worker: The Negro and*

the Labor Movement (New York: Columbia University Press, 1931; reprint ed., New York: Atheneum, 1969), pp. 337–9.

32 Robert Ozanne, *The Negro in the Farm Equipment and Construction Machinery Industries*, Report no. 26, Racial Policies of American Industry Series (Philadelphia: Wharton School of Finance and Commerce, University of Pennsylvania, 1972), pp. 19–22; Ozanne, *Century of Labor*, pp. 183–7.

33 On the Chicago race riot of 1919, see Chicago Commission on Race Relations, *The Negro in Chicago: A Study of Race Relations and A Race Riot* (Chicago: University of Chicago Press, 1922); Tuttle, *Race Riot*; Philpott, *Slum and Ghetto*, pp. 168–80, 273–5; Drake and Cayton, *Black Metropolis*, pp. 65–73; Anthony M. Platt, ed., *The Politics of Riot Commissions, 1917–1970: A Collection of Official Reports and Critical Essays* (New York: The Macmillan Company, 1971), pp. 93–158.

34 Interview with American Worker, Gary, IN, 17 August 1920, Saposs Papers, Box 26, Folder 6, SHSW, p. 3; Frank H. Serene, "Immigrant Steelworkers in the Monongahela Valley: Their Communities and the Development of a Labor Class Consciousness" (Ph.D. dissertation, University of Pittsburgh, 1979), pp. 275–6.

35 William Z. Foster to P. J. Morrin, 16 July 1919, attached to William Z. Foster to John Fitzpatrick, 15 July 1919, FITZ, Box 8, Folder 61.

36 National Committee for Organizing Iron and Steel Workers, Minutes of Meeting in Pittsburgh, 20 July 1919, FITZ, Box 8, Folder 61, p. 6. For other mention of steelworkers' independence, see Commission of Inquiry, Interchurch World Movement, *Report on the Steel Strike of 1919* (New York: Harcourt, Brace and Howe, 1920), pp. 170–2; Telegram from National Committee to President Wilson, 4 September 1919, quoted in David Brody, *Steelworkers in America: The Nonunion Era* (New York: Harper Torchbooks, 1969), p. 239.

37 National Committee for Organizing Iron and Steel Workers, Minutes of Meeting in Pittsburgh, 20 July 1919, FITZ, Box 8, Folder 61, p. 6.

38 Mendel Packard, "C.I.O.," 3 August 1937, FWP, Box A121, pp. 6–7.

39 Interchurch World Movement, *Report on Steel Strike*, p. 178; "Fitzpatrick Tells Steel Strike Facts," *New Majority*, 11 October 1919.

40 Interchurch World Movement, *Report on Steel Strike*, pp. 135–41, includes immigrant workers' testimony about how they were discriminated against in job advancement, often being told "that the good jobs are not for hunkies."

41 "Conditions at Wisconsin Steel, September and October 1919," Daily reports including workers' complaints about harassments, File 214, IH.

42 Mrs. M. A. Gadsby, "The Steel Strike," *Monthly Labor Review* 14 (December 1919): 85.

43 The following were the general demands of the strike: (1) right of collective bargaining; (2) reinstatement of all men discharged for union activities with pay for time lost; (3) eight-hour day; (4) one day's rest in seven; (5) abolition of twenty-four-hour shift; (6) increase in wages sufficient to

guarantee American standard of living; (7) standard scales of wages in all trades and classifications of workers; (8) double rates of pay for all overtime after eight hours, holiday, and Sunday work; (9) check-off system of collecting union dues and assessments; (10) principles of seniority to apply in the maintenance, reduction, and increase of working forces; (11) abolition of company unions; (12) abolition of physical examination of applicants for employment. National Committee for Organizing Iron and Steel Workers, Minutes of Meeting in Pittsburgh, 20 July 1919, FITZ, Box 8, Folder 61, p. 8.

44 "Steel Trust Spy Chiefs Try to Start Race Riot," *New Majority*, 11 October 1919; Taylor, *Mexican Labor in Chicago*, pp. 116–19.

45 William Z. Foster, *The Great Steel Strike and its Lessons* (New York: B. W. Huebsch, 1920), pp. 198–9; Interview with Edward J. Evans, 27 December 1918, Saposs Papers, Box 21, Folder 5, SHSW. See also statement by John Fitzpatrick quoted in Elizabeth Balanoff, "A History of the Black Community of Gary, Indiana, 1906–1940" (Ph.D. dissertation, University of Chicago, 1974), pp. 154–5, and comment by a Gary organizer that "the average American should be ashamed of himself for his lack of interest." Brody, *Steelworkers*, p. 223.

46 Foster, *Great Steel Strike*, pp. 198–9.

47 Gary Works Circle, August – September 1919, quoted in David Brody, *Labor in Crisis: The Steel Strike of 1919* (Philadelphia: J. B. Lippincott Company, 1965), p. 158; "John W. O'Leary Talks of 'Strike Facts' and Principles," *Chicago Commerce* 16 (4 October 1919).

48 Spero and Harris, *Black Worker*, p. 200; Spear, *Black Chicago*, pp. 163–4; Foster, *Great Steel Strike*, p. 205; The Workers' Bureau, National Urban League, "The Negro Workers' Councils, Bulletin No. 12," 7 August 1936, BAR, Box 280, Folder 1, pp. 3–4.

49 Pacyga, "Villages of Packinghouses and Steel Mills," pp. 310–12; Spero and Harris, *Black Worker*, p. 261; Brody, *Labor in Crisis*, p. 163.

50 Balanoff, "Black Community in Gary," pp. 152–3.

51 "Conditions at Wisconsin Steel, September and October 1919," Daily reports, File 214, IH. From the start, Wisconsin Steel workers had responded in fewer numbers to the national strike call than employees of the U.S. Steel plants in the Chicago area. Brody, *Steelworkers*, p. 262.

52 "The Immigrant and the Labor Movement," Saposs Papers, Box 6, Folder 30, SHSW, p. 81; "The U.S. Steel Corporation: III," *Fortune Magazine* 13 (May 1936): 138.

53 At a mass meeting kicking off the campaign in June 1917, organizer John Kikulski spoke eloquently of "this great campaign" in which "Polish, Irish, Lithuanian, and in fact every race, color, creed, and nationality is to be included," quoted in Tuttle, *Race Riot*, p. 134. For the most thorough treatments of the packinghouse situation from wartime through the strike of 1921–2, see David Brody, *The Butcher Workmen: A Study of Unionization* (Cambridge, MA: Harvard University Press, 1964), pp. 75–105, and Barrett, *Work and Community*, pp. 188–268.

54 For discussion of black resistance to unionism and the union's effort to

overcome it, see Tuttle, *Race Riot*, pp. 136–7, 142–56; Spear, *Black Chicago*, pp. 161–4; Barrett, *Work and Community*, pp. 208–24; Spero and Harris, *Black Worker*, pp. 271–6; Labor's Conference Committee, "Meetings Held with Ministers in an Attempt to Secure Their Cooperation in the Interest of Community Welfare," August 1920, FITZ, Box 9, Folder 64; John Riley, "Suppression of Free Speech on the South Side in Chicago," July 1920, FITZ, Box 9, Folder 64.

Kate Adams, "Humanizing a Great Industry" (Chicago: Armour and Company, 1919), p. 21, advertises Armour's establishment, in collaboration with the YMCA, of Armour efficiency clubs during June 1917 "for the promotion of welfare among colored workers." Also, "as an incentive to its colored workers to join the YMCA, the company gives an annual membership to each worker at the end of his first year of service."

55 Drake and Cayton, *Black Metropolis*, p. 304. Fitzpatrick acknowledged, "The breach [is] so broad that it is almost impossible now to cement or bridge it over." *Chicago Tribune*, 28 July–3 August 1919, quoted in Brody, *Butcher Workmen*, p. 87.

56 "Yards Employees' Parade Inspires Colored Workers With Union Ideals," *New Majority*, 10 July 1919. On black strikebreakers and the 1921–2 strike, see Spero and Harris, *Black Worker*, pp. 280–3; Dominic Pacyga, "Crisis and Community: The Back of the Yards 1921," *Chicago History* 6 (Fall 1977): 172–4; "Negroes in the Packing House Strike in Chicago," December 1921, NAACP Papers, LC, Box 320, pp. 1–2.

57 For hazards of this organizational structure, see F. Smolenlki to Hon. John Fitzpatrick, 18 January 1919, FITZ, Box 7, Folder 54; William M. Leiserson, *Adjusting Immigrant and Industry* (New York: Harper & Brothers Publishers, 1924), pp. 193–6. Even the approximately two thousand Jewish stockyard workers organized in their own locals. See from the CFLPS: "Jewish Stock-yard Workers Will Meet Sunday," *The Forward*, 1 February 1919, Box 23; "Jewish Stockyard Workers to Parade Today," *Sunday Jewish Courier*, 8 June 1919, Box 23; "From Workmen's Interest," *Daily Jewish Courier*, 4 August 1919, Box 27.

58 Quoted in Brody, *Butcher Workmen*, p. 89. For further discussion of growing xenophobia within the Amalgamated, see Arthur Kampfert, Manuscript, UPWA, p. II-167, and Barrett, *Work and Community*, pp. 224–30. Barrett charts the union's shift in attitude from its commitment at the 1917 convention to publish organizers' reports in the *Butcher Workman* in Polish, Lithuanian, Bohemian, German, and English (and later Spanish) to its action at the 1920 convention, when a "100 percent Americanism" resolution passed requiring all officers to be U.S. citizens. By the end of 1921, the foreign-language columns had disappeared entirely from the newspaper. For details on the split between the Amalgamated and the SLC see Heitman, "Controversy Between Labor and Capital in the Slaughtering and Meatpacking Industries in Chicago," 29 March 1934, MCD, Box 3, Folder 15; Interview with Herbert March, San Pedro, CA, 16–17 November 1970, ROHP, pp. 38–9.

59 For details of the plan, see Industrial Relations Department, "Harvester

Industrial Council Personnel of Works Councils, March 1919," 2 April 1919, File 214, IH. On the plan's limitations, see Toni Gilpin, "Fair and Square: International Harvester's Industrial Council Plan and the Works Councils at McCormick and Tractor Works," Unpublished seminar paper, Yale University, 1982, pp. 22–33, and Ozanne, *Century of Labor–Management Relations*, pp. 116–31. On strikes, see "Arrests and Deception for Harvester Help: 'Company Union' Says It Will Call Employes Back to Work When Its Plans Are Laid," *New Majority*, 9 August 1919; "Harvester Officials Try to Trick Strikers," *New Majority*, 23 August 1919. For the company's viewpoint, see "The Plain Truth about Industrial Disturbances at IHC Chicago Plants," *Harvester World*, August 1919.

60 From the Saposs Papers, SHSW: "The Mind of Immigrant Communities," Box 8, Folder 22, pp. 3–4; Statement of David Saposs, Box 21, Folder 5, pp. 5, 9; Interview with Anzuino D. Marimpietri, President of Coat Makers' Local, 2 December 1918, Chicago, Box 22, Folder 2; Interview with Sam Levin, Business Agent, Chicago Council, Amalgamated Clothing Workers, 26 December 1918, Box 21, Folder 5; Interview with Joseph Schlossberg, General Secretary, Amalgamated Clothing Workers, New York, NY, 27 February 1919, Box 21, Folder 6. Spero and Harris, *Black Worker*, pp. 337–8.

61 On the organization of the garment industry in the 1919 era, see Newell, *Chicago and Labor*, pp. 54, 61–4; Chicago Joint Board, Amalgamated Clothing Workers of America, *Amalgamented Centre: The Tailor Re-Tailored – A Story of Surging Humanity* (Chicago: ACWA, May Day, 1928), pp. 10, 22, 34, 56–9; Leiserson, *Adjusting Immigrant*, pp. 206–14; Carroll Binder, "Chicago, Hotbed of American Labor," *Survey Graphic* 23 (October 1934): 487, 513; Wilfred Carsel, *A History of the Chicago Ladies' Garment Workers Union* (Chicago: Normandie House, 1940), pp. 65–125; "Contributions to the General American Labor Movement," *American Jewish Historical Society* 41 (June 1952).

62 "Western Electric's Federal 'Aid,'" *New Majority* 4 (January 1919).

63 Arthur Kampfert, Manuscript, UPWA, p. II-156.

64 Interview with German Worker, South Chicago, IL, 19 August 1920, Saposs Papers, Box 26, Folder 6, SHSW. On the Labor Party, its municipal campaign, and voter response, see David Ficke Simonson, "The Labor Party of Cook County, Illinois, 1918–1919" (M.A. thesis, University of Chicago, 1959); Harry Bird Sell, "The A.F. of L. and the Labor Party Movement of 1918–1920" (M.A. thesis, University of Chicago, 1922), particularly pp. 66–94; David Dolnick, "The Role of Labor in Chicago Politics Since 1919" (M.A. thesis, University of Chicago, 1939), pp. 4–17; Truman Cicero Bingham, "The Chicago Federation of Labor" (M.A. thesis, University of Chicago, 1925), pp. 129–50; John Howard Keiser, "John Fitzpatrick and Progressive Unionism, 1915–1925" (Ph.D. dissertation, Northwestern University, 1965), pp. 127–54; Edward R. Kantowicz, *Polish–American Politics in Chicago 1888–1940* (Chicago: University of Chicago Press, 1975), pp. 140–2; Materials on Labor Party, FITZ;

Daily News, *Almanac and Yearbook, 1920* (Chicago: Daily News, 1920), section entitled "Chicago City Election, April 1, 1919, Vote for Mayor by Wards and Precincts," pp. 847–57.

65 Typical treatments that stress the cultural escapism of the 1920s include Frederick Lewis Allen, *Only Yesterday: An Informal History of the 1920's* (New York: Harper and Row, 1931); George E. Mowry, ed., *The Twenties: Fords, Flappers and Fanatics* (Englewood Cliffs, NJ: Prentice-Hall, 1963); Isabel Leighton, *The Aspirin Age: 1919–1941* (New York: Simon and Schuster, 1949); Daniel J. Boorstin, *The Americans: The Democratic Experience* (New York: Random House, 1973). The standard work on labor in the 1920s is Irving Bernstein, *The Lean Years: A History of the American Worker, 1920–1933* (Boston: Houghton Mifflin Company, 1960).

2. ETHNICITY IN THE NEW ERA

1 *Chicago Chronicle*, 16 January 1925, quoted in Louis Wirth, *The Ghetto* (Chicago: University of Chicago Press, 1928), p. 257.

2 For anxiety over ethnic assimilation, see Jakub Horak, "Assimilation of Czechs in Chicago" (Ph.D. dissertation, University of Chicago, 1920), p. 126; *Immaculate Conception B.V.M. Parish, South Chicago, 1882–1957, Diamond Jubilee* (Chicago: Immaculate Conception B.V.M., 1957), p. 41; Mary McDowell, "The Foreign Born," c. 1928, MCD, Box 12, p. 5; Mary Lydia Zahrobsky, "The Slovaks in Chicago" (M.A. thesis, University of Chicago, 1924), p. 52; Eugene McCarthy, "The Bohemians in Chicago and Their Benevolent Societies: 1875–1946" (M.A. thesis, University of Chicago, 1950), p. 96; and from the CFLPS: "Build a Dam," *Daily Jewish Courier*, 23 March 1923, Box 27; "Jews Marrying Italians Now a Common Occurrence," *Forward*, 27 July 1924, Box 22; Dr. S. M. Melamed, "The Mothers Are At Fault," *Daily Jewish Courier*, 18 August 1922, Box 22.

Much work remains to be done on the leadership of ethnic communities. For a start, see Ewa Morawska, "The Internal Status Hierarchy in the East European Immigrant Communities of Johnstown, PA 1890–1930's," *Journal of Social History* 16 (Fall 1982): 75–107; Josef J. Barton, "Eastern and Southern Europeans," in John Higham, ed., *Ethnic Leadership in America* (Baltimore: Johns Hopkins University Press, 1978), pp. 150–75; Victor R. Greene, *American Immigrant Leaders, 1800–1910: Marginality and Identity* (Baltimore: Johns Hopkins University Press, 1987); John J. Bukowczyk, "The Transformation of Working-Class Ethnicity: Corporate Control, Americanization, and the Polish Immigrant Middle Class in Bayonne, New Jersey, 1915–1925," *Labor History* 25 (Winter 1984): 53–82; John Bodnar, *The Transplanted: A History of Immigrants in Urban America* (Bloomington: Indiana University Press, 1987), pp. 117–43.

3 The nationalism of Italians and Jews followed a slightly different timetable, with events during the 1920s, around Mussolini's fascism and an invigo-

rated Zionism, rousing nationalistic feeling. Neither group, however, viewed support for Italy or Palestine as requiring a denunciation of American loyalty. As a Chicago delegate to the Fascisti League of North America put it, "We love America as one could love his own wife; we love Italy as one loves his own mother." Chev. Mario Lauro, 11 November 1927, quoted in Giovanni E. Schiavo, *The Italians in Chicago: A Study in Americanization* (Chicago: Italian American Publishing Company, 1928; reprint ed. New York: Arno Press, 1975), p. 64; also pp. 70, 118–19. A similar point about the compatibility of American and Zionist loyalties was made in J. Leibner, "From the Public Rostrum," *Sunday Jewish Courier*, 28 March 1920, CFLPS, Box 23. For more on Italian nationalism during the twenties, see John P. Diggins, *Mussolini and Fascism: The View from America* (Princeton: Princeton University Press, 1972), pp. 78–86; Humbert S. Nelli, *Italians in Chicago* (New York: Oxford University Press, 1979), pp. 239–42. On Jewish Zionism, see Sentinel's Golden Jubilee Committee, *History of Chicago Jewry, 1911–1961* (Chicago: Sentinel, 1961), pp. 19–29, 199; Jewish newspaper articles from the 1920s, CFLPS, Boxes 22–7, *passim*, e.g., "Chicago Junior Hadassah," *Sunday Jewish Courier*, 8 January 1928.

On nationalism during World War I and its decline afterward among other eastern Europeans, see *Immaculate Conception Jubilee*, pp. 31–8; Joseph John Parot, *Polish Catholics in Chicago, 1850–1920* (DeKalb: Northern Illinois Press, 1981), pp. 161–78; Edward R. Kantowicz, *Polish – American Politics in Chicago, 1888–1940* (Chicago: University of Chicago Press, 1975), pp. 110–20, 168–70; Joseph A. Wytrwal, *America's Polish Heritage: A Social History of the Poles in America* (Detroit: Endurance Press, 1961), pp. 236–42; Thaddeus Radzialowski, "The View From a Polish Ghetto," *Ethnicity* 1 (1974): 129; Lindquist, "Lithuanians in Chicago, 1922," BUR, Box 190A.

4 On ethnic schools and clubs in the 1920s, see, e.g., "How to Keep the Youth in the Ranks of the Polish National Alliance," *Weekly Zgoda*, 15 January 1931, CFLPS, Box 37, which recommends the establishment of youth clubs, amateur theaters, and choirs, all carried on in the Polish language.

5 Sponsoring athletic teams was at the heart of all ethnic groups' strategy to keep members, particularly young people, within the fold. For example, see John Daniels, *America Via the Neighborhood* (New York: Harper & Brothers Publishers, 1920), pp. 126–33; John T. Reichman, *Czechoslovaks of Chicago: Contributions to a History of a National Group with an Introduction on the Part of Czechoslovaks in the Development of Chicago* (Chicago: Czechoslovak Historical Society of Illinois, 1937), pp. 32, 43–5; Helen Hrachovska, "Study of Czech Sokols in Chicago," Paper for Sociology 268, June 1931, BUR, Box 144, Folder 1; Schiavo, *Italians*, pp. 60–61; "History of Italian Soccer Teams in Chicago," n.d., IC, Box 8, Folder 2; "Study of the Jewish People's Institute," 1937, WC, Box 26, Folder "JPI 1937–38"; Casimir J. B. Wronski, "Early Days of Sport Among Polish Americans of Chicagoland," in *Poles of Chicago, 1837–1937: A History of One Century of Polish Contribution to the City of Chicago* (Chicago: Polish

Pageant, 1937), pp. 145–8; and many articles from the foreign-language press in the CFLPS collection.

6 Ethnic organizations and parishes involved themselves in helping members file papers and pass citizenship tests throughout the 1920s. They justified the importance of becoming a citizen on several grounds: as a necessary response to nativism and Americanization pressures; to hold onto jobs; to protect the reputation of unions; to own real estate without risk; and most frequently, to gain influence in American politics. See Reverend Arcady Piotrowsky to Executive Committee of Americanization Council, 8 April 1924, WC, Box 230, Folder "Citizenship and Naturalization," and many articles from the CFLPS, including: "Poles Organize Naturalization League. They Will Conduct Schools in All Parts of the City," *Dziennik Zjednoczenia*, 8 May 1922, Box 36; "Every Jewish Union Member Should Become An American Citizen," *Jewish Forward*, 25 May 1924, Box 23; "Citizenship School," *Bulletin Italo–American National Union*, 27 August 1927, Box 22; "A New School for Czechoslovak Aliens," *Denni Hlasatel*, 26 April 1922, Box 3.

7 This is not to say that these ethnic groups were monolithic entities in themselves. Poles had origins in Germany, Austria, and Russia and were further divided here between Roman Catholics and members of the smaller Polish National Catholic Church. Italians held onto identities rooted in their native towns and regions and also were in conflict as Catholics and anticlericals, many of whom were socialists. Jews, too, identified very strongly with their regional backgrounds, not only German Jews as opposed to eastern European, and more Orthodox, Jews, but also as Polish, Russian, Hungarian, Roumanian, and so forth. Jewish socialists created their own community within the larger Jewish one. Bohemians or Czechs divided into two camps, Roman Catholics and free-thinkers. Most of these factions, however, established institutions of their own within larger ethnic communities in the years before the war, so that ethnicity had a very specific meaning for people. These narrowly focused communities more often than not developed in parallel ways.

8 Sophonisba P. Breckinridge, *New Homes for Old* (New York: Harper & Brothers Publishers, 1921), pp. 277–304; Chicago Council of Social Agencies, "A Study of Association House, Chicago, Illinois," 1922, WC, Box 249, Folder "Association House 1922–66," p. 7.

9 Interview with Christine Ellis (alias Katherine Hyndman), in Alice and Staughton Lynd, eds., *Rank and File: Personal Histories of Working-Class Organizers* (Princeton: Princeton University Press, 1981), p. 15.

10 Phyllis H. Williams, *South Italian Folkways in Europe and America: A Handbook for Social Workers, Visiting Nurses, School Teachers, and Physicians* (New York: Russell & Russell, 1938; reissued 1969), pp. 172, 184–97.

11 Anthony Sorrentino, *Organizing Against Crime* (New York: Human Sciences Press, 1977), p. 53. For other evidence of the stigma Italians attached to public charity, see Interview with Margaret Sabella, Chicago, IL, 29

March 1980, IC, pp. 31–2, and Gaetano DeFilippis, "Social Life in an Immigrant Community," Paper for Sociology 264, n.d. but c. 1930, BUR, p. 19. On Czech efforts to avoid becoming objects of public charity, see McCarthy, "Bohemians in Chicago," p. 9.

12 J. Lulinski, "Report on South Chicago Area Project," n.d., CAP, Box 36, Folder 3, p. 4.

13 J. Leibner, "From the Public Rostrum," *Sunday Jewish Courier*, 28 March 1920, CFLPS, Box 23.

14 For descriptions of taking up neighborhood collections for needy Italians, see the following interviews, Chicago, IL, IC: Lina Tarabori, 5 June 1980, pp. 16–17; Sylvio Petri, 8 June 1981, p. 18; Alfred Fantozzi, 27 May 1980, p. 13; Margaret Sabella, 29 March 1980, p. 31.

15 Sydelle Kramer and Jenny Masur, eds., *Jewish Grandmothers* (Boston: Beacon Press, 1976), p. 99.

16 William I. Thomas and Florian Znaniecki, *The Polish Peasant in Europe and America: Monograph of an Immigrant Group*, vol. 5 (Boston: Richard G. Badger, Dorham Press, 1920), pp. 37, 51–5, 182, 214–15; Father Abramowicz, priest at Five Holy Martyrs Church, recalled that he decided to be a priest in sixth grade because that seemed the best way to help people in trouble. Interview with Most Reverend A. Abramowicz, Polonia Archives, CHS, p. 16.

17 George Hanas, "Study of Slovak Church Group, Northwest Side," Paper for Sociology I, Winter 1925, BUR, Box 149, Folder 3, p. 18.

18 Breckinridge, *New Homes for Old*, p. 303; Edna Dumaresq, "Report on Bohemian Charitable Association by Family Welfare Study," 6 May 1936, WC, Box 253, Folder "Bohemian Charitable Association, 1936–39," pp. 1–2.

19 Other ethnic groups envied Jews their welfare institutions. Interview with Father Bassi, in Robert E. Park and Herbert A. Miller, *Old World Traits Transplanted* (New York: Harper & Brothers Publishers, 1921), p. 239; President's Research Committee, *Recent Social Trends in the United States*, vol. 2 (New York: McGraw-Hill Book Company, 1933; reprint ed. Westport, CT: Greenwood Press, 1970), pp. 1183–4. Lillian Herstein, who worked with a Jewish welfare agency in Illinois, pointed out a negative result of the greater availability of relief for Jews: "The Jewish husbands didn't beat their wives and they didn't get drunk, but they deserted. They knew the Jewish Charities would take care of their families." Interview with Lillian Herstein, Chicago, IL, 1970–1, ROHP, p. 25.

On Jewish welfare activities in Chicago, see Edward Mazur, "Jewish Chicago: From Diversity to Community," in Peter d'A. Jones and Melvin G. Holli, eds., *Ethnic Frontier* (Grand Rapids: William B. Eerdmans Publishing Company, 1977), pp. 280–1; Irving C. Bilow, "Federation: The Challenge of Human Welfare, 1911–1961," in Sentinel, *History of Chicago Jewry*, pp. 162–5; "Memorandum Regarding the Jewish Vocational Service and Employment Center," 26 August 1928, WC, Box 356, Folder "Jewish Vocational Service, 1939–1959," pp. 40–1; "On the Public Rostrum," *Daily Jewish Courier*, 22 June 1923, CFLPS, Box 25; "Organization of Federated Orthodox Jewish Charities of Chicago," *Forward*, 23 April 1922, CFLPS, Box 27.

20 "Too Much Charity – Too Little Tzdokoh," *Sunday Jewish Courier*, 18 February 1923, CFLPS, Box 26.

21 William Arthur Hillman, "Urbanization and the Organization of Welfare Activities in the Metropolitan Community of Chicago" (Ph.D. dissertation, University of Chicago, 1940), pp. 19–22; Daniels, *American Via the Neighborhood*, pp. 133–6; "Homes for the Aged, Maintained by Religious Organizations," *Monthly Labor Review* 28 (March 1929): 13–21; "Old People's Homes Maintained by Nationality Groups," *Monthly Labor Review* 28 (April 1929): 1–13. Paul Starr, *The Social Transformation of American Medicine* (New York: Basic Books, 1982), pp. 171, 173–5, suggests how important discrimination was in the formation of separate religious and ethnic hospitals.

On Polish charity activities, see Al. Bak, "Polish Contribution to Social Welfare in Chicago," in *Poles of Chicago*, pp. 115–20; Merrill F. Krughoff, "Polish Welfare Association," 1 August 1934, WC, Box 390, Folder "Polish Welfare Association, 1925–54," pp. 1–2; and many articles in the CFLPS, particularly: "Welfare Festival Opens," *Dziennik Chicagoski*, 5 December 1921, Box 340; "Meeting of Polish Welfare Association," *Dziennik Chicagoski*, 8 February 1922, Box 35; "Many Polish Families Suffer Great Privations in Town of Lake," *Dziennik Chicagoski*, 7 January 1928, Box 32; "Benefit Ball for Polish Welfare Association Planned," *Dziennik Chicagoski*, 7 January 1928, Box 35; "Christmas Donations at the Polish National Alliance Benevolent Association," *Weekly Zgoda*, 1 January 1931, Box 35; Interview with Father Wojtalewicz, 9 December 1936, Box 35.

On Czech charity activities, see Reichman, *Czechoslovaks of Chicago*, pp. 13, 32; McCarthy, "Bohemians in Chicago," p. 23; "Annual Report of the Ladies' Auxiliary of the Bohemian Charitable Association," *Denni Hlassatel*, 3 February 1920, CFLPS, Box 4.

On Italian charity activities, see Raymond Sayler, "A Study of Behavior Problems of Boys in Lower North Community," n.d., BUR, Box 135, Folder 4, p. 26; Williams, *South Italian Folkways*, pp. 195–6; "The Progress of the Italian–Americans, Their Contribution to This Country's Growth," *Chicago Daily Forward*, 31 December 1926, CFLPS, Box 21.

On Jewish charity activities, see previous two footnotes. For other eastern European groups, see "Slovenian Women's Benefit Society," *American Slovenec*, 22 January 1926, CFLPS, Box 10; "The Celebration at the National Cemetery," *Vilnis*, 5 June 1925, CFLPS, Box 29; Algimantas Kezys, ed., *A Lithuanian Cemetery: St. Casimir Lithuanian Cemetery in Chicago, Ill.* (Chicago: Lithuanian Photo Library and Loyola University Press, 1976); Joseph Stipanovich, "Collective Economic Activity among Serb, Croat, and Slovene Immigrants in the United States," in Scott Cummings, ed., *Self-Help in Urban America: Patterns of Minority Business*

Enterprise (Port Washington, NY: National University Publications, Kennikat Press, 1980), p. 174.

22 Schedules of standard of living data for semiskilled and unskilled Chicago workers, 1924–5, in two volumes, UCSC, collected for study by Leila Houghteling, *The Income and Standard of Living of Unskilled Laborers in Chicago* (Chicago: University of Chicago Press, 1927).

23 For how Chicago social agencies dealt with the depression of 1920–2, see Philip Klein, *The Burden of Unemployment: A Study of Unemployment Relief Measures in Fifteen American Cities, 1921–22* (New York: Russell Sage Foundation, 1923), pp. 225–7; Materials on the Unemployment Conference, 1921–2, WC, Box 75, Folder "Unemployment 1921–28"; Gudrun Rom, "Centennial History of the United Charities," 1936, UNCH, Box 17, Folder 2, pp. 252–7; Minutes of Board Meeting, Federated Orthodox Jewish Charities, 31 January 1922, CFLPS, Box 25; *The New World (Official Organ of Archdiocesan Union of Chicago)*, 1919–22, *passim.*

24 "Vast Throng at Auditorium Cheer Opening of Charity Drive," *Daily Jewish Courier*, 8 May 1923, CFLPS, Box 26; "Charity Work Put on a Business Basis," *The New World*, 16 June 1922; "Associated Charities as Bulwark Against Socialism and Anarchy," *The New World*, 8 August 1919.

25 On the merger of the Federation of Jewish Charities and the Associated Jewish Charities, see Sentinel, *History of Chicago Jewry*, pp. 30, 163–4; and *Daily Jewish Courier*, CFLPS, Box 26: "Chaos in Our Philanthropy," 15 June 1919; "Chicago and Other Cities in America: Proposal to Unite the Two Charity Organizations," 10 September 1922.

26 On the establishment of the Associated Catholic Charities and the Central Charity Bureau and their first years of operation, see "The Catholic Charities of the Archdiocese of Chicago" (Chicago: Archdiocese of Chicago, 1940) Reverend Monsignor Harry C. Koenig, S.T.D., ed., *Caritas Christi Urget Nos: A History of the Offices, Agencies, and Institutions of the Archdiocese of Chicago*, 2 vols. (Chicago: Archdiocese of Chicago, n.d.), pp. 304–6, 811–13, 871; Charles Shanabruch, "The Catholic Church's Role in the Americanization of Chicago's Immigrants, 1853–1928" (Ph.D. dissertation, University of Chicago, 1975), pp. 435–6; *The New World*, January 1919–June 1922, *passim.*

27 Wirth, *The Ghetto*, pp. 274–7.

28 Helen R. Jeter and A. W. McMillen, "Some Statistics of Family Welfare and Relief in Chicago – 1928," *Social Service Review* 3 (September 1929): 452.

29 Harriet Clark Cade, "Statistics of Chicago Relief Agencies" (M.A. thesis, University of Chicago, 1927), p. 110. For ethnic group presence in the Chicago population in 1920 and 1930, see City of Chicago, Department of Development and Planning, "The People of Chicago: Who We Are And Who We Have Been," n.d. (mimeo), pp. 30–6. This ethnic breakdown of the welfare case load is born out in a United Charities' study done in 1925,

"Five Hundred Seventy Four Families Known to United Charities," UNCH, Box 50, Folder 1, p. 34.

30 Jeter and McMillen, "Some Statistics of Family Welfare," p. 452; Cade, "Chicago Relief Agencies," p. 36; Hillman, "Urbanization and the Organization of Welfare Activities in the Metropolitan Community of Chicago," pp. 58–9. On mothers' pensions, see Schiavo, *Italians*, p. 122; Mary F. Bogue, *Administration of Mothers' Aid in Ten Localities with Special Reference to Health, Housing, Education and Recreation*, Children's Bureau publication no. 184, (Washington, DC: U.S. Government Printing Office, 1928), pp. 7, 67–9.

31 Houghteling, *Income and Standard of Living of Unskilled Laborers*, p. 124.

32 Schiavo, *Italians*, p. 122.

33 On the role of ethnic groups in the development of Chicago's machine politics, a subject to be further examined in Chapter 6, see Harold F. Gosnell, *Machine Politics Chicago Model* (Chicago: University of Chicago, 1937, reprinted 1968); John W. Allswang, *A House For All Peoples: Ethnic Politics in Chicago, 1890–1936* (Lexington: University Press of Kentucky, 1971); Charles Edward Merriam, *Chicago: A More Intimate View of Urban Politics* (New York: Macmillan Company, 1929), pp. 134–77; Kantowicz, *Polish–American Politics in Chicago*, pp. 133–95; John P. White, "Lithuanians and the Democratic Party: A Case Study of Nationality Politics in Chicago and Cook County" (Ph.D. dissertation, University of Chicago, 1953), pp. 10–14, 27–8; Schiavo, *Italians*, pp. 104–5; Nelli, *Italians in Chicago*, pp. 91–3, 123.

34 Gosnell, *Machine Politics*, p. 71; Sonya Forthal, *Cogwells of Democracy: A Study of the Precinct Captain* (New York: William-Frederick Press, 1946), pp. 56–7, 60, 63–5; "Three Hundred Christmas Baskets Given Out by the Polish Democratic Club of the Thirty-third Ward," *Dziennik Chicagoski*, 3 January 1928, CFLPS, Box 35; Interview with George M. Tearney, 25 November 1925, in Paul F. Cressey, "Survey of McKinley Park Community," 20 October 1925, BUR, Box 129, Folder 7, p. 3. Alfred Fantozzi, a precinct captain for thirty years in the Italian neighborhood at 24th and Oakley near International Harvester, served both the Republican and Democratic parties. He described the job in great detail in his interview, including how people came to him for help getting public medical assistance. Interview with Alfred Fantozzi, Chicago, IL, 27 May 1980, IC, pp. 37–41.

35 Harriet E. Vittum, "Politics from the Social Point of View," *Proceedings of the National Conference of Social Work*, 1924, pp. 423–5, quoted in Harvey Warren Zorbaugh, *The Gold Coast and the Slum: A Sociological Study of Chicago's Near North Side* (Chicago: University of Chicago Press, 1929), pp. 178–80.

36 For historical background on mutual benefit societies and fraternal insurance see Richard De Rasimes Kip, *Fraternal Life Insurance in America*

(Philadelphia: Wharton School of Finance and Commerce, University of Pennsylvania, 1953), pp. 1–25, 98–107; Educational Committee of the National Fraternal Congress of America, *Fraternal Life Insurance* (Indianapolis: Insurance Research and Review Service, c. 1939), pp. 14–29; Daniels, *America Via the Neighborhood*, pp. 98–110.

Some groups had had comparable organizations in the Old World, but among all ethnicities these institutions proliferated in America. For experience with mutual benefit societies in Europe, see, e.g., on Italians, Josef J. Barton, *Peasants and Strangers: Italians, Rumanians and Slovaks in an American City* (Cambridge, MA: Harvard University Press, 1975), pp. 64–71, and Interview with Joseph Ungari, Shaumburg, IL, 8 March 1980, IC, p. 32; and on Jews, Park and Miller, *Old World Traits*, pp. 126–7.

37 Interview with Nina Dal Cason, Chicago, IL, 3 December 1979, IC, p. 23; Interview with Lillian Cwik, Chicago, IL, 1976, Polonia Archives, CHS, p. 28. Also see Breckinridge, *New Homes for Old*, pp. 96–8; Williams, *South Italian Folkways*, pp. 206–9; Joseph Chalasinski, "Polish and Parochial School among Polish Immigrants in America: A Study of a Polish Neighborhood in South Chicago," n.d. but c. 1930, CAP, Box 33, Folder 2, pp. 23, 25–6; Michael R. Weisser, *A Brotherhood of Memory: Jewish Landsmanshaftn in the New World* (New York: Basic Books, 1985); Judith E. Smith, *Family Connections: A History of Italian and Jewish Immigrant Lives in Providence, Rhode Island, 1900–1940* (Albany: State University of New York Press, 1985), pp. 124–65.

38 *Report of the Health Insurance Commission of the State of Illinois* (Springfield: State of Illinois, May 1, 1919), particularly: "Summary Statement of Facts, with the Commission's Findings and Recommendations," pp. 4–174; "A Study of Chicago Wage-earning Families" by Ernest W. Burgess, pp. 179–317; "Fraternal Insurance" by W. M. Duffus, pp. 443–82; and "Foreign Benefit Societies in Chicago" by Jakub Horak, pp. 523–31.

The findings of the Illinois Health Insurance Commission confirm the data collected on insurance among workingmen's families by the Bureau of Labor Statistics in 1918–19. See "What Is the American Standard of Living?" *Monthly Labor Review* 9 (July 1919): 10–12; "Cost of Living in the United States – Clothing and Miscellaneous Expenditures," *Monthly Labor Review* 9 (November 1919): 15–17; Bureau of Labor Statistics, Bulletin 357, *Cost of Living in the United States* (Washington, DC: U.S. Government Printing Office, May 1924), pp. 420–1.

39 For example, a study of the budget of a Bohemian family living in South Lawndale revealed that the husband, who earned $35 a week in a dye plant, gave his wife a weekly allowance from which she paid for household necessities, including $2.50 a month for his $1,500 insurance policy, and $1 for a $500 policy of her own. Helen Hrachowska, Paper for Sociology 264, 15 March 1931, BUR, Box 156, Folder 2, pp. 7, 17.

40 *Laws of the State of Illinois Enacted by the Fifty-fifth General Assembly*

at the Regular Biennial Session (Springfield: State of Illinois, 1927), pp. 557–90.

41 President's Research Committee, *Recent Social Trends,* vol. 1, p. 594; Breckinridge, *New Homes for Old*, pp. 194–5; Daniels, *America Via the Neighborhood*, pp. 148–51; *Illinois Health Insurance Commission Report*, p. 126.

42 "Nationalistic Insurance Organizations or Insurance Companies Only," *The Weekly Zgoda*, 8 January 1931, CFLPS, Box 36.

43 William Rutherford Ireland, "Young American Poles" (written but not submitted as M.A. thesis, University of Chicago, 1932), UCSC, pp. 31–3; Anonymous, "The New Year," *Chicago Society News*, January 1924, CFLPS, Box 36; "Reforms Demanded in Fraternal Aid Societies," *Dziennik Zwiazkowy*, 8 December 1910, CFLPS, Box 35; Polish Falcons of America, "60 Years of District IV: 1904–1964," 25 September 1965, Polish Falcons Papers, Folder 3, UICC; "Polish Organizations of Chicago," in *Poles of Chicago,* pp. 149–82; Frank Mocha, ed., *Poles in America: Bicentennial Essays* (Stevens Point, WI: Worzalla Publishing Company, 1978), pp. 634–48; Thomas and Znaniecki, *The Polish Peasant*, vol. 5, pp. 38–40, 106–62; Frank Renkiewicz, "The Profits of Nonprofit Capitalism: Polish Fraternalism and Beneficial Insurance in America," in Cummings, ed., *Self-Help in Urban America*, pp. 113–29; Wytrwal, *America's Polish Heritage*, pp. 156–7, 170–235.

44 Horak, "Assimilation of Czechs," pp. 60–73, 81–2; McCarthy, "Bohemians in Chicago and Their Benevolent Societies"; Alex Gottfried, *Boss Cermak of Chicago: A Study of Political Leadership* (Seattle: University of Washington Press, 1962), pp. 44–5; and the following from *Denni Hlasatel*, CFLPS, Box 4: "Czecho Slavonic Benevolent Societies," 11 January 1920; "Unification of Bohemian Free Thought Benevolent Societies," 8 August 1920; "Unification of All Czech Catholic Jednoty," 20 October 1920; "Convention News Affecting the Fraternal Societies of the Chicago Czechs," 9 September 1922.

45 Wirth, *The Ghetto*, pp. 222–4, 254; Irving Howe, *World of Our Fathers* (New York: Simon & Schuster, 1976), pp. 183–90, 357–9; Sidney Sorkin, Unpublished research notes on Jewish fraternal organizations with a focus on Chicago, Summer 1983; Arthur Liebman, *Jews and the Left* (New York: John Wiley & Sons, 1979), pp. 284–355; "April Meeting Learns of Changes in Direction over Past 40 Years," *Society News of the Chicago Jewish Historical Society* 7 (June 1984): 9; "Lost Waldheim Cemetery Rediscovered," *Society News of the Chicago Jewish Historical Society* 8 (September 1984): 9; and the following from the CFLPS: "The Progressive Order of the West," *Chicago Forward*, 25 May 1919, Box 25; "From the Public Rostrum," *Sunday Jewish Courier*, 17 August 1919, Box 25; "The Question of Economy at the Workmen's Circle Convention," *Forward*, 10 May 1922, Box 26; "What the Health Department of the Workmen's Circle Does for Its Members," 12 February 1932, Box 25.

46 Schiavo, *Italians*, pp. 55–9, 65; Nelli, *Italians in Chicago*, pp. 170–7, 239; Dominic Candeloro, "Suburban Italians: Chicago Heights 1890–1975," in Peter d'A. Jones and Melvin G. Holli, eds., *Ethnic Chicago* (Grand Rapids, MI: William B. Eerdmans Publishing Company, 1981), p. 194; Interviews, Chicago, IL, IC: Mario Avignone, 12 and 14 July 1979, pp. 10–11; Rosamond Mirabella, 23 May 1980, pp. 43–4; Leonard Giuliano, 2 January 1980, p. 79; "Laws and Regulations of the Grand Lodge of Illinois of the Sons of Italy in America as Approved at the Grand Extraordinary Convention of January the 17th, 1937, Chicago, Illinois," Folder 145.1, IC; "Ritual of the Roseland Lodge No. 1723, Sons of Italy in America," c. 1934, Folder 145.2 IC; Material on the Unione Veneziana, Folder 55.65, IC; the following from CFLPS: "The Order Sons of Italy," *Vita Nuova*, April 1925, Box 22; "Pro-Federation to the Members of Every Italian Mutual Benefit Society," *Il Bollettino Sociale*, 20 March 1929, Box 22; "Ten Years of Life," *Bulletin Order Sons of Italy in America, State of Illinois,* 15 December 1934, Box 21; and from the *Bulletin Italo–American National Union*, Box 22: "The Italo–American National Union," May 1926; "Rise of 'Italo–American National Union,'" March 1927; "Italians and Sicilians," March 1927.

47 *Illinois Health Insurance Report*, p. 139.

48 "How Should One Live?" *Dziennik Zjednoczenia*, 12 January 1929, CFLPS, Box 35.

49 From the CFLPS: "Progressive Order of the West Convention," *Daily Jewish Courier*, 29 July 1919, Box 27; "B'Nai Brith Woman Auxiliary Organized," *Sunday Jewish Courier*, 22 April 1923, Box 26; "Growing Organization," *Denni Hlasatel*, 17 September 1922, Box 4; "Branch of the Slovenian Women's Society," *American Slovenic*, 4 December 1926, Box 40; "The Italo–American National Union Is Now a Legal Reserve Fraternal Insurance Society," *Bulletin Italo–American National Union*, January 1933, Box 22. Material on the Women's Piemontese Society for Mutual Benefit, IC, Folders 55 and 63; National Fraternal Congress, *Fraternal Life Insurance*, pp. 109–12; Breckinridge, *New Homes for Old*, pp. 205–15.

50 National Fraternal Congress, *Fraternal Life Insurance*, pp. 103–7; and the following from the CFLPS: "Forging Ahead," *Bulletin Italo–American National Union*, January 1928, Box 22; "Membership Drive," *Dziennik Zjednoczenia*, 30 July 1926, Box 37; "The Polish Roman Catholic Union and Its Home," *Dziennik Zjednoczenia*, 15 November 1926, Box 35; "Workmen's Circle To Win Jewish Youth," *Jewish Forward*, 7 February 1926, Box 27.

51 "Rise of the SNPJ: A Brief Historical Summary Compiled by Ivan Molek" (n.p.: SNPJ, c. 1934), p. 32; and the following from the CFLPS: "Sixth Convention of the Bohemian Sisterhood," *Denni Hlasatel*, 25 August 1922, Box 4; "Notice," *Bulletin Italo–American National Union*, December 1924, Box 21; "All Members Please Note," *Bulletin Italo–American National Union*, February 1925, Box 22.

52 President's Research Committee, *Recent Social Trends,* vol. 2, pp. 935–6; Kip, *Fraternal Life Insurance in America*, pp. 12–20.

53 Schedules of standard of living data for semiskilled and unskilled Chicago workers, 1924–5, in two volumes, UCSC, collected for study by Houghteling, *Income and Standard of Living of Unskilled Laborers.*

54 Felicia Tarski and Marie Jasmski, "St. Casimir's Parish," Paper for Sociology 264, 17 March 1931, BUR, Box 156, Folder 3.

55 J. Lulinski, "Report on South Chicago Area Project," n.d., CAP, Box 36, Folder 3, pp. 12–14; James R. Barrett, *Work and Community in the Jungle: Chicago's Packinghouse Workers, 1894–1922* (Urbana: University of Illinois Press, 1987), p. 82.

56 Mary McDowell, "The Foreign Born," c. 1928, MCD, Box 12, p. 4; Interview with Joseph J. Elias, 1934, MCD, Folder 12, pp. 1–2.

57 Quoted in Howe, *World of Our Fathers,* p. 136. The U.S. Immigration Commission also noted that inconvenient hours at American banks in addition to their intimidating atmosphere assured the immigrant banker of ethnic workers' business. Report of the U.S. Immigration Commission, vol. 37, p. 216, quoted in Park, *Old World Traits*, p. 122.

58 Interview with Salvatore Cosentino, Berwyn, IL, 13 July 1979, IC, p. 14.

59 On immigrants' desire to own homes, see Edward R. Kantowicz, "Polish Chicago: Survival through Solidarity," in Holli and Jones, eds., *Urban Frontier*, p. 185; J. Lulinski, "Report on South Chicago Area Project," n.d., CAP, Box 36, Folder 3, p. 4; Breckinridge, *New Homes for Old*, pp. 105–8. Because Jews were less likely than Bohemians, Poles, and Italians to purchase homes and more likely to invest capital in small businesses and education, they had fewer building and loan associations. They feared that these securities could not be readily converted if it proved necessary to sell the property. Chicago Council of Social Agencies, "A Study of Association House, Chicago, Illinois," 1922, WC, Box 249, Folder "Association House 1922–66," p. 62.

60 For details on how building and loan associations actually operated and their history in Chicago, see Victor Greene, *For God and Country: The Rise of Polish and Lithuanian Ethnic Consciousness in America, 1860–1910* (Madison: State Historical Society of Wisconsin, 1975), pp. 54–8; Breckinridge, *New Homes for Old*, pp. 109–11; Gottfried, *Boss Cermak of Chicago*, pp. 44–5; Horak, "Assimilation of Czechs in Chicago," pp. 74–80; Dr. Peter P. Hletko, "Slovaks of Chicago," in *Slovak Catholic Souvenir Book* (Chicago: n.p., 1967); "Bohemian League of Building and Loan Associations of Chicago: The Annual Report," *Denni Hlasatel*, 7 December 1920, CFLPS, Box 2; "Albert Wachowski's Building and Loan Association Celebrates Silver Anniversary," *Dzienik Chicagoski*, 4 January 1928, CFLPS, Box 34.

61 Daniels, *America Via the Neighborhood*, pp. 315–18; Margaret H. Schoenfeld, "Trend of Wage Earners' Savings in Philadelphia," *Annals of the American Academy of Political and Social Science*, Supplement to vol. 121 (September 1925): 52–4.

62 *The Czechoslovak Review* 3 (June 1919), p. 175, CFLPS, Box 2; "Liberty Loan Campaign Workers Meet," *Denni Hlasatel*, 12 October 1918, CFLPS, Box 2; Horak, "Assimilation of Czechs in Chicago," p. 71.

63 Miecislaus Haiman, "The Poles in Chicago," in *Poles of Chicago*, p. 7; "Buy Victory Liberty Loan Bonds," *Narod Polski*, 23 April 1919, CFLPS, Box 34.

64 Louis Wirth, Notes for Study of Monroe District c. 1919, BUR, Box 139, Folder 6; and from the CFLPS, Box 28: "Lithuanians Participate in Parade," *Lietuva*, 18 October 1918; "What Place Will the Lithuanians Take This Time?" *Lietuva*, 27 September 1918.

65 Report by Stockyards Community Clearing House, 1918–19, MCD, Box 40, Folder 20.

66 Interview with Salvatore Cosentino, Berwyn, IL, 13 July 1979, IC, p. 22.

67 "Unusual Growth of Savings Deposits in Bohemian Banks," *Denni Hlasatel*, 15 January 1920, CFLPS, Box 2; Report by Stockyards Community Clearing House, 1918–19, MCD, Box 40, Folder 20; Chicago Council of Social Agencies, "A Study of Association House, Chicago, Illinois," 1922, WC, Box 249, Folder "Association House 1922–66," pp. 58–60. Numerous investigations into the impact of Prohibition in working-class neighborhoods in the early 1920s identified an increase in bank savings, which social workers liked to credit to a new Puritanism brought on by Prohibition. It is more likely, however, that the newfound interest in banks was responsible. See Marian Winthrop Taylor, "The Social Results of Prohibition: A Study Made in the Central District of the United Charities" (M.A. thesis, University of Chicago, 1923); Norman Sylvester Hayner, "The Effect of Prohibition in Packingtown" (M.A. thesis, University of Chicago, 1921). For discussion of similar growth in savings deposits among Philadelphia workers, see Schoenfeld, "Trend of Wage-earners' Savings," pp. 15–16. On the national level, Paul T. Cherington, "Where Are You Going – My Pretty Market?" *J. Walter Thompson News Bulletin* (November 1926): 10, JWT, RG 11.

68 Savings in the Postal Banking System peaked in 1919 and then declined. Paul Nystrom, *Economic Principles of Consumption* (New York: Ronald Press Company, 1929), p. 492; Breckinridge, *New Homes for Old*, pp. 111–14; Schoenfeld, "Trend of Wage Earners' Savings," pp. 47–52.

69 The monthly journal of Lord & Thomas (Chicago's largest advertising company in the period), *Judicious Advertising*, chronicles the growing marketing interest of banks. See, e.g., "The Relation of Bank Advertising to War Finance," 16 (September 1918); "Fifteen Million New Bondholders as Prospects," 16 (January 1919); "The Man in the Street and Financial Advertising," 19 (July 1921); "10,000 New Accounts in Four Months," 22 (January 1924); "This New Advertising Increased Our Savings Deposits," 23 (January 1925).

70 F. Cyril James, *The Growth of Chicago Banks*, vol. 2 (New York: Harper & Brothers Publishers, 1938), pp. 943–59; Arthur H. Winakor, *Banking*

Turnover and Facilities in Illinois, Bulletin no. 55 of the Bureau of Business Research (Urbana: University of Illinois, 1937), pp. 7–22.

71 Quoted in Renkiewicz, "The Profits of Nonprofit Capitalism," in Cummings, ed., *Self-Help in Urban America*, p. 113.

72 "The Schiavone State Bank," *Chicago Chamber of Commerce*, May 1924, CFLPS, Box 21. Also see from CFLPS: "New Czech Bank Opens in Berwyn, Illinois," *Denni Hlasatel*, 14 December 1922, Box 2; "Meeting of the Polish Bankers at Chicago," *Dziennik Zjednoczenia*, 29 November 1922, Box 24.

73 E. N. Baty, "The Story of the Outlying Banks of Chicago" (Chicago: Chicago and Cook County Bankers Association, 1924), pp. 5–29.

74 "The First National Bank of Cicero Celebrates Grand Opening," *Denni Hlasatel*, 8 May 1921, CFLPS, Box 2; Mary Zahrobsky, "The Slovaks in Chicago" (M.A. thesis, University of Chicago, 1924), p. 54; "Consider the Czechoslovaks," *Judicious Advertising* 21 (December 1923): 64; "Less Recognized Cities in the United States: The Polish City of Chicago," J. Walter Thompson Company newsletter no. 75 (April 1925): 2, JWT, RG 11; and for a full list of Chicago banks through the 1920s, *Handbook of the Banks of Chicago*, vols. 16–23 (Chicago: Chicago Evening Post, 1922–9).

75 George Hanas, "Study of Slovak Church Group, Northwest Side," Paper for Sociology I, Winter 1925, BUR, Box 149, Folder 3; from the CFLPS: "Chicago Avenue Businessmen's Association Completes Arrangements for Holiday Season," *Dziennik Chicagoski*, 2 December 1921, Box 36; "Growth of Kaspar State Bank," *Denni Hlasatel*, 24 December 1920, Box 2; "We Have Direct Communications with Poland," *Forward*, 19 July 1919, Box 26; "Foreign Exchange," *Forward*, 17 July 1919, Box 26; "Where and For What Italians Spend Their Money," *Il Bolletino Sociale*, 2 June 1930, Box 22; "Chicago's Pageant of Nations: Italians and Their Contributions," *Chicago Evening Post*, 16 November 1929, Box 22.

76 Interview with Thomas Perpoli, Chicago, IL, 26 June 1980, IC, pp. 10–11.

77 Interview with Angelo Patti, Chicago, IL, 14 July 1980, IC, pp. 24–5.

78 From the CFLPS: "The Big Historical Day: Opening of 16th Street Bank," *Forward*, 2 February 1919, Box 23; Advertisement 16th Street Bank, *The Daily Jewish Courier*, 4 July 1919, Box 24; "16th Street Bank Closed, President and Cashier Held," *Daily Jewish Courier*, 21 March 1923, Box 26; "Meeting of Depositors," *Daily Jewish Courier*, 17 April 1923, Box 23.

79 Polish Welfare Association of Chicago, "Yearbook 1925," WC, Box 390, Folder "Polish Welfare Association, 1925–1954."

80 Nystrom, *Economic Principles*, pp. 491–2; "Development of Building and Loan Associations in 1928," *Monthly Labor Review* 29 (November 1929): 58–9; Chicago Council of Social Agencies, "A Study of Association House, Chicago, Illinois," 1922, WC, Box 249, Folder "Association House 1922–66," p. 61; *Poles of Chicago*, pp. 6, 15, 184; Stipanovich, "Collec-

tive Economic Activity Among Serb, Croat, and Slovene Immigrants in the United States," in Cummings, ed., *Self-Help in Urban America*, p. 173; and from the CFLPS: "Annual Meeting of the Polish Building and Loan Associations," *Dziennik Zjednoczenia*, 13 March 1928, Box 34; "Annual Meeting of the Members of the Building and Loan Association," *Sandara*, 3 January 1930, Box 28; "Poland's Historic Struggle," *Chicago Evening Post*, 30 November 1929, Box 37.

81 Arthur H. Winakor, *State-chartered Savings, Building, and Loan Associations in Illinois, 1920 to 1936*, Bulletin no. 58 of the Bureau of Business Research (Urbana: University of Illinois, 1939), p. 33; Julius John Ozog, "A Study of Polish Home Ownership in Chicago" (M.A. thesis, University of Chicago, 1942); and from CFLPS, Box 34: "Meeting of League of Polish Building and Loan Association of Illinois," *Dziennik Zwiazkowy*, 9 September 1918; "New Building and Loan Association," *Dziennik Chicagoski*, 11 February 1922. For a list and financial statement of all building and loan associations in Chicago, see Illinois Auditor of Public Accounts, *Annual Report of Mutual Building, Loan and Homestead Associations* (Springfield: State of Illinois, 1919–29).

82 *The New World*, 28 July 1922; and see 23 April 1920, 1 October 1920, 22 October 1920, 4 March 1921, 11 March 1921, 18 March 1921, 22 April 1921, 17 June 1921, and 11 August 1922 for further discussion of the necessity of making the church a social center that could compete with commercial recreation. Also, *All Saints Church Diamond Jubilee Book, 1875–1950* (Chicago: All Saints Church, 1950), and "New Slovenian Hall in Chicago," *Amerikanski Slovenec*, 21 April 1926, CFLPS, Box 40.

83 On church efforts to establish its own sports programs, see *The New World*, 9 April 1920, 17 June 1921, 21 March 1922, 16 February 1923.

84 Concerning the church's opposition to other private and public welfare programs, see *The New World*, 11 July 1919, 29 August 1919, 5 December 1919, 5 May 1922, 26 May 1922, 28 July 1922.

85 Edward R. Kantowicz, "Cardinal Mundelein of Chicago and the Shaping of Twentieth-Century American Catholicism," *Journal of American History* 68 (June 1981): 64; Charles Shanabruch, "The Catholic Church's Role in the Americanization of Chicago's Immigrants: 1853–1928" (Ph.D. dissertation, University of Chicago, 1975), pp. 506–9.

86 Kantowicz, "Cardinal Mundelein," p. 63.

87 For an extensive examination of Archbishop, and after 1924 Cardinal, Mundelein's leadership in Chicago, see Edward R. Kantowicz, *Corporation Sole: Cardinal Mundelein and Chicago Catholicism* (Notre Dame: University of Notre Dame Press, 1983). For discussion of Mundelein's early policies, see Parot, *Polish Catholics in Chicago*, pp. 179–232. The one exception to Mundelein's opposition to nonterritorial parishes was his creation of a separate black Catholic parish in the Black Belt in 1917.

88 Thomas and Znaniecki, *The Polish Peasant*, vol. 5, pp. 41–51. Also see Jay Dolan, *The American Catholic Experience: A History from Colonial*

Times to the Present (Garden City, NY: Doubleday & Co., 1985), pp. 181–5; Wytrwal, *America's Polish Heritage*, pp. 159–69; Radzialowski, "The View from a Polish Ghetto," pp. 131–2; Greene, *For God and Country*, for early history of Polish Catholic Church in Chicago.

89 Joseph Chalasinski, "Polish and Parochial School among Polish Immigrants in America: A Study of a Polish Neighborhood in South Chicago," n.d. but c. 1930, CAP, Box 33, Folder 2.

90 Ireland, "Young American Poles," p. 58. Perhaps the most insulting of Mundelein's actions was his effort to get Polish churches to drop from the ritual the Polish national anthem, prompting one man to angrily argue, "Poles have spirit. Coercion doesn't work with us. You tell us to stop singing our Polish song in Church, and we won't do it. Why should we?"

91 Reverend John Lange to Associated Catholic Charities, 19 August 1919, quoted in Shanabruch, "The Catholic Church's Role," p. 556.

92 On the effort to create a Holy Name Society at St. Michael's, see *The New World*, 27 May 1921, 21 October 1921, 28 October 1921. On Mundelein's ambitions for the Holy Name Societies, see Koenig, ed., *Caritas Christi Urget Nos*, vol. 1, pp. 174–9. A survey of parish jubilee books clearly reveals the resistance of Polish parishes to Holy Name Societies. Typical are St. Stanislaus Kostka, Chicago's earliest Polish church, which did not have a Holy Name Society until 1935, and Immaculate Conception, B.V.M. in South Chicago, which resisted one until 1943. In contrast, St. Augustine's, a German church in Back of the Yards, established a Holy Name Society in 1917, began to preach English sermons in 1918, and founded its first Boy Scout Troop in 1920. *St. Stanislaus Kostka Diamond Jubilee Book, 1867–1942* Chicago: St. Stanislaus Kostka, 1957), p. 78; *Immaculate Conception B.V.M. Parish, South Chicago, 1882–1957, Diamond Jubilee,* p. 138; *Program and Chronological History: Souvenir of St. Augustine's Parish Golden Jubilee, 1880–1936* (Chicago: St. Augustine, 1936), pp. 147, 159, 161, 265.

93 On the Polish National Catholic Church in Chicago during the 1920s, see from *Przebudzenie*, CFLPS: "Americanization or 'Irishization,'" 20 November 1927, Box 37; "The Power of the Polish National Catholic Church," 3 January 1928, Box 36; "Roman Catholic Church Tightening Grip," 3 June 1928, Box 36; "Two National Parishes Established in Chicago," 13 January 1929, Box 36; "Committee for the Protection of the Polish Lanauge," 12 January 1930, Box 36; "O Lord, Forgive Them, They Know Not What They Do," 29 October 1931, Box 32. Also "Parish of All the Saints Church," *Memorial Book '33' – Polish National Catholic Church*, p. 395, CFLPS, Box 36. For background on the Polish National Catholic Church, see Theodore L. Zawistowski, "The Polish National Catholic Church: An Acceptable Alternative," in Mocha, ed., *Poles in America*, pp. 423–34.

94 James W. Sanders, *The Education of an Urban Minority: Catholics in Chicago, 1833–1965* (New York: Oxford University Press, 1977), pp. 118–19.

95 Joseph Chalasinski, "Polish and Parochial School Among Polish Immigrants in America: A Study of a Polish Neighborhood in South Chicago," n.d. but c. 1930, CAP, Box 33, Folder 2.

96 Parot, *Polish Catholics in Chicago*, p. 230.

97 "Poles Want Exclusive Parish in 'New Poland'," *Dziennik Chicagoski*, 10 January 1928, CFLPS, Box 37.

98 For number of souls and churches by ethnicity in the Chicago Archdiocese between 1919 and 1929, see Marvin Reuel Schafer, "The Catholic Church in Chicago, Its Growth and Administration" (Ph.D. dissertation, University of Chicago, 1929), pp. 16–17, 49–51. For ethnic enrollments in Catholic elementary schools between 1910 and 1930, see Sanders, *Education of an Urban Minority*, p. 45. Whereas all Catholic elementary school attendance grew an average of 22 percent between 1920 and 1930, territorial parish schools increased 26 percent and Polish parish schools 28 percent. On the growth of Polish high schools during the 1920s, see *Poles of Chicago*, pp. 128–34, and Sanders, *Education of an Urban Minority*, pp. 161–9.

99 On Italian relations with the church in Italy and difficulties with the Irish-dominated American Catholic Church, see Rudolph Vecoli, "Prelates and Peasants: Italian Immigrants and the Catholic Church," *Journal of Social History* 2 (Spring 1969): 217–68; Nelli, *Italians in Chicago*, pp. 181–7; Williams, *South Italian Folkways*, pp. 146–8; Dolan, *American Catholic Experience*, pp. 173–5, 237; James S. Olson, *Catholic Immigrants in America* (Chicago: Nelson-Hall, 1987), pp. 84–8, 118–25, 131–4, 139–41.

100 For the fate of Italian Catholicism under Archbishop Quigley, see Stephen Joseph Shaw, "Chicago's Germans and Italians, 1903–1939: The Catholic Parish as a Way-station of Ethnicity and Americanization" (Ph.D. dissertation, University of Chicago, 1981), pp. 208–10; Nelli, *Italians in Chicago*, pp. 188–94; Schafer, "The Catholic Church in Chicago," pp. 30–3, 51; Sanders, *Education of an Urban Minority*, pp. 45, 67–71; Zorbaugh, *The Gold Coast and the Slum*, p. 177.

101 The composite picture of patron saint feasts in Italy and in Chicago presented here has been derived from numerous sources, including: *75th Anniversary History of the Blessed Mother St. Maria Incoronata Church, 1897–1972* (Chicago: St. Maria Incoronata, 1972); Ann Zaloha, "A Study of the Persistence of Italian Customs Among 143 Families of Italian Descent, Members of Social Clubs at Chicago Commons" (M.A. thesis, Northwestern University, 1937), pp. 89, 96–9; diverse materials about feasts in the IC collection, including films of feasts in Italy and Chicago, record books of society feast committees, photographs, newspaper clippings, publicity handbills and press releases, and numerous interviews; Alice L. Anderson, "The Chicago Commons: Its Contribution to the Community," Sociology paper, University of Nebraska, May 1940, COM, Box 18, pp. 11–12; Schiavo, *Italians*, pp. 56–7; Zorbaugh, *Gold*

Coast and the Slum, pp. 167–8; Williams, *South Italian Folkways*, pp. 135–40, 149–51. For a fascinating, in-depth study of the changing celebration of the feast in Italian Harlem, see Robert Anthony Orsi, *The Madonna of 115th Street: Faith and Community in Italian Harlem, 1880–1950* (New Haven: Yale University Press, 1985).

102 Interviews from IC: Leonard Giuliano, Chicago, IL, 2 January 1980, pp. 40–1, 49; Carmella Zoppetti, Chicago, IL, 9 June 1980, pp. 38–9; Florence Parise, Chicago, IL, 20 June 1980, pp. 12–17; Paul Penio, Itasca, IL, 30 June 1980, p. 49.

103 *The New World*, 12 September 1919; "Social Work Aids Italians ," *The New World*, 14 September 1923; *The Scoop* (West Side Community newspaper) 1 (September 1924): 7; Shaw, "Chicago's Germans and Italians," p. 233.

104 *70th Anniversary of St. Anthony's Parish* (Chicago: St. Anthony, 1973); *Golden Jubilee Book, Mt. Carmel School, Chicago Heights, Illinois, 1912–1962* (Chicago Heights, IL: Mt. Carmel School, 1962); Vecoli, "Prelates and Peasants," pp. 253–60. For 1939 statistics, see *The Official Catholic Directory* (New York: P. J. Kennedy and Sons, 1940).

105 *Il Calendario Italiano* (Church Bulletin of St. Philip Benizi), September 1925, quoted in Shaw, "Chicago's Germans and Italians," pp. 242–3.

106 *Il Calendario Italiano*, May 1924, quoted in Shaw, "Chicago's Germans and Italians," pp. 236–7; also see Gaetano DeFilippis, "Social Life in an Immigrant Community," n.d. but c. 1930, Paper for Sociology 264, BUR, Box 130, Folder 2, pp. 31–2; Schiavo, *Italians*, p. 81.

107 Shaw, "Chicago's Germans and Italians," p. 205; *Golden Anniversary Saint Michael's Church, November 1, 1953* (Chicago: St. Michael, 1953); Interviews, Chicago, IL, IC: Maria Valiani, 10 June 1980, pp. 36, 40; Alfred Fantozzi, 27 May 1980, p. 15; Lina Tarabori, 5 June 1980, p. 25.

108 Interviews, IC: Theresa De Falco, Downers Grove, IL, 28 April 1980, p. 2; Florence Roselli, Villa Parks, IL, December 1980, pp. 57, 62; Frank DeLiberto, Chicago, IL, 17 April 1980, p. 28; Nick Zaranti, Chicago Heights, IL, 5 March 1980, p. 4. Italians were particularly involved with Hull House and the Chicago Commons Settlement.

109 Sanders, *Education of an Urban Minority*, pp. 45, 70; Nelli, *Italians in Chicago*, p. 192; Shaw, "Chicago's Germans and Catholics," p. 240; and Interviews, Chicago, IL, IC: Carmella Zoppetti, 9 June 1980, p. 30; Nina Dal Caron, 3 December 1979, p. 8.

110 See, e.g., the work of Victor Turner, such as *The Ritual Process: Structure and Anti-Structure* (London: Routledge and Kegan Paul, 1969) and *Dramas, Fields, Metaphors: Symbolic Action in Human Society* (Ithaca, NY: Cornell University Press, 1974). For a similar kind of analysis of the Mexican fiesta, see Octavio Paz, *The Labyrinth of Solitude: Life and Thought in Mexico* (New York: Grove Press, 1961), pp. 47–64.

111 Interview with Rosa Clementi, Chicago, IL, 7 April 1980, IC, pp. 54–6.

112 *Chicago Tribune*, 11 May 1924, quoted in Shanabruch, "Catholic

Church's Role," p. 552; Interview with Most Reverend A. Abramowicz, Chicago, IL, Polonia Archives, CHS.

113 Kantowicz, "Polish Chicago," p. 204.

114 Schiavo, *Italians*, p. 81.

3. ENCOUNTERING MASS CULTURE

1 J. Walter Thompson Company newsletter no. 139 (1 July 1926), JWT, RG 11, pp. 157–9; Howard Henderson, "Behind the Doorbell: Sifting Out the Basic Desires Which Control the Consumer Family's Choice of a Product," *J. Walter Thompson News Bulletin* no. 101 (January 1923): 5–9, JWT, RG 11.

2 Gregory Mason, "Satan in the Dance Hall," *The American Mercury* (June 1924): 177–80, quoted in Notes for Sociology 34 on "The Public Dance Hall," BUR, Box 31, Folder 4, p. VI-17.

3 *Balaban & Katz Magazine* 1 (13 July 1925, 27 July 1925).

4 "The 5-Day Week in Ford Plants," *Monthly Labor Review* 23 (December 1926): 10–14.

5 "The Trend of Commercialized Recreation," 13 September 1928, BUR, Box 15, Folder 5, p. 2.

6 Some present-day sociologists have shared the assumptions of contemporary observers who were confident of the homogenizing powers of mass culture. They have posited what has come to be called "the embourgeoisement thesis," arguing that mass consumption and leisure have blurred the divisions between social classes, assimilating workers into mainstream patterns and a middle-class identity. Daniel Bell, *The End of Ideology* (New York: Free Press, 1962); John Goldthorpe and David Lockwood, *The Affluent Worker in the Class Structure* (Cambridge: Cambridge University Press, 1969). For criticism of the embourgeoisement thesis, see John Clarke, Chas Critcher, and Richard Johnson, *Working Class Culture: Studies in History and Theory* (University of Birmingham, Centre for Contemporary Cultural Studies and London: Hutchinson & Company, 1979), and James E. Cronin, *Labour and Society in Britain, 1918–1979* (London: Batsford Academic and Educational, 1984), pp. 146–72.

Ironically, many present-day, radical historians also have endorsed the notion that mass culture was a homogenizing force. They tend, however, to criticize movies, radio, or chain stores for being agents of social control, out to destroy a truer popular culture and to homogenize cultural life along "American," middle-class lines. Many of these studies fall into this pattern partly because their major focus is on the late nineteenth and early twentieth centuries; treatment of mass culture in the 1920s serves as a kind of epilogue, "the fall" following "the rise" of working-class culture, which is their primary interest. See particularly Stuart Ewen, *Captains of Consciousness: Advertising and the Social Roots of the Consumer Culture* (New York: McGraw-Hill Book Company, 1976); Richard Wightman Fox and T. J.

Jackson Lears, eds., *The Culture of Consumption* (New York: Pantheon Books, 1983).

Although this is also the general thrust of historian Roy Rosenzweig's argument, he suggests that in bringing diverse groups of workers together, the movies unintentionally may have helped them mount a more unified political challenge in the 1930s. But they did not organize out of a working-class consciousness. Having shared in middle-class culture during the 1920s, workers fought to sustain and expand their access to it, which was being endangered by the depression. Roy Rosenzweig, *"Eight Hours For What We Will": Workers and Leisure in Worcester, Massachusetts, 1870–1930* (New York: Cambridge University Press, 1984). A similar perspective informs the work of Ronald Edsforth's *Class Conflict and Cultural Consensus: The Making of a Mass Consumer Society in Flint, Michigan* (New Brunswick: Rutgers University Press, 1987), particularly pp. 32–6. Francis Couvares's work does not fit these generalizations. He makes an interesting argument that participating in mass culture became a working-class strategy of defiance against pietistic, reformist alternatives. His analysis ends, however, around 1920. Francis G. Couvares, "The Triumph of Commerce: Class Culture and Mass Culture in Pittsburgh," in Michael H. Frisch and Daniel J. Walkowitz, eds., *Working-Class America: Essays on Labor, Community, and American Society* (Urbana: University of Illinois Press, 1983), pp. 123–52, and "The Remaking of Urban Culture in Late Nineteenth and Early Twentieth Century America," Paper delivered at the Lowell Industrial History Conference, Lowell, MA, 29–30 April 1983.

7 True Story Magazine, *The American Economic Evolution*, vol. 1 (New York: Macfadden Publications, 1930), pp. 32–4, 67. Also see Paul T. Cherington, "New Practices in the Construction of Sales Quotas," *J. Walter Thompson News Bulletin* no. 126 (January 1927), for optimism about how much money American workingmen had to spend "for the less imperative uses" after necessities were covered.

8 Frank Stricker, "Affluence for Whom? – Another Look at Prosperity and the Working Classes in the 1920s," *Labor History* 24 (Winter 1983): 33.

The *Chicago Tribune Survey*, a monthly report on current business conditions in the Chicago territory, which was started in 1927 to inform potential advertisers, recognized the relationship between industrial unemployment and purchasing power. Every issue included an article on the industrial economy in the area and its impact on employment. *Chicago Tribune Survey*, vols. 1–3 (May 1927–December 1929).

I will investigate the issues of wages and unemployment further in Chapter 4. Meanwhile, other sources that substantiate the economic struggles of manufacturing workers during the 1920s include the following for the national picture: Irving Bernstein, *The Lean Years: A History of the American Worker, 1920–1933* (Baltimore: Penguin Books, 1966), pp. 57–74; Walter Pitkin, *The Consumer: His Nature and His Changing Habits* (New York: McGraw-Hill Book Company, 1932), pp. 157–9; Peter H. Lindert and Jeffrey G. Williamson, "Three Centuries of American Inequality," in P.

Uselding, ed., *Research in Economic History*, vol. 1 (Greenwich, CT: JAI Press, 1977); "Index of Pay-roll Totals in Manufacturing Industries," *Monthly Labor Review* 20 (March 1925): 130–5; "Labor-absorbing Power of American Industry," *Monthly Labor Review* 28 (June 1929): 222–4.

On the economic position of industrial workers in Chicago during the 1920s, see Leila Houghteling, *The Income and Standard of Living of Unskilled Laborers in Chicago* (Chicago: University of Chicago Press, 1927); Franc Lewis McCluer, "Living Conditions among Wage Earning Families in Forty-one Blocks in Chicago" (Ph.D. dissertation, University of Chicago, 1928); Elizabeth A. Hughes, *Living Conditions for Small-Wage Earners in Chicago* (Chicago: Department of Public Welfare, City of Chicago, 1925); Florence Nesbitt, "The Chicago Standard Budget for Dependent Families," Prepared under the supervision of the Division on Family Welfare of the Chicago Council of Social Agencies, revised September 1, 1920, January 1925, June 1, 1929; Robert Ozanne, *Wages in Practice and Theory: McCormick and International Harvester, 1860–1960* (Madison: University of Wisconsin Press, 1968), pp. 8, 11, 44–53, 134–6, 139; U.S. Department of Labor, Bureau of Labor Statistics, *Changes in the Cost of Living in Large Cities in the United States, 1913–41*, Bulletin no. 699 (Washington, DC: U.S. Government Printing Office, 1941), pp. 53, 105; "Memorandum of Informal Conference Called by Director of the Chicago Council of Social Agencies at the Request of Representatives of Organizations Concerned with Employment for Men and Women in Chicago . . .," 18 June 1924, WC, Box 75, Folder "Unemployment 1921–28"; Illinois Department of Labor, *Tenth Annual Report, July 1, 1926 to June 30, 1927* (Springfield: State of Illinois, 1928), pp. 96–115.

9 Wilbur C. Plummer, "Social and Economic Consequences of Buying on the Instalment Plan," *Annals of the American Academy of Political and Social Science*, Supplement to vol. 129 (January 1927): 2. Edwin Seligman refuted figures as high as Plummer's, claiming that at the close of 1926, $4.5 billion, or a little less than 12 percent of total retail sales, were by installment. Edwin R. A. Seligman, *The Economics of Installment Selling: A Study in Consumers' Credit with Special Reference to the Automobile* (New York: Harper & Brothers Publishers, 1927), pp. 14–23, 28–33, 92–119, 260–77.

10 Plummer, "Buying on Instalment," pp. 10, 33–9; Paul T. Cherington, "Where Are You Going – My Pretty Market?" *J. Walter Thompson News Bulletin* (November 1926): 9–14, JWT, RG 11.

11 Wilbur D. Plummer, "The Effects of Instalment Selling on Stability," *Annals of the American Academy of Political and Social Science* 139 (September 1928): 160–5; and discussion of employers' attitudes to worker savings and thrift in my Chapter 4. The Lynds identified the double message that businessmen were giving, to spend and to save, in their study of Muncie, Indiana, during the 1920s. Robert S. Lynd and Helen Merrell Lynd, *Middletown: A Study in American Culture* (New York: Harcourt, Brace & World, 1929), p. 88.

12 Houghteling, *Unskilled Laborers*, pp. 120–1; Chicago Tribune, *Chicago Tribune Fact Book, 1928* (Chicago: Tribune Publishers, 1928), p. 46; Stricker, "Affluence for Whom?" pp. 30–2. Stricker also makes the point that workers were much less likely to own automobiles than the popular imagery of the 1920s suggests. He estimates that by 1929 a working-class family had no more than a 30 percent chance of owning a car.

13 President's Research Committee, *Recent Social Trends in the United States*, vol. 2 (New York: McGraw-Hill Book Company, 1933; reprinted Westport, CT: Greenwood Press, 1970), p. 862; Plummer, "Buying on Instalment," pp. 2–3, 12–13.

14 Plummer, "Buying on Instalment," p. 11; Mildred John, "Why Workers Borrow: A Study of Four Thousand Credit Union Loans," *Monthly Labor Review* 25 (July 1927): 6–16, which has some limitations because it provides no information on any additional installment debts the families might have had; Marie De Vroet Kobrak, "Consumer Installment Credit and Factors Associated with It" (M.A. thesis, University of Chicago, 1958), particularly pp. 21–4.

15 Heller Committee for Research in Social Economics, *Cost of Living Studies*, vol. 4, *Spending Ways of a Semi-Skilled Group: A Study of the Incomes and Expenditures of Ninety-Eight Street-car Men's Families in the San Francisco East Bay Region* (Berkeley: University of California Publications in Economics, 1931), p. 345, quoted in Stricker, "Affluence for Whom?" p. 33; also see Pitkin, *The Consumer*, pp. 332–3.

16 John Dollard, "The Changing Functions of the American Family" (Ph.D. dissertation, University of Chicago, 1931), pp. 137–8.

17 Interview with Rena Domke, Chicago, IL, 28 April 1980, IC, p. 3. For other discussion of how Italians valued the phonograph as a way to enjoy their native culture, see Gaetano DeFilippis, "Social Life in an Immigrant Community," Paper for Sociology 264, n.d. but c. 1930, BUR, Box 130, Folder 2, p. 42; C. W. Jenkins, "Chicago's Pageant of Nations: Italians and Their Contribution," *Chicago Evening Post*, 16 November 1929, CFLPS, Box 22; Autobiography of an Italian Immigrant, n.d., CAP, Box 64, Folder 24, p. 18; and interviews with the following from IC: Mario Avignone, Chicago, IL, 12 July 1979, p. 24; Thomas Perpoli, Chicago, IL, 26 June 1980, p. 34; Theresa De Falco, Downers Grove, IL, 28 April 1980, p. 17; Leonard Giuleano, Chicago, IL, 2 January 1980, p. 19; Rena Morandin, Chicago, IL, 22 July 1980, p. 18; Ernest Dalle-Molle, Downers Grove, IL, 30 April 1980, p. 76; Edward Baldacci, Chicago Heights, IL, 29 May 1980, p. 17.

18 Anthony Sorrentino, *Organizing Against Crime: Redeveloping the Neighborhood* (New York: Human Sciences Press, 1977), pp. 40–1.

19 Richard K. Spottswood, "The Sajewski Story: Eighty Years of Polish Music in Chicago," in American Folklife Center, *Ethnic Recordings in America: A Neglected Heritage*, Studies in American Folklife, no. 1 (Washington, DC: Library of Congress, 1982), pp. 133–73, and two others in the anthology: Pekka Gronow, "Ethnic Recordings: An Introduction," pp.

1–99, and Richard K. Spottswood, "Commercial Ethnic Recordings in the United States," pp. 51–66.

20 Robert C. Jones and Louis R. Wilson, *The Mexican in Chicago* (Chicago: Comity Commission of the Chicago Church Federation, 1931), p. 7; Manuel Gamio, *Mexican Immigration to the United States: A Study of Human Migration and Adjustment* (Chicago: SSRC, 1930; reprinted New York: Dover Publications, 1971), Appendix 5, "Objects Brought into Mexico Free of Custom Duty by 2,104 Returned Immigrants in the Year 1927 . . . ," pp. 224–9.

21 *Supreme Court of the District of Columbia in Equity No. 37623, United States of America Petitioner vs. Swift & Company, Armour & Company, Morris & Company, Wilson & Co., Inc., and the Cudahy Packing Co., et al., Defendants, on Petitions of Swift & Company, and Its Associate Defendants, and Armour & Company, and Its Associate Defendants, for Modification of Decree of February 27, 1920, Petitioning Defendants Statement of the Case* (Washington, DC: Press of Byron S. Adams, 1930), p. 14. For more on chain stores as a way of streamlining distribution to make it equal in efficiency to mass production, see *Chain Store Progress* 1 (November – December 1929), *Chain Store Progress* 2 (January 1930).

22 For basic information on the development of chain stores, see James L. Palmer, "Economic and Social Aspects of Chain Stores," *Journal of Business of the University of Chicago* 2 (1929): 172–290; Paul H. Nystrom, *Economic Principles of Consumption* (New York: Ronald Press Company, 1929), pp. 518–22; Walter S. Hayward, "The Chain Store and Distribution," *Social Service Review* 115 (September 1924): 220–5; Daniel J. Boorstin, *The Americans: The Democratic Experience* (New York: Vintage Books, 1974), pp. 109–18; Time-Life, *This Fabulous Century, 1920–1930*, vol. 3 (New York: Time-Life Books, 1971), pp. 104–6; J. Walter Thompson Company newsletters nos. 3, 83, 94, 97, 132 (4 June 1925, 20 August 1925, 10 September 1925, 13 May 1926), JWT, RG 11.

23 For discussion of the spread of standard brands, see President's Research Committee, *Recent Social Trends*, vol. 2, pp. 874–7, which includes the results of a consumer survey in Milwaukee charting the increased use of packaged and branded goods from 1924 to 1930; the following articles from Lord & Thomas Advertising Agency, *Judicious Advertising*: "The Danger in the 'Bulk Goods' Movement," 16 (September 1918): 91–5; "Advertising is the Consumers' Guarantee," 19 (March 1921): 105; "Consider the Consumer," 19 (July 1921): 65–71; "What the Trade-Mark Means to Merchandising: How Manufacturers, Retailers and the Public Benefit," 21 (July 1923): 40–4; and from JWT, RG 11: J. Walter Thompson Company newsletter nos. 4, 10, 7, 8, 9, 100, 115 (27 June 1916, 8 August 1916, 27 December 1923, 3 January 1924, 10 January 1924, 1 October 1925, 14 January 1926); "The Value of a Trade Mark," *J. Walter Thompson News Bulletin* no. 91-A (16 October 1922); "What Makes Turnover and What It Means," *J. Walter Thompson News Bulletin* no. 97 (April 1923).

24 For details on Chicago chain stores, see Ernest Hugh Shideler, "The Chain

Store: A Study of the Ecological Organization of a Modern City" (Ph.D. dissertation, University of Chicago, 1927), particularly pp. 13–21 for enumeration of chain stores in Chicago as of 1923; Paul H. Nystrom, *Chain Stores* (Washington, DC: Chamber of Commerce of the United States, 1930), pp. 4, 27–8, for 1926 figures; Committee on Business Research, "Study Sales of Groceries in Chicago," *Chicago Commerce* 25 (14 April 1928): 16; "Analyze Sales of Drugs in Chicago," *Chicago Commerce* 25 (4 August 1928): 15, "Analyze Variety Store Sales Here," *Chicago Commerce* 25 (1 September 1928): 23.

25 On Sears's move into the retail store business, see Boris Emmet and John E. Jeuck, *Catalogues and Counters: A History of Sears, Roebuck and Company* (Chicago: University of Chicago Press, 1950), pp. 338–57; "Sears Yesterday and Today: A Brief History of the Origins and Development of Sears, Roebuck and Co." (Chicago: Sears, Roebuck, 1982), pp. 9–12; Advertisement "We Open Tomorrow," *Chicago Sunday Tribune*, 1 February 1925; Photo book of Sears, Roebuck and Company's Kansas City, Missouri, store, 1 September 1925, Sears Archives, Chicago, IL; Advertisement "Chicago's Four Retail Department Stores," *Chicago Daily News*, 6 November 1929; Tom Mahoney and Leonard Sloane, *The Great Merchants: America's Foremost Retail Institutions and the People Who Made Them Great* (New York: Harper & Row, 1966), pp. 236–8. On Montgomery Ward's see "1872–1972: A Century of Serving Consumers, the Story of Montgomery Ward's" (Chicago: Montgomery Ward & Company, 1972), pp. 65–74.

26 For detailed information on the explosion of chain stores during the 1920s, see:

On grocery chains: Raymond Rosco Gregg, "Organization for Executive Control in Chain Stores" (M.A. thesis, University of Chicago, 1923), pp. 38–100, 158–74; Mahoney and Sloane, *Great Merchants*, pp. 171–86; Einer Bjorklund and James L. Palmer, *A Study of the Prices of Chain and Independent Grocers in Chicago* (Chicago: University of Chicago, 1930); Lionel Ralph Martin, "Grocery Chain Competition in Chicago as Reflected Through Newspaper Advertising" (M.A. thesis, University of Chicago, 1931); J. Walter Thompson Company newsletter nos. 106, 168, 171 (12 November 1925, 20 January 1927, 10 February 1927), JWT, RG 11; Special issue of *Progressive Grocer*, "A&P Study," February 1970, pp. 3, 7–12; *A&P: Past, Present and Future* (New York: Progressive Grocer Magazine, n.d.), pp. 4, 16–29; Richard Clinton Massell, "The A&P: Large-Scale Operations in the Food Industry" (M.A. thesis, University of Chicago, 1947); National Tea Company, *Annual Reports*, December 31, 1921 – December 31, 1929; Shideler, "The Chain Store," pp. 10 – 11; and the following articles from Lord & Thomas, *Judicious Advertising*: "Piggly Wiggly Stores and Their Unique Advertising Copy," 16 (April 1918); "Queer But Productive Advertising," 16 (July 1918); "Sky-Rocket Growth from Newspaper Advertising: The Advertising Campaign Conducted by the Piggly Wiggly Corporation," 18 (October 1920).

On drug chains, particularly Walgreen's, which originated in Chicago:

Ernest Frederic Witte, "Organization, Management, and Control of Chain Drug Stores" (Ph.D. dissertation, University of Chicago, 1932); Gregg, "Organization for Executive Control," pp. 116–17; Robert Greenwell Knight, "A Study of the Organization and Control Methods of the Walgreen Company's Chain of Drug Stores" (M.A. thesis, University of Chicago, 1925); *Walgreen Pepper Pod, 50th Anniversary Issue* (June 1951): 9–14 particularly; *Walgreen World* 43 (September–October 1976): 4–7; and from JWT, RG 11: "How Strong Are the Chain Drug Stores in the Larger Cities?" *J. Walter Thompson News Bulletin* (July 1926): 11–18; J. Walter Thompson Company newsletter nos. 87, 120 (June 1922, 18 February 1926).

On five-and-ten-cent or variety chains, see: Mahoney and Sloane, *Great Merchants*, pp. 198–205; *Woolworth's First 75 Years: The Story of Everybody's Store* (New York: F. W. Woolworth Co., 1954), p. 28; F. W. Woolworth Co., *100th Anniversary: 1879–1979* (New York: F. W. Woolworth Co., 1979), pp. 19–30.

27 Virginia Pattison, "A Report of Minimum Budget Study: A Term Paper for Sociology 264," March 1931, BUR, Box 156, Folder 2, p. 4. Two of her fellow students also observed the paucity of chain groceries in poor neighborhoods. Isabella Shapera, "Chicago Standard Budget and Dependent Families," Paper for Sociology 264, March 1931, BUR, Box 156, Folder 2, p. 8; Florence Andrews, "The Minimum Budgeting of Poor Families," Paper for Sociology 264, 16 March 1931, BUR, Box 156, Folder 2, p. 8.

Tabulations of A&P and National Tea grocery stores based on *Chicago Telephone Directory*, 1927, and *Polk's Directory of Chicago*, 1928–29; stores located in census areas with help of Charles S. Newcomb, *Street Address Guide by Census Area of Chicago, 1930* (Chicago: University of Chicago Press, 1933); identification of census tracts by economic level through Economic Status of Families Based on Equivalent Monthly Rentals, Table 10, "Census Data of Chicago, 1930," BUR, Box 51, Folder 8.

28 Louis Schefke, "Immigrant to America," March 1931, BUR, Box 155, Folder 5, pp. 9–10, and Map 1, Map of Store Locations on 71st Street. A study of the Wilson Avenue high-grade apartment district six miles north of the Loop along Lake Michigan made similar findings in 1924. Here one in three stores belonged to a chain at a time when less than 15 percent of all retail units citywide did. Shideler, "The Chain Store," Chapter 8.

29 "How Strong Are the Chain Groceries in the Leading Cities?" *J. Walter Thompson News Bulletin* (June 1926): 14–21, JWT, RG 11; U.S. Department of Commerce, Bureau of the Census, *Fifteenth Census of the United States: 1930*, vol. 1, *Retail Distribution* (Washington, DC: U.S. Government Printing Office, 1934), p. 662.

30 Studies of various neighborhoods indicate that there were often as many as three or four stores on a typical street, and more, of course, in a more defined shopping district. Mary Adams, "Present Housing Conditions in South Chicago, South Deering, and Pullman" (M.A. thesis, University of Chicago, 1926), pp. 68, 81; Gaetano DeFelippis, "Social Life in an Immi-

grant Community," Paper for Sociology 264, n.d. but c. 1930, BUR, Box 130, Folder 2, pp. 12, 24–5; "Business in South Chicago," c. 1930, BUR, Box 37, Folder 12; Annie Gosenpud, "Study of South Chicago," 1932, BUR, Box 158, Folder 3, p. 2. On differences in prices, see Bjorkland and Palmer, *Study of Prices of Chain and Independent Grocers in Chicago.*

When Italians interviewed for the Italian–American oral history project were asked to talk about their old neighborhoods, almost without fail they emphasized the local stores, often referring to them by the proprietor's name. From IC, see interviews with: Angelo Patti, Chicago, IL, 14 July 1980, pp. 19–20; Edward Baldacci, Chicago Heights, IL, 29 May 1980, p. 24; Alfred Fantozzi, Chicago, IL, 27 May 1980, pp. 24–7; Frank Corradetti, Chicago Heights, IL, 13 May 1980, p. 1; Angeline Tonietto, Chicago, IL, 1 July 1980, p. 21.

31 Quoted in Robert A. Slayton, "'Our Own Destiny': The Development of Community in Back of the Yards" (Ph.D. dissertation, Northwestern University, 1982), p. 126.

32 Sophonisba P. Breckinridge, *New Homes for Old* (New York: Harper & Brothers, 1921), pp. 122–3.

33 Quoted in Paul S. Taylor, *Mexican Labor in the United States, Chicago and the Calumet Region*, vol. 7, no. 2, University of California Publications in Economics (Berkeley: University of California Press, 1932), p. 169.

34 On how ethnic stores contributed to the perpetuation of ethnic foodways, see Louis Wirth, *The Ghetto* (Chicago: University of Chicago Press, 1928), p. 224; Mark Rosentraub and Delbert Taebel, "Jewish Enterprise in Transition: From Collective Self-Help to Orthodox Capitalism," in Scott Cummings, ed., *Self-Help in Urban America: Patterns of Minority Business Enterprise* (Port Washington, NY: Kennikat Press, 1980), p. 195; Breckinridge, *New Homes for Old*, pp. 126–8; Andrews, "Minimum Budgeting of Poor Families," p. 8.

35 On local stores as a social center for women, see Slayton, "Our Own Destiny," p. 130. Other neighborhood shops served a similar purpose for men. Italian men used barbershops as a place to gather, particularly after Prohibition closed many saloons. Harvey Warren Zorbaugh, *The Gold Coast and the Slum: A Sociological Study of Chicago's Near North Side* (Chicago: University of Chicago Press, 1929), p. 165; the following interviews from IC: Sylvio Petri, Chicago, IL, 8 June 1981, p. 30; Louis Panico, Melrose Park, IL, 25 March 1980, p. 39. Mexican men used neighborhood pool rooms as social club, bank, and employment office. Manuel Bueno, "The Mexican in Chicago," 1923, BUR, Box 187, Folder 4, p. 25; Edward Hayden, "Immigration, the Second Generation, and Juvenile Delinquency," n.d., BUR, Box 131, Folder 3, p. 10.

36 R.D. McCleary, "General Survey of Attitudes Involved in the Formation of a Youth Council on the Near-West Side," n.d., CAP, Box 101, Folder 10, p. 2. Patronizing trusted local merchants also allowed parents to send children to pick up items at the store. See Interviews in Chicago, IL, IC, with: Angeline Tonietto, 1 July 1980, p. 6; Joe Gentili, 2 June 1980, p. 30;

Frank De Liberto, 17 April 1980, p. 42; Nina Dal Casin, 3 December 1979, p. 16.

Specific data on the ethnicity of Chicago grocers is spotty. One general investigation of the ethnic breakdown of urban grocers in America claimed that out of 100 representative city grocers, 38 were Italians, 16 Jews, 12 Germans, 4 Greeks, and 2 Russians, whereas only 28 referred to themselves as Americans. David N. Walker, Jr., "The Great American Cupboard," *J. Walter Thompson News Bulletin* no. 103 (November 1923): 8.

37 Interview by author with Bernice Novak, New Lenox, IL, 4 August 1983.

38 Paul Frederick Cressey, "The Succession of Cultural Groups in the City of Chicago" (Ph.D. dissertation, University of Chicago, 1930), pp. 154, 195.

39 Marion Cutler, "How A Widowed Shopkeeper Became the Unofficial Mayor of Bridgeport Community," *Society News of the Chicago Jewish Historical Society* 6 (June 1983): 6.

40 *Dziennik Chicagoski*, 7, 9, 18 January 1922, CFLPS, Box 33.

41 *Dziennik Zjednoczenia*, 28 November 1932, quoted in Joseph Chalasinski, "Polish and Parochial School among Polish Immigrants in America: A Study of a Polish Neighborhood in South Chicago," n.d. but c. 1930, CAP, Box 33, Folder 2, p. 20. For other calls to demonstrate ethnic loyalty by patronizing the right stores – some of which were community cooperatives – see from CFLPS: Vaclavas Karuza, "An Unexploited Branch of Commerce," *Lietuva*, 6 September 1918, and "Alliance of Polish Mercantile Corporations," *Dziennik Zwiazkowy*, 14 September 1918; Louis Wirth, "Notes for Study of Monroe District," c. 1919, BUR, Box 139, Folder 6; and interviews, IC, with: Maria Valiani, Chicago, IL, 10 June 1980, p. 34; Lina Tarabori, Chicago, IL, 5 June 1980, pp. 20–1; Nick Zaranti, Chicago Heights, IL, 5 March 1980, pp. 15–16.

Among Mexican immigrants, who came to Chicago in increasing numbers during the 1920s, loyalty to Mexico entered into the selection of stores to patronize. It was not enough that a merchant be Mexican; he also had to be a Mexican citizen. One storekeeper complained, "I have a store in the Mexican district. If I become a citizen of the United States the Mexicans won't trade with me, because they wouldn't think I was fair to them or loyal to my country. I read the papers and I would like to vote, but I must not become a citizen. I have to have the Mexican trade to make a living." Quoted in Edward Hayden, "Immigration, The Second Generation, and Juvenile Delinquency," n.d., BUR, Box 131, Folder 3, p. 12.

42 Adeline Milano Zappa, "East Sider Recalls Life in the Old Days," *Daily Calumet*, 19 July 1982; for more on the credit system, see Breckinridge, *New Homes For Old*, p. 124.

43 Interview with Paul Penio, Itasca, IL, 30 June 1980, IC, p. 17. Some grocers, aware of their customers' financial plights, helped them out by sending over extra food or Christmas presents for the children. In this way, the merchant became viewed as a caretaker of the ethnic community. Interview with Emilia Scarpelli, Chicago, IL, 2 July 1980, IC, pp. 8, 27.

44 Ling Me Chen, "The Development of Chain Stores in the United States"

(M.A. thesis, University of Chicago, 1929), pp. 12, 102; William J. Baxter, "The Future of the Chain Store," *Chicago Commerce* 25 (29 September 1928): 24; Palmer, "Economic and Social Aspects of Chain Stores," p. 275; Witte, "Chain Drug Stores," pp. 392–3; "The Science of Chain Store Locations," *Chain Store Progress* 1 (March 1929): 5.

45 Guy C. Smith, "Selective Selling Decreases Costs: Market Analysis Enables Seller to Choose His Customer, Saving Costly Distribution Wastes," *Chicago Commerce* 25 (14 April 1928): 24. Also see similar findings that chain stores in Fort Wayne, Indiana, secured a greater number of customers from the moderate-income class than from the wealthier or poorer classes in Russell Leas Furst, "Grocery Chains in Fort Wayne, Indiana" (M.A. thesis, University of Chicago, 1931).

46 James Reeves in *New York Evening Post*, 12 June 1925, quoted in "Is the Chain Store Still in Its Infancy?" *J. Walter Thompson News Bulletin* no. 114 (July 1925): 19, JWT, RG 11.

47 A few observers did record, however, that chain stores in poor neighborhoods looked somewhat different from those in more prosperous ones, suggesting that management responded to a poorer clientele by omitting certain merchandise and occasionally adding other items. University of Chicago students investigating the prices of goods in different neighborhoods of the city noted that A&P and National Tea stores in poor neighborhoods were smaller and dirtier and had fewer clerks, food luxuries, and window displays than the ones near their homes, presumedly in the middle-class neighborhood of Hyde Park. They also reported the prevalence of cheaper items, for instance, more oleomargarine than butter, and more dried fruit and bulk articles. Betty Wright, Paper for Sociology 264, March 1931, BUR, Box 156, Folder 2, p. 9; Florence Andrews, "The Minimum Budgeting of Poor Families," Paper for Sociology 264, 16 March 1931, BUR, Box 156, Folder 2, p. 7; Virginia Pattison, "A Report of Minimum Budget Study: A Term Paper for Sociology 264," March 1931, BUR, Box 156, Folder 2, p. 1.

48 Stanley Resor, "What Do These Changes Mean?" *J.Walter Thompson News Bulletin* no. 104 (December 1923): 12–13, JWT, RG 11.

49 Sidney Sorkin, "A Ride Down Roosevelt Road, 1920–1940," *Society News of the Chicago Jewish Historical Society* 3 (October 1979): 6.

50 From JWT, RG 11: "It Takes Too Much Time To Sell Bulk Goods," newsletter no. 95 (27 August 1925); "Chicago Office News: Libby, McNeill & Libby Plays Santa Claus," newsletter no. 11 (24 January 1924). From *Judicious Advertising*: "Featuring the Package in Selling Sugar," 17 (June 1919): 67–8; "How Trademarked Carton Helps Grocer Sell Merchandise," 22 (June 1924): 81.

51 For evidence of advertising company awareness of untapped ethnic and working-class markets, see in J. Walter Thompson publications, JWT, RG 11: David N. Walker, Jr., "The Great American Cupboard," *J. Walter Thompson News Bulletin* no. 103 (November 1923): 4–14; William A. Berridge, "An Index of the Incomes of Factory Workers," *J. Walter*

Thompson News Bulletin no. 106 (March 1924): 7–15; "Cities Within a City – And Each One a Worthwhile Market" and "Colgate Makes a Drive for the Jewish Market," newsletter no. 13 (7 February 1924); "Unrecognized Cities in the United States: Polish City in Buffalo," newsletter no. 17 (6 March 1924); "The Foreign Born Market in New York City," newsletter no. 19 (20 March 1924); "Unrecognized Cities in the United States: Jewish City of New York," newsletter no. 24 (24 April 1924); "Facts About America's Foreign Population," newsletter no. 27 (15 May 1924); "Unrecognized Cities in the United States: The Czechoslovak City of Chicago," newsletter no. 22 (22 May 1924); "Unrecognized Cities in the United States: The German City of Philadelphia," newsletter no. 31 (12 June 1924); "Unrecognized Cities of the United States: The Polish City of Chicago," newsletter no. 75 (9 April 1925); "Families with Incomes of Under $2,000 Number 79% of the Total," newsletter no. 129 (23 April 1926).

In *Judicious Advertising*, the publication of The Lord & Thomas Advertising Agency: "What the Foreigner Means to America: The Necessity of the Foreign Press and Its Value as an Advertising Medium," 19 (March 1921): 62–4; "What Social Standing Should the Advertisement Show?" 19 (April 1921): 39–41; "A Great Clacking of Strange Tongues: The Story of the Foreign Language Press in America," 21 (February 1923): 66–70; "Consider the Czechoslovaks," 21 (December 1923): 64; "Chicago – The World's Market Place," 22 (June 1924): 101.

52 Samuel A. Riebel, "A Yuban Salesman – Plus," *J. Walter Thompson News Bulletin* no. 85-A (10 April 1922): 1–4; see also "Make a Sale Every Time You Get an Interview: Twenty Minutes from the Average Day of a Specialty Salesman," J. Walter Thompson Company newsletter no. 115 (14 January 1926), JWT, RG 11.

53 The Chicago Tribune, "Consumer Survey: An Investigation into the Shopping Habits of 2205 Chicago Housewives, October 1929" (mimeo). A study of one hundred working-class Chicagoans found that in 1927, "curiously enough, canned goods and American inventions – the cheaper ways of filling an empty stomach . . . – seem to have invaded the ranks but little." Laura Friedman, "A Study of One Hundred Unemployed Families in Chicago, January 1927 to June 1932" (M.A. thesis, University of Chicago, 1933), p. 112. The growing use of packaged and branded goods among mostly middle-class consumers during the 1920s was documented in studies of Milwaukee consumption in 1924, 1927, and 1930. President's Research Committee, *Recent Social Trends*, vol. 2, pp. 874–7.

54 Sophonisba Breckinridge spoke with a Croatian woman who pointed out that in her neighborhood store she could ask the grocer about new things she saw and did not know how to use, whereas elsewhere she could not inquire and hence would not buy unfamiliar products. Breckinridge, *New Homes for Old*, p. 123.

55 Louis Weinstein, "The Maxwell Street Market," Paper for Sociology 270, 9 December 1929, BUR, Box 142, Folder 5. For more description of the

Maxwell Street market during the 1920s, see Isabella Shapera, "Chicago Standard Budget For Dependent Families," Paper for Sociology 264, March 1931, BUR, Box 156, Folder 2, p. 5; Wirth, *The Ghetto*, pp. 229–40.

56 President's Research Committee, *Recent Social Trends*, vol. 2, pp. 877–80.

57 Interview by author with Sheldon Robinson, Chicago, IL, 2 August 1983. For other testimony that lower-class, ethnic consumers valued quality over style, see George Hanas, "Study of Slovak Church Group Northwest Side," 1925, BUR, Box 149, Folder 3, p. 8; Louis Wirth, "Study of Monroe District," c. 1919, BUR, Box 139, Folder 2, where he claimed that storekeepers on Milwaukee Avenue "sell merchandise which the downtown stores have to get rid of at a sacrifice price."

58 Louis Wirth, "Study of Monroe District," c. 1919, BUR, Box 139, Folder 2.

59 *Ibid.*; Leo J. May, "Observations of a Halsted Street Salesman," Paper for Sociology 264, March 1930, BUR, Box 154, Folder 6, pp. 8–11.

60 JoEllen Goodman and Barbara Marsh, "The Goldblatt's Story: From Poverty to Retailing Riches to Ch. 11 Disgrace," *Crain's Chicago Business* 4 (19–25 October 1981): 17–27; "Four Boys and a Store," 30 June 1960, mimeographed press release acquired from Goldblatt's headquarters; "Goldblatt Brothers Fifth Store Comes to West Town," *West Town News*, 15 November 1929; David S. Oakes, "Selling All Creation," *Central Manufacturing District Magazine* 18 (December 1934); "Goldblatt Bros. Investment, One Million," *Daily Calumet Centennial Edition*, 6 June 1936. On how a revitalized Goldblatt's is employing the same merchandising strategies in Chicago's immigrant neighborhoods today, see Steve Weiner, "Poor Customers, Rich Profits," *Forbes* 6 (March 1989).

61 Betty Wright, Student Paper for Sociology 264, March 1931, BUR, Box 156, Folder 2, pp. 4–6. Similar observations of Goldblatt's and Klein's were made by Virginia Pattison, "A Report of Minimum Budget Study: A Term Paper for Sociology 264," March 1931, BUR, Box 156, Folder 2, p. 7; Florence Andrews, "The Minimum Budgeting of Poor Families," Paper for Sociology 264, 16 March 1931, BUR, Box 156, Folder 2, pp. 3–5; Bertha Ellman, "The Standard of Living and the Minimum Budget," Paper for Sociology 264, Winter 1931, BUR, Box 156, Folder 2, pp. 4–7. William Ireland noted that the Wieboldt's Store on Milwaukee Avenue lost its lower-class customers to Iverson's across the street when it expanded and sought out more middle-class customers. "'The lower class' Poles will only trade where the store puts out on the sidewalk baskets of wares through which customers can rummage." William Rutherford Ireland, "Young American Poles" (written but not submitted as M.A. thesis, University of Chicago, 1932), UCSC, p. 26.

62 In the 1950s, market research became more sophisticated. Researchers began to investigate the subjective side of consumer experience, particularly to recognize that consumer response to symbols varied. Moving away from a simple psychological explanation for an individual's reaction,

moreover, they stressed the importance of social "reference groups," reflecting people's real and aspirant identifications, for explaining and predicting consumer response. For a good collection of the pathbreaking studies in market research along these lines, see Louis E. Boone, *Classics in Consumer Behavior: Selected Readings Together With the Authors' Own Retrospective Comments* (Tulsa, OK: The Petroleum Publishing Company, 1977).

63 On the increase in mergers among chains in the late 1920s, see *Progressive Grocer*'s "A&P Study," p. 29; Harper Leech, "The Individual Store's Future," *Chicago Commerce* 25 (29 September 1928): 11; Witte, "Chain Drug Stores," p. 63; Chen, "Development of Chain Stores in U.S.," pp. 16–17; *Walgreen's Pepper Pod*, p. 13; National Tea Company, *Annual Report, 1927.*

64 Martin, "Grocery Chain Competition in Chicago as Reflected through Newspaper Advertising," pp. 80–3.

65 Smith, "Selective Selling Decreases Costs," *Chicago Commerce*, p. 13.

66 Kitty Joy Jamison, "The Drug Business," 1932, BUR, Box 157, Folder 2; *Walgreen's Pepper Pod*, p. 13; *Progressive Grocer's* "A&P Study," p. 12; National Tea Company, *Annual Report, 1929; Supreme Court of the District of Columbia in Equity No. 37623*, pp. 18–29.

67 Maurice Van Hollebeke to Mr. William Green, American Federation of Labor, 26 May 1930, FITZ, Box 18, Folder 127, p. 2.

68 Quoted in Harold M. Mayer and Richard C. Wade, *Chicago: Growth of a Metropolis* (Chicago: University of Chicago Press, 1969), p. 344. On the development of these outlying shopping districts, see Homer Hoyt, *One Hundred Years of Land Values in Chicago: The Relationship of the Growth of Chicago to the Rise in Its Land Values, 1830–1933* (Chicago: University of Chicago Press, 1933), pp. 225–7, 249–55, 320–44, 445; Shideler, "The Chain Store," Chapters 6, 9, 10; Malcolm J. Proudfoot, "The Major Outlying Business Centers of Chicago" (Ph.D. dissertation, University of Chicago, 1936); Chicago Tribune, *Bigger Profits: Book of Sunday Tribune Advertising Facts* (Chicago: Chicago Tribune, 1929); *The Fourth Estate Market Guide for November 23, 1929* (New York: The Fourth Estate, 1929), p. 100.

69 J. C. Penney, "Are Chain Stores Good Citizens? A Test of Human Relations," *Chicago Commerce* 27 (4 October 1930): 7–8; also see Francis G. Gibson, "Chain Personnel Pleases Women," *Chain Store Progress* 1 (October 1929): 5; "Come to Chicago," *Chain Store Progress* 1 (August 1929): 1. For a good summary of the attacks on chain stores and the defenses usually offered, see James L. Palmer, "Economic and Social Aspects of Chain Stores," *Journal of Business of the University of Chicago* 2 (1929): 272–90.

70 Walker, "Great American Cupboard," *J. Walter Thompson News Bulletin*, p. 8; Palmer, "Economic and Social Aspects of Chain Stores," pp. 287–8, for study that determined that the rate of turnover of retail grocers in Buffalo, New York, between 1918 and 1926 exceeded 30 percent annually.

71 Jean Brichke, "Report on Term Paper under Miss Nesbitt's Direction," Paper for Sociology 264, c. 1931, BUR, Box 156, Folder 2, pp. 15–18.

72 Louis Weinstein, "The Maxwell Street Market," Paper for Sociology 270, 9 December 1929, BUR, Box 142, Folder 5. A study of grocery chains in Fort Wayne, Indiana, in 1931 found that there were more chain grocery stores in the lower-income sections of town in 1930 than in 1920 or 1925. Furst, "Grocery Chains in Fort Wayne," p. 28.

73 V. H. Pelz and the editorial and research staff, *The Voluntary Chains* (second of a series of reports to be issued on this subject) (New York: American Institute of Food Distribution, 1930), pp. 3, 8, 17–18, 23, 63; *Supreme Court of the District of Columbia in Equity No. 37623*, pp. 18–23, 450–7; Paul Nystrom, *Chain Stores* (Washington, DC: Chamber of Commerce of the United States, 1930), pp. 17–18, 43–4; and from *Printers' Ink Monthly*: Albert E. Haase and V. H. Pelz, "The Rapid Rise of National Voluntary Chains" 18 (April 1929): 52–6, 98–103; Haase and Pelz, "The Significance of the Voluntary Chain" 18 (May 1929): 52–6, 90–2; C. B. Larrabee, "Will the Independent Save Himself by Losing His Independence?" 19 (September 1929): 38, 92–100.

74 Vincent Salamoni, Photographs of North Side groceries and commentary, IC, 185.13; "Interview with Mr. Stanislaus Dunin, Advertising Manager of the Midwest Grocery Company, by Thomas Nowacki, June 23, 1937," CFLPS, Box 34.

75 Alice Miller Mitchell, *Children and Movies* (Chicago: University of Chicago Press, 1929), p. 66.

76 "Cost of Living in the United States – Clothing and Miscellaneous Expenditures," *Monthly Labor Review* 9 (November 1919): 16.

77 Mary F. Bogue, *Administration of Mothers' Aid in Ten Localities with Special Reference to Health, Housing, Education and Recreation*, Children's Bureau Publication no. 184 (Washington, DC: U.S. Government Printing Office, 1928), p. 90.

78 President's Research Committee, *Recent Social Trends*, vol. 2, p. 895.

79 For a study that analyzes film content for insight into audience response, see Lary May's fascinating *Screening Out the Past: The Birth of Mass Culture and the Motion Picture Industry, with a New Preface* (Chicago: University of Chicago Press, 1983).

80 "Trip to Calumet Theatre Brings Back Memories," *Daily Calumet*, 23 November 1981; "South Chicago Was Home to Many Theaters," *Daily Calumet*, 25 April 1983; Felipe Salazar and Rodolfo Camacho, "The Gayety: A Theatre's Struggle for Survival," Project for Metro History Fair, n.d. (manuscript), CHS; "Southeast Chicago Theatres Filled Entertainment Need," *Daily Calumet*, 3 January 1983; "Theaters Plentiful on the Southeast Side," *Daily Calumet*, 10 January 1983.

81 "In Memoriam: Edward E. Eichenbaum (1894–1982)," *Marquee (Journal of the Theatre Historical Society)* 15 (First quarter 1983): 21; Douglas Gomery, "Movie Audiences, Urban Geography, and the History of the American Film," *The Velvet Light Trap Review of Cinema* no. 19 (Spring

1982): 23–9. I am indebted to Professor Gomery for the application of urban geography to the problem of motion picture audience. In this article, he takes the cases of Manhattan and Chicago and demonstrates how picture palace locations reveal that they were intended for "the Yuppies of the 1920s," young, well-educated, upwardly mobile people living in new, outlying residential areas. Also see by him "The Growth of Movie Monopolies: The Case of Balaban & Katz," *Wide Angle* 3 (1979): 54–63, and "History of the (Film) World, Part II," *American Film* 8 (November 1982): 53–7, 89.

For general information on picture palaces, see Karen J. Safer, "The Functions of Decoration in the American Movie Palace," *Marquee* 14 (Second quarter 1982): 3–9; Ben M. Hall, *The Best Remaining Seats* (New York: Clarkson N. Potter, 1961); Robert Sklar, *Movie-Made America: A Cultural History of American Movies* (New York: Vintage Books, 1975), pp. 86–7; May, *Screening Out the Past*, pp. 147–66.

For specifics on Chicago's picture palaces, see Lois Halley, "A Study of Motion Pictures in Chicago As a Medium of Communication" (M. A. thesis, University of Chicago, 1924), pp. 32–8, 44–5; Theatre Historical Society, *Official Souvenir Booklet, Conclave 1977, Chicago* (Notre Dame, IN: Marquee, 1977); "Built with Moving Stairs," *Marquee* 14 (Third quarter 1982): 1–24; Theatre Historical Society, *The Paradise Theatre*, Annual no. 4 (Notre Dame, IN: Marquee, n.d.); Theatre Historical Society, *The Chicago Theatre: A Sixtieth Anniversary Salute*, Annual no. 8 (Chicago: Theatre Historical Society, 1981); Ira Berkow, "The Nickelodeon That Grew," *Chicago Magazine*, October 1977, pp. 191–3; Lloyd Lewis, "The Deluxe Picture Palace," *The New Republic*, 27 March 1929, p. 175, reprinted in George E. Mowry, ed., *The Twenties: Fords, Flappers and Fanatics* (Englewood Cliffs, NJ: Prentice-Hall, 1963), pp. 56–9.

82 Interview with Jim Fitzgibbon, Chicago, IL, 16 July 1981, SECHP, p. 14.

83 My own survey of the motion pictures playing in three theaters in South Chicago (Pete's International, the Gayety, and the Commercial) on the ninth day of every month during 1926 revealed that only on rare occasions was a film held over a second day. Otherwise, the program changed daily. *Daily Calumet*, 1926.

84 Interview with Ernest Dalle-Molle, Chicago, IL, 30 April 1980, IC, p. 76. In these ways the neighborhood theater of the 1920s differed little from the nickelodeons of the prewar period. Kathy Peiss, *Cheap Amusements: Working Women and Leisure in Turn-of-the-Century New York* (Philadelphia: Temple University Press, 1986), pp. 149–51.

85 Slayton, "Our Own Destiny," pp. 59–60.

86 For a description of amateur night, see "Fitzgibbons Was Important Part of Southeast Historical Project," *Daily Calumet*, 13 June 1983. On "Garlic Opera House," see Zorbaugh, *Gold Coast and the Slum*, pp. 164–5.

87 Interview with Anna Blazewicz, Polonia Archives, CHS, pp. 64–5.

88 Anonymous, Student paper, n.d. but c. 1930, BUR, Box 154, Folder 5, p. 26; for more evidence of the discrimination blacks encountered at movie

theaters, see the Chicago Commission on Race Relations, *The Negro in Chicago: A Study Of Race Relations And A Race Riot* (Chicago: University of Chicago Press, 1922), pp. 318–20.

89 Quoted in Taylor, *Mexican Labor in Chicago*, p. 232.

90 Dempsey J. Travis, *An Autobiography of Black Chicago* (Chicago: Urban Research Institute, 1981), p. 32; also see Morris Lewis to Robert Bognall, 3 March 1923, NAACP Papers, LC, Box 48, Folder "Chicago, Illinois, March 1923–June 1923," pp. 2–3.

91 Florence Lyon Gaddis, "Conflict between Mexicans and Poles Living Near Ashland Avenue and 45th Street," Term paper for Sociology 270, 1928, BUR, Box 142, Folder 3, p. 8.

92 Joseph P. Kennedy, *The Story of the Films (As Told By Leaders of the Industry to the Students of the Graduate School of Business Administration, George F. Baker Foundation, Harvard University)* (Chicago: A. W. Shaw Company, 1927), p. 276.

93 "Ruf Recalls Area History," *Daily Calumet*, 9 November 1982, special section on the SECHP, pp. 18, 20.

94 For a wonderful description of what it was like to be a palace usher, see "It Was October 26, 1921 – And McNeil Smith Was There!" Theatre Historical Society, *Chicago Theatre*, pp. 46–7. Smith was hired for a part-time ushering job as a college student when the Chicago Theatre was about to open.

95 Barney Balaban and Sam Katz, *The Fundamental Principles of Balaban & Katz Theatre Management* (Chicago: Balaban & Katz Corporation, 1926), pp. 19–20, 22–3, 105–7.

96 *Ibid.*, pp. 15, 17–20. The reality may have differed from this ideal, however. I have seen references to picture palaces that discriminated against blacks, though they would probably not have been so obvious as to segregate theaters. They just turned them away at the door.

97 Motion Picture Producers and Distributors of America, Annual attendance estimates, in Rice, *Communication Agencies*, p. 179.

98 On the subject of vertical integration, see Douglas Gomery, *The Hollywood Studio System* (New York: St. Martin's Press, 1986); Sklar, *Movie-Made America*, pp. 144–8; Tino Balio, ed., *The American Film Industry* (Madison: University of Wisconsin Press, 1976), pp. 113–16, 213–14; Mae Huettig, "The Motion Picture Industry Today," in *Economic Control of the Motion Picture Industry* (Philadelphia: University of Pennsylvania Press, 1944), reprinted in Gerald Mast, ed., *The Movies in Our Midst* (Chicago: University of Chicago Press, 1982), p. 391; Kennedy, ed., *The Story of the Films*, pp. 273–5, 281; Harold B. Franklin, *Motion Picture Theater Management* (Garden City, NY: Doubleday, Doran & Company, 1928), pp. 28–9; Jan-Christophe Horak, *Dream Merchants: Making and Selling Films in Hollywood's Golden Age* (Rochester: International Museum of Photography at George Eastman House, 1989). For the historical development and integration of the five major producer–distributor–exhibitor companies and the three satellite producer–distributor companies

(United Artists, Columbia Pictures, and Universal), see "Appendix 1: The Eight Major Companies," in Temporary National Economic Committee, *Investigation of Concentration of Economic Power: The Motion Picture Industry – A Pattern of Control*, Monograph no. 43 (Washington, DC: U.S. Government Printing Office, 1941), pp. 59–62.

99 On the growth of the Balaban & Katz chain, see Douglas Gomery, "The Movies Become Big Business: Publix Theatres and the Chain-Store Strategy," in Gorham Kindem, ed., *The American Movie Industry: The Business of Motion Pictures* (Carbondale: Southern Illinois University Press, 1982), pp. 104–16; Berkow, "The Nickelodeon That Grew," p. 193; Halley, "Study of Motion Pictures in Chicago," p. 49. On the growth of the Schoenstadt theater chain in Back of the Yards during the 1920s, see Slayton, "Our Own Destiny," p. 57.

100 The expression "chaining up" was used by William A. Johnston, the editor of *Motion Picture News*, in "The Motion Picture Industry," *Annals of the American Academy of Political and Social Science* 127 (September 1926): 100.

101 On block-booking, see Temporary National Economic Committee, *Motion Picture Industry*, pp. 23–34; Sklar, *Movie-Made America*, pp. 145–6, 152; Carl E. Milliken, "Who Selects America's Movies? The Facts About 'Block Booking,'" Pamphlet, 1937; Jowett, *Film: The Democratic Art*, pp. 199–203. For other kinds of complaints raised by small exhibitors, see Simon N. Whitney, "Antitrust Policies and the Motion Picture Industry," in Kindem, ed., *The American Movie Industry*, p. 166. For a dispute in the Chicago area between a large studio and an independent theater owned by "a Greek who does not speak English," see United Artists Corporation to Mr. Lichtman, 7 May 1935, United Artists Papers, Box 3, Folder 5, SHSW.

102 William J. Blackburn, "A Brief Report of a Study Made of the Organization Program, and Services of the University of Chicago Settlement, 1927–28", MCD, Box 2, Folder 7, p. 5.

103 Malcolm M. Willey and Stuart A. Rice, *Communication Agencies and Social Life* (one of a series of monographs prepared under the direction of the President's Research Committee on Social Trends) (New York: McGraw-Hill Book Company, 1933), p. 180.

104 Information from the Motion Picture Producers and Distributors of America (more commonly known as the Hays Organization, after Will H. Hays, its president), cited in *ibid.*, p. 178. This point, that some theaters had to close because they were not equipped with sound equipment, was made specifically in reference to Chicago by Amelia Rinkenberger, "Effect of Depression on Relaxation and Recreation," Paper for Sociology 358, July 1934, BUR, Box 176, Folder 2, p. 1.

105 J. Douglas Gomery, "The Coming of the Talkies: Invention, Innovation, and Diffusion," in Balio, ed., *The American Film Industry*, pp. 193–211; Gomery, "Movies Become Big Business," pp. 113–14; Jowett, *Film: The Democratic Art*, pp. 190–7, 260; Harry Geduld, "The Voice of Vitaphone," from *The Birth of the Talkies* (Bloomington: Indiana Uni-

versity Press, 1975), in Mast, ed., *Movies in Our Midst*, pp. 243–54; Douglas Gomery, "Rewriting the History of Film in the United States: Theory and Method," *Wide Angle* 5 (1983): 79.

106 My calculations based on "Theatres Wired for Sound in the United States," *The Film Daily Yearbook of Motion Pictures, 1930,* p. 717; Arthur J. Todd et al., *The Chicago Recreation Survey, 1937,* vol. 2, *Commercial Recreation* (Chicago: Chicago Recreation Commission and Northwestern University, 1938), p. 32; theater lists in CHS library.

107 Salazar and Camacho, "The Gayety: Theatre's Struggle" (Metro history fair manuscript); Interview Schedules, "How Boys Spend Their Time," 1934, BUR, Box 48, Folder 2. The quality of sound in a theater made such a difference to the public that even a four-thousand-seat picture palace could be forced to close because of poor sound equipment. The Paradise Theater was near to the slightly larger Marbro. As talkies became common, the Marbro quickly gained popularity because of its better acoustics, and the Paradise closed from late 1931 to early 1934. Theatre Historical Society, *Paradise Theatre*, p. 37.

108 Sklar, *Movie-Made America*, pp. 152–3.

109 Todd et al., *Chicago Recreation Survey*, vol. 2, pp. 29–30.

110 *Ibid.*, pp. 31–3; Halley, "Study of Motion Pictures," pp. 35–7; "Theater Chains – U.S. & Canada," *The Film Daily Yearbook of Motion Pictures, 1928,* pp. 680–1; "Theatre Directory," listing theater name, address, and owner, early 1930s, CHS, Arthur G. Levy Collection; Gilbert Seldes, *The Great Audience* (New York: Viking Press, 1950), p. 17. By 1945, the majors controlled at least 70 percent of first-run theaters in cities of more than 100,000 population and about 60 percent of those in cities of 25,000–100,000. United States v. Paramount Picutres, 334 U.S. 131, 150 n. 9, 167–8 (1948), cited in Whitney, "Antitrust Policies," in Kindem, ed., *The American Movie Industry*, p. 166.

111 Interview with Joseph Provenzano, Brookfield, IL, 17 March 1980, IC, pp. 24–5; also interview with Thomas Perpoli, Chicago, IL, 26 June 1980, IC, p. 59, for a similar memory. For further discussion of early radio as a hobby, see J. Fred MacDonald, *Don't Touch That Dial: Radio Programming in American Life from 1920 to 1960* (Chicago: Nelson-Hall, 1979), p. 3; Alfred N. Goldsmith and Austin C. Lescarboura, *This Thing Called Broadcasting* (New York: Henry Holt and Company, 1930), pp. 301–21.

112 Anita Edgar Jones, "Conditions Surrounding Mexicans in Chicago" (Ph.D. dissertation, University of Chicago, 1928), p. 85; *Hawthorne Microphone*, 1 September 1922, 19 January 1923, 23 April 1923.

113 Hiram L. Jome, *Economics of the Radio Industry* (Chicago: A. W. Shaw Company, 1925), pp. 116–17.

114 *Radio Broadcast*, October 1922, quoted in Erik Barnouw, *A Tower in Babel: A History of Broadcasting in the United States*, vol. 1 to 1933 (New York: Oxford University Press, 1966), p. 88; also Paul F. Cressey, "Survey of McKinley Park Community," 20 October 1925, BUR, Box 129, Folder 7, p. 1.

115 Lynd and Lynd, *Middletown*, pp. 269–70. For an amusing picture of "DX fishing," see Bruce Bliven, "The Legion Family and the Radio: What We Hear When We Tune In," *Century Magazine* 108 (October 1924): 811–18.

116 On Chicago's silent night see Barnouw, *Tower in Babel*, p. 93.

117 "Merry Jests and Songs Mark Radio Party," *Chicago Commerce* 21 (5 April 1924): 17; "Radio Marvels Will Be Seen at Show," *Chicago Commerce* 23 (2 October 1926): 9.

118 Clifford Kirkpatrick, *Report of a Research into the Attitudes and Habits of Radio Listeners* (St. Paul: Webb Book Publishing Company, 1933), p. 25; Pitkin, *The Consumer*, pp. 322–4; Hadley Cantril and Gordon W. Allport, *The Psychology of Radio* (New York: Peter Smith, 1941), pp. 86–8.

119 Daniel Starch, "A Study of Radio Broadcasting Made for the National Broadcasting Company, Inc.," 1928, Edgar James Papers, Box 8, Folder 4, SHSW, p. 23; American Telephone and Telegraph Company, "The Use of Radio Broadcasting as a Publicity Medium," 1926, Edgar James Papers, Box 1, Folder 8, SHSW, p. 4 (mimeo); Kirkpatrick, *Report of a Research*, p. 26; Willey and Rice, *Communication Agencies and Social Life*, p. 202.

Many descriptions of workers' homes during the 1920s mention the presence of a radio, usually in a prominent place. See, e.g., Felicia Tarski and Marie Jasinski, "St. Casimir's Parish," Paper for Sociology 264, 17 March 1931, BUR, Box 156, Folder 3, p. 15; Margaret Artman, "Observations on the Causes for the Prevalence of Delinquency among the Children of Immigrants in the City Slums," December 1931, BUR, Box 144, Folder 2, portrait of "Frank"; Laura A. Friedman, "A Study of One Hundred Unemployed Families in Chicago January, 1927, to June, 1932" (M.A. thesis, University of Chicago, 1933), p. 113; Alice Theresa Theodorson, "Living Conditions of Fifty Unemployed Families" (M.A. thesis, University of Chicago, 1935), p. 44; Raymond Edward Nelson, "A Study of an Isolated Industrial Community: Based on Personal Documents Secured by the Participant Observer Method" (M.A. thesis, University of Chicago, 1929), p. 162.

120 Lynd and Lynd, *Middletown*, p. 270.

121 Interview with Joseph Provenzano, Brookfield, IL, 17 March 1980, IC, p. 25. For other testimony about communal radio listening, see Interview with Anthony Novak by author, Park Ridge, IL, 18 August 1983; Interview with Bernice Novak by author, New Lenox, IL, 4 August 1983; and Interviews in Chicago, IL, IC, with: Mario Avignone, 12 and 14 July 1979, pp. 24–5; Phil Rafaelli, 23 June 1980, p. 26.

122 Daniel Starch, "A Study of Radio Broadcasting Made for the National Broadcasting Company, Inc.," 1928, Edgar James Papers, Box 8, Folder 4, SHSW, p. 28. As late as 1926, a study prepared for the AT&T station asserted that "no one station can at present render regular dependable service, day and night, summer and winter, to an audience more than 100

miles distant from its antenna." American Telephone and Telegraph Company, "The Use of Radio Broadcasting as a Publicity Medium," Edgar James Papers, Box 1, Folder 8, SHSW.

123 Willey and Rice, *Communication Agencies and Social Life*, pp. 196, 200.

124 From *Chicago Commerce*: "Chicago Radio Makers Unite Big Plants" 21 (26 April 1924): 7–8; "Radio Show Profitable to Dealers and Exhibitors" 21 (29 November 1924): 10; "Chicago – Nation's Radio Capital: *Commerce* Survey Shows This City as a Leader in Manufacturing, Wholesaling and Retailing" 25 (15 September 1928): 8–11; "Chicago to Celebrate Radio Week" 28 (15 September 1928): 15; "Tells City's Part in Radio History" 25 (13 October 1928): 15–16.

125 Willey and Rice, *Communication Agencies and Social Life*, pp. 195–9; Bruce Linton, "A History of Chicago Radio Station Programming, 1921–1931, with Emphasis on Stations WMAQ and WGN" (Ph.D. dissertation, Northwestern University, 1953), pp. 61–2, 121; Barnouw, *Tower in Babel*, pp. 99–101; Arthur Frank Wertheim, *Radio Comedy* (New York: Oxford University Press, 1979), pp. 3–7; Christopher H. Sterling and John M. Kittross, *Stay Tuned: A Concise History of American Broadcasting* (Belmont, CA: Wadsworth Publishing Company, 1978), pp. 71–8.

The participatory character of early radio had the benefit of demystifying the media, but it also gave stations less control over programming. For example, a local man who asked to give a talk on Americanism on Station KYW in Chicago turned out to be a potentate of the Ku Klux Klan bent on extolling the virtues of white supremacy and the Klan. Barnouw, *Tower in Babel*, p. 102.

126 Mark Newman, "On the Air with Jack L. Cooper: The Beginnings of Black-Appeal Radio," *Chicago History* 12 (Summer 1983): 53–4; Linton, "History of Chicago Radio Station Programming," p. 155; Chicago Tribune, *WGN: Picture Book of Radio* (Chicago: Tribune Publishing Company, 1928), pp. 75–86; *WGN: A Pictorial History* (Chicago: Tribune Publishing Company, 1961), p. 28; *Poles of Chicago, 1837–1937: A History of One Century of Polish Contribution to the City of Chicago* (Chicago: Polish Pageant, 1937), p. 240; Martha E. Gross, "The 'Jolly Girls' Club: Report and Diary," March 1933, BUR, Box 158, Folder 5, p. 28; Joseph Kisciunas, "Lithuanian Chicago" (M.A. thesis, DePaul University, 1935), p. 40; Interview with Margaret Sabella, Chicago, IL, 29 March 1980, IC, p. 8; *Immaculate Conception, B.V.M. Parish, South Chicago, Diamond Jubilee: 1882–1957* (Chicago: Immaculate Conception, B.V.M., 1957); Peter C. Marzio, ed., *A Nation of Nations: The People Who Came to America as Seen Through Objects and Documents Exhibited at the Smithsonian Institution* (New York: Harper & Row, Publishers, 1976), p. 443.

127 Linton, "A History of Chicago Radio Station Programming," pp. 180–1, 202–3, 247; Chester F. Caton, "Radio Station WMAQ: A History of Its Independent Years (1922–1931)" (Ph.D. dissertation, Northwestern University, 1951), pp. 306–8; William James DuBourdieu, "Religious Broad-

casting in the United States" (Ph.D. dissertation, Northwestern University, 1933), pp. 25–9, 128–31, 153; "Factual Information on Radio Station WLS," 1946, Sears Archives (mimeo); "Little Brown Church in the Vale," Memo from Harold A. Safford, WLS, 20 December 1927, Sears Archives; Samuel L. Rothafel and Raymond Francis Yates, *Broadcasting: Its New Day* (New York: Arno Press reprint, 1971; originally published 1925), pp. 117–36; Goldsmith and Lescarboura, *This Thing Called Broadcasting*, pp. 260–72.

128 Goldsmith and Lescarboura, *This Thing Called Broadcasting*, p. 265. See also Quinn A. Ryan, "The New Sky Pilots or Tuning In Your Religion," Reprint from WGN's *Liberty Weekly*, quoted in *WGN Picture Book of Radio, 1928*, pp. 40–4.

129 George Hanas, "Study of Slovak Church Group, Northwest Side," 1925, BUR, Box 149, Folder 3, p. 16. Catholics also used the radio. For example, several years before Father Coughlin emerged as a political orator, he preached traditional Catholic sermons over the radio from his pulpit in Royal Oak, Michigan. Alan Brinkley, *Voices of Protest: Huey Long, Father Coughlin, and The Great Depression* (New York: Alfred A. Knopf, 1982), pp. 90–3.

130 Joel A. Carpenter, "From Retreat to Revival: Fundamentalist Renewal and the Postwar Evangelical Resurgence, 1930–1950" (Institute for the Study of American Evangelicals, Wheaton College, September 1983), p. 12. On other Fundamentalist radio programming, see Bliven, "Legion Family and the Radio," p. 815, and Marion Kells's fascinating description of a visit in the late 1930s to The Reverend J. C. O'Hair, who made daily and Sunday radio broadcasts for the previous fourteen years. Marion Kells, "Survey of Protestant Churches on Chicago's Northwest Side: North Shore Church, Sheridan and Wilson, J. C. O'Hair, Pastor," n.d. but c. 1938, BUR, Box 132, Folder 1.

131 Secretary Edward Nockels to Trade Union Secretaries, 23 December 1926, FITZ, Box 15, Folder 106.

132 William J. H. Strong, "Report on Radiocasting for the Special Committee, Mssrs. Fitzpatrick, Nockels and Olander, of the Chicago Federation of Labor and the Illinois Federation of Labor, November 5th, 1925," FITZ, Box 14, Folder 100, p. 1.

133 "The Aims, Objects and History of WCFL," *WCFL Radio Magazine* 1 (Spring 1928): 58–9; "Labor Presents Splendid Record," *WCFL Magazine* 2 (Spring 1929): 15; Nathan Godfried, "The Origins of Labor Radio: WCFL, the 'Voice of Labor,' 1925–1928," *Historical Journal of Film, Radio and Television* 7, no. 2 (1987): 143–59.

134 Erlign Sejr Jorgensen, "Radio Station WCFL: A Study in Labor Union Broadcasting" (M.A. thesis, University of Wisconsin, 1949), pp. 59–60, 79, 97; "WCFL, Voice of Labor Marks 50 Years on Air," *Federation News*, June 1976, p. 12; article in *Chicago Herald*, 3 December 1927, in *WCFL Scrapbook*, CHS.

135 "W-C-F-L Program for the Week, Saturday, July 23, 1927 to Friday, July 29, 1927," FITZ, Box 15, Folder 111.

136 *The Federation News*, 23 January 1926, quoted in Jorgensen, "Radio Station WCFL," p. 44.

137 "W-C-F-L Program for the Week, Saturday, July 23, 1927 to Friday, July 29, 1927," FITZ, Box 15, Folder 111; "How WCFL Serves the Public: Voice of Labor Aids Many Public Movements," *WCFL Radio Magazine* 1 (Spring 1928): 57; "Tune in on Station WCFL," *WCFL Radio Magazine* 2 (Spring 1929): 74–5; Fannia M. Cohn to John Fitzpatrick, 13 May 1927, FITZ, Box 15, Folder 109; "Dziennik Chicagoski's Polish Hour to Be Broadcast over WCFL Tonight, 8 p.m.," *Dziennik Chicagoski*, 6 January 1928, CFLPS, Box 32; "Program of the Federation of Italian Societies and Clubs of Chicago," *Il Bolletino Sociale*, 15 June 1929, CFLPS, Box 22; "Spanish – American Radio Hour WCFL," *Mexico*, 6 May 1930, CFLPS, Box 40; Article, *Daily News*, 11 October 1926, in *WCFL Scrapbook*, CHS; Interview with Mollie Levitas, Chicago, IL, July 1970, ROHP, p. 55; Jorgensen, "Radio Station WCFL," pp. 90, 104, 122–4.

138 "Why Labor Needs a Radio Station," *WCFL Radio Magazine* 1 (Spring 1928): 44–5; Chicago Federation of Labor form letter on aid to miners, n.d., FITZ, Box 17, Folder 125, CHS; Interview with Mollie Levitas, Chicago, IL, July 1970, ROHP, pp. 7–9.

139 From FITZ: Mrs. Mary Schultz to WCFL Broadcasting Station, 29 September 1927, Box 16, Folder 113; Anonymous to Mr. John Fitzpatrick, 20 February 1927, Box 15, Folder 107; M. J. O'Brien to American Federation of Labor, 12 October 1927, Box 16, Folder 113; A. N. Holmes to WCFL Broadcasting Radio Station, Chicago, IL, Box 16, Folder 114; Dan Niksic to WCFL, 19 May 1930, Box 18, Folder 127; M. Van Hollebeke to Mr. John Fitzpatrick, 16 June 1930, Box 18, Folder 127; Mrs. E. Erisman to "Voice of Labor and Farmer," 26 June 1930, Box 18, Folder 127.

140 Goldsmith and Lescarboura, *This Thing Called Broadcasting*," p. 296. For the expression of a similar expectation for radio, see "Recent Economic Changes," Summary of *Recent Economic Changes in the United States: Report of the Committee on Recent Economic Changes of the President's Conference on Unemployment* (Washington, DC, 1929), in *Monthly Labor Review* 28 (June 1929): 105.

141 MacDonald, *Don't Touch That Dial*, p. 17; Sterling and Kittross, *Stay Tuned*, p. 63.

142 Caton, "Radio Station WMAQ," p. 46; Giraud Chester and Garnet K. Garrison, *Television and Radio: An Introduction* (New York: Appleton-Century-Crofts, 1956), p. 24; "Sees Chicago as Radio Broadcast Capital: David Sarnoff of the Radio Corporation of America Suggests That a National Super-Station May Be Established Here," *Chicago Commerce* 21 (26 April 1924): 10–11.

143 J. Walter Thompson Company newsletter no. 107 (19 November 1925): 5, JWT, RG 11; MacDonald, *Don't Touch That Dial*, pp. 18, 21. It took some time for advertising companies to become convinced themselves that radio was a suitable medium for advertising. An article in a February

1925 issue of J. Walter Thompson's newsletter, for example, concluded that radio was a questionable medium at present. The company worried that the spoken word lacked the authority of the printed word and that radio advertising lacked the "various color and diagrammatic possibilities of the printed page." It feared as well that the spoken message was more likely to be misinterpreted than the printed one. J. Walter Thompson Company newsletter no. 65 (5 February 1925): 17, JWT, RG 11.

144 Wertheim, *Radio Comedy*, pp. 8–11; Boorstin, *The Americans*, p. 474; MacDonald, *Don't Touch That Dial*, p. 31.

145 Alice Goldfarb Marquis, "Written on the Wind: The Impact of Radio During the 1930s," *Journal of Contemporary History* 19 (1984): 386–8; Barnouw, *Tower of Babel*, pp. 185–93; Sterling and Kittross, *Stay Tuned*, pp. 68–9, 105–10; MacDonald, *Don't Touch That Dial*, pp. 16–24.

146 "Radio Rays," J. Walter Thompson Company newsletter no. 1 (1 January 1928): 20–1, JWT, RG 11. For further discussion of the benefits of radio advertising and the companies who pioneered in radio campaigns early on, see J. Walter Thompson Company newsletter no. 117 (28 January 1926): 25–6; J. Walter Thompson Company newsletter no. 178 (31 March 1927): 270; Aminta Casseres, "Radio Today is Not Just a Good-Will Medium," *J. Walter Thompson News Bulletin* (October 1929): 5–8; "J. Walter Thompson Radio Programs," *J. Walter Thompson Bulletin* 2 (April 1930): 42–3; "Declares Radio Broadcasting to Be Big Feature in Advertising," *Chicago Commerce* 25 (14 July 1928): 10; "Advertisers Make Our Programs Possible," *WLS Family Album: 1930 Edition* (Chicago: Tribune Publishing Co., 1930), p. 39.

147 A good source on the growing role of advertising companies in radio is Stephen Fox, *The Mirror Makers: A History of American Advertising and Its Creators* (New York: William Morrow and Company, 1984), pp. 150–62. See also J. Walter Thompson Company, "An Analysis," 1938, JWT, RG 3. MacDonald includes the following statistics documenting how radio program production moved out of the hands of the networks:

Accounts of one network, 1929

33 percent of the programs produced by advertising agencies
28 percent produced by networks (for its sponsors)
20 percent produced by sponsors themselves
19 percent produced by special program builders

By 1937, the 28 percent produced by the networks plus the 20 percent produced by the sponsors was gradually swallowed by the advertising agencies. "Currently, network commercial program production stands virtually at zero," a critic for *Variety* wrote. Edgar A. Grunwald, "Program-Production History, 1929–1937," *Variety Radio Directory, 1937–1938* (New York, 1937), p. 19, quoted in MacDonald, *Don't Touch That Dial*, p. 32.

The amount of money spent for broadcast advertising over the two national networks increased by one calculation 167.5 percent between 1927 and 1928, 80.6 percent between 1928 and 1929, and 43.2 percent between 1929 and 1930. Another study by Media Records of 129 chain-broadcast advertisers in 1929 and 1930 concluded that there had been a 74.1 percent gain. Daniel Lee Doeden, "The Press-Radio War: A Historical Analysis of Press-Radio Competition 1920–1940" (Ph.D. dissertation, Northwestern University, 1975), pp. 38, 66–7. Although radio made this 74.1 percent gain, newspapers lost 11.7 percent and magazines 7.3 percent. Buel W. Patch, "Radio Competition with Newspapers," *Editorial Research Reports* 1 (May 1931): 332–3.

148 John Black, "Twelve Years of Radio – the Story of A&P," *Broadcasting* (15 July 1935): 19; J. Walter Thompson Company, JWT, RG 11: newsletter no. 67 (19 February 1925); 5; newsletter no. 124 (1 April 1928): 134; newsletter no. 18 (15 September 1928): 1; newsletter no. 25 (15 December 1928): 1.

149 For the struggle over the regulation of the airwaves, culminating in the Radio Act of 1927, see "Radio Progress in 1926," *Daily News Almanac and Year-book for 1927* (Chicago: Daily News, 1927), pp. 365–6; "Radio Progress in 1927," *Daily News Almanac and Year-book for 1928* (Chicago: Daily News, 1928), pp. 571–2; WGN, "Mamma's Little Helper" (pamphlet for potential advertisers on station WGN); Linton, "History of Chicago Radio Station Programming," pp. 148, 220, 291; Chicago Tribune, *WGN: Picture Book of Radio, 1928*, pp. 1–7; Chester and Garrison, *Television and Radio*, pp. 30–2; Sterling and Kittross, *Stay Tuned*, pp. 66, 83–8, 110–11, 127–31; Barnouw, *Tower of Babel*, pp. 175, 211–19.

Specifically on WCFL's struggles, see "Destroy the Radio Trust," *WCFL Magazine* 1 (Spring 1928): 11, 98; "Radio Commission Turns Deaf Ear to Toilers' Plea," *WCFL Magazine* 2 (Spring 1929): 14; "Labor Reviews Its Struggles for Justice in Radio," *WCFL Magazine* 3 (Fall 1930): 10–11, 17, 22–3, 26–7; Frank J. Shillin (Janitors' Union No. 11) to Mr. Ira E. Robinson, Chairman FRC, n.d. but c. 1928, FITZ, Box 17, Folder 125; John Fitzpatrick to Sir and Brother (form letter), 11 November 1930, FITZ, Box 18, Folder 130; Jorgensen, "Radio Station WCFL," pp. 63, 76–7, 83–9, 92–4, 98–101, 105–9, 117.

150 Jorgensen, "Radio Station WCFL," pp. 90–1. On the growth of network radio in Chicago by the late 1920s, see Caton, "Radio Station WMAQ," pp. 382, 394–9; Linton, "History of Chicago Radio Station Programming," pp. 286, 314–38; and for a sophisticated analysis, Nathan Godfried, "Corporatism and Broadcasting: The Case of WCFL, 1928–1932," Unpublished paper presented to the Ohio Academy of History, 22 April 1989.

151 Jorgensen, "Radio Station WCFL," pp. 78–9; Joseph Chalasinski, "Polish and Parochial School among Polish Immigrants in America: A Study of a Polish Neighborhood in South Chicago," n.d. but c. 1930, CAP, Box 33, Folder 2, p. 19; "Legend of Wanda Homeland Music on Radio

Chain," *Dziennik Zwiazkowy*, 15 July 1929, CFLPS, Box 32; Interview with Mr. Charles Nurczyk, Secretary of the Polish Men's Association, 4 May 1937, CFLPS, Box 34; Robert D. W. Bartels, "The Use of Radio Advertising by Retailers in Chicago, Illinois" (M.B.A. thesis, Northwestern University, 1936).

152 "The Little Brown Church in the Vale," *WLS: The Prairie Farmer Station* (Chicago: WLS, 1929); *Chicago Radio Weekly*, 8 February 1931, back cover; William F. Fore, "A Short History of Religious Broadcasting," William F. Fore Collection, SHSW; DuBourdieu, "Religious Broadcasting in the United States," pp. 27–9, 128–31, 153; "Chicago Helps Put Breath of Life Into Radio," *Chicago Commerce* 27 (6 December 1930): 8; Goldsmith and Lescarboura, *This Thing Called Broadcasting*, pp. 269–71; Brinkley, *Voices of Protest*, p. 92.

153 Mary Helen Daly, "Community Study: The West Side through the Metropolitan Section of the Chicago Sunday Papers," Paper for Sociology 264, 17 March 1931, BUR, Box 157, Folder 1; Chicago Tribune, *WGN: Picture Book of Radio, 1928*, p. 73; Wertheim, *Radio Comedy*, p. 14; National Broadcasting Company, *A Study of the Relative Effectiveness of Major Advertising Media, Based on Results Observed by 1803 Retail Dealers in 26 Cities and Towns* (New York: NBC, 1934); Arnold Shankman, "Black Pride and Protest: The Amos 'N' Andy Crusade," *Journal of Popular Culture* 12 (February 1979): 238; Lester A. Weinrott, "Chicago Radio: The Glory Days," *Chicago History* 3 (Spring–Summer 1974): 19.

154 *Chicago Daily News*, 24 March 1927, p. 30, cited in Linton, "A History of Chicago Radio Station Programming," pp. 153–4.

155 James L. Palmer, "Radio Advertising," *Journal of Business of the University of Chicago* 1 (1928): 495–6.

156 *Before the Federal Radio Commission. In re Application of WMAQ, Inc., Docket No. 686. Reply Argument for WMAQ, Inc. Following Oral Argument and Printed Exceptions* (Chicago: WMAQ, n.d.), p. 11, quoted in Caton, "Radio Station WMAQ," p. 396.

157 Steve Nelson, James R. Barrett, and Rob Ruck, *Steve Nelson: American Radical* (Pittsburgh: University of Pittsburgh Press, 1981), p. 68.

158 Mary E. Shemerdiak to Miss Masley, Chicago, IL, 24 March 1931, BUR, Box 156, Folder 6. For further observations of the cultural divide between the generations in ethnic communities, see Gaetano DeFilippis, "Social Life in an Immigrant Community," Paper for Sociology 264, n.d. but c. 1930, BUR, Box 130, Folder 2, pp. 6–10; Zorbaugh, *The Gold Coast and the Slum*, pp. 176–7; Joseph Chalasinski, "Polish and Parochial School among Polish Immigrants in America: A Study of a Polish Neighborhood in South Chicago," n.d. but c. 1930, CAP, Box 33, Folder 2, p. 35.

159 There are many excellent sources on delinquency among ethnic youth in Chicago during the 1920s and 1930s since the subject fascinated the city's sociologists and social workers. In retrospect, many of the crimes these "deviant" youth committed can be viewed as "crimes of mass culture," extralegal strategies to participate in the consumer society without any

money. A study by the University of Chicago Settlement, for example, determined that shoplifting at the nearby Goldblatt's Department Store was the most common kind of delinquency in the neighborhood. "Back of the Yards Area," n.d. but c. 1934, MCD, Box 1, Folder "Historical Data," p. 29, and Interview with Goldblatt's detectives, MCD, Box 2, Folder 10. Other sources on juvenile delinquency include many documents in CAP and BUR and the classics, Clifford Shaw and Henry D. McKay, *Juvenile Delinquency and Urban Areas: A Study of Rates of Delinquency in Relation to Differential Characteristics of Local Communities in American Cities* (Chicago: University of Chicago Press, 1942), and Clifford R. Shaw, *The Jack-Roller: A Delinquent Boy's Own Story* (Chicago: University of Chicago Press, 1930).

High school attendance nationwide jumped during the twenties. In Chicago, public high school enrollment increased 121 percent between 1920 and 1930 (85,031 in 1930), whereas Catholic high school enrollment went up 76 percent between 1925 and 1930 (20,212 in 1930). Investigations of high school attendance in working-class neighborhoods make clear that young people from these areas contributed to the increase. Ralph E. Heilman, "How Chicago Prepares Its Young Citizens for Industry," *Chicago Commerce* 27 (15 November 1930): 129–30; "Study of Junior High and High School Students in Chicago, 1930," BUR, Box 83, Folder 7; Joseph Chalasinski, "Polish and Parochial School among Polish Immigrants in America: A Study of a Polish Neighborhood in South Chicago," n.d. but c. 1930, CAP, Box 33, Folder 2, p. 57.

160 Breckinridge, *New Homes for Old*, p. 173; Ireland, "Young American Poles," p. 96; Interview with Female in Technical Branch, 11 November 1930, HSMF, Fiche no. 184. There is much evidence indicating Chicago working-class youths' interest in the latest clothing fashions and their extravagance in purchasing them. Gaetano DeFelippis, "Social Life in an Immigrant Community," Paper for Sociology 264, n.d. but c. 1930, BUR, Box 130, Folder 2, p. 23; Louis Wirth, "Study of Monroe District," c. 1919, BUR, Box 139, Folder 2; Interview with Lillian Cwik, Polonia Archives, Box 2, CHS, p. 40; "The Mexican in Chicago, 1928–31," CFLPS, Box 41.

161 Mitchell, *Children and Movies*, pp. 18–19, 43–4, 67–9, 159, 162; Seldes, *The Great Audience*, p. 12, argues that the most reliable audience for movies was children between the ages of ten and nineteen.

162 Martha E. Gross, "The 'Rangers Club': A Group of Italian Boys at Chicago Commons," Paper for Social Pathology, 21 December 1931, BUR, Box 144, Folder 2, p. 25; Martha E. Gross, "The 'Jolly Girls' Club: Report and Diary," March 1933, BUR, Box 158, Folder 5, p. 25; Estelle Cooper, "How Polish Adolescents Spent Evenings," Paper for Sociology 137, c. 1930, BUR, Box 85, Folder 8; Sorrentino, *Organizing Against Crime*, p. 46; Interview with Frank Broska, Polonia Oral History Project, CHS, p. 22; and Interviews with the following in Chicago, IL, IC: Rena Morandin, 22 July 1980; Emilia Scarpelli, 2 July 1980.

163 Ireland, "Young American Poles," p. 83.

164 "Study of the Jewish People's Institute," n.d., WC, Box 95, Folder "JPI, 1937–38," pp. 70, 70a.

165 For vivid descriptions of club life, see Isadore Zelig, "A Study of the 'Basement' Social Clubs of Lawndale District," Paper for Sociology 270, 1928, BUR, Box 142, Folder 3; S. Kerson Weinberg, "Jewish Youth in the Lawndale Community: A Sociological Study," Paper for Sociology 269, n.d., BUR, Box 139, Folder 3, pp. 50–79; Meyer Levin, *The Old Bunch* (New York: Viking Press, 1937), pp. 3–9, 18–26, 121–39, a novel about Jewish youth in Lawndale during the 1920s; Ireland, "Young American Poles," pp. 72–5; "The Ragen's Colts and the Sherman Park District" and "The Neighborhood," 1924, MCD, Box 2, Folder 10; Guy DeFillipis, "Club Dances," 1935, CAP, Box 91, Folder 7; Robert Sayler, "A Study of Behavior Problems of Boys in Lower North Community," n.d., BUR, Box 135, Folder 4, pp. 24–7; William J. Dempsey, "Gangs in the Calumet Park District," Paper for Sociology 270, c. 1928, BUR, Box 148, Folder 5; Donald Pierson, "Autobiographies of Teenagers of Czechoslovakian Backgrounds from Cicero and Berwyn," 1931, BUR, Box 134, Folder 5; Slayton, "Our Own Destiny," pp. 87–8, 92–5.

166 Levin, *Old Bunch*, p. 125; Ireland, "Young American Poles," p. 74; Slayton, "Our Own Destiny," p. 88; Miscellaneous programs from club dances at rented neighborhood halls, 1927–30, in possession of author. Evidence also suggests that young people attending high school participated in extracurricular activities according to their ethnicity, which curbed the integrative impact of that experience. Paula S. Fass, *Outside In: Minorities and The Transformation of American Education* (New York: Oxford University Press, 1989), Chapter 3.

167 On parental disapproval of commercial dance halls, see Interview with Mrs. Z, 5 May 1925, in Report by University of Chicago students under Professor Burgess, "The Lower Northwest Side," n.d., com, Box 23, Folder "Lower Northwest Side Study, Burgess Project," p. 24; Song "El Enganchado," in Taylor, *Mexican Labor in Chicago*, p. vii; S. Mucha, Interview with Kozhowski, May 1932, BUR, Box 133, Folder 7, pp. 1–2.

On Chicago's commercial dance halls, see "'An Evening in a Dance Palace,' Adapted from Materials on *The Natural History of Vice Areas in Chicago* by Walter C. Reckless," Handout for Sociology 34, BUR, Box 31, Folder 4, pp. VI-18–19; Theatre Historical Society, "The Aragon Ballroom," *Program of Conclave + 1977 + Chicago* (Notre Dame, IN: Marquee, 1977); Richard Wright, "White City Recreation Center," FWP, Box A526, pp. 8–10; Children's Bureau, *Public Dance Halls: Their Regulation and Place in the Recreation of Adolescents*, Publication no. 189 (Washington, DC: U.S. Government Printing Office, 1929); Daniel Russell, "The Road House: A Study of Commercialized Amusements in the Environs of Chicago" (M.A. thesis, University of Chicago, 1931), pp. 115–27; John Ashenhurst and Ruth L. Ashenhurst, *All About Chicago* (Boston: Houghton Mifflin Company, 1933), pp. 252–4.

For fascinating descriptions of the ethnic dynamics within commercial dance halls, see Constance Weinberger and Saul D. Alinsky, "The Public

Dance," 1928, BUR, Box 126, Folder 10; "A Study of Gaelic Park," n.d. but late 1920s, BUR, Box 129, Folder 7; Clara G. Row, Paper on dance halls for Sociology 34, 1924, BUR, Box 129, Folder 6.

168 Interviews with Florence Roselli, Villa Park, IL, December 1980, IC, pp. 43–4, and Margaret Sabella, Chicago, IL, March 1980, IC, p. 30.

169 On the fragmentation of black churches in Chicago, see St. Clair Drake, "Churches and Voluntary Associations in the Chicago Negro Community," Report of Official Project 465-54-3-386 conducted under the auspices of the Works Projects Administration, Chicago, IL, 1940 (mimeo), pp. 147–50, 183–7, 190–205, 219, Appendix 4; Chicago Commission on Race Relations, *Negro in Chicago*, pp. 142–5; Robert Sutherland, "An Analysis of Negro Churches in Chicago" (Ph.D. dissertation, University of Chicago, 1930); Allan H. Spear, *Black Chicago: The Making of a Negro Ghetto, 1890–1920* (Chicago: University of Chicago Press, 1967), pp. 91–7, 174–9; St. Clair Drake and Horace R. Cayton, *Black Metropolis: A Study of Negro Life in a Northern City* (New York: Harcourt, Brace and Company, 1945), pp. 412–29; Harold F. Gosnell, *Negro Politicians: The Rise of Negro Politics in Chicago* (Chicago: University of Chicago Press, 1935), pp. 94–100; E. Franklin Frazier, "Chicago: A Cross-Section of Negro Life," *Opportunity* 7 (March 1929): 71–2; Harold Kingsley, "The Negro Goes to Church," *Opportunity* 7 (March 1929): 90–1.

For further discussion of the class divisions within the black community of Chicago, see Drake, "Churches and Voluntary Associations," pp. 215–19; E. Franklin Frazier, *The Negro Family in Chicago* (Chicago: University of Chicago Press, 1932), pp. 82–3; Gunnar Myrdal, *An American Dilemma: The Negro Problem and Modern Democracy*, vol. 2 (New York: Harper & Row, 1944; reprint ed. McGraw-Hill Book Company, 1964), pp. 695–705; James R. Grossman, *Land of Hope: Chicago, Black Southerners, and the Great Migration* (Chicago: University of Chicago Press, 1989), Chapter 5.

170 St. Clair Drake and Horace R. Cayton used the expression "black metropolis" in their monumental study of black Chicago. Even if the phrase was not in use before the 1940s, many people during the 1920s shared the goal of a thriving, independent black world within Chicago. Drake and Cayton, *Black Metropolis*.

171 On the philosophy of a separate black economy, see Spear, *Black Chicago*, pp. 111–18, 192–200; M. S. Stuart, *An Economic Detour: A History of Insurance in the Lives of American Negroes* (New York: Wendell, Malliet and Company Publishers, 1940), pp. xvii–xxv, 101; Richard I. Durham, "Don't Spend Your Money Where You Can't Work," n.d. but c. 1939, BAR, Box 149, Folder 4.

172 Drake and Cayton, *Black Metropolis*, p. 430.

173 Stuart, *Economic Detour*, p. 74; J. H. Harmon, Jr., "The Negro as a Local Business Man," *The Journal of Negro History* 14 (April 1929): 139.

174 On black businesses that flourished in Chicago and in the nation in gener-

al, with special attention to successful trades like undertaking, barber and beauty shops, cosmetics, and newspapers, see Drake and Cayton, *Black Metropolis*, pp. 433–6, 456–62; Spear, *Black Chicago*, pp. 112–15, 184–5; Chicago Commission on Race Relations, *Negro in Chicago*, pp. 140–1; Thomas E. Hunter, "Problems of Colored Chicago," 1930, BUR, Box 154, Folder 4; Abram L. Harris, *The Negro as Capitalist: A Study of Banking and Business among American Negroes* (Philadelphia: American Academy of Political and Social Science, 1936), pp. 170–2; Harmon, "Negro as Local Business Man," pp. 137–8, 140–1, 144–51; Myrdal, *American Dilemma*, vol. 1, pp. 309–10, 317; Jervis Anderson, *This Was Harlem, 1900–1950* (New York: Farrar Straus Giroux, 1981), pp. 92–8; Camille Cohen-Jones, "Your Cab Company," *The Crisis* 34 (March 1927): 5–6.

175 W. E. B. Dubois, "Marcus Garvey," *Crisis* 21 (January 1921): 113, quoted in Edmund David Cronon, *Black Moses: The Story of Marcus Garvey and the Universal Negro Improvement Association* (Madison: University of Wisconsin Press, 1968), p. 52, also see 50–61, 174–5; Drake, "Churches and Voluntary Associations," pp. 234–40; Spear, *Black Chicago*, pp. 193–7; August Meier and Elliott Rudwick, *From Plantation to Ghetto* (New York: Hill and Wang, 1976), pp. 246–8.

176 On the decline of fraternals and the rise of social clubs, see Drake, "Churches and Voluntary Associations," pp. 152–3, 189, 208–11; Frazier, *Negro Family*, pp. 74–5, 115; Drake and Cayton, *Black Metropolis*, pp. 520–1; Spear, *Black Chicago*, pp. 107–10; Gosnell, *Negro Politicians*, pp. 110–11; Chicago Commission on Race Relations, *Negro in Chicago*, pp. 141–2; Leo M. Bryant, "Negro Insurance Companies in Chicago" (M.A. thesis, University of Chicago, 1934), pp. 1–4; Myrdal, *American Dilemma*, vol. 2, pp. 952–5; Stuart, *Economic Detour*, pp. 11–34; Harris, *Negro as Capitalist*, pp. 46–7; Todd et al., *Chicago Recreation Survey*, vol. 3, p. 105.

177 On black commercial insurance companies, see Bryant, "Negro Insurance Companies in Chicago," pp. 1–80; Hylan Garnet Lewis, "Social Differentiation in the Negro Community" (M.A. thesis, University of Chicago, 1936), pp. 98–101; Robert C. Puth, "Supreme Life: The History of a Negro Life Insurance Company" (Ph.D. dissertation, Northwestern University, 1967), pp. 1–93; Drake and Cayton, *Black Metropolis*, pp. 462–4; Spear, *Black Chicago*, pp. 181–3; C. G. Woodson, "The Insurance Business among Negroes," *Journal of Negro History* 14 (April 1929): 202–26; Stuart, *Economic Detour*, pp. 35–62, 72–108; "The North's Largest Negro Business: Supreme Liberty Life Insurance Company," *Ebony* 12 (November 1956): 64–9; President's Research Committee, *Recent Social Trends*, vol. 1, p. 598.

178 Drake and Cayton, *Black Metropolis*, p. 440, and general discussion on pp. 439–43. Although Greeks, Italians, and others also ran shops in black neighborhoods, the great preponderance of white merchants were Jews. The best figures I have located indicate that a decade later, in 1938,

Jews made up three-fourths of the merchants in the Black Belt, which made them the scapegoat of antiwhite feeling among blacks. Drake and Cayton, *Black Metropolis*, p. 432. See also "Business Leaders Discuss Should Negroes Buy from Negroes?" n.d., BAR, Box 277, Folder 7.

179 On Jesse Binga's and Anthony Overton's Chicago banks, see Harris, *Negro as Capitalist*, pp. 48–9, 144–64, 175, 191, 193; Spear, *Black Chicago*, pp. 74–5, 184; F. Cyril James, *The Growth of Chicago Banks* (New York: Harper & Brothers Publishers, 1938), p. 959; Drake and Cayton, *Black Metropolis*, p. 82, 464–5; Arnett G. Lindsay, "The Negro in Banking," *Journal of Negro History* 14 (April 1929): 180–96; Madrue Chavers-Wright, *The Guarantee – P.W. Chavers: Banker, Entrepreneur, Philanthropist in Chicago's Black Belt of the Twenties* (New York: Wright-Armstead Associates, 1985). On obstacles black businesses faced getting mortgages, see H. O. Stone and Company, First Mortgage Bonds, to C. U. Turpin Company, 25 April 1928, NAACP Papers, Box 49, Folder "Chicago, Illinois, 1927–28," LC.

180 For discussion of the difficulties of black businessmen, see Drake and Cayton, *Black Metropolis*, pp. 438–56; Thomas E. Hunter, "Problems of Colored Chicago," 1930, BUR, Box 154, Folder 4, p. 12; Spear, *Black Chicago*, pp. 183–4; Paul K. Edwards, *The Southern Urban Negro as a Consumer* (New York: Prentice-Hall, 1932), pp. 126, 135–9; Harris, *Negro as Capitalist*, pp. 54–5, 172; Myrdal, *American Dilemma*, vol. 1, pp. 307–12; Harmon, "Negro as a Local Business Man," pp. 131, 140, 142, 144–5, 147, 152–5; "Business in Bronzeville," *Time* 31 (18 April 1938): 70–1.

181 Dianne M. Pinderhughes, *Race and Ethnicity in Chicago Politics: A Reexamination of Pluralist Theory* (Urbana: University of Illinois, 1987), p. 24; Albert Anderson, "What's This Thing the Business League Is Trying to Do?" n.d., BAR, Box 277, Folder 7; Edwards, *Southern Urban Negro as Consumer*, pp. 153–66, 209–13. Several years after this study was published, Edwards expanded his investigation into urban black consumption habits to include the North. He concluded that northern blacks showed the same predisposition to brand names as southern urbanites. Also see Raymond A. Bauer and Scott M. Cunningham, *Studies in the Negro Market* (Cambridge, MA: Marketing Science Institute, 1970), pp. 11–14, and Raymond A. Bauer, Scott M. Cunningham, and Lawrence H. Wortzel, "The Marketing Dilemma of Negroes," *Journal of Marketing* 29 (July 1965), reprinted in Boone, *Classics in Consumer Behavior*, pp. 353–64.

182 *Chicago Defender*, 10 September 1927, quoted in Drake, "Churches and Voluntary Associations," p. 247. On boycott campaigns also see Oliver Cromwell Cox, "The Negroes Use of Their Buying Power in Chicago as a Means of Securing Employment," Prepared for Professor Millis, University of Chicago, 1933, cited extensively in Drake, "Churches and Voluntary Associations," pp. 230, 247–51; Richard F. Durham, "Don't Spend Your Money Where You Can't Work," n.d. but c. 1939, BAR, Box 149,

Folder 4; "Newspaper Vows Fight Against Chain Stores," 1 March 1930, BAR, Box 260, Folder 7; "Butler Stores Cheat," *Messenger* 7 (April 1925): 156; T. Arnold Hill, "Picketing for Jobs," *Opportunity* 8 (July 1930): 216; Claude A. Barnett, "We Win a Place in Industry," *Opportunity* 7 (March 1929): 84–5; Address by Joseph D. Bibb, Editor Chicago *Whip*, at employment mass meeting, 24 April 1930, Urban League Papers, Series 7, Box 21, Folder "Voc Scrapbook-Report, City Reports 1930," LC; Arvarh E. Strickland, *History of the Chicago Urban League* (Urbana: University of Illinois Press, 1966), p. 92; Elizabeth Balanoff, "A History of the Black Community of Gary, Indiana, 1906–1940" (Ph.D. dissertation, University of Chicago, 1974), pp. 200–2; Harris, *Negro as Capitalist*, p. 179; Myrdal, *American Dilemma*, vol. 1, pp. 313–14; President's Research Committee, *Recent Social Trends*, vol. 1, p. 580.

183 John L. Tilley, *A Brief History of the Negro in Chicago, 1779–1933 (from Jean Baptiste DeSaible – to "A Century of Progress")* (Chicago: Century of Progress, 1933), pp. 16–18, 25–6; Thomas E. Hunter, "Problems of Colored Chicago," 1930, BUR, Box 154, Folder 4, p. 10; "Woolworth Employs Colored Girls, Pickets Are Removed," 6 October 1930, BAR, Box 260, Folder 7; Stephen Breszka, "And Lo! It Worked: A Tale of Colored Harmony," *Opportunity* 11 (November 1933): 342–4, 350.

184 Drake and Cayton, *Black Metropolis*, p. 428.

185 Thomas Lee Philpott, *The Slum and the Ghetto: Neighborhood Deterioration and Middle-Class Reform, Chicago, 1880–1930* (New York: Oxford University Press, 1978), p. 158; Chicago Commission on Race Relations, *Negro in Chicago*, pp. 343–4; Mike Rowe, *Chicago Blues: The City & the Music* (New York: Da Capa Press Paperback, 1975), pp. 34, 40.

186 My treatment of the Chicago jazz scene was derived from the following sources: Thomas Joseph Hennessey, "From Jazz to Swing: Black Jazz Musicians and Their Music, 1917–1935" (Ph.D. dissertation, Northwestern University, 1973); Robert L. Brubacker, *Making Music Chicago Style* (Chicago: Chicago Historical Society, 1985), pp. 16–25, 148–55; Dempsey Travis, *An Autobiography of Black Jazz* (Chicago: Urban Research Institute, 1983); Burton W. Peretti, "White Hot Jazz," *Chicago History* 17 (Fall and Winter 1988–9): 26–41; Thomas G. Aylesworth and Virginia L. Aylesworth, *Chicago: The Glamour Years (1919–1941)* (New York: Gallery Books, 1986), pp. 55–89; LeRoi Jones, *Blues People: The Negro Experience in White America and the Music That Developed from It* (New York: William Morrow and Company, 1963), pp. 95–165; Marshall W. Stearns, *The Story of Jazz* (New York: Oxford University Press, 1956); Louis Armstrong, *Swing That Music* (New York: Longmans, Green & Co., 1936), excerpted in Albert Halper, ed., *This Is Chicago: An Anthology* (New York: Henry Holt and Company, 1952), pp. 88–96; Rowe, *Chicago Blues*; William Kenney, "Chicago Jazz and

City Culture: The South Side Cabaret, 1915–1930," Paper presented to the American Studies Association, 28 October 1988; J. A. Rogers, "Jazz at Home," *Survey* (1 March 1925): 665, reprinted in Mowry, ed., *The Twenties*, pp. 67–9; Time-Life Books, *This Fabulous Century: 1920–1930*, vol. 3, pp. 76–93; David Levering Lewis, *When Harlem Was in Vogue* (New York: Vintage Books, 1982), pp. 170–5; Lewis A. Erenberg, *Steppin' Out: New York Nightlife and the Transformation of American Culture, 1890–1930* (Chicago: University of Chicago Press, 1981), pp. 250–2; Anderson, *This Was Harlem*, pp. 128–33; "Earl 'Fatha' Hines – A Giant of Jazz," *San Francisco Chronicle*, 23 April 1983.

187 Stearns, *Story of Jazz*, pp. 167–8.

188 A survey of a 1929 out-of-town edition of the *Chicago Defender* revealed that 18.7 percent of the 1,070 advertisements were for race records. Edwards, *Southern Urban Negro as Consumer*, p. 185. On race records, see Robert M. W. Dixon and John Godrich, *Recording the Blues* (New York: Stein and Day Publishers, 1970), pp. 7–63; Lawrence W. Levine, *Black Culture and Black Consciousness: Afro–American Folk Thought from Slavery to Freedom* (New York: Oxford University Press, 1977), pp. 224, 231; Jones, *Blues People*, pp. 99–103, 128–9; Stearns, *Story of Jazz*, pp. 167–8, 190; Barnouw, *Tower in Babel*, pp. 128–31; Brubacker, *Making Music Chicago Style*, pp. 50–1; Lewis, *When Harlem Was in Vogue*, pp. 173–5.

4. CONTESTED LOYALTY AT THE WORKPLACE

1 For more about these particular workers, see Interview with Betty Piontkowsky by Betty Burke, in Ann Banks, ed., *First-Person America* (New York: Vintage Books, 1981), pp. 59–60; Interview with Bernice Novak by author, New Lenox, IL, 4 August 1983; Phillip F. Janik with Phyllis Janik, "Looking Backward From 'The Bush' to the Open Hearth," *Chicago History* 10 (Spring 1981): 49–56; Employment packet of Moses Parker, Employee no. 39998, McCormick Works Employee Records, Box 1, IH.

2 To appreciate how prewar welfare programs emphasized "moral uplift," see Mary Irwin, "Welfare Work in Industries of Chicago," Paper for Sociology 1, 10 December 1918, BUR, Box 131, Folder 5; Gerd Korman, "Americanization at the Factory Gate," *Industrial and Labor Relations Review* 18 (April 1965): 396–419; Stuart D. Brandes, *American Welfare Capitalism, 1880–1940* (Chicago: University of Chicago Press, 1976), pp. 10–24, 111–18; Daniel Nelson, *Managers and Workers: Origins of the New Factory System in the United States, 1880–1920* (Madison: University of Wisconsin Press, 1975), pp. 101–21; Sanford Jacoby, "The Development of Internal Labor Markets in American Manufacturing Firms," in Paul Osterman, ed., *Employment Practices in Large Firms* (Cambridge, MA: MIT Press, 1984), pp. 31–2.

3 Sumner H. Slichter, "The Current Labor Policies of American Industries," *Quarterly Journal of Economics* 43 (May 1929): 396–7.
4 National Industrial Conference Board (NICB), *Industrial Relations: Administration of Policies and Programs* (New York: NICB, 1931), p. 63.
5 L. Grace Powell Sitzer, M.D., Manager of Medical and Welfare Department, William Wrigley Jr. Company, as told to Kathleen North in "Factory and Industrial Management," *Central Manufacturing District Magazine* 13 (April 1929): 9.
6 Cyrus McCormick, Jr., "Employee Representation as Affecting the Attitude of Labor and Business," Address before the American Management Association, Kansas City, MO, 30 November 1925, IH, Document file 16756.
7 Swift & Company, *Yearbook of 1923, Covering Activities for the Year 1922* (Chicago: Swift & Company, 1923), p. 47. For a full statement of Swift & Company's commitment to welfare capitalism, see Harold H. Swift, "Guaranteed Time in the Stock Yards," *Survey* 67 (1 November 1931): 121–6.
8 Edwin B. Parker, "The Fifteen Commandments of Business," *Nation's Business* 12 (June 1924): 16 ff, quoted in Morrell Heald, "Business Thought in the Twenties: Social Responsibility," *American Quarterly* 13 (Summer 1961): 133.
9 It is difficult to know exactly how widespread these attitudes were, but most studies agree that large-scale mass production employers were in the forefront of the welfare capitalist movement. After surveying 1,500 of the largest companies in the United States in 1926, a researcher reported that 80 percent had adopted at least one form of welfarism and about half had comprehensive programs. At the very least, four million people worked for companies engaged in welfare practices. Brandes, *American Welfare Capitalism*, p. 28. It is usually assumed that small manufacturers were less prone to run innovative industrial relations programs because of their cost, but a study of 4,500 establishments employing 250 or less wage earners, carried out by the National Industrial Conference Board in 1929, revealed that activities were more frequent in these firms than had been expected. National Industrial Conference Board (NICB), *Industrial Relations in Small Plants* (New York: NICB, 1929).

There has been some debate among historians about whether welfare capitalism persisted throughout the 1920s or declined after a peak of antiunion fervor in 1920–1. Sanford Jacoby, for example, argues this latter position. My findings, however, suggest that among the kind of employers most enthusiastic about welfare capitalism, the large mass production manufacturers, welfare capitalism remained a compelling ideology throughout the decade. Smaller companies who experimented with welfare capitalist schemes in the early twenties may have been more likely to let programs lapse. I agree with Jacoby that the rate of growth of welfare capitalism plans slowed in the second half of the decade, but I think that is because the major industries for whom the philosophy made the most sense had already adopted them. Figures on welfare capitalist programs like Employee Representation Plans reveal a peak in the number of plans by the mid-1920s but a continued growth in the number of employees affected, reflecting their greater incidence in large firms. A search through *Chicago Commerce*, the weekly journal of the Chicago Association of Commerce, over the decade shows a continued interest in welfare capitalism through the late 1920s, with some intensification at the end of that period. See Sanford Jacoby, "The Origins of Internal Labor Markets in American Manufacturing Firms, 1910–1940" (Ph.D. dissertation, University of California, Berkeley, 1981), p. 476.

10 NICB, *Industrial Relations*, pp. 5, 23. For secondary sources that explore business's larger conception of "welfare capitalism" during the 1920s, see Ellis W. Hawley, *The Great War and the Search for a Modern Order, a History of the American People and Their Institutions, 1917–1933* (New York: St. Martin's Press, 1979), pp. 10–11, 47–8, 52–5, 68–71, 100–4, which argues that employers, and government leaders like Herbert Hoover, were antistatist and sought a weak, cooperative association between the federal government and business; David Brody, "The Rise and Decline of Welfare Capitalism," in *Workers in Industrializing America: Essays on the Twentieth Century Struggle* (New York: Oxford University Press, 1980), pp. 48–81; Theda Skocpol and John Ikenberry, "The Political Formation of the American Welfare State in Historical and Comparative Perspective," Unpublished paper presented at the Annual Meeting of the American Sociological Association, 7 September 1982, pp. 48–51; Edward Berkowitz and Kim McQuaid, *Creating the Welfare State: The Political Economy of Twentieth Century Reform* (New York: Praeger, 1980); Kim McQuaid, "Corporate Liberalism in the American Business Community, 1920–1940," *Business History Review* 52 (Autumn 1978): 342–52; Heald, "Business Thought in the Twenties."

Some primary sources that also recognize this new attitude among employers are J. David Houser, *What the Employer Thinks: Executives' Attitudes toward Employees* (Cambridge, MA: Harvard University Press, 1927); Slichter, "The Current Labor Policies of American Industries"; "No Companionate Marriage!" in True Story Magazine, *The American Economic Evolution*, vol. 2 (New York: Macfadden Publications, 1931), pp. 21–4. Chicago's early place in the forefront of the welfare capitalism movement was asserted in Arthur Frederick Sheldon, "Cure for Bolshevism: Mutual Service Cures Bolshevism," *Chicago Commerce* 16 (5 April 1919): 23–4. For the closest thing to a treatise on enlightened personnel policies produced by a Chicago employer, see J. W. Dietz, "Some Aspects of Personnel Research in a Manufacturing Organization," *Annals of the American Academy of Political and Social Science* 119 (May 1925): 103–7.

11 Phyllis Bate, "The Development of the Iron and Steel Industry of the Chicago Area, 1900–1920" (Ph.D. dissertation, University of Chicago, 1948), p. 131.

12 John R. Commons et al., *History of Labor in the United States*, vol. 3 (New York: Macmillan, 1935), p. xxv, quoted in David M. Gordon, Richard Edwards, and Michael Reich, *Segmented Work, Divided Workers: The Historical Transformation of Labor in the United States* (New York: Cambridge University Press, 1982), p. 257.

13 Arthur H. Young to Special Conference Committee, 9 August 1919, IH, Document file 19753, pp. 6–7.

14 On Americanization and naturalization efforts in Chicago industries, see William M. Leiserson, *Adjusting Immigrant and Industry* (New York: Harper & Brothers, 1924), pp. 124–5; Frank D. Loomis, *Americanization in Chicago: The Report of a Survey Made by Authority and under Direction of the Chicago Community Trust* (Chicago: Chicago Community Trust, n.d. but c. 1920), pp. 22, 24–5; and many articles from 1919 to 1926 in *Chicago Commerce*, among them: "Visit to Americanization Classes, International Harvester and Sing Company," 16 (31 May 1919); "How Men Are Made Loyal Americans, Chairman Tells of Americanization Committee's Work to Make Foreigners Contented and Patriotic Citizens," 16 (28 June 1919); "Americanization Committee Issues Primer for Non-English Speaking Adults in Factory Classes," 17 (12 June 1920); "United Americans Working at Yards," 17 (31 July 1920); "Reports Show Growth of Americanization Work," 17 (2 October 1920); "Rank and File of Americanization Workers Talk of Problems That Confront Them in Their Daily Work," 17 (20 November 1920); "Foreign Language Editors Discuss Americanization Work with Association Committee," 18 (12 March 1921); "Thousands to Be Made Citizens Tomorrow: Impressive Americanization Ceremonies at Lake Front Stadium Will Mark Rededication of Chicago," 18 (8 October 1921).

15 Paul S. Taylor, *Mexican Labor in the United States: Chicago and the Calumet Region*, vol. 7, no. 2, University of California Publications in Economics (Berkeley: University of California Press, 1932), p. 93.

16 Raymond Edward Nelson, "A Study of an Isolated Industrial Community: Based on Personal Documents Secured by the Participant Observer Method" (M.A. thesis, University of Chicago, 1929), p. 130. Discussion of the necessity of dividing ethnic workers within the factory was widespread among employers. See Taylor, *Mexican Labor in Chicago*, pp. 93–4, 114, 121; "The Iron and Steel Industry of the Calumet District," *University of Illinois Studies in the Social Sciences* 12 (June 1925): 93, quoted in Horace B. Davis, *The Condition of Labor in the American Iron and Steel Industry* (New York: International Publishers, 1934), p. 32; Robert Ozanne, *A Century of Labor–Management Relations at McCormick and International Harvester* (Madison: University of Wisconsin Press, 1967), p. 184.

17 On the growth of Mexican and black labor in Chicago factories during the 1920s, see Edward Greer, "Racism and U.S. Steel, 1906–1974," *Radical America* 10 (September–October 1976): 50–1; Walter A. Fogel, *The Negro in the Meat Industry*, Report no. 2, Racial Policies of American Industry Series (Philadelphia: Wharton School of Finance and Commerce,

University of Pennsylvania, 1970) pp. 46–7; Jacoby, "The Origins of Internal Labor Markets," p. 536; Chicago Commission on Race Relations, *The Negro in Chicago: A Study of Race Relations and a Race Riot* (Chicago: University of Chicago, 1922), pp. 357–403; Taylor, *Mexican Labor in Chicago*, pp. 35–7, 40, 42, 46–7, 87; Robert Ozanne, *The Negro in the Farm Equipment and Construction Machinery Industries*, Report no. 26, Racial Policies of American Industry Series (Philadelphia: Wharton School of Finance and Commerce, University of Pennsylvania, 1972), pp. 19–22; Elizabeth Balanoff, "A History of the Black Community of Gary, Indiana, 1906–1940" (Ph.D. dissertation, University of Chicago, 1974), pp. 158, 189; Ozanne, *Century of Labor–Management Relations*, pp. 184–7; Robert Ozanne, *Wages in Practice and Theory: McCormick and International Harvester, 1860–1960* (Madison: University of Wisconsin Press, 1968), pp. 47–8; Marcia Kijewski, David Brosch, and Robert Bulanda, *Three Chicago Millgates*, "South Chicago," Illinois Labor History Society, 1972 (mimeo), p. 53; Eunice Felter, "The Social Adaptations of the Mexican Churches in the Chicago Area" (M.A. thesis, University of Chicago, 1941), pp. 18–19; Anita Edgar Jones, "Conditions Surrounding Mexicans in Chicago" (Ph.D. dissertation, University of Chicago, 1928), p. 37; Francisco A. Rosales and Daniel T. Simon, "Chicano Steel Workers and Unionism in the Midwest, 1919–1945," *Aztlan* 6 (Summer 1975): 267–9; Ciro Sepulvedo, "Research Note: Una Colonia de Obreros, East Chicago, Indiana," *Aztlan* 7 (Summer 1976): 327–36; Mark Reisler, *By the Sweat of Their Brow: Mexican Immigrant Labor in the United States, 1900–1940* (Westport, CT: Greenwood Press, 1976), pp. 96–126; Juan Garcia, "History of Chicanos in Chicago Heights," *Aztlan* 7 (Summer 1976): 292–8.

18 "The Melting Pot," Student paper, n.d. but c. 1930, BUR, Box 154, Folder 4, p. 21, also see pp. 7, 27. For further discussion of the low-level jobs of most Mexicans and blacks, see Dempsey J. Travis, *An Autobiography of Black Chicago* (Chicago: Urban Research Institute, 1981), pp. 90–1; Greer, "Racism and U.S. Steel," p. 51; Nelson, "Study of Isolated Industrial Community," pp. 84, 134; Catherine Elizabeth Lewis, "Trade Union Policies in Regard to the Negro Worker in the Slaughtering and Meatpacking Industry of Chicago" (M.A. thesis, University of Chicago, 1945), pp. 73–4; St. Clair Drake and Horace R. Cayton, *Black Metropolis: A Study of Negro Life in a Northern City* (New York: Harcourt, Brace and Company, 1945), pp. 218–31, 252–62.

19 Taylor, *Mexican Labor in Chicago*, pp. 87–90, 93–4; Balanoff, "History of the Black Community of Gary," pp. 190–1.

20 William L. Evans, "The Negro in Chicago Industries," *Opportunity* 1 (February 1923): 15–16. For discussion of the job mobility that some Mexicans and blacks enjoyed as a result of being "strike insurance," see Alma Herbst, *The Negro in the Slaughtering and Meat-packing Industry in Chicago* (New York: Arno & The New York Times, 1971), pp. xxii, 75–6; Herbert R. Northrup, *Organized Labor and the Negro* (New York:

Harper, 1944), pp. 176–7; Herman Feldman, *Racial Factors in American Industry* (New York: Harper, 1931), pp. 24, 38–9, which calls attention to the comparatively large number of skilled jobs available to blacks in steel; and Taylor, *Mexican Labor in Chicago*, pp. 155–7, who calculated that at the Gary Works and South Works of Illinois Steel Company (subsidiary of U.S. Steel), although almost 80 percent of Mexicans and blacks were unskilled, 19 percent of Mexicans and 16 percent of blacks were semiskilled and roughly 2 percent of Mexicans and 5 percent of blacks were skilled. Paul Taylor's survey of the skill levels of Mexicans in seven large industrial plants (Armour, Swift, Buffington plant of Universal Atlas Cement Company, Gary Works, South Works, McCormick Works, and Inland Steel) was consistent: 81.9 percent unskilled, 16.6 percent semiskilled, and 1.5 percent skilled.

21 Taylor, *Mexican Labor in Chicago*, pp. 40, 42, 114, 220–55; Kijewski, Brosch, and Bulanda, *Three Chicago Millgates*, "South Deering," p. 35; "The Melting Pot," Student paper, n.d. but c. 1930, BUR, Box 154, Folder 4, pp. 13–16.

22 Katherine Stone, "The Origin of Job Structures in the Steel Industry," *Radical America* 7 (November – December 1973): 43–8. The number of foremen in manufacturing increased 300 percent between 1900 and 1920, from 90,000 to 296,000, which contrasted with an increase of only 96 percent in total manufacturing employment. Gordon, Edwards, and Reich, *Segmented Work*, p. 135. See also Nelson, *Managers and Workers*, pp. 34–54.

23 Bate, "Development of Iron and Steel Industry," p. 148.

24 Irving Bernstein, *The Lean Years: A History of the American Worker, 1920–1933* (Baltimore: Penguin Books, 1970), pp. 174–8; Nelson, *Managers and Workers*, p. 81; Richard Edwards, *Contested Terrain: The Transformation of the Workplace in the Twentieth Century* (New York: Basic Books, 1979), pp. 63–5, for complaints by steel workers about their foremen during testimony to the Senate committee investigating the 1919 strike.

25 Nelson, "Study of an Isolated Industrial Community," p. 69; Swift & Company, *The Meatpacking Industry in America* (Chicago: Swift & Company, 1931), p. 103; Kate J. Adams, *Humanizing a Great Industry* (Chicago: Armour and Company, 1919), p. 3; Arthur H. Carver, *Personnel and Labor Problems in the Packing Industry* (Chicago: University of Chicago Press, 1928), pp. 90–103; "Introducing the Personnel Men," *Hawthorne Microphone*, 19 January 1923; "Industrial Relations Department," *Harvester World*, December 1918; Ozanne, *Century of Labor–Management Relations*, pp. 163, 174–6; Jacoby, "Development of Internal Labor Markets," pp. 37–8, 46.

26 Slichter, "Current Labor Policies," pp. 411–13; Carver, *Personnel and Labor Problems*, p. 93; Illinois Manufacturers' Association, *Annual Reports, 1919*, p. 8, quoted in Alfred H. Kelly, "A History of the Illinois Manufacturers' Association" (Ph.D. dissertation, University of Chicago, 1938), p. 179; "Industrial Relations," MCD, Box 15, Folder "Swift &

Company"; Swift & Company, *Yearbook of 1920, Covering the Activities for Year 1919* (Chicago: Swift & Company, 1920), p. 16, 58; James R. McIntyre, "The History of Wisconsin Steel Works of the International Harvester Company," 1951 (typescript), SECHP, p. 48; P. W. Willard, "Basic Principles and Trends in Personnel Administration," 1928, WE, HC-121, p. 13; Nelson, "Study of an Isolated Industrial Community," p. 70; NICB, *Industrial Relations*, pp. 43–4, 67–8; "Plant Foremen Dine," *Hawthorne Microphone*, 27 January 1922; "1000 Factory Foremen Celebrate Completing Foremen's Development Course," *Harvester World*, July 1920; "Foremen Get Weekly Newsletter," *Tractor Interester*, March 1920; "Teach – Don't Boss," *South Works Review*, January 1919; "A Leader, Not a Driver," *South Works Review*, July–August 1919; "Foreman's Forum," *South Works Review*, November 1928, May 1929.

27 A. P. Ogilvie, President, National Foremen's Institute, Chicago, "Your Foremen: How They Can Help You Meet 1930 Competition," *Illinois Manufacturers' Costs Association Monthly Bulletin* no. 86 (7 February 1930): 1–2.

28 Jacoby, "Development of Internal Labor Markets," p. 44. A study of women workers in meatpacking carried out by the Women's Bureau of the Department of Labor in 1928–9 revealed that three-fourths of the 5,101 women surveyed worked for firms that paid bonuses, and three-fourths of this group had received one in the current week. Women's Bureau, U.S. Department of Labor, *The Employment of Women in Slaughtering and Meatpacking*, Bulletin no. 88 (Washington, DC: U.S. Government Printing Office, 1932), p. 10.

29 National Industrial Conference Board (NICB), *Systems of Wage Payments* (New York: NICB, 1929), p. 25, quoted in Stone, "Origin of Job Structures in Steel," p. 39. For details on wage incentive schemes, see Women's Bureau, *Women in Slaughtering*, pp. 63–70; Herbst, *Negro in Slaughtering and Meat-Packing*, pp. 69, 114–16; Carver, *Personnel in Packing*, pp. 119–34; Theodore V. Purcell, *The Worker Speaks His Mind on Company and Union* (Cambridge, MA: Harvard University Press, 1953), pp. 236–41, 299; "A Survey of Harvester Industrial Relations Progress," *Harvester World*, July 1924, p. 5; F. J. Roethlisberger and William J. Dickson, *Management and the Worker: An Account of a Research Program Conducted by the Western Electric Company, Hawthorne Works, Chicago* (Cambridge, MA: Harvard University Press, 1929; reprinted 1976), pp. 409–12; Reinhard Bendix, *Work and Authority in Industry: Ideologies of Management in the Course of Industrialization* (Berkeley: University of California Press, 1974), pp. 279–87, 312–13; Ronald W. Schatz, *The Electrical Workers: A History of Labor at General Electric and Westinghouse, 1923–60* (Urbana: University of Illinois Press, 1983), pp. 18–19, 22–4; Edwards, *Contested Terrain*, pp. 97–104; David Montgomery, *Workers' Control in America: Studies in the History of Work, Technology, and Labor Struggles* (New York: Cambridge University Press, 1979), pp. 37–8, 123.

30 Franklyn Meine, "Promotions of Factory Employees," in Daniel Bloom-

field, ed., *Problems in Personnel Management* (New York, 1923), quoted in Jacoby, "Development of Internal Labor Markets," p. 38. For more on promotions, see Charles Reitell, "Machinery and Its Effect upon the Workers in the Automotive Industry," *Annals of the American Academy of Political and Social Science* 116 (November 1924): 37–43; Schatz, *Electrical Workers*, pp. 19–20; Gordon, Edwards, and Reich, *Segmented Work*, p. 138.

31 Hawthorne Works, "A Good Place to Work" (Chicago: Western Electric Company, n.d. but c. 1923–4), p. 6; "Mechanical Drawing Classes," *The Magnet*, October 1920; *Hawthorne Microphone*, 1922–30, *passim; Western Electric News*, 1920–30, *passim; South Works Review*, 1920–30, *passim*; Swift & Company, *Yearbooks* (Chicago: Swift & Company, 1920–30), *passim.*

32 Elbert Gary, *Addresses and Statements* 6 (29 March 1922), quoted in Stone, "Origin of Job Structures in Steel," p. 42. A similar statement appeared in an editorial in *Hawthorne Microphone*, 19 January 1923, "Introducing the Personnel Man."

33 Adams, *Humanizing a Great Industry*, p. 31; "From the Bottom of the Ladder," Swift & Company advertisement, *Saturday Evening Post*, 29 December 1929; Hawthorne Works, "A Good Place to Work," p. 3.

34 The work of William A. Sundstrom suggests another motive behind the standardization of jobs that I will not go into here. As mergers in the first decades of the twentieth century created larger and more decentralized firms, management valued more standardized job categories to permit more centralized operations and better comparisons across plants. "Cooperation and Contract: Tradition and Innovation in the Emergence of Internal Labor Markets in the United States, 1900–1930," Unpublished paper, Stanford University Economic History Seminar, October 1984; "Rules vs. Contracts in Wage Determination: The Case of Atlas Powder, 1913–1921," Unpublished paper, Stanford University Economic History Seminar, April 1985. For just this motivation in a Chicago firm, see discussion of Harvester's implementation of a companywide "occupational rating plan" in the early 1920s. "A Survey of Harvester Industrial Relations Progress," *Harvester World*, July 1924, p. 5.

35 Paul F. Brissenden and Emil Frankel, *Labor Turnover in Industry* (New York: Macmillan, 1922), pp. 36–7; "Memorandum: Labor Turnover," in Industrial Relations Section, Department of Economics and Social Institutions, Princeton University, *Memoranda of the Industrial Relations Section, Princeton University, 1926–1929* (bound mimeos), p. 1. The memorandum cites other studies with similar findings of extraordinarily high turnover rates. See also Emil Frankel, "Labor Turnover in Chicago," *Monthly Labor Review* 9 (September 1919): 44–59.

36 M. W. Alexander, "Hiring and Firing: Its Economic Waste and How to Avoid It," *Annals of the American Academy of Political and Social Science* 65 (May 1916): 136–9, cited in Princeton University, *Memoranda of Industrial Relations*, "Memorandum: Labor Turnover," pp. 2–3.

37 On the mechanization of Chicago's mass production plants during the 1920s, see Harold Platt, "City Lights: The Electrification of Chicago, 1880–1930," Lecture to Chicago Urban History Seminar, Chicago Historical Society, 15 March 1984; "Productivity of Labor in Slaughtering and Meat Packing and in Petroleum Refining," *Monthly Labor Review* 23 (November 1926): 30–4; Fogel, *Negro in Meat Industry*, p. 45; "Significant Events in History of South Works," (mimeo), SECHP; McIntyre, "History of Wisconsin Steel Works," pp. 41–2; Reitell, "Machinery and Its Effect upon the Workers"; "Memorandum on Condition of Labor in the Iron and Steel Industry in the United States," NRA, Consolidated Approved Code Iron and Steel, Files 16 – Labor, p. 1; William T. Hogan, S. J., *Economic History of the Iron and Steel Industry in the United States*, vol. 3 (Lexington, MA: Lexington Books, 1971); Davis, *Condition of Labor in American Iron and Steel*, pp. 116–23; Irving S. Olds, *Half a Century of United States Steel: An Address at New York on Occasion of U.S. Steel Corporation's 50th Anniversary* (New York: Newcomen Society in North America, 1951), pp. 11–12.

38 *South Works Review*, 2 January 1920; *The Magnet*, June 1920, August 1920, September 1920.

39 Employers claimed that they respected seniority during the 1920s. During the brief recession of 1927, 40 percent of the firms surveyed by the Special Conference Committee reported that seniority had been the primary factor in determining layoffs. Jacoby, "Development of Internal Labor Markets," p. 54. In 1924, Swift & Company began a program of departmental and divisional seniority, which ensured employees with five years of service that they could not be laid off without a supervisor making every effort to find them another job. Purcell, *Worker Speaks His Mind*, p. 304. Western Electric developed an elaborate system of service awards to celebrate milestones in employee seniority: a certificate at the end of two years, a 10-karat gold lapel pin at the end of ten years and thereafter every five years, a luncheon for completing 25 years and each 5 years after that, and a 14-karat gold and diamond-inset pin to men after 45 and 50 years and women after 40, 45, and 50 years. "Recognition of Service Anniversaries in the Western Electric Co.," WE, History of Personnel Practices, HC-121.

40 McIntyre, "History of Wisconsin Steel Works," p. 40. See Swift & Company, *Yearbook of 1922, Covering Activities for the Year 1921* (Chicago: Swift & Company, 1922), p. 49, for a similar statement.

For more details on how various employee representation plans worked, the history of how they were implemented – particularly in Chicago plants – and estimates of the number of workers covered, see Swift & Company, *Yearbook of 1922*, pp. 8, 49–50; James R. Barrett, *Work and Community in the Jungle: Chicago's Packinghouse Workers, 1894–1922* (Urbana: University of Illinois Press, 1987), pp. 248–54; "Harvester Industrial Council, Report of an Inquiry Conducted under the Direction of the Special Conference Committee," 10 August 1928, IH, Document file 213-B; Ozanne, *Century of Labor–Management Relations*, pp. 116–43;

Bureau of Labor Statistics, U.S. Department of Labor, *Characteristics of Company Unions, 1935*, Bulletin no. 634 (Washington, DC: U.S. Government Printing Office, 1938), pp. 1–26; Daniel Nelson, "The Company Union Movement, 1900–1937: A Reexamination," *Business History Review* 56 (Autumn 1982): 335–57; Brandes, *American Welfare Capitalism*, pp. 119–34; Bernstein, *Lean Years*, pp. 157, 160–72.

41 Harold F. McCormick to Cyrus Hall McCormick, Memorandum, 7 May 1919, McCormick Papers – H. F. McCormick, Box 38, SHSW, copy in IH, Document file 19754.

42 On the way that works councils cooperated with companies to lower wages, dismiss strikers, and the like as well as for details on the kinds of issues that councils handled during the 1920s, see "High Points in Armour & Company," *Armour Magazine* 16 (April 1927): 8; W. F. McClennan of Armour & Company, Chicago, "Employees' Representation With Reference to Safety," *Monthly Labor Review* 15 (November 1922): 22–5; Swift & Company, *Yearbook of 1922*, p. 8; James Rogers Holcomb, "The Union Policies of Meat Packers, 1929–1943" (M.A. thesis, University of Illinois, 1957), p. 29; McIntyre, "History of Wisconsin Steel Works," p. 41; Nelson, "Study of Isolated Industrial Community," pp. 63–4; Wisconsin Steel Works Council, *Harvester Industrial Council Minutes of Regular Meetings* (published monthly and bound by years), IH, Document file 5495; McCormick Works Council, *Harvester Industrial Council Minutes of Regular Meetings* (published monthly and bound by years), IH, Document file 18322; International Harvester companywide and in-plant newspapers: *Harvester World, Tractor Interester, The Magnet.*

43 Swift & Company, *Yearbook of 1923,* p. 46.

44 Nelson, "Study of Isolated Industrial Community," p. 300. Edwards, *Contested Terrain*, p. 109, also notes how employee representation individualized workers' grievances and kept foremen under control.

45 Swift & Company, *Yearbook of 1925, Covering Activities for the Year 1924* (Chicago: Swift & Company, 1925), p. 51. For details on the kinds of cases brought before the assembly, see Swift & Company, *Yearbook of 1922*, p. 51; Swift & Company, *Yearbook of 1923,* p. 45; Swift & Company, *Yearbook of 1924, Covering Activities for the year 1923* (Chicago: Swift & Company, 1924), p. 51.

46 F. W. Willard, "Basic principles and Trends in Personnel Administration," 1928, WE, HC-121.

47 On Hawthorne's employee interview program, see Roethlisberger and Dickson, *Management and the Worker*, pp. 190–205, 270–91; F. J. Roethlisberger, *The Elusive Phenomenon: An Autobiographical Account of My Work in the Field of Organization Behavior at the Harvard Business School* (Boston: Graduate School of Business Administration, Harvard University, 1977), p. 47; D. D. Davisson, Chief of Personnel Counseling Section, Western Electric Company, Chicago, "Western Electric's Experimental Interviewing Program, 1928–40," WC, Box 75, Folder "Unemployment 1921–28"; and the remarkable raw data from the interviewing program, including administrative memos and interview transcripts, which

have been put on microfiche (along with other data from the Hawthorne studies) and can be consulted at the Baker Library, Harvard Business School, and at Regenstein Library, University of Chicago, Microfilm Reading Room.

48 On company pension programs, see Swift & Company, *Yearbook of 1920*; Hawthorne Works, "Good Place to Work"; R. E. McEwen, "The Why of Our Benefit Plan," 1927, WE, HC-121, p. 7; O. C. Richter, "Bell System Employee Security Plans," 31 July 1935, WE, HC-121, pp. 5–6; *South Works Review*, February–March 1922; Jack M. Stein, "A History of Unionization in the Steel Industry in the Chicago Area" (M.A. thesis, University of Chicago, 1948), p. 38; *Harvester World* twentieth anniversary issue (paste-up, may never have been printed), September–October 1922, IH, Document file 3212, p. 15; Mary Conyngton, "Industrial Pensions for Old Age and Disability," *Monthly Labor Review* 22 (January 1926): 21–45; Brandes, *American Welfare Capitalism*, pp. 103–10; National Industrial Conference Board, (NICB) *Industrial Pensions in the United States* (New York: NICB, 1925); Murray Webb Latimer, *Industrial Pension Systems in the United States and Canada*, vols. 1 and 2 (New York: Industrial Relations Counselors, 1932).

49 On mutual benefit programs, see almost every issue of *Hawthorne Microphone, South Works Review*, and *Harvester World*; Hawthorne Works, "A Good Place to Work," p. 6; P. W. Willard, "Basic Principles and Trends in Personnel Administration," 1928, WE, HC-121, p. 7; R. E. McEwen, "The Why of Our Benefit Plan," 1927, WE, HC-121, p. 7; O. C. Richter, "Bell System Employee Security Plans," 31 July 1935, WE, HC-121, p. 4; Nelson, "Study of an Isolated Industrial Community," p. 43; Meyer Bloomfield, "A Way to Greater Employe Efficiency: Find Employe Mutual Benefit Associations, to Be Effective in Strengthening Industrial Relations," *Chicago Commerce* 25 (3 November 1928): 11, 29; "Establishment Funds for the Benefit of Disabled Workers," *Monthly Labor Review* 25 (July 1927): 20–6; Robert W. Dunn, *The Americanization of Labor: The Employers' Offensive against the Trade Unions* (New York: International Publishers, 1927), pp. 243–7; National Industrial Conference Board (NICB), *The Present Status of Mutual Benefit Associations* (New York: NICB, 1931); Princeton University, *Memoranda of Industrial Relations*, "Memorandum: Mutual Benefit Associations," p. 15; Brandes, *American Welfare Capitalism*, pp. 92–102.

50 When International Harvester finally decided to grant its shop workers paid vacations in 1929, it joined ranks with Western Electric, the Chicago area's pioneer in this area, and Armour and Swift. See "Harvester Vacation Plan for Hourly-Paid Employes, Piece-Workers, and Employes Working on a Similar Basis," 1 January 1929, IH, Document file 13140. File 13140 contains a wealth of material documenting International Harvester's decision-making process on the vacation issue beginning in 1919, including surveys of the vacation policies of other employers in Chicago, the nation, and even western Europe.

For additional material on paid vacations, Hawthorne, "Good Place to

Work"; *Hawthorne Microphone*, 25 February 1929, 12 July 1929; *Illinois Manufacturers' Costs Association Monthly Bulletin* no. 82 (12 September 1929): p. 2; Industrial Relations Association of America, "Vacations: A Summary," n.d., IH, Document file 13140; "Vacations with Pay for Wage Earners," *Monthly Labor Review* 22 (May 1926): 1–7; "Vacations with Pay for Industrial Workers," *Monthly Labor Review* 25 (September 1927): 49; "Wage Earners' Vacations," *Monthly Labor Review* 25 (December 1927): 63.

51 *The Magnet*, September 1920, back cover.

52 Quoted in Brandes, *American Welfare Capitalism*, p. 86.

53 Swift & Company, *Yearbook of 1924*, p. 20.

54 *Hawthorne Microphone*, 25 April 1927. On stock ownership plans, see in IH: Howard McCormick to Cyrus McCormick, 17 March 1919, Document file 19755; Cyrus McCormick, "Notes of Division Managers and Other Meetings," 14 June 1920, Document file 17587; "International Harvester Company Profit-Sharing Plan," 2 January 1920, Document file 18235; Cyrus McCormick, "Special Notes," 26 June 1923, Document file 17587; "Thoughts on the Stock Plan," Cyrus McCormick memo, 29 October 1929, and G. A. Ranney response, "More Thoughts on the Stock Plan," 1 November 1929, Document file 19178; C. E. Jarchow and W. R. Odell, Jr., "Investigation of Employe Security Plans: General Electric Company, American Telephone & Telegraph Company, United States Steel Company, Standard Oil Co. of New Jersey," 26 February 1930, Document file 19178; "Recommendations: Security Plan for Harvester Employes," 28 February 1930, Document file 19178; "Stock Ownership and Savings Plan of 1930 for Employees of International Harvester Company, Effective May 1, 1930, Questions and Answers," 1 May 1930, Document file 19178; "History of International Harvester Company Employee Benefit Plans," n.d. but after 1940, Document file 15246.

Also, many articles in *Western Electric News, Hawthorne Microphone, South Works Review*, 1922–9; Leroy Dean Stinebower, "Employee Stock Ownership in Chicago" (M.A. thesis, University of Chicago, 1927), pp. 24–5, 27, 29–30; Kelly, "History of the Illinois Manufacturers' Association," p. 181; Swift & Company, *Yearbooks of 1918, 1919, 1921, 1922, 1923, 1930, Covering Activities for the Years 1917, 1918, 1920, 1921, 1922, 1929* (Chicago: Swift & Company, 1918, 1919, 1921–3, 1930); Armour and Company, *Annual Report for 1923*, 1 March 1924; Hawthorne, "Good Place to Work"; "Stock Ownership in Twenty Important Companies," *Monthly Labor Review* 24 (January 1927): 55–6; "Employee Stock Ownership," *Monthly Labor Review* 27 (August 1928): 99–103; "Essay on Lifting Up a Man's Chin," in True Story Magazine, *The American Economic Evolution* (New York: True Story Magazine, 1930), pp. 15–19; Slichter, "Current Labor Policies," p. 408; Dunn, *Americanization of Labor*, pp. 147–68; Brandes, *American Welfare Capitalism*, pp. 83–91.

55 Ozanne, *Century of Labor–Management Relations*, pp. 176–7. A fascinat-

ing series of letters between Harold McCormick and Alex Legge, Cyrus McCormick, and E. S. Simpson, expressing the latters' displeasure at some prolabor comments that Harold made, reveal how paranoid Harvester executives still felt in 1928. Alex Legge to Harold F. McCormick, 27 February 1928; Cyrus McCormick to Harold McCormick, 27 February 1928; Harold F. McCormick to Alex Legge, 2 March 1928; E. S. Simpson to Harold F. McCormick, 28 March 1928; IH, Document file 19753, originals in McCormick Papers, SHSW.

56 "Committee on Vacation" to A. L. Owen, Superintendent, McCormick Twine Mill, 28 February 1920, IH, Document file 13140; *Illinois Manufacturers' Association, Labor Review* no. 11 (July 1923): 1; Minutes of discussion "Vacations with Pay for Hourly Paid Employes," 28 September 1927, IH, Document file 13140.

57 Taylor, *Mexican Labor in Chicago*, p. 121.

58 On Hawthorne's Building and Loan Association, see Hawthorne, "Good Place to Work"; *Hawthorne Microphone*, 24 February 1922, 7 April 1922, 2 June 1922, 10 November 1922, 16 February 1923, 9 November 1923, 15 February 1924, 7 November 1924, 31 January 1927, 28 February 1927, 28 March 1927, 7 November 1927; *Western Electric News*, January 1921, June 1923.

Chicago employers liked the idea of workers owning their own homes for the way it stabilized the work force. They all featured photographs of workers' homes in company magazines and congratulated homeowners for their thrift and diligence. *Chicago Commerce* frequently discussed how to encourage the city's workers to become homeowners. See, e.g., "Build Homes to Make Good Citizens," 16 (2 August 1919); "Own Your Own Home Show to Open Next Week: President Coolidge and Secretary Hoover Are among Those Who Back Movement to Encourage Building of Small Residences," 21 (15 March 1924); "Rapid Advance Made in Home Building," 23 (14 August 1926).

On group insurance plans, see *Hawthorne Microphone*, 26 March 1928, 14 January 1929, 23 September 1929; Swift & Company, *Yearbook of 1927, Covering Activities for the Year 1926* (Chicago: Swift & Company, 1927); Discussion of "life insurance" in materials on history of personnel practices, WE, HC-121; *South Works Review*, September 1926, November 1926, January 1927, April 1927, August 1927, December 1927, November 1929, September 1930; Advertisement by Charles V. Jewell, "Mr. Employer! Reduce Labor Turnover – Stimulate Efficiency – Create Good Will – with Group Insurance," *Chicago Commerce* 17 (11 December 1920): 34; Advertisement by Marsh & McLennan, "Employees' Group Insurance: We Will Gladly Counsel with You in All Matters Pertaining to Group Life, Weekly Disability, Salary Allotment Insurance and Pensions," *Chicago Commerce* 25 (30 June 1928), inside cover; Sections on group insurance in State of Illinois, *Annual Insurance Reports of the Department of Trade and Commerce, Division of Insurance* (Springfield: State of Illinois, 1919–29); Report of the *Health Insurance Commission of the State of Illinois* (Springfield: State of Illinois, May 1, 1919), pp. 135–40, 498–521, 532–49, 640–1; William J. Graham, "Group Life Insurance," *Annals of American Academy of Political and Social Science* 130 (March 1927): 27–33; Harry Alvin Millis, *Sickness and Insurance: A Study of the Sickness Problem and Health Insurance* (Chicago: University of Chicago Press, 1937), pp. 25–7; Princeton University, *Memoranda of Industrial Relations*, "Memorandum: Group Insurance"; "Workmen's Compensation and Social Insurance: Experience with Group Life Insurance in the Metal Trades," *Monthly Labor Review* 23 (July 1926): 64–6; "Workmen's Compensation and Social Insurance: A Survey of Industrial Group Insurance," *Monthly Labor Review* 25 (September 1927): 84–5; National Industrial Conference Board (NICB) *Industrial Group Insurance* (New York: NICB, 1927); National Industrial Conference Board (NICB), *Recent Developments in Industrial Group Insurance* (New York: NICB, 1934); Brandes, *American Welfare Capitalism*, pp. 97–8.

59 *Harvester World*, February 1920.

60 Princeton University, *Memoranda of Industrial Relations*, "Memorandum: Group Insurance," p. 13.

61 "Ball League Will Be Perfected Tuesday: Great Meeting of Teams and Players in Every Line of Industry Will Convene at the Morrison Hotel," *Chicago Commerce* 16 (31 January 1920); also see "Baseball League Starts with a Rush, 40 Teams Join at Meeting," *Chicago Commerce* 17 (7 February 1920).

Employers also promoted athletics to keep their work forces healthy. Not only would healthy workers attend work more regularly and produce more effectively, they felt, but also the costs of sick benefits would decline. Gulick, *Labor Policy of the United States Steel Corporation*, p. 174, cited in Dunn, *Americanization of Labor*, p. 224.

For more on employers' use of sports, consult almost every issue of *Hawthorne Microphone, Western Electric News, South Works Review,* and *Harvester World*; Hawthorne, "Good Place to Work"; Wisconsin Steel Works Council, *Minutes of Regular Meetings* for 8 January 1929, 2 April 1929, 10 September 1929; McIntyre, "History Wisconsin Steel," p. 46; Adams, *Humanizing a Great Industry;* Dunn, *Americanization of Labor*, pp. 223–4; Bureau of Labor Statistics, U.S. Department of Labor, *Health and Recreation Activities in Industrial Establishments, 1926*, Bulletin no. 458 (Washington, DC: U.S. Government Printing Office, 1928); "Outdoor Recreation for Industrial Employees," *Monthly Labor Review* 24 (May 1927): 1–16; "Indoor Recreation for Industrial Employees," *Monthly Labor Review* 25 (September 1927): 1–14.

62 On radio at Hawthorne, see *Hawthorne Microphone*, 10 March 1922, 18 August 1922, 1 September 1922, 13 November 1922, 2 February 1923, 14 September 1923, 1 February 1924, 23 May 1924, 29 August 1924, 3 March 1927, 29 December 1927, 7 May 1928; *Western Electric News*, May 1922; Kelly, "History of Illinois Manufacturers' Association," p. 180; *Illinois Manufacturers' Association Labor Review* no. 21 (October 1924): 1.

63 For motion pictures at Hawthorne, see *Hawthorne Microphone*, 24 October 1927, 16 January 1928, 14 January 1929, 10 March 1930; Gerald Mast, ed., *The Movies in Our Midst* (Chicago: University of Chicago, 1982), p. 246. On interest in motion pictures by other employers, see Lois Kate Halley, "A Study of Motion Pictures in Chicago as a Medium of Communication" (M.A. thesis, University of Chicago, 1924), pp. 87–90.

One employer told a Bureau of Labor Statistics investigator that "we have them [movies] everyday at noon hour. They are remarkably successful. There is something about the movies that the employees can't resist. Even if they think that you are trying to put something over on them, they come in anyway. In this way, we fill up the employees' time during the noon hour and keep them from getting together in little groups and talking about their troubles." Bureau of Labor Statistics, *Health and Recreation*, p. 41.

64 Dances are mentioned in almost every issue of the *Hawthorne Microphone*; see also Constance Weinberger and S. D. Alinsky, "The Public Dance Hall," 1928, BUR, Box 126, Folder 10, Harmon's Dreamland poster.

65 At least an issue a month of the *Hawthorne Microphone* discussed the items for sale in the Hawthorne store, the volume of sales, and stores that would sell to employees at a discount with a special identification card. See also Hawthorne, "Good Place to Work"; "Employees' Cooperative Buying," *Monthly Labor Review* 19 (December 1924): 162–4.

66 *Hawthorne Microphone*, 9 May 1927.

67 F. W. Willard, "Basic Principles and Trends in Personnel Administration," 1928, WE, HC-121, p. 12.

68 "Introduce Music in Chicago Industries: Western Electric Company and Other Plants Provide for Workers' Recreation," *New York City Musical America*, 24 April 1920, WC; *Hawthorne Microphone*, 27 January 1922.

69 "First Bowling Tournament Gets a Flying Start," *Chicago Commerce* 18 (14 May 1921). In the late 1920s, employers were still promoting bowling for the same ends. "There is not another recreation or sport of any kind that approaches the cosmopolitanism with the social leveling of good-fellowship qualities as does bowling. Large corporations have adopted the game as a welfare unit and appropriate large sums annually for conducting leagues." "Good Will That Pays Its Own Way: American Bowling Congress Will Attract 50,000 Visitors – Entries Close February 1," *Chicago Commerce* 25 (26 January 1929): 36. For discussion of the integrative benefits of bowling at the Hawthorne Works, see Roethlisberger and Dickson, *Management and the Worker*, p. 541.

70 On company magazines, see *Harvester World*, May 1021; *South Works Review*, July 1924; Advertisement by Inter Ocean Bureau, Publicity Engineers, "The Age of House Organs," in *Chicago Commerce* 17 (12 June 1920): 11; National Industrial Conference Board (NICB), *Employee Magazines in the United States* (New York: NICB, 1925); a series of articles by Henry Boyd McKelvey in *Judicious Advertising*: "Uses of the House Organ," 21 (October 1923): 19–22; "A Study of House Organs," 21

(November 1923): 64–7; "Successful House Organs," 21 (December 1923): 30–6; Dunn, *Americanization of Labor*, pp. 247–51; Brandes, *American Welfare Capitalism*, pp. 62–5.

71 NICB, *Industrial Relations*, pp. 17–18; Conger Reynolds, "Industry and the Public: How Big Business Bids for Popular Favor," *Chicago Commerce* 27 (16 August 1930): 9–10; "1919 Contributions to Advertising," Editorial, *Judicious Advertising* 17 (December 1919): 23–4; "Armour's New Campaign Sells an Industry: To Win Public's Good Will for the Entire Packing Business, National Campaign Is Launched. Company's Products Are Not Featured," *Judicious Advertising* 22 (April 1924): 13–16; "Why Swift & Company Use Two Types of Advertising: Results from an Institutional Campaign to Combat Prejudice and from Copy That Sold Company's Products," *Judicious Advertising* 22 (May 1924): 79–85.

72 "Y.M.C.A. Stimulates Morale of Workers," *Chicago Commerce* 21 (5 July 1924): 15; Interview with George Patterson, December 1970, ROHP, p. 17; Ozanne, *Century of Labor–Management Relations*, p. 132; *South Works Review*, February 1919, August–September 1921, December 1924, October 1925, December 1925, December 1926, October 1929; in SECHP: "History of the South Chicago Department YMCA, 1882–1934" (mimeo); "Tenth Anniversary South Chicago YMCA, 1920–1936," 12 November 1936; "South Chicago Dept. YMCA Silver Anniversary, 1926–1951," 7 November 1951; "Golden Anniversary Dinner, 1926–1976: South Chicago YMCA," 17 November 1976. For industry–YMCA connections in another part of town, see "A Study of Association House, Chicago, Illinois Made by the Chicago Council of Social Agencies," 1922, WC, Box 249, Folder "Association House 1922–66," pp. 49–51.

73 On employers' contributions to local churches, see "Report on South Chicago Area Project," n.d., CAP, Box 36, Folder 3, "Chapter 3: The Community Organizes," p. 19; Eunice Felter, "The Social Adaptations of the Mexican Churches in the Chicago Area" (M.A. thesis, University of Chicago, 1941), p. 36; McIntyre, "History of Wisconsin Steel Works," p. 30; Dominic Pacyga, "Story of Wisconsin Steel Is Story of U.S. Industry," *Daily Calumet*, 3 December 1982; Fogel, *Negro in the Meat Industry*, p. 35.

74 Taylor, *Mexican Labor in Chicago*, p. 93.

75 Interview with George Patterson, December 1970, ROHP, pp. 18–19.

76 On company activities in various communities, see "Community Service Urged as a Remedy for Unrest – Marshall Field III Makes Plea," *Chicago Commerce* 17 (29 May 1920): 18; Judge Elbert Gary, Speech to presidents of subsidiary companies of U.S. Steel in Marshall Olds, *Analysis of the Interchurch World Movement Report on the Steel Strike* (New York: G. P. Putnam, 1923), quoted in William Kornblum, *Blue Collar Community* (Chicago: University of Chicago Press, 1974), pp. 94–5; "Bulletin of the South Chicago Neighborhood House," 1939, SECHP; Jean C. Rosenbluth, "An Attempt to Study Child Life at the Russell Square Field House," Paper for Sociology 270, n.d., BUR, Box 148, Folder 2, pp. 6–7; "Boy Scouts,"

The Magnet, September 1920; "Boy Scouts," *South Works Review*, July 1925; McIntyre, "History of Wisconsin Steel Works," pp. 45–6; Matthew C. Wagner, "The Community Council of the Stockyards District of Chicago," 1935, WC, Box 296, Folder "Community Council of Stockyards District, 1936–44," pp. 9–10; Interview with Nick Zaranti, Chicago Heights, IL, 5 March 1980, IC, p. 3.

77 Swift & Company, *Yearbook of 1919*, pp. 30, 37; Swift & Company, *Yearbook of 1921*, p. 13; Swift & Company, *Yearbook of 1922*, p. 7; Swift & Company, *Yearbook of 1924*, pp. 7, 48; Swift & Company, *Yearbook of 1926, Covering Activities for the Year 1925* (Chicago: Swift & Company, 1926), pp. 8, 47; Swift & Company, *Yearbook of 1927*, p. 7; *Harvester World*, August 1923, September–October 1923, May 1925; William T. Moye, "The End of the 12-Hour Day in the Steel Industry: Fifty-four Years Ago, After Pressure by the Harding Administration, the Steel Industry Finally Agreed to Reduce the Workday in the Mills," *Monthly Labor Review* 100 (September 1977): 21–6; Bate, "Development of Iron and Steel Industry," pp. 138–9.

78 "Business Tends toward Self-Government: Secretary Hoover Addresses National Chamber on Signs of Capacity of Commerce and Industry to Correct Own Abuses," *Chicago Commerce* 21 (10 May 1924): 19–20.

79 William Chenery, "Unemployment at Washington," *Survey* (8 October 1921): 42, quoted in Skocpol and Ikenberry, "The Political Formation of the American Welfare State in Historical and Comparative Perspective," pp. 50–1; Materials on depression 1921–2, WC, Box 75, Folder "Employment 1921–8"; Philip Klein, *The Burden of Unemployment: A Study of Unemployment Relief Measures in Fifteen American Cities, 1921–22* (New York: Russell Sage Foundation, 1923), pp. 63–70, 144–5, 225–7; and many articles from *Chicago Commerce*, including: "Civic Cooperation for Public Works," 16 (13 February 1919): 7; "Unemployment: Returns on an Association Survey of Chicago Conditions," 16 (13 February 1919): 22; "This Is the Public Welfare Department Which Is in Close Touch with Chicago Charities," 17 (1 January 1921): 16.

80 *Greater Chicago: Official Bulletin of the Chicago Booster's Publicity Club* 1 (July 1921, Special Pageant of Progress Issue; August–September 1921), 2 (March–April 1922); "How Chicago Stimulates Business: The Pageant of Progress Exposition: Its Inception, Organization and Purpose," *Judicious Advertising* 19 (August 1921): 23–5; Perry R. Duis and Glen Holt, "Big Bill's Pageant of Progress," *Chicago Magazine*, September 1980; and *Chicago Commerce*, February 1921 to April 1922, *passim.*

81 Clifford W. Barnes, "Subscriptions Investigating," *Chicago Commerce* 26 (19 January 1929): 45; "Charity Endowment by Community Trust," *Chicago Commerce* 27 (26 July 1930): 53; Frank Denman Loomis, *The Chicago Community Trust: A History of Its Development, 1915–62* (Chicago: Chicago Community Trust, n.d.), pp. 13–16; Gudron Rom, "Centennial History of the United Charities," 1936, UNCH, Box 17, Folder 2, p. 275; "Memorandum of Informal Conference Called by Direc-

tor of the Chicago Council of Social Agencies at the Request of Representatives of Organizations Concerned with Employment of Men and Women in Chicago," 18 June 1924, WC, Box 75, Folder "Unemployment 1921–1928."

82 Alfred H. Kelly, *A History of Illinois Manufacturers' Association* (part of dissertation) (Chicago: University of Chicago Libraries, 1940), pp. 12–22; "Addresses Delivered before the Employers' Association of Chicago," 24 October 1923; National Conference on Mutual Benefit Associations," *Monthly Labor Review* 27 (December 1928): 104–5; A. Epstein, "Present Status of Old-Age Pension Legislation in the United States," *Monthly Labor Review* 19 (October 1924): 26–33; Edwin Amenta, Elisabeth Clemens, Jefren Olsen, Sunita Parikh, and Theda Skocpol, "From Workers' Compensation to Unemployment Insurance: A Comparison of Four States of the United States, 1910–1937," Unpublished paper, University of Chicago, February 1985, pp. 16–17, on the ineffectiveness of Illinois's Industrial Board, charged with administering the Illinois Workmen's Compensation law.

83 P. W. Willard, "Basic Principles and Trends in Personnel Administration," 1928, WE, HE-121, p. 12. See also NICB, *Industrial Relations*, pp. 21–2.

84 Slichter, "Current Labor Policies," pp. 433–4.

85 Interview with Dan Delluch, Arthur O'Leary, Dr. Romeo Pallutto, and Alexander Savastano on life in South Deering, by Jim Martin and Dominic Pacyga, Chicago, IL, n.d., SECHP, p. 6.

86 Swift & Company, *Yearbook of 1925*, p. 52; Swift & Company, *Yearbook of 1927*, pp. 13, 54; Swift & Company, *Yearbook of 1928, Covering Activities for the Year 1927* (Chicago: Swift & Company, 1928), pp. 50–1; Swift & Company, *Yearbook of 1931, Covering Activities for the Year 1930* (Chicago: Swift & Company, 1931), p. 55. International Harvester had a similarly high rate of membership in its Employes' Benefit Association, 83 percent of all employees in the manufacturing department. *The Harvester World: Twentieth Anniversary Issue*, September–October 1922, paste-up, IH, p. 15.

87 See *Hawthorne Microphone, passim*, for rising attendance figures at Hawthorne Evening School and growing participation in Hawthorne Building and Loan Association. Also, in HSMF: Interview with Male from Inspection Branch, 22 November 1929, Fiche no. 109; Interview with Male from Technical Branch, 22 August 1930, Fiche no. 184.

88 Swift & Company, "Swift & Company and the American Meat Industry," 1932, p. 30; Swift & Company, *Yearbook of 1922*, p. 4; Swift & Company, *Yearbook of 1924*, p. 22; Swift & Company, *Yearbook of 1925*, p. 34; Swift & Company, *Yearbook of 1927*, p. 5; Swift & Company, *Yearbook of 1929, Covering Activities for the Year 1928* (Chicago: Swift & Company, 1929), p. 56; Swift & Company, *Yearbook of 1931*, p. 55; Dunn, *Americanization of Labor*, p. 153. Armour and Company claimed in its 1926 annual report that a majority of its 60,000 employees owned stock in the company.

89 Interview with George Patterson, December 1970, ROHP, p. 5; on em-

ployee stock ownership at U.S. Steel also see C. E. Jarchow and W. R. Odell, Jr., "Investigation of Employe Security Plans," 26 February 1930, IH, Document file 19178, "Exhibit E: Outline of Stock Plan, United States Steel Corporation," p. 2; *South Works Review*, January 1919, January 1923.

90 Nelson, "Study of an Isolated Industrial Community," p. 70; also pp. 105, 108, 111, for workers' testimony about buying stock. For more on stock ownership among Harvester workers see Interview with Augie Ruf by Dominic Pacyga, Chicago, IL, 8 April 1982, SECHP, p. 8; Cyrus McCormick, Jr., "Employee Representation as Affecting the Attitude of Labor and Business," Address before the American Management Association, Kansas City, MO, 30 November 1925, IH, Document file 16756, pp. 14–20; McCormick Works Council, *Harvester Industrial Council Minutes of Regular Meetings*, IH, Document file 18322, 11 May 1928, p. 8; and from IH, Document file 19178: "Stock Ownership and Saving Plan of 1930: Analysis of Monthly Payments," "Stock Ownership and Savings Plan of 1930: Analysis Showing Denominations of Subscriptions," "Stock Ownership and Savings Plan of 1930: Subscriptions Approved to June 6, 1930"; Dunn, *Americanization of Labor*, p. 153.

91 "The Woman Pays – and Finds It Pays," *Western Electric News*, July 1928; "Western Electric Reports for Year," *Chicago Commerce* 25 (7 April 1928): 18; *Western Electric News*, May 1928; from HSMF: Interview with Male from Technical Branch, 19 June 1930, Fiche no. 186; Interview with Male from Operating Branch, 19 April 1929, Fiche no. 104; Interview with Female from Technical Branch, 11 November 1930, Fiche no. 184; and Interview with Male from Inspection Branch, 7 January 1929, Fiche no. 109.

92 Historians differ on the issue of whether or not welfare capitalism worked. Two opposing positions have been staked out. One, by Stuart Brandes and more recently, Richard Edwards, argues that welfare capitalism failed to win the support of workers. The other view, that workers endorsed welfare capitalism and benefited from it, has been suggested in a speculative essay by David Brody. Brody argues that the depression, and not flaws in welfare capitalism, doomed it. The work of Gerald Zahavi on the shoeworkers of Endicott Johnson argues for a more intermediate position, that management and labor worked out a compact where workers remained loyal but helped negotiate the terms. Brandes, *American Welfare Capitalism*, pp. 136–41; Edwards, *Contested Terrain*, pp. 95–7; Brody, "The Rise and Decline of Welfare Capitalism," in *Workers in Industrial America*, pp. 48–81; Gerald Zahavi, "Negotiated Loyalty: Welfare Capitalism and the Shoeworkers of Endicott Johnson, 1920–1940," *Journal of American History* 70 (December 1983): 602–20.

93 Nelson, "Study of an Isolated Industrial Community," p. 109. At a September 1929 works council meeting at Wisconsin Steel, a manager routinely reported, "Last month, in No. 2 and No. 5 Mills, we had to go ahead and hire a lot of new men and when we got through with the work,

we had to release them." Wisconsin Steel Works, *Harvester Industrial Council Minutes of Regular Meetings*, IH, Document file 5495, 10 September 1929, p. 22. See also Jacoby, "Development of Internal Labor Markets," p. 43; Frank Stricker, "Affluence for Whom? – Another Look at Prosperity and the Working Classes in the 1920's," *Labor History* 24 (Winter 1983): 17–20; "Unemployment Seasonal and Otherwise," *Chicago Commerce* 21 (4 October 1924): 30; "Reviewers Are Optimistic for Present and Future as Unemployment Decreases," *Chicago Commerce* 25 (7 April 1928):12; "Chicago Has 200,000 Unemployed," *Dziennik Zjednoczenia*, 15 March 1928, CFLPS, Box 33; Illinois Department of Labor, *Annual Reports* for the 1920s, employment data by industries and by years.

A particular kind of unemployment that attracted a lot of attention during the 1920s was called "technological unemployment." New machinery and organizational approaches were blamed for increasing the productivity of some workers while decreasing industry's need for others. Despite the creation of some new work as a result of technological advances, workers who lost their jobs this way found it hard to recover. A study in 1928 by the Institute of Economics of the Brookings Institute substantiated that displaced workers had trouble relocating: Nearly half who got new jobs had been unemployed more than six months, and some were still looking after a year. Even then, the dispossessed frequently took new jobs at a sacrifice in income. "Labor Absorbing Power of American Industry," *Monthly Labor Review* 28 (June 1929): 222–4.

For contemporary discussion of "technological unemployment," see in the *Monthly Labor Review*: James J. Davis, "Efficiency and Wages in the United States," 20 (May 1925): 2–5; James J. Davis, "The Problem of the Worker Displaced by Machinery," 25 (September 1927): 32–5; "Trade Union Press on Displacement of Labor by Machinery," 27 (May 1928): 36–41; and James J. Davis, "'Old Age' at Fifty," 27 (June 1928): 1–6; "History of Benefit Plan," n.d., WE, HC-121, p. 6; from *Chicago Commerce*: "Industrial Standardization Growth: Private Interests and Government Working toward Lower Costs to Public by Making Mass Production Possible," 23 (28 August 1926): 17; "Factors in Profitable Prosperity: Find Rapid Growth of New and Old Industries Offsets Elmination of Workers by Machines," 25 (7 April 1928): 7; "The Educational Influence of Power: Walter Dill Scott Tells How Machines Are Bettering the American Standard of Living," 25 (26 May 1928): 13; and "Machine Age Men and Their Life's Compensations," 27 (12 April 1930): 11; "Speech of a Prominant Economist," *Dziennik Zjednoczenia*, 1 October 1928, CFLPS, Box 33; Harry A. Millis and Royal A. Montgomery, *Labor's Risks and Social Insurance* (New York: McGraw-Hill Book Company, 1938), pp. 27–39; President's Research Committee, *Recent Social Trends in the United States* (New York: McGraw-Hill Book Company, 1933; reprint ed. Westport, CT: Greenwood Press, 1970), vol. 1, pp. 310–11, vol. 2, pp. 806–8.

94 Davis, *Condition of Labor in American Iron and Steel Industry*, pp. 91–8.

95 Purcell, *Worker Speaks His Mind*, p. 54; see also Women's Bureau, *Women in Slaughtering*, p. 85; and Leslie F. Orear and Stephen H. Diamond, *Out of the Jungle: The Packinghouse Workers Fight for Justice and Equality* (Chicago: Hyde Park Press, 1968), quote from worker: "Sixty days laid off and your service was broken. . . . Then you started in again as a new employee. That's why people hardly ever got their week's vacation."

96 On seasonal unemployment in general, see Jacoby, "Origins of Internal Labor Markets," pp. 521–4; "Stability of Employment in the Iron and Steel Industry," *Monthly Labor Review* 27 (November 1928): 1–3; and from *Chicago Commerce*: "General Business – A Weekly Analysis," 21 (17 May 1924): 36; "What Does Hand-to-Mouth Buying Mean? Does the New Purchasing Practice Tend to Equalize the Flow of Goods and Stabilize Both Production and Distribution?" 23 (27 November 1926): 13; "Show Favorable Employment Factors: Survey Shows New Industries Absorbing Men Otherwise Unemployed through Seasonal Drop," 25 (10 March 1928): 9.

On seasonal unemployment in packing, see Purcell, *Worker Speaks His Mind*, p. 22; Women's Bureau, *Women in Slaughtering*, pp. 86–7. International Harvester's seasonal problems were compounded by the depression in agriculture, which kept farmers from purchasing new equipment. *Harvester World*, May 1922, December 1922, April 1923, January 1928, May 1928; "Memorandum of Informal Conference, 18 June 1924," WC, Box 75, Folder "Unemployment 1921–28," p. 3, International Harvester testimony.

97 Herbst, *Negro in Slaughtering and Meat-packing*, p. 99. A study by Simon S. Kuznets, *Seasonal Variations in Industry and Trade* (New York: National Bureau of Economic Research, 1932), argued that seasonal instability had increased in a number of industries by the late 1920s.

98 Women's Bureau, *Women in Slaughtering*, pp. 86–7, 102–3.

99 Taylor, *Mexican Labor in Chicago*, p. 105; "Unemployment Problem," *Mexico*, 13 November 1928, CFLPS, Box 40; Herbst, *Negro in Slaughtering and Meat-packing*, pp. 99–103. My sampling of employee records of workers who had remained with the company until the McCormick Works closed down in the early 1960s, a particularly stable group of people, showed that black workers experienced many more layoffs before the depression-era difficulties than their white co-workers. McCormick Works employee records, IH.

100 Leila Houghteling, *The Income and Standard of Living of Unskilled Laborers in Chicago* (Chicago: University of Chicago Press, 1927), pp. 31–2.

101 Slichter, "Current Labor Policies," p. 428; "Index of Pay-roll Totals in Manufacturing Industries," *Monthly Labor Review* 20 (March 1925): 130–5; Jacoby, "Origin of Internal Labor Markets," p. 531; Bernstein, *Lean Years*, pp. 66–8, 180; Brody, *Workers in Industrial America*, p. 59; Gordon, Edwards, and Reich, *Segmented Work, Divided Workers*, p. 150. Concerning International Harvester, Ozanne, *Century of Labor–*

Management Relations, pp. 237–8; Ozanne, *Wages in Practice and Theory*, pp. 134–6.

102 Roethlisberger and Dickson, *Management and the Worker*, pp. 232–3.

103 *Ibid.*, p. 141.

104 On workers' desire for shorter hours, see "Five-Day Work Week," Editorial, *Dziennik Zjednoczenia*, 13 April 1928, CFLPS, Box 32; "The Stockyards Workers," *Vilnis*, 12 January 1926, CFLPS, Box 28; Interview with Male from Operating Branch, 19 April 1929, HWMF, Fiche no. 104; Mrs. M. A. Gadsby, "The Steel Strike," *Monthly Labor Review* 14 (December 1919): 86. Complaints about hours were high on Hawthorne workers' list of grievances. Roethlisberger and Dickson, *Management and the Worker*, pp. 232–3.

On hours worked during the 1920s and employers' resistance to cutting them, see Ozanne, *Century of Labor–Management Relations*, p. 241; Brody, *Workers in Industrial America*, p. 59; Bernstein, *Lean Years*, pp. 71–2; David R. Roediger, "The Limits of Corporate Reform: Fordism, Taylorism and the Working Week in the U.S., 1914–1929." Paper presented to Chicago Area Labor History Seminar, Newberry Library, 1986. On hours in the steel industry specifically, see Martha Shiells, "Collective Choice in Labor Markets: Hours Reductions in British and U.S. Iron and Steel Industries, 1890–1923," Paper delivered at Social Science History Workshop, Stanford University, 16 April 1985, p. 4; Moye, "End of the 12-Hour Day," p. 25; "Wages and Hours in the Blast-Furnace, Open-Hearth, and Bar-Mill Departments of the Iron and Steel Industry, 1926," *Monthly Labor Review* 23 (September 1926): 76; Davis, *Condition of Labor in American Iron and Steel Industry*, pp. 80–1; Jones, "Conditions Surrounding Mexicans in Chicago," p. 45; Interview with Robert H. Bork by William Bork, Chicago, IL, 28 January 1982, SECHP, p. 12.

105 For working conditions in the packing plants, see Interviews with Estelle Zabritz, Victoria Kramer, and Anna Novak in Banks, *First-Person America*, pp. 57–8, 60–3, 65; Interview with Stella Nowicki in Alice and Staughton Lynd, eds., *Rank and File: Personal Histories by Working-Class Organizers* (Princeton: Princeton University Press, 1981), p. 78; Women's Bureau, *Women in Slaughtering*, pp. 8, 34; Travis, *An Autobiography of Black Chicago*, p. 90.

106 For working conditions in steel, Janik, "Looking Backward from 'The Bush' to Open Hearth," pp. 51, 53; Anonymous, "The Melting Pot," Student paper, n.d. but c. 1930, BUR, Box 154, Folder 4, p. 25; Bate, "Development of Iron and Steel Industry," pp. 149, 154; and from the *Monthly Labor Review*: Lucian W. Chaney, "Accident Occurrence in the Iron and Steel Industry, 1922," 17 (October 1923): 131–41; Lucian W. Chaney, "Accident Experience of the Iron and Steel Industry," 19 (November 1924): 195–201; "Accident Rates for the Iron and Steel Industry in Specified State Jurisdictions, 1922 to 1925," 25 (August 1927): 43–5.

107 Workers frequently put the inadequacy of lockers at the top of their list of complaints about factory conditions. It upset them greatly that their personal possessions, particularly their street clothes, could not be kept safe and sanitary. Interview with Male from Operating Branch, 12 April 1929, HSMF, Fiche no. 104; Wisconsin Steel Works Council, *Harvester Industrial Council Minutes of Regular Meetings*, IH, Document file 5495, 12 November 1929, p. 10, where an employee representative said, "We are short of lockers. . . . I have heard that a great many men have quit on that account."

108 Nelson, "Study of an Isolated Industrial Community," p. 71. Even the National Industrial Conference Board admitted the failure of many foremenship training programs; NICB, *Industrial Relations*, pp. 67–8. Also see Jacoby, "Origins of Internal Labor Markets," p. 487, for contemporary analyst Simon Slichter's assessment of how foremen opposed welfare capitalism.

109 Workers' testimony about their jobs is filled with references to the favoritism of foremen. Some mention nepotism: Interview with George Patterson, December 1970, ROHP, p. 4, and "The Melting Pot," Student paper, n.d. but c. 1930, BUR, Box 154, Folder 4, p. 7. Others recount numerous incidents of harassment and special treatment. See, e.g., in HSMF: Interview with Male from Operating Branch, 12 April 1929, Fiche no. 104; Interview with Male from Technical Branch, 2 June 1930, Fiche no. 184; Interview with Male from Technical Branch, 21 August 1930, Fiche no. 184; Interview with Female from Technical Branch, 11 November 1930, Fiche no. 184.

110 On workers' offers of gifts and bribes, see Interview with George Patterson, December 1970, ROHP, p. 7; "The Melting Pot," Student paper, n.d. but c. 1930, BUR, Box 154, Folder 4, p. 11; Taylor, *Mexican Labor in Chicago*, pp. 102–4; Interview with Anna Novak, in Banks, *First-Person America*, p. 63; Interview with Male from Operating Branch, 12 April 1929, HSMF, Fiche no. 104.

111 "The Melting Pot," n.d. but c. 1930, BUR, Box 154, Folder 4, p. 6; also see pp. 7, 25–6; Taylor, *Mexican Labor in Chicago*, pp. 92, 100–1, 103, 113–14; Interview with Male in Operating Branch, 12 April 1929, HSMF, Fiche no. 104.

112 Interview with Anna Novak, in Banks, ed., *First-Person America*, p. 63; Interview with Female in Operating Branch, 10 April 1929, HSMF, Fiche no. 104; Interview with Male in Operating Branch, 10 April 1929, HSMF, Fiche no. 104.

113 Purcell, *Worker Speaks His Mind*, p. 319; also see pp. 55, 190 on abuses of seniority.

114 Interview with Estelle Zabritz, in Banks, ed., *First-Person America*, pp. 58, 62.

115 Houser, *What the Employer Thinks*, p. 129. For more on the limited opportunities for promotion see Nelson, "Study of an Isolated Industrial Community," pp. 30, 102, 106; "The Melting Pot," Student paper, n.d.

but c. 1930, BUR, Box 154, Folder 4, pp. 6, 20, 23. A new obstacle that workers complained about after the war was the growing presence of college-educated men in the factory. They were hired to do skilled work, with an eye toward their becoming supervisors someday. One working in the Gary Works of U.S. Steel after four years of high school and two of college told Rose Feld, "I'm not going to tend furnace all my life. I'm going to follow this molten metal right through," an ambition that the typical worker would not dared to have held. Rose Feld, "Steelworkers at Leisure?" *Century Magazine* 108 (October 1924): 752.

116 Taylor, *Mexican Labor in Chicago*, p. 101.

117 Houser, *What the Employer Thinks*, p. 82.

118 Taylor, *Mexican Labor in Chicago*, p. 101.

119 "How Employe Representation Is Working," Swift & Company, *Yearbook of 1924*, p. 50; Catherine Elizabeth Lewis, "Trade Union Policies in Regard to the Negro Worker in the Slaughtering and Meatpacking Industry" (M.A. thesis, University of Chicago, 1945), p. 36. Barrett, *Work and Community*, pp. 251–2, provides evidence of employer intimidation to get packinghouse workers to vote.

120 Ozanne, *Century of Labor–Management Relations*, pp. 114–17.

121 All three employers required that employee representatives be American citizens, at least 21 years of age, who had worked continuously for the company at least one year. Representatives also had to be able to read, write, and speak English. Although these qualifications may not seem stiff, when applied to work forces as heavily immigrant as those in packing, steel, and agricultural equipment, they narrowed the field of eligible candidates dramatically. The men who were elected representatives at Armour and International Harvester overwhelmingly turned out to be native born, long employed with the company, and property owning. "Harvester Industrial Council Personnel of Works Councils, March 1919," IH, Document file 214; Toni Gilpin, "Fair and Square: International Harvester's Council Plan and the Works Councils at McCormick and Tractor Works," Unpublished seminar paper, Yale University, December 1982, pp. 27–8; Barrett, *Work and Community*, pp. 250–1, "Appendix B: Personal Data on the First Group of Elected Employee Representatives at Armour & Company, Chicago Plant, March 1921," pp. 283–4.

On the early efforts of employee representatives to raise grievances, see Ozanne, *Century of Labor–Management Relations*, pp. 138–9; *Tractor Interester*, May 1920, August 1920, December 1920; Gilpin, "Fair and Square," pp. 35–9; Barrett, *Work and Community*, pp. 252–3.

122 Interview with Edward Hassett, in Purcell, *Worker Speaks His Mind*, p. 288.

123 Nelson, "Study of an Isolated Industrial Community," pp. 47–51; also see pp. 33, 51–6 for other workers' opinions of the works council at Wisconsin Steel. Some of the obstacles employee representatives encountered were structural. For example, plans in packing and International

Harvester required unit voting: Management and employee representatives voted separately but a majority of votes in each unit was recorded as unanimous. A tie between the two blocks went to the company president. Holcomb, "Union Policies of Meatpackers," p. 28; Gilpin, "Fair and Square," p. 26.

124 Cyrus McCormick, Jr., "Employee Representation as Affecting the Attitude of Labor and Business," Address before the American Management Association, Kansas City, MO, 30 November 1925, Document file 16756, IH, p. 11.

125 Herbst, *Negro in Slaughtering and Meat-packing*, pp. 116–17.

126 Purcell, *Worker Speaks His Mind*, p. 248; for investigators' discoveries that workers found wage incentive plans confusing, see Purcell, *Worker Speaks His Mind*, pp. 236–54; Women's Bureau, *Women in Slaughtering*, pp. 69–71; Nelson, "Study of an Isolated Industrial Community," p. 34.

127 On workers' complaints about the negative effects of the system, see Purcell, *Worker Speaks His Mind*, pp. 236–54, *passim*; Women's Bureau, *Women in Slaughtering*, pp. 69–70; and from HSMF: Interview with Female from Operating Branch, 10 April 1929, Fiche no. 104; Interview with Male from Operating Branch, 12 April 1929, Fiche no. 104; Interview with Female from Operating Branch, 17 April 1929, Fiche no. 104; Interview with Female from Operating Branch, 17 April 1929, Fiche no. 104.

128 Interview with Male from Inspection Department, 28 November 1928, HSMF, Fiche no. 109.

129 "Conclusion from Supervisors' Conference Groups," HSMF, Fiche no. 109.

130 Nelson, "Study of an Isolated Industrial Community," p. 184; Anna Masley, "Term Paper, Research Project: Study of Ukranians, a Nationality Group of Chicago and Vicinity," Paper for Sociology 264, n.d. but c. 1930, BUR, Box 156, Folder 6, "Document 11," pp. 7–9.

131 Dunn, *Americanization of Labor*, pp. 172–5; Davis, *Conditions of Labor in American Iron and Steel*, pp. 159–63.

132 *South Works Review*, November 1926.

133 "Rules of Group Insurance," *South Works Review*, December 1926.

134 Cyrus McCormick, Jr., "Employee Representation as Affecting the Attitude of Labor and Business," Address before the American Management Association, Kansas City, MO, 30 November 1925, IH, Document file 16756, p. 18.

135 Ray Stannard Baker, *The New Industrial Unrest: Reasons and Remedies* (Garden City: Doubleday, Page & Company, 1920), pp. 139–40; *South Works Review*, October 1926.

136 *Western Electric News*, May 1928.

137 C. E. Jarchow and W. R. Odell, Jr., "Investigation of Employe Security Plans," IH, Document file 19178, "Exhibit E: Outline of Stock Plan, United States Steel Corporation," p. 2; McCormick Works Council,

Harvester Industrial Council Minutes of Regular Meetings, IH, Document file 18322, 10 September 1929, p. 9.

138 "Employee's Part in Industry," Editorial, *Dziennik Zjednoczenia*, 2 July 1928, CFLPS, Box 32.

139 Stinebower, "Employee Stock Ownership in Chicago," p. 91.

140 Luther Conant, Jr., *A Critical Analysis of Industrial Pension Systems*, 1922, quoted in Dunn, *Americanization of Labor*, p. 185.

141 Davis, *Condition of Labor in American Iron and Steel*, p. 157; Ozanne, *Century of Labor–Management Relations*, pp. 84–5.

142 Interview with Anna Novak, in Banks, ed., *First-Person America*, p. 64.

143 "Employment Personnel Records and Reports," WE, "History of Personnel Practices," HC-121, p. 2; Davis, "'Old Age' at Fifty," *Monthly Labor Review*, p. 1; "Age Limits on Employment by American Manufacturers," *Monthly Labor Review* 28 (May 1929): 110–11; Millis and Montgomery, *Labor's Risk and Social Insurance*, pp. 353–60; President's Committee, *Recent Social Trends*, vol. 1, pp. 320–2.

144 Jack M. Stein, "A History of Unionization in the Steel Industry in the Chicago Area" (M.A. thesis, University of Chicago, 1948), p. 35. Despite grandiose plans by the AFL to organize in the steel mills, not much more than a few mass meetings of steel workers in Gary, Indiana Harbor, and South Chicago resulted. For evidence of the low number of work stoppages between 1923 and 1930, see Bureau of Labor Statistics, Department of Labor, *Handbook of Labor Statistics* (Washington, DC: U.S. Government Printing Office, 1950), p. 142, Table E-2.

145 Taylor, *Mexican Labor in Chicago*, p. 122; "The Stockyards Workers," *Vilnis*, 12 January 1926, CFLPS, Box 28; Dunn, *Americanization of Labor*, pp. 255–61; "Harvester Industrial Council: Report of an Inquiry Conducted under the Direction of the Special Conference Committee," 10 August 1928, IH, Document file 213, pp. 3–4; "Report on the Study of the Background and Development of the United Farm Equipment and Metal Workers' Union," 25 April 1952, IH, p. 4, Appendix D, Document 1, p. 1; Harold D. Lasswell and Dorothy Blumenstock, *World Revolutionary Propaganda: A Chicago Study* (New York: Alfred A. Knopf, 1939), pp. 58–60.

146 Slichter, "The Current Labor Policies of American Industries," pp. 396, 429–31; Jacoby, "Origins of Internal Labor Markets," p. 534; Bernstein, *Lean Years*, p. 62.

147 Nelson, "Study of an Isolated Industrial Community," p. 125; see also pp. 106, 112–3, 135, 157. For further examples of workers' "casual" behavior, see "The Problem of the Unskilled Laborer with a Large Family," *Monthly Labor Review* 25 (November 1927): 34; and job histories during the 1920s of International Harvester employees who in the end remained with the company until the McCormick Works closed in the early 1960s, McCormick Works employee records, IH.

148 From IH: Industrial Relations Department, "Vacation Statistics," Document file 13140; George J. Kelday, "Memo: 1927 Labor Stability and

Turnover Report," 15 December 1927, Document file 19429, p. 3 and table at end; George J. Kelday, "Memo 10 December 1928," Document file 19429; Memo to Cyrus McCormick, Jr. from Industrial Relations Department, "Labor Turnover and Stability Report for 1929 Manufacturing Season, October 1, 1928–September 30, 1929," 25 April 1930, Document file 19429.

149 Memo to Cyrus McCormick, Jr. from Industrial Relations Department, "Labor Turnover and Stability Report for 1929 Manufacturing Season, October 1, 1928–September 30, 1929," 25 April 1930, IH, Document file 19429. On turnover in other industries, see Herbst, *Negro in Slaughtering and Meat-packing*, pp. 71–5, 130–47; Thomas Wesley Rogers, "An Analysis of the Nature and Use of Labor Turnover Data among Chicago Industries" (M.A. thesis, University of Chicago, 1928), pp. 66–70, 86, 91; *Western Electric News*, January 1928, November 1928; Industrial Relations Department, Wharton School of Finance and Commerce, University of Pennsylvania, *Four Years of Labor Mobility: A Study of Labor Turnover in a Group of Selected Plants in Philadelphia, 1921–1924* (American Academy of Political and Social Science, 1925); and from the *Monthly Labor Review*: "Recent Conclusions Concerning Labor Turnover," 24 (February 1927): 17–18; "Factory Labor Turnover – Two New Monthly Indexes," 24 (March 1927): 9–13; "Labor Turnover," 24 (December 1927): 26–7; "Labor Turnover in American Factories, 1927 and 1928," 27 (July 1928): 27.

150 Wisconsin Steel Works Council, *Harvester Industrial Council Minutes of Regular Meeting*, IH, Document file 5495, 13 August 1929, p. 14. See literally all minutes of Wisconsin Steel Works Council meetings between 8 January 1929 and 10 December 1929 for discussion of the vacation plan and frustration with workers' response to it.

151 Nelson, "Study of an Isolated Industrial Community," p. 58.

152 On Western Electric's struggles against worker absenteeism and tardiness at Hawthorne, see *Hawthorne Microphone*, 31 August 1923; Interview with Male from Technical Branch, 17 April 1930, HSMF, Fiche no. 184; Rogers, "Analysis of the Nature and Use of Labor Turnover Data among Chicago Industries," p. 73.

153 Myra Hill Colson, "Negro Home Workers in Chicago," *Social Service Review* 2 (September 1928): 407–10.

154 "The Melting Pot," Student paper, n.d. but c. 1930, BUR, Box 154, Folder 4, p. 22.

155 For other studies documenting Chicago working-class families' dependence on multiple sources of income, see Houghteling, *Income and Standard of Living of Unskilled Laborers*; Franc Lewis McCleur, "Living Conditions among Wage Earning Families in Forty-One Blocks in Chicago (1923)" (Ph.D. dissertation, University of Chicago, 1928); Women's Bureau, *Women in Slaughtering*, pp. 14, 55, 118; "Women in the Candy Industry in Chicago and St. Louis," *Monthly Labor Review* 16 (April 1923): 89–91; "Hours and Working Conditions of Women in Illinois

Industries," *Monthly Labor Review* 23 (July 1926): 48; "Report by Stockyards Clearing House on Women Workers," 1919, MCD, Box 4, Folder 20, Section "Reasons for Working"; Chicago Federation of Settlements, "Study of the Educational and Industrial Life of Girls in Settlement Groups, Ages 14–18," 1923, Lea Taylor Papers, Box 8, Folder "Chicago Federation of Settlements, 1923," CHS; Elizabeth A. Hughes, *Living Conditions of Small-Wage Earners in Chicago* (Chicago: Department of Public Welfare, 1925), p. 45; Irene J. Graham, "Family Support and Dependency among Chicago Negroes: A Study of Unpublished Census Data," *Social Service Review* 3 (December 1929): 544–5.

For details about the kind of work women often did, see Leila Houghteling, "Charity and Women's Wages," *Social Service Review* 1 (September 1927): 399; Mary McDowell, "Our Proxies in Industry," n.d., MCD, Box 15, p. 8; "Child Labor – Industrial Home Work Investigations, November 1925–June 1927," Juvenile Protective Association Papers, Folder 33, UICC; Helen Russell Wright, *Children of Wage-earning Mothers: A Study of Selected Groups in Chicago*, Children's Bureau bulletin no. 102 (Washington, DC: U.S. Government Printing Office, 1922); from Polonia Oral History Project, CHS: Interview with Lillian Cwik, p. 10, whose mother did maintenance work in their apartment building, and Interview with Helen Bajkowski, whose mother cooked for a caterer; and Interviews in IC, Chicago, IL, with Rose Clementi, 7 April 1980, whose mother sewed collars at home; Rena Domke, 28 April 1980, whose mother shelled nuts; Rena Morandin, 22 July 1980, who worked as a presser in a laundry as a young woman; and Angeline Tonietto, 1 July 1980, whose mother went to work at Hart, Schaffner & Marx during the seasons her father was unemployed.

156 Interview with Anna Novak, in Banks, ed., *First-Person America*, pp. 64–5.

157 Women's Bureau, *Women in Slaughtering*, p. 102.

158 Jones, "Conditions Surrounding Mexicans in Chicago," p. 45.

159 Interview with Stella Nowicki, in Lynd and Lynd, *Rank and File*, p. 79; also see Purcell, *Worker Speaks His Mind*, p. 241, for a Swift foreman's description of how fear of loss in earnings and jobs made his men slow down.

160 Roethlisberger and Dickson, *Management and the Worker*, pp. 418, 421, 522–3.

161 Interview with Stella Nowicki, in Lynd and Lynd, *Rank and File*, p. 79; see also Nelson Algren's story, "Highpockets," which satirized the efficiency expert's dream worker. Algren collected industrial folklore in Chicago for the Federal Writers' Project during the depression. It is likely that this humorous tale of the diligent operative and his hostile co-workers was based on stories Algren heard. "Highpockets," in Banks, ed., *First-Person America*, pp. 90–2.

162 Roethlisberger and Dickson, *Management and the Worker*, p. 386. For

extensive reminiscences of how Hawthorne workers handled the bogey, see my interview with retired employee John Mega, Chicago, IL, 27 January 1987.

163 Roethlisberger and Dickson, *Management and the Worker*, p. 426; Stanley B. Mathewson, *Restriction of Output among Unorganized Workers* (Carbondale, IL: Southern Illinois University Press, 1969; originally published 1931), pp. 78–83, 107. Stanley Mathewson traveled around the country during the late 1920s, often disguised as a worker, observing output restriction in factories. He was one of the first to identify how widespread the phenomenon was among unorganized workers. Previously, people had associated the tactic with organized workers in labor unions.

164 The actual findings of the Hawthorne Studies are summarized in Roethlisberger and Dickson, *Management and the Worker*; T. N. Whitehead, *The Industrial Worker: A Statistical Study of Human Relations in a Group of Manual Workers* (Cambridge, MA: Harvard University Press, 1938); and Elton Mayo, *The Human Problems of an Industrial Civilization* (New York: Macmillan Company, 1933), pp. 55–98. A useful summary of the studies can be found in Loren Baritz, *The Servants of Power: A History of the Use of Social Science in American Industry* (Middletown, CT: Wesleyan University Press, 1960), pp. 77–116.

165 Roethlisberger and Dickson, *Management and the Worker*, pp. 404, 461–2, 473–4, 477.

166 Nelson, "Study of an Isolated Industrial Community," pp. 28–9; see also "The Melting Pot," Student paper, n.d. but c. 1930, BUR, Box 154, Folder 4, pp. 20, 26.

167 Comment by Toni Gilpin, Chicago Area Labor History Seminar, Newberry Library, 29 January 1987.

168 David Montgomery, *The Fall of the House of Labor* (New York: Cambridge University Press, 1987), p. 458; Louise Lamphere, "Bringing the Family to Work: Women's Culture on the Shop Floor," *Feminist Studies* 11 (Fall 1985): 519–40.

169 Houser, *What the Employer Thinks*, p. 35; Sterling D. Spero and Abram L. Harris, *The Black Worker: The Negro and the Labor Movement* (New York: Atheneum, 1969), p. 283; Holcomb, "The Union Policies of Meat Packers," p. 30; "Memorandum of Address Made June 17th before the Interracial Committee of the Union League Club," 17 June 1926, Julius Rosenwald Papers, Box 40, Folder 2, UCSC, p. 3.

170 Herbst, *Negro in Slaughtering and Meat-packing*, pp. 75–80.

171 Interview with Mary Hammond, in Banks, ed., *First-Person America*, p. 54.

172 Travis, *Autobiography of Black Chicago*, p. 91.

173 Blacks' lower wages resulted from a combination of their low-level jobs and pay that was less than whites earned for equivalent labor. Houghteling, *Income and Standard of Living*, pp. 24–6; Herbst, *Negro in Slaught-*

ering and Meat-packing, pp. 81–3, 85–7, 111–12, 114–15, 118–19, 120–5, 168–71; Ozanne, *Wages in Practice and Theory*, pp. 47–8, 52, 95.

174 Ozanne, *Century of Labor–Management Relations*, pp. 184–7; Taylor, *Mexican Labor in Chicago*, p. 93; Herbst, *Negro in Slaughtering and Meat-packing*, pp. 127–47; Hughes, *Living Conditions for Small-Wage Earners*, pp. 49–56; Chicago Commission on Race Relations, *Negro in Chicago*, pp. 372–91.

175 Interview with Anna Novak, in Banks, ed., *First-Person America*, p. 64; "Excerpt from a Larger Study Sent from Ira De A. Reid, Dir. of Dept. of Research and Investigation, National Urban League, to Mr. Robert W. Bagnell, NAACP," 30 September 1930, NAACP Papers, Box 321, File "Labor – General, May 12–December 31, 1930," LC, p. 20.

176 Interview with Philip Weightman, Chicago, IL, 7 and 8 October 1986, UPWA Oral History Project, Tape 284, Side 2.

177 Purcell, *Worker Speaks His Mind*, pp. 81–2; also see pp. 83, 85, 88–9, 91, 93–5, 293. Mary Hammond told interviewer Betty Burke that "I used to think Swift's was the cream." Interview with Mary Hammond, in Banks, ed., *First-Person America*, p. 55.

178 Jones, "Conditions Surrounding Mexicans in Chicago," p. 45; Nelson, "Study of an Isolated Industrial Community," p. 27.

179 Jacoby, "Origins of Internal Labor Market," p. 510.

180 Nelson, "Study of an Isolated Industrial Community," p. 54.

181 McCormick Works Council, *Harvester Industrial Council Minutes of Regular Meetings*, IH, Document file 18322, 14 October 1927, pp. 1–3.

182 Taylor, *Mexican Labor in Chicago*, p. 109.

183 Interview with Male from Technical Branch, 22 August 1930, HSMF, Fiche no. 184; also from HSMF: Interview with Male from Inspection Branch, 21 October 1928, Fiche no. 109; Interview with Male from Operating Branch, 12 April 1929, Fiche no. 104; Interview with Male from Technical Branch, 26 March 1930, Fiche no. 184; Interview with Male from Technical Branch, 17 April 1930, Fiche no. 184; Interview with Male from Technical Branch, 21 August 1930, Fiche no. 184; Interview with Female from Technical Branch, 11 November 1930, Fiche no. 184.

184 "General Outline of Interviewing Methods Followed by the Interviewer in the Inspection Branch," HSMF, Fiche no. 104; "Summary Outline of Employee Interview Program, Inspection Branch – Hawthorne Works – Western Electric Company, September 1928–February 1929," HSMF, Fiche no. 109.

185 Roethlisberger and Dickson, *Management and the Worker*, p. 303; see also "Employee Interviewing Program Comment and Reactions," HSMF, Fiche no. 104.

186 Turnover data cited in note 149; Rogers, "Analysis of the Nature and Use of Labor Turnover Data among Chicago Industries," pp. 86, 91; "Vacations for Factory Workers," Memo to Miss A. M. Holt from Geo. J.

Kelday, 12 March 1926, IH, Document file 13140; Memo to Cyrus McCormick, Jr. from Industrial Relations Department, 25 April 1930, IH, Document file 19429, p. 2; *Western Electric News*, January 1928.

187 Materials on the Union Labor Life Insurance Company and Union Cooperative Insurance Association in FITZ, Boxes 13–16; Materials on Union Motor Club, FITZ, Boxes 15–17; "Health, Wealth and Happiness for You! Valmar By the Lake," Promotional Pamphlet, FITZ, Box 15, n.d.; and from FITZ on home ownership: Geo. R. MacNeill, President, Progressive Home Builders of Illinois, to John Fitzpatrick, 24 August 1927, Box 15, Folder 112; *Home Hits*, published by the Progressive Home Builders of Illinois, n.d., Box 15, Folder 108; "Break Ground for... WCFL Home in Lombard," Box 16, Folder 115; Telegram to CFL From Chicago Heights Trade & Labor Assembly, 1927, Box 16, Folder 115.

On similar labor union activities nationwide, see Bureau of Labor Statistics, U.S. Department of Labor, *Beneficial Activities of American Trade Unions*, Bulletin no. 465 (Washington, DC: U.S. Government Printing Office, 1928); from the *Monthly Labor Review*: "Trade-Union Provision for Sick, Aged, and Disabled Members, and for Dependents," 26 (January 1928): 1–15; "Trade-Union Old-Age Pensions and Homes for the Aged and Tubercular," 26 (February 1928): 1–27; "Recreational Activities of Labor Organizations," 26 (May 1928): 5–20; "General Health Work of Labor Organizations," 27 (December 1928): 11.

188 Chicago Joint Board, Amalgamated Clothing Workers of America, *Amalgamated Centre: The Tailor Re-Tailored – A Story of Surging Humanity, May Day 1928 on the Occasion of the Dedication of the Amalgamated Centre in the Cause of Labor* (Chicago: Chicago Joint Board, Amalgamated Clothing Workers of America, 1928); Interview with Jacob Potofsky, President of the Amalgamated Clothing Workers of America, 4 August 1970, Chicago, IL, ROHP, pp. 24–6; Morris Ziskind, "In the Chicago Amalgamated Clothing Workers Union," *Forward*, 31 December 1922, CFLPS, Box 23; Sentinel's Golden Jubilee Committee, *History of Chicago Jewry 1911–1961* (Chicago: The Sentinel, 1961), pp. 82–3; "Experience of Unemployment Insurance Fund in Chicago Clothing Industry," *Monthly Labor Review* 21 (November 1925): 133–4; "Condition of Labor Banks as of December 31, 1925," *Monthly Labor Review* 22 (May 1926): 104–5; Hyman H. Bookbinder and Associates, *To Promote the General Welfare: The Story of the Amalgamated* (New York: Amalgamated Clothing Workers of America, 1950), pp. 74–103; Charles Elbert Zaretz, *The Amalgamated Clothing Workers of America: A Study of Progressive Trade-Unionism* (New York: Ancon Publishing Company, 1934), pp. 263–84; Daniel Nelson, "'While Waiting for the Government': The Needle Trades Unemployment Insurance Plans, 1919–28," *Labor History* 11 (Fall 1970): 482–99.

189 Robert S. Lynd and Helen Merrell Lynd, *Middletown: A Study in American Culture* (New York: Harcourt, Brace & World, 1929; reprint ed. 1956), p. 34.

190 "On Behalf of Personal Freedom," *Denni Hlasatel*, 4 October 1922, and "Czechoslovaks Protest against Prohibition," *Denni Hlasatel*, 6 October 1922, CFLPS, Box 1.

191 John M. Allswang, *A House For All Peoples: Ethnic Politics in Chicago, 1890–1936* (Lexington: University of Kentucky Press, 1971), pp. 118–28; Harold F. Gosnell, *Machine Politics Chicago Model* (Chicago: University of Chicago Press, 1937; reprint ed. 1968), pp. 144–9; Edward R. Kantowicz, *Polish–American Politics in Chicago 1888–1940* (Chicago: University of Chicago Press, 1975), pp. 145–8; Humbert S. Nelli, *Italians in Chicago: A Study in Ethnic Mobility* (New York: Oxford University Press, 1979), pp. 233–4; Eugene McCarthy, "The Bohemians in Chicago and Their Benevolent Societies: 1875–1946" (M.A. thesis, University of Chicago, 1950), pp. 87–9; "Interview with Mr. Ewald on Prohibition" in Lindquist, "Lithuanians in Chicago," 1922, BUR, Box 190A; Nelson, "Study of an Isolated Industrial Community," pp. 144–9, 167–9, 183, 241; Norman S. Hayner, "The Effect of Prohibition in Packingtown" (M.A. thesis, University of Chicago, 1921); Marian Winthrop Taylor, "The Social Results of Prohibition: A Study Made in the Central District of the United Charities" (M.A. thesis, University of Chicago, 1923); Articles against prohibition in CFLPS: *Denni Hlasatel*, 6 March 1922, 20 March 1922, 27 August 1922, 5 November 1922, Box 1; "People's Sentiment Against Prohibition," *Amerikanski Slovenec*, 17 February 1926, Box 40; "A Glance at Prohibition," 1 May 1919, and "The Reformers Went Too Far," 7 September 1922, *Polonia*, Box 32; "Italophobia," *Bulletin Italian American National Union*, April 1925, Box 21.

5. ADRIFT IN THE GREAT DEPRESSION

1 Jeannette Margaret Elder, "A Study of One Hundred Applicants for Relief the Fourth Winter of Unemployment" (M.A. thesis, University of Chicago, 1933), p. 71.

2 Lyle Spencer, "Case Study of a Destitute Immigrant Family," Paper for Sociology 310 and 264, 16 August 1932, BUR, Box 156, Folder 4.

3 Dempsey J. Travis, *An Autobiography of Black Chicago* (Chicago: Urban Research Institute, 1981), pp. 33, 41, 47.

4 Genevieve Ann Lensing, "An Unemployment Study in the Stockyards District" (M.A. thesis, University of Chicago, 1932), pp. 89–90.

5 Interview with George Patterson, December 1970–January 1971, ROHP, pp. 5–7; George Patterson, "Autobiography," Book 1, "Embryo Steelworker," PAT, Box 9, File 6, pp. 1–7.

6 Alice Theresa Theodorson, "Living Conditions of Fifty Unemployed Families" (M.A. thesis, University of Chicago, 1935), pp. 90–1; Lensing, "Unemployment Study," pp. 18, 33.

7 Elder, "Study of One Hundred Applicants for Relief," pp. 86–9; also see Lensing, "Unemployment Study," pp. 20, 29.

8 Mary G. Midura to Mr. B. Panoff, 6 November 1934, in B. Panoff, "Effect of the Depression on Poles," BUR, Box 130, Folder 4.

9 For a sampling of the vast materials on how ethnic welfare agencies tried to cope with the Great Depression, see Edna Dumaresq, "Report on Bohemian Charitable Association by Family Welfare Study," n.d., WC, Box 253, Folder "Bohemian Charitable Association, 1936–39"; "Danish Aid and Relief Society: Description of Work 1930–36 and Plans for 1937," 1937, WC, Box 310, Folder "Danish Aid and Relief Society, 1936–42"; and from CFLPS: "We Need More Welfare Centers within the Polish National Alliance," *Weekly Zgoda*, 8 January 1931, Box 36; "Slovenian Relief Organization," *Amerikanski Slovenec*, 26 January 1928, Box 40.

10 *Program and Chronological History: Souvenir of St. Augustine's Parish Golden Jubilee, 1880–1936* (Chicago: St. Augustine, 1936), p. 229.

11 *Ibid.*, p. 231.

12 "Society of St. Vincent de Paul," in Reverend Monsignor Harry C. Koenig, S.T.D., ed., *Caritas Christi Urget Nos: A History of the Offices, Agencies, and Institutions of the Archidocese of Chicago* (Chicago: Roman Catholic Archdiocese of Chicago, n.d.), vol. 1, pp. 811–13; *The New World* (Chicago Archdiocese weekly newspaper), 24 July 1931, 18 December 1931, 29 April 1932, 6 May 1932, 13 May 1932, 10 December 1932, 16 June 1933; "Study of Central Charity Bureau, the Catholic Charities, March 27th–April 8th, 1933," UNCH, Box 8, Folder 4; *Our Lady of Pompeii Church 65th Anniversary Book, 1911–1976* (Chicago: Our Lady of Pompeii, 1976); *St. Mary Magdalene Anniversary Book* (Chicago: St. Mary Magdalene, n.d.); and other anniversary books of Polish and Italian parishes for evidence that they established St. Vincent de Paul Societies in the early years of the depression.

13 *Osadne Hlasy*, 31 August 1934, CFLPS, Box 40.

14 *Mexico*, 5 December 1928, CFLPS, Box 40.

15 Memo to all districts of the United Charities, 2 December 1931, UNCH, Box 8, Folder 1.

16 Sentinel's Golden Jubilee Committee, *History of Chicago Jewry, 1911–1961* (Chicago: Sentinel Publishing Company, 1961), pp. 32, 165; "Report 50,000 Jews Being Supported," *Forward*, 25 January 1932, CFLPS.

17 Merrill F. Krughoff, "Study of Polish Welfare Association," c. 1934, WC, Box 390, Folder "Polish Welfare Association, 1925–54," p. 2. For a similar decline in income, see "The Needs of the Jewish People's Institute: The Financial Situation," *Chicago Jewish Chronicle*, 8 September 1933. Even individual churches were hard hit by declines in revenue. At St. Augustine's in Back of the Yards, for example, collections on Sundays and holidays and for charities and school tuition during 1933 were far below those of 1929. As a result, parishes like this one had trouble keeping up mortgage payments, to say nothing of running programs.

18 For background on the interaction of public and private welfare agencies in the early depression, see William Arthur Hillman, "Urbanization and the Organization of Welfare Activities in the Metropolitan Community of Chicago" (Ph.D. dissertation, University of Chicago, 1940); Frank Z. Glick, "The Illinois Emergency Relief Commission" (Ph.D. dissertation, University of Chicago, 1940); Edward L. Ryerson, Jr., "Out of the Depression," *The Survey* 70 (January 1934): 3–7; Florence W. Hutsinpillar, "Report of Study of the United Charities of Chicago, Made for the Council of Social Agencies," 10 June 1936, UNCH, Box 50, Folder 6; P. Mathew Titus, "A Study of Protestant Charities in Chicago: History, Development, and Philosophy" (Ph.D. dissertation, University of Chicago, 1939); "Minutes of the Meeting of the Advisory Board of the Cook County Bureau of Public Welfare," 24 September 1931, 10 December 1931, BUR, Box 6, Folder 10; "Governor's Commission on Unemployment Relief," Community Fund Papers, Folders 30-5, 30-7, 30-8, 30-10, UICC; Files "Salvation Army, 1936" and "Salvation Army 1938–69," WC, Box 397; "77th Annual Report of the German Aid Society, 1931," German Aid Society Papers, Folder 8, UICC.

19 *The New World*, 23 October 1931; "Memo to All Districts of the United Charities from Florence Nesbitt," 2 December 1931, UNCH, Box 8, Folder 1.

20 *First Annual Report of the Illinois Emergency Relief Commission for the Year Ending February 5, 1933, Issued Jointly with a Report of the Illinois Emergency Relief Commission (Federal) Covering the Period July 27, 1932 through February 5, 1933* (Springfield: State of Illinois, 1933), p. 4.

21 Clorinne McCulloch Brandenburg, "Chicago Relief and Service Statistics, 1928–1931" (M.A. thesis, University of Chicago, 1932), pp. 35, 49; for similar published conclusions see Clorinne McCulloch Brandenburg, "Chicago Relief Statistics, 1928–31," *Social Service Review* 6 (June 1932): 270–9.

22 Lensing, "Unemployment Study," pp. 73–4.

23 *St. Augustine's Parish Golden Jubilee*, pp. 230–1.

24 Joseph Chalasinski, "Polish and Parochial School among Immigrants in America: A Study of a Polish Neighborhood in South Chicago," n.d. but c. 1930, CAP, Box 33, Folder 2; W. H. Sutherland, "Notes on My Work at the Bush," c. 1932, BUR, Box 138, Folder 7; Interview with Lillian Cwik, Polonia Oral History Project, Box 2, CHS; *The New World*, 13 June 1933; *Golden Jubilee of Holy Cross Lithuanian Roman Catholic Parish, 1904–54* (Chicago: Holy Cross, 1954), pp. 108, 123–4; *Golden Jubilee of St. Hyacinth Church, 1894–1944* (Chicago: St. Hyacinth, 1944), "Statistics 1894 to 1944"; *The 75th Anniversary Year Commemoration Book of Saint Michael's Church, 1892–1967* (Chicago: St. Michael's Church, 1967), pp. 23–5, 28; *Holy Trinity Jubilee Book, 1893–1943* (Chicago: Holy Trinity, 1943), p. 87; *The Diamond Years of St. Ailbe's Parish, 1894–1969* (Chicago: St. Ailbe's Church, 1969).

25 *Fiftieth Anniversary, 1919–1969, St. Archangel Michael Serbian Ortho-*

dox Church, South Chicago, Illinois, 22–23 November 1969 (Chicago: St. Archangel Michael Serbian Orthodox Church, 1969).

26 "The Nature and Characteristics of Delinquents and Delinquency in the South Chicago Area Project, as Revealed by Three Group Diaries," Chapter 5: "Attitudes of Delinquents," CAP, Box 110, Folder 1, p. 19.

27 Raymond Sayler, "A Study of Behavior Problems of Boys in the Lower North Community," n.d. but c. 1934, BUR, Box 135, Folder 4, p. 51.

28 Interview with the Reverend J. B. Redmond, in Robert McMurray, "Study of the Effect of the Depression on a Three-Block Area: Federal, Wabash and Calumet between 47th and 51st Streets," 1934, BUR, Box 133, Folder 1, p. 1.

29 Interview with the Reverend W. L. Petty and the Reverend Mary Evans, in Robert McMurray, "Study of the Effect of the Depression on a Three-Block Area: Federal, Wabash and Calumet between 47th and 51st Streets," 1934, BUR, Box 133, Folder 1, p. 1.

30 St. Clair Drake and Horace R. Cayton, *Black Metropolis: A Study of Negro Life in a Northern City* (New York: Harcourt, Brace and Company, 1945), pp. 418–24.

31 Interview with the Reverend W. L. Petty and the Reverend Mary Evans, in Robert McMurray, "Study of the Effect of the Depression on a Three-Block Area: Federal, Wabash and Calumet between 47th and 51st Streets," 1934, BUR, Box 133, Folder 1, p. 2; "A Report of the Status of Spiritualism in the Area as Reported in an Interview with R. F. C. Tonelle," in *ibid.*; Herbert Morrisohn Smith, "Three Negro Preachers in Chicago: A Study in Religious Leadership" (M.A. thesis, University of Chicago, 1935); Orang Winkfield, "Religious Institutions on the South Side for Colored People," FWP, Box A521; A. Friend to President, Chicago Branch, NAACP, 6 May 1933, NAACP Papers, Box G-51, File "Chicago, Illinois, July 1933," LC; Drake and Cayton, *Black Metropolis*, p. 671.

32 Mrs. Joseph T. Bowen, Report on District Offices, 13 October 1931, UNCH, Box 8, Folder 1; "Distribution of Persons on Relief, March 1933," BUR, Box 52, Folder 1; "Report of South Side Survey, April 1931, Compiled under the Joint Auspices of the Council of Social Agencies and the Graduate School of Social Service Administration, University of Chicago," WC, Box 145, Folder "Minorities 1926–42." Black fraternal organizations suffered as well in the depression, with many of them going out of existence. Arthur J. Todd et al., *The Chicago Recreation Survey, 1937*, vol. 3, *Private Recreation* (Chicago: Chicago Recreation Commission and Northwestern University, 1938), p. 105.

33 Studs Terkel, *Hard Times: An Oral History of the Great Depression* (New York: Avon Books, 1971), p. 180; also see Irving Bernstein, *The Lean Years: A History of the American Worker, 1920–1933* (Baltimore: Penguin Books), p. 467.

34 "Unione Veneziana," IC, Ephemera Collection, Item 55.65.

35 *Rise of the SNPJ: A Brief Historical Summary, Compiled by Ivan Malek* (Chicago: Slovene National Benefit Society, 1934), pp. 36–9. For other

accounts of difficulties, see Polish Falcons of America, "60 Years of District IV, 1904–1964," Polish Falcons Papers, Folder 3, UICC; "Memo by Heitmann on Visit to Lithuanian Unity Club," 18 April 1934, MCD, Box 12, Folder "Politics, Back of the Yards, 1928–34," and *Monthly Reporter*, Official Organ of Gegenseitigen Unterstutzungs Vereins (GUV), January 1929–December 1939, CHS, for a particularly good view of how a Chicago mutual benefit society struggled during the Great Depression.

36 Frank Renkiewicz, "The Profits of Nonprofit Capitalism: Polish Fraternalism and Beneficial Insurance in America," in Scott Cummings, ed., *Self-Help in Urban America: Patterns of Minority Business Enterprise* (New York: Kennikat Press, 1980), pp. 128–9; Moshe Yanovsky, "Recent Life Insurance Company Failures in the State of Illinois" (M.A. thesis, University of Chicago, 1935), p. 52; *Sixty-Second Annual Insurance Report of the Department of Trade and Commerce, Division of Insurance, of the State of Illinois* (Springfield: State of Illinois, 1930), pp. 358–67.

37 "Nationalistic Insurance Organizations or Insurance Companies Only," Editorial, *Weekly Zgoda*, 8 January 1931, CFLPS.

38 "Chapter 6: Boys' Own Reasons for Indulging in Delinquency," in "The Nature and Characteristics of Delinquents and Delinquency in the South Chicago Area Project, as Revealed by Three Group Diaries," CAP, Box 110, Folder 1, p. 5.

39 Lensing, "Unemployment Study," pp. 72–3.

40 *Ibid.*, p. 17; Theodorson, "Living Conditions," pp. 48–51; Helen Wright, "The Families of the Unemployed in Chicago," *Social Service Review* 8 (March 1934): 27; Laura Friedman, "A Study of One Hundred Unemployed Families in Chicago, January 1927 to June 1932" (M.A. thesis, University of Chicago, 1933), p. 143; Ruth Schonle Cavan and Catherine Howland Ranck, *The Family and the Depression: A Study of One Hundred Chicago Families* (Chicago: University of Chicago, 1938), p. 51.

Personal testimonies that suggest the same lapse in insurance include: Interview with Lillian Cwik, Polonia Archives, Box 2, CHS, p. 10; George W. Collins, "Effect of the Depression on Adult Recreation," Paper for Sociology 358, 3 July 1934, BUR, Box 176, Folder 3; P. C. Maurer, "Effect of the Depression on Play and Recreation," Paper for Sociology 358, 3 July 1934, BUR, Box 176, Folder 3, p. 2; "Jimmy: School and All That Shit," Institute for Juvenile Research Papers, CHS, p. 80.

41 Flora Slocum, "A Study of Life Insurance Adjustments in 275 Relief Families," *Social Service Review* 8 (June 1934): 302–25.

42 Elder, "Study of One Hundred Applicants for Relief," p. 80. Blacks felt a similar kind of disillusionment when they were forced to abandon long-standing policies with black insurance firms like the Supreme Life Insurance Company. Interview with George W. O'Bee and Ernest H. Williamson, in Robert McMurray, "Study of the Effect of the Depression on a Three-Block Area: Federal, Wabash and Calumet between 47th and 51st Streets," 1934, BUR, Box 133, Folder 1; Leo M. Byrant, "Negro Insurance Companies in Chicago" (M.A. thesis, University of Chicago, 1934), pp.

33–5; Robert C. Puth, "Supreme Life: The History of a Negro Life Insurance Company" (Ph.D. dissertation, Northwestern University, 1967), pp. 92–124; M. S. Stuart, *An Economic Detour: A History of Insurance in the Lives of American Negroes* (New York: Wendell Malliet and Company Publishers, 1940), pp. 44–8.

43 Homer Hoyt, *One Hundred Years of Land Values in Chicago: The Relationship of the Growth of Chicago to the Rise of Its Land Values, 1830–1933* (Chicago: University of Chicago Press, 1933), pp. 268–72; F. Cyril James, *The Growth of Chicago Banks*, vol. 2 (New York: Harper & Brothers Publishers, 1938), pp. 993, 1159–419; Arthur H. Winakor, *Banking Turnover and Facilities in Illinois*, Bulletin no. 55, Bureau of Business Research (Urbana: University of Illinois, 1937), pp. 9, 11, 16, 22; Melchior Palyi, *The Chicago Credit Market: Organization and Institutional Structure* (Chicago: University of Chicago Press, 1937), pp. 263–9, 346–8, 357–9, 371; A. T. Hizinga, "Stabilizing the Neighborhood Bank: A Dramatic Story of How Deflation Weeded Out the Weak from Chicago's Fantastic Structure," *Chicago Commerce* 29 (March 1932); *World's Fair Memorial of the Czechoslovak Group (Czechs and Slovaks), International Exposition, Chicago, 1933* (Chicago: n.p., 1933), p. 34; John T. Reichman, *Czechoslovaks of Chicago* (Chicago: Czechoslovak Historical Society of Illinois, 1937), p. 31; Peter P. Hletko, "Slovaks of Chicago," in *Slovak Catholic Sokol Souvenir Book, July 23, 1967*, Slovak League of America Papers, UICC; Joseph Wagner, "Berwyn: A Short Study of a Residential Suburb of Chicago," Sociology paper, Winter 1933, BUR, Box 159, Folder 3, p. 17; Abram L. Harris, *The Negro as Capitalist* (Philadelphia: American Academy of Political and Social Science, 1936), pp. 59–61, 144–64; and from *Osadny Hlasy*, CFLPS, Box 40: "From among Our Circles," 3 June 1932, and "Conditions of Closed Slovak Bank," 10 August 1934.

44 Drake and Cayton, *Black Metropolis*, pp. 466–7, also 721–2; Madrue Chavers-Wright, *The Guarantee – P.W. Chavers: Banker, Entrepreneur, Philanthropist in Chicago's Black Belt of the Twenties* (New York: Wright-Armstead Associates, 1985), pp. 354–5.

45 Terkel, *Hard Times*, pp. 493–4.

46 Interview with Ernest Dalle–Molle, Chicago, IL, 30 April 1980, IC, pp. 46–7. For other instances of people losing money in bank failures, see Friedman, "Study of One Hundred Unemployed Families," p. 142; Edith Abbott assisted by Sophonisba P. Breckinridge, *The Tenements of Chicago, 1908–1935* (Chicago: University of Chicago Press, 1936), p. 459; Mary Rupcinski to B. Panoff, n.d. but c. 1934, Panoff Project, "The Effect of Depression on Poles," BUR, Box 130, Folder 4; and from interviews in IC: Rena Domke, Chicago, IL, 28 April 1980, p. 59; Thomas (Chick) Perpoli, Chicago, IL, 26 June 1980, pp. 21–2; Rena Morandin, Chicago, IL, 22 July 1980, p. 32; Salvatore Cosentino, Berwyn, IL, 13 July 1979, pp. 30–1; Umberto Mugnaini, Chicago, IL, 17–18 July 1979, p. 2; Rosalie Augustine, Chicago, IL, 5 August 1980, p. 23.

47 Hoyt, *One Hundred Years of Land Values*, p. 270.

48 Pastor Brazinski to B. Panoff, n.d. but c. 1934, Panoff Project, "The Effect of Depression on Poles," BUR, Box 130, Folder 4; "A Negro Bank Closes Its Doors," *Opportunity* 8 (September 1930): 264.
49 Lensing, "Unemployment Study," p. 22.
50 Auditor of Public Accounts, *Annual Reports of Mutual Building, Loan and Homestead Associations, State of Illinois*, 33rd–49th (Springfield: State of Illinois, 1924–40).
51 Friedman, "Study of One Hundred Unemployed Families," p. 145; Lensing, "Unemployment Study," pp. 21–3; Hoyt, *One Hundred Years of Land Values*, p. 369, which gives statistics on the rapid mounting of home foreclosures in Chicago: 3,148 in 1929, 5,818 in 1930, 10,075 in 1931, 15,021 in 1932.
52 S. George Jacobzak to B. Panoff, 17 October 1934, Panoff Project, "The Effect of Depression on Poles," BUR, Box 130, Folder 5.
53 Background research for "Metropolitan Chicago, Illinois: Re-Survey Report Vol. 1, 1940," HOLC, pp. 72–3; Interview with S. C. Mazonkowski, HOLC, Folder "Chicago Report No. 3, 1936," pp. 145–53; also see Division of Research and Statistics, Federal Home Loan Bank Board, "Metropolitan Chicago: A Summary of Economic, Real Estate and Mortgage Finance Survey," 1940, HOLC, "City Survey File," for very high rates of foreclosures in Cook County compared to U.S. average during 1930–6.
54 Mary Rupcinski to B. Panoff, n.d. but c. 1934, Panoff Project, "The Effect of Depression on Poles," BUR, Box 130, Folder 4.
55 "Evictions during the Depression Period," "The Rent Moratorium of the Chicago Relief Agencies, 1931–33," and "Housing Deterioration," in Abbott, *The Tenements of Chicago*, pp. 426–75; Interview with Frank De Liberto, Chicago, IL, 17 April 1980, IC, p. 36; Testimony from L. Johnson, 1934, Panoff Project, "The Effect of Depression on Poles," BUR, Box 130, Folder 3.
56 W. H. Sutherland, "Notes on my work at the Bush," 1932, BUR, Box 138, Folder 7.
57 Interview with Theresa Giannetti, Chicago Heights, IL, 16 April 1980, IC, pp. 5–6.
58 On storekeepers' efforts to limit credit, see Lensing, "Unemployment Study," pp. 17–18, 77; Mrs. Adamczyr to B. Panoff, 5 November 1934, Panoff Project, "The Effect of Depression on Poles," BUR, Box 130, Folder 3, p. 2; Elder, "Study of One Hundred Applicants for Relief," p. 81; Theodorson, "Living Conditions of Fifty Unemployed Families," p. 79.
59 Roland S. Vaile, *Research Memorandum on Social Aspects of Consumption in the Depression* (New York: Arno Press, reprint ed. 1972; originally published 1937), pp. 33–5; "Chain Store Expansion in 1930: A Survey of Chain Store Leasing Activities from Coast to Coast as Reported by Chain Store Specialists," *Chain Store Age* 7 (January 1931): 88; "Chain Store Modernization Active, Survey Reveals," *Chain Store Age (General Merchandise Edition)* 8 (November 1932): 635, 667; Hugh M. Foster, "The Chain Store Comes of Age: They Progress from Depths of Depression to

New Heights in 1936," *Printers' Ink Monthly* 34 (April 1937): 79–94; Godfrey M. Lebhar, "Position and Outlook of Chain Stores," *Chain Store Age* 15 (August 1939): 69–70, 138; Nils Hansell, "American Food Counter," *Printers' Ink Monthly* 40 (February 1940): 5–8, 52; "Business Secrets," BUR, Box 7, Folder 11; *Walgreen Pepper Pod, 50th Anniversary Issue* (June 1951): pp. 14–19; *Seventy-Five Years of Walgreen Progress,* Special Issue of *Walgreen World* 43 (September–October 1976): 7–10; "A&P Goes to the Wars," *Fortune* 17 (April 1938): 92; *Woolworth's First 75 Years: The Story of Everybody's Store* (New York: F. W. Woolworth Co., 1954), pp. 29–30; *A&P, Past, Present and Future* (New York: Progressive Grocer Magazine, n.d.), pp. 4–5, 36–9; Richard Clinton Massell, "The A&P: Large-Scale Operations in the Food Industry" (M.A. thesis, University of Chicago, 1947), pp. 6, 13–15, 127–9; John P. Nichols, *The Chain Store Tells Its Story* (New York: Interstate Distributors, 1940), pp. 89–95; J. Walter Thompson Co., "Analysis of Retail Grocery Sales by Type of Outlet," February 1936, JWT, RG 5; Edwin P. Hoyt, *That Wonderful A&P* (New York: Hawthorne Books, Publishers, n.d.), pp. 157–74; Swift & Company, *Yearbook of 1932, Covering Activities for the Year 1931* (Chicago: Swift & Company, 1932), p. 34.

60 "Minutes of Supervisors' Meeting," 31 March 1931, UNCH, Box 8, Folder 1, p. 3; "Minutes of Districts' Committee Meeting, April 15, 1932," 4 May 1932, UNCH, Box 8, Folder 2, p. 1; "People on Relief May Choose Their Own Grocers," *Osadne Hlasy*, 24 February 1933, CFLPS, Box 40; Friedman, "Study of One Hundred Unemployed Families," pp. 165–6.

61 Joseph Golcz to Honorable Frances Perkins, 4 August 1933, NRA, "Meat Packing and Meat Stockyards."

62 "An Urban Famine: Suffering Communities of Chicago Speak for Themselves. Summary of Open Hearings Held by the Chicago Workers' Committee on Unemployment, January 5–12, 1932," COM, Box 24, pp. 16–17.

63 Interview with Anna Blazewicz, Polonia Oral History Project, CHS, Box 1, pp. 92–3.

64 Mrs. Carl Doyle to Harry Hopkins, 10 June 1933, FERA, "Illinois Complaints, N–Q"; Raymond Sayler, "A Study of Behavior Problems of Boys in the Lower North Community," n.d. but c. 1934, BUR, Box 135, Folder 4, p. 49.

65 Illinois State NRA Office, "Compliance Status of the Retail Food and Grocery Industry in the Chicago Area with Particular Emphasis on the Large Chain Organizations," n.d. but c. 1935, NRA, Region VI Papers.

66 John H. Cover, *Business and Personal Failure and Readjustment in Chicago* (Chicago: University of Chicago Press, 1933); Hoyt, *One Hundred Years of Land Values*, p. 275; Gunnar Myrdal, *An American Dilemma: The Negro Problem and Modern Democracy* (New York: Harper & Brothers Publishers, 1944), pp. 306–7; Interview with Ruth Katz, in Sydelle Kramer and Jenny Masur, eds., *Jewish Grandmothers* (Boston: Beacon Press, 1976), p. 150; Interview with Lillian Cwik, Polonia

Archives, Box 2, CHS, p. 20; and from interviews in IC: Joe Gentili, Chicago, IL, 2 June 1980, p. 19; Margaret Sabella, Chicago, IL, 29 March 1980, p. 13; Rosalie Augustine, Melrose Park, IL, 5 August 1980, p. 29.

67 Godfrey M. Lebhar, "Chain Store Progress in 1930," *Chain Store Age* 7 (January 1931): 33; also see "To Bring Out Hoarded Dollars," *Chain Store Age* 8 (March 1932): 172, and Godfrey M. Lebhar, "Looking Ahead with The Chains," *Chain Store Age (General Merchandise Edition)* 9 (January 1933): 76.

68 L. M. McDermott, "Food Chains and the Housewife," *Chicago Commerce* 33 (June 1936): 22–4; Arthur C. Nielsen, "Solving Marketing Problems of Food Retailers and Manufacturers," Based on an Address to the National Association of Food Chains, Chicago, 11 October 1939, p. 24.

69 "Memo to Members of the Special Conference Committee Summarizing the Relief Activities of the International Harvester Company," 1 June 1932, with two attachments: "Harvester Loan Plan for Unemployment Relief, with an Address by Cyrus McCormick, Jr." and "The Harvester Plan for Unemployment Relief," IH, Document file 15247; Carroll R. Daugherty, Melvin G. De Chazeau, and Samuel S. Stratton, *The Economics of the Iron and Steel Industry*, vol. 1 (New York: McGraw-Hill Book Company, 1937), pp. 177–9; Robert R. R. Brooks, *As Steel Goes, ... Unionism in a Basic Industry* (New Haven: Yale University Press, 1940), pp. 44–5; Horace Davis, *The Condition of Labor in the American Iron and Steel Industry* (New York: International Publishers, 1933), pp. 103, 107; "Works Employe Gardeners Harvest Big Crops," *Harvester World*, September–October 1932, pp. 16–17; Lensing, "Unemployment Study," pp. 12, 79–80; Theodorson, "Living Conditions of Fifty Unemployed Families," p. 12; "Employment Committee," *Industrial Review (published by the Illinois Manufacturers' Association)* 7 (August 1931): 1.

From *Chicago Commerce*: "Business Tackles Relief for Jobless through Association of Commerce," 27 (25 October 1930): 7; Arthur H. Young, "Can Private Initiative Solve the Unemployment Problem?" 27 (27 December 1930): 1; Arthur H. Young, "How Industry 'Feeds the Kitty' to Aid the Jobless," 28 (21 February 1931): 21; Arthur H. Young, "How Industry Protects Its Workers and Gains Efficiency," 28 (14 March 1931): 14; William J. Graham, "Management Takes a Human Look at Itself," 28 (6 June 1931): 14; William Mauthe, "Beating the Dole by Corporation Team Work," 28 (January 1932): 33.

70 Elder, "Study of One Hundred Applicants for Relief," pp. 79–80; also p. 77 on AT&T stocks sold at a great loss; "Minutes of Meeting between Unemployed Groups and Cook County Bureau of Public Welfare Advisory Board," 4 May 1932, Hilliard Papers, Section 2 – Unemployment, Folder "Unemployment Relief, 1927–1932," CHS, p. 1; Friedman, "Study of 100 Unemployed Families," p. 157; "Important Notice to Policy Holders, Good Fellow Club Group Insurance," *South Works Review*, September 1930; "Amendments to Plan of United States Steel Company," in "Information Regarding Pensions, Personnel Conference, Southern Pines,

North Carolina, October 29–November 2, 1940," WE, File HC-121; Davis, *Condition of Labor in American Iron and Steel*, pp. 107, 109, 158; "The U.S. Steel Corporation III," *Fortune* 13 (May 1936): 147; Robert Ozanne, *A Century of Labor–Management Relations at McCormick and International Harvester* (Madison: University of Wisconsin Press, 1967), p. 94; Sanford Jacoby, *Employing Bureaucracy: Managers, Unions, and the Transformation of Work in American Industry, 1900–1945* (New York: Columbia University Press, 1985), pp. 210–11; President's Research Committee, *Recent Social Trends in the United States* (New York: McGraw-Hill Book Company, 1933; reprint ed. Westport, CT: Greenwood Press, 1970), vol. 2, pp. 845–6; and from *Chicago Commerce*, by a director of personnel as told to George Applegren, "Ten Thousand Losers, The Story of a Pension Plan," 30 (December 1933): 21; George Applegren, "Hidden Contingency Harassing to Employer," 30 (January 1934): 27.

71 Interview with Herbert March by Roger Horowitz, San Pedro, CA, 15 July 1985, UPWA Oral History Project.

72 "Chicago Commons Tuesday Discussion Group, Boys and Girls, 'How Does It Feel to be Unemployed,'" 1929, COM, Box 23a, Folder "April 5–December 1929"; Jack M. Stein, "A History of Unionization in the Steel Industry in the Chicago Area" (M.A. thesis, University of Chicago, 1948), p. 38; Swift & Company, *Yearbook of 1932,* p. 5; Swift & Company, *Yearbook of 1933, Covering Activities for the Year 1932* (Chicago: Swift & Company, 1933), p. 5; "Chicago Area Statistics: 8316 Plants in 1933," *Chicago Commerce* 32 (June 1935): 2; Interview with Joseph Arendlt, Polonia Oral History Project, CHS, p. 6; Interview with Anthony Cassano, Burnham, IL, 22 March 1980, IC, p. 39; Interview with Nina Dal Casson, Chicago, IL, 3 December 1979, IC, p. 13; Irving Bernstein, *A Caring Society: The New Deal, the Worker and the Great Depression* (Boston: Houghton Mifflin Company, 1985), pp. 18, 277, 293; Don D. Lescohier, "And the 'Lucky' Who Kept Their Jobs," in John R. Commons, ed., *History of Labor in the United States, 1896–1932*, vol. 3, (New York: Macmillan Company, 1935), pp. 92–6, reprinted in David A. Shannon, ed., *The Great Depression* (Englewood Cliffs, NJ: Prentice-Hall, 1960), pp. 7–10.

73 Drake and Cayton, *Black Metropolis*, pp. 83, 261–2; Raymond A. Mohl and Neil Betten, *Steel City: Gary, Indiana, 1906–1950* (New York: Holmes & Meier, 1986), p. 75; Ozanne, *Century of Labor–Management Relations*, p. 187; Interview with Elmer Thomas by Betty Burke, Chicago, IL, 11 May 1938, FWP, Folklore, Life Histories, A707; Richard L. Rowan, *The Negro in the Steel Industry*, Report no. 3 in the Racial Policies of American Industry (Philadelphia: Wharton School of Finance and Commerce, University of Pennsylvania, 1968), pp. 26–9; Walter A. Fogel, *The Negro in the Meat Industry*, Report no. 12, Racial Policies of American Industry Series (Philadelphia: Wharton School of Finance of Commerce, University of Pennsylvania, 1970), pp. 50–1; Theodore V. Purcell, *The Worker Speaks His Mind on Company and Union* (Cambridge, MA:

Harvard University Press, 1953), p. 17; Janet Laura Weiss, "Industrial Relations in the Calumet District of Indiana" (M.A. thesis, University of Chicago, 1937), p. 45; Edward Greer, "Racism and U.S. Steel, 1906–1974," *Radical America* 10 (September–October 1976): 53.

74 Paul Taylor, *Mexican Labor in the United States: Chicago and the Calumet Region*, vol. 7, no. 2, University of California Publications in Economics (Berkeley: University of California Press, 1932), p. 35; Edward Jackson Bauer, "Delinquency among Mexican Boys in South Chicago" (M.A. thesis, University of Chicago, 1938), pp. 35–6, 291; "Mexican Work Reports," October 1930 and annual report 1930–1, MCD, Box 21; Louise Ano Nuevo Kerr, "The Chicano Experience in Chicago: 1920–1970" (Ph.D. dissertation, University of Illinois at Chicago, 1976), pp. 69–83; in *Aztlan* 7 (Summer 1976): Francesco Arturo Rosales, "The Regional Origins of Mexican Immigrants to Chicago during the 1920's," p. 191, and Gilbert Cardenas, "Los Desarraigados: Chicanos in the Midwestern Region of the United States," p. 162; and from the CFLPS: "Act of Barbarism" and "Assaulted Mexican," *La Lucha*, 28 April 1934, Box 40; "Return of Mexicans to Homeland," *El Nacional*, 28 May 1932, Box 41; "Immigration," *Chicago Daily Tribune*, 28 June 1932, Box 41; "Message from the Mexican Consul," *El Nacional*, 14 May 1932, Box 41; "A Repatriation Program," *La Defensa*, 18 January 1936, Box 41.

75 For work sharing more broadly, see Jacoby, *Employing Bureaucracy*, pp. 212–14. On Western Electric's treatment of its employees during the depression, see "The Great Depression," *Western Electric*, September–October 1981: Special Issue "100 Years in the Bell System," p. 16. From HC-121, WE: "Termination of Employment," "Comparison of Termination Allowance Schedules 1/1/30 to 10/13/46 Hourly Rated Employees," "Hours of Work," and "History of Western Electric Company's Termination Allowance Plans," in "History of Personnel Practice File"; O. C. Richter, "Bell System Employee Security Plans," 31 July 1935, p. 14; "Employment Stabilization and Aid to Employees during Periods of Reduced Activity"; "History of Vacation Provisions, Hourly Rated Employees," 15 April 1938, p. 3; "Thrift: Employers' Stock Plan," p. 2. Interview with Dominick Di Mucci, Chicago, IL, 19 July 1979, IC, pp. 45–6; Mildred M. Beard, "That's Where Their Money Goes: This Tale of the Pay Envelope Discloses Some Surprising and Unusual Ways in Which Western Electric Women Spend Their Wages," *Western Electric News*, February 1931, pp. 14–15; and many articles in *Hawthorne Microphone*, including: "Works Committee Formed to Assist Relief Programs," 1 December 1930; "Outline Works Charity Plan," 19 October 1931; "Record $800,000 Gain in Works Life Insurance," 29 January 1932; "Cancellation Privileges under the Employers AT&T Stock Plan," May 1932; "Building and Loan Association to Have Federal Loan Funds Available November 1," October 1932; "Expert Skilled Craftsmen at Works Will Do Work at Home" and "Plan Project to Make Work for Our Shops," January 1933.

76 Interview with John Mega by author, Chicago, IL, 27 January 1988.

77 Interview about South Deering with Dan Delluch, Arthur O'Leary, Dr. Romeo Pallutto, and Alexander Savastana by Jim Martin and Dominic Pacyga, Chicago, IL, n.d. but c. 1982, SECHP, p. 6.

On U.S. Steel's poorer record, see Interview with George Patterson, December 1970–January 1971, ROHP, pp. 7–9; George Patterson, Autobiography, Book 1 – "Embryo Steelworker," PAT, Box 9, Files 6 and 7, p. 7; Jim Fitzgibbon, "Tracing Baseball to Great Depression," *Daily Calumet*, Special SECHP Section, 9 November 1982, p. 10; "The U.S. Steel Corporation III," *Fortune* 13 (May 1936): 138, 141.

78 Interview with Justin Cordero by Jim Martin, Chicago, IL, 2 October 1981, SECHP, p. 12; Ozanne, *Century of Labor–Management Relations*, pp. 52, 93–4, 143–4; James R. McIntyre, "The History of Wisconsin Steel Works of the International Harvester Company," 1951, Typescript, SECHP, p. 52; Industrial Relations Department, "Manufacturing Divisions International Harvester Company: Labor Turnover and Labor Stability Report," 1930–5, IH, Document file 19431; Interview with Harry O. Bercher by author, Chicago, IL, 26 January 1988, Tape 1, Side 2; see Tape 2, Side 1, on the autonomy of Wisconsin Steel's management within Harvester.

79 David Bensman and Roberta Lynch, *Rusted Dreams: Hard Times in a Steel Community* (New York: McGraw-Hill Book Company, 1987), pp. 39, 43–4; Barbara Marsh, *A Corporate Tragedy: The Agony of International Harvester Company* (New York: Doubleday & Company, 1985), p. 58.

80 Robert McElvaine, *The Great Depression: America 1929–1941* (New York: Times Books, 1984), p. 172.

81 Nada Chupkavich, "Yugoslavs in Chicago and Depression," 26 February 1935, BUR, Box 130, Folder 4; Interview with George Beal, in Robert McMurray, "Study of the Effect of the Depression on a Three-Block Area: Federal, Wabash and Calumet between 47th and 51st Streets," 1934, BUR, Box 133, Folder 1; L. Hickok to A. Williams, 31 October 1935, Harry Hopkins Papers, FDR Library, cited in Bernstein, *A Caring Society*, p. 146. Also see "Report of the Work of Chicago Commons Association for the Year 1940," COM, Box 5, p. 1; "Aged Unemployed Workers Cannot Find Work," *Dziennik Zjednoczenia*, 8 January 1929, CFLPS; President's Research Committee, *Recent Social Trends*, vol. 2, p. 311; Eugene Lyman Fisk, M.D., "The Man Over Forty, *Chicago Commerce* 27 (20 September 1930): 9.

82 Gladys L. Palmer and Katherine D. Wood, *Urban Workers on Relief*, Part 1 – "The Occupational Characteristics of Workers on Relief in Urban Areas, May 1934" (Washington, DC: Works Progress Administration, 1936), pp. xx, 286–9; "Report of the Work of Chicago Commons Association For the Year Ended September 30, 1935," COM, Box 5, p. 1; Interview with Pastor Brazinski, Panoff Project, "The Effect of Depression on Poles," 1934, BUR, Box 130, Folder 4; Interview with Marie Czamouski, Polonia Archives, CHS, p. 36; Clinch Calkins, *Some Folks Won't Work* (New York: Harcourt, Brace and Company, 1930), pp. 113–14; Ruth

Milkman, "Women's Work and the Economic Crisis: Some Lessons from the Great Depression," in Nancy F. Cott and Elizabeth H. Pleck, *A Heritage of Her Own* (New York: Simon & Schuster, 1979), pp. 507–41; Lois Scharf, *To Work and To Wed: Female Employment, Feminism, and the Great Depression* (Westport, CT: Greenwood Press, 1980).

83 From the Panoff Project, "The Effect of Depression on Poles," 1934, BUR: Statement from Harriet A. Lesniak, Box 130, Folder 4; Statement of Altina Rumyzewicz, Box 130, Folder 3, p. 3; Statement of Mrs. Adamczyk, 5 November 1934, Box 130, Folder 3, p. 2. Also, Interview with Margaret Bradburn, truant officer, in Robert McMurray, "Study of Effect of Depression on Three-Block Area: Federal, Wabash and Calumet between 47th and 51st Streets," 1934, BUR, Box 133, Folder 1, pp. 3–4; Cavan and Ranck, *The Family and the Depression*, pp. 161–78; Weiss, "Industrial Relations in the Calumet District of Indiana," p. 45; from IC: Interview with Frank Corradetti, Chicago Heights, IL, 13 May 1980, p. 11; Interview with Teresa De Falco, Chicago, IL, 28 April 1980, p. 28; Interview with Rena Morandin, Chicago, IL, 22 July 1980, p. 32; and Robert S. Lynd and Helen Merrell Lynd, *Middletown in Transition: A Study in Cultural Conflicts* (New York: Harcourt, Brace and Company, 1937), pp. 149–52.

84 Mirra Komarovsky, *The Unemployed Man and His Family: The Effect of Unemployment upon the Status of the Man in Fifty-nine Families* (New York: Dryden Press, 1940), pp. 74–7, quoted in David Kennedy, ed., *The American People in the Depression* (West Haven, CT: Pendulum Press, 1973), p. 74.

85 "Collection of Life Histories of Italians," BUR, Box 172, Folder 3; Cavan and Ranck, *The Family and the Depression*, p. 131; from Panoff Project, "The Effect of Depression on Poles," 1934, BUR, Box 130: Interview with President of Local #5 Unemployed Council, 24 December 1934, Folder 4, and Statement from Dr. M. J. Kostrzewski, Folder 3.

86 Interview with Father Victor, Panoff Project, "The Effect of Depression on Poles," 1934, BUR, Box 130, Folder 4.

87 Statement of Clara Odeski, 15 November 1934, Panoff Project, "The Effect of Depression on Poles," 1934, BUR, Box 130, Folder 4.

88 Interview with Bernice Wozniak, Panoff Project, "The Effect of Depression on Poles," 1934, BUR, Box 130, Folder 4.

89 Eli Ginzberg, *The Unemployed* (New York: Harper and Brothers, 1943), pp. 76–9, reprinted in Kennedy, ed., *American People in the Depression*, pp. 65–8; also see quotation in Bernstein, *Caring Society*, p. 21.

90 Ernest W. Burgess, "The Effect of Unemployment upon the Family and the Community," n.d. but c. 1942, BUR, Box 52, Folder 1, p. 4.

91 Interview with Larry Van Dusen, in Terkel, *Hard Times*, p. 131. Also see statement of S. George Jacobzak, Attorney, 17 October 1934, Panoff Project, "The Effect of Depression on Poles," 1934, BUR, Box 130, Folder 5; Coral Brooke, "Youth Engulfed," *The Survey* 71 (January 1935): 10–12, reprinted in Kennedy, ed., *American People in the Depression*, pp.

35–42; Komarovsky, *Unemployed Man and His Family*, pp. 97–101, reprinted in Kennedy, ed., *American People in the Depression*, pp. 69–73; Interview with Sister Mary Augustine, Chicago, IL, 7 August 1980, IC, p. 43.

92 Mary G. Midura to B. Panoff, 6 November 1934, Panoff Project, "The Effect of Depression on Poles," 1934, BUR, Box 130, Folder 4, UCSC, p. 2. Also see Institut de Recherches Sociales (Geneva), "Enquiry on Influence of Unemployment on Family Life" (20 surveys of Chicago families), BUR, Box 100, Folder 6; Florence Nesbitt, "Present Relief Policies and Their Effect on Family Relationships," *Journal of Home Economics* 27 (December 1935): 627; Esther S. Swerdloff, "The Effect of the Depression on Family Life," *The Family* 13 (January 1933): 310–14; Samuel A. Stouffer and Paul F. Lazarsfeld, *Research Memorandum on the Family in the Depression* (New York: Social Science Research Council, 1937).

6. WORKERS MAKE A NEW DEAL

1 Mrs. Olga Ferk to Franklin D. Roosevelt, 11 April 1935, FERA, Illinois 460, "Special Folder Cook County."

2 Arthur W. Kornhauser, "Analysis of 'Class Structure' of Contemporary American Society – Psychological Bases of Class Divisions," in George W. Hartmann and Theodore Newcomb, *Industrial Conflict: A Psychological Interpretation* (First Yearbook of the Society for the Psychological Study of Social Issues, Affiliate of the American Psychological Association) (New York: Cordon Company, 1940), pp. 251–2, 255.

3 My analysis of voting behavior in Chicago from 1924 to 1940 depends heavily on Kristi Anderson, *The Creation of a Democratic Majority, 1928–1936* (Chicago: University of Chicago Press, 1979), pp. 83–120. I have also been helped by Dianne M. Pinderhughes, *Race and Ethnicity in Chicago Politics: A Reexamination of Pluralist Theory* (Urbana: University of Illinois Press, 1987), pp. 39–108, and John M. Allswang, *A House For All Peoples: Ethnic Politics in Chicago 1890–1936* (Lexington: University Press of Kentucky, 1971). For an analysis of voting on the national level that comes to similar conclusions about low voter turnout in the 1920s and the mobilization of voters in the 1930s in major cities like Chicago, see Paul Kleppner, *Who Voted? The Dynamics of Electoral Turnout, 1870–1980* (New York: Praeger Publishers, 1982), pp. 55–111.

4 Interview with George Patterson, December 1970, ROHP, p. 155.

5 Anderson, *Democratic Majority*, pp. 90–2; Sonya Forthal, *Cogwells of Democracy: A Study of The Precinct Captain* (New York: William-Frederick Press, 1946); Dianne Marie Pinderhughes, "Interpretations of Racial and Ethnic Participation in American Politics: The Cases of the Black, Italian and Polish Communities in Chicago, 1910–1940" (Ph.D. dissertation, University of Chicago, 1977), pp. 171, 177–81, 194–209;

Edward Mazur, "Jewish Chicago: From Diversity to Community," in Melvin Holli and Peter d'A. Jones, eds., *The Ethnic Frontier: Essays in the History of Group Survival in Chicago and the Midwest* (Grand Rapids, MI: William B. Eerdmans Publishing Company, 1977), pp. 284–5.

6 John M. Allswang, *Bosses, Machines and Urban Voters* (Baltimore: Johns Hopkins University Press, revised ed., 1986), pp. 105–16; Alex Gottfried, *Boss Cermak of Chicago: A Study of Political Leadership* (Seattle: University of Washington Press, 1962); Humbert S. Nelli, *Italians in Chicago, 1880–1930: A Study in Ethnic Mobility* (New York: Oxford University Press, 1979), p. 234; Pinderhughes, "Interpretations," p. 166; and interviews that attest to people's new Democratic identification, IC, Chicago, IL: Interview with Sylvio Petri, 8 June 1981, p. 10, and Alfred Fantozzi, 27 May 1980, p. 37.

7 Harold F. Gosnell, *Machine Politics Chicago Model* (Chicago: University of Chicago Press, 1937; Midway reprint 1968), p. 145.

8 Allswang, *House for All Peoples*, pp. 118–28; Gosnell, *Machine Politics Chicago Model*, pp. 144–9; Douglas Bukowski, "William Dever and Prohibition: The Mayoral Elections of 1923 and 1927," *Chicago History* 7 (Summer 1978): 109–18; Raymond Edward Nelson, "A Study of an Isolated Industrial Community: Based on Personal Documents Secured by the Participant Observer Method" (M.A. thesis, University of Chicago, 1929), pp. 144–50, 167–9, 233–4, 241–2, 246–7; Nelli, *Italians in Chicago*, p. 234; Gottfried, *Boss Cermak*, pp. 115–19, 157–61; from FITZ: Mrs. Leslie Wheeler to John Fitzpatrick, 17 October 1930, Box 18, Folder 129; "What Prompted Prohibition?" n.d., Box 25, Folder 169A; John Fitzpatrick to Mrs. Glenn Plumb, 26 October 1928, Box 17, Folder 123; and from CFLPS: "The Reformers Went Too Far," *Polonia*, 7 September 1922, Box 32; "Both Sides of the Prohibition Problem: An Interesting Debate between Alderman Anton J, Cermak and John A. Lyle," *Denni Hlasatel*, 6 March 1922, Box 1; "Italophobia," *Bulletin Italian American National Union*, April 1925, Box 21; "People's Sentiment against Prohibition," *Amerikanski Slovenec*, 17 February 1926.

Evidence abounds that drinking did not stop in Chicago's ethnic, working-class neighborhoods during the 1920s despite harassment; in other words, workers and their families ignored the Volstead Act. See Marie Waite, "Prohibition Survey of the Stockyards Community Made by the University of Chicago Settlement," December 1926, MCD, Box 7; "Study of Prohibition for the National Federation of Settlements," 1926, COM, Box 24, Folder "Prohibition"; Norman Sylvester Hayner, "The Effect of Prohibition in Packingtown" (M.A. thesis, University of Chicago, 1921); Marian Winthrop Taylor, "The Social Results of Prohibition: A Study Made in the Central District of the United Charities" (M.A. thesis, University of Chicago, 1923); Anonymous, "The Lower Northwest Side," n.d. but c. 1928, Student paper for Professor Burgess, COM, Box 23, p. 24; Esther Crockett Quaintance, "Rents and Housing Conditions in the Italian District of the Lower North Side of Chicago, 1924" (M.A. thesis, University of

Chicago, 1925), p. 8; John Valentino, "Of the Second Generation," *Survey* (18 March 1922), reprinted in Wayne Moquin and Charles Van Doren, *A Documentary History of the Italian Americans* (New York: Praeger Publishers, 1974), pp. 355–7; Interviews, Chicago, IL, IC, with Mario Avignone, 12 July 1979, Tape 1 (pp. 25–6), Tape 2 (pp. 15–16), and Joe LaGuidici, 21 July 1980, p. 59; Marie Bensley Bruere, *Does Prohibition Work? A Study of the Operation of the Eighteenth Amendment Made by the National Federation of Settlements, Assisted by Social Workers in Different Parts of the United States* (New York: Harper & Brothers, 1927).

For evidence that Chicago's manufacturers promoted Prohibition and let their workers know it, see *Harvester World*, July 1919, Editorial; *South Works Review*, March–April 1919, Cartoon; Taylor, "Social Results of Prohibition," pp. 108–17; Hayner, "Effect of Prohibition in Packingtown"; Eugene J. Benge, "The Effect of Prohibition on Industry from the Viewpoint of an Employment Manager," *Annals of the American Academy* 109 (September 1923): 110–20; Herman Feldman, *Prohibition: Its Economic and Industrial Aspects* (New York: D. Appleton and Company, 1927).

9 *Fifteenth Census of the United States, 1930* and *Census of Religious Bodies, 1928*, compiled by Allswang, *Bosses, Machines, and Urban Voters*, p. 93.

10 Quoted in Allswang, *Bosses, Machines, and Urban Voters*, p. 110. For more on the operation of the Democratic machine in Chicago during the 1930s and its links to Roosevelt's New Deal, see "The Kelly–Nash Political Machine," *Fortune* 14 (August 1936): 47; Paul M. Green and Melvin G. Holli, eds., *The Mayors: The Chicago Political Tradition* (Carbondale: Southern Illinois University Press, 1987), pp. 99–125; Gene Delon Jones, "The Local Political Significance of New Deal Relief Legislation in Chicago: 1933–1940" (Ph.D. dissertation, Northwestern University, 1970); William Roger Biles, "Mayor Edward J. Kelly of Chicago: Big City Boss in Depression and War" (Ph.D. dissertation, University of Illinois at Chicago, 1981).

11 Anderson, *Democratic Majority*, pp. 92–120. The elections of 1928–36 have received a good deal of attention from political scientists and historians who have tried to identify which was the "critical election" when the balance of political power was realigned. My own preference is to downplay the debate over whether 1928, 1932, or 1936 was the "critical election" and consider a "critical period" during which not only were voters converted to the Democratic party but also new people were mobilized as voters. For the debate, see Bernard Sternsher, "The New Deal Party System: A Reappraisal," *Journal of Interdisciplinary History* 15 (Summer 1984): 53–81, and Alan J. Lichtman, "Critical Elections Theory and the Reality of American Presidential Politics, 1916–40," *American Historical Review* 81 (April 1976): 317–48.

12 "Report of the Head Resident for the Year Ending September 30, 1933," COM, Box 5, Folder "Annual Reports 1933–35," p. 3. Also see Heitmann, "Report on Americanization Classes in Chicago Public Schools," 28 April 1934, MCD, Box 2, Folder 11.

13 Interview with Ed Paulsen, in Studs Terkel, *Hard Times: An Oral History of the Great Depression* (New York: Avon Books, 1971), p. 49.

14 Interview by author with John Mega, Chicago, IL, 27 January 1988. A retired sheetmetal worker, who was born in Yugoslavia but spent most of his life in Southeast Chicago, told a *New York Times* reporter right before the Illinois primary in March 1988 that by following machine boss Edward Vrdolyak into the Republican Party and voting for him for circuit court clerk and George Bush for president, he will be voting Republican for the first time since he cast his first ballot for Roosevelt in 1932. R. W. Apple, Jr., "Where the Political Vista Is Not of the White House," *New York Times*, 14 March 1988.

15 Celie Carradina to Mr. Roosevelt, 30 December 1935, WPA 693, "Illinois C–D."

16 Edward Hornbeck to Mrs. Franklin D. Roosevelt, n.d. but c. December 1935, WPA 693, "Illinois H–K."

17 Mr. and Mrs. Richard Memenga to The President, 4 December 1935, WPA 693, "Illinois M," and (Mrs.) Freda L. Smith to His Excellency Franklin D. Roosevelt, 29 October 1935, WPA 693, "Illinois S-T."

18 Anderson, *Creation of a Democratic Majority*, pp. 104–6; Pinderhughes, *Race and Ethnicity*, pp. 71, 86.

19 Harold F. Gosnell, *Politicians: The Rise of Negro Politics in Chicago* (Chicago: University of Chicago Press, 1935); Harold Gosnell, "The Chicago 'Black Belt' as a Political Battlefield," *American Journal of Sociology* 29 (November 1933): 329–41; Dempsey J. Travis, *An Autobiography of Black Politics* (Chicago: Urban Research Press, 1987), pp. 56–91.

20 Ralph J. Bunche, "The Thompson–Negro Alliance," *Opportunity* 7 (March 1929): 78–80. On blacks' shift from the Republican to the Democratic Party during the 1930s, see Elmer William Henderson, "A Study of the Basic Factors Involved in the Change in the Party Alignment of Negroes in Chicago, 1932–1938" (M.A. thesis, University of Chicago, 1939); Rita Werner Gordon, "The Change in the Political Alignment of Chicago's Negroes During the New Deal," *Journal of American History* 56 (December 1969): 584–603; Biles, "Mayor Edward J. Kelly of Chicago," pp. 154–72; St. Clair Drake and Horace R. Cayton, *Black Metropolis: A Study of Negro Life in a Northern City* (New York: Harcourt, Brace and Company, 1945), pp. 346–55, 370–7; Travis, *Autobiography of Black Politics*, pp. 92–159; Nancy J. Weiss, *Farewell to the Party of Lincoln: Black Politics in the Age of FDR* (Princeton: Princeton University Press, 1983), *passim* and particularly pp. 228–9; Pinderhughes, "Interpretation," pp. 209–41; Interview with Mrs. Willye Jeffries, in Terkel, *Hard Times*, p. 461.

21 "Jelly" was slang meaning "getting by or taking advantage of an opportunity"; the inference in the poem is to a bribe. Grace Outlaw, "Folk-lore – Negro Lore," FWP, Folklore, Box A587, p. 3. For Democratic efforts to capitalize on blacks' dependence on New Deal Programs, see the Colored Division of the Democratic National Campaign Committee, "Take Your Choice: New Deal and the Negro," 1936, BAR, Box 341, Folder 1.

22 An extremely valuable source on the activities of the Communist Party in Chicago during the first half of the 1930s is Harold D. Lasswell and Dorothy Blumenstock, *World Revolutionary Propaganda: A Chicago Study* (New York: Alfred A. Knopf, 1939). On the membership of the Chicago party, see particularly pp. 47, 139–40, 196–204, 307; 391–3; also Harvey Klehr, *The Heyday of American Communism: The Depression Decade* (New York: Basic Books, 1984), pp. 162, 329–33, 469; and Harry Haywood, *Black Bolshevik: Autobiography of an Afro–American Communist* (Chicago: Lake View Press, 1978), pp. 441–66. On the party's appeal to blacks, see Michael Gold, "The Communists Meet," *New Republic* 71 (15 June 1932): 117–19; Frank L. Hayes, "Chicago's Rent Riot," *Survey* 66 (15 September 1931): 548–9; Mark Naison, *Communists in Harlem during the Depression* (New York: Grove Press, 1984), pp. 279–84. On the party's Popular Front strategy, see Klehr, *Heyday*, pp. 167–280, and Naison, *Communists in Harlem*, p. 256.

23 For background on the Communist Unemployed Councils in Chicago, see Lasswell and Blumenstock, *World Revolutionary Propaganda, passim*, but particularly pp. 170–2; Steve Nelson, James R. Barrett, and Rob Ruck, *Steve Nelson: American Radical* (Pittsburgh: University of Pittsburgh Press, 1981), pp. 70–87; Description of conditions in United Charities' district offices, 13 October 1931, and minutes of superintendents' meeting, 31 March 1931, UNCH, Box 8, Folder 1; Materials on Unemployed Council activities, 1932–4 and *The Chicago Hunger Fighter* (biweekly newspaper of the Unemployed Council of Chicago), random issues, 1932–4, Hilliard Papers, Section 2, CHS; Jack Martin, *On Relief in Illinois* (Chicago: Chicago Pen and Hammer, n.d. but c. 1935); Daniel J. Leab, "'United We Eat': The Creation and Organization of the Unemployed Councils in 1930," *Labor History* 8 (Fall 1967): 300–14. For vivid descriptions of eviction protests see Interview with Katherine Hyndman, 1970, ROHP, pp. 51–4.

On the Socialist Chicago Workers' Committee on Unemployment, see Robert E. Asher, "The Influence of the Chicago Workers' Committee on Unemployment upon the Administration of Relief, 1931–1934" (M.A. thesis, University of Chicago, 1934); Robert E. Asher, "Chicago's Unemployed Show Their Fist," *Revolt* (December 1932): 15; Gertrude Springer, "Shock Troops to the Rescue: Chicago Settlement Houses Have Become Centers for a New Kind of Life for Those Who Must Live on 'The Relief,'" *Survey* 69 (January 1933): 9–11; Materials on the activities of the Chicago Workers' Committee on Unemployment and *New Frontier* (biweekly newspaper of the Chicago Workers' Committee on Unemployment), 12 December 1932, Hilliard Papers, Section 2, CHS; Karl Borders, "When Unemployed Organize," *The Unemployed*, no. 5 (publication of the League for Industrial Democracy), 1931, pp. 22–3, 34; Karl Borders, "The Unemployed Strike Out for Themselves: 1. They Speak Up in Chicago," *Survey* 67 (15 March 1932): 663–5; from COM: Annual reports, 1932, 1933, 1934, Box 5 and Minute Book of Local #5, Workers' Committee on Unemployment, 1933–7 (in Italian), Box 25, and miscellaneous papers concerned with the Workers' Committee, Boxes 24–7; "Record of the Development of the Clubs for Unemployed Men and Women," c. 1933, University of Chicago Settlement Papers, Box 20, Folder "Adult Dept. Reports, 1922–1934," CHS; Materials on Chicago Workers' Committee on Unemployment, c. 1934, MCD, Box 3, Folder 15; Mollie Ray Carroll, "The University of Chicago Settlement, Report for January 1933," BUR, Box 18, Folder 11; Walter C. Hart, "Relief – As the Clients See It" (M.A. thesis, University of Chicago, 1936); "An Urban Famine: Suffering Communities of Chicago Speak for Themselves: Summary of Open Hearings Held by the Chicago Workers' Committee on Unemployment, January 5–12, 1932," COM, Box 24, Folder "July 1931–January 1932"; Judith Ann Trolander, *Settlement Houses and the Depression* (Detroit: Wayne State University Press, 1975), pp. 91–106; Roy Rosenzweig, "'Socialism in Our Time': The Socialist Party and the Unemployed, 1929–1936," *Labor History* 20 (Fall 1979): 485–508.

A few sources deal with both unemployed organizations within Chicago. My interpretation has been influenced particularly by Roy Rosenzweig's "Organizing the Unemployed: The Early Years of the Great Depression, 1929–1933," *Radical America* 10 (July–August 1976): 36–60. Also see Helen Seymour, "The Organized Unemployed" (M.A. thesis, University of Chicago, 1937); Mario Manzardo, "Christmas, 1934," *South End Reporter*, 11 December 1974, IC, Item 69.17; Hilliard Papers, Section 2, *passim*, particularly 1932–3; Franz Z. Glick, "The Illinois Emergency Relief Commission" (Ph.D. dissertation, University of Chicago, 1939; published by University of Chicago Press, 1940), pp. 117–37; "Minutes of a Hearing for the Unemployed arranged by Miss Breckenridge of the Advisory Committee of the County Board," 4 May 1932, Hilliard Papers, Section 2, CHS; Lasswell and Blumenstock, *World Revolutionary Propaganda*, p. 273.

24 The 1932 citywide vote for Socialist, Communist, and Socialist Labor presidential candidates may be of some help in estimating membership in unemployed groups: 31,133 Socialist; 11,879 Communist; and 1,592 Socialist Labor. These numbers are four times the Socialist vote of 1928, six-and-a-half times the Communist, and two-and-a-half times the Socialist Labor. Still, however, they together only total 3 percent of the vote for president, whereas 97 percent of the vote went for the candidates of the two major parties. Philip Booth, "The Socialist and Communist Vote in Chicago: A Summary Study," 1933, MCD, Box 3, Folder 19.

25 Nelson et al., *Steve Nelson*, p. 78.

26 *Ibid.*, p. 76; Lasswell and Blumenstock, *World Revolutionary Propaganda*, pp. 91–2.

27 Paul Hutchinson, "Hunger on the March," *Christian Century* (9 November 1932): 1377–88; "The Workers' Committee and the Hunger March of October 31, 1932," MCD, Box 25, Folder "Adult Dept. 1932–1938"; Trolander, *Settlement Houses*, pp. 97–8; and miscellaneous papers concerning the hunger march, COM, Box 25.

28 Materials on the Illinois Workers' Alliance and the Workers' Alliance of America in Victor Olander Papers, File 157, UICC; "How to Win Work at a Living Wage Or a Decent Standard of Relief with the Workers Alliance of America," Workers Alliance of America, 1937; Rosenzweig, "Socialism in Our Time," pp. 503–8; Asher, "Influence of Chicago Workers' Committee," pp. 27–9; Frances Fox Piven and Richard A. Cloward, *Poor People's Movements: Why They Succeed, How they Fail* (New York: Vintage Books, 1979), pp. 85–92.

29 Seymour, "Organized Unemployed," p. 58.

30 On the involvement of blacks in the unemployed organizations, particularly the Communist Unemployed Councils, see Lasswell and Blumenstock, *World Revolutionary Propaganda*, p. 280; Gosnell, *Negro Politicians*, pp. 325–52; St. Clair Drake, "Churches and Voluntary Associations in the Chicago Negro Community," Report of Official Project 465-54-3-386 Conducted under the Auspices of the Works Projects Administration, December 1940, pp. 257–64; Drake and Cayton, *Black Metropolis*, pp. 86–8, 734–40; Edith Abbott, *The Tenements of Chicago* (New York: Arno Press and The New York Times, 1970), pp. 442–3; Dempsey Travis, *An Autobiography of Black Chicago* (Chicago: Urban Research Institute, 1981), pp. 48–52; Terkel, *Hard Times*, pp. 455–62, 498–502; Elizabeth Balanoff, "A History of the Black Community of Gary, Indiana, 1906–1940" (Ph.D. dissertation, University of Chicago, 1974), pp. 205–6; "Reds! Chicago's Communists: Nothing to Lose But Their Chains," *Chicago Tribune Magazine*, 23 May 1982.

31 Annie Gosenpud, "The History of the Chicago Workers' Committee on Unemployment Local #94 Until February 1933," Paper for Social Pathology 270, February 1933, BUR, Box 144, Folder 7; Nelson et al., *Steve Nelson*, pp. 75–8. For other discussion of how unemployed groups appealed to ethnic organizations, see interviews with Mario Manzardo and Nick Migas in Alice and Staughton Lynd, eds., *Rank and File: Personal Histories by Working-Class Organizers* (Princeton: Princeton University Press, 1981), pp. 138–9, 166–7.

32 Two examples of revisionist works that stress the conservative character of the New Deal are Barton Bernstein, "The New Deal: The Conservative Achievements of Liberal Reform," in Bernstein, ed., *Towards a New Past: Dissenting Essays in American History* (New York: Vintage Books, 1969), pp. 263–88, and Mark Leff, "Taxing the 'Forgotten Man': The Politics of Social Security Finance in the New Deal," *Journal of American History* 70 (September 1983).

33 See the many letters of complaint to the president and to Harry L. Hopkins in the FERA files, particularly Mr. and Mrs. John Jerzyk to "Sir", 30 November 1933, FERA 460, "Illinois Complaints J," and Chicago Workers' Committee on Unemployment to Mr. Harry L. Hopkins, 10 May 1935, FERA 460, "Illinois Complaints C." Also, Jones, "Local Political Significance of New Deal Relief," particularly p. 145; Harry L. Hopkins, *Spending to Save: The Complete Story of Relief* (New York: W. W.

Norton & Company, 1936); Arthur P. Miles, "Federal Aid and Public Assistance in Illinois" (Ph.D. dissertation, University of Chicago, 1940); Henderson, "Study of Basic Factors Involved in Change in Party Alignment of Negroes," pp. 54–6.

34 Grace Abbott, *From Relief to Social Security: The Development of the New Public Welfare Services and Their Administration* (New York: Russell & Russell, 1966), pp. 134–5; United Charities, "A Friend of the Family: United Charities of Chicago, 1857–1957," 1957, UNCH, Box 1, Folder 1; United Charities, "United Charities of Chicago: Eighty Years of Service," 1937; Minutes of Subscriptions Investigating Committee of Chicago Association of Commerce Meeting 16 December 1937," 4 January 1938, WC, Box 260; Jeannette Margaret Elder, "A Study of One Hundred Applicants for Relief the Fourth Winter of Unemployment" (M.A. thesis, University of Chicago, 1933), pp. 9–10; William Hillman, "Urbanization and the Organization of Welfare Activities in the Metropolitan Community of Chicago" (Ph.D. dissertation, University of Chicago, 1940); David J. Maurer, "Unemployment in Illinois during the Great Depression," in Donald F. Tingley, ed., *Essays in Illinois History in Honor of Glenn Huron Seymour* (Carbondale, IL: Southern Illinois University Press, 1968), pp. 120–32.

35 *The Catholic Charities of the Archdiocese of Chicago* (Chicago: Archdiocese of Chicago, 1940); Reverend Monsignor Harry C. Koenig, *Caritas Christi Urget Nos: A History of the Offices, Agencies, and Institutions of the Archdiocese of Chicago* (Chicago: Archdiocese of Chicago, n.d.), vol. 2, pp. 814–15; Jennie Rovner Zetland, "Private Agencies and the Development of Public Assistance in Chicago, 1911–1935" (M.A. thesis, University of Chicago, 1947), pp. 69, 72; Edward Kantowicz, "Cardinal Mundelein of Chicago and the Shaping of Twentieth-Century American Catholicism," *Journal of American History* 68 (June 1981): 65–6. On Mundelein's personal determination to keep the government from providing welfare to Catholics, see Edward Kantowicz, *Corporation Sole: Cardinal Mundelein and Chicago Catholicism* (Notre Dame: University of Notre Dame Press, 1983), pp. 145–6.

For the Chicago social work establishment's criticism of this deal between the church and the IERC, see "Memo to the Board of Directors, Council of Social Agencies of Chicago from the Chairman, Family Welfare Division, Council of Social Agencies," 10 August 1933, UNCH, Box 8, Folder 4; "Resolution of the Board of Directors of the Council of Social Agencies of Chicago Protesting the Policy of the Illinois Emergency Relief Commission in Making a Portion of the Staff of the Central Charity Bureau and the Society of St. Vincent de Paul Integral Part of the Cook County Bureau of Public Welfare," 10 August 1933, and Chicago Chapter of the American Association of Social Workers to Harry L. Hopkins, 21 August 1933, WC, Box 256, Folder "Catholic Charities 1933–59."

36 Genevieve Ann Lensing, "An Unemployment Study in the Stockyards District" (M.A. thesis, University of Chicago, 1932), p. 78; Interview with

Mrs. Gatz in S. Mucha, "Interviews with Polish Families," 1932, BUR, Box 133, Folder 7.

37 William T. Bowles to the Honorable F. D. Roosevelt, President of These United States of America, 23 May 1933, FERA 460, "Illinois Complaints B."

38 Edward J. Newman to President Franklin Roosevelt, 20 January 1935, FERA 460, "Special Folder Cook County."

39 John Walsh to Dear Friend, Mr. President Franklin Delano Roosevelt, 10 August 1933, FERA 460, "Illinois Complaints W–Z." See also Henry B. Young to Federal Emergency Relief Commission, Washington, DC, 26 August 1935, FERA 460, "Illinois Complaints W–Z," and Mrs. Carl Doyle to Mr. Harry Hopkins, 22 June 1933, FERA 460, "Illinois Complaints D–E."

40 Interview with Miss Albina Runyzewicz, Panoff Project, "Effect of the Depression on Poles," 1934, BUR, Box 130, Folder 3, p. 1; Interview with Mrs. Margaret Bradburn, Truant officer for the Colman and Farren Schools, in Robert McMurray, "Study of the Effect of the Depression on a Three-Block Area: Federal, Wabash, and Calumet between 47th and 51st Streets," 1934, BUR, Box 133, Folder 1, p. 5.

41 John Modell, "Public Griefs and Personal Problems: An Empirical Inquiry into the Impact of the Great Depression," *Social Science History* 9 (Fall 1985): 399–427; Wayne Parrish to Harry Hopkins, 11 November 1934, Hopkins Papers, Box 61, quoted in James T. Patterson, *America's Struggle Against Poverty: 1900–1980* (Cambridge, MA: Harvard University Press, 1981), p. 51.

42 Robert H. Bremner, "The New Deal and Social Welfare," in Harvard Sitkoff, ed., *Fifty Years Later: The New Deal Evaluated* (Philadelphia: Temple University Press, 1985), p. 75.

43 Irving Bernstein, *A Caring Society: The New Deal, the Worker, and the Great Depression* (Boston: Houghton Mifflin Company, 1985), pp. 43–71, 175–88; Barry Karl, *The Uneasy State: The United States from 1915 to 1945* (Chicago: University of Chicago Press, 1983), pp. 139–42; Edward Berkowitz and Kim McQuaid, *Creating the Welfare State: The Political Economy of Twentieth Century Reform* (New York: Praeger, 1980), pp. 101, 104; "A Seminar on Unemployment Compensation and Placement Service, under Auspices of Division of Employment and Guidance, Council of Social Agencies of Chicago, 12 April 1938," WC, Box 76, Folder "April 1938–December 1938, Employment"; League of Women Voters, "Toward Unemployment Insurance for Illinois," n.d. but c. 1935, COM, Box 12, Folder "Adult Education."

44 "Report of the Work of the Chicago Commons Association for the Year Ending September 30, 1937," COM, Box 5, p. 1.

45 Interview with Florence Parise, Chicago, IL, 20 June 1980, IC, p. 4; Lee K. Frankel, Jr., "The Twilight of Industrial Life Insurance," *Survey Midmonthly* 74 (June 1938): 204–5.

46 Interview with Salvatore Cosentino, Berwyn, IL, 13 July 1979, IC, p. 30;

Susan Estabrook Kennedy, *The Banking Crisis of 1933* (Lexington, KY: The University of Kentucky Press, 1975), pp. 175–223; Interviews with Raymond Moley and David Kennedy, in Terkel, *Hard Times*, pp. 289, 313–15.

47 Melchior Palyi, *The Chicago Credit Market: Organization and Institutional Structure* (Chicago: University of Chicago Press, 1937), pp. 31, 268–9; Background research for "Metropolitan Chicago, Illinois: Re-survey Report Vol. 1, 1940," HOLC, pp. 74–5; "Confidential Report of a Survey of Chicago, Illinois and Its Metropolitan Area for the Home Owners' Loan Corporation, Washington, D.C., Division of Research and Statistics," 1 November 1936, HOLC, Folder "Chicago Report No. 3, 1936," p. 77.

48 Interview with Salvatore Cosentino, Berwyn, IL, 13 July 1979, IC, p. 1. For general background on the HOLC, see C. Lowell Harriss, *History and Policies of the Home Owners' Loan Corporation* (New York: National Bureau of Economic Research, 1951); Kenneth T. Jackson, *Crabgrass Frontier: The Suburbanization of the United States* (New York: Oxford University Press, 1985), pp. 195–203; Morton Bodfish, "The Depression Experience of Savings and Loan Associations in the United States," Address delivered in Salzburg, Austria, September 1935, pp. 20–3.

On the HOLC in Chicago, see Division of Research and Statistics, Federal Home Loan Bank Board, "Metropolitan Chicago: A Summary of Economic, Real Estate and Mortgage Finance Survey," 1940, HOLC, "City Survey File," pp. 20, 29; Background Research for "Metropolitan Chicago, Illinois: Re-survey Report Vol. 1, 1940," HOLC, pp. 84–5; "Summary Analysis of HOLC Loans in the Metropolitan Area of Chicago, Ill.," n.d. but c. 1940, HOLC, Folder "Chicago, Illinois No. 3." For more cases of individuals benefiting from the HOLC, see Edith Abbott, *The Tenements of Chicago, 1908–1935* (New York: Arno Press and New York Times, 1970; originally published by the University of Chicago Press, 1936), pp. 396–8; Interview with Mrs. Bradburn, Truant officer for the Colman and Farren Schools, in Robert McMurray, "Study of the Effect of the Depression on a Three-Block Area: Federal, Wabash, and Calumet between 47th and 51st Streets," 1934, BUR, Box 133, Folder 1, p. 5; Interview with Mildred Bonavolonta, Melrose Park, IL, 21 July 1980, IC, p. 49.

49 "Security Area Map Folder of Metropolitan Chicago, Ill.," October 1939–April 1940, HOLC, Folder "Chicago Ser. I, No. 2"; "Summary Analysis of HOLC Loans in the Metropolitan Area of Chicago, Ill.," n.d. but c. 1940, HOLC, Folder "Chicago, Illinois No. 3"; "Applications for Home Loans Now Being Accepted," *Berwyn Life*, 4 August 1933.

50 Anna Cohen to Franklin D. Roosevelt, 5 November 1934; Mr. Flory Calzaretta to Hon. Franklin Delano Roosevelt, 14 May 1936; Barbara Ann Carter to Hon. Franklin D. Roosevelt, 19 September 1936; Sample of general loan correspondence of regional offices, "C" File, HOLC.

51 "Chicago Report No. 3. Interviews," 1940, HOLC, pp. 145, 148–9.

52 "Area Description of Southwest Chicago, D-44," in "Security Area Map

Folder of Metropolitan Chicago, Ill.," February 1940, HOLC, Folder "Chicago Ser. I, No. 2," p. I-355. For discussion of red-lining in neighboring Gary, Indiana, see Raymond A. Mohl and Neil Betten, *Steel City: Urban and Ethnic Patterns in Gary, Indiana, 1906–1950* (New York: Holmes & Meier, 1986), pp. 66–70.

53 Laura Friedman, "A Study of One Hundred Unemployed Families in Chicago, January 1927 to June 1932" (M.A. thesis, University of Chicago, 1933), p. 185.

54 Thaddeus J. Lubera, "Hundred Years of Economic Contribution of the Poles to Chicago's Progress," in *Poles of Chicago, 1837–1937: A History of One Century of Polish Contribution to the City of Chicago* (Chicago: Polish Pageant, 1937), p. 18.

55 For a good background on the NRA, see Ellis W. Hawley, *The New Deal and the Problem of Monopoly: A Study in Economic Ambivalence* (Princeton: Princeton University Press, 1966). Also see Carroll R. Daugherty, *Labor under the NRA* (Boston: Houghton Mifflin Company, 1934); Janet Laura Weiss, "Industrial Relations in the Calumet District of Indiana" (M.A. thesis, University of Chicago, 1937), pp. 42, 52; Sidney Hillman, "The NRA, Labor and Recovery," in *Annals of the American Academy of Political and Social Science* 172 (March 1934): 70–5; Theda Skocpol and Kenneth Finegold, "State Capacity and Economic Intervention in the Early New Deal," *Political Science Quarterly* 97 (Summer 1982): 264–8.

56 Rich sources on the range in Chicago workers' experiences under the NRA are interviews done in a survey by the National Federation of Settlements in 1936 on the impact of the NRA. Case profiles compiled by the Chicago Commons Settlement for the study examine the variety of experiences workers had before, during, and after the NRA. "Industrial Study," 1936, Lea Taylor Papers, Box 4, Folder "National Federation of Settlements, 1936," CHS. Also see Interview with Frank Bertucci, Chicago, IL, 3 March 1980, IC, pp. 20–2; Workers Education Bureau of America, Proceedings of conferences on the impact of the NRA, February–March 1935, Chicago, IL, FITZ, Box 18, Folder 132. Blacks in Gary, Indiana, felt that the NRA codes in many cases led to the displacement of black labor by white; Balanoff, "History of the Black Community of Gary," p. 213.

57 Files for all the industry codes and for codes that never were adopted are in the NRA records in the National Archives. For the industries important in Chicago, see NRA, Consolidated Approved Codes Industry File for Farm Equipment, Iron and Steel, and Electrical Manufacturing, as well as Files of National Steel Labor Relations Board, Region VI (Chicago), and Division of Review Approved Code Histories. Materials on meatpacking are located in the Consolidated Unapproved Code Industry File.

58 See large number of letters from steelworkers in the Chicago area in Consolidated Approved Code Iron and Steel, NRA, Files 16 – Labor.

59 For the typical kinds of jobs Chicago workers performed, see *Achievements of WPA Workers in Illinois, July 1, 1935 to June 30, 1938*, in WPA, Illinois 610, January 1939–March 1939; "Highlights in Works Progress

Administration Construction Program, Illinois District Number Three, Chicago," WPA, Illinois 610, July–November 1936.

60 Mrs. Ellen De Lisle to Mr. F. D. Roosevelt, 29 November 1935, WPA, 693 Illinois C–D.

61 Friedman, "Study of One Hundred Unemployed Families," p. 186. For more about workers' attitudes toward federal job programs and the programs themselves, see Interview with Theresa Giannetti, Chicago Heights, IL, 14 April 1980, IC, p. 8; Dorothy Mack, "Some Effects of Civil Works Administration: A Study of Sixty-One Families Known to the Unemployment Relief Service in Chicago Before and After Their Assignment" (M.A. thesis, University of Chicago, 1936); Margaret Cochran Bristol, "Changes in Work Relief in Chicago," *Social Service Review* 9 (June 1935): 243–55; Margaret C. Bristol, "W.P.A. in Chicago, Summer 1936: A Study of 550 Cases Assigned to W.P.A. Now Under Care by the Chicago Relief Administration," *Social Service Review* 11 (September 1937): 372–94; Margaret C. Bristol, "Personal Reactions of Assignees to W.P.A. in Chicago," *Social Service Review* 12 (March 1938): 69–100; Loretta Laczynski, "Is WPA a Success?" *St. Michael's Study Club Chronicle* 3 (February 1939): 8, in Stephen Bubacz Papers, UICC; Ruth Shonle Cavan and Katherine Howland Ranck, *The Family and the Depression: A Study of One Hundred Chicago Families* (Chicago: University of Chicago Press, 1938), p. 157; Jones, "Local Political Significance of New Deal Relief Legislation," pp. 53–66, 224–32; Bonnie Fox Schwartz, *The Civil Works Administration, 1933–1934: The Business of Emergency Employment in the New Deal* (Princeton: Princeton University Press, 1984), particularly p. 43; Hopkins, *Spending to Save*, pp. 108–25; Robert McElvaine, *The Great Depression, 1929–1941* (New York: Times Books, 1984), pp. 264–8; Bernstein, *A Caring Society*, pp. 37–40, 149–64, 168–75.

There were many charges of corruption in the way the WPA was administered in Chicago: Supposedly jobs were traded for votes, certain nationalities were favored over others, job assignments and pay scales varied unfairly, and contacts rather than training earned one a foremanship. Gene Delon Jones made a careful examination of how Kelly's machine may have unduly influenced the operation of FERA and WPA in Chicago and concluded that their administration, particularly in the crucial area of certifying applicants, was surprisingly clean. Even when people had legitimate complaints, the fact that they could appeal to the federal government over their corrupt local administrators kept them invested in the program. Letters from Chicago residents, WPA, Illinois 610, Political Coercion, A–Z; Jones, "Local Political Significance of New Deal Relief Legislation," pp. 140–55; also see Biles, "Mayor Kelly," pp. 126–34 for a similar conclusion.

62 Grace Outlaw, Interviews for Chicago Folkstuff, 26 April 1939, FWP, Folklore, Box A707. For more on blacks and the WPA, see Alfred O. Philipp, "Robbins, Illinois – A Folklore in the Making," 6 April 1939, FWP, Folklore, Box A707; Henderson, "Study of Basic Factors Involved in

Change in Party Alignment of Negroes," pp. 57–8; Interview with Earl Fitch, in Robert McMurray, "Study of the Effect of the Depression on a Three-Block Area: Federal, Wabash and Calumet between 47th and 51st Streets," 1934, BUR, Box 133, Folder 1; Drake and Cayton, *Black Metropolis*, p. 512; Arvarh E. Strickland, *History of the Chicago Urban League* (Urbana: University of Illinois Press, 1966), pp. 109–10; Harvard Sitkoff, *A New Deal for Blacks: The Emergence of Civil Rights as a National Issue*, vol. 1, *The Depression Decade* (New York: Oxford University Press, 1978), pp. 69–72.

63 Franklin Rudder, Walter Williams, O'Bryant Smith, Henry W. Hayes, Clarence Howard, Nelson Livingston, and William Harrison to President Roosevelt, 4 November 1938, WPA, 693, Illinois A–Z, January–June 1939.

64 A WPA Worker, Project 776, to Mr. Harry L. Hopkins, 13 August 1936, WPA, 693, Illinois A–C, July 1936–June 1937.

65 Richard I. Durham, "Don't Spend Your Money Where You Can't Work," BAR, Box 149, Folder 4, p. 14.

66 Kenneth Holland and Frank Ernest Hill, *Youth in the CCC* (prepared for the American Youth Commission) (Washington, DC: American Council on Education, 1942), particularly p. 87. CCC materials, c. 1939, in BUR, Box 99, Folders 4–6: Ruth Shonle Cavan to Dr. E. W. Burgess, 9 September 1940; Interview with John Peyton; Interview with Joe A. Mikos; Statements Made by Kenneth Holland to American Youth Commission of American Council on Education, "My Experiences at CCC." "Attitudes Toward the CCC Camps," in Chapter 4, "Attitudes of Delinquents," in "The Nature and Characteristics of Delinquents and Delinquency in the South Chicago Area Project, as Revealed by Three Group Diaries," CAP, Box 110, Folder 1, p. 34. From IC: Interview with Mario Avignone, Chicago, IL, 12 July 1979, pp. 30–2; Interview with Paul Penio, Itasca, IL, 30 June 1980, pp. 36–7. Henry Coe Lanpher, "The Civilian Conservation Corps: Some Aspects of Its Social Program for Unemployed Youth," *Social Service Review* 10 (December 1936): 623–36.

67 "The Fortune Survey," *Fortune* 12 (July 1935): 67.

68 Geo. E. Sokolsky, "Labor's Fight for Power," *Chicago Commerce* 34 (December 1937).

For the "corporate liberal" argument about the New Deal, see Ronald Radosh, "The Myth of the New Deal," in Ronald Radosh and Murray Rothbard, eds., *A New History of Leviathan: Essays on the Rise of the American Corporate State* (New York: E. P. Dutton & Company, 1972), pp. 146–87. For refutations of this position, see Theda Skocpol, "Political Response to Capitalist Crisis: Neo-Marxist Theories of the State and the Case of the New Deal," *Politics and Society* 10 (Spring 1980): 155–201, and Stanley Vittoz, *New Deal Labor Policy and the American Industrial Economy* (Chapel Hill: University of North Carolina Press, 1987). For a more nuanced argument that some businessmen from capital-intensive firms joined international bankers in supporting New Deal reforms, see

Thomas Ferguson, "Industrial Conflict and the Coming of the New Deal: The Triumph of Multinational Liberalism in America," in Steve Fraser and Gary Gerstle, *The Rise and Fall of the New Deal Order, 1930–1980* (Princeton: Princeton University Press, 1989), pp. 3–31.

On Chicago employers' opposition to the New Deal, see Employers' Association of Chicago, "Begin at the Toe," c. 1948, CHS, p. 9; Illinois Manufacturers' Association, "Government Competition with Private Enterprise, Chicago, 1936, CHS; Krestnbaum, vice-president of Hart, Schaffner & Marx Company, "The 'Progressive' Business View of Unemployment," 1938, WC, Box 76, Folder "Employment April 1938–December 1938"; George Neesham to Joseph Keenan, 26 October 1937, FITZ, Box 23, Folder 155; "A Seminar on Unemployment Compensation and Placement Service," panel discussion, 6 May 1938, WC, Box 76, Folder "April 1936–December 1938"; *Illinois Manufacturers' Costs Association Monthly Bulletin*, 1934–40; *Industrial Review published by the Illinois Manufacturers' Association*, 1932–40; Alfred H. Kelly, "A History of the Illinois Manufacturers' Association" (Ph.D. dissertation, University of Chicago, 1938), pp. 254–318.

On the Fair Labor Standards Act, see "Digest of the Federal Fair Labor Standards Act of 1938," in "Digest of Laws Affecting Workers in Illinois," 1939, WC, Box 76, Folder "Employment 1939," pp. 6–9; Jonathan Grossman, "Fair Labor Standards Act of 1938: Maximum Struggle for a Minimum Wage," *Monthly Labor Review* 101 (June 1978): 22–30; Bernstein, *A Caring Society*, pp. 134–43.

A good way to follow the attitudes of Chicago employers toward the New Deal is to survey *Chicago Commerce*, the journal of the Chicago Association of Commerce, from 1933 to 1939. Sample articles that convey the tone of business's attitude include: "The Dole Catches Hold: Wisconsin Started Something; Now Twenty-One Other States Face Legislative Action on Unemployment Insurance and Provide Employers with a Problem as Big as the War Debts," 29 (January 1933); "Social Insurance – Maker of Parasites," 32 (March 1935); "How Much Government?" 32 (November 1935); "State vs. Private Business – Where Government Sniping May Lead: The Outlook for American Enterprise," 34 (June 1937); "Social Security – So What?" 34 (September 1937); "Unemployment Compensation – Boon or Burden?" 34 (December 1937); "Labor's Fight for Power: A Recognized Authority Finds That the Big Labor Question Is Who Will Control the Worker and through Him Control the Government," 34 (December 1937); "The 'Floor' under Wages and 'Ceiling' over Hours: An Analysis of the New Wage and Hour Bill Passed by the Last Congress Which Business Men Must Provide for by October 24," 35 (August 1938).

69 McElvaine, *The Great Depression*, p. 280; also see William E. Leuchtenburg, *Franklin D. Roosevelt and the New Deal, 1932–1940* (New York: Harper & Row Publishers, 1963), pp. 331–2.

70 Eli Ginzberg, *The Unemployed* (New York: Harper and Brothers, 1943), pp. 76–9, quoted in David Kennedy, ed., *The American People in the Depression* (West Haven, CT: Pendulum Press, 1973), p. 66.

71 Case of Henrietta Malone, in Robert McMurray, "Study of the Effect of the Depression on a Three-Block Area: Federal, Wabash and Calumet between 47th and 51st Streets," 1934, BUR, Box 133; Anonymous to Mrs. Roosevelt, Chicago, IL, 21 November 1934, and Anonymous to Mr. and Mrs. Roosevelt, Chicago, IL, February 1936, in Robert S. McElvaine, ed., *Down and Out in the Great Depression: Letters from the Forgotten Man* (Chapel Hill: The University of North Carolina Press, 1983), pp. 112, 117. Also see the files of such New Deal agencies as the NRA, FERA, HOLC, and WPA for letters.
72 Weiss, *Farewell to the Party of Lincoln*, p. 227.
73 Lorena Hickok to Harry Hopkins, 18 May 1936, Hopkins Papers, quoted in Bernard Sternsher, "Victims of the Great Depression: Self-Blame/Non-Self-Blame, Radicalism, and Pre-1929 Experiences," *Social Science History* 1 (Winter 1977): 150. Also see "Notes for Annual Report of Adult Education Dept., 1933–34" and "Reports of Meetings of Current Discussion Group," COM, Box 12.
74 Quoted in McElvaine, *Great Depression*, p. 113; also see pp. 175–6.
75 Bernard Asbell, *When FDR Died* (New York, 1961), p. 161, quoted in Leuchtenburg, *Roosevelt and the New Deal*, pp. 330–1.
76 Martha Gellhorn to Harry Hopkins, 19 November 1934, Hopkins Papers, quoted in Bernstein, *A Caring Society*, p. 307.
77 "The Fortune Survey: XXVII, The People of the U.S.A. – a Self-Portrait," *Fortune* 21 (February 1940): 134.
78 Charles Farace to the President, 25 November 1935, WPA, 693, Illinois E–G, and see many other letters in the WPA complaint files that make the same appeal for a need-determined wage. Ben Whitehurst to Mr. Louis Picalek, 23 December 1935, WPA, 693, Illinois N–P, Sample of form letter the WPA sent in reply.
79 For material on the Labor Party of Chicago and Cook County and the Illinois Labor Party, 1935–6, see FITZ, Boxes 19 and 20. An important essay that probes how the New Deal diffused working-class radicalism is Melvyn Dubofsky, "Not So 'Turbulent Years': Another Look at the American 1930s," in Charles Stephenson and Robert Asher, eds., *Life and Labor: Dimensions of American Working-Class History* (Albany: State University of New York Press, 1986), pp. 205–23.
80 F. Wight Bakke, *Citizens Without Work* (New Haven: Yale University Press, 1940), p. 101.
81 See, e.g., John Wozniak to Hon. Frances Perkins, n.d. but c. September 1933, and Andy Kakuris to Hugh S. Johnson, 9 January 1934, NRA, Consolidated Approved Code Iron and Steel, Files 16 – Labor.
82 Kleppner, *Who Voted?* pp. 102–3; McElvaine, *Great Depression*, pp. 280–1.
83 John Connolly to Mr. President Roosevelt, 28 July 1933, NRA, Consolidated Approved Code Iron and Steel, Files 16 – Labor.
84 Interview with Eva Barnes, in Studs Terkel, *Division Street: America* (New York: Avon Books, 1968), p. 90.
85 Kornhauser, "Analysis of 'Class' Structure of Contemporary American

Society," in Hartmann and Newcomb, eds., *Industrial Conflict*, pp. 234, 237. On class divisions in the 1936 vote nationally, see McElvaine, *Great Depression*, pp. 281–2.

86 Interview with Win Stracke, in Terkel, *Hard Times*, p. 195.

87 Dorothy M. Flowers to Hon. Franklin D. Roosevelt, 30 November 1935, WPA, 693, Illinois E–G.

88 Biles, "Mayor Edward J. Kelly," p. 132.

7. BECOMING A UNION RANK AND FILE

1 Interview with John Sargent in Alice and Staughton Lynd, eds., *Rank and File: Personal Histories of Working-Class Organizers* (Princeton: Princeton University Press, 1981), pp. 105–6.

2 Mary Heaton Vorse, "Organizing the Steel Workers, " in *The New Republic* (1936), reprinted in Dee Garrison, ed., *Rebel Pen: The Writings of Mary Heaton Vorse* (New York: Monthly Review Press, 1985), p. 173.

3 On organizing steel, see George Patterson, Autobiography, Book 1 and Book 2 and Miscellaneous Items, PAT; Interview with George Patterson, December 1970–January 1971, ROHP; Interviews in Labor Archives, Pennsylvania State University: Interview with George Patterson, Indiana, 31 October 1967; Interview with Dorothy and George Patterson, State College, PA, 1 February 1969; Interview with George Patterson, State College, PA, 2 February 1969; Interview with Sam Evett, East Chicago, IN, 1 April 1971; Interview with Joseph Germano, Chicago, IL, 16 February 1972; Interview with Joseph Germano, Chicago, IL, 21 June 1972. United Steelworkers of America, District 31 Papers, SECHP; USWA, District 31 Papers; *Steel Labor*, 1936–40; "Illinois Steel Company," National Steel Labor Relations Board, 11E–396, and Labor, 11–16, NRA; Lynd and Lynd, eds., *Rank and File*, pp. 89–110; Barbara Newell, *Chicago and the Labor Movement: Metropolitan Unionism in the 1930s* (Urbana: University of Illinois Press, 1961), pp. 115–47; Robert R. R. Brooks, *As Steel Goes... Unionism in a Basic Industry* (New Haven: Yale University Press, 1940); Frederick Harbison, "Steel," in Harry A. Millis, ed., *How Collective Bargaining Works: A Survey of Experience in Leading American Industries* (New York: Twentieth Century Fund, 1942), pp. 508–70. A recent collection of essays that defines very well the central issues in the steel campaign is Paul Clark, Peter Gottlieb, and Donald Kennedy, *Forging a Union of Steel: Philip Murray, SWOC, & the United Steelworkers* (Ithaca, NY: ILR Press, 1987).

4 On the struggle to organize the packing plants, see Arthur Kampfert, Manuscript, UPWA, vols. 2 and 3; Materials on the PWOC, UPWA, Boxes 8–10; Interviews with Herbert March, Milton Norman, James Samuel, Richard Saunders, Vicky Starr, Todd Tate, Jesse Vaughn, Philip Weightman, Chicago, IL, 1985–6, UPWA Oral History Project; Interview with Herbert March, Los Angeles, CA, 16 and 17 November 1970, ROHP; Conciliation and Strikes PWOC and Armour & Co., 1939, General Records of the

Department of Labor, Office of the Secretary Frances Perkins, General subject file 1933–41, RG 174, NA; *CIO News – Packinghouse Workers' Organizing Committee (PWOC) Edition*, October 1938–December 1940, *passim*; Case files 199–4449, 199–6913, Federal Mediation and Conciliation Service, RG 280, NA – Suitland; National Labor Relations Board, *Decisions and Orders*, vols. 8, 10, 13, 14, 18 (Washington, DC: U.S. Government Printing Office, 1938–9); Armour & Co., Case files R-584, R-1388, R-1561, NLRB. From MCD, Box 15: Heitmann, Memo on Stockyards Labor Council, March 1934; Heitmann, Memo on Amalgamated Meat Cutters and Butcher Workmen of North America, April 1934; Thomas Powers, Memo on Stockyards Labor Council, May 1934. From COM, Boxes 26 and 27: Meeting of Citizens' Emergency Committee on Industrial Relations, 19 November 1937; Chicago Citizens' Committee on Industrial Relations, "The Dispute between Armour and Company and the CIO...," August 1939. Newell, *Chicago and the Labor Movement*, pp. 152–203; Paul Street, "'Breaking Up' Old Hatreds and Breaking Through 'The Fear': The Rise of the Packinghouse Workers Organizing Committee in Chicago," Unpublished paper delivered at the North American Labor History Conference, Wayne State University, 24 October 1985 [published later in *Studies in History and Politics* 5 (1986): 63–83]; David Brody, *The Butcher Workmen: A Study of Unionization* (Cambridge, MA: Harvard University Press, 1964), pp. 152–203; James Roger Holcomb, "The Union Policies of Meat Packers, 1929–1942" (M.A. thesis, University of Illinois, 1957), pp. 33–198.

5 For the unionization of International Harvester, see "Report on Study of Background and Development of the United Farm Equipment and Metal Workers Union," 25 April 1952, IH; *CIO News – Farm Equipment Workers' Organizing Committee (FE) Edition*, 1939–40; Case files 196–740, 196-2373, 196-2376, Federal Mediation and Conciliation Service, RG 280, NA – Suitland; International Harvester Company – McCormick Works Case File XIII-C-1482, NLRB; National Labor Relations Board, *Decisions and Orders*, vols. 2, 5, 29, 33 (1936, 1938, 1941); Interview with Clarence Stoecker by Julia Reichert, Chicago, IL, 12 August 1978; Robert Ozanne, *A Century of Labor–Management Relations at McCormick and International Harvester* (Madison: University of Wisconsin Press, 1967), pp. 85–6, 94–5, 146–53, 178–9, 194–208, 224–5, 249–51, 271; Barbara Marsh, *A Corporate Tragedy: The Agony of International Harvester Company* (New York: Doubleday & Company, 1985), pp. 59–76.

6 Studies that stress the crucial role played by "facilitators," the state, and union leaders include: Irving Bernstein, *The Turbulent Years: A History of American Workers, 1933–1941* (Boston: Houghton-Mifflin, 1969); Theda Skocpol, "Political Response to Capitalist Crisis: Neo-Marxist Theories of the State and the Case of the New Deal," *Politics and Society* 10 (1980): 155–201; David Brody, *Workers in Industrial America: Essays on the 20th Century Struggle* (New York: Oxford University Press, 1980), pp. 120–72; Christopher L. Tomlins, *The State and the Unions: Labor Relations, Law,*

and the Organized Labor Movement in America, 1880–1960 (New York: Cambridge University Press, 1985). For a useful treatment of the historiography about the CIO, as it pertains to the story of steel, see Ronald L. Filippelli, "The History is Missing, Almost: Philip Murray, the Steelworkers, and the Historians," in Clark et al., *Forging a Union of Steel*, pp. 1–12.

7 Secondary studies too numerous to mention detail these government actions on behalf of labor. For a good analysis, see the essays on the 1930s in Brody, *Workers in Industrial America*, pp. 82–172. On the Department of Labor's intervention, see General Records of the Department of Labor, Office of the Secretary Frances Perkins, General subject file 1933–41, "Conciliation – Strikes: PWOC & Armour Co., 1939, " RG 174, NA; and file 196–2376 on International Harvester Company, 1940, Federal Mediation and Conciliation Service, RG 280, NA – Suitland. For quote from Swift organizer, see *People's Press*, 13 November 1937, quoted in Arthur Kampfert, Manuscript, UPWA, p. 33.

8 Edward Andrew Zivich, "Fighting Union: The CIO at Inland Steel, 1936–1942" (M.A. thesis, University of Wisconsin – Milwaukee, 1972), pp. 27–8; William Roger Biles, "Mayor Edward J. Kelly of Chicago: Big City Boss in Depression and War" (Ph.D. thesis, University of Illinois at Chicago, 1981), pp. 99–100; *CIO News – PWOC Edition*, 6 March, 20 March, 17 April 1939; Interview with Herbert March, Los Angeles, CA, 16 and 17 November 1970, ROHP, p. 76.

9 Arthur Kampfert, Manuscript, UPWA, p. 33; "Memorandum from Mr. Dewey on Steel Situation," 1 June 1934, and Memo to Hon. Frances Perkins from Edw. F. McGrady, 28 December 1934, Department of Labor general files, Office of the Secretary Perkins, Conciliation–Steel, RG 174, NA; J. Carroll Moody, "U.S. v. Weirton Steel: Capital, Labor and Government under the NRA," Unpublished paper, 1987, pp. 52–8; letters from workers to Roosevelt and Johnson in NRA, Region VI (Chicago) 551 pt. 9; NRA Unapproved Codes, Meatpacking 199; and NRA Approved Codes, Steel, Files 16 – Labor.

10 Patterson quotation from Linnet Myers, "The Birth of USWA Local 65," Term paper, 15 December 1977, SECHP, p. 23; also see petition from Elected Employee Representatives of the Illinois Steel Works, South Works, to General Hugh S. Johnson, 29 August 1933, NRA Approved Codes, Steel, Files 16 – Labor.

11 Interview with Herbert March, San Pedro, CA, 15 July 1985, UPWA Oral History Project, Tape 1, Side 1.

12 *CIO News – PWOC Edition*, 5 November 1938, Editorial; Interview with Leslie Orear by author, Chicago, IL, 27 July 1983, Tape 1, Side 2. For frequent discussion of workers' need to support prolabor legislation and candidates through the Non-Partisan League, see *CIO News – PWOC Edition*, 1938–40, *passim*, which particularly documents the Chicago CIO's growing relationship with Mayor Kelly; *Steel Labor*, 1936–9, *passim; People's Press (National Edition)*, 1936–9, *passim*; Interview with Herbert March, Los Angeles, CA, 16 and 17 November 1970, ROHP, pp. 93–5; and PAT, Boxes 6 and 7.

13 Ozanne, *Century of Labor–Management Relations*, p. 197.

14 Quotation from *CIO News–PWOC Edition*, 5 November 1938. Many sources document the numerous job actions that took place during this period of union organization. See, particularly, Interview with Herbert March, Los Angeles, CA, 16 and 17 November 1970, ROHP, pp. 50–1; Interview with Richard Saunders, Todd Tate, and Annie Collins Jackson, Chicago, IL, 13 September 1985, UPWA Oral History Project, Tape 11, Side 1; Interview with Milton Norman, Richard Saunders, Todd Tate, and James Samuel, Chicago, IL, 1 October 1985, UPWA Oral History Project, Tape 19, Side 2; Interviews with Jesse Perez and Elmer Thomas, in Ann Banks, ed., *First-Person America* (New York: Vintage Books, 1981), pp. 66, 70; "Sweeps 12 Armour Depts," *CIO News – PWOC Edition*, 4 September 1939; Interviews with Stella Nowicki, Jesse Reese, and Nick Migas, in Lynd and Lynd, *Rank and File*, pp. 87, 99, 168; Minutes of SWOC District 31 Field Workers' Meeting, 1 February 1937, USWA, District 31, p. 1. Workers in the Gary plant of Carnegie–Illinois burned the sugar barrels put out by the company union to collect their contributions, necessitating a "24–hour watch" being placed on them. *Steel Labor*, 6 February 1937.

Note that "Stella Nowicki" (interviewed by the Lynds in *Rank and File*) and "Vicky Starr" (interviewed in UPWA Oral History Project) is the same person; Nowicki is an alias. For the purposes of simplicity, I have continued to use both names.

15 Interview with Clarence Stoecker by Julia Reichert, Chicago, IL, 12 August 1978, Side 2; Ozanne, *Century of Labor–Management Relations*, pp. 198–9.

16 Interview with Joseph Germano, Chicago, IL, 16 February 1972, Labor Archives, Pennsylvania State University, p. I-135.

17 SWOC Circular Letter, 31 March 1937, quoted in David Brody, "The Origins of Modern Steel Unionism: The SWOC Era," in Clark et al., *Forging a Union of Steel*, p. 25. Several months later, in late July, Philip Murray circulated another letter cautioning against rank-and-file actions in violation of the contract, suggesting that such shop floor agitations were still going on. Quoted in Staughton Lynd, "What the Productivity Clause Means to the Steelworker," Speech, n.d., PAT, Box 10, Folder 2, p. 14.

18 Interview with John Sargent, in Lynd and Lynd, *Rank and File*, pp. 107–9.

19 "300 Leave Jobs in Armour Plant During Dispute," *Chicago Tribune*, 12 January 1940, and "350 Armour Men Return to Jobs After Walkout," *Chicago Daily News*, 12 January 1940.

20 "Company Flunkyism Didn't Work in the I.C.S. Department," *Swift's CIO Flash*, 26 June 1939 (mimeo), UPWA, Box 9, Folder 4, p. 3. Albert Towers told of a similar experience at South Works. He was illegally fired by his department superintendent, but at the plant gate he was met by a superintendent of industrial relations, who, realizing that Thomas would have an NLRB case against the company, told him to go back to work. "He talked me into going back – he brought me into the Superintendent and he really bawled the Superintendent out... 'Don't you ever go telling

anybody they're fired without checking with us first,'" he scolded. Myers, "The Birth of the USWA Local 65," p. 28.

21 Mary Heaton Vorse, "Organizing the Steel Workers," *The New Republic* (1936), in Garrison, ed., *Rebel Pen*, pp. 170–1. Also see *Steel Labor*, 5 September 1936, for the argument that the big difference between 1919 and now is a "unified command" with "centralized, responsible leadership."

22 For insights into how Communist organizers operated in Chicago plants, see Interview with Stella Nowicki, in Lynd and Lynd, *Rank and File*, pp. 74–6; Interview with Vicky Starr, Chicago, IL, 4 August 1986, UPWA Oral History Project, Tape 235, Side 2; Interviews with Herbert March, San Pedro, CA, 15 July 1985 (Tape 1, Side 1, and Tape 2, Side 1), and Madison, WI, 21 October 1986 (Tape 294, Side 1), UPWA Oral History Project; Harold D. Lasswell and Dorothy Blumenstock, *World Revolutionary Propaganda: A Chicago Study* (New York: Alfred A. Knopf, 1939), pp. 142–64, 391–3; "Report on Study of Background and Development of the United Farm Equipment and Metal Workers Union," 25 April 1952, IH. For the larger picture, see Bert Cochran, *Labor and Communism: The Conflict That Shaped American Unions* (Princeton: Princeton University Press, 1977).

23 Many plant-level leaders in Chicago conformed to the pattern that Ronald Schatz has identified for General Electric and Westinghouse: They tended more often to be native born, skilled, and from radical backgrounds than the average worker. The latter characteristic was most evident among Chicago militants. Herbert March, Vicky Starr, and Clarence Stoecker had fathers who had supported Eugene Debs; George Patterson, Nick Migas, Albert Towers, and Steve Ulanowski had fathers who had been strong unionists. Interview with George Patterson, Chicago, IL, December 1970–January 1971, ROHP, p. 31; Myers, "The Birth of USWA Local 65," p. 23; Ronald W. Schatz, *The Electrical Workers: A History of Labor at General Electric and Westinghouse, 1923–60* (Urbana: University of Illinois Press, 1983), pp. 80–101.

24 "Chicago Armour Stewards Plan Final Drive," *CIO News – PWOC Edition*, 19 December 1938.

25 House Report 1311, 78th Congress, 2nd Session, p. 13, quoted in "Report on Study of Background and Development of the United Farm Equipment and Metal Workers Union," IH, p. 77; Interview with Vicky Starr, Chicago, IL, 4 August 1936, UPWA Oral History Project, Tape 236, Side 1.

26 Interview with Clarence Stoecker by Julia Reichert, Chicago, IL, 12 August 1978, Side 2; Interview with Leslie Orear by author, Chicago, IL, 27 July 1983, Tape 2, Side 1; Patterson, Autobiography, Book 1, PAT, p. 44; Interview with Philip Weightman, Chicago, IL, 7 and 8 October 1986, UPWA Oral History Project, Tape 286, Sides 1 and 2.

27 Arthur Kampfert, Manuscript, UPWA, Part 3, p. 62. Van Bittner also interpreted the CIO's victory as a deliberate rejection of the Dies Committee's accusations. Van A. Bittner, "Our Magnificent Armour Victory in

Chicago," *CIO News – PWOC Edition*, 27 November 1939. Steelworkers at South Works chose to ignore the red-baiting of their foremen and superintendents, who called the CIO the "Communist International Organization," and of the company union, the Steel Employees' Independent Labor Organization of South Works, which contrasted itself to the SWOC by claiming it was "not subject to foreign influence and dictatorship." Myers, "The Birth of USWA Local 65," p. 49, and flyer, "Greetings from Steel Employees' Independent Labor Organization of South Works," USWA, District 31, SECHP, Box 20.

28 Interview with Stella Nowicki, in Lynd and Lynd, *Rank and File*, p. 85.

29 Jack Martin, "Shop Papers in the Chicago Area," *Party Organizer* (February 1938): 15–19, included in "Report on Study of Background and Development of the United Farm Equipment and Metal Workers Union," 25 April 1952, IH, as Appendix D, Document 10.

30 Interview with Herbert March, Madison, WI, 21 October 1986, UPWA Oral History Project, Tape 295, Side 1.

31 Interview #97 with Peter K., 14 July 1981, quoted in Ewa Morawska, *For Bread with Butter: Life-Worlds of East Central Europeans in Johnstown, Pennsylvania, 1890–1940* (New York: Cambridge University Press, 1985), p. 273.

32 Interview with Philip Weightman, Chicago, IL, 7 and 8 October 1986, UPWA Oral History Project, Tape 285, Side 2.

33 My perspective here differs from both that of John Bodnar, who argues that workers' involvement in the CIO grew out of a traditional desire to safeguard a minimum of economic security for their families, and that of Sidney Verba and Kay Lehman Schlozman, who claim that workers had internalized the American ideology of individual success and were seeking economic mobility. John Bodnar, "Immigration, Kinship, and the Rise of Working-Class Realism in Industrial America," *Journal of Social History* 14 (Fall 1980): 45–65; Sidney Verba and Kay Lehman Schlozman, "Unemployment, Class Consciousness and Radical Politics: What Didn't Happen in the Thirties," *Journal of Politics* 39 (May 1977): 291–323.

34 Minutes of USWA–SWOC Grievance Committee Meetings, Inland Steel, Indiana Harbor, IN, 1937–41, USWA District 31 Papers, Labor Archives, Pennsylvania State University; "Is There Going to Be a Strike in the Meat-packing Industry?" 1939, UPWA, Box 9, Folder 4.

35 Clifton McKinney, quoted in Arthur Kampfert, Manuscript, UPWA, p. 27; Heitmann, Memo on Stockyards Labor Council, 18 March 1934, MCD, Box 15; E. W. Anderson, "The Amalgamated Association Is the Organization for Steel Workers," *Amalgamated Journal*, 5 December 1935; Minutes NLRB Evening Session, 18 February 1937, PAT, Box 3, Folder 5, pp. 141–2; Benjamin Fairless to Employee Representatives of South Works, 8 September 1936, and General and Wages Committee, Employee Representation Plan, South Works, to Benjamin Fairless, 14 September 1936, PAT, Box 2, Folder 3; and from *People's Press (National Edition)*: "Steel Stocks Soar, But Pay Stands Still," 17 October 1936; "U.S. Steel Jumps

Income 50 Times from '35 to '36," 6 February 1937; "Packers Profits Top Record, Says Hushed Exposure," 6 November 1937.

36 John B. Driscoll to General Hugh Johnson, 21 January 1934, Approved Codes Steel, NRA, Files 16 – Labor, "Labor Saving Machinery"; also see W. J. Van Tassel and E. J. Piatt to Mr. Franklin D. Roosevelt, 6 December 1933, in same file; "Special Memorandum to Mr. Barnett," 1937, BAR, Box 280, Folder 1.

37 "Consumer Goods Market for Steel," *Steel Facts*, April 1936, and "Activity in Consumer Goods Lifts Three Steels to New Peak," *Steel Facts*, May 1937; Irving S. Olds, *Half a Century of United States Steel: An Address at New York on the Occasion of U.S. Steel Corporation's 50th Anniversary* (New York: Newcomen Society in North America, 1951); *Steel and Metal Notes* 4 (August 1936): 3; "The Rise of Inland," *Chicago Commerce* 32 (January 1936): 22; "Speed-up in South Chicago Blast Furnace Kills Three," *People's Press*, 2 October 1937; "The Corporation," *Fortune* 13 (March 1936). For a very detailed picture of technological improvements in steelmaking and their impact on worker productivity, see William T. Hogan, *Economic History of the Iron and Steel Industry*, vol. 3 (Lexington, MA: D. C. Heath and Company, 1971), pp. 1133–65, 1180–1, 1194–1205, 1269–78.

Interview with Mary Siporin, 19 April 1939, FWP, Chicago Folklore, Box A707; Heitmann, Memo on Stockyards Labor Council, 18 March 1934, MCD, Box 15; Extensive discussion of speed-ups in the packing plants during the 1930s, in Chicago interviews, UPWA Oral History Project.

38 Laura Weiss, "Industrial Relations in the Calumet District of Indiana" (M.A. thesis, University of Chicago, 1937), p. 42; "Industrial Study of the Impact of the NRA on Workers" (interviews with workers in the Commons neighborhood), COM, Box 4, Folder "National Federation of Settlements: January–June 1936"; L. O. Harper, "Strikes Spread in Chicago Area," 22 March 1937, FWP, American Guide File – Illinois, Box A122.

39 Interview with Nick Migas, in Lynd and Lynd, *Rank and File*, p. 167. Arthur Kampfert made a similar comment: "Most of the men, and the women, too, in Armour's didn't need coaxing, they signed the blue cards eagerly." Kampfert, Manuscript, UPWA, p. 24.

40 "Report on Study of Background and Development of the United Farm Equipment and Metal Workers Union," 25 April 1952, IH, pp. 26–7, 30.

41 George Patterson, Autobiography, Book 1, PAT, pp. 11–12, 34.

42 *CIO News – PWOC Edition*, 10 June 1940, also see 13 November 1937 and 27 November 1937; Interview with Stella Nowicki, in Lynd and Lynd, *Rank and File*, pp. 78–81; Interview with Herbert March, Los Angeles, CA, 16 and 17 November 1970, ROHP, pp. 50–1; Purcell, *Worker Speaks His Mind*, p. 178.

43 Interview with Stella Nowicki, in Lynd and Lynd, *Rank and File*, p. 81; Interview with Jesse Perez, in Banks, *First-Person America*, p. 66; also see "Chicago Girls Stage Own Book Day," *CIO News – PWOC Edition*, 30 October 1939.

44 Clinton Golden and Harold Ruttenberg, *The Dynamics of Industrial Democracy* (New York: Harper & Brothers, 1942), p. 182; Joel Seidman, Jack London, Bernard Karsh, and Daisy L. Tagliacozzo, *The Worker Views His Union* (Chicago: University of Chicago Press, 1958), Chapter 4: "Steel Workers, Militant Unionism," p. 77.

45 Interview with Stella Nowicki, in Lynd and Lynd, *Rank and File*, pp. 74–5; Interview with Philip Weightman, Chicago, IL, 7 and 8 October 1986, UPWA Oral History Project, Tape 285, Side 2.

46 Golden and Ruttenberg, *Dynamics of Industrial Democracy*, p. 112; Interview with George Patterson, Chicago, IL, December 1970–January 1971, ROHP, pp. 4–5.

47 Interview with Herbert March, San Pedro, CA, 15 July 1985, UPWA Oral History Project, Tape 1, Side 1; Interview with Todd Tate, Chicago, IL, 2 October 1985, UPWA Oral History Project, Tape 23, Side 1.

48 *Survey Magazine* 73 (December 1937): 385.

49 Articles from *People's Press (National Edition)*: "Steel Union to Fight for More Relief," 13 November 1937; "CIO Unions Map Relief Slate Here," 28 May 1938; "Seek Relief Allotments in Cicero" and "UFEW Studies Relief Tactics," 24 September 1938. Also, Flyer for Unemployment and Relief Mass Meeting Sponsored by Sub-District Council of the SWOC, November 1937, and SWOC, "Resolution on a More Adequate Number of Case Workers at South Eastern Relief Station," 26 November 1937, PAT, Box 6, Folder 7; Herbert March, "Testimony on Behalf of the American Youth Administration before Sub-Committee of Senate Committee on Education and Labor," 11 March 1938, MCD, Box 7, Folder "General Papers 1938–39," p. 1.

50 Sanford M. Jacoby, *Employing Bureaucracy: Managers, Unions, and the Transformation of Work in American Industry, 1900–1945* (New York: Columbia University Press, 1985), p. 219; Interview with Clarence Stoecker by Julia Reichert, Chicago, IL, 12 August 1978, Side 1.

51 Arthur Kampfert, Manuscript, UPWA, Part 2, p. 5.

8. WORKERS' COMMON GROUND

1 Horace Davis, *The Condition of Labor in the American Iron and Steel Industry* (New York: International Publishers, 1933), pp. 18–21; "The 31,000,000 Workers," *Fortune* 21 (February 1940): 128.

2 On the racial and ethnic makeup of Chicago's steel and meatpacking work forces in 1928, see Paul Taylor, *Mexican Labor in the United States: Chicago and the Calumet Region,* vol. 7, no. 2, University of California Publications in Economics (Berkeley: University of California Press, 1932), pp. 40, 42. According to the steel industry's publication, *Steel Facts*, in December 1937 the average age of all steel employees was 38, up two years from 1930. Twenty percent were 25 years or younger; 40 percent were between 26 and 40; and 40 percent were ages 41 and over. At Republic Steel, 55 percent of the workers were under 35. "Two Out of Every Five

Steel Employees Are More than Forty Years Old," *Steel Facts*, December 1937, was an effort of the steel industry to defend itself against charges that it favored younger over older men; Chicago SWOC Report on Carnegie–Illinois and Republic Steel, n.d. but c. 1936, USWA District 31 Papers, SECHP, p. 2. On workers' ages, also see Sanford M. Jacoby, *Employing Bureaucracy: Managers, Unions, and the Transformation of Work in American Industry, 1900–1945* (New York: Columbia University Press, 1985), p. 219, and "The 31,000,000 Workers," *Fortune* 21 (February 1940): 64. For data on Mexican CIO militants, see Francisco Arturo Rosales, "The Regional Origins of Mexicano Immigrants to Chicago during the 1920s," *Aztlan* 7 (Summer 1976): 197.

3 For more detail than is given in Chapter 3 on movie distribution in the 1930s, see Douglas Gomery, *The Hollywood Studio System* (New York: St. Martin's Press, 1986), and Lary May with the assistance of Stephen Lassonde, "Making the American Way: Moderne Theatres, Audiences, and the Film Industry 1929–1945," *Prospects* 12 (1987): 89–124. May and Lassonde document how weekly movie attendance grew during the Great Depression, from 37.6 million in 1929 to 45.1 million in 1931 to 54.6 million in 1941, and argue that working-class people made up a large part of this expanded audience. Other studies also show that the depression did not keep workers out of movie houses. Lloyd Warner and Paul Lunt discovered, in their *Yankee City* study of Newburyport, Massachusetts, that in the midst of the depression, "upper–lower class" people (which would include employed workers) went to the movies in the largest numbers. These findings were corroborated in a study of movie going in San Francisco, where it was found that workers allocated twice as much money for movies as the professional class. Both studies are cited in Garth Jowett, *Film: The Democratic Art* (Boston: Little, Brown and Company, 1976), pp. 263–5.

4 Martha E. Gross, "The 'Jolly Girls' Club: A Report and Diary of Meetings," Term paper for "The Growth of Cities," 24 March 1933, BUR, Box 158, Folder 5, p. 27; John L. Brown, Report on Group of Boys Living in the Russell Square, South Chicago, Community, n.d. but mid-1930s, CAP, Box 95, Folder 12, p. 67; Ethel Shanas, *Recreation and Delinquency: A Study of Five Selected Chicago Communities* (Chicago: Chicago Recreation Commission, 1942), p. 76. Also see Reeva Cohen, "Effect of the Depression on Recreation," Paper for Sociology 358, July 1934, BUR, Box 176, Folder 4, UCSC.

5 Arthur Frank Wertheim, *Radio Comedy* (New York: Oxford University Press, 1979), p. 46; James Douglas Johnson, "A Comparative Study of Newspaper Reading and Radio News Listening in the Chicago Area" (M.S. thesis, Northwestern University, 1941), Fig. 31.

6 "The Culture of Democracy," *Fortune* 21 (February 1940): 83; "Fortune Quarterly Survey," *Fortune* 17 (January 1938): 88.

7 H. M. Beville, Jr., "Social Stratification of the Radio Audience" (mimeo distributed by the Princeton Office of Radio Research, transferred to Columbia University in 1940), 1939–40; Paul F. Lazarsfeld, *Radio and the Printed Page: An Introduction to the Study of Radio and Its Role in the*

Communication of Ideas (New York: Duell, Sloan and Pearce, 1940), pp. 16–20, 133–9; Frederick H. Lumley, *Measurement in Radio* (Columbus, OH: Ohio State University, 1934), pp. 194–5; National Association of Broadcasters in Cooperation with CBS and NBC based on a study conducted by Crossley, Inc., *Urban Radio Listening in the United States*, 1941, in the Edgar James Papers, Box 8A, SHSW; Cooperative Analysis of Broadcasting, Inc., Semi-annual Reports, 1934–40, SHSW. Survey research was certainly less sophisticated in the 1930s and 1940s than it is today, but its findings are still useful to the historian, particularly when consistent patterns emerge.

8 Cited in Daniel J. Czitrom, *Media and the American Mind from Morse to McLuhan* (Chapel Hill: University of North Carolina Press, 1982), p. 86; "Fortune Quarterly Survey 12," *Fortune* 17 (April 1938): 106; Johnson, "Comparative Study of Newspaper Reading and Radio News"; Lazarsfeld, *Radio and Printed Page*, pp. 218–25.

9 Radio's ability to take over the job from foreign-language newspapers of delivering news was aided by the folding of some of those publications during the 1930s. The *People's Press*, a labor newspaper that served the steel unionists of South Chicago before SWOC began publishing *Steel Labor*, identified this situation and hoped its own circulation might be helped by it. "The times shift in the field of newspapers as surely as changes occur in all fields, as one after another of the old established foreign language weeklies and dailies pass into the void." "People's Press Meets New Need," *People's Press*, June 1936.

10 Czitrom, *Media and the American Mind*, p. 80; see William S. Hedges, "30 Years in Broadcasting!" (transcript of Columbia Oral History interview, 1951), William S. Hedges Papers, Box 2, Folder 2, SHSW, for story of how Chicago station WMAQ was purchased by NBC in 1931; Correspondence between NBC executives and WCFL in NBC Papers, Box 99, Folder 77, SHSW; Profiles of Chicago radio stations in 1930 and 1938 compiled from *WLS Family Album: 1930 Edition* (Chicago: Station WLS, 1930); *Chicago Tribune Picture Book of Radio* (Chicago: Tribune Publishing Co., 1928); and John S. Hayes and Horace J. Gardner, *Both Sides of the Microphone: Training for the Radio* (Philadelphia: J. B. Lippincott Co., 1938), p. 149.

11 Lazarsfeld, *Radio and the Printed Page*, pp. 102–4; Theodore C. Grame, *Ethnic Broadcasting in the United States*, Publications of the American Folklife Centre, no. 4 (Washington, DC: American Folklife Center, 1980), particularly pp. 93–9; "Radio," *Time* 33 (1 May 1939): 44; Ads for Italian, Polish, and Czech radio programs on station WGES (500 watts) and WHFC (100 watts) in local and ethnic papers.

12 Abe Aaron, Interview with Philip Marcus (sign painter), 11 May 1939, FWP, Folklore Project – Life Histories, Box A707.

13 "The Culture of Democracy," *Fortune* 21 (February 1940): 83; NBC, "This Fight Should Have Been Broadcast," 1937, Pamphlet in Edgar James Papers, Box 17, Folder 4, SHSW; Elmo Roper, "A Study Made among 1207 Buyers of 'Women's Day,'" August 1939, p. 32.

14 Lumley, *Measurement in Radio*, pp. 186–7; Lazarsfeld, *Radio and the*

Printed Page, pp. 29–47; Beville, "Social Stratification of the Radio Audience"; Charles Hall Wolfe, *Modern Radio Advertising* (New York: Funk and Wagnalls Company in Association with Printers' Ink Publishing Company, 1949), pp. 101–78.

15 H. M. Beville, Jr., "The ABCD's of Radio Audiences," *Public Opinion Quarterly*, June 1940, p. 196. The Office of Radio Research, under the direction of Paul Lazarsfeld, was funded by the Rockefeller Foundation in 1937 to investigate the social impact of mass communication. In 1939, the Office moved to Columbia University, later to be transformed into the Bureau of Applied Social Research. For a fascinating history of the office and its director, see Paul F. Lazarsfeld, "An Episode in the History of Social Research: A Memoir," in Donald Fleming and Bernard Bailyn, eds., *The Intellectual Migration: Europe and America, 1930–1960* (Cambridge, MA: Harvard University Press, 1969), pp. 270–337.

16 *Amalgamated Journal* (23 May 1935): 20; Interview with George Patterson, State College, PA, 2 February 1969, Labor Archives, Pennsylvania State University, p. 12.

17 Al Monroe quotation from *Chicago Defender*, in Chris Mead, *Champion – Joe Louis, Black Hero in White America* (New York: Charles Scribner's Sons, 1985), p. 204; Jonathan Mitchell quotation from the *New Republic*, in Mead, *Champion*, p. 74. For more on the fight, see Mead, *Champion*, pp. 65–74, and Jeffrey T. Sammons, *Beyond the Ring: The Role of Boxing in American Society* (Urbana: University of Illinois Press, 1988), pp. 96–117. For discussion of steelworkers' interest in the fight, see Interview with George Patterson, State College, PA, 2 February 1969, Labor Archives, Pennsylvania State University. Clarence Stoecker remarked that the CIO at Harvester often made initial contact with men by talking sports. Interview with Clarence Stoecker by Julia Reichert, Chicago, IL, 12 August 1978, Tape 1, Side 1.

18 Robert S. Lynd and Helen Merrell Lynd, *Middletown in Transition: A Study in Cultural Conflicts* (New York: Harcourt, Brace and Company, 1937), p. 264; Hadley Cantril and Gordon W. Allport, *The Psychology of Radio* (New York: Peter Smith, 1941), p. 18. For a general discussion of the nationalization of culture during the 1930s, see Warren I. Susman, *Culture as History: The Transformation of American Society in the Twentieth Century* (New York: Pantheon Books, 1984), pp. 158–9.

19 Minutes of SWOC District 31 Field Workers' Meetings, 5 November 1936, USWA; George Patterson, Autobiography, Book 1, PAT, p. 100; J. Fred MacDonald, *Don't Touch That Dial! Radio Programming from 1920 to 1960* (Chicago: Nelson-Hall, 1979), pp. 40–1. Also see Employee Representative Newsletter, Pittsburgh District, Joint Representatives Council (12 November 1936), SECHP; Linnet Myers, "The Birth of USWA Local 65," Term paper, 15 December 1977, SECHP, p. 28 which includes a poem written by Jim Stewart, the second president of Local 65, in June 1937:

> Hope was almost down to zero,
> Pleas for work and food were vain,

When arose that mighty hero
Franklin Roosevelt, bless his name.
First he fed the hungry nation,
Then he gave men work to do,
Stopped mankind's degeneration
Lit the spark of hope anew.

20 Interview with Herbert March, Madison, WI, 21 October 1986, UPWA Oral History Project, Tape 294, Side 2; *Amalgamated Journal*, 31 January 1935; "Is There Going to be a Strike in the Meat-Packing Industry?" 1939, UPWA, p. 10.

21 *People's Press*, 13 February 1937; Minutes of SWOC District 31 Field Workers' Meeting, 8 February 1937, USWA; "Nation-wide Aid to Union, Negro Pledge," *Steel Labor*, 20 February 1937. On blacks' anger toward AFL unions in the 1930s, see from the NAACP Papers, LC: "Memorandum. John P. Davis to Rose M. Coe, Proposed Study of Negro Workers and Organized Labor," 10 February 1934, Box 413, File "Unions – AF of L, Feb. 10–Nov. 22, 1934"; Roy Wilkins to Horace R. Cayton, 30 October 1934, Box 322, File "Labor, General, June 16–Dec. 17, 1934"; Walter White to John L. Lewis, 27 November 1935, Box 413, File "Unions – AF of L, June 27–Dec. 13, 1935."

22 Minutes of SWOC District 31 Field Workers' Meetings, 16 November 1936, 28 December 1936, 15 March 1937, USWA. A representative from the National Urban League who visited the Chicago SWOC headquarters got a good report from black organizer Henry Johnson on the SWOC's sincerity in organizing without discrimination and insistence that black workers be employed at higher paid and more skilled jobs. Lester B. Granger to Mr. Hill, 30 October 1936, National Urban League Papers, Series 4, Box 9, Folder "Workers' Bureau Reports, 1936," LC.

23 On blacks and the PWOC in Chicago, see Arthur Kampfert, Manuscript, UPWA, vol. 3, pp. 2–7; Interview with Philip Weightman, Chicago, IL, 7 and 8 October 1986, UPWA Oral History Project, Tape 286, Side 2; Interview with Stella Nowicki, in Lynd and Lynd, *Rank and File*, p. 87; Interview with Anna Novak, in Ann Banks, ed., *First-Person America* (New York: Vintage Books, 1981), p. 64; Interviews with Elmer Thomas, 11 May 1939, and Pat Christie, 14 June 1939, FWP, Folklore, Box A707; Catherine Elizabeth Lewis, "Trade Union Policies in Regard to the Negro Worker in the Slaughtering and Meatpacking Industry of Chicago" (M.A. thesis, University of Chicago, 1945); St. Clair Drake and Horace R. Cayton, *Black Metropolis: A Study of Negro Life in a Northern City* (New York: Harcourt Brace and Company, 1945), pp. 284, 308–9, 312–41; Oscar D. Hutton, Jr., "The Negro Worker and the Labor Unions of Chicago" (M.A. thesis, University of Chicago, 1939), pp. 7–16, 90–114.

24 Interview with Sophie Kosciolowski, ROHP, pp. 20, 33.

25 Interview with Clarence Stoecker by Julia Reichert, Chicago, IL, 12 August 1978, Side 1.

26 Correspondence between Claude A. Barnett and John A. Stephens (Manager of Industrial Relations, Chicago District, Carnegie–Illinois Steel Cor-

poration) and drafts of reports and memoranda to Barnett and Stephens, 1936–7, BAR, Box 280, Folder 1. For information on Claude Barnett, see Linda J. Evans, "Claude A. Barnett and the Associated Negro Press," *Chicago History* 12 (Spring 1983): 44–56.

27 The Workers' Bureau of the National Urban League, "The Negro Workers' Councils Bulletin No. 12," 7 August 1936, BAR, Box 280, Folder 1; also clipping "CIO Drives to Organize Race Steel Workers" in same file.

28 Interview with Leslie Orear by author, Chicago, IL, 27 July 1983, Tape 1, Side 2; Interview with Jim Cole, 18 May 1939, FWP, Folklore, Box A707, p. 2; Hutton, "Negro Worker and the Labor Movement," pp. 99–100.

29 Interview with Elmer Thomas, 11 May 1939, FWP, Folklore, Box A707.

30 The ethnic line-up in Local 65 of SWOC (South Works) was similarly diverse: Stanley Baczsinski (Polish), Charlie Henry (black), Charlie Jankus (Lithuanian), Alfredo Avila (Mexican), Joe McNellis (Irish), James Stewart (American).

Minutes from SWOC District 31 Field Workers' Meetings, November 1936–March 1942, USWA, are filled with mention of ethnic organizing committees and events oriented toward particular ethnic groups. There is also extensive material on the ethnic orientation of CIO unions in: PAT, Box 2, Folders 1–3, Box 6, Folders 3, 5, 7, 8; George Patterson, Autobiography, Book 1, PAT, pp. 107–9; Interview with Leon Beverly, 16 November 1970, ROHP, pp. 6–7; Interview with Frank Coradetti, Chicago Heights, IL, 13 May 1980, IC, p. 28; Arthur Kampfert, Manuscript, UPWA, p. 26; Myers, "Birth of the USWA Local 65," pp. 34–9. Articles in all CIO newspapers also report on special events for different ethnic groups, some even written in foreign languages, such as "Wielki Wiec!" *CIO News – Farm Equipment Workers' (FE) Edition*, 3 April 1939.

31 Minutes of SWOC District 31 Field Workers' Meeting, 5 November 1936, note that "fraternal organs are now really taking the drive more seriously. Sentiment of Church organizations is changing in our favor now," USWA. For more on support from the Catholic Church, see "An Invocation by His Excellency Most Reverend Bernard J. Sheil, Senior Auxiliary Bishop of Chicago on the Occasion of the National Policy Convention of the Packinghouse Workers' Organizing Committee (C.I.O.)," 16 July 1939, pp. 3–7; "Thank God for CIO, Prelate Tells Rally," *People's Press*, 27 November 1937.

32 "Fraternal Orders and Societies of Foreign Born Americans Pledge Help to Steel Drive," *Steel Labor*, 20 August 1936; "500,000 'Fraternals' to Aid SWOC," *Steel Labor*, 20 November 1936; Harvey Klehr, *The Heyday of American Communism: The Depression Decade* (New York: Basic Books, 1984), p. 232; George Patterson, Autobiography, Book 1, PAT, p. 109; "Chicago: Name Committee to Aid Chicago Drive," *Steel Labor*, 5 December 1936.

33 For Mexican support, see Interview with Herbert March, Los Angeles, CA, 16 and 17 November 1970, ROHP, pp. 67–8; Interview with Nick Migas, in Lynd and Lynd, *Rank and File*, pp. 167, 169; Interview with Jesse Perez,

in Banks, ed., *First-Person America*, p. 66; George Patterson, Autobiography, Book 1, PAT, pp. 116–17, and other materials in PAT showing efforts to recruit Mexicans into SWOC; Interview with Mr. John V. Riffe, Director and Office Manager of SWOC, South Chicago, by Nicholas Hernandez, 14 December 1936, CFLPS, Box 49; Frank X. Paz, "Report of Committee on Mexican–American Interests, Council of Social Agencies, January 1948," SECHP; "Mexicans in PWOC," *CIO News – Packinghouse Workers' Organizing Committee (PWOC) Edition*, 12 June 1939; Francisco A. Rosales and Daniel T. Simon, "Chicano Steelworkers and Unionism in the Midwest, 1919–1941," *Aztlan* 6 (1975): 270–3.

34 Zivich, "Fighting Unions," p. 25; Patterson, Autobiography, Book 1, PAT, p. 146. One of the best testaments to the new ethnic unity in the packinghouses was the formation of the Back of the Yards Council, a self-help community organization that brought together ethnic groups within the neighborhood, the PWOC, and the Catholic Church. It was founded in 1939 by sociologist–organizer Saul Alinsky, Davis Square Park Director Joseph Meegan, and Catholic Bishop Bernard Sheil. For a thorough treatment of the council, see Robert A. Slayton, *Back of the Yards: The Making of a Local Democracy* (Chicago: University of Chicago Press, 1986). Also, "Annual Report of the Back of the Yards Council, 1941," WC, Box 251, Folder "Back of the Yards Council, 1940–67"; Kathryn Close, "Back of the Yards: Packingtown's Latest Drama in Civic Unity," *Survey Graphic* (December 1940); Walter Heitzman, "The Back of the Yards Neighborhood Council: A Study of the Community Organizing Approach to Juvenile Delinquency" (M.A. thesis, University of Chicago, 1946); Fred K. Hoehler, Jr., "Community Action by the United Packinghouse Workers of America – CIO in the Back of the Yards Neighborhood of Chicago" (M.A. thesis, University of Chicago, 1947).

35 Arthur Kampfert, Manuscript, UPWA, vol. 3, p. 27, also pp. 33, 40, 48, 67, and Phil Weightman, "Why I Joined the CIO," in Kampfert, vol. 3, part 2, p. 5; Al Tower, quoted in Myers, "The Birth of USWA Local 65," p. 61; "Armour CIO On War Path," *CIO News – PWOC Edition*, 5 December 1938; "SWOC Men See Armour Chicago Plant," *CIO News – PWOC Edition*, 27 May 1940. On workers wearing buttons and managers' response to them, see Interview with Herbert March, Los Angeles, CA, 16 and 17 November 1970, ROHP, p. 60; "Buttons Show at 31st Street," *CIO News – PWOC Edition*, 21 November 1938; Interview with Stella Nowicki, in Banks, *First-Person America*, p. 62; Theodore V. Purcell, *The Worker Speaks His Mind on Company and Union* (Cambridge, MA: Harvard University Press, 1953), p. 55; "Armour and Company and Packing House Workers Organizing Committee for United Packing House Workers, Local 347, Cases Nos. R-584 and C-695, Decided September 15, 1938," in *Decisions and Orders of the NLRB*, vol. 8 (Washington, DC: U.S. Government Printing Office, 1938), pp. 1109, 1111.

36 Interview with Jim Cole, 18 May 1939, FWP, Folklore, Box A707; Interview with Herbert March, Los Angeles, CA, 16 and 17 November 1970,

ROHP, p. 59a; Interview with George Patterson, ROHP, December 1970–January 1971, pp. 94–5; Interview with Stella Nowicki, in Lynd and Lynd, *Rank and File*, p. 80; Statement of Herbert March, 14 November 1938, MCD, Box 3, Folder 15, p. 2; Rick Halpern, "Race and Radicalism in the Chicago Stockyards," Paper delivered at the Organization of American Historians' Meeting, 1987, p. 14. On the return of taverns to Chicago after Prohibition ended, see Arthur J. Todd et al., *The Chicago Recreation Survey, 1937*, vol. 2 (Chicago: Chicago Recreation Commission and Northwestern University, 1938), pp. 143–59.

37 The following is only a sampling of the multitude of articles on union-sponsored recreation in the Chicago area to appear in the CIO press: "First Annual Tractor Dance Planned Jan. 8," *People's Press*, 25 December 1937; "SWOC Lodges to Hold Dance On New Year's," *People's Press*, 1 January 1938; "Armour Team Leads League," *CIO News – PWOC Edition*, 16 January 1938; "SWOC To Open Training 'School': Union Members Given Chance to Hear Outstanding Speakers and Enjoy Mountain Vacation," *Steel Labor*, 17 June 1938; "Soft Ball Series Opens," *CIO News – PWOC Edition*, 12 June 1939; "Mardi Gras and Victory Ball," *CIO News – PWOC Edition*, 11 December 1939; "Chicago to Have Annual Picnic At Berutes Grove, June 12," *CIO News – PWOC Edition*, 27 May 1940. On the explosion of the interest in softball during the 1930s, see Frederick Lewis Allen, *Since Yesterday: The 1930s in America* (New York: Harper & Row, Publishers, 1939), p. 120. On CIO recreation, see Elizabeth Fones-Wolf, "Industrial Unionism and Labor Movement Culture in Depression-Era Philadelphia," *Pennsylvania Magazine of History and Biography* 109 (January 1985): 3–26.

38 "PWOC Sports Program," *CIO News – PWOC Edition*, 28 November 1938; Minutes of SWOC District 31 Field Workers' Meeting, 9 August 1937, USWA; "PWOC Sports League," *CIO News – PWOC Edition*, 10 June 1938; "Open Chicago Softball League," *CIO News – PWOC Edition*, 10 June 1940.

39 William Z. Foster, *Organizing Methods in the Steel Industry* (New York: Workers' Library Publishers, 1935). In many other ways as well – such as his advice on recruiting blacks, ethnic groups, and women and on dealing with company unions – Foster's pamphlet became a blueprint for CIO policy.

40 "SWOC Memo to All Field Workers," 28 December 1936, PAT, Box 6, Folder 3. A sampling of articles about radio programming in the labor press: "Lewis To Speak on Big Hookup," *People's Press*, 2 January 1936; "What This 1936 Election Means to You and to Your Family: A Dramatic Presentation Via a Radio Broadcast of the Campaign Issues Which Are Important to You, Philip Murray, Chairman of the SWOC, Answers Questions from the Audience," *Steel Labor*, 3 November 1936; "Lewis to Give Radio Speech over a Coast-to-Coast Network of the Columbia Broadcasting System," *Steel Labor*, 26 August 1937; "Wider Use of Radio Urged at Convention; Broadcasts Criticized," *CIO News – PWOC Edition*, 30

October 1939; "CIO Broadcasts Jobs, Security, Peace Program," *CIO News – FE Edition*, 8 January 1940; "Carey on NBC Network Jan. 29; Has Your Station Scheduled Speech?" *CIO News – PWOC Edition*, 22 January 1940; "CIO Leaders Programs Popular," *CIO News – FE Edition*, 25 March 1940.

Employers also used the radio to reach workers with their antiunion message, through programming sponsored by the National Association of Manufacturers. Rick Fantasia, *Cultures of Solidarity: Consciousness, Action and Contemporary American Workers* (Berkeley: University of California Press, 1988), pp. 43–4.

41 Minutes of SWOC District 31 Field Workers' Meetings, 26 November 1936 and 7 December 1936, USWA.

42 "PWOC on the Air," *CIO News – PWOC Edition*, 22 May 1939; "Industry-Wide PWOC All Set to Go," *CIO News – PWOC Edition*, 15 May 1939.

43 For example, every issue of *People's Press* included "Mike Talk by Lee Kay," "In the Field of Sports by Ken Allen," and "The Film Corner by the New Film Alliance."

44 George A. Patterson to John L. Lewis, 23 January 1936, PAT, Box 2, Folder 2.

45 Clinton Golden and Harold Ruttenberg, *The Dynamics of Industrial Democracy* (New York: Harper & Brothers, 1942), p. 170.

46 Executive Boards of Lodges 65 and 1068 to Fellow Steel Workers," n.d., PAT, Box 6, Folder 3; also see PAT for frequent mention of use of patriotic symbolism in the CIO organizing campaign in steel.

47 Zivich, "Fighting Unions," p. 22; Minutes of SWOC District 31 Field Workers' Meeting, 11 July 1937, USWA.

48 "Whirlwind Drive on in Wilson and Swift; Armour Tightens Grip," *CIO News – PWOC Edition*, 21 August 1939.

49 "CIO Sets Up Farm Machine Campaign," *CIO News – PWOC Edition*, 30 July 1938; Arthur Kampfert, Manuscript, UPWA, vol. 3, pp. 35–6; "Harvester Workers on Strike," *Swift Flash*, 25 February 1941, UPWA, p. 2. Steelworkers also reinforced the picket lines during the big McCormick strike of 1941, according to Robert Ozanne, *A Century of Labor–Management Relations at McCormick and International Harvester* (New York: Doubleday & Company, 1985), p. 200.

50 Benjamin Appel, *The People Talk: American Voices from the Great Depression* (New York: Simon & Schuster, 1940; republished 1982), p. 180; Interview with Sam Evett, State College, PA, 1 April 1971, Labor Archives, Pennsylvania State University, p. 5. Journalist Mary Heaton Vorse felt that "this sense of unity – the identity of interest of all workers of whatever union, making them in truth members of one body – is the C.I.O.'s greatest source of power. It begins in the industrial union which embraces all the workers of an industry, then leaps the bounds of the industry and sees the interrelation of all industries." Mary Heaton Vorse, *Labor's New Millions* (New York: Modern Age Books, 1938), p. 221.

51 "Local 1010 Auxiliary," *CIO News – FE Edition*, 18 March 1940.

52 "'Steel Labor' Is Now Being Mailed Direct to Members," *Steel Labor*, 13 December 1937; Vorse, *Labor's New Millions*, pp. 153–4, 234.

53 "And Dad, Too, Knows That Is True," Cartoon, *Steel Labor*, 19 November 1937; also column "The Owl," *Steel Labor*, 5 September 1936, and "Why Is My Man on Strike?" *Steel Labor*, 5 June 1937.

54 Interview with Dorothy and George Patterson, State College, PA, 1 February 1969, Labor Archives, Pennsylvania State Archives, pp. 5–6; Hutton, "Negro Worker and the Labor Movement," pp. 99–100; Extensive material on women's auxiliaries in PAT, Box 9, Folder 3; Ingersoll report on women's success signing men into union, Minutes of SWOC District 31 Field Workers' Meeting, 23 November 1936, USWA; "Women Push Drive in Chicago Area," *Steel Labor*, 5 September 1936; "Auxiliaries Active in Enlisting Support for Organizing Drive," *Steel Labor*, 20 November 1936; Interview with George Patterson, December 1970–January 1971, ROHP, p. 72; Interview with George Patterson, State College, PA, 31 October 1967, Labor Archives, Pennsylvania State University, pp. 35–7; William Foote Whyte, *Pattern for Industrial Peace* (New York: Harper & Brothers, 1951), p. 15.

SWOC was not alone in recognizing the important influence of steelworkers' wives. At Inland Steel, the independent (company) union also canvassed door-to-door to reach them. Zivich, "Fighting Union," p. 23. The *People's Press* printed an article warning women that companies were sending professional "strikebreakers" into workers' homes disguised as door-to-door salesmen trying to sell women some "shiny new dojigger for the kitchen." When the woman of the home informed the "salesman" that she could not make such a purchase now because her husband or father was on strike, he launched into a tirade about how outsiders have been stirring up trouble and women ought to take things in their own hands and order the men back to work. *People's Press – Workers' Alliance Edition*, 17 October 1936.

55 Kosciolowski, quoted in Arthur Kampfert, Manuscript, UPWA, vol. 3, pp. 28–9; Barnes, quoted in Studs Terkel, *Division Street: America* (New York: Avon Books, 1968), pp. 89–90; also see "Fight Speedup," *CIO News – PWOC Edition*, 19 March 1938; "Women's Organizing Committee Formed," *CIO News – PWOC Edition*, 7 August 1939.

56 Office Memorandum from John G. Shott, 23 November 1934, NRA, Meatpacking, File 199.

57 "The Perils of Packinghouse Patty: For Women Only! Read This True Story," Leaflet, n.d. but notation "found between letters dated May and June 1941" (mimeo), CHS.

58 "We Women," vol. 1, nos. 1 and 2 (October 1937 and November 1937), CHS; also see Arthur Kampfert, Manuscript, UPWA, vol. 3, pp. 2, 13–14.

59 Although I do not discuss it as extensively here, the FE also had a women's auxiliary similar to those in the SWOC and PWOC; see *CIO News – FE Edition*, 24 April 1939, 26 June 1939, and 18 March 1940, for more

details. For related discussion of women's involvement in the union drives of the 1930s, see Marjorie Penn Lasky, "'Where I Was a Person': The Ladies' Auxiliary in the 1934 Minneapolis Teamsters' Strikes," and Ruth Meyerowitz, "Organizing the United Automobile Workers: Women Workers at the Ternstedt General Motors Parts Plant," both in Ruth Milkman, ed., *Women, Work and Protest: A Century of U.S. Women's Labor History* (Boston: Routledge & Kegan Paul, 1985), pp. 181–205, 235–58; Ruth Milkman, *Gender at Work: The Dynamics of Job Segregation by Sex during World War II* (Urbana: University of Illinois Press, 1987), pp. 27–48.

60 Interview with Elmer Thomas, in Banks, *First-Person America*, pp. 70–1. For other examples of employers trying to divide workers along racial and ethnic lines, see *Amalgamated Journal*, 2 July 1936; "The U.S. Steel Corporation III," *Fortune* 13 (May 1936): 142; Interview with Herbert March, Madison, WI, 21 October 1986, UPWA Oral History Project, Tape 294, Side 2; Interview with Anna Novak and Jim Cole, in Banks, *First-Person America*, pp. 64, 67; Interview with Philip Weightman, Chicago, IL, 7 and 8 October 1986, UPWA Oral History Project, Tape 285, Side 2; "But True Nature of Co. Union Is Revealed," *CIO News – FE Edition*, 10 April 1939.

61 Interview with Leslie Orear by author, Chicago, IL, 27 July 1983, Tape 1, Side 2. On sources of militance in packing, see Interview with Herbert March, Los Angeles, CA, 16 and 17 November 1970, ROHP, p. 195; Interview with Stella Nowicki, in Lynd and Lynd, *Rank and File*, p. 87; Interview with Philip Weightman, Chicago, IL, 7 and 8 October 1986, UPWA Oral History Project, Tape 287, Side 2.

62 Interview with Mary Hammond, in Banks, ed., *First-Person America*, p. 55. For more on the difficulty of organizing Swift and anticommunism there, see Purcell, *Worker Speaks His Mind*; Interview with Stella Nowicki, in Lynd and Lynd, *Rank and File*, pp. 77–8; Interview with Philip Weightman, Chicago, IL, 7 and 8 October 1986, UPWA Oral History Project, Tape 285, Sides 1 and 2.

63 On the SWOC's purge of Communists, see PAT and interviews in Labor Archives, Pennsylvania State University: Joseph Germano, Chicago, IL, 21 June 1972, pp. II-27–30, and Sam Evett, East Chicago, IN, 1 April 1971, pp. 13–14. On the Communist Party's involvement in the organization of the McCormick Works of International Harvester, see "Report on Study of Background and Development of the United Farm Equipment and Metal Workers Union," 25 April 1952, IH.

64 In both plants, union "activists" often received promotions to supervisors. At Western Electric, many union stewards ended up as plant foremen. At Wisconsin Steel, the first president of the Progressive Steel Workers' Union, Bill Reilly, had been active in the works council and finished his career at Harvester on the staff of the company's industrial relations department.

65 From 1937 until the mid-1950s, Hawthorne workers had their own independent union. In the early 1940s, the United Electrical, Radio and

Machine Workers of America (UE-CIO) tried to organize Hawthorne but was not successful, though it broke into some smaller plants in Cicero. See correspondence between Ernest De Maio and James J. Matles, 1941–2, O-FF148, 151, 152, 164, and "Report on Organization For November 1943, Western Electric Company," by T. L. Majors, D-11 #142, UE Archives, University of Pittsburgh, Pittsburgh, PA. Also, "Meet Tomorrow for Wage–Hour Mediation Effort," *Berwyn Life*, 21 March 1937, and "UE Certified in Westinghouse's Chicago Plant," *People's Press*, 31 December 1938. Finally, in the fifties, workers voted to leave the independent and join the IBEW, selecting it from among more militant unions.

On the history of union organization at the Hawthorne Works, see Interview with Hugh Young (President of 1851, International Brotherhood of Electrical Workers) by author, Chicago, IL, 7 December 1983; Loren Baritz, *The Servants of Power: A History of Social Science in American Industry* (Middletown, CT: Wesleyan University Press, 1960), p. 106; Jeanne L. and Harold L. Wilensky, "Personnel Counseling," *American Journal of Sociology* 57 (November 1951); "Interview with Mr. Ralph Johnson and Mr. Nixon, Western Electric Company, Cicero, Ill.," 15 April 1940, HOLC, Background research for "Metropolitan Chicago, Illinois. Re-Survey Report," 1940.

On union history at Wisconsin Steel, including the SWOC's many efforts to organize there, see Minutes of SWOC District 31 Field Workers' Meetings, USWA, Reports at almost every meeting; File 4035, Wisconsin Steel, 1942, and File 13-R-2800, International Harvester Company–Wisconsin Steel Works, 1944, NLRB; Marshall A. Pipin to William J. Reilly, Progressive Steel Workers' Union, 18 June 1937, and Van A. Bittner to Marshall A. Pipin, 19 June 1937, USWA District 31 Papers, SECHP; James R. McIntyre, "The History of Wisconsin Steel Works of the International Harvester Company, 1951" (typescript), SECHP, pp. 51, 53–5; "Steelyard Blues: The Death of a Chicago Mill," *Chicago Tribune Magazine*, 13 June 1982; William Kornblum, *Blue Collar Community* (Chicago: University of Chicago Press, 1974), pp. 98–101; Robert Bulanda, "South Deering," in "The Historical Development of Three Chicago Millgates," by Marcia Kijewski, David Brosch, and Robert Bulanda, Illinois Labor History Society, 1972, pp. 56–64 (mimeo); Labor Relations newsletter no. 90 (8 July 1942) and no. 102 (28 August 1942), IH, Undocumented NLD files; David Bensman and Roberta Lynch, *Rusted Dreams: Hard Times in a Steel Community* (New York: McGraw-Hill Book Company, 1987), p. 41; "Employes of Wisconsin to Have Union," *Daily Calumet*, 24 April 1937.

66 Interview with Carl Koch and his wife, Chicago, IL, 20 October 1981, SECHP.

67 "Report on Study of Background and Development of the United Farm Equipment and Metal Workers Union," 25 April 1952, IH, pp. 28–9, and Appendix D, Document 17, p. 1.

68 Letter to the Editor from Henry Caler, *Berwyn Life*, 18 January 1933; "Roosevelt Road Trade Campaign Called Success," *Berwyn Life*, 19 April

1933; "Unfair Competition," *Cicero Life*, 24 November 1933; "Says Serdiak" column, *Cicero Life*, 24 April 1935; Joseph Epstein, "Blue Collars in Cicero," in Irving Howe, ed., *The World of the Blue Collar Workers* (New York: Quadrangle Books, New York Times Company, 1972), p. 95; also see Frank D. Finlay, "Cicero Survey 1937: A Survey of the Town of Cicero, Illinois, Conducted under the General Supervision of the Department of Statistics and Research of the Council of Social Agencies of Chicago," 1937, WC, Box 292, p. 11.

69 "Recreational Interest Schedules" for WPA Project no. 3743 (Illinois), "Recreational Delinquency Study," BUR, Boxes 47 and 48; Results published in Shanas, *Recreation and Delinquency*.

70 Interview with Clarence Stoecker by Julia Reichert, Chicago, IL, 12 August 1978, Tape 1, Side 1; Minutes of SWOC District 31 Field Workers' Meeting, 29 July 1937, USWA.

71 Press release on black workers at Western Electric's Hawthorne Works, n.d. but c. November 1942, BAR, Box 260, Folder 6; Draft of article on black workers at International Harvester, n.d. but early 1940s, BAR, Box 280, Folder 2, p. 2; Robert Ozanne, *The Negro in the Farm and Construction Machinery Industries*, Report no. 26, Racial Policies of American Industry Series (Philadelphia: Wharton School of Finance and Commerce, University of Pennsylvania, 1972), pp. 22, 25.

72 Report sponsored by Chicago Council Against Racial and Religious Discrimination, "The Cicero Riots of 1951," compiled by Dr. Homer A. Jack (2 ed., revised 22 July 1951), BAR, Box 351, Folder 6; Camille DeRose, *The Camille DeRose Story: The True Story of the Cicero Race Riots* (Chicago: Erle Press, 1953); Materials on Trumbull Park Race Riots, UPWA, Box 353, Folder 11, including Carl Hirsch, *Terror at Trumbull* (New York: New Century Publishers, 1955), and Chicago Commission on Human Relations, "The Trumbull Park Homes Disturbances," Documentary report nos. 1 (August 1953–March 1954) and 2 (April–June 1954) (mimeo); "Trumbull Park Branch: South Chicago Community Center," 1 May 1956, Community Fund Papers, Box 95, Folder 2, UICC; Bulanda, "South Deering," in "Three Chicago Millgates," pp. 44–51; Arnold R. Hirsch, *Making the Second Ghetto: Race & Housing in Chicago, 1940–1960* (New York: Cambridge University Press, 1983).

73 Interview with George Patterson, December 1970–January 1971, ROHP, p. 84.

74 Fantasia, *Cultures of Solidarity: Consciousness, Action, and Contemporary American Workers*, pp. 3–24.

75 J. Walter Thompson Company, *People*, October 1937; also see July 1937 and November 1937; *Chain Store Age*, 1935–40, *passim*; "Oven Meals Win Prize for Toledo, Ohio, Woman," *A&P Menu, a Weekly Food Supplement to Woman's Day*, 16 December 1937.

76 Bittner instructions, quoted in Barbara Newell, *Chicago and the Labor Movement: Metropolitan Unionism in the 1930s* (Urbana: University of Illinois Press, 1961), p. 133; Patterson, Autobiography, PAT, Book 1,

pp. 113, 129–30, 146–7, Book 2, pp. 15, 89, 121, 128, 142; Patterson, quoted in Myers, "The Birth of USWA Local 65," pp. 65, 73; Interview with Nick Migas, in Lynd and Lynd, *Rank and File*, pp. 170–5; Bensman and Lynch, *Rusted Dreams*, pp. 130–2; Staughton Lynd, "What the Productivity Clause Means to the Steelworkers," speech, n.d., PAT, Box 10, Folder 2, pp. 113–15; Robert R. R. Brooks, *As Steel Goes... Unionism in a Basic Industry* (New Haven: Yale University Press, 1940), pp. 255–60; David Brody, "Origins of Modern Steel Unionism," and Mark McColloch, "Consolidating Industrial Citizenship," in Paul Clark, Peter Gottlieb, and Donald Kennedy, *Forging a Union of Steel: Philip Murray, SWOC & the United Steelworkers* (Ithaca, NY: ILR Press, 1987), pp. 27, 77.

77 Interview with Stella Nowicki, in Lynd and Lynd, *Rank and File*, p. 83; "The Dressing Room Gossip Corner," *CIO News – PWOC Edition*, 20 March 1939; Banks, *First-Person America*, p. 67; Interview with Sophie Kosciolowski, ROHP, p. 28; Sharon Hartman Strom, "Challenging 'Women's Place': Feminism, the Left, and Industrial Unionism in the 1930's," *Feminist Studies* 9 (Summer 1983): 359–86; Milkman, *Gender at Work*, pp. 27–48.

78 Vorse, *Labor's New Millions*, p. 133; Myers, "Birth of USWA Local 65," pp. 63–4; George Patterson, Autobiography, PAT, Book 2, pp. 16–72; Interview with George Patterson, December 1970–January 1971, ROHP, pp. 96–134, particularly pp. 117 and 134; Interview with Anthony Cassano, Burnham, IL, 22 March 1980, IC, pp. 47–8; William Hal Bork, "The Memorial Day 'Massacre' of 1937 and Its Significance in the Unionization of Republic Steel Corporation" (M.A. thesis, University of Illinois, 1975); Donald G. Sofchalk, "The Chicago Memorial Day Incident: An Episode of Mass Action," *Labor History* 6 (Winter 1965): 3–43.

79 Interview with Leslie Orear by author, Chicago, IL, 27 April 1983, Tape 2, Side 1.

CONCLUSION

1 On ethnic politics in the 1930s, see William W. Link, "The Activities and Accomplishments of the Polish American Democratic Organization, Inc., of Illinois," in *Poles of Chicago, 1837–1937: A History of One Century of Polish Contributions to the City of Chicago* (Chicago: Polish Pageant, 1937), pp. 166–8; Anna Masley, "Term Paper, Research Project: Study of Ukranians, A Nationality Group of Chicago and Vicinity," Paper for Sociology 264, BUR, Box 156, Folder 6, Document 10, p. 4; Thomas P. Powers, Memo on Polish Democratic Club, 17 May 1934, MCD, Box 19, Folder 3; "James S. Jabczynski Elected President of Polish Democratic Club of Seventh; Henry Lenard Heads Committee," *Daily Calumet*, 10 April 1937; from the CFLPS: "Mass Meeting of Democrats," *Osadne Hlasy*, 28 October 1932, Box 40; Record Books of Political Clubs, 1937, in the possession of

the Secretary of Political Clubs (Lithuanian), Box 28; "American Lithuanians in Politics," *Sandara*, 14 March 1930, Box 28; Interview with Representative of the 21st Ward American Lithuanian Citizens Club, Chicago, IL, by Theo Kucinskas, 11 June 1937, Box 28; Edward R. Kantowicz, *Polish–American Politics in Chicago, 1888–1940* (Chicago: University of Chicago Press, 1975), pp. 189–95; John P. White, "Lithuanians and the Democratic Party: A Case Study of Nationality Politics in Chicago and Cook County" (Ph.D. dissertation, University of Chicago, 1953), pp. 10–14, 54–8.

For cases of Italians buying and selling commercial insurance policies in their Chicago neighborhoods during the 1930s, see interviews in Chicago, IL, in IC with: Lina Tarabori, 5 June 1980, p. 22; Emilio Scarpelli, 2 July 1980, pp. 82, 126; Alfred Fantozzi, 27 May 1980, pp. 49–50.

2 On the 1940s see Alan Brinkley, "The New Deal and the Idea of the State," in Steve Fraser and Gary Gerstle, *The Rise and Fall of the New Deal Order, 1930–1980* (Princeton: Princeton University Press, 1989), pp. 85–121; Nelson Lichtenstein, *Labor's War at Home: The CIO in World War II* (New York: Cambridge University Press, 1982); Ronald W. Schatz, *The Electrical Workers: A History of Labor at General Electric and Westinghouse, 1923–60* (Urbana: University of Illinois Press, 1983); Joshua B. Freeman, *In Transit: The Transport Workers Union in New York City, 1933–1966* (New York: Oxford University Press, 1989); James R. Green, *The World of the Worker: Labor in Twentieth-Century America* (New York: Hill and Wang, 1980), pp. 174–209; David Brody, *Workers in Industrial America: Essays on the Twentieth Century Struggle* (New York: Oxford University Press, 1980), pp. 82–119, 173–257; Sumner M. Rosen, "The CIO Era, 1935–55," in Julius Jacobson, *The Negro and the American Labor Movement* (Garden City, NY: Anchor Books, Doubleday & Company, 1968), pp. 188–208; August Meier and Elliott Rudwick, *Black Detroit and the Rise of the UAW* (New York: Oxford University Press, 1979).

3 Interview with Jim Cole, Chicago, IL, 18 May 1939, FWP, Folklore, Box A707, p. 2.

Index

A&P, 106, 107, 112, 119, 407n47; and blacks, 154; expansion of, 116, 117, 326, 356–7; Hawthorne pay checks cashed at, 178; and radio, 140; store locations of, 109
Abbott, Edith, 7
Abramowicz, Rev., 94, 384n16
Akron, Ohio, 2, 297
Alabama, 262
Alinsky, Saul, 501n34
Alschuler, Judge Samuel, 44
Amalgamated Association of Iron, Steel and Tin Workers, 3, 39, 294
Amalgamated Clothing Workers of America (ACWA), 47–8, 210, 308
Amalgamated Meat Cutters and Butcher Workmen of North America, 4, 43–6, 296, 379n58
American Federation of Labor (AFL), 333; and blacks, 336; in competition with CIO, 300; in 1919, 3, 13, 39
Americanization programs, 165
American Red Cross, 223
"Amos 'n' Andy Show," 142, 328, 329
anti-Semitism, 29, 151–2, 427n178
Armour and Company, 13, 27, 160; blacks at, 35, 166, 206, 379n54; and community outreach, 180; company and plant magazines at, 179; compared to Swift, 207; employee representation at, 171–3, 190, 205, 297, 452n121, n123; ethnicity of work force at, 28; foremen at, 188; in Great Depression, 239, 240, 316; longstanding resistance to unionism at, 4; NLRB election at, 311; PWOC at, 2, 302, 305, 307–8, 310, 320, 321, 349, 350; PWOC contract with, 297–8, 307–8; response to PWOC by, 297, 305; and stock ownership plans, 175, 445n88; unionization at, in early 1930s, 296–7; vacations at, 439n50; welfare capitalism at, 163–4; and women, 347
Armstrong, Louis, 155
Associated Catholic Charities, 60–1, 84, 86; and government relief, 269; in Great Depression, 219, 221, 222, 223, 224–6
Associated Grocers of Chicago, 119
Associated Jewish Charities, 60
automobiles: owned by workers, 103, 143, 401n12; purchased by installment, 103
Avalon Park, 134t
Avila, Alfredo, 500n30

Back of the Yards, 17, 27–30; employers compared in, 207; ethnic banking in, 75; in Great Depression, 1; movie theaters in, 123, 124, 127, 131; radio in, 134t; stores in, 107, 110, 115
Back of the Yards Council, 501n34
Baczsinski, Stanley, 500n30
Baer, Max, 330
Balaban & Katz, 100, 122, 124–5, 126, 128, 129
Barczak family, 234
Barnes, Eva, 287, 347
Barnett, Claude, 335–6
Barrett, Joseph, 338
Beiderbacke, Leon "Bix," 156
Bekker's Cleaners, 109
Berwyn, 31, 80; cultural isolation of, in 1930s, 353; and Hawthorne Works, 33, 49; stores in, 353
Binga State Bank, 152; closed in Great Depression, 215, 231–2, 233
Bittner, Van, 297, 299, 309, 338, 343, 358
B. Kuppenheimer Company, 31
Black Belt, 21, 33–8, 148–56; as "black metropolis," 425n170; and CIO organizing, 334; in Great Depression, 215, 226, 270, 271; movie theaters in, 131; radio in, 134t; stores in, 151–3, 427n178
blacks: in agricultural implements industry, 18; attitude toward unions of, 42,

blacks (*cont.*)
45; banks among, 152, 215, 233; churches among, 148, 226, 394n87; and CIO, 334–6, 335, 337, 338, 363, 499n22, 500n30; and Communist Party, 261–2; and consumption, 148–54; and employee representation, 205–6; employer attitude toward, 45; and FERA, 268; fraternals among, 151; in garment industry, 18, 20, 35, 48; in Great Depression, 226–7, 242, 331–2, 363; increase within industrial work force during 1920s of, 165–6; and insurance, 150–1, 464n42; isolated from coworkers, 36; and jazz, 154–6; job discrimination toward, 36, 165–7, 205–6, 207–8, 242, 354, 457n173; at McCormick Works, 32, 35, 449n99; and mass culture, 147–57; and movie theaters, 123, 125, 131, 413n96; in 1919 steel strike, 42; and NRA, 260; in packinghouses, 17, 18, 20, 28, 35, 166; in packinghouse strike of 1921–2, 45; and politics, 254, 257, 258–61; prefer brand-name goods, 152, 427n181; prefer chain stores, 152–4; residential patterns of, 34, 376n26; and separate black economy, 148–52; skill of, 167, 434n20; in steel, 17, 18, 20, 35, 165–7, 335–6, 442–3; as strikebreakers, 35, 42, 45; and unemployed movement, 266; and unemployment, 185–6, 242, 449n99; and WPA, 260–1, 279–81; *see also* Black Belt; Democratic Party; Republican Party; Roosevelt, Franklin D.; welfare capitalism; *by names of employers*
Blazewicz, Anna, 236
Blue Island, Illinois, 342
Bohemian Charitable Association, 58, 219
Bohemians, 29; anxiety about assimilation among, 54; avoidance of public assistance in 1920s among, 62–3; conflicts within, 383n7; and consumption, 111, 114; and dance palaces, 146; in garment industry, 47; at Hawthorne Works, 33, 49, 203; new settlements of, 31, 32; old community of, 30; opposition to Prohibition among, 210–11; in packinghouses, 28; and politics, 254; in unemployed movement, 266; and United Charities, 62; *see also* ethnic and religious welfare organizations in 1920s; ethnic banks in 1920s; ethnic banks in 1930s; ethnic building and loan associations in 1920s; ethnic mutual benefit societies in 1920s; Liberty Loans
Boston, 104, 107
Bowles, William, 270
Brachs Candy Company, 277
Brazinski, Father, 232
Breckinridge, Sophonisba, 7, 110, 144, 408n54
Brichke, Jean, 118
Bridgeport, 28; *see also* Back of the Yards
Brighton Park, 32; in Great Depression, 236; movie theaters in, 123; *see also* Southwest Corridor
British, 373n12
Brown, Mary, 263
Buffalo, 410n70
building and loan associations, *see* ethnic building and loan associations in 1920s; ethnic building and loan associations in 1930s
Bunche, Ralph, 260
Burgess, Ernest, 7, 101, 248
Bush, the, 24

Calumet region, 21–6
Calzaretta, Flory, 274
Canadians, 373n12
Canaryville, 28
capitalism: and "moral capitalism," 209, 253, 286, 289, 291, 292, 315, 366; worker attitude toward, 209, 252, 263–4, 286, 315–17, 356, 365–6
Carnegie-Illinois Steel Corporation, *see* U.S. Steel
Carnegie Steel Company, *see* U.S. Steel
Carradina, Celie, 258
Carter, Barbara Ann, 274
Caruso, Enrico, 105
Caruso, Tony, 197
Castiglia, Agnes, 277
Catholic Church: Associated Catholic Charities established by, 60–1; attack on national parishes by, 55, 83–4; among blacks, 394n87; and CIO, 338, 500n31; criticism of, in Great Depression, 224–6; Five Holy Martyrs, 384n16; and government relief, 269–70; Holy Name Societies in, 84, 86, 91, 221, 395n92; Immaculate Conception, B.V.M., 395n92; Italian feasts and, 88–90; and Italians, 87–94; Our Lady of Guadalupe, 24; Our Lady of Pompeii, 221; parochial schools of, 86, 87, 92, 225, 374n12, 396n98, 423n159; and Poles, 85–7, 94, 395n90; and radio, 135, 418n129; Sacred Heart, 24; St. Adelbert, 222; St. Anthony, 90; St. Augustine, 225, 395n92, 461n17; St. Casimir, 73, 222; St. George, 26; St. Joseph, 24; St. Kevin, 180; St. Marina, 232; St.

Mary Magdalene, 221; St. Michael, 24, 85, 86, 180, 225; St. Patrick, 24; St. Philip Benizi, 91; S.S. Peter and Paul, 26; St. Stanislaus Kostka, 395n92; San Callisto, 90; San Rocco, 90, 92; in South Chicago, 24, 26; *see also* ethnic and religious welfare organizations in 1920s
Cayton, Horace, 226
Central Charity Bureau, *see* Associated Catholic Charities
Cermak, Anton, 63, 255, 259
chain stores, *see* consumption
Chalasinski, Joseph, 86
Chatham, 134t
Cheltenham, 24
Chicago: chain stores in, 107–9; CIO in, 291; class polarization in, during 1930s, 287–8; economic characteristics of, 7, 13, 21, 27–8; employment in, 13, 14–15, 16, 371n6; HOLC in, 274; industrial work force composition in, 7, 17, 18, 20, 35, 324–5; movie theaters in, 130; in 1919, 12; outlying shopping areas in, 117; postal savings rates in, 273, 392n68; unemployment in, 102, 217, 241, 243t, 246–9, 399n8; unionization in, by 1940, 292; U.S. savings bonds sales in, 273
Chicago Commons Settlement, 31, 256, 272
Chicago Council of Social Agencies, 102
Chicago Defender, 149, 153, 155, 231, 330, 429n188
Chicago Federation of Labor, 4, 43, 50, 261, 286; and Hawthorne Works in 1919, 49; in 1919 steel strike, 39; in packinghouse industrial conflicts, 1917–22, 45; and WCFL, 136–8, 140, 141–2, 327; welfare programs of, 210
Chicago Heights, Illinois, 21, 88, 90
Chicago Urban League, 167, 242
Chicago Workers' Committee on Unemployment, *see* Workers' Committee on Unemployment
Churches, *see* Catholic Church; Protestant churches
Cicero, 21, 31, 137, 320, 506n65; cultural isolation of, in 1930s, 352–4; and Hawthorne Works, 33, 49; stores in, 109, 111, 353
Cieslak, Stanley and Natalie, 73
Civilian Conservation Corps (CCC), 252, 258, 278; class composition of, 281; impact of, on youth, 281; program of, 281
Civil Works Administration (CWA), 278, 279
Clementi, Rose, 92
Cleveland, 274
Cohen, Anna, 274
Cole, Jim, 337, 367
Colson, Myra Hill, 200
Columbia Broadcasting System (CBS), 141, 327
Communist Party: efforts to attract blacks by, 261–2; during 1920s, 196, 261; during 1930s, 261–4, 296, 309–12, 319; votes for, 478n24; *see also* Unemployed Councils
communities, *see* neighborhoods
Congress of Industrial Organizations (CIO), 2, 5; and blacks, 334–6, 363; in Chicago, 291, 292; Communist support of, 262, 309–12; and "culture of unity," 324, 333–49, 365; demands of, 314, 315; diversity in militance within, 349–50; early history of, 294; employer response to, 350; ethnic and racial solidarity within, 323, 324, 333–40, 348–9, 361, 367; family orientation of, 346–8, 358–9; helped by ethnic and religious organizations, 338; historical debate over workers' motives for, 493n33; influence of unemployed movement on, 265, 320; internal conflicts within, 357–8, 367; leadership of, 308–13, 318–19, 492n23; limitations of, 357–60, 366; after 1940, 367–8; and radio, 341, 343, 344; and rank and file, 310–13, 367; red-baiting of, 493n27; and Roosevelt, 302, 332, 359; shared culture among workers in, 324–33, 352–3, 356–7, 365; shop floor strategies of, 339; social and recreational programs of, 340–1, 342; and union buttons, 339–40; use of bars in organizing by, 340; workers' goals for, 292–3, 493n33; worker solidarity nationally in, 308, 331–3, 343–5, 367, 503n50; worker solidarity within Chicago in, 345–6, 503n49; *see also* Farm Equipment Workers' Organizing Committee (FE); Packinghouse Workers' Organizing Committee (PWOC); Steel Workers' Organizing Committee (SWOC)
consciousness, *see* political consciousness of industrial workers
Consumers' Store, 154, 236
consumption: of automobiles, 103, 143, 401n12; among blacks, 148–54; of brand-name goods, 106–7, 113, 115, 119, 152, 402n23, 408n53, n54; through chain stores, 106–9, 112–13, 116–20, 152–4, 235–8, 325, 404n28, 407n45, n47, 411n72; changing patterns

consumption (*cont.*)
of, between 1920s and 1930s, 108, 116, 234–8; credit needed for, 112, 234–5; distinctive patterns among classes in, 103–4, 109–16, 120, 356–7, 404n28, 407n45, n47, 408n53, 409n61; distinctive patterns between races in, 154; of foreign-language records, 105–6; and Great Depression, 234–8, 325; through independent stores, 107, 117–18, 234–8, 405n36, 410n70, 427n178; by installment, 102–4; market research in, 116, 409n62; of phonographs, 104–6; social impact of, 104–6, 119, 143, 154; tied to ethnicity, 110–12, 406n41; through voluntary chains, 118–19; *see also by names of stores*
Cook County Bureau of Public Welfare: and Mothers' Pensions, 62, 120; in 1920s, 57, 62, 63; in 1930s, 216, 224, 265
Cosentino, Salvatore, 76, 78, 275
Coughlin, Charles E. (Father), 418n129
Croatian Falcons, 53
Croatians: and CIO, 338; and consumption, 408n54; ethnic organizations among, 53; in steel, 24, 163, 203; *see also* ethnic building and loan associations in 1920s
"culture of unity," *see* Congress of Industrial Organizations (CIO)
Cwik, Lillian, 65
Czechs, *see* Bohemians

Dal Cason, Nina, 65
Daley, Richard J., 255
Dalle-Molle, Ernest, 123
dance palaces, 146–7, 177
Danes, 165
Davis, John W., 256
Debs, Eugene, 492n23
De Lisle, Ellen, 278
Democratic Party, 5; and blacks, 259–61, 363; in Chicago, 254–61, 387n34; compared to European parties, 365–6; and Lithuanians, 362; and Poles, 362; worker support of, 2, 255–61, 287–9, 304, 332, 364, 366, 476n14
Dennison family, 233
depression of 1920–1, 60, 103, 161, 181–2, 185
depression of 1930s, *see* Great Depression
Detroit, 2, 273, 274, 330
Dies, Martin, 311
Dollard, John, 104
Domke, Rena, 105
Douglass National Bank, 152
Doyle, Mrs. Carl, 236
Drake, St. Clair, 226
Dubinsky, David, 308
Dynamics of Industrial Democracy, The, 318–19

East Chicago, Indiana, 21
East Side, 24; *see also* Southeast Chicago
elections, *see* voting
Elias, Joseph, 75
Ellington, Duke, 156
Elson, Gab, 193
Emergency Banking Act of 1933, 275
employee representation plans: and blacks, 205; in Chicago factories, 164; established, 171–3; as launching pad for CIO, 293–5, 299, 304; prevalence of nationally, 431n9; reality of, 172–3, 190–1, 452n121, 453n123; *see also by name of company*
employee stock ownership plans, *see* stock ownership plans
Employers' Association of Chicago, 182
Englewood, 134t
ethnic and religious welfare organizations in 1920s, 55, 56–64, 219–27; among Bohemians, 58; among Catholics, 60–1, 219, 221–2; consolidation of, 60–1; and hospitals, 63, 385n21; among Jews, 57, 58–61, 384n19; among Poles, 61, 219
ethnic and religious welfare organizations in 1930s: among Catholics, 224–6; crisis in, 222–7, 461n17
ethnic banks in 1920s, 56, 75–83; attitudes toward, 80–2, 391n57; among Bohemians, 80, 82; changes over decade in, 83; competing with employee stock ownership plans, 195; financial weakness of, 79–80, 82, 230–1; and higher savings rate, 103, 392n67; impact of World War I on, 76–9; among Italians, 80, 81; among Jews, 76, 80, 81–2; among Lithuanians, 75; location of, 79–80; motives behind creation of, 80; people's banking experiences prior to, 75–6; among Poles, 80; among Slovaks, 80
ethnic banks in 1930s: among Bohemians, 231; crisis in, 230–3; and federal government, 272–3; among Italians, 231, 232; among Jews, 231; among Lithuanians, 231; among Poles, 231, 232; postal savings preferred to, 273; among Slovaks, 231; U.S. savings bonds preferred to, 273
ethnic building and loan associations in 1920s: among Bohemians, 76, 82;

changes over decade of, 82–3; among Croatians, 82; among Jews, 391n59; among Lithuanians, 82; people's experiences prior to, 76; among Poles, 76, 82; among Serbians, 82; among Slovaks, 82; among Slovenians, 82
ethnic building and loan associations in 1930s: in crisis, 233, 274–6; and HOLC, 274–6; among Italians, 233; among Lithuanians, 233; among Poles, 233, 275
ethnic groups: anxiety about assimilation within, 54–6, 75, 96, 144–7, 382n5; assist CIO, 338, 362; avoidance of public assistance in 1920s among, 57, 62–4; avoidance of United Charities in 1920s among, 62; change in their institutions during 1920s, 94–5; citizenship within, 55, 383n6; class relations within, during 1920s, 96; class tensions within, during Great Depression, 223, 230, 232, 238, 362–3; decline in their newspapers, 497n9; dependence on precinct captains in 1920s by, 63–4, 387n34; dispersed on shop floor under welfare capitalism, 163, 165, 167, 202–4; displaced by state in 1930s, 289, 362; European nationalism in, 54, 68; generational conflict in, 144–7; help own needy, 58, 218; leaders of, 54–6, 96, 362, 381n2; as mediators between workers and state, 362–3; mobility within Chicago of, 31, 32, 55; and movies, 123–4; and radio, 135–6; role of merchants in, 57, 111–12, 146, 406n41; support for Liberty Loans among, 76–9; and unemployed movement, 265–6; *see also by name of ethnic group*
ethnicity: as defined by second generation, 147, 424n166; importance to workers of, 26, 28, 29, 31, 95, 362; as problem for employers, 163, 165, 167, 176–9; reinforced through foreign-language records, 104–6; reinforced through neighborhood theaters, 123–5; reinforced through radio, 135; tensions over, 24, 29–30, 167, 243; *see also by name of ethnic group*
ethnic mutual benefit societies in 1920s, 64–75, 227–8; among Bohemians, 65, 66, 68–9, 388n39; competing with commercial insurance companies, 55, 64–5, 67, 71, 72; competing with employers' group insurance, 55, 65, 70–1, 72, 193–4; consolidation of, during 1920s, 68–70; difficulties faced by, 67–8; history of, 65; Illinois Health Insurance Commission Report on, 65–7, 71; among Italians, 65, 66, 69; among Jews, 65, 66, 69; among Mexicans, 176; new benefits to children by, 71–2; new benefits to women by, 71–2; among Poles, 65, 66, 68, 73; among Ukrainians, 193
ethnic mutual benefit societies in 1930s: assist CIO, 500n31; crisis in, 227–30, 362; and Social Security, 272
Evans, Rev. Mary, 226
Evanston, Illinois, 109

factory conditions, *see* working conditions
Fair Labor Standards Act, 267, 282, 288
family: in crisis during Great Depression, 214–17, 246–9; *see also* wages
Fannie May Candies, 109
Fantasia, Rick, 356
Fantozzi, Alfred, 387n34
Farm Equipment Workers' Organizing Committee (FE): and blacks, 335; Communists in, 310, 311, 351; and contract with International Harvester, 299; demands of, 299; family orientation of, 346; history of, at International Harvester, 298–300; organizing strategies of, 498n17; and relief, 320; role of employee representatives in founding of, 299; shop floor strategies of, 306, 317; social and recreational programs of, 341; *see also* International Harvester; seniority
Federal Deposit Insurance Corporation (FDIC), 267, 275
Federal Emergency Relief Administration (FERA), 265, 268–9, 271, 484n61
federal government: and Catholic Church, 269–70; feeling of entitlement toward, 258, 270–1, 274, 280–1, 285–6, 364; growing dependence on, 251–2, 252–3, 257–8, 260–1, 268, 270–1, 272–7, 278, 281–2, 282–5, 359–60, 364; postal savings with, 392n68; under pressure from workers, 303–8; Roosevelt administration view of, 267–8, 271–2, 286, 289; support for unionization by, 301–3, 308, 491n17; worker attitude toward, 2, 5, 210–11, 252, 253–5
Federal Writers' Project, 279
Federation of Jewish Charities, 60
Feld, Rose, 452n115
Ferk, Olga, 252
Fielde, Gerald, 309
Fitzpatrick, John, 39, 42, 43, 49–50, 261
Flint, Michigan, 297, 328
Flowers, Dorothy, 288
Fontecchio, Nicholas, 309

Ford, Henry, 100
Ford, James, 262
foremen: under drive system, 167–8, 434n22; in Great Depression, 216, 244–5, 316; training programs in Chicago factories for, 164; under welfare capitalism, 168–9, 172–4, 187–9, 202, 451n108, n109
Fort Wayne, Indiana, 407n45, 411n72
Foster, William Z., 39, 42, 43, 261, 262, 319, 341, 502n39
Fox Film Corporation, 126
fraternals, *see* blacks; ethnic mutual benefit societies in 1920s; ethnic mutual benefit societies in 1930s

garment industry: economic importance of, 31; ethnicity of workers in, 31; female dominance in, 17; importance of Jews in, 47–8; lack of ethnic and racial fragmentation in, 48; location of factories in, 31; nativity of workers in, 20; organizing success in 1919 in, 47; prevalence of local employers in, 31, 49; race of workers in, 35
Garvey, Marcus, 149–50
Gary, Indiana, 21, 42, 109, 153, 454n144
Gary, Judge Elbert, 170, 175
Gellhorn, Martha, 285
German Aid Society, 223
Germano, Joseph, 306, 358
Germans, 17, 32; and Catholic Church, 87; and consumption, 406n36; at Hawthorne Works, 203; in packinghouse industrial conflicts, 1917–22, 45; in packinghouses, 28, 373n12; in steel, 24, 26
Gillies, Fred, 315
Goich family, 214–15
Goldblatt's Department Store, 107, 115, 423n159
Golden, Clinton, 318–19, 344–5
Goldsmith, Samuel A., 222
Goodman, Benny, 156
Gosnell, Harold, 7, 255
Grand Boulevard, 34; *see also* Black Belt
Grande family, 26
Grant's Dollar Store, 118
Great Atlantic and Pacific Tea Company, *see* A&P
Great Depression: bank failures in, 215, 230–3; credit refused in, 216, 234–5; crisis of authority in, 249; evictions in, 213, 263, 266; insurance lost in, 216, 229–30, 264, 464n42; mortgage foreclosures in, 214, 233–4, 273–7; strategies of coping with, 2, 214–17; *see also* blacks; ethnic and religious welfare organizations in 1930s; ethnic banks in 1930s; ethnic building and loan associations in 1930s; ethnic mutual benefit societies in 1930s; hours of work; relief in Great Depression; unemployment; wages; *companies by name; ethnic groups by name; neighborhoods by name*
Greater Grand Crossing, 134t
Greeks, 406n36
Greenbay, 24

Hammond, Mary, 205
Hardin, Lil, 155
Harding, Warren G., 181, 283
Hart, Schaffner and Marx, 13, 31, 48
Hassett, Edward, 190
Hawthorne studies, 7, 173–4, 202, 208
Hawthorne Works (Western Electric), 13, 21, 31–3, 160; age limits in hiring at, 196; and CIO, 506n65; and community outreach, 33, 180, 182; company and plant magazines at, 179; company union at, 300–1, 351, 505n64; compared to other employers, 208, 243–4; discrimination against blacks at, 36, 207, 354; ethnic groups dispersed on shop floor at, 202–3; ethnicity of workers at, 33, 202; foremen at, 169, 202, 208; in Great Depression, 217, 240, 243–4; Hawthorne Building and Loan Association, 176, 183; Hawthorne Evening School, 170, 177, 183; human relations approach to workers at, 173–4; mass culture at, 177–9; motives for working at, 144; in 1919, 49, 180; NRA at, 277; output restriction at, 201–2; paternalism pre-1920 at, 32–3, 36, 49; and radio, 132; recreation and social programs at, 177–9; seniority at, 437n39; sick benefits at, 174; and stock ownership plans, 175, 184, 195; success of welfare capitalism at, 207–8, 243–4, 351–4; vacations at, 244, 439n50; wage incentives at, 169, 192; wages at, 186; welfare capitalism at, 163–4; worker response to welfare capitalism at, 159, 183; *see also* Hawthorne studies
Haymarket, 4, 32, 300
Hegewisch, 24, 78, 207, 326; *see also* Southeast Chicago
Henderson, Fletcher, 155, 156
Henry, Charlie, 500n30
Herbst, Alma, 191
Hickok, Lorena, 246, 284
Hillman, Sidney, 308, 336
Hindelwicz family, 229
Hines, Earl "Fatha," 155
Holy Name Societies, *see* Catholic Church

homeownership: in Great Depression, 233–4, 273–6; influence on worker politics of, 315; promoted by employers, 273–4, 441n58; among workers, 76
Home Owners' Loan Corporation: on building and loan associations, 233, 275–6; discriminatory ratings of, 276; mortgages from, 252, 273–7; program of, 273–4
Hoover, Herbert, 181, 431n10; in Great Depression, 223, 227, 242, 283; and radio, 139, 140
Hopkins, Harry, 236, 268, 269, 271, 280, 284, 285
Horbatcz family, 224–5
Houghteling, Leila, 60, 62, 102, 103, 151, 186, 200
hours of work, 186–7; in Great Depression, 215, 216, 217, 234, 240, 243–4, 292; under PWOC contract, 298; under SWOC contract, 295; and work sharing, 243–5; *see also* Fair Labor Standards Act
House Committee on Un-American Activities, 310, 311
Houser, J. David, 189
Houston, 259
Humboldt Park, 31
Hungarians, 24, 261–2
Hyde Park, 407n47

identity, *see* social identity of industrial workers
Illinois Manufacturers' Association, 169, 177, 182
Illinois State Federation of Labor, 49
Illinois Steel Company, *see* U.S. Steel
Immigration Acts of 1921 and 1924, 54
Independent Grocers' Alliance (IGA), 119
Independent Order Brith Abraham, 69
Indiana Harbor, Indiana, 42, 454n144
Indianapolis, 271
Industrial Workers of the World (IWW), 4, 333
Infant Welfare Society of Chicago, 344
Inland Steel, 13, 21, 166, 333; company union at, 504n54; SWOC at, 292, 296, 303, 306, 315, 338
installment buying, *see* consumption
International Eucharistic Congress, 135
International Harvester, 13; antistatism of, 181; blacks at, 35, 449n99; Chicago plants compared, 207; Communists at, 312; and community outreach, 180, 182; company and plant magazines at, 179, 298; early unionization at, 4; Employee Benefit Association at, 174–5, 446n86; employee representation at, 47, 171–3, 190, 298, 452n121, 453n123; ethnicity and race of workers at, 32–3, 375n21; FE at, 2, 298–300, 302, 350; FE contract with, 299; foremen at, 168, 298; in Great Depression, 240, 245; industrial relations philosophy pre-1920 at, 32–3, 160; insurance held by workers at, 73–4, 151; McCormick Works of, 4, 21, 31–3, 46–7, 87–8, 160, 184, 190, 207, 242, 299–300, 321, 335, 350, 353, 375n21, 449n99; NLRB election at, 299; pensions at, 195–6; recreation and social programs at, 178; response to FE by, 298–300, 305; shop floor strategies at, 317; and stock ownership plans, 175, 183–4; strikes in 1919 at, 12, 47, 163; Tractor Works of, 193, 204, 299, 304, 317–18, 350; turnover at, 197–8; unemployment at, 270, 449n99; vacations at, 174, 199, 298, 439n50; wages at, 186, 298; welfare capitalism at, 163–4; work discipline at, 198–9; *see also* unionization; Wisconsin Steel
International Ladies' Garment Workers' Union (ILGWU), 48, 138, 308
Irish, 17, 29, 32; and Catholic Church, 87; and CIO, 338, 500n30; and consumption, 111; at Hawthorne Works, 203; in packinghouses, 28, 45, 373n12; and radio, 138; in steel, 24, 165
Italians, 17, 34; avoidance of public assistance in 1920s among, 57, 62–3; and Catholic Church, 87–94; and CIO, 338, 339; conflicts within, 383n7; and consumption, 105, 110, 114, 152, 405n30, 406n36; and dance palaces, 146; feasts of, 88–90, 92–3; and foremen, 188; in garment industry, 47–8; in Great Depression, 225–6; help own needy, 58; at McCormick Works, 32, 375n21; and movies, 123; nationalism of, 381n3; new settlements of, 31; in 1919 steel strike, 41; old community of, 30; in packinghouses, 373n12; and politics, 254, 387n34; prejudice against, in Southeast Chicago, 24; in steel, 165; and United Charities, 62; *see also* ethnic banks in 1920s; ethnic banks in 1930s; ethnic building and loan associations in 1930s; ethnic mutual benefit societies in 1930s
Italo–American National Union, 69–70
Iverson's Department Store, 409n61

Jablonski, Thomas, 270
Jacovich, Frank, 207

Janik, Phillip, 160, 187
Jankus, Charlie, 500n30
jazz, 104, 154–6
Jewish Charities of Chicago, 60, 61, 62, 219, 221, 222
Jewish Home for the Aged, 59
Jewish People's Institute, 145
Jewish Progressive Order of the West, 69, 71
Jewish synagogue, Anshe Sholom, 54
Jews, 29; anxiety about assimilation among, 54; avoidance of public assistance in 1920s among, 57; in Communist Party, 261–2; conflicts within, 58–9, 61, 383n7; and consumption, 110, 111, 406n36; and dance palaces, 146; in garment industry, 31, 47; help own needy, 58; nationalism of, 381n3; new settlements of, 31; old community of, 30; and politics, 254; and radio, 135; and United Charities, 62; *see also* ethnic and religious welfare organizations in 1920s; ethnic banks in 1920s; ethnic banks in 1930s; ethnic mutual benefit societies in 1920s
Johnson, General Hugh, 304, 316
Johnson, Henry (Hank), 312, 338, 499n22
Johnstone, Jack, 319
Joliet, Illinois, 103, 109
Jungle, The, 2
J. Walter Thompson Company, 100, 139, 356, 420n143

Kampfert, Arthur, 28–9, 303, 339
Katz, Sam, 124, 126
Kell, Stanley, 232
Kelly, Edward, 221, 255, 259, 260; and CIO, 303, 304, 335; operation of New Deal programs by, 269, 484n61
Keppard, Freddy, 155
Kikulski, John, 49, 378n53
Klein's Department Store, 115
Knights of Labor, 4, 333
Kornhauser, Arthur W., 252
Kosciolowski, Sophie, 335, 347
Ku Klux Klan, 417n125

Labor Party of Chicago and Cook County, 286
Labor Party of Cook County, 12, 49–50
Labor's Nonpartisan League, 288, 304
labor unions, *see* unionization
LaFollette, Robert, 302
Landon, Alfred, 288
Lane, Dennis, 46
Lange, Rev. John, 86
Latkovich, Estelle Uzelac, 26
Lawrence Strike of 1912, 4
Lazarsfeld, Paul, 329, 498n15
Leader Store, 115
League for Industrial Democracy, 262
Lee, Owensby, 185
Levin, Sam, 48
Lewis, John L., 294–5, 308, 309, 336, 341, 343, 359–60
Liberty Life Insurance Company, 151
Liberty Loans, 76–9, 84, 175
Linker, Mollie, 58
Lisle Manual Training School, 61
Lithuanians, 17, 29; and CIO, 500n30; in Communist Party, 261–2; and consumption, 114; and Democratic Party, 362; in 1919 steel strike, 40; in packinghouses, 28, 373n12; and politics, 254; in race riot of 1919, 37; racism among, 281; and radio, 328; in steel, 26; *see also* ethnic banks in 1920s; ethnic banks in 1930s; ethnic building and loan associations in 1920s
Little Bohemia, 30
Little Italy, 30
Little Sicily, 30, 91, 105, 112, 119, 123
"Little Steel," 296, 303, 359
Loew's, Inc., 126
Los Angeles, 107, 274
Louis, Joe, 260, 328, 330
Love, Crawford, 321
Lubliner & Trinz, 129
Lynd, Helen and Robert, 7, 133, 330–1

McCarty, Frank, 338
McCormick, Cyrus, Jr., 161, 171, 172, 191, 194–5, 198
McCormick, Harold Fowler, 172
machine politics, 5, 63–4, 254, 255, 257, 387n34
McKinley Park, 32; *see also* Southwest Corridor
McKinney, Clifton, 316
McNellis, Joe, 500n30
Majewski, Rose, 215–16
Malone, Henrietta, 283
March, Herbert, 304, 311, 312, 320, 333, 338, 492n23
Margolis, Ida, 111
Marquette Park, 281
Martin, Jack, 312
Martinez, Aida, 348
Martinez, Refugio, 338
mass consumption, *see* consumption
mass culture: changes between 1920s and 1930s in, 157–8, 325; distinctive patterns among ethnic groups, races, and classes in, 144–7, 156; expectations of,

96–7, 100–1, 142–3, 154; popular among second-generation immigrants, 144–7, 422n159; social impact of, 156–7, 177–9, 356–7, 364, 365; and theories of its impact, 398n6; *see also* consumption; motion pictures; movie theaters; radio
Mathewson, Stanley, 457n163
Maxwell Street, 30, 113–14, 118
Mayer, Oscar, 239
Mayo, Elton, 7, 173
Mazankowski, S. C., 233, 275
mechanization of work process, 171, 185, 204, 316–17, 324, 448n93
Meegan, Joseph, 501n34
Mega, John, 244, 257
Memenga family, 258
Memorial Day Massacre, 303, 304, 323, 340, 359
men: segregated in factory, 204; shared culture at work among, 204, 328–9, 498n17; socializing in neighborhood by, 110, 405n35; as victims of Great Depression, 246–9
Merriam, Charles, 7
Metropolitan Life, 139, 140, 151
Mexicans, 33; and CIO, 324–5, 338–9, 500n30; and consumption, 106, 406n41; and foremen, 188; in Great Depression, 222, 242–3, 331–2; increase within industrial work force during 1920s of, 165–6; and job discrimination, 165–7; and movie theaters, 123–4; in packinghouses, 28, 165, 166; and radio, 132; skill of, 167, 434n20; in steel, 24, 35, 165–7, 201, 203; as strikebreakers, 41, 46; unemployment among, 185–6; and welfare capitalism, 184; *see also* ethnic mutual benefit societies in 1920s
Middletown, 7, 133
Middletown in Transition, 7, 330–1
Midura, Mary, 219
Migas, Nick, 317, 338, 492n23
Milwaukee, 104, 402n23, 408n53
Milwaukee Avenue, 31, 114, 115, 409n57, n61
minimum wage, *see* Fair Labor Standards Act
Minneapolis, 303
Mitchell, Arthur, 260
Mitchell, Jonathan, 330
Monroe, Al, 330
Montgomery Ward's, 107
Mooney, Tom, 12
"moral capitalism," *see* capitalism
Morris & Company, 27, 229
Morton, Jelly Roll, 155
motion pictures: promoted by employers, 443n63; social impact of, 121, 124–5
movie industry, vertical integration of, 126–8, 414n101, 415n110
movies, *see* motion pictures
movie theaters: distinctive patterns among classes in, 124–5, 127, 129, 496n3; impact of sound on, 127–9, 414n104, 415n107; in neighborhoods, 99, 121–6, 145; patronage of, 120–2, 125, 145, 353, 496n3; as picture palaces, 121–2, 124–5, 412n81, 413n94; popular among youth, 145; seating capacity of, 120, 129–31; and shift from neighborhood to chain, 126–9, 325
Mundelein, Archbishop (later Cardinal) George: and Americanization, 84, 87, 90–1, 93, 94; Associated Catholic Charities established by, 60–1; attitude toward relief in Great Depression of, 223, 269; and blacks, 394n87; opposition to national parishes by, 83, 221
Murray, Philip, 294, 334, 341, 491n17
Mussolini, Benito, 69, 135, 381n3
mutual benefit societies, *see* ethnic mutual benefit societies in 1920s; ethnic mutual benefit societies in 1930s
Mutual Broadcasting System, 327

National Association of Manufacturers, 503n40
National Broadcasting Company (NBC), 139, 141, 143, 327, 341
National Cash Register Company, 160
National Industrial Conference Board, 162, 451n108
National Industrial Recovery Act (NIRA), 333; Section 7a of, 278, 292, 293–4, 302, 303; *see also* National Recovery Administration (NRA)
National Labor Relations Act (Wagner Act), 5, 288, 292, 298, 301, 307; employer attitude toward, 282; impact of, 302, 305–8
National Labor Relations Board (NLRB), 302; elections supervised by, 297, 299, 301, 307, 311; rulings of, 300, 305
National Metal Trade Association, 168
National Negro Business League, 148
National Negro Congress, 336
National Recovery Administration (NRA): employer attitude toward, 282; as experienced by workers, 277–8; favored chain stores, 237; program of, 277; and steel industry, 303–4; *see also* National Industrial Recovery Act (NIRA)

National Tea Company, 407n47; expansion in Great Depression of, 118, 235–6; Hawthorne pay checks cashed at, 178; store locations of, 109
National Urban League, 233, 499n22
National Youth Administration (NYA), 278, 281
neighborhoods: as assessed by HOLC, 276; divided by skill, 24, 28; ethnic segregation of, 24, 28, 30–3, 374n16; isolated in 1919, 21; located near factories, 17; male socializing in, 110, 405n35; movie theaters in, 99, 121–6, 145, 412n83; needy helped within, 57; physical barriers separating, 24, 28; racial segregation of, 33–8; and radio, 133; role of employers in, 26, 30, 33, 45; stores within, 110–12, 117–18, 146, 404n30; unemployed movement in, 265–6; youth clubs in, 145–6; *see also by name*
Neilsen, A. C., Company, 237
Neisner's 5 Cents to A Dollar Store, 154
Nelson, Steve, 264
Newburyport, Massachusetts, 496n3
New Deal: Communist support of, 262; "corporate liberal" analysis of, 282; employer attitude toward, 282, 486n68; impact of, on worker attitudes, 289; limitations of, 267–8, 289; worker support of, 252, 286, 289; *see also names of individual programs*
Newman, Edward J., 270
New Orleans, 155
New York, 107, 126, 139, 143, 274, 412n81
Nofrio, 105
Norris, John, 214
Norris–LaGuardia Act, 302
North Lawndale, 31, 81; *see also* Southwest Corridor
North Side, 113, 145, 225
Northwest Side, 58
Novak, Anna, 188, 196
Novak, Bernice, 110–11, 160
Nowicki, Stella, 339, 359, 491n14; *see also* Starr, Vicky

Oak Park, Illinois, 109
Odeski, Clara, 248
O'Hair, Rev. J. C., 418n130
old immigrant neighborhoods of West and Northwest Sides, 17, 30–1; movie theaters in, 131; and radio, 134t
Oliver, King, 155
Orear, Leslie, 305, 337, 350, 360
Oregon, 281
Ostroski, Michael, 343
Outlaw, Grace, 279
output restriction: and CIO organizing, 317–19; as response to welfare capitalism, 201–5, 457n163; wage incentives to limit, 170

packinghouse industrial conflicts, 1917–22, 43–6; employer response to, 45, 46; ethnic fragmentation in, 45, 379n58; racial conflict in, 45
packinghouses: citizenship status of workers in, 373n12; economic importance of, 27–8; ethnicity of workers in, 28, 163, 373n12; labor turnover in, 171; location of, 27–8; nativity of workers in, 18, 20, 167, 373n12; NRA at, 277; race of workers in, 35, 242; seasonal unemployment in, 185–6; seniority in, 189; skill of workers in, 28; wage incentives in, 192; working conditions in, 187; *see also* unionization
Packinghouse Workers' Industrial Union, 296, 309
Packinghouse Workers' Organizing Committee (PWOC): achievements of, 297–8; and blacks, 334–5, 337; Communists in, 310–11, 351; and contract with Armour, 297–8; and contract with Swift and Wilson, 298; ethnic and racial solidarity in, 334, 338, 361; family orientation of, 347–8; history of, 296–8; membership of, 298; Mexicans in, 338; and rank and file, 307, 310; and relief, 320; shop floor strategies of, 305, 307–8; small packing plants organized by, 298; social and recreational programs of, 341; use of radio by, 343; women in, 359; women's auxiliaries of, 347–8; worker solidarity nationally in, 345, 361; and worker solidarity within Chicago, 345; *see also* Armour and Company; hours of work; seniority; Swift & Company; wages
Packingtown, *see* Back of the Yards
"Pageant of Progress," 182
Palumbo, Antonio, 277
Paramount Pictures, 126
Parise, Florence, 272
Park, Robert, 7
Parker, Moses, 160
Patterson, Dorothy, 347
Patterson, George, 183, 216, 254, 304, 309, 311, 318, 319, 330, 338, 339, 343, 356, 358, 492n23
Patterson, William, 266
Patti, Angelo, 81

Pattison, Virginia, 107
Pavero, Father, 232
Penio, Paul, 112
Penney, J. C., 117
Perez, Jesse, 318
Perkins, Frances, 302
Perpoli, Thomas, 81
Petty, Rev. W. C., 226
Philadelphia, 107, 274
phonographs, *see* consumption
Piggly Wiggly Stores, 106, 109
Pilsen, 32
Piontkowsky, Betty, 160
Pittsburgh, 2, 40, 296, 334, 338, 345, 370n1
Poles, 17, 29, 31; anxiety about assimilation among, 54; avoidance of public assistance in 1920s among, 57, 62–3; and Catholic Church, 85–7, 94, 395n90; and CIO, 338, 339, 500n30; in Communist Party, 261–2; conflicts within, 383n7; and consumption, 111, 112, 114–15, 152, 409n61; and dance palaces, 146; and Democratic Party, 362; and foremen, 188; in garment industry, 47–8; in Great Depression, 223, 225, 243, 247–8; at Hawthorne Works, 203; help own needy, 58; and movies, 123, 124, 145; New Deal viewed by, 277; new settlements of, 31, 32; in 1919 steel strike, 40; old community of, 30; in packinghouses, 28, 373n12; and politics, 254; and radio, 138, 325; in steel, 24, 163, 165, 203; and stock ownership plans, 195; in unemployed movement, 266; and United Charities, 62; *see also* ethnic and religious welfare organizations in 1920s; ethnic banks in 1920s; ethnic banks in 1930s; ethnic building and loan associations in 1920s; ethnic mutual benefit societies in 1920s; Liberty Loans
Polish Alma Mater, 68
Polish Falcons of America, 68
Polish Manual Training School, 61
Polish National Alliance, 68, 85, 219, 228–9
Polish National Catholic Church, 86, 383n7
Polish National Union, 68
Polish Roman Catholic Union, 68, 71, 85
Polish Welfare Association, 219, 222–3
Polish Women's Alliance, 68, 228
political consciousness of industrial workers: changes between 1920s and 1930s in, 5, 252, 257–8, 362; class character of, in 1919, 50; and class in 1930s, 286–9, 355–6, 362–4, 366; importance of cultural realm in defining, during 1920s, 51; localistic orientation of, in 1919, 38; as obstacle to Labor Party success in 1919–20, 50; *see also* capitalism
Pomorski, Ted, 110
Pressed Steel Car Company, 78
Progressive Steelworkers' Union, *see* Wisconsin Steel
Prohibition, 28, 79, 364; encouraging worker antistatism, 210–11, 254, 255; impact of, 29, 405n35; and impact of its repeal, 340; linked to higher savings rate, 392n67; supported by employers, 255; worker opposition to, 210–11, 254, 255, 474n8
Protestant churches: among blacks, 148, 226; Cosmopolitan Community Church, 226; East Side Baptist, 26; Evangelical United Methodist, 26; Fourth Presbyterian, 288; in Great Depression, 220, 226; Immanuel Baptist, 220; Mount Messiah Baptist, 226; Olivet Baptist, 148; and radio, 135–6, 418n130; St. Marks Methodist Episcopal, 226
Provenzano, Joseph, 132, 133
Pryblzka, John, 272
Public Works Administration (PWA), 278
Publix Theatres Corporation, 126, 128, 139
Pulitzer family, 219
Pullman Company, 13, 160, 372n6

Quigley, Archbishop James Edward, 84, 88
Quinn, Mike, 190

Raboy, I., 76
racial violence: in Chicago Race Riot of 1919, 36–7; in Cicero Race Riots of 1951, 354; in Trumbull Park Riots of 1953, 354
racism: among employers, 205–6, 242; in 1930s, 279–81; after 1940, 354, 363, 367–8; in packinghouses, 1917–22, 44–6; in steel strike of 1919, 42; among whites, 36–7
radio: changes between 1920s and 1930s in, 138–43, 326–9; and consumption, 329–31; contributing to shared culture among workers, 325–31; distinctive patterns among classes in, 133, 134t, 143, 327, 329–31; early history of, 129, 132, 140; growth of commercial sponsorship of, 139–43, 325, 420n143, n147; growth of networks in, 139–43, 325,

radio (*cont.*)
420n147; impact of Radio Act of 1927 on, 141–3; and jazz, 155; local orientation of, in 1920s, 133–5, 416n122; market research in, 326–9, 497n7; national orientation of, in 1930s, 330–1; popularity among workers of, 132–3, 416n119; programming of, 133–8, 327–8, 417n125; reinforcing ethnicity, 135–6, 353; social impact of, 133, 138, 142–3; used by employers against unions, 503n40; in youth clubs, 145
rationalization, *see* mechanization of work process
Reconstruction Finance Corporation, 265, 268
record industry, 105–6, 155, 429n188
Redman, Don, 156
Redmond, Rev. J. B., 226
Red Scare, 5, 13, 38
Reeves Stores, 112
Reilly, William, 505n64
relief in Great Depression: administration of, 252, 263, 265, 283, 484n61; appeals to federal government for, 227, 251, 264–7; appeals to State of Illinois for, 227; balance of federal, state, and local funding of, 268; balance of public and private funding of, 224, 269; and Catholic Church, 269–70; and CIO, 319–20; favored chain stores, 235–7; informal alternatives to, 218–19; need among blacks for, 226–7; provided by employers, 238–40, 243–5; recipient attitude toward, 270–2, 278; role of private welfare in, 223–4, 269
Republican Party, 304; and blacks, 254, 259–61, 363; in Chicago, 254, 256, 288, 387n34; and view of Roosevelt and New Deal, 287, 288
Republic Steel, 13, 21, 316, 495n2; SWOC at, 296, 303, 323
RKO, 126
Robinson's Department Store, 114
Roman Catholic Church, *see* Catholic Church
Roosevelt, Eleanor, 285; letters to, 258, 283; and radio, 332
Roosevelt, Franklin D., 246, 255, 269, 304; admired by Poles, 277; black support for, 260; letters to, 258, 268, 270, 274, 278, 279, 283; and "New Democratic Coalition," 2; as paternal figure, 283–5; and radio, 332; as workers' hero, 287–8, 332, 359, 499n19; worker support for, 256
Roselli, Florence, 147
Roumanians, 373n12
Royal Oak, Michigan, 418n129
Rupcinski, Mary, 233
Russians, 114, 261–2, 373n12, 406n36
Ruttenberg, Harold, 318–19, 344–5
Ryerson, Edward, 227

Sabella, Margaret, 147
Sacco and Vanzetti, 175
St. Vincent de Paul Societies, *see* Associated Catholic Charities
Salamoni, Vincent, 119
Salvation Army, 223
San Francisco, 274, 303, 496n3
Schiavo, Giovanni, 94
Schmeling, Max, 328
Schoenstadt Theatre Company, 129
Schultz, Mrs. Mary, 138
scientific management, 169, 317
Scottsboro Boys, 262
Sears Roebuck, 107, 154
Senate Sub-Committee Hearings on Violations of Civil Liberties, 302
seniority: under FE contract, 299; in Great Depression, 244–5, 292; as major CIO demand, 320–1; under PWOC contract, 298; and race relations, 368; reality of, under welfare capitalism, 188–9; under SWOC contract, 295; with welfare capitalism, 174, 437n39
Senise, Daniel, 342
Serbians, 40, 41; *see also* ethnic building and loan associations in 1920s
settlement houses, 55, 83, 91, 264; *see also* Chicago Commons Settlement; University of Chicago Settlement
Severino family, 216–17
Sheet and Metal Workers Industrial Union, 309
Sheil, Bishop Bernard, 501n34
Shemerdiak, Mary, 144
Silber, Rabbi Saul, 54, 55
Silver, Adolph and Max, 81
Sinclair, Upton, 2
Sinclair Gasoline, 109
Siporin, Mary, 317
Slovaks: in Great Depression, 221; help own needy, 58; in packinghouses, 28, 373n12; and radio, 136; *see also* ethnic banks in 1920s; ethnic banks in 1930s; ethnic building and loan associations in 1920s
Slovene National Benefit Society, 228
Slovenian Relief Organization, 219
Slovenians, 26; *see also* ethnic building and loan associations in 1920s
Smith, Alfred E., 255

social identity of industrial workers, 6; as citizens, 285–6, 364–5; in crisis during Great Depression, 249; ethnicity in, 26, 29, 31, 94–6, 362–4; impact of mass culture on, 157–8, 356–7, 363–4, 399n6; as working class, 286–9, 362–3
Socialist Labor Party, votes for, 478n24
Socialists: among Italians, 88, 353, 383n7; among Jews, 383n7; and unemployed movement, 262; votes for, 478n24
Social Security Act, 267, 272, 275, 288; employer attitude toward, 282
Sons of Italy, 69
Sorkin, Sidney, 113
Sorrentino, Anthony, 57, 105
South Center Department Store, 154
South Chicago, 24, 29, 40, 42, 57, 75, 85, 86; CCC popularity in, 281; CIO in, 291, 337; and dance palaces, 146; ethnic organizations in, 53; in Great Depression, 225, 229, 234, 265; movie theaters in, 121, 123, 124, 128, 412n83; radio in, 132, 325–6; steel organizing in 1923 in, 454n144; stores in, 115; symbols of, 11; *see also* Southeast Chicago
South Deering, 24, 26–7, 42; cultural isolation of, in 1930s, 352–4; in Great Depression, 245; *see also* Southeast Chicago
Southeast Chicago, 17, 21–6; employers compared in, 207, 244–5; in Great Depression, 214; movie theaters in, 131, 353; radio in, 134t; stores in, 112, 326; *see also* Hegewisch; South Chicago; South Deering
South Lawndale, 31, 33, 73, 388n39; *see also* Southwest Corridor
Southwest Corridor, 21, 31–3; movie theaters in, 131; radio in, 134t; *see also* Berwyn; Brighton Park; Cicero; North Lawndale; South Lawndale
Soviet Union, 264
Special Conference Committee, 437n39
Stanislawowo, 30
Starr, Vicky, 311, 312, 491n14, 492n23; *see also* Nowicki, Stella
state, *see* federal government
steel industry: age of workers in, 495n2; economic importance of, 21; ethnicity of workers in, 24, 163, 377n40; location of plants in, 21–5; Mexicans employed in, 35; nativity of workers in, 18, 20, 167; race of workers in, 35; skill of workers in, 24; working conditions in, 187; *see also* unionization
steel strike of 1919, 38–43; and blacks, 42–3, 336; demands of, 187, 377n43; employer response to, 40, 41; ethnic fragmentation in, 40–3; isolation of union locals in, 39–40; lessons learned from, 43; recalled in 1930s, 319; role of AFL craft unions in, 39
Steeltown, *see* Southeast Chicago
Steel Workers' Organizing Committee (SWOC): achievements of, 292–3, 295–6; and blacks, 334–5, 337, 499n22; in Calumet region, 295; collective bargaining established with, 295–6; Communists in, 309, 351; and contract with U.S. Steel, 295–6; ethnic solidarity in, 500n30; family orientation of, 346; grievance procedures under contract with, 295–6; history of, 294–6, 343–4; internal conflicts within, 358; and "Little Steel" strike, 359; membership of, 295; and Mexicans, 338–9; and radio, 330, 341, 343; and rank and file, 306–7, 310, 358, 491n17; role of employee representatives in founding of, 294–5; shop floor strategies of, 305, 306; social and recreational programs of, 341; vacations under contract with, 295; women's auxiliaries of, 294, 295, 346–7; worker solidarity nationally in, 344–5; and WPA, 320; *see also* hours of work; Inland Steel; Republic Steel; seniority; U.S. Steel; wages
Stewart, James, 498n19, 500n30
stock ownership plans: in Great Depression, 216, 240; reality of, 194–5; under welfare capitalism, 164, 175, 183–4, 194–5; *see also by name of company*
Stockyards Labor Council: in 1930s, 296, 319; in packinghouse industrial conflicts, 1917–22, 46
Stoecker, Clarence, 311, 321, 335, 492n23, 498n17
stores, *see by name*
strikes: in 1919, 12, 161, 163; *see also* International Harvester; packinghouse industrial conflicts, 1917–22; steel strike of 1919
Swedes, 17, 24, 26, 163
Swift & Company, 13, 27; blacks at, 35, 166; and community outreach, 180, 182; company and plant magazines at, 179; compared to Armour, 207; employee representation at, 171–3, 190, 205, 297, 452n123; ethnicity of work force at, 163; foremen at, 168; in Great Depression, 216–17, 239; group insurance at, 183; insurance held by workers at, 73–4, 151; longstanding resistance to unionism at, 4; output restriction at,

Swift & Company (*cont.*)
201; PWOC at, 2, 302, 308, 314, 318, 340, 350–1; PWOC contract with, 298; seniority at, 437n39; shop floor strategies at, 318; sick benefits at, 183; and stock ownership plans, 175, 183; unemployment at, 185; unionization at, in early 1930s, 296–7; vacations at, 185, 439n50; wage incentives at, 169, 191, 318; welfare capitalism at, 161, 163–4, 207
Swiss, 373n12
synagogues, *see* Jewish synagogue

Taft–Hartley Act, 360, 366–7
Taylor, Frederick Winslow, 169, 191, 192
Taylor, Myron, 239, 295
Terkel, Studs, 248
Thomas, Elmer, 242
Thomas, William, 85
Thompson, William Hale "Big Bill," 256, 259
Toledo, Ohio, 303
Tortolano, Antonio and Angeline, 111
Towers, Albert, 340, 491n17, 492n23
Traficanti Noodle Company, 277
Travis, Dempsey, 123, 205, 215
True Story Magazine, 101–2
Truman, Harry S, 366
turnover of labor, 170–1, 174–5, 186, 197–8, 292, 436n35

Ulanowski, Steve, 492n23
Unemployed Councils, 251, 262–7; and blacks, 266; encouraging worker alliances, 266–7
unemployment: among blacks in Great Depression, 242; due to age, 196, 246, 320–1; due to technology, 448n93; in Great Depression, 214, 217, 222, 234, 240–3, 245; in 1920s, 102, 182, 184; psychological impact on family of, 246–9; seasonal, 185–6, 197; *see also by company name*
Union Bag Company, 217
Unione Veneziana, 69, 228
unionization: as affected by paternalism of employers, 1919–22, 38; AFL response to, in 1919–22, 3, 38; between 1923–30, 454n144; employer response to, in 1919–22, 38; in garment industry in 1919, 47–8; hurt by ethnic and racial fragmentation of work force, 1919–22, 38; at International Harvester, early history of, 4; at International Harvester, 1919, 3; in packinghouses, early history of, 3–4; in packinghouses, 1917–22, 3, 29, 43–6; in steel, early history of, 3; in steel, 1918–20, 3, 38–43; in steel, 1923, 196, 454n144; support for, in Great Depression, 252–3, 292–3, 301–21, 364; *see also* Congress of Industrial Organizations (CIO); Farm Equipment Workers' Organizing Committee (FE); Packinghouse Workers' Organizing Committee (PWOC); Steel Workers' Organizing Committee (SWOC)
United Auto Workers (UAW), 300
United Charities of Chicago, 61–2, 63, 223, 226
United Electrical, Radio and Machine Workers of America (UE), 505–6 n65
United Mine Workers (UMW), 294, 334, 336, 351
United Packinghouse Workers of America (UPWA), 298, 307, 368
United Steelworkers of America (USWA), 296, 298
University of Chicago Settlement, 225, 423n159
Urban League of Chicago, 45
U.S. Chamber of Commerce, 162, 168, 181
U.S. Steel, 2, 13, 24; antistatism of, 181; and blacks, 35, 166, 335–6, 434n20; Communists at, 312; and community outreach, 180; company and plant magazines at, 179; company union at, 305, 340, 491n14; compared to Wisconsin Steel, 207, 244–5; employee representation at, 293–4; foremen at, 207, 244–5; Gary Works of, 21, 42, 166, 242, 293–5, 312, 316, 335, 341, 452n115; in Great Depression, 239–40, 242, 316; group insurance at, 193–4; longstanding resistance to unionism at, 4; Mexicans at, 242, 434n20; and 1919 steel strike, 41–2; pensions at, 195–6; race of workers at, 242; response to SWOC by, 295; shop floor strategies at, 318; South Works of, 21, 42, 86, 165, 166, 168, 180, 183, 187, 201, 207, 216, 240, 242, 244, 293–5, 304, 309, 312, 318, 319, 335, 341, 358, 491n20; and stock ownership plans, 175, 183, 195; and subsidiaries, 370n1; SWOC at, 305, 306, 350–1; SWOC contract with, 291, 295–6; unemployment at, 270; vacations at, 316; wage incentives at, 318; welfare capitalism at, 163–4

Victor, Father, 247
Victory Life Insurance Company, 151

Voorhis, Bill, 192
Vorse, Mary Heaton, 295, 308, 503n50
voting: and historical debate over critical elections of 1928–36, 475n11; during 1920s, 5, 63, 254–6, 258–9; during 1930s, 2, 5, 256–61, 262, 283, 304, 332, 476n14, 478n24

wages: cut in Great Depression, 217, 240, 242–3, 245, 292; and family economy, 200, 218, 246–9; in 1920s, 102, 186; by piecework, 299, 317–18; under PWOC, 298; under SWOC, 295; and wage incentives, 164, 169–70, 191–2, 201–2, 318, 435n28; *see also* Fair Labor Standards Act
Walgreen Drugs, 106, 116, 117, 118, 139, 153, 154
Waller, "Fats," 155
Walsh, John, 270
Warner Brothers, 126, 128, 129
Washington, Booker T., 148
Washington, Elizabeth, 207
Washington Park, 34; *see also* Black Belt
Washington (state), 281
WCFL, *see* Chicago Federation of Labor
Weber, Joseph, 299, 309, 312
Weightman, Philip, 311, 314, 339–40
Weinstein, Louis, 118
welfare capitalism: antistatism of, 181–3; and blacks, 205–6; community outreach in, 179–80; company and plant magazines in, 164, 179; in competition with ethnic identity, 176–9; as employer defense against labor militance, 175–6; employer ideology before, 160–1, 167–8; encouraging worker alliances, 202–5, 209, 211, 317–19, 324, 364–5; fate of, in Great Depression, 238–46, 292, 298–9, 351–4; to fight labor turnover, 170–1; gap between promise and reality of, 184, 189, 196, 206, 208–9, 238, 246; group insurance in, 72–4, 164, 183, 193–4, 240; historical debate about, 447n92; ideology of, 161–83, 430n9; to individualize employer–employee relations, 163–9, 172–4; as influence on workers in 1930s, 209, 314–19, 321, 324, 350; job ladders in, 170, 188–9, 436n34, 452n115; and mass culture, 177–9, 443n63, n69; output restriction as response to, 170, 201–5, 457n163; pensions in, 164, 174, 195–6, 240; prevalence of, 162, 430n9; reality of, 184–211; recreation and social programs in, 164, 176–9, 204–5, 442n61; sex segregation under, 204; and shift to welfare state in 1930s, 289, 365; sick benefits in, 164, 174, 183, 193; success at Hawthorne Works, Swift, and Wisconsin Steel, 206–8; vacations in, 164, 174, 185, 199, 240; wage incentives in, 164, 169–70, 191–2, 435n28; work discipline under, 198–9, 209; worker response to, 183–211, 246, 446n86, n88; *see also* employee representation plans; foremen; seniority; stock ownership plans; wages; *by names of companies*
welfare state, 3, 283, 289; compared to Europe, 267–8, 365–6
Western Electric Independent Labor Association, *see* Hawthorne Works (Western Electric)
Western Union, 109
West Side, 58, 76, 80, 110, 125, 256; stores on, 113–14, 115; *see also* old immigrant neighborhoods of West and Northwest Sides
West Town, 30; *see also* old immigrant neighborhoods of West and Northwest Sides
Whiteman, Paul, 104, 156
Wieboldt's Department Store, 107, 409n61
Willard, P. W., 182
Wilson & Company, 27, 298, 307
Wisconsin, 281
Wisconsin Steel, 13, 160; and community outreach, 26, 180; company union at, 300–1, 310, 351, 505n64; compared to other Chicago Harvester plants, 207; compared to U.S. Steel, 207, 244–5; discrimination against blacks at, 36, 207, 354; employee representation at, 173, 190–1, 199, 207; ethnic groups dispersed on shop floor at, 165; ethnicity of workers at, 203; foremen at, 188, 207, 245; in Great Depression, 243–6; history of, 26; 1919 steel strike at, 40, 42; NLRB elections at, 301; paternalism, pre-1920, at, 26, 36; sick benefits at, 193; steel strike of 1919 at, 180; and stock ownership plans, 184; success of welfare capitalism at, 207, 243–6, 351–4; turnover at, 174–5, 197; unemployment at, 184, 214, 447n93; *see also* International Harvester
Woldarozyk, Sigmond, 338
women: in CIO, 346–8, 358–9; as citizens, 256; as consumers, 110–11; as contributors to family income, 200, 215–17, 246–9; as factory workers, 17, 20, 200, 204; and family roles in Great Depression, 246–9; and foremen, 188, 347; in garment industry, 20; as influ-

women (*cont.*)
ence on husbands' unions, 346–7, 504n54; and insurance, 67, 71–2, 229, 388n39; in packinghouses, 20, 28, 29, 347–8, 373n12, 435n28; and radio, 329; recruited by Labor Party in 1919, 50; segregated in factory under welfare capitalism, 204; shared culture at work among, 204, 328–9; unemployed in Great Depression, 241, 244; in union auxiliaries, 294, 295, 346; and welfare capitalism, 184
Woolworth's Five-and-Ten-Cent-Store, 118, 154
work discipline, lack of, 198–9, 209
Workers Alliance of America, 265, 288
Workers' Committee on Unemployment, 251, 262–7; and blacks, 266; encouraging worker alliances, 266–7
working conditions, 187, 451n107
Works Progress Administration (WPA): administration of, 484n61; and employer attitude toward, 282; jobs with, 258, 260–1, 265, 271, 278–81, 320
World War II and unionization, 291, 293, 368
Wright, Betty, 115
Wrigley Company, 161
Wyle's Hat Shop, 109

YMCA, 55, 83, 91; supported by employers, 26, 45, 168, 180, 379n54
Young, Arthur H., 163
Youngstown, Ohio, 370n1
Youngstown Sheet and Tube, 13, 21, 296
youth: and fashion, 144, 423n160; high school attendance among, 144, 423n159, 424n166; juvenile delinquency among, 144, 422n159; and mass culture, 143–7
Yugoslavs, 57, 214, 254

Zappa, Adeline Milano, 112
Znaniecki, Florian, 85